Philippe Barbour

LOIRE

'...a region which isn't a region
with an accent which is without accent'

CADOGANguides

Contents

About the author

Philippe Barbour's greatest delight in life is exploring France and French culture. Half-English and half-French by birth, he once spent a year living very close to the Loire, in Tours. When he wasn't teaching, he was rushing around with friends from great château to great church to great city, but also going in search of less well-known sights, which proved equally rewarding. Since then he has returned to the Loire Valley on many occasions for Cadogan Guides. He adores this, one of the most richly cultural regions in Europe.

Philippe has written several other books for Cadogan, including their guide to *Brittany*, and is the main author of the Cadogan Guide to *France*.

Cadogan Guides
Network House, 1 Ariel Way, London W12 7SL
cadoganguides@morrispub.co.uk
www.cadoganguides.com

The Globe Pequot Press
246 Goose Lane, PO Box 480, Guilford,
Connecticut 06437–0480

Copyright © Philippe Barbour 1997, 2001

Cover and photo essay design by Kicca Tommasi
Book design by Andrew Barker
Cover photographs by John Ferro Sims
Maps © Cadogan Guides,
    drawn by Map Creation Ltd
Editorial Director: Vicki Ingle
Series Editor: Linda McQueen
Editor: Christine Stroyan
Editorial Assistant: Tori Perrot
Design: Sarah Rianhard-Gardner and
    Tracey Ridgewell
Proofreading: Susannah Wight
Indexing: Isobel McLean
Production: Book Production Services

Printed in Italy by Rotolito Lombarda, Milan
A catalogue record for this book is available
    from the British Library
ISBN 1-86011-834-8

Loire
a photo essay

by John Ferro Sims

01

Loire River,
Champtoceaux

Château de Langeais

Abbey of Fontevraud

Vineyard in the Chinonais

Cathédrale St-Maurice,
Angers

Shop window, Amboise

Lutes, Fontevraud

Place St-Pierre, Saumur

Half-timbered building,
Tours

Château de Montreuil-
Bellay

Cathédrale Ste-Croix,
Orléans

Château de Chenonceau

Mosaic menu, Saumur

Market, Azay-le-Rideau

Baker's sign,
Montreuil-Bellay

Château d'Ussé

Church of Notre-Dame,
Cunault

About the photographer
John Ferro Sims was born of Anglo-Italian parents in Udine, Italy. He worked successfully for five years as an investment analyst before quitting the world of money for a career as a professional photographer which has taken him around the world. He has published nine books.

Introduction

The Loire inspires romantic images of pure white fairytale palaces along France's longest river. The Château d'Ussé supposedly even inspired Charles Perrault's story of Sleeping Beauty. In this guide we aim to show the glory of the châteaux of the Loire Valley, but also that they and the region aren't as spotless, innocent or limited as their popular image. We peer behind the charming stone fronts of the châteaux, which conceal tales of obscene extravagance, political intrigue, courtly corruption, murders even.

It is often thought that the Loire's châteaux date almost exclusively from the late 15th and early 16th centuries, when late Gothic exuberance was fused with new Renaissance fashions rushed back from French military campaigns in Italy. However, dramatic Loire castles in the form of formidable fortifications remain in great number from well before this time. Some of these donjons date back one thousand years, as do the other fine buildings which make another significant contribution to the Loire Valley's outstanding cultural and architectural legacy – its great religious

Chapter Divisions

institutions. These mushroomed up along the Loire and its tributaries in vast numbers and were embellished with fine works of art, the enriching manure of money once again provided by royals and aristocrats. The city cathedrals and the famed churches at Fontevraud, St-Benoît, Cunault and Candes-St-Martin offer fine examples.

Successive royal dynasties – the Capetians, the Plantagenets and the Valois – all left their mark along the Loire Valley; the section of the Loire covered in our guide is in fact commonly known as France's Valley of the Kings. But you might equally talk, if

The Best of the Loire

Major Châteaux
Amboise; Angers; Azay-le-Rideau; Blois; Brissac; Chambord; Chaumont; Chenonceau; Cheverny; Chinon; Loches; Montgeoffroy; Le Plessis-Bourré; Saumur; Serrant; Sully-sur-Loire; Ussé, Valençay, Villandry.

Lesser-known Châteaux
Beauregard; Bouges; Brézé; Chamerolles; Du Moulin; Gizeux; Le Grand-Pressigny; Gué-Péan; Langeais (for the interiors); Luynes; Montrésor; Montreuil-Bellay; Le Plessis-Macé; Talcy (for the interiors); Troussay; Villesavin.

Towns
Amboise; Angers; Briare; Beaugency; Blois; Bourges; Chinon; Clisson; Loches; Nantes; Orléans; Richelieu; Sancerre; Saumur; Tours.

Museums
Jean Lurçat's *Chant du Monde* tapestries at the Hôpital St-Jean in Angers; Musée David d'Angers in Angers; Tapestries of the Apocalypse in the Château d'Angers; Maison de la Magie in Blois; Musée des Beaux-Arts in Blois; Palais Jacques Cœur in Bourges; Musée du Berry in Bourges; Musée Maurice Estève in Bourges; Musée International de la Chasse in the Château de Gien; Musée de la Préhistoire in the Château du Grand-Pressigny; Musée des Beaux-Arts in Nantes; Musée Dobrée in Nantes; Musée des Beaux-Arts in Orléans; Escal' Atlantic in St-Nazaire; Musée Archéologique in Tours; Musée des Beaux-Arts in Tours.

Religious Buildings and Art
Cathédrale St-Maurice in Angers; Church of St-Nicolas in Blois; Cathédrale St-Louis in Blois; Church of St-Aignan in Brinay; Cathédrale St-Etienne in Bourges; Church of St-Martin in Candes-St-Martin; St-Louis Chapel in Champigny-sur-Veude; Basilique de

not of the Valley of the Queens, at least of the Vallée des Dames. Joan of Arc triumphs as the heroine of Loire history. Catherine de' Medici has been portrayed too easily as its greatest villain. Diane de Poitiers was the rival who beat Catherine in King Henri II's affections. Agnès Sorel, a famed and infamous earlier royal mistress, didn't manage to win the country's affections with her extravagant ways and fashions, but Charles VII appears to have found her much more appealing than moralizing Joan. Then there were the wives of the lords who commissioned the châteaux; their husbands were so often away with the peripatetic court that these *châtelaines* were frequently left to help oversee the building plans.

However, the Loire isn't all about royalty and aristocracy, you may be relieved to hear. Down on the cobbled riverside quays, where so much of the commerce in the region was carried out over so many centuries, you can try to re-create in your mind the sound and bustle of carts loading and unloading all manner of goods which

Cléry-St-André; Church of Cunault; Abbey of Fontevraud; Carolingian Oratory in Germigny-des-Prés; Church of St-Ours in Loches; religious legacy east of Loches; Cathédrale St-Pierre in Nantes; Cathédrale Ste-Croix in Orléans; Crypt of St-Aignan in Orléans; Abbaye de Pontlevoy; Church of Le Puy-Notre-Dame; Church of St-Aignan in St-Aignan-sur-Cher; Abbey of St-Benoît-sur-Loire; Abbey Church of St-Florent-le-Vieil; Church of St-Pierre in Saumur; Church of Notre-Dame de Nantilly in Saumur; Notre-Dame-des-Ardilliers in Saumur; Church of St-Nicolas in Tavant (for its Romanesque frescoes); Cathédrale St-Gatien in Tours; churches along the Vienne.

River Stretches

The Loire by Sancerre; the Loire south bank from Gien to Châteauneuf-sur-Loire; the Loire south bank from Muides-sur-Loire to Blois; either bank of the Loire from Blois through to Nantes; the Loire estuary; the Cher valley; the Cisse valley between Blois and Tours; the Indre and Indrois valleys; the Creuse and Claise valleys; the Vienne and Manse valleys; the Aubance and Layon valleys; the Sèvre Nantaise through Muscadet country.

Gardens

Château de Chamerolles gardens; Festival International des Jardins at the Château de Chaumont; Maulévrier Parc Oriental; Prieuré de St-Cosme garden; Château de Villandry gardens.

Curiosities

Pagode de Chanteloup near Amboise; Beaugency Town Hall embroideries; Briare's Pont-Canal; Musée du Vieux Chinon et de la Batellerie in Chinon; Zoo de Doué-la-Fontaine; Aquarium de Touraine in Lussault; Celtic animal statues in Orléans' Musée Archéologique; Ecole Nationale d'Equitation/Cadre Noir outside Saumur; troglodyte sites south of Saumur; La Mine Bleue slate museum in the Segréen; Zooparc de Beauval near St-Aignan-sur-Cher; Espadon submarine in St-Nazaire; Musée du Compagnonnage in Tours; Musée du Gemmail in Tours.

travelled along the river, barrels of wine in particular. Sancerre, Touraine and Anjou remain important French wine-producing areas, while the Orléanais and the Blésois yield lesser-known Loire wines that you could discover. Touraine is popularly known as the Jardin de la France, the Garden of France, in recognition of its general fertility. The whole of the Loire Valley is highly productive, fruit orchards densely planted in parts, vegetables thriving on the alluvial river sands. As well as the game that proliferates in the Loire forests, freshwater fish land on many a restaurant plate.

Thoughts of water bring us to a popular misconception about the Loire Valley that should be dispelled: that it's all about the one river. This is far from the case. Several major tributaries add not just to the weight of the Loire's waters, but also to the greater Loire Valley's cultural importance. The splendid trio of the Cher, the Indre and the Vienne join the Loire from the south. The main river to merge with the Loire from the north along our stretch is the mighty Maine. Lesser-known little rivers steal up more surreptitiously, like the meadowy Cisse, the sun-drenched Authion and the vine-growing Layon.

The finest limestone of Bourré on the Cher, from which some of the greatest Loire châteaux were built, is especially praised for its whiteness – it's said to grow even whiter with age. You might draw a comparison with the way that these modern tourist times have cleaned and beautified the reputation of the Loire châteaux and the Loire Valley. Look more closely, however, at the region and at the tints of the tufa blocks so characteristic of the Loire buildings and you'll realize they're much more complex than you may have thought at first sight. You'll see that the stones aren't a uniform colour at all; some of the blocks may be white still, some grey, some yellowing, some positively brown with age. Many have been replaced. We've tried to take a slightly closer, slightly more realistic, look at the Loire's history and cultural heritage than is generally the case in tourist guides. But we have to admit that it's still utterly impossible not to be immediately seduced by the region's exceptional gentle beauty.

A Guide to the Guide

The first stretch of river on the planet to have been declared a World Heritage Site by UNESCO, the Loire covered by this guidebook has long been a world-famous tourist destination, with very good reason. Our guide also covers in detail the river valleys which help make up the greater Loire Valley region and which share many characteristics with the mighty Loire: majestic meanders, splendid châteaux, courtly towns, vine-covered slopes, and a plethora of dramatic underground caverns.

The guide starts, in the east, with the favoured land of the Capetians, the **Orléanais**, so close to Paris and at the Loire's crowning point, and the **eastern Berry** (including the Sancerrois), early acquired by the first French medieval dynasty. Next come the **Blésois** and **Touraine**, haunts and great hunting grounds of the Valois kings – Charles VII came here after running away from Paris at the start of the 1420s, and his successors stayed on for a century and more. Then comes **Anjou**, most famously connected with an English, not a French, royal dynasty, as the birthplace of the Plantagenets. Approaching the Atlantic coast we arrive at **Nantes**, once capital of the independent duchy of Brittany, but swallowed up by the Valois in the late medieval period.

For this second edition, we have added descriptions of striking new places open to the public, such as the Château de Brézé and the Château du Rivau, and new troglodyte attractions along the Cher and in the Saumurois. We have also included the sensuous vine-covered hills around **Sancerre**, one of the the loveliest stretches along the Loire (for some mysterious reason left out of the UNESCO classification), as well as the magnificent medieval city of **Bourges**, whose cathedral rivals Chartres and has been declared a World Heritage Site in its own right.

History

03

Prehistory
How Gregory of Tours, misled by the Bible, underestimates the age of the world and completely ignores the roots of civilization along the Loire

Gregory of Tours, that unique and splendidly inaccurate recorder of the history of the world as seen from the end of the 6th century, told a particularly mean tale about the dog-eat-dog world of the early Merovingians. He wasn't so hot, though, when it came to recounting earlier Loire history in his extraordinary book, *The History of the Franks*. His aim was more grandiose than the title suggests: he wished in fact to relate the history of the world from its beginnings up to his day. Unfortunately, he relied much too heavily on the very limited, very irrelevant stories contained in the Bible as a source for the millennia before the Franks or, to be more imprecise, the 5,792 years he calculated had passed between the beginning of the world to the time he finished his work.

The Bible has little to say on men and civilizations along the Loire. So the well-intentioned bishop, who lived by the great river, failed to mention the neolithic dolmens and menhirs scattered around the region, most densely in the Saumurois. Mind you, even specialist archaeologists today have trouble telling us much about the civilization behind these megaliths, beyond vaguely dating their construction to between 5000 and 2000 BC. Nor is there any explanation by Gregory of the commercial activities of prehistoric man along the valleys in this region, and at Le Grand Pressigny in southern Touraine in particular. Their tool-making business here became thoroughly European from 2800 to 2400 BC at least, the high-quality flints being exported across the continent.

c.500 BC–AD 260
Celtic Druids gather along the Loire before Caesar has the Gauls' guts for garters

Gregory also omitted to mention the arrival of the Celts. An influx from the east into what became known as Gaul occurred from around 500 BC or earlier. The main Celtic (or Gaulish) groups to settle along the Loire Valley were the Carnutes in the Orléans region, the Turones in the vicinity of Tours, the Andes in the Angers area, and the Namnetes around Nantes. The Bituriges were the powerful group that settled around Bourges, down the Cher. The Loire river constituted, for a good many centuries before the Roman and Christian eras, a trade route with the Greeks, who had founded Marseille on the Mediterranean as early as 600 BC.

Gregory even failed to give any account of Julius Caesar conquering Gaul! The Roman megalomaniac did the job himself, of course, in his *Conquest of Gaul*, subtly distancing himself from the glorifying accounts of his campaigns by writing in the third person. Caesar relates some interesting details about the Celtic way of life, including a reference to the great annual gathering of druids from the various tribes across Gaul, supposed to have taken place around St-Benoît-sur-Loire, east of Orléans (*see* p.123). Caesar's subjugation of Gaul in 56 BC caused the rival Celtic tribes to unite, and in 52 BC a unified Gaulish uprising took place. The Carnutes were the first to show their defiance. Caesar returned to wreak revenge for the widespread insubordination. The terrible devastation of Cenabum, as the Romans called the Carnutes' capital on the site of present-day Orléans, is dispassionately retold by Caesar. His legacy was several hundred years of supposed Pax Romana – with occasional abortive uprisings – in the Gallo-Roman society created in his wake. Under Roman and Roman-style administration, Italian customs became mixed with Celtic ones, religious practices included. Big Gallo-Roman towns grew up in the region, Aurelianis (Orléans), Caesarodunum (Tours), Juliomagus (Angers), Portus Namnetum (Nantes) and Avaricum (Bourges) being the most important ones. Gallo-Roman roads connected the towns, while villas sprang up in the countryside and, after a long period of Roman protectionism, it was permitted to cultivate vines in the Empire's provinces.

260–732
Barbarian leaders and brave bishops

As the Roman Empire gradually weakened, pagan hordes began flowing into Gaul from the east, as did Christianity, which slowly but steadily established itself. The first Frankish incursions took place in the mid-3rd century, mainly in the east of Gaul. Under threat of these invaders, the Gallo-Roman towns erected defensive walls, fragments of which can still be seen in some of the big Loire cities.

Certainly as early as the 3rd century, preachers and bishops were spreading the Christian message in the Loire. St Gatien, for example, is reckoned to have been established in Tours in the second half of the 3rd century, at a time when the Roman Empire was still persecuting Christians. The big cities all had a bishop comparatively early. A Christian from the 4th century became one of the most important figures in French and European Church history: St Martin. Some of his deeds and the unseemly dispute at Candes over his dead body in 397 are memorably recounted by Gregory of Tours. In fact, such is the importance Gregory ascribes to the saint that for the first section of *The History of the Franks* he takes as his parameters the beginning of the world down to the death of St Martin. Before becoming a committed Christian, Martin was a soldier in the service of the Roman Empire. He underwent a Pauline conversion on a road in Amiens in northeastern France. Seeing a miserable unclothed wretch of a pauper along the way, he unsheathed his sword, cut his cloak in two and shared it. This image recurs time and again in churches in the region. Martin zealously set about converting Gaul and helped establish the first religious communities in France, one near Poitiers, some way south of the Loire Valley, and a second in 372 at Marmoutier, on the northern Loire bank outside Tours.

Another particularly celebrated early Loire saint was Aignan, bishop of Orléans, a man who helped save his city from barbaric invaders long before Joan of Arc. The enemy, one in a line of the great 5th-century waves of invaders, was the dreaded

Attila the Hun. St Aignan raised the alarm early enough for Roman legions under Aetius to come to Orléans' rescue, and the Hun was repulsed in 451.

The Frankish Merovingian dynasty had recently been founded, and it is on the bloody history of the beginnings of this dynasty that Gregory of Tours concentrates his writing. The tales are of rivalry in high places, the factions resorting to the lowest of methods to gain power. Clovis was the most important figure in the dynasty, ruling from just after the Western Roman Empire officially disappeared in 476. Clovis' wife, Clotilde, crucially converted him to Christianity, with a little help from St Martin. Hard pressed by the Alamanni, Clovis paused at St Martin's tomb in Tours in 496 and promised to adopt the new religion if he was granted victory. He won and converted. In 511 the Council of Orléans importantly enshrined the alliance between the royal family and the Church in the Frankish territories. Gregory of Tours believed St Martin helped him too, curing him of a bad illness when he visited his shrine. The grateful Auvergnat stayed to become bishop of the place and write his fabulous history.

Around and after Gregory's time, important new religious institutions sprang up along the Loire. The one which acquired the most fame, due to a highly prized relic, was the abbey of Fleury, which later became known as the abbey of St Benoît (Benedict in English). In the 670s a party of monks from the abbey travelled over to the southern Italian mountain where the deeply venerated and influential saint had died and claimed that they had gathered his bones and brought them back to their abbey, a great pilgrimage draw for the future.

732–987
A brief Carolingian Renaissance before the violent Vikings

Virtually nothing remains of the Merovingian civilization along the Loire. Nor does much from the Carolingian dynasty which followed. At the start of the Carolingian times, Charles Martel halted the Arab surge northwards, beating the Moors in an important battle somewhere between Poitiers and Tours in 732 – some reckon it may have taken place on the southern Touraine plain of Ste-Maure. Charlemagne, Martel's grandson, became the great conquering, Christianizing, first Holy Roman Emperor. In the Carolingian renaissance of learning during his reign, both Tours and the abbey of Fleury became enormously influential centres of intellectual life in Europe. The scholar Alcuin of York, based at St-Martin's in Tours from 796, made this the centre of a renowned school. Théodulfe became the powerful Spanish head of Fleury at the start of the 9th century, appointed by Charlemagne.

The mid-9th century saw the rapid collapse of the Carolingian empire. The Vikings raided, Norse (or Norman) long boats penetrating far up the Loire. Nantes was taken in 842, Angers was sacked in 853–4, and the Vikings continued upriver to Orléans. No respecters of religion, by way of example of their brutality, they slashed the bishop of Nantes' throat at his cathedral altar. Loire monks fled east, taking their relics with them. Much was pillaged or destroyed. A Breton chief, Barbetorte (Twisted Beard), finally managed in 937 to dislodge the Normans from Nantes and Brittany.

ing in 1096. A few nobles would bring back precious relics from the long-running campaigns, firing their own and the populace's credulous imaginations. Staying at home in France, one of the most charismatic religious figures of the times, the preacher Robert d'Arbrissel, founded the great abbey of Fontevraud in 1101.

1101–1328
The Plantagenêts of Anjou win England and an empire after accusations of adultery in Antioch

After the Black Falcon, a later Foulques, Foulques V of Anjou (also King of Jerusalem), had a son Geoffroy, who showed a predilection for placing a piece of broom in his helmet. From this came his famous nickname, Plantagenêt (genêt being French for broom). Foulques V having already got his hands on Maine through marriage in 1109, arranged for Geoffroy to wed Mathilda, daughter of Henry I of England and Normandy. Geoffroy, impatient for his inheritance, simply took control of Normandy in 1144. His son and heir was Henri Plantagenet.

The French king in the middle of the 12th century, Louis VII, had married Eleanor of Aquitaine, heiress to a vast swathe of southwest France. The two proved incompatible and there were even rumours that Eleanor had committed adultery in Antioch during the second Crusade. The royal couple was granted a divorce in 1152, at Beaugency on the Loire, and Eleanor took back her dowry. Two years later it was presented to Henri Plantagenet in one of the most significant marriages in western European medieval history. A year after his marriage, Henri exerted pressure on the pathetically weak English king, another figure stemming from the Loire and a grandson of William the Conqueror, Etienne de Blois (alias King Stephen I). The latter recognized Henri as the rightful heir to the English throne. One year later Stephen died and in 1154 Henri became King Henry II of England, first in the Plantagenet dynasty that was to rule briefly, but memorably, on both sides of the Channel.

Thanks to Eleanor of Aquitaine's dowry, Henry II controlled an empire stretching from the Pyrenees to the border with Scotland. Chinon in Touraine became a favoured seat of power, with its excellent defensive position above the Vienne river and its location reasonably close to the centre of his territories. Henri appointed an able administration and ruled very firmly, imposing a good measure of centralized control. He also tried to take away some of the Church's independent powers, especially its right to try its own members, quarrelling bitterly and disastrously with his former friend Thomas à Becket. The latter's murder by knights of the king in Canterbury Cathedral in 1170 led Henry to perform acts of expiation, which included commissioning the building of religious foundations, some in the Loire Valley.

It was hard for Henry II to keep his diverse regions together, especially with his wife and eldest son Richard (the Lionheart) plotting against him. Richard pledged his allegiance to the new French king from 1180, Philippe II Auguste. This Capetian was a formidable fighter. His close friendship with Richard the Lionheart came to an end when the two fell out on the third Crusade. Returning to France, they fought bitterly. Richard was mortally injured in fighting in 1199, dying in Chinon. His body was taken to nearby Fontevraud abbey to be buried alongside those of his parents. Richard's brother and successor, John, proved no match for the capable Capetian. John famously lost practically all his French territories and is best known in French as Jean sans Terre (Lackland). Anjou and Touraine quickly came into Philippe Auguste's possession, in 1202 and 1205 respectively. The Blésois, too, entered the royal domains.

The Capetians were now really beginning to assert their authority as kings of France. Blanche de Castille was queen regent for another of the important unifying Capetian kings after Philippe Auguste, the pious Louis IX, or Saint Louis. She ordered work on the massive new defences of Angers castle, begun in 1230. Brittany, that thorn in the side for the acquisitive French royal family for a couple of centuries to come, lay all too close.

Over the 13th and 14th centuries, the Capetian kings granted royal appanages to brothers or sons, territories for them to look after for their lifetime, a useful way of maintaining royal family control of the provinces. Louis IX gave the duchy of Anjou to his brother Charles. The latter, as Charles I of Anjou and also count of Provence, was actually more interested in warring for the papacy and in self-aggrandizement abroad than staying put; in fact, he became the head of another extraordinary Angevin empire, being declared king of Naples and Sicily by the pope in 1266. Charles' descendants ruled over Naples for some time, and held on to Provence. France during this period was by no means a unified entity, but was split into semi-autonomous regions where all sorts of different powers, royal, noble and religious, flexed their muscles and tested each other's strength.

The Church had some particularly powerful branches. At the start of the 14th century, King Philippe IV le Bel (the Handsome), suppressed the Knights Templars, a Church-backed military religious order which had amassed extraordinary powers and riches from its role in administering the finances of the Crusades. They were imprisoned in Chinon castle, and then tortured and executed them on the most infamous of trumped-up charges.

1328–80
The Valois succession sparks off the Hundred Years' War between France and England

Philippe le Bel's heirs were cursed. By 1328 his three sons had ruled and died, leaving behind only girls. His daughter Isabelle had married the English king, Edward II. Who was to inherit the French throne when females had been declared ineligible? Philippe, a grandson of the Capetian King Philippe III, represented the Valois claim. Edward III, son of Isabelle and Edward II, argued that even if women could not succeed, the inheritance could be passed down via a female line. The French barons, however, elected the Valois candidate, who became King Philippe VI of France, and thus set in motion the terrible Hundred Years' War between England and France.

King Jean le Bon, Philippe VI's son and successor, was captured by the English in Poitou in 1356, and taken over to England as a prisoner for a time. He had created appanages for his sons (apart from the eldest, who would succeed him as Charles V). One had become Louis Duc d'Anjou, another Jean Duc de Berry and a third the Duc de Bourgogne (Burgundy). These powerful provincial princes were all wilful and cruel rulers, vying do outdo each other as patrons of the arts (the works they commissioned survive to this day), while outbreaks of plague and famine and widespread poverty drove common people to the desperate uprisings of the Jacquerie. The Loire mariners and merchants, however, managed to form a strong body to defend their common interests in the 14th century.

1380–1431
King Charles VII flees to the Loire in the second phase of the Hundred Years' War, and Joan of Arc brings timely relief

While Charles V consolidated French royal power, this crumbled under his son and successor Charles VI, who was prone to increasing fits of madness through the first two decades of the 15th century. His weakness precipitated the second bout of the Hundred Years' War, as rival provincial royal factions, the princes of Orléans and Burgundy, started a civil war. The parties each called on the English to support their cause, not realizing the danger of such an appeal until it was too late. The English Crown had decided to exercise its own rights in France. The first great English victory was at Agincourt in northern France in 1415. Charles Duc d'Orléans was the most important French figure of royal lineage taken prisoner. In 1418 the French dauphin Charles, heir to the French Crown and duke of Touraine and Berry through his uncle Jean, fled from Paris. Forced south of the Loire, he headed first for the Berry and then for Chinon and Loches in Touraine.

This enforced move would give rise to the great royal period in the Loire Valley. A line of French kings who followed Charles VII – Louis XI, Charles VIII, Louis XII and, for a time, François I – would stay based in the valley even after the English had been ousted from most of France. With their courtiers, the last three would see in the French Renaissance and other massive changes in lifestyle from around the start of the 16th century. As the court shifted centre according to the preference of the particular reigning monarch, a handful of Loire Valley cities became royal, prosperous and beautiful in their turn – Amboise, Blois, Bourges, Chinon Loches, Tours. The kings and courtiers encouraged merchants, particularly of luxury goods, who in turn were made wealthy and enriched the Loire's cultural legacy.

However, first the dauphin Charles had to extricate himself from dire straits. The English King Henry V was declared heir to the French throne by the 1420 Treaty of Troyes. Charles had himself proclaimed king of France at the Duc de Berry's château of Mehun-sur-Yièvre in 1422. But a man of action was needed to help him out with the English enemy. Joan of Arc proved herself to be that man. She arrived in Chinon from Lorraine in 1429, instructed, she said, by heavenly voices to help the French forces free Orléans and boot the English out of France. With her extraordinary powers of persuasion she convinced people in authority of the righteousness of her cause. The French powers were desperate for a miracle; most importantly, Orléans was being besieged by English troops.

Joan of Arc picked out the king in the Chinon court crowd and in a private hearing with him persuaded him to back her. After undergoing tests of her beliefs and virginity, she joined the French troops marching to the beleaguered Loire city. Her dogged part in the subsequent fight led to the release of Orléans, which adopted her as its Maid. She then participated in a string of French victories in the Orléanais that summer, at Jargeau, Meung, Beaugency and Patay. The French fortunes seemed to be changing. (Historically speaking, however, it should be noted that before Joan there had already been French victories at Baugé in 1421, beating the English in Anjou, and at Montargis, in the northern Loiret, in 1426.)

The independently minded Joan continued in her campaigns, despite frictions with Charles VII's favourite La Trémoille, who stopped her briefly at the Château de Sully. She was soon captured by the enemy and we know the fate that awaited her at Rouen in Normandy in 1431. The ungrateful French king didn't lift a finger to rescue her from the flames.

1431–61
The late Gothic chivalric courts of the Loire Valley

Charles VII had been married to Marie d'Anjou when they were both children, as was the custom. Marie's was the more typical lot of the contemporary female, stuck in a perpetual cycle of childbearing. Most of the 14 children she bore didn't survive long. Charles VII, his family and court spent a time exiled from Paris in the beautiful city of Bourges, and in fact the king was mockingly called Le Petit Roi de Bourges. In the second part of his reign, Charles installed his influential and beautiful mistress, Agnès Sorel, at Loches. She was feted as a great beauty and fashion-setter of her times, and the king splashed out a fortune from the public purse and taxes on the poor for her exotic furs and silks. Vast sums would equally be poured into increasingly sumptuous châteaux.

In these chivalric times, hunting, falconry, jousting and real tennis were favourite pastimes of many of the Loire kings. One courtly companion of Charles VII, René d'Anjou, or Le Bon Roi René as he is popularly known in French history, was the grandson of Louis I d'Anjou, count of Provence and legitimate heir to the kingdom of Naples, for which he unsuccessfully fought. René was renowned for his love of chivalric culture, in particular jousting, poetry and roses. Moving from little castle to little castle in Anjou, he and Charles VII enjoyed their refined pleasures together while Charles neglected his wife.

Charles d'Orléans, a hero of Joan of Arc's, was finally released from captivity in England in 1440 and went back to his home in Blois to establish another artistic chivalric court there. Late in life, Charles d'Orléans was blessed with a son, Louis d'Orléans, who would eventually inherit the throne in extraordinary circumstances. As for Joan, in a rehabilitation trial in Orléans in 1456, three years after the end of the Hundred Years' War, her part in freeing France from the English was recognized.

It was the ordinary people in France who suffered most terribly in the Hundred Years' War. One tax census in the Orléanais, dating from 1450, close to the end of the conflict, records that there was no tax to be paid in one walled town: '*Néant, parce que tout est en désert. Il n'y a que petits enfants mendiant* (Nothing, because all is deserted. There are only little beggar children there).'

1461–83
Louis XI, king of France 1461–83, paranoid but well prepared

Louis XI, Charles VII's son and successor, has suffered particularly badly from adverse fictionalization of his character by Walter Scott in *Quentin Durward*. Recent history has tried to redress the balance with serious studies of this difficult man's actions. He was brought up in Touraine, hated Agnès Sorel, and twice tried to rise up against his father, running off to live in Flanders for a time. Louis was first married to Margaret of Scotland (daughter of King James I) at the Château de Tours in 1436, but detested her too – the young couple had no children before Margaret died. His second wife was

Charlotte de Savoie. Crowned king in 1461 after his father's death, Louis effectively chose Tours as the capital of France. He lavished favours on the Touraine, encouraging all sorts of business enterprises. Most notorious for his *fillettes* (not little girls, but dreadful iron prison cages) at his châteaux at Plessis-lès-Tours and Loches, he is now more roundly depicted as a king who successfully advanced the unification of the provinces for the French Crown (Anjou became his at the end of the Roi René's life, for example), helping bind the nobles to the royal cause by creating the exclusive Order of St Michael (*see* p.241). His administration was pragmatically business-minded, developing such important industries as the French postal service and a silk trade based in Touraine, where mulberries were planted in large numbers.

Louis XI was also extremely vigilant about the provisions he made for his children. While his heir, Charles, was meticulously groomed for kingship at the Château d'Amboise, he arranged for the marriage of his intelligent, crippled daughter Jeanne de France to another Louis, the son of Charles Duc d'Orléans, in 1476. The idea was apparently to put a halt to the ambitions of that branch of the royal family.

Louis XI was a deeply superstitious man in a deeply superstitious age. His belief in divine intervention, especially by the Virgin Mary, was extremely powerful and his paranoia seems to have grown with age. He asked for the Italian Christian mystic, François de Paule, to come to his bedside as death approached, and this influential religious figure would remain close to the monarchy for some time to come.

1483–98
Charles VIII, king of France 1483–98, discovers Italy and deals Brittany a marriage blow

Under Charles VIII, the Château d'Amboise would become the French royal head-quarters. But at the start of his reign his sister, Anne de Beujeu, with her new brick-patterned castle at Gien, east of Orléans, acted as regent for a brief period until her little brother came of age. Louis d'Orléans became rebellious, forming an alliance with the independent Duc François II de Bretagne, based at his castle in Nantes, to revolt against the regency in what's known in French as the Guerre Folle (the Mad War). Brittany's independence was drawing to an unhappy end, however. At the Traité du Verger in 1488, François II de Bretagne was forced to accept – among other constraints – not to marry his daughters without French royal consent. The Breton leader died the same year, leaving the 11-year-old Anne as his successor. Two years later, in a bid to ensure the duchy's independence, she was betrothed by proxy to Maximilian of Austria. Charles VIII's troops marched into Brittany, and Anne de Bretagne, in surely one of the least romantic proposals in French royal history, was forced to marry the young French king in 1491. The ceremony took place in the Château de Langeais along the Loire.

Charles soon went galloping off to Italy to assert inheritance rights there. He was unsuccessful, but fell for Naples and gathered together cartloads of art as booty. He also bought the services of a whole bunch of specialist Italian artists, from architects to a parrot trainer. Charles and his army only just made it back to France, almost wiped out when trapped by an alliance of enemies at Fornova in 1495. Philippe de Comines, servant to both Louis XI and Charles VIII, recorded a famous history of the period in his *Mémoire*.

Just a few years after his lucky escape in Italy, Charles VIII ended his life in the most banal of household accidents in 1498; he banged his head on a door in the Château d'Amboise and promptly died. Anne's marriage contract forced her to marry his successor, his cousin Louis d'Orléans, who became Louis XII. The latter was pleased to find an excuse to spurn the crippled Jeanne for a better prize.

1498–1515
Louis XII, king of France 1498–1515, sees in the French Renaissance

Louis XII moved the court to his home town of Blois, while continuing to pursue French royal claims and ambitions in Italy, again unsuccessfully. But the defeated nobles came back with their heads crammed full of ideas on Italian decoration and these were adopted in new Loire architecture in particular. Declared the Le Père du Peuple (the Father of the People), Louis XII was relatively popular at home. Many of the acts of his reign took place at the Château de Blois. By Anne de Bretagne, Louis had a daughter, Claude, who would become the wife of the next French king as Louis and Anne had no son. A short time before he died, Louis was briefly married to the young beauty Mary Tudor, sister of King Henry VIII of England.

1515–47
François I, king of France 1515–47, the French answer to Henry VIII

The monumental French king of the 16th century was Louis XII's successor in 1515, his nephew and son-in-law François d'Angoulême, who became François I on his accession. François had been brought up at Amboise by his mother, Louise de Savoie. His sister, the bright and well-educated Marguerite d'Angoulême, was taught with him. She became a reputed writer and married into the De Navarre family. François I proved a match for Henry VIII of England, but not for Habsburg Charles who, with the backing of the massively wealthy Fugger family bankers, won the fight between them in for the post of Holy Roman Emperor, as well as becoming Charles V of Spain.

François continued the violent French royal love affair with Italy. The first foray was successful, the Battle of Marignano securing Milan. Leonardo da Vinci was among the treasures brought back. François got himself into terrible difficulties in another Italian campaign, and was captured at the Battle of Pavia in 1525, the year after his first wife had died. While in captivity in Spain, his marriage to his captor's sister, Eleanor of Austria, was agreed.

In 1532, Brittany was officially signed over to France at the Château de Nantes. But conflict was spreading across the country as the debate on religious reform started by Luther in Germany caught on. The radical reformer Calvin studied in the Loire region in the 1530s before heading for the safety of Geneva. François I became interested and then embroiled in the grave matter of Church reform. Then someone had the audacity, in the so-called Affaire des Placards (not cupboards here, but pamphlets), to pin up a piece attacking the Catholic Mass on the king's very bedroom door, and François I suddenly decided to suppress the would-be reformers, who became known as Huguenots, or Protestants. The seeds were being sown for the terrible French Wars of Religion later in the century. Meanwhile François I moved his attentions more and more towards Paris and away from the Loire.

1547–89
Henri II, Catherine de' Medici, their three kingly sons and the French Wars of Religion

The religious situation got worse under François' son, Henri II, who married Catherine de' Medici, notorious in history. She wasn't the only forceful woman in his life; his mistress, Diane de Poitiers, was also a strong influence. While the extravagance of the court was somewhat curbed in Henri's time, Protestantism was spreading like wild fire and Henri ordered the Huguenots' persecution. Although the royal children were brought up at Amboise, the Loire became less and less the centre of royal and court life, although it was there that Henri II died from an accident in a tournament in 1559, leaving only young sons. Religious factions and powerful families on both sides had become more entrenched in their positions during his reign.

The sickly King François II, married so briefly to Mary Queen of Scots, was a puppet ruler who wouldn't last long. Mary Queen of Scots' uncles, the ultra-Catholic Duc and Cardinal de Guise, had acquired considerable power and began exercising it. Catherine de' Medici tried at first to pacify the feuding parties. The Conjuration d'Amboise, a plot by leading Protestant nobles to kidnap François II and assassinate the De Guises, was uncovered in 1560. François de Guise was then given permission to quell the revolt and those caught were treated ruthlessly, many drowned in the Loire, many hung up for public display at Amboise. François II died of illness at the Hôtel Groslot in Orléans in 1560. Catherine de' Medici remained several years as regent for the new French king, Charles IX.

The bloody Wars of Religion really got under way in 1562 and would last until the end of the century. The Wars of Religion weren't only about the bitter struggle between Catholics and Protestants, but also about the battle for power between the great families of France, the De Guises, the Chastillons/Colignys and the Bourbons/ Condés; even the royal family itself was threatened. Orléans became one of the strongholds of the Protestants in the first war. The De Guise troops were massed against them, but François de Guise was killed in the battle. The first bout of fighting ended with the peace of Amboise in 1563. The infamously cowardly St Bartholomew's Day massacres of Protestants took place in a later outburst in 1572 and were particularly bloody in some of the major Loire towns.

King Henri III took over the reins from 1574, after his brother Charles IX died. The ultra-Catholic Ligue was founded in 1576 by the mighty Henri de Guise le Balafré (Scarface), that family's faction threatening royal authority still further. Such was Henri III's fear that he snapped, ordering Henri de Guise's execution in his own royal château of Blois at the meeting of the Estates General in 1588. Henri was assassinated in his turn in 1590, dying without heirs. His pious wife was left to mourn in royal white at Chenonceau. The Valois line was at an end.

1589–1789
Bourbon kings begin with Henri IV and move away from the Loire

The Protestant Henri de Navarre became king as Henri IV, as Henri III had agreed. But the religious wars were still raging. Henri IV was much aided in the task of reviving French fortunes by his trusted companion in arms and minister Maximilien de Béthune, who became Duc de Sully and was given that splendid château on the Loire. The Edict of Nantes of 1598 famously allowed for freedom of religion for the Huguenots – a new official tolerance had been proclaimed. In Saumur, the reforming Duplessis-Mornay was even able to set up the Protestant Academy, which became for a short time a great centre of new learning.

Political power had moved firmly to Paris, however. The Loire was a place of retreat. Blois even became something of a town for exiles, Henri IV's wife, Marie de' Medici, being sent there as an awkward queen mother under Louis XIII. This king's rebellious brother, and for a long time heir presumptive, Gaston d'Orléans, would follow later. He took part in all attempts to oust Cardinal Richelieu, Louis XIII's extraordinary counsellor, who amassed phenomenal power and wealth, including enough to create a whole town and massive château on the border with Touraine, named – surprise, surprise – Richelieu. Before Cardinal Richelieu, it was the Duc de Luynes, with his old-established country château in Touraine, who had held the strings of power.

The mid-17th century saw a revolt of princes and nobility, the Fronde, as little Louis XIV came to the throne. Inheriting her obstreperous nature from her father, Gaston d'Orléans, La Grande Mademoiselle caused havoc, even marching on Orléans. As absolutist monarchy took a firmer hold on the country and centralized control, the Loire became still further distanced from political action. Royal representatives, the *intendants* appointed by the king, were sent out to rule the new regions or *généralités*, the important administrative towns of the time in the Loire Valley being Orléans and Tours. Louis XIV did enjoy the odd jaunt down to Chambord, built to his scale of pomp. His Revocation of the Edict of Nantes in 1685 was the culmination of the French Counter-Reformation, stamping the authority of Catholicism on the country. The previously Protestant Saumur, for example, was swamped by Catholic foundations in the 17th century. The Revocation and the persecution of Protestants that ensued led a large number of them, in particular merchants, to leave France.

The western end of the Loire, however, found itself with several sources of great prosperity in the 17th century. Anjou wine and fruit were very successfully exported in this period. Slate mining also became important there. And from the mid-17th century the French colonies began to bring vast riches to some of the Loire towns, most especially to Nantes. This town's top merchants grew fabulously wealthy on the triangular slave trade in the 18th century. Louis XV paid little attention to the Loire, except to send his many daughters packing to religious school at the abbey of Fontevraud – the place had maintained connections with royal blood through a long line of well-connected and wealthy abbesses. The foolish king, swayed by his favourite women, also sent his most able minister, the Duc de Choiseul, into exile in the Loire.

And what of the more ordinary people through these centuries of tales of kings, counts and nobility? A former trades union activist turned monk sent me this impassioned little late 19th-century text on the inhabitants at the foot of the Château de Montrésor in Touraine:

This carefully graded populace moulded goblets, fashioned glasses and stuffed pillows for its masters; it made their breeches and tied together their valets' whips; it mixed their dogs' food, forged the dungeon bars, then the battle lances, then the horse-shoes...doing its best to grovel in the shadow of the great wall which hid the oubliettes, slithering on its stomach just as it had seen the sticky slugs do in the mud down below. Cunningly, cleverly, desperately, with deft moves and leaps this populace became the bourgeoisie. And so people grow up...through the same acts of humility, the same stupefaction, the same terror, the same crawling.

An aristocratic young Briton staying at Chanteloup before the Revolution noted the poverty of the masses more simply.

A fat goose was 15p English, and a fat fowl 4p, yet in spite of fat geese and fat fowls, the poor live on bread and water from Monday to Sunday.

1789–1800
Revolution and the Guerre de Vendée

The Loire was meek and marginalized by the end of the Ancien Régime and wasn't rocked particularly violently by the Revolution, although in towns like Blois many churches were taken down. Orléans briefly became the seat of a high court investigating so-called crimes against the nation. Slave-trading was banned, and the new geographical administrative units of France, the *départements*, were created during this period. Many châteaux and religious buildings, rather than being destroyed through hatred, were pragmatically turned into barracks or prisons (most notoriously Fontevraud abbey) or, temporarily, 'temples of reason'.

The anti-Republican Guerre de Vendée (Vendée War), which deeply affected the west of Anjou and Nantes as well as the Vendée just to the south, belies the general impression that the French Revolution wasn't challenged by Frenchmen on their own soil. An uprising by staunchly Catholic peasants supporting their clergy gained momentum when pro-royalist nobles joined their cause. They swept northwards, passing through the Cholet area in southwestern Anjou and from there up to Maine, the province between the Loire Valley and Normandy, before being savagely halted by Revolutionary troops. The bitter memories of these events remain vivid in the Choletais as well as the Vendée, places where the bicentenary of the Revolution was certainly not a time of celebration. The local fighters of the Guerre de Vendée are regarded as heroic figures there.

1800–1900
Nineteenth-century upheaval

The 19th century was characterized by radically shifting regimes and bouts of social upheaval. After the end of Napoleon's follies, the Prussians briefly marched as far as Tours and the French monarchy was restored. Republicanism, though, continued to fight its patch, the second and third French republics divided by the mid-century Second Empire, which ended with a disastrous but brief war with Prussia. The Prussians under Bismarck provoked the French into attacking them in 1870. Very quickly the French troops had to retreat and a new emergency government was forced to flee Paris as the Germans advanced, Léon Gambetta memorably escaping by hot air balloon to Tours. Two armies along the Loire, led by d'Aurelle and Chanzy, were put out of action by the Prussians, who came as far as Tours once again. France was forced to give in to terms very favourable to the enemy. The cantankerous Comte de Chambord failed to take his chance to restore the monarchy immediately afterwards. Instead came the Third Republic, which expelled the would-be French royals and lasted until the outbreak of the Second World War.

Loire trade was profoundly disturbed and altered in the 19th century, in particular by the arrival of the railway mid-century. The great river itself and its network of tributaries had served as extremely important trade routes from before recorded history began. Ships had been growing larger and larger through the Ancien Régime, which meant that full-scale Loire navigation had become more awkward before the Revolution; even Nantes was no longer easily accessible to the large seafaring trading vessels, and river activity moved out towards the estuary. Suddenly, with the railways, the waterways were abandoned. Many riverside towns along the Loire Valley have retained their picturesque cobbled quays, which went quiet practically overnight. Urban expansion further altered the towns, as did industrialization, although this was limited along the Loire. Phylloxera blighted its vines at the end of the century, as elsewhere across France.

1900–
The 20th century – from world wars to nuclear energy

The theme of the German threat dominated the history of France for the first half of the 20th century. The First World War emptied the French countryside of its young sons, remembered in monuments and plaques in every village. Soviet-style communism was somewhat surprisingly the subject of debate at the Congrès de Tours of

1920. At this meeting the French Left split into two, with the formation of the Socialist and Communist parties which went on to dominate that half of politics throughout the century.

Tours became the fleeting capital of the French government on the run at the beginning of the Second World War, Winston Churchill flying over for a last desperate meeting before the Germans overran the country. The few attempts to halt the advance, such as that by 300 North African snipers in Tours, were doomed. The shipbuilding stretch of the Loire by St-Nazaire, where many of the great French transatlantic liners were built, was taken over for German uses and U-boats. During the war, most of the river crossings were bombed. The scars of this new type of warfare, inflicted by Germans and Allies alike, are obvious to this day in several Loireside towns, notably along Tours' riverbanks, or in the centre of historic Orléans, while smaller riverside towns, such as Gien and Sully to the east, had to be almost entirely rebuilt. The Cher river running through Touraine served as part of the dividing line between German-occupied and Vichy France until the close of 1942, the château of Chenonceau even acting as a bridge by which Resistance workers could pass from one territory to the other.

It hasn't all been plain sailing for the Loire since the war. Despite the general growing prosperity , major industries, such as shipbuilding close to the estuary, have dwindled. The new French regions were created in the 1960s, when some bizarre divisions were made along the Loire. The stretch covered in this book is split between the Région Centre and the Région Pays de la Loire – all a bit of a mess and going against historical affiliations. On the Loire itself, the installation of a string of nuclear plants went ahead relatively unchallenged, until the authorities tried to build one near Nantes, in a more combative area which was once a part of independent Brittany.

The image of the Loire Valley held by other French people is of a deeply bourgeois culture still, and a strongly Catholic one. Church attendance remains relatively high on Sundays. The towns, though, have been swinging between the Right and the Left recently. In the 2001 local elections, to the whole country's surprise, the flamboyant socialist minister Jack Lang lost control of Blois, while traditionally deeply conservative Saumur amazed everyone even more, electing an ecologist as mayor. Economically, unemployment as everywhere in France became an increasing problem in the 1990s. But the Loire Valley has some very solid business strengths. The Orléanais benefits from its proximity to Paris, taking the overspill from the capital and offering space for green-field sites. The cosmetics industry flourishes here, to such an extent that one area next to Orléans has been comically nicknamed Cosmetics Valley. Selling the Loire's history has, of course, become a major part of the valley's economy since the war, and the Blésois, Touraine and Anjou have profited enormously from the tourist boom. At the same time, the high-speed French trains, the TGVs, have brought the major Loire towns much closer to the capital, encouraging people to move around more easily; some even commute daily from Tours to Paris, for instance, able to return to the peace of the Loire every evening. In 1996, the pope came to Tours, along with his special *papamobile* car. He came to celebrate the past, and the 16th centenary of the death of Gregory's hero, St Martin.

Art and Architecture

04

Introduction: Architecture that's Not Quite as Empty as You May Think

Architecture stands head and shoulders above the other arts in the Loire. But can we just forget for a while the gracious and turreted 16th-century châteaux, their ever-so-pretty heads vainly reflected in rivers, and hold off fantasizing about Chenonceau, Chambord and Azay-le-Rideau just for a few moments? Loire architecture isn't simply about the so-called French Renaissance châteaux. The region has a rich legacy of 500 years of well-preserved remains from before their time, with one of the densest concentrations in France of fine medieval architecture.

In fact, the Loire experienced three great periods of architecture; very roughly speaking these are: the Romanesque, in the 11th and 12th centuries; the Gothic, emerging from around the mid- to late 12th and lasting to the very end of the 15th century; and the French Renaissance, through the 16th century, after which grandiose building projects grew less common, although there are some notable exceptions. As well as the secular architecture – the fortified castles, the more delicate châteaux and the boastfully ornate town houses – religious architecture was prominent in each period. The Church, after all, was a massively powerful multinational in those times, commissioning a wealth of new building. Along the Loire Valley you'll find a few fine cathedrals, the remains of extensive abbeys, great churches, and splendid little chapels. Crude capital carvings, delicate rib-vaulting, more or less naive statues of saints, the odd more sophisticated tomb or reliquary, even some rich tapestries, all add visual interest to these spiritual houses. Stained-glass windows contribute further to the religious and decorative effects, although many of the original works in this art were lost through time and periods of violence; the Hundred Years' War, the French Wars of Religion, the Revolution and Second World War bombings destroyed substantial amounts of Loire art and architecture.

What happened to all the original art that adorned the château interiors? Time and again you'll be reminded by guides on visits that up until the Bourbons, the courts and courtiers rushed from one property to another, taking their prized possessions with them in chests. Then there is the recurring problem of the French Revolution; some castles were ransacked, others were sold, and thus many were emptied as aristocrats fled into exile abroad. Some châteaux lost their lives, dismembered, in many cases, a fair few years after the Revolution. A good number of others suffered the ignominy of becoming barracks or prisons. However, people tend to underestimate the number that actually remained relatively unscathed, or that reverted to aristocratic proprietors; and in recent times, regional authorities that have acquired others have worked hard to promote their châteaux in the battle for tourist numbers, revamping the interiors with important acquisitions. Artefacts from châteaux were also saved and pooled in certain cases, and the fine arts museums in both Orléans and Tours, for example, contain extravagant works plucked from châteaux.

A brief word of warning about that broad term 'château' in French – this can refer just as well to a massive medieval fort as to a dainty morceau of Ancien Régime masonry. And be on the lookout for the occasional towering donjon, the word for a keep, not a dungeon, the centrepiece of the *château-fort*, or fortress. As to the building materials used for châteaux and noble houses, in the east of the area covered in this guide, brick was used as readily as stone, and the masons became quite playful with it, incorporating motifs in darker brick. Moving westwards, lime-stone, *the* Loire stone *par excellence*, soon comes to dominate the architectural scene, the buildings generally topped by slate roofing. Only around Angers, where the slate was quarried, does limestone give way to a darker, ugly-named stone, schist, often used in grand Anjou buildings with a mixture of limestone.

Prehistory–AD 1000

Very little remains of Loire architecture or art from before the year 1000, but the legacy of neolithic civilization in the region, in the form of dolmens, can be found scattered around, notably in the Saumurois, southern Touraine and southwestern Anjou. One of the most impressive, and the largest, of the so-called Angevin dolmens is now captured within a café's confines, the **dolmen de Bagneux** on the southern outskirts of Saumur. The **Château du Grand-Pressigny** in southern Touraine has an interesting museum on prehistory.

Although the major Loire cities grew out of the most important settlements formed by the Gauls, developing considerably after the Roman invasion, virtually nothing from Celtic times has survived, and very few vestiges of Gallo-Roman civilization along the Loire remain. **Gennes** has an overgrown amphitheatre, the **Château de Pont-Chevron** a couple of period mosaics, **Luynes** the arches of a relatively low aque-duct, **Cinq-Mars-la-Pile** a funerary tower, and **Thésée-la-Romaine** remnants of a market as well as a little museum, but these are pretty small affairs. Hardly anything made it through the pillaging and devastation wrought by the hordes of invaders in the late Gallo-Roman period and the much later raids of the Vikings. One superb cache, though, unearthed at Neuvy-en-Sullias, contained splendid animal-deities sculpted in bronze, probably from the 2nd century, now displayed in the Musée Archéologique in **Orléans**.

The great religious buildings of the first millennium have also disappeared, leaving us with the Dark Ages. One colourful exception of a fragment survives at **Germigny-des-Prés**, the rare early 9th-century Carolingian church, originally built to a Greek cross plan and with one apse still decorated with a blue and gold mosaic showing angels surrounding the Ark of the Covenant, God's hand reaching down from the sky.

Military Architecture at the Start of the Second Millennium

Suddenly, from the start of the second Christian millennium solid stone structures went up in large numbers and many have survived. The Angevin count Foulques Nerra, at the end of the 10th century and the start of the 11th, left his mark on the

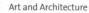

region in the form of a ring of towering donjons, square stone defensive keeps. This type of architecture superseded the earth-mound, wood-fenced forts of the previous period, the latter inevitably more temporary constructions. Many of the stone keeps in this new military fashion have crumbled, but important ones dating back to the 11th and 12th centuries can be seen along the Loire west from Orléans, with **Loches** (the most interesting), **Beaugency** and **Montrichard** counting among the finest examples. These are impressive, severe-looking pieces of architecture, with sheer, cliff-like walls, particularly dramatic when jackdaws circle round them. There's some debate as to whether the oldest stone keep in France is the impressive one being restored at Montbazon, or the more dilapidated one at Langeais, dated by some to the very end of the 10th century. The skeletal keep at Le Grand-Pressigny, another fine example, again within a later château's walls, dates from the 12th century.

Romanesque Architecture and Art

Generally, the image of Romanesque architecture is of squat little churches with rounded arches and rounded apses, lost in the countryside. In this part of France, these charming rural churches are often crowned by a slate-covered tower which looks like a tough, pointed helmet, giving them a slightly defensive look. Dark inside, with few window openings and fat arches supporting barrel vaults, their walls and pillars would originally have been decorated, the walls with two-dimensional paintings in shades of ochre depicting mainly New Testament Biblical scenes, the pillar capitals carved with a weirder, warring medieval menagerie, including stylized depictions of mythical creatures and frequent references to that ever-so-influential book in the early medieval period, *The Revelation to John*, alias *The Apocalypse*.

The best example of surviving Romanesque wall paintings can be found in the church of St-Nicolas at **Tavant**, the curves of the tiny room serving to impart a rare degree of movement to the figures. In fact, the Vienne valley region near Chinon, where you'll find St-Nicolas, has the distinction of a number of more or less restored Romanesque churches with murals. Other significant, if sometimes small, remnants of busy, gauche, yet powerful Romanesque art can be seen at the crypt of St-Aignan in **Orléans**, that of St-Aignan in **St-Aignan-sur-Cher**, St-Jean-du-Liget near **Loches**, and the Préfecture of **Angers**.

But while the widespread image of Romanesque church architecture may be of small-scale buildings, in the Loire Valley the period saw some truly remarkable and substantial religious architecture. You just have to look at the height and bulk of the Tour Charlemagne in **Tours** to picture the vastness of the edifice of which it once formed a part. Or most famously, admire the entrance tower to the abbey church of **St-Benoît-sur-Loire**. This influential building is propped up by superbly decorated capitals from the end of the 11th century.

At this time and from the beginning of the next century (when the Crusades began) other vast edifices were being erected to reinforce the power of the Church at home: **Fontevraud**'s abbey church, Le Ronceray in **Angers**, the church of Notre-Dame in

Cunault, St-Laumer (now St-Nicolas) in **Blois**, St-Mexme in **Chinon**, Notre-Dame-de-Nantilly in **Saumur**...these were impressive works, reflecting the might of the Church. Although on the whole sombre, architecturally they brought in innovations, generally from southwest France, in various ways, developing the height and space of church building and, in particular, the expansion of the choir end. Fontevraud's abbey church interior is spanned by a row of cupolas. Several other churches, such as Le Ronceray and Notre-Dame in Cunault, adopted a new, hall style, with aisles reaching to same height as the nave. Notre-Dame-de-Nantilly used the altogether simpler plan of an aisle-less nave. St-Ours in **Loches** adopted a unique feature, its nave bays topped by a roof with pyramidal towers, dubbed *dubes*.

Some of these grandiose churches were more highly decorated than others; the church of Cunault had hundreds of carvings on its capitals. St-Nicolas was given some fine decoration, as were two further churches not so far mentioned, that of Notre-Dame of **Beaugency**, with its delightful choir ambulatory, and that of **Candes-St-Martin**. This last was built on the spot where the great French saint Martin had died in the 4th century. Pilgrimage, and relics in particular, motivated large numbers to travel to spots like this in the Middle Ages, and you can see at the church of Candes-St-Martin how the splendidly ornate porch, miraculously held up in the middle by just one slender finger of a column, faces the Loire, as though to greet and amaze the pilgrims, many of whom would have arrived by boat and walked up from the quays. One of the major routes to Santiago de Compostela passed this way, the Route d'Or. Architecture could be highly practical at that time too. The kitchen of the abbey of Fontevraud, although its mushrooming silhouette and scaly roof may not be entirely true to the original, shows how the builders of the period could mix invention with practicality.

Bourges and Anjou Vault into Gothic Forms

The most extraordinary development in religious architecture in the region in the 12th century occurred at two cathedrals. With its five statue-filled portals on the front and its ranks of flying buttresses, St-Etienne in Bourges ranks as one of the very finest cathedrals in Christendom, a rival to Chartres, which was begun at the same time, at the close of the 12th century.

The cathedral of St-Maurice in Angers was where the Angevin vault was born a little earlier in the century. This splendidly elegant vaulting, with its particularly light look, spread far and wide as a model, but the finest examples are to be found in Anjou, and Angers in particular. The church of St-Serge in Angers, the remnant of the abbey of Asnières and the church of Le Puy-Notre-Dame (built to honour a relic of the girdle of the Virgin Mary, a typical object of veneration in the medieval period) all show off the style. As well as its novel vaulting, Angers' cathedral contains some of the oldest stained-glass windows along the Loire. The tombs of Henri Plantagenêt, his wife Eleanor of Aquitaine and their son Richard the Lionheart lie serenely not in Angers, but in the abbey church of Fontevraud.

Early Medieval Secular Architecture

Interestingly, the greatest example of Angevin vaulting is in a secular building, one of the oldest hospitals to survive in France, the Hôpital St-Jean in **Angers**, ordered by Henri Plantagenêt to be run by lay authorities. The vaulting and slender columns combine to create surely one of the lightest pieces of architecture of medieval times. In stark, heavy contrast, one of Henri Plantagenêt's greatest power bases was the **Château de Chinon**. Although the buildings have mostly disappeared, the series of fortified walls and ditches remain extraordinarily impressive, reckoned to have formed the largest fortress in Europe for its time.

The early medieval châteaux were formidable *châteaux forts*. None of these fortresses along the Loire looks more impenetrable than the **Château d'Angers**, with its heavy schist walls and elephantine towers, constructed to help guard the border of the royal territories against Brittany. Sharing its mix of schist and tufa constructions, the **Château du Plessis-Macé** in Anjou acted as a further regional outpost. To the east, the knobbly towered exterior of the **Château de Luynes** in Touraine also dates back to the 13th century.

For the next couple of centuries, châteaux would remain defensive military strongholds, with sturdy corner towers, high guards' walkways (*chemins de ronde*) with machicolations through which to throw down projectiles, arrow slits for windows, and drawbridge-protected entrances. But gradually they would be constructed with a little more consideration to comfort and refinement, using neater blocks of stone, letting in a bit more light, and allowing a bit more room for good living. Some Loire châteaux are curious and charming accretions from various centuries, of course, such as the delightful **Château de Montrésor** or the fabulously turreted **Château de Montreuil-Bellay**, itself set within the 15th-century town walls that have survived.

Louis d'Anjou's Artistic Commissions

Exquisite pieces of decorative art started being made for the lords who lived within the region's strongholds. The second half of the 14th century saw the making of some of the finest medieval French art, brought on by brotherly rivalry between the sons of King Jean le Bon. This was while the first part of the Hundred Years' War was raging and the Black Plague was striking regular terror into the populace. Louis, who became Duc d'Anjou, concerns us most here. His brother, Jean Duc de Berry, would have some of the greatest châteaux of the times portrayed in one of the most famous and fabulous of all medieval manuscripts, the *Très Riches Heures du Duc de Berry*. Among the depictions, the splendid silhouette of the **Château de Saumur** stands out, with its Disney-inspiring magical look, built for Louis d'Anjou after 1360. The second monumental work this lord commissioned, in the 1370s, was a tapestry cycle of the **Apocalypse**, made in Paris in Nicolas Bataille's studios after the cartoons of Jean Bondol, court painter to King Charles V. The tapestry, most often housed in Angers when it wasn't on tour, now hangs imprisoned in the château there. Tapestry had become popular in the medieval period, the methods of weaving brought over from the East. This art form would be commonly adopted in châteaux through to the Revolution to help adorn, embellish and even warm chambers. The attention to detail and the colours of the tapestry of the Apocalypse reflect some of the qualities of illuminated manuscript, the major painting form of the period (panel painting would only become popular a little later). The other great piece of art we owe to Louis d'Anjou's massive wealth is relatively miniature – he had a piece of Christ's **True Cross**, which had been brought back to the region in the mid-13th-century by an Angevin Crusader, wholly inappropriately and extravagantly smothered in precious jewels (see p.415).

In Bourges, Louis d'Anjou's equally extravagant brother, the cruel Jean de Berry, commissioned fabulous art, the most famous remaining vestige being his tomb, in **Bourges cathedral**.

Outstanding among the châteaux of this century, apart from Saumur, is the **Château de Sully**, like the former reflected in the Loire. It's thought that Raymond du Temple, the architect to Charles VI whose name is most commonly associated with the Louvre, played a part in this splendid construction, much added to during later centuries.

The Royal Family Moves to the Loire in the 15th Century

After the would-be Charles VII ran off to the Loire, court in tow, to escape the English army's arrival to fight the second half of the Hundred Years' War, the Loire Valley became the main base of the French royals until the 1520s. This led to an extraordinary flowering of architecture and art along the Loire. While most of the buildings of this period have had their interiors emptied, many of the exteriors, although often tampered with or substantially altered or amputated, still stand. During this time of the Loire Valley kings, a massively important new artistic influence would arrive from Italy at the very end of the 15th century, spelling the end of Gothic and the transformation to the so-called Renaissance style, reviving and developing models found in the ancient Greek and Roman worlds.

Each king wanted to stamp his mark on his own palatial homes. Charles VII, having spent a stint in his uncle's city of Bourges, developed the châteaux of **Chinon** and **Loches**, both rather vacant now, but still full of atmosphere. Louis XI favoured the **Château du Plessis-lès-Tours** and the **Château de Langeais**, the first reduced to a sad stump, the second grimly grey on the outside, but containing perhaps the finest and most colourfully varied collection of tapestries of any Loire château, albeit not from the period but gathered together at much later date. Charles VIII moved his full attentions to the **Château d'Amboise**, where he had been brought up and which the previous two kings had been slowly expanding. He also added a wing to the Château de Loches. Louis XII, from a different branch of the royal lineage, transferred the builders of Amboise to the **Château de Blois**. François I was such an oversized character that not surprisingly he's associated with countless châteaux, including the expansion of the Château de Blois and the Château d'Amboise (although it was his mother, Louise de Savoie, who really saw to the development of the latter), and of course the construction of the totally new and totally absurd but awe-inspiring **Château de Chambord**. But before considering the transition architecture of places like Chambord, let's focus on the beautiful elaboration of late Gothic.

15th-century Religious Architecture and Art

In terms of religious architecture in this royal period along the Loire, Louis XI's deep anxieties left the greatest marks, most notably through encouraging the completion of the **Basilique Notre-Dame-de-Cléry**, where he was buried, but also by helping to pay for the expansion of such churches as Notre-Dame-de-Nantheuil in **Montrichard** and Notre-Dame-de-Nantilly in **Saumur**. The late Gothic jewel of a chapel at the **Château d'Amboise** also stands out among royal commissions. Other aristocrats had chapels built or embellished for themselves and sometimes the community. Death encouraged fine art; artistic attention was lavished on the tombs of the ultra-wealthy royals and aristocrats. In many cases they were badly damaged during the Wars of Religion or the Revolution, as for example the tomb of Jean de Berry in **Bourges** or that of Agnès Sorel at **Loches**. Sadly, little religious art in the form of panel painting from this period has remained in the Loire. A couple of exceptions do stand out. Nondescript **Nouans-les-Fontaines** in eastern Touraine mysteriously boasts a rare painting by Jean Fouquet, Charles VII's court painter, often considered the first known great French painter. His *Deposition of Christ* is a vast and harrowing work. The **Château de Loches** contains a triptych attributed to another outstanding period painter, Jean Bourdichon.

The great court composer of the late 15th century, who wrote for three French kings, was Johannes Ockeghem, an example of the Flemish influence of the times, the inter-twining of voices in his music somewhat comparable to the intriguing tracery of late Gothic church windows.

15th-century Châteaux and Civic Architecture

While grand Gothic religious architecture seemed very carefully and geometrically planned, secular architecture appeared less meticulously and mathematically conceived in the late Gothic period. Certainly symmetry of façades and windows wasn't a major concern as it was in important Gothic churches and would be gener-ally in the new Renaissance style. But the style was often wonderfully exuberant.

The Loire châteaux of the period were particularly distinguished by their prettifying towers and *lucarnes*, the latter the pointed dormer windows reaching increasingly extravagantly skywards through the slate roofs. Many courtiers would build country seats to suit their rank. The **Château de Baugé** offers a typical example of early 15th-century architecture, built for Le Bon Roi René's parents, and one of his favourite residences. The **Château du Plessis-Bourré** is the image of an ordered late medieval castle, constructed between 1468 and 1473 for Louis XI's most trusted minister. On a square plan, marked with round towers on each corner, encircled by the protective belt of a moat, its flat walls dotted with mullion windows, it is one of finest examples of the well-planned late Gothic castle. From a little earlier, the remnant of the **Château de Montsoreau** is another example of the period, with typical *lucarnes* breaking through the slate roofs. The **Château de Chaumont**, majestically situated in woods above the Loire, bears typical late Gothic punning symbols on its massive entrance towers, reached by a drawbridge.

Most interior decoration inside these late Gothic châteaux has been lost, except for travelling chests. **Le Plessis-Bourré** is one of the 15th-century castles to have retained some original wall paintings, with its shocking painted ceiling. At the dilapidated **Château de Pimpéan**, it's the chapel that has retained its murals. Often the private chapels or oratories attached to the castles constitute their most ornate and best-preserved rooms. The **Château de Montreuil-Bellay**, for example, has a ceiling on which angels still sing – apparently to a tune by a Scottish composer! It's not usual to think of brick châteaux in the Loire Valley, but there are quite a number to the east, the **Château de Gien**, with its mysterious brick patterns, and the **Château du Moulin**, one of the most romantically moated of all Loire châteaux, among the finest.

Courtly towns grew up around the royal châteaux, becoming wealthy from the demand for luxury goods. You can admire a particularly important, dense and pictur-esque set of late medieval houses in **Chinon**. Here, as in the old courtly and mercantile quarters of Tours and Blois, the Gothic staircases attached to the exterior in the form of towers make the urban architecture particularly appealing. Playful, often lewd, Gothic carved figures clamber up the outer beams of some of the grandest town houses. Jesters play their tricks on the Maison des Acrobates in **Blois**, while a riot of figures and carvings attack the façade of the Maison d'Adam in **Angers**, both amazing examples of this kind of house.

Transition Architecture from Late Gothic to French Renaissance

The late Gothic was often exuberant, imaginative, playful. The châteaux which began to fuse traditional French forms with newer Italian-inspired features at the start of the 16th century would cling on to certain cherished forms, although the Renaissance would, in general, reduce the imaginative play – and the potential for utterly charming chaos – of the great French 15th century.

With some of the late medieval châteaux, the kind of decorative but indecorous carving seen on the outside of some late Gothic town houses can be viewed inside, particularly in carved *culs-de-lampe* at the bottom of vaults or ribs. Even **Azay-le-Rideau**'s kitchen shows a stone dog chewing on a bone, and a bare bottom sticking out prominently into the air, while the **Château d'Amboise** conceals a wealth of comic grotesques. 'Filthy' Gothic forms did live on, even in the clean-up act of the Renaissance.

Family heraldic devices, charged symbols (the most famous and repeated royal ones being the fleur-de-lys for all, the ermine's tail and Franciscan cords for Anne de Bretagne, the porcupine for Louis XII, the salamander for François I, the arrow-pierced swan for his mother, Louise de Savoie, and the full ermine for his wife, Claude de France) and intertwined initials, particularly over door entrances or on the monumental fireplaces (which added grace and warmth to so many château interiors) also survived for some time in the shift from one style to another. The Loire *lucarnes* not only stayed a while, but also became increasingly ornate as late Gothic gave way to Renaissance. Sometimes they bore arms or allegorical symbols.

Perhaps the greatest distinguishing feature of French Gothic secular architecture, the tower – either in the form of the solid round towers of defence or of the spiral staircases set out from the building – survived for a time as well. The apogee of the Gothic tower is to be seen at the **Château d'Amboise**, the massive Tour des Minimes and Tour Heurtault, 20m in diameter, built at the very end of the 15th century and large enough to allow carriages to ascend the 150m of ramps within.

Even several of the greatest so-called French Renaissance châteaux of the Loire, **Chenonceau**, **Azay-le-Rideau** and **Villandry**, retained pieces of Gothic towers, in the case of the first two separated from the main building. **Chambord**'s corners were marked by the largest towers of all. Some châteaux juxtaposed late Gothic forms with the Renaissance, such as the **Château d'Ussé** and the **Château de Blois**. The last, along with Chambord, contains the most extravagant stair tower on the Loire – both feats of architecture in their own right.

These buildings also reflect a set of new, derivative influences. Built (or started in Chenonceau's case) in the first half of the 16th century, they actually combine French Gothic and Italian Renaissance forms. In the last decade of the 15th century Charles VIII had rushed hot-headedly off to Italy with his army to lay claim to certain inheritances there. Seduced by the Italian way of living, he tried to bring some of it back with him, not only in the form of booty, but also in the form of artists. Among the first wave of Italians imported into the Loire to put an Italian stamp on French architecture were Domenico da Cortona and Fra Giocondo, not to mention the landscape gardener Dom Pacello da Mercoliagno. Charles VIII's successor, Louis XII, added further French royal claims on Italy, and further Italian influences were carried back after his failed invasion. François I continued the trend. Courtiers started to change the styles of their houses.

One of the clearest examples of the way Italianate features were absorbed into Loire architecture is provided by the François I wing at the **Château de Blois**, built by the 1520s. You can see how several ultramontane details have encroached: on the inner side, in the network of horizontal bands dividing up the façade and diminishing the vertical lines, in the heavily decorated cornice, in the putti in niches and in the openwork of the staircase; on the outer side, in the rows of loggias imitating what was going on in Rome. These elements are grafted onto French Gothic. The façades are stamped with the salamander symbols, the putti are placed in the typical Loire *lucarnes*, and, most outstanding of all, the great stair tower protrudes proudly from the building.

Like a nanny tidying up the mess after children have been playing, or as in Rabelais' *Gargantua* (written around this time) when the humanist teacher comes to impose order on the chaotic studies of the initially unruly giant, the Renaissance would quickly tame the exuberant, show-off delight of late Gothic. Of course, behind the Italian forms lay higher ideals of harmony and order. The most famous Italian import of them all had the most advanced mind of his time. **Leonardo da Vinci** was enticed over by François I to Amboise, where the genius died in 1519. He may have been involved in the planning of the **Château de Chambord**, which had just got underway, with its ingenious stair tower, its extravagant roofscape and its stamp of massive royal power. Its great Greek cross form (normally reserved for churches) combined with that of the typical square fortress was deliberately built in the middle of a forest teeming with game. Sadly, of the many great works of art that François I collected to decorate his palaces, none are left in the Loire.

Many smaller Gothic-to-Renaissance buildings lie scattered around the countryside, a few lesser-known ones open to visitors, like the charming **Château de Villesavin**, hidden in woods. Also near to Cheverny, **Troussay**, a *gentilhommière* rather than a château, offers a good example of the kind of home that noblemen a step down the social ladder had built for themselves in this transition period. (Inside, Troussay lovingly preserves a collection of wonderful Renaissance scraps.)

The **Château de Villandry**, back among the most famous châteaux of the period, is now particularly celebrated for its formal gardens (actually an early 20th-century re-creation of a Renaissance garden). The **Château de Chamerolles** and the **Château de Beauregard** count among other châteaux to have recent Renaissance-style *jardins*. The carefully planned garden had developed in medieval monasteries in France, but Italian finesse imposed further influences which came to dominate in the châteaux. Many aristocratic Loire homes were surrounded by ultra-neat *parterres* laid out in carefully controlled geometric patterns, such as those also to be seen at the **Château de Chenonceau**. Delightful château chapels are another place where you can often admire Italianate touches. The chapel of the **Château d'Ussé** offers a fine example of the Renaissance in the Loire. Greatest of all in this sphere is the chapel of the **Château de Champigny-sur-Veude**. Most of this château has been pulled down, but the chapel survives with its period stained glass.

The Renaissance stamped its mark on religious architecture in towns and villages as well, for example in the tops of Tours cathedral's towers, or with the work of Jean de l'Espine in Angers. The **abbey of Fontevraud** was substantially altered to reflect the new fashion and given the largest Renaissance cloister in France, with a painted chapterhouse to boot. Rich tombs continued to be commissioned. Anne de Bretagne ordered a particularly moving tomb for her children, which now lies in **Tours cathedral**, reckoned to be a joint work of the much respected Tours sculptor Michel Colombe and an Italian artist. Colombe's name crops up on several occasions as an admired Loire artist. Other examples of funerary art for aristocrats can be seen in chapels close to châteaux, for example at Montrésor or Gizeux.

This early 16th-century period of transition left many delightful and particularly memorable buildings. But was the French Renaissance a good thing for Loire architecture? It depends on your taste, of course, but the exuberance, eccentricity and individuality that the late Gothic exhibited is hard to surpass even if, intellectually and mathematically, the Renaissance appears more robust. On reflection, the majority of great Loire châteaux date from the time just before rigid Renaissance discipline had imposed itself on the French imagination, when the fusion of late Gothic and Renaissance produced marvellous results.

In literature, the beautiful mixing of classical forms and the French language counted among the aims of the so-called Pléiade poets, including two great Loire writers, Joachim du Bellay and Pierre de Ronsard, the latter arguably the greatest lyric poet in French, a marvel to read, his verse flowing like a majestic river.

The Second French Renaissance

The châteaux of what the French sometimes refer to as the *seconde Renaissance*, roughly speaking in the second half of the 16th century, are more sober than those of the first. Examples in the Loire Valley include the **Château de Beauregard** and the central section of the **Château du Grand-Pressigny**. This architecture looks much more restrained, and rather duller. However, the most exciting addition to Loire Valley castles in this period produced the most enticing of all French châteaux – the **Château de Chenonceau**, whose wing spanning the river Cher was commissioned by the Queen Mother of the time, Catherine de' Medici, in the 1570s. The controlled elegance of the bays contrasts with the unpredictable shimmering light thrown up it from the water below. Jacques Androuet du Cerceau, both architect in Orléans and recorder of royal châteaux, executed splendid black-and-white bird's-eye drawings of this and other French royal châteaux at the end of the 16th century, giving an excellent idea of their forms in that time, and of their gardens. Some fine Renaissance town façades survive too, notably in Blois and Tours.

A much less well-known and less refined piece of art thought to date from the mid- to late 16th century survived underground in the **Caves Sculptées de Denezé**, the carvings seemingly crammed with satirical or critical references to contemporary politics. The limestone in many parts of the Loire Valley had long been exploited for town and château building; the quarries were then used for storage and, in the coming centuries, increasingly for housing. Some of the oldest, most diverse troglodyte housing in the Loire Valley can be seen along the Loire east of Saumur and along the Cher around Bourré. As for the **Château de Brézé**, recently opened to the public, it boasts not just 16th-century architecture, but also the most impressive underground world of the lot.

The Classical Period of the 17th and 18th Centuries

Great architecture didn't simply fizzle out in the Loire after the Renaissance. Several splendid Loire châteaux date from the 17th century, reflecting developments in classical forms. The Mannerist **Château de Brissac**, breaking out of medieval chains, the supremely ordered Gaston d'Orléans wing of the **Château de Blois** by the illustrious François Mansart, and the **Château de Cheverny**, the last perhaps the most perfect of the Loire châteaux, all date from the first half of the 17th century. Cheverny has retained outrageously rich interiors, Jean Mosnier the main painter-cum-interior decorator associated with it, as well as one of the finest art collections in a Loire château. Some of Brissac's beams are also smothered with a mass of miniature landscapes.

A much grander Loire château than Cheverny once held a far more extraordinary art collection, one of the most important ever gathered in Europe by an individual. That man was Armand du Plessis, the Cardinal de Richelieu. Only one measly pavilion of his vast 1630s home remains, but the model new town of **Richelieu**, a utopian geometric plan, with a staggering covered market place and a noble church, stands almost intact, if a little desolate, in southern Touraine. The innumerable works of art collected in the château were dispersed. Some of the finest, such as Michel-angelo's *Dying Slaves*, were packed off to the Louvre, while a fair number, including the paintings of the elements seen through aristocratic fantasies by Deruet, ended up in the excellent Orléans Fine Arts Museum, which also houses a rich collection of 18th-century religious paintings seized from local religious establishments during the Revolution.

An interesting development down the centuries was the popularity of the portrait. It became a trend in certain swanky homes to commission a whole room full of portraits of famous men. The **Château de Beauregard** contains one of these portrait galleries, offering a visual history of great men (and their fashions) over several centuries. The Château de Blois displays works from other such portrait galleries.

Some châteaux developed as a mix of parts from different centuries, for example the delightful **Château du Gué-Péan**, where the mid-16th-century form, including one very eccentric bell-shaped tower, encloses a 17th-century hunting lodge. Most splen-didly harrowing, the chapel within the elegant mix of tufa and schist of the **Château de Serrant** displays a family tomb by the sculptor Coysevoix. Serrant also has the rare distinction of a park landscaped in the English style. Still more exaggerated in emotion than Serrant's tomb, one of the most compellingly hideous mixes of sickly-sweet and morbid art you're likely to have the shock of encountering hangs out in the church of **Châteauneuf-sur-Loire**.

Little art exists around the Loire Valley from the Ancien Régime except that produced for or portraying aristocrats. One exception meriting attention is the 17th-century engravings by Abraham Bosse, displayed in the museum of fine art in his home town of **Tours**. Bosse's works not only show prissy people at art and play in a renowned allegorical series on the senses, they also depict a wide variety of profes-sions and backgrounds.

Many Loire châteaux have undergone facelifts and aesthetic cuts in their time. In the 17th and 18th centuries several were altered in the same manner – one wing demolished to open up their views – two of the most obvious examples being the **Château d'Ussé** (also given a whole extra 17th-century wing out of keeping with the rest), and the **Château de Chaumont**. At the start of the 18th century, Roger de

Gaignières charmingly illustrated many Loire châteaux and religious edifices as they looked in his day.

Town and village houses of both the 17th and 18th centuries survive, but you'll find very few grand buildings from the 18th century in the Loire Valley. Worthy of mention is the elongated Loire-side **Château de Ménars** (not open to the public), while all that remains of the even longer **Château de Chanteloup is** its adorable, clownish pagoda. One fine château from this period does survive almost intact inside as well as out, though: the **Château de Montgeoffroy** dates from just before the French Revolution, built for the Marquis de Contade, the table still set as though it has just been left. Another château which displays the finery and new refinements of the century inside is the **Château de Talcy**, but its outer forms are much older.

Jacques V Gabriel left his mark on the cityscape of **Blois** in the 18th century, designing, among other things, the most elegant bridge over the Loire. To see more of 17th- and 18th-century painting and sculpture, the fine arts of museums of Orléans, Blois, Tours and Angers merit a visit. And go to the **Château de Gien** to admire a collection of hunting paintings by royal-commissioned Desportes and Oudry among the many topical precious objects on display.

Catholicism Triumphant

In the period between the Wars of Religion and the Revolution, combative Catholic architecture was used as another instrument to crush Protestantism. Henri IV, the king at the end of the Wars of Religion, did however try to patch up differences and supported the rebuilding of the Protestant-bombed **cathedral of Orléans** in the outdated but original Gothic style. But after Henri IV, the centralizing powers used church construction and the foundation of new religious orders as important means of reinforcing Catholicism. The one-time Loire Protestant capital **Saumur** was swamped with Catholic propaganda, including a Catholic pilgrimage church with an enormous and spectacular breast of a dome, Notre-Dame des Ardilliers. **Blois'** church of St-Vincent-de-Paul is a typically overdone piece of Jesuit Counter-Reformation grandeur, and the town's Cathédrale St-Louis offers the curious sight of a late 17th-century Gothic form. Dating from the early 18th-century, the **abbey of Pontlevoy** looks as much like a military school as a religious establishment. Still more surprising are the Ancien Régime parts of the **Chartreuse du Liget**, a foundation in the forests east of Loches with ruins dating back to Henri Plantagenêt's time.

19th-century Nostalgia

The 18th century ended, of course, with the French Revolution, which attacked châteaux and churches as part of the political action. Many major châteaux and religious buildings went through a terrible period during the Revolution and the Napoleonic era which followed so fast on its heels. Some châteaux were destroyed. Several were turned into prisons or barracks, their fabric scarcely respected by their new inhabitants. Some were sold off, only to be dismantled by entrepreneurs who would sell the stone.

On a more edifying note, many of the leading men of the first half of the 19th century are recalled in David d'Angers' medallions. He also sculpted many historic heroes for various French towns, including Le Bon Roi René for Angers. But his most famous work is the sculpture on the tomb of Bonchamps at **St-Florent-le-Vieil**, one of the most powerful and moving of images of the century, recalling one rare charitable moment in the terribly violent and divisive anti-Republican Guerre de Vendée. A vast range of more diverse types is brought to life in Balzac's fictional *Comédie Humaine*, a huge interconnecting series of novels set in this period, many of them in the Loire Valley.

Another writer, Prosper Mérimée, as minister of culture, went around the country in the middle of the century frantically making lists of the great mass of French architectural heritage that needed to be saved. After the terrifying and exhausting fantasies for the future in the aftermath of the Revolution, the French looked back nostalgically to the past. Commemorative work came into its own, especially recalling the unifying, strong heroine Joan of Arc. Romanticization of the past included building neo-Gothic and neo-Renaissance châteaux and restoring the real things more or less successfully. René Hodé was particularly prolific in Anjou, creating new castles in the countryside. Joly-Leterme was a rather less successful restorer in most cases. Rather better than him were de la Morandière and Sanson, both of whom did their neo-Gothic best, for example, on the **Château de Chaumont**, Sanson adding the monumental stables. The most famous name in Loire restoration work is undoubtedly Félix Duban, who led the restoration of the **Château de Blois**, both inside and out. Of course, it's understandable that the period's proprietors wished to install some modern comforts, so don't be surprised to bump into the odd heating system, even a lift in the Château de Serrant, while at the frankly over-bulky Château de Brissac the *châtelaine* removed one floor to install a theatre!

New civic projects were instigated, especially the opening up of major arteries or boulevards, following the example of Haussman in Paris, while the railways also demanded new provisions from mid-century. **Tours**, for example, boasts the most splendid railway, by Victor Laloux. Laloux also designed the Romano-Byzantine new basilica of St-Martin in the city and the Hôtel de Ville (and, more famously, the Gare d'Orsay in Paris). The Tours Hôtel de Ville entrance is held up by vast telamons, the work of the Tourangeau sculptor François Sicard, quite well represented in the region, who worked into the early 20th century. One notable project which combined engineering with art and which is associated with the name of the great Gustave Eiffel is the supremely elegant Pont-Canal de Briare.

Stained glass revived as an art, with the likes of Lobin decorating **Blois cathedral**, and the churches of Les Mauges commissioning much work to commemorate the pro-Catholic uprising of the Guerre de Vendée, most notably at the church of Le Pin-en-Mauges. At **Blois** and **Gien**, pottery thrived, Gien's production still well known, while in **Briare** tiles for mosaics and more prosaic uses became an important local industry.

20th Century

In postwar times, the distinguishing feature, rather than innovation, has perhaps been the demonstration of greater respect for the Loire's rich legacy. There have been disasters too, such as the 1950s concrete bunker in which **Angers'** Apocalypse tapestry was placed, but the city can be proud of one of the most successful transformations of a partly ruined church building in Pierre Prunet's conversion of the Eglise Toussaint into the David d'Angers museum.

In the Loire-side cities many of the stained-glass windows were blown out during war bombing. The name of Max Ingrand crops up time and again in the work to replace them. For example, he did many of the windows for **Gien's** church of Ste-Jeanne d'Arc, an interesting brick-patterned reconstruction in a town that was devastated, with modern ceramic saints from the Gien pottery factory.

Two places focus particularly on novel 20th-century art forms: the Musée du Gemmail in **Tours**, where paintings, often by famous artists such as Picasso, are interpreted in a new light in shards of stained glass; and the Musée de l'Objet in **Blois**, with challenging presentations of – yes – objects. There are artists' studios dotted all around the Loire and exhibition spaces such as the Centre de Création Contemporaine in Tours and the Bouvet-Ladubay gallery in St-Hilaire-St-Florent near Saumur. Few are more curious than the troglodyte homes of Richard Rak and Jacques Warminski in **Anjou**, the latter referred to as *l'Hélice terrestre*, a more-or-less successful work of art outside and in. A few pieces of modern architecture stand out in Orléans and Tours, notably the new baseball-hatted conference centre by Jean Nouvel (who designed the extraordinary Institut du Monde Arabe in Paris) in **Tours**. The art of modern and futuristic gardening is celebrated at the annual international garden festival of the Château de Chaumont, with some garden designs that look like prototypes not simply for the 21st century on this planet, but for a different planet altogether.

Topics

The Loire River

...often my eyes were attracted to the horizon by the beautiful gold strip of the Loire where, among the waves, the sails drew fantastic figures that then fled, carried off by the wind.

Balzac, Le Lys dans la vallée

Green to Baudelaire's eyes, silvery for Flaubert, blonde to Péguy, blue to Lemaître, of crystal for La Fontaine, the Loire could seem golden to Balzac. All these great writers would have witnessed a quite different Loire from the one you see today, a river teeming with boats going about their business. While today it's the busy roads hemming in the Loire along great stretches that carry the traffic, it was the river itself that was the major trade route for so many centuries. Museums at Châteauneuf-sur-Loire, Chinon and Montjean-sur-Loire recall the importance of commerce along the *fleuve* (the French word for a great river) and its tributaries. They show the variety of boats that plied the rivers, from primitive dugouts to the improbable paddle steamers of the early 19th century. But the days of Loire shipping were numbered anyway by the time of the steamers as the railways arrived in the mid-19th century. Today the enormous quays in the major towns and the surprisingly substantial ones in little riverside villages along the Loire (often with a cluster of mariners' cottages left standing nearby) bear witness to the former importance of the river trade.

The Loire is an enormously long river, just over 1,000km in length. We cover a good section of it in this guide book, going from Sancerre in central France (just north of Nevers) to the Atlantic at St-Nazaire. But it actually starts not far from the Mediterranean, a mere 160km north as the crow flies from where the Rhône spews out into that sea via its marshy Camargue estuary. For a surprising distance the Loire and the Rhône roughly parallel each other – only flowing in opposite directions. At their closest, the two rivers lie just 30km apart. Goods could be transported from one to the other, making possible a river trading link between the Mediterranean and the Atlantic. The Loire is thought to have been a route which connected the Celtic and Greek trading worlds, Cornish tin apparently among the products making its way from one to the other in this manner.

The banks of the Loire have long been open to civilization then. Celtic settlements sprang up early along the river, foundations for the later Gallo-Roman cities. The Romans knew the Loire well, but as the Liger (the people who live along the Loire are still known in French as Ligériens). St Martin founded the second Christian monastery in France along its banks in the 4th century. The Viking invaders came up it to create havoc and devastation in the 9th century, providing a suitably gory ending to the Dark Ages. In the 13th century Loire mariners set up an association to protect their rights along the length of the trading river and to ensure its good maintenance. Created in 1215 and lasting until 1773, the Communauté des Marchands Fréquentant la Rivière de Loyre et Fleuves Descendant en Icelle defended its members' joint interests in the face of the tolls imposed by different proprietors along the river. The association also tried to make sure that dredging and the marking of navigation channels were carried out.

Memorable images of the Loire and its vessels stand out through history:
St Martin's body carried by boat up to Tours, the November trees so surprisingly
springing into flower; pilgrims arriving on the quays of Candes-St-Martin to visit the
place where the great evangelizer died; Viking longships bringing heathen terror;
Anne de Bretagne coming from Nantes to Langeais by boat for her enforced marriage
to King Charles VIII, her extravagant belongings in tow; the plotters of the
Conjuration d'Amboise in the 16th century being drowned in bags; tens of thousands
of anti-Republicans crossing the river at St-Florent-le-Vieil in the Guerre de Vendée,
others being drowned by the Revolutionary leaders of Nantes in dreadful couplings;
the Second World War bombings...

As the contemporary Loire artist Jacques Warminski described it to me once, the
Loire is a capricious creature whose course resembles that of an Anjou *boule de fort*,
the unevenly weighted bowl that makes its unpredictable, drunkenly swerving way
towards its destination. Actually, the Loire's extreme natural waywardness was
curbed from medieval times on with the building of levees, the riverside banks that
generally stop it from overspilling. These levees were begun under Henri Plantagenêt
in the 12th century. Many of the Loire roads were built on top of them, affording good
views of the river and countryside around, as you'll see. These days the Loire only
rarely tries to act in unruly manner. Although the French often refer to the Loire as *le
dernier fleuve sauvage de France* (the last great wild river in France), it is relatively well
behaved most of the time – to the extent that nuclear power stations have been ever-
so-reassuringly placed along its length. The Loire Valley has become the Nuclear Loire
Valley. If you followed the journey right through this book you'd see four such power
stations spewing their cloud-sized plumes of smoke into the air.

While nuclear power has flourished in the postwar period, fish numbers have dwindled. Pollution has been a problem, but seems to be improving slightly. The Loire
salmon, despite a number of obstacles conspiring against them along the way, are
starting to reappear slowly and in very small numbers make their laborious journey
upstream. You're much more likely to be able to eat shad fished from the Loire, or eel,
although *sandre*, considered *the* Loire Valley fish *par excellence*, will probably come
from way out east in Europe. Aquariums at Lussault and near Romoranthin-
Lanthenay allow you to see some of the types of fish that may land up on your
holiday plate while they're still happily swimming around. On the river itself you may
see *carrelets*, the square nets lowered into the water, or, in summer, men out in their
little *barques* (the punt-like Loire boats) fishing with rods. In Anjou, large numbers of
fishermen take to the jetties that emerge as the water level drops in the heat, and in
season a few privileged hunters erect floating camouflaged cabins on the water for
duck shooting.

The gravelly and sandy shores and numerous islands of the Loire provide good
havens for birds, particularly when they're migrating. Species you may see along the
Loire include terns (like refined, petite gulls), sandpipers and ringed plovers. You may
spot the odd kingfisher shooting past, or sand martins flitting to and from their nests
dug into the sandy banks. Mallards, teal, coots and moorhens swim around the
quieter waters. Ospreys, hovering on the spot before diving, put in an appearance, as

do grebes and large cormorants, which can be seen fishing from August to April. The grey heron stands out as the most majestic bird you can spot on the Loire. You'd be lucky to catch sight of the European beaver, which doesn't build dams here, but digs a home only accessible by water. Weasels and polecats count among the less popular inhabitants, but the little metallic-blue Hoplia beetles peculiar to the Loire were once prized as jewels. Of the trees that give the Loire banks their particularly lovely appearance, the willows are the most distinctive, the purple variety a Loire speciality. Ash and elm also often line the river bank.

In summer and the major tourist season, you'll see a very different Loire from that of the rainier months. In winter the Loire can become massively bloated. I've also witnessed the rare sight of it clogged with huge chunks of ice cracking painfully apart – this exceptional occurrence in the mid-1980s destroyed the bridge at Sully. In summer the river looks much less formidable. The waters dwindle and split into branches, following much narrower courses and sometimes abandoning whole portions of the river bed, leaving *boires*, isolated pools of trapped water, and great sandy expanses. Avoid the temptation of walking on these unless you see the locals doing so – they can hide quicksands (*sables mouvants*). The advice for you should you come across such dangers is to turn round immediately and follow your tracks back to where you started from. Swimming is forbidden in the Loire as even in summer its currents can be treacherous. The river bed also goes down in deceptive shelves. But you can go canoeing on the Loire in places and a few of the old-fashioned boats have been revived for little tourist outings.

Despite busy roads rushing along large stretches of the Loire, this remains a magnificent and majestic river. Recognizing this, in the year 2000 UNESCO declared most of the section covered in this guide book a World Heritage Site, just barring those parishes containing nuclear power stations. The Loire is the first river to have received this UNESCO distinction. But although such official admiration and tourist attention is focused on the Loire river, in fact the majority of the so-called Loire châteaux, Loire churches and Loire courtly towns were built beside tributaries of the great river, in the so-called Loire Valley, a region which needs some clarification.

The Loire Valley – Purest of French Regions?

Le fleuve le plus national pour nous est la Loire (our most national river is the Loire).
Balzac

The Loire Valley is the most French of regions and yet not an administrative region at all. It's traditionally considered to stretch from somewhere east of Orléans to the western end of Anjou, and thus is split between two official administrative French regions, Centre and Pays de la Loire. (To confuse you just a little further, there's a *département* called quite simply the Loire, but this isn't in the tourist region of the Loire Valley at all; it's far away in the Rhône-Alpes region, with St-Etienne as its capital!) Foreign students flock to the Loire Valley, as the purest of French is supposed to be spoken here – there's said to be no regional accent. So the Loire Valley is a region which isn't a region with an accent which is without accent (the educated urban Loire Valley accent could maybe be compared to BBC or Oxford English). If the Loire region covered here has an overall, clichéd identity, it is of purity: purity of accent, purity of typically French countryside, purity of traditional French food and wine, purity of archetypal French châteaux.

Many tourist guides define the Loire Valley as the region of the Châteaux de la Loire. But where do the châteaux of the Loire begin and end? More of the Loire Valley châteaux lie along tributaries of the Loire than along the great river itself. There is a typical look to the heart of the Loire Valley region, though, which might help to define it: the gentle slopes and gentle meanders of the rivers, the limestone banks and caves, the Romanesque churches and blonde châteaux, the vineyards and orchards, the soft light. And looking at the buildings of the region, you can't help but notice the importance of limestone and slate, devoted their own topic below.

One aspect that makes the Loire Valley such a very French region is suggested in Balzac's line quoted above. Historically, the Loire Valley is indissociable from certain vital moments and movements of national pride. Joan of Arc's leading role in this is indisputable. And whatever the shortcomings of the Valois kings who settled in the Loire Valley for a while, during their stint here defining events took place. Despite King Charles VII's weakness, in his time the English were sent packing, losing most of their continental baggage; during Louis XI's reign from Touraine, the notion of the French nation was cemented by the acquisition of new provinces and by important new economic measures; wild Brittany was tamed and brought into the fold by the actions of Charles VIII and François I. These kings all encouraged and sponsored a vibrant culture in the Loire Valley that has become a source of great pride for the whole country, and instantly recognized abroad. They and their entourage commissioned their sumptuous and unforgettable châteaux and caused many beautiful courtly towns to be built. The Loire Valley does represent something of a psychological divide in the French mind, though: this is where western France divides between north and south.

A few hugely influential French writers stemmed from the Loire Valley and have been adopted as national icons. If Balzac was right in saying that the Loire is the most national of France's rivers, then it's probably fair to say that Balzac, from Touraine, is now considered the most national of French writers. Rabelais, too, is a figure who, however little read or understood, has become a French hero. Ronsard and Du Bellay, a couple of the most influential poets from the group of 16th-century versifiers referred to as the Pléiade and seen as early champions of the French language, are strongly associated with the Loire Valley. Ronsard even embarked on what he vainly hoped would be a great epic for the nation and the language, the *Franciade*.

All told, many consider that the seeds of modern France sprang up in the Loire Valley. It's hard to pin down specifically Loire Valley traditions, Loire Valley cuisine doesn't really exist as such and it's impossible to imagine a Loire Valley separatist movement! Even if the Loire Valley is hard to define precisely, it just feels so quintessentially French.

Black and White Loire

Going underground in the Loire Valley, you'll find the sources for the main materials from which not just the Loire Valley châteaux, but also most of the Loire Valley towns and villages were built – limestone and slate. Tufa, or *tuffeau* in French, is the special type of limestone that dominates. But before digging deeper into the subject, first let's dismiss the distracting side issues here, brick and schist.

In the east of the region covered in the guide, in the Orléanais and Blésois in particular, you will find brick in a good number of castles, often put to decorative effect. The Château de Gien offers a fine example, with its mysterious patternings; the Louis XII wing of the Château de Blois another. One of the most romantic of all the châteaux covered here, the Château du Moulin, reflects its ruddy complexion in its moat. Many grand town houses in Orléans and Blois were also built of brick.

In the west of the Loire Valley, around Angers, the limestone hits schist. The contrast between the pale, soft, typical Loire Valley stone and the much grittier, darker rock could scarcely be stronger. The local architecture immediately reflects the change to schist, although many of the châteaux west of the geological dividing line did insist on a little limestone to lighten their looks, for example at Angers, Serrant, Brissac and Le Plessis-Macé. Schist isn't actually as ugly as it sounds, containing tinges of oranges and browns, but it does come as a bit of a shock after all that lovely light limestone.

The tufa was quite easily extracted from the Loire Valley riverside cliffs. You can visit numerous limestone grottoes and former quarries in the region. Hermits and religious communities apparently discovered the advantages of the limestone caves in these parts in the Dark Ages. The monastery of Marmoutier, founded by St Martin outside Tours, was built in part into the Loire cliff. At Chinon by the Vienne you can still visit the wonderful cave with its magical well where Jean le Reclus settled. Loire Valley tufa became increasingly excavated for construction through the medieval centuries. Some in the region say it was used to build Westminster Abbey in London; certainly vast numbers of fine churches as well as châteaux were built in limestone along the Loire and its tributaries, a tradition which continued through the Ancien Régime.

The careful quarrying of neat blocks left a whole mass of caves in the region. These caves have been put to an ever-growing number of uses. In wine-producing areas like Vouvray and Montlouis, the Saumurois or along the Cher and the Vienne, they've been adapted to store wine, even to serve as wineries. More extraordinarily, many were transformed into troglodyte homes, particularly in the Saumurois. While the more common type of quarry was dug into cliffsides, around Doué-la-Fontaine the quarries were dug straight down into the ground, galleries leading off central craters. The Doué caves have also been turned to a multitude of uses: for homes, for farms, for silk production, for a zoo even. As to Les Perrières' huge interconnecting chambers, their weird forms resemble an Art Nouveau cathedral. Close to Saumur, horse town *extra-ordinaire*, the manure the beasts produce is put to good use by the mushroom growers who have taken over many of the cliffside caves. Conditions are ideal for growing fungi. More fragrantly, squashed apples (*pommes tapées*) are smoked and bashed in a cave at Le Val Hulin, on the other side of Saumur. After the Saumurois, the

Cher valley is the second most important troglodyte area. Bourré along the Cher is reputed to produce the purest white Loire Valley stone. Several of its former quarries have been turned into tourist attractions similar to those in the Saumurois.

Some have turned their caves to very artistic use. The eccentric late Jacques Warminski dug out a disorientating set of chambers, including one intriguing circular one that emits a musical note as you stamp around inside it. Richard Rak exhibits his paintings in a cave at Coutures, southeast of Angers, while extraordinary centuries-old silos in the grounds of the posh Le Choiseul hotel in Amboise are turned into an art gallery in high season. The most mysterious Loire troglodyte art is to be found in a scruffy cave at Denezé-sous-Doué, where a panoply of messily carved figures appear to present an irreverent, possibly masonic view of 16th-century life. More recently, more accomplished sculptors have specifically created new tourist sights by carving quarry walls in Bourré and in St-Hilaire-St-Florent.

In the caves east of Tours and in the Saumurois you can even seek out the odd former quarry or cave converted into a superbly atmospheric restaurant or hotel where you can sample the troglodyte life briefly for yourself. You probably wouldn't be so excited about staying down a Loire slate mine. While virtually all the limestone quarries of the Loire Valley have shut, some slate mines in Anjou are still producing the material which adds the black to the typical black-and-white Loire Valley buildings. Although limestone extraction can never have been a piece of cake, somehow the multitude of diverting uses to which the former stone quarries have been transformed romanticizes them. The memories of slate mining in the two Anjou pits turned into tourist sights remain working class and miserable, with a pronounced interest on the guided tour (by former miners) in poor working conditions and ill health. The Mine Bleue, in particular, serves as a reminder of all the sweat, toil and suffering that went into the production of the Loire Valley's architectural legacy.

Joan of Arc in the Arts

One of the other great heroes of the Loire Valley beyond the limestone and slate, the builders and their works, rather less anonymous and much more frequently sung, is Joan of Arc. The Loire is where she knew her great triumphs. It was at Chinon in Touraine that she persuaded the dauphin, the future King Charles VII, to trust in her, while it was in the Orléanais that she inspired a string of victories that helped in the long process of booting the English out of France to end the Hundred Years' War.

Sensible Orléans gets slightly carried away over its favourite Maid in the annual celebrations to mark the liberation of the town from the English siege of 1429. But beyond a little museum devoted to Joan in the town and one in the Château de Chinon, and the commemorative statues and plaques to her that litter the Loire Valley, there's no serious and profound tribute paid to Joan in the region. If this stretch of the Loire along which she knew her finest hours of glory fails to do her justice as one of the most extraordinary figures in French history, then literature at least has played its part in devoting to her the attention she deserves.

Some fine fiction, and some very silly stuff, has been written using her as the source of inspiration. Bernard Shaw entertainingly dismissed, in the preface to his play *Saint Joan*, some of the mounds of more famous writings in which she's been reinvented. According to Shaw, Shakespeare's portrayal of Joan in *Henry VI* 'ends in mere scurrility'. In Schiller's *Die Jungfrau von Orleans* she's 'drowned in a witch's caldron of raging romance...it is not about Joan at all, and can hardly be said to pretend to be, for he makes her die on the battlefield, finding her burning unbearable'. On Voltaire's outrageous *La Pucelle d'Orléans*, he writes: 'I certainly cannot defend it against the charge of extravagant indecorum. But its purpose was not to depict Joan, but to kill with ridicule everything that Voltaire righteously hated in the institutions and fashions of his own day.' To give you a taste of this work, in one of Voltaire's scenes Joan is courted by, and narrowly avoids giving up her virginity, to an ass!

Shaw rubbishes Mark Twain's interpretation of Joan of Arc: 'Mark Twain's Joan, skirted to the ground, and with as many petticoats as Noah's wife in a toy ark, is an attempt to combine Bayard with Esther Summerson from [Dickens'] *Bleak House* into an unimpeachable American school teacher in armor.' Twain was inspired by the highly influential republication in 1841 by Quicherat of the reports of Joan's trial and rehabilitation. 'Later on,' continues Shaw, 'another man of genius, Anatole France, reacted against the Quicheratic wave of enthusiasm, and wrote a *Life of Joan* in which he attributed Joan's ideas to clerical prompting and her military success to an adroit use of her by Dunois as a *mascotte*: in short, he denied that she had any serious military or political ability. At this Andrew saw red, and went for Anatole's scalp in a rival *Life* of her which should be read as a corrective to the other.' That still leaves, among numerous other writers to have been inspired by Joan, such notable worthies as Paul Claudel, Charles Péguy and Maurice Maeterlinck to plough through. Shaw's own depiction hasn't been without its critics, although the confused conviction of his Joan character comes across with great force.

It's ironic to observe that while the pens of so many notable literary figures have got carried away by her stirring life and legend, Joan herself was illiterate, or as a contemporary put it more quaintly, knew not A from B. But there's no doubt that Joan knew the power of the word when it came to winning people over. For an in-depth present-day interpretation of Joan, which places her brilliantly in her historical context and in the context of the subsequent interpretations of her by a very wide variety of causes, Marina Warner's *Joan of Arc: The Image of Female Heroism* proves engrossing. The author adds her own feminist reading of the Maid: 'She has extended the taxonomy of female types; she makes evident the dimension of women's dynamism. It is urgent that this taxonomy be expanded further...we must develop a richer vocabulary for female activity than we use at present, with our restrictions of wife, mother, mistress, muse.' Such is the profusion of readings of Joan's character that she remains a totally fascinating figure, extremely difficult to grasp – Bernard Shaw once described her as 'the queerest fish among the eccentric worthies of the Middle Ages'.

The 'queerer' side of Joan's wearing of men's clothing and armour was suppressed in the plethora of paintings of her executed in the 19th century, which tried to improve her wholesomeness and re-establish her femininity, putting her back in a dress, sometimes giving her an ostentatiously plumed hat. The numerous civic statues of Joan, in stark contrast, tend to show her triumphantly in her armour, a bellicose leader, often on horseback, full of heroic action, ready to mow down a whole army of Englishmen – although she claimed at her trial never to have killed a man. You may spot many further conflicting renderings of Joan in stained glass and tapestry along the Loire Valley. The depictions of Joan most people recall are those in films. In this medium Joan inspired a handful of 20th-century classics, including Carl Théodor Dreyer's *La Passion de Jeanne d'Arc*, Marco de Gastyne's *La Merveilleuse Vie de Jeanne d'Arc*, Robert Bresson's *Procès de Jeanne d'Arc* and Cecil B. De Mille's *Joan the Woman*.

It may surprise you to learn that it was only in the early 20th century that Joan was canonized by the Catholic Church. But Joan has always been a difficult figure for that church to deal with; after all, it condemned her to death, causing her to become such an emblematic figure.

Dogs' Paws in Wine

Among the recipes cooked up by King Louis XI's talented cook Jean Pastourel, such as pomegranate soup, white pudding, rock partridge, royal bread soup, stork and hedgehog, is a dish of '*branches de bois de jeunes cerfs coupés menus et frits dans du saindoux avec des sauces au citron, au vin vieux, à la dodine – incorporant le jus de volailles rôties*' – basically, young stags' antlers served in a complex and exotic sauce. Hunting was one of the great courtly pursuits and excesses to excite the kings of France and there were always culinary joys to follow the thrill of the kill.

Louis XI was one of the Loire Valley kings particularly, perhaps pathologically, impassioned by hunting. It was a heady hobby when there was no warring. Royal activities, both at work and at play, were often basically barbaric it seems in the Middle Ages. Louis XI wrote in one telling letter: 'I have been informed from Normandy that the English army has disbanded for this year. I am returning to take and kill wild boar, not wishing to miss the end of the season while awaiting the other one to take and kill Englishmen.' Louis' hunting dogs were treated to obscene luxury, their collars decorated with gold studs, their food prepared by apothecaries, their paws sometimes bathed in hot wine, poor darlings – they could be utterly exhausted by a hard day's work romping through the forests. Louis' favourite, Mistodin, was dressed in robes and slept in a bed. Offerings and prayers for the hounds were made to Saint Hubert. When Louis was ageing and ill, he even organized a miniature hunt in his room to distract him from his neurotic superstitions – rats were released as he gave instructions to his dogs to catch them. Hunting was something of a religion for the Loire kings. Louis had his original tomb effigy portray him kneeling in huntsman's gear in front of the Virgin, a greyhound with gold-studded collar by his side.

Some of the greatest Loire châteaux have been described as glorified hunting lodges, not least Chambord. Chambord's park, on the edge of the Sologne, the hunting region *par excellence* in France, became the official hunting reserve of the French presidents. Former president Giscard d'Estaing even set an embarrassingly tacky novel against the hunting background of the Sologne, with adultery as a main theme. It's possible to imagine adulterous François Mitterrand, a French politician who liked to have it both ways if ever there was one, selling his principles again here. Several other châteaux have taken up the hunting theme as a tourist attraction. They're certainly not critical of the sport, but what they show is revealing. Gien's Musée de la Chasse particularly so, presenting a vast collection of works of art inspired by hunting, from guns encrusted with delicately carved ivory and huge polished brass horns to pieces of fine art including canvases by official hunt painters to Louis XIV. The Château de Montpoupon's feisty old owner, Mlle de la Motte St-Pierre, recently opened a hunt museum in her château's outhouses with the help of her nephew, an art dealer, and from a more personal collection – several faded photos show her standing triumphantly over dead stags. The Château de Cheverny's pack, a formidable bunch of long-legged hounds who run across virtually every postcard of the château, can often be seen languishing in their kennels. Antlers, tusks and various hunting trophies are used to decorate rooms in innumerable Loire Valley castles. A living reminder of hunting in the region is the displays of falconry, another great passion among many of the Loire Valley kings, at the Zoo de Beauval near St-Aignan.

When there's a formal hunt in the Loire Valley, local people turn out not to protest but to cheer. While in the British countryside pro-hunt and anti-hunt campaigners are savagely trying to tear each other apart, in the French provinces there seems to be little awareness that this might be an issue at all. Although France is often considered a relatively liberal country, the debate on such issues can seem to lag well behind much of the rest of northern Europe. The passions of your average Frenchman come into play here. You'd have thought hunting was in the blood, it's such a strong pull. It may be understandable that the hunting of animals was an instinct in prehistoric men, some of whose hunting implements you can see well displayed at the Château du Grand-Pressigny's museum on prehistory. And explaining the niceties of animal rights might have been a problem for Gauls, who worshipped the creatures they hunted – the fabulous find of Celtic bronze animals, including stags and wild boar, displayed in Orléans' archaeological museum is well worth going to see. But your average contemporary French provincial man would no doubt argue that hunting down animals is still in the genes today, an irresistible urge.

While the cliché may be that half of Frenchmen are out fornicating at weekends (an image which French presidents have hardly helped dispel), in autumn and winter a huge proportion of them will genuinely be out roaming the countryside with their guns and their dogs, looking for any game they can have a go at; as a tourist you may find that the noise of gunfire can quite spoil a trip out into the countryside at this time of year. The nearest you may come to the kill on a summer visit to the Loire Valley, though, is eating in a restaurant where a stuffed doe's head looks irritatingly innocently out from the wall above you. And, glancing up at the ceiling, you may be delighted to see one of those tasteful wagonwheel candelabras, the bulbs fixed in place in upturned does' hooves.

Food and Drink

06

Were you to go by the giants' diet in Rabelais' books, you'd expect to be served cart-loads of tripe at every meal in the Loire Valley, washed down with your personal barrel or two of wine. And you wouldn't be surprised to eat the odd stray pilgrim in a salad. The one Rabelaisian food you may still taste in the Loire Valley today is *fouaces* or *foués*, dough balls that puff up when cooked in a baker's oven. In reality, the common features of Loire cuisine include freshwater river and lake fish, goat's cheese in a variety of shapes resembling children's building blocks, orchard fruits, a plethora of vegetables (such as the asparagus grown on the alluvial valley river sands), game in autumn, and Loire wine sauces at any time of year. There isn't a particularly typical Loire cuisine. The region, with its great trade route of the Loire river, was open to all sorts of culinary influences across the centuries. Standards of cuisine are pretty high across the board.

Regional Specialities

Food

Meats: With its fair number of forests, you'll find plenty of game around the Loire Valley in autumn, with the likes of duck and venison on most menus and, increasingly, given their explosion in numbers, wild boar (*sanglier* in French) or the baby *marcassin*. *Rillons* are a pork speciality in Touraine, cooked in their fat, and to be distinguished from *rillettes*, which is a kind of coarse pâté. *Géline de Touraine*, the black hen of that region, is reckoned to be particularly tasty. *Andouillettes*, tripe sausages, are the food of Rabelais, while *cul de veau* from Montsoreau is veal rump. The Maine-Anjou cow is a special breed that was developed across those two provinces. You may find meat dishes incorporating some of the fruits of the region (for example pork with apples or prunes) as well as local mushrooms and wines, even honey sometimes.

Freshwater fish: *The* Loire fish dish is *sandre*, or zander, often translated as pikeperch. *The* fish sauce along the Loire is *beurre blanc*, made with shallots, butter, dry white wine and vinegar. (Orléans, by the way, used to be very well known in France for its vinegar.) Other fleshy freshwater fish you'll come across include pike (*brochet*), bream (*brème*) and shad (*alose*). Eels (*anguilles*) are quite a speciality along the rivers. *Matelote d'anguilles* is a stew incorporating both eels and red wines, and possibly prunes. You may also find lamprey (*lamproie*) around the place. *Friture*, little fried fish, is popular. Salmon, which used to swim upriver in large numbers, have had an increasingly tough time in the last century, but some still manage to return to their breeding grounds. In traditional manner, a Loire salmon might be poached in a *court-bouillon* of Vouvray wine. Sea fish and seafood feature on most menus nowadays, rapidly transported from the Atlantic, so the choice should be good.

Vegetables tend to be especially fine in the Loire Valley. Asparagus grows particularly well on the alluvial sands. So, too, does a large variety of other vegetables. Those grown locally in large numbers include onions, leeks, beans, cabbage and artichokes.

Cardon is a rare relative of the last, its stem served in white sauce. Fresh lettuces of all sorts also flourish. *Champignons de Paris*, button mushrooms, are grown in vast profusion in the darkness of the caves of the Saumurois. Apparently, over three-quarters of the production for the whole of France is here. Now the producers are branching out, supplying other mushrooms such as *pleurotes* and *pieds bleu*. Much rarer, the occasional truffle can be found in southern Touraine.

Cheese in the Loire means goat's cheeses essentially. The most reputed come from the Sancerrois (with its temptingly named *crottins*, or 'droppings', of Chavignol), from Olivet in the Orléanais, from Selles-sur-Cher in the Blésois, and from Ste-Maure in Touraine. Olivet also produces some cow's milk cheese, as do other little locations.

Fruit: From the orchards of the Loire Valley, pears and apples are made into some lovely desserts. Pears are a speciality of both the Orléanais and of Anjou. *Tarte Tatin*, a native dish of the Sologne in the Loir-et-Cher, invented by accident by an absent-minded woman, is an apple tart with a caramelized top which you'll find on menus everywhere. *Pommes tapées* and *poires tapées* are apples and pears dried using old techniques. Excellent strawberries, raspberries, blackberries and even kiwis grow along the Loire Valley. Quinces from Ay in the Orléanais are made to into a jelly known as *cotignac*. Plums and prunes were once found in profusion, but are rarer now.

Among pastries and puddings, other than *tarte Tatin*, almond pastries are popular, such as the Pithiviers, an almond-based *pâtisserie* named after a town north of Orléans. Cormery is known for its macaroons. *Crémets d'Anjou*, a fresh cream cheese concoction with cream and sugar added makes for a deliciously light dessert. Some of the liqueurs of the region, such as Cointreau made in Angers or Combier made in Saumur, or local wines can add delicate flavours to fine desserts. You'll find local chocolate specialities across the region. Among the most amusing are *crottins de cheval*, 'horse-dropping' chocolates from Saumur, and chocolate 'slates' in Anjou, covered with a blue-dyed coating.

Wine

The map in the colour map section at the back of the book shows the different Loire wine regions, and the following wine areas are devoted more detailed descriptions in the text: in the Cher *département*, Sancerre; in the Blésois, Cheverny and Cour-Cheverny, Cher valley wines and Touraine-Mesland; in Touraine, Vouvray, Montlouis, Chinon, and Bourgueil and St-Nicolas-de-Bourgueil; in Anjou, Saumur-Champigny, Saumur sparkling, the Coteaux du Layon and the Coteaux de l'Aubance.

You'll realize from the map and if you travel along the Loire that the region produces a wide variety of wines from vineyards dotted along hundreds of miles. Many of the wine areas produce red, white and rosé wines. Some produce sparkling. The Loire Valley region is probably best known abroad for its distinctive white wines, such as Sancerre, Pouilly-Fumé, Vouvray and Muscadet; for the rosé of Anjou; and for the reds of Chinon, Bourgueil and Saumur. The last also produces a sparkling wine that you may well be familiar with, Saumur *mousseux*.

But Loire wines have a misleadingly limited reputation abroad. Anjou, the most diverse of all the Loire wine regions, is particularly badly served by its popular imaged outside France. It's rather disappointing that, outside the country, it's difficult to find a wide selection of Loire wines in most wine merchants' shops – the choice is often poor. There are actually many discoveries to be made. The advantage of few wines being available abroad is that you wine buffs out there can have the pleasure of bringing back your own exclusives if you buy on the spot.

The wines of the Loire can seem very complex at first, but almost all the white wines are made from either Sauvignon Blanc or Chenin Blanc grapes, while Cabernet Franc largely wins in the reds. The Loire's vine-growing areas are far north in terms of French viticulture, and this means that they're particularly susceptible to the variations in weather from year to year; as a consequence, quality tends to vary more than in regions where the climate is slightly more reliably warm. Spring frosts and cooler summers can clearly affect a vintage. The lie of the land counts for a good deal at such times, although better winemaking techniques have made Loire wines more reliable in recent years. Considering recent vintages along the Loire, 1996 was a good year, producing quality wines across the board, while 1997 has proved a great vintage, with superb results, particularly in the reds and the finest sweet white wines. 1998 was a good year once again, with some very good reds. The wines of 1999 turned out to be more average, and those of 2000 won't be remembered long.

Under the national classification system for French wines, the best vine-growing parts of France are controlled and tightly restricted by the designation of particularly suitable areas as distinct *appellations d'origine contrôlée*, abbreviated to AOCs. These *appellations* vary greatly in size – what counts is the suitability of the particular terrain chosen, the distinctiveness of the grapes it produces and the quality of the wines these give. Anjou alone has almost 30 different *appellations*, Touraine some 10. The title of *appellation d'origine contrôlée* is generally a guarantee of a good-quality wine. AOC wine labels on the whole state the vintage, or year the grapes were harvested, and will often bear the name of an individual property and vine-grower, showing that the wine is made on the estate (*domaine*, *clos* and château are the most common terms for a wine estate). There are also generic AOC wines, in France almost always regarded as being of a lesser quality than the estate-produced AOC wines. Beneath the AOCs come wines called *vin délimité de qualité supérieure*, abbreviated to VDQS, and below them simple *vin de pays*.

Sections of the official French wine authorities have laid out wine routes through the region and can send you useful brochures on them. For information on the wine routes and *appellations* of Sancerre, the Berry and the Giennois, contact the Bureau Interprofessionnel des Vins du Centre, 9 Route de Chavignol, 18300 Sancerre, **t** 02 48 78 51 07, **f** 02 48 78 51 08, *contact@vins-centre-loire.com*, *www.vins-centre.com*. For information about the wine routes of Touraine and the Blésois, contact Interprofessionnel des Vins du Val de Loire, Bureau des Vins de la Touraine, 19 Saure Prosper Mérimée, B.P.1921, 37019 Tours Cedex 1, **t** 02 47 05 40 01, **f** 02 47 66 57 32, *touraine@interloire.com*. The many wine *appellations* and routes in Anjou are covered by the Comité Interprofessionnel des Vins d'Anjou-Saumur, Hôtel Godeline, 73 Rue

Planagenêt, 49000 Angers, **t** 02 41 87 62 57, **f** 02 41 86 71 84. Finally, the vineyards of the west around Nantes are dealt with by the Comité Interprofessionnel des Vins du Pays Nantais, Maison des Vins, Bellevue, 44690 La Haye Fouassière, **t** 02 40 36 90 10, **f** 02 40 36 95 87.

Wine writer Hubrecht Duijker has written a little practical book devoted exclusively to wine-touring along the Loire, *Loire: A Wine Lover's Touring Guide*.

Other Drinks

French coffee is strong and black but lacklustre compared with the aromatic brews of Italy or Spain. If you order *un café* you'll get a very small *express*. If you want more than these few drops of caffeine, ask for *un grand café*. If you like milk in your coffee, order *un café crème*. The French tend to order *café au lait*, which contains only a small amount of coffee topped up with a large quantity of hot milk, at breakfast. The word for decaffeinated is *déca*. If you order *un thé* you'll most likely get a tea bag in a cup of hot water. You'll probably have to specify *au lait* (with milk) or *au citron* (with lemon) if that's what you're after. *Chocolat chaud*, hot chocolate, is also available. An *infusion* or *tisane* is a herbal tea; *camomille*, *menthe* (mint), *tilleul* (lime or linden blossom) and *verveine* (verbena) count among the most popular types.

Mineral water (*eau minérale*) comes either sparkling (*gazeuse* or *pétillante*) or still (*non-gazeuse* or *plate*). The usual international corporate soft drinks are easy to find, as well as a variety of bottled fruit juices (*jus de fruit*). Some bars also do refreshing freshly squeezed lemon and orange juices (*citron pressé* or *orange pressée*), served with plenty of chilled water. The French are fond of sweet fruit syrups, for example red *grenadine*, *sirop d'orgeat* (barley-water) or ghastly green *diabolo menthe*.

Beer (*bière*) in most bars and cafés is run-of-the-mill big brands from Alsace, Belgium or Germany. Draft beer (*pression*) is cheaper than bottled beer. Pastis and red wine flavoured with spices make popular apéritifs. The French, by the way, offer *porto* (port) before a meal, not as a *digestif*. Cognac is drunk across France, while Cointreau and Combier are two orange liqueurs actually made in Anjou.

Restaurant Generalities

Most restaurants, unless they're very small, will normally offer a choice of set-price menus with two to five (or even more) courses. The menus are usually posted by the entrance, so that you can peruse the options and check the prices. Many restaurants offer a lunch menu at a good price, a fine way of trying out the more exclusive gourmet addresses. Opening hours tend to be from 12 or 12.30 to 2pm and 7 to 9pm, though many places stay open later on summer evenings.

A proper full French restaurant meal normally begins with an apéritif served with little savoury snacks known as *amuses-gueules* (a *gueule* is a rather vulgar word for a mouth). The hors-d'oeuvre are the starters. The entrées or *plats/pièces de résistance* or *plats principaux* are the main courses. (If you order a side salad it will normally come before or after the main course, so if you want it with the main course, explain this.) *Les fromages*, cheeses, are served before the *desserts*, the puddings. You could finish a meal with a *digestif* or a coffee, tea or an *infusion* or *tisane*, the last two herbal teas. Drinks to end a meal are often accompanied by *petits fours*, or chocolates. More ordinary meals consist of a starter, a main course and either cheese or pudding. A *plat du jour*, sometimes also referred to as the *plat du marché*, is the day's special, which could be eaten by itself. A *menu dégustation* is a selection of the chef's or the region's specialities. Eating à la carte will always be much more expensive than opting for a set menu, so avoid that extravagance unless you're not worried about your budget. A fair number of restaurants don't accept credit cards, so check if you're unsure.

Menus in cheaper restaurants sometimes include a bottle or a carafe of house wine in the price (signalled by the phrase *vin compris*). With the exception of some house wines, generally speaking wine in French restaurants isn't good value – it normally carries a very substantial mark-up. But French families would expect to splash out on a reasonable bottle when eating out. With the increasingly severe action to stop drink-driving some places now serve *le vin au verre*, wine by the glass. By contrast, with certain very sumptuous menus you may get a glass of a different type of wine with each course! For choosing your type of wine, see the wine section below.

Service should be automatically included in the price of set menus nowadays, indicated by *service compris* (service included), sometimes abbreviated to s.c. *Service non compris* means service is not included. If eating à la carte, add a 10 per cent tip.

The restaurants recommended in this guide almost exclusively serve French food. Where prices are quoted for menus they're only there to give you a rough guide and will inevitably change in time. In towns especially you'll find a growing number of fast-food chains and ethnic restaurants. North African restaurants (i.e. Moroccan, Tunisian or Algerian – the generic term is *maghrébin*) serving couscous (steamed semolina topped with spicy meat and vegetables) as the stock speciality are the most popular and numerous, along with Vietnamese and Italian restaurants. Crêperies are rarely noted in this book, but are easy to find.

To avoid disappointment with restaurants which have a well-established reputation or which are well located, call at least a day in advance to book a table. With *fermes-auberges* (farms-turned-inns) and a few other special types of restaurant, you have to call in advance to be served.

Vegetarians may have a tough time in France. Generally speaking, the French seem extraordinarily unaware about some people's desire to eat vegetarian food. Normally you can find a choice among the starters, and ordering two or more of these à la carte may allow you to make up your own vegetarian menu. However, it can be difficult to know exactly what ingredients have gone into the preparation. You should be warned that while many people will be helpful, others may be uncomprehending ('well, you can eat the chicken then, or there's plenty of fish and seafood') or, worse still, not eating meat may be taken as a personal insult – in provincial France, vegetarianism can, like other new choices in ways of living, be seen by some as an attack on French tradition.

French Menu Vocabulary

Starters and Soups
(*Hors-d'œuvre et Soupes*)
amuse-gueule appetizers
assiette assortie plate of mixed cold hors d'oeuvre
bisque shellfish soup
bouchée mini vol-au-vent
bouillon broth
charcuterie mixed cold meats, salami, ham, etc.
consommé clear soup
potage thick vegetable soup
velouté thick smooth soup, often fish or chicken

Fish and Shellfish
(*Poissons et Coquillages*)
aiglefin little haddock
alose shad
anchois anchovies
anguille eel
bar sea bass
barbue brill
baudroie anglerfish
belon flat oyster
beurre blanc sauce of shallots and wine vinegar whisked with butter
bigorneau winkle
blanchailles whitebait
brème bream
brochet pike
bulot whelk
cabillaud cod
calmar squid
carrelet plaice
colin hake
congre conger eel
coque cockle
coquillages shellfish
coquille St-Jacques scallop
crabe crab
crevette grise shrimp
crevette rose prawn
cuisses de grenouilles frogs' legs
darne slice or steak of fish
daurade sea bream
ecrevisse freshwater crayfish
eperlan smelt
escabèche fish fried, marinated and served cold

escargot snail
espadon swordfish
esturgeon sturgeon
flétan halibut
friture deep-fried fish
fruits de mer seafood
gambas giant prawn
gigot de mer a large fish cooked whole
grondin red gurnard
hareng herring
homard Atlantic (Norway) lobster
huître oyster
lamproie lamprey
langouste spiny Mediterranean lobster
langoustines Norway lobster (often called Dublin Bay prawns or scampi)
limande lemon sole
lotte monkfish
loup (de mer) sea bass
maquereau mackerel
matelote d'anguilles eels in a wine sauce
merlan whiting
morue salt cod
moules mussels
omble chevalier char
oursin sea urchin
pagel sea bream
palourde clam
petit gris little grey snail
piballe elver
poulpe octopus
praire small clam
raie skate
rouget red mullet
St-Pierre John Dory
sandre zander or pikeperch
saumon salmon
sole (meunière) sole (with butter, lemon and parsley)
telline tiny clam
thon tuna
truite trout
truite saumonée salmon trout

Meat and Poultry
(*Viandes et Volailles*)
agneau (de pré-salé) lamb (grazed in fields by the sea)
andouillette chitterling (tripe) sausage
autruche ostrich
biftek beefsteak
blanc breast or white meat

blanquette stew of white meat, thickened with egg yolk
bœuf beef
boudin blanc sausage of white meat
boudin noir black pudding
brochette meat (or fish) on a skewer
caille quail
canard, caneton duck, duckling
carré the best end of a cutlet or chop
cassoulet haricot bean stew with sausage, duck, goose, etc.
cervelle brains
chapon capon
chateaubriand porterhouse steak
cheval horsemeat
chevreau kid
chevreuil venison
chorizo spicy Spanish sausage
civet meat (usually game) stew, in wine and blood sauce
cœur heart
confit meat cooked and preserved in its own fat
contre-filet sirloin steak
côte, côtelette chop, cutlet
cou d'oie farci goose neck stuffed with pork, foie gras, truffles
crépinette small sausage
cuisse thigh or leg
dinde, dindon turkey
entrecôte ribsteak
epaule shoulder
estouffade a meat stew marinated, fried and then braised
faisan pheasant
faux-filet sirloin
foie liver
foie gras goose liver
frais de veau veal testicles
fricadelle meatball
géline de touraine rare black hen of the region
gésier gizzard
gibier game
gigot leg of lamb
graisse, gras fat
grillade grilled meat, often a mixed grill
grive thrush
jambon ham
jarret knuckle
langue tongue
lapereau young rabbit
lapin rabbit

lard (lardons) bacon (diced bacon)
lièvre hare
maigret/magret (de canard) breast (of duck)
manchon duck or goose wing
marcassin young wild boar
merguez spicy red sausage
mouton mutton
museau muzzle
navarin lamb stew with root vegetables
noix de veau (agneau) topside of veal (lamb)
oie goose
os bone
perdreau, perdrix partridge
petit salé salt pork
pieds trotters
pintade guinea fowl
plat-de-côtes short ribs or rib chops
porc pork
pot au feu meat and vegetables cooked in stock
poulet chicken
poussin baby chicken
quenelle poached dumplings made of fish, fowl or meat
queue de bœuf oxtail
rillons pork pieces cooked in their fat; a speciality from Touraine
ris (de veau) sweetbreads (veal)
rognon kidney
rosbif roast beef
rôti roast
sanglier wild boar
saucisse sausage
saucisson salami-like sausage
selle (d'agneau) saddle (of lamb)
steak tartare raw minced beef, often topped with a raw egg yolk
suprême de volaille fillet of chicken breast and wing
taureau bull's meat
tournedos thick round slices of beef fillet
travers de porc spare ribs
tripes tripe
veau veal
venaison venison

Vegetables, Herbs, etc. (Légumes, Herbes, etc.)
ail garlic
aneth dill
anis anis
artichaut artichoke

asperge asparagus
aubergine aubergine (eggplant)
avocat avocado
basilic basil
betterave beetroot
blette Swiss chard
cannelle cinnamon
céleri (-rave) celery (celeriac)
cèpe ceps, wild boletus mushroom
champignon mushroom
chanterelle wild yellow mushroom
chicorée curly endive
chou cabbage
chou-fleur cauliflower
choucroute sauerkraut
choux de bruxelles Brussels sprouts
ciboulette chives
citrouille pumpkin
clou de girofle clove
cœur de palmier heart of palm
concombre cucumber
cornichon gherkin
courgette courgette (zucchini)
cresson watercress
échalote shallot
endive chicory (endive)
epinards spinach
estragon tarragon
fenouil fennel
fève broad (fava) bean
flageolet white bean
fleur de courgette courgette blossom
frites chips (French fries)
galipette large round mushroom
genièvre juniper
gingembre ginger
haricot bean
 (rouge, blanc) (kidney, white)
haricot vert green (French) bean
jardinière mixed vegetables
laitue lettuce
laurier bay leaf
lentilles lentils
macédoine diced vegetables
maïs (épis de) sweetcorn (on the cob)
marjolaine marjoram
menthe mint
mesclun salad of various leaves ·
morille morel mushroom
navet turnip
oignon onion
oseille sorrel

panais parsnip
persil parsley
petits pois small peas
pied bleu wood blewit (type of mushroom)
piment pimento
pissenlits dandelion greens
pleurote type of mushroom
poireaus leeks
pois chiche chickpeas
pois mange-tout sugar pea, mangetout
poivron sweet pepper (capsicum)
pomme de terre potato
potiron pumpkin
primeurs young vegetables
radis radish
riz rice
romarin rosemary
roquette rocket
safran saffron
salade verte green salad
salsifis salsify
sarriette savory
sarrasin buckwheat
sauge sage
seigle rye
serpolet wild thyme
thym thyme
truffe truffle

Fruit and Nuts
(*Fruits et Noix*)

abricot apricot
amande almond
ananas pineapple
banane banana
bigarreau black cherries
brugnon nectarine
cacahouète peanut
cassis blackcurrant
cerise cherry
citron lemon
citron vert lime
coco (noix de) coconut
coing quince
dattes dates
figue (de Barbarie) fig (prickly pear)
fraise (des bois) strawberry (wild)
framboise raspberry
fruit de la passion passion fruit
grenade pomegranate
griotte morello cherry
groseille redcurrant

lavande lavender
mandarine tangerine
mangue mango
marron chestnut
merise black cherry
mirabelle mirabelle plum
mûre (sauvage) mulberry, blackberry
myrtille bilberry
noisette hazelnut
noix walnut
noix de cajou cashew
pamplemousse grapefruit
pastèque watermelon
pêche (blanche) peach (white)
pignon pinenut
pistache pistachio
poire pear
pomme apple
prune plum
pruneau prune
raisin (sec) grape (raisin)
reine-claude greengage plum

Desserts

Bavarois mousse or custard in a mould
biscuit biscuit, cracker, cake
bombe ice-cream dessert in a round mould
bonbon sweet, candy
brioche light sweet yeast bread
charlotte sponge fingers and custard
  cream dessert
chausson turnover
clafoutis batter fruit cake
compote stewed fruit
corbeille de fruits basket of fruit
coulis thick fruit sauce
coupe ice cream: a scoop or in cup
crème anglaise egg custard
crème caramel vanilla custard with
  caramel sauce
crème Chantilly sweet whipped cream
crème fraîche slightly sour cream
crème pâtissière thick pastry cream filling
  made with eggs
crémets fresh cream cheese, normally
  from Anjou and mixed with fresh cream
  and sugar
gâteau cake
gaufre waffle
génoise rich sponge cake
glace ice cream
macaron macaroon

madeleine small sponge cake
miel honey
mignardise same as petits fours
œufs à la neige floating island/meringue
  on a bed of custard
pain d'épice gingerbread
parfait frozen mousse
petits fours sweetmeats; tiny cakes and
  pastries
profiteroles choux pastry balls, often filled
  with crème pâtissière or ice cream, and
  covered with chocolate
sablé shortbread
savarin a filled cake, shaped like a ring
tarte, tartelette tart, little tart
truffe chocolate truffle
yaourt yoghurt

Cheese (Fromage)

brebis (fromage de) ewe's milk cheese
chèvre goat's cheese
doux mild
fromage (plateau de) cheese (board)
fromage blanc yoghurty cream cheese
fromage frais a bit like sour cream
fromage sec general name for solid cheeses
fort strong

Cooking Terms and Sauces

à point medium steak
aigre-doux sweet and sour
aiguillette thin slice
à l'anglaise boiled
au feu de bois cooked over a wood fire
au four baked
barquette pastry boat
beignet fritter
béarnaise sauce of egg yolks, shallots and
  white wine
bien cuit well-done steak
bleu very rare steak
bordelaise red wine, bone marrow and
  shallot sauce
broche roasted on a spit
chaud hot
cru raw
cuit cooked
émincé thinly sliced
en croûte cooked in a pastry crust
en papillote baked in buttered paper
épice spice

farci stuffed
feuilleté flaky pastry
flambé set aflame with alcohol
fourré stuffed
frais, fraîche fresh
frappé with crushed ice
frit fried
froid cold
fumé smoked
galantine cooked food served in cold jelly
galette savoury pancake
garni with vegetables
(au) gratin topped with melted cheese
    and breadcrumbs
grillé grilled
haché minced
marmite casserole
médaillon round piece
mijoté simmered
pané breaded
pâte pastry, pasta
pâte brisée shortcrust pastry
pâte à chou choux pastry
pâte feuilletée flaky or puff pastry
paupiette rolled and filled thin slices of
    fish or meat
pavé slab
piquant spicy hot
poché poached
sanglant rare steak
salé salted, spicy
sanglant rare steak
sucré sweet
timbale pie cooked in a dome-shaped mould
tranche slice
vapeur steamed
vinaigrette oil and vinegar dressing

Miscellaneous

addition bill (check)
baguette long loaf of bread
beurre butter
carte menu
confiture jam
couteau knife
crème cream
cuillère spoon
formule/menu set menu
fouace (or fouée) doughball which puffs up
    when cooked
fourchette fork
huile (d'olive) oil (olive)

lait milk
menu set menu
moutarde mustard
nouilles noodles
pain bread
œuf egg
poivre pepper
sel salt
service compris/non compris service included/
    not included
sucre sugar
vinaigre vinegar

Drinks
(Boissons)

bière (pression) beer (draught)
bouteille (demi) bottle (half)
brut very dry
café coffee
café au lait white coffee
café express espresso coffee
café filtre filter coffee
chocolat chaud hot chocolate
citron pressé fresh lemon juice
demi a third of a litre
doux sweet (wine)
eau water
  gazeuse sparkling
  minérale mineral
  plate still
eau-de-vie brandy
eau potable drinking water
glaçon ice cube
infusion/tisane herbal tea
  menthe mint
  tilleul lime flower
  verveine verbena
jus juice
lait milk
moelleux semi-dry
mousseux sparkling (wine)
orange pressée fresh orange juice
pichet pitcher
pression draught
sec dry
thé tea
verre glass
vin wine
  blanc white
  mousseaux sparkling
  rosé rosé
  rouge red

Markets and Picnic Food

In most villages, the market day is the event of the week, a social occasion for the locals. Celebrated for their fresh farm produce, French markets are fun to visit in their own right, but become even more enticing if you're cooking for yourself or gathering the ingredients for a picnic. In the larger towns you may find a market every day. Most markets finish around noon, when, in villages, the lunch siren goes off at the *mairie* (an old custom, designed to reach farm workers out in the field). In cities you can also find more established covered markets, *les halles*. Other good sources for picnic food are *boulangeries* (selling bread, but also tarts and pastries often), *charcuteries* (selling meat specialities, especially pork), *traiteurs* (delicatessens, selling a diversity of elaborate prepared dishes) and *pâtisseries*.

Cafés

That venerable French institution, the café, isn't only a place for a drink, but for many people also a home away from home, somewhere to read the papers, play cards, write letters, read a book, meet friends, or just unwind and watch the world go by. You can sit for hours over one coffee and shouldn't feel hurried by the staff. Prices for drinks are listed on the *tarif des consommations*; they go up according to whether you're served at the bar (*le comptoir*), at a table inside (in the *salle*) or outside (*en terrasse*).

Travel

07

Getting There

By Air

Arriving from overseas, be it Britain, the US or elsewhere in the world, Paris-Orly airport, south of the French capital, is the most convenient international airport to fly in to for the eastern Loire – Orléans lies around 100km southwest of Orly. Paris Charles-de-Gaulle (also known as Roissy), north of the capital, also has very good train links with the major railway stations along the Loire Valley.

The cities of Tours, Angers and Nantes along the Loire itself have airports offering a few international flights to and from Britain. Nantes has the most significant airport of the three. Flights from Britain to Angers go via the hub of Clermont-Ferrand, which is slightly awkward, but the service is still quite swift. The other airport to consider if flying from Britain is Poitiers, just south of the Loire Valley, to which you can get cheap flights on no-frills carrier Buzz.

Although the likes of Buzz are slightly cheaper, **charter flights** can be good value, and offer the added advantage of departing from

Airline Carriers

UK

Air France, t 0845 0845 111, **f** (020) 8782 8115, *www.airfrance.co.uk*. Offers flights from London-Gatwick to Nantes as well as to the major Paris airports. Between Gatwick (North Terminal) and Nantes there are two flights in both directions each day, three on Saturdays. The flight lasts around one hour. The Gatwick Express rail link departs every 15mins from London-Victoria station during the day, the journey taking 30mins. Air France also flies from London-City Airport to Nantes and Angers via Clermont-Ferrand, the whole journey to and from either of these Loire Valley airports lasting around 2 hours 40mins.

British Airways, t 0845 773 3377, **f** (0161) 247 5707, *www.britishairways.com*. As well as all the flights to the major Paris airports, operates two flights a day from London-Gatwick to Nantes.

British Midland, t 0870 607 0555, *www.flybmi.com*. Large range of flights from various British airports to Paris.

Buzz, t 0870 240 7070, *www.buzzaway.com*. Low-cost flights from London-Stansted to Poitiers.

USA and Canada

Air France, 125 West 55th St, New York, NY 10019, **t** 800 237 2747, Canada **t** 800 667 2747, *www.airfrance.com*. Non-stop flights from New York to Lyon, daily flights to Paris from Philadelphia, twice a day from Cincinnati, and three times a day from Atlanta. Regular services also from Boston, Chicago, Houston, Miami, San Francisco and Washington.

American Airlines, t 800 433 7300, *www.im.aa.com*. Flights from Boston, Chicago, Dallas, JFK, Los Angeles and Miami.

British Airways, t 800 AIRWAYS, *www.britishairways.com*.

Continental, t 800 231 0856, **t** 800 343 9195 (hearing impaired), Canada **t** 800 525 0280, *www.continental.com*. Flights from Houston and Newark.

Delta, t 800 241 4141, *www.delta.com*. Flights from Cincinnati and Atlanta to Paris, and regularly from New York to Nice.

Northwest Airlines, t 800 225 2525, *www.nwa.com*. Flights from Detroit to Paris.

TWA, t 800 892 4141, *www.twa.com*.

United Airlines, t 800 241 6522, *www.ual.com*.

Students, Discounts and Special Deals

UK

Besides saving 25% on regular flights, young people under 26 have the choice of flying on special discount charters. Students with the relevant ID cards are eligible for considerable reductions, not only on flights but also on trains and admission fees to museums, concerts and more. Agencies specializing in student and youth travel can supply ISIC cards. Try:

Europe Student Travel, 6 Campden St, London W8, **t** (020) 7727 7647. Caters to non-students as well.

a wider range of regional UK airports. Companies such as Thomson, Airtours and Unijet can offer return flights from as little £80. Check out your local travel agency, the Sunday papers and TV Teletext. In London, look in the *Evening Standard* and *Time Out*. Remember, there are no refunds for missed flights – most travel agencies sell insurance so that you don't lose all your money if you become ill.

If you are flying from North America, it may be cheaper to fly to London and pick up an onward flight from there, especially in the low season.

By Train

Travelling by high-speed train is an attractive alternative to flying from the UK. There are very good train links between London and the Loire Valley, but book more than a fortnight in advance (and much longer in advance if possible) to get tickets at a decent price; otherwise rail travel can be uncomfortably expensive.

Using the Eurostar service (**t** 08705 186 186, *www.eurostar.com*), the best way of getting to the Loire Valley is to go from either London-Waterloo or Ashford in Kent to Lille;

STA, 6 Wright's Lane, London W8 6TA, *www.statravel.com*, **t** (020) 7361 6161. Also many other branches in the UK, including: 117 Euston Rd, London NW1 2SX, Bristol, **t** (0117) 929 4399; Cambridge, **t** (01223) 366 966; Leeds, **t** (0113) 244 9212; Manchester, **t** (0161) 834 0668; Oxford, **t** (01865) 792 800. Telesales 08701 600599.

Trailfinders, 194 Kensington High St, London W8 6BD, **t** (020) 7937 1234, *www.trailfinder.com*.

Usit Campus Travel, 52 Grosvenor Gardens, London SW1 0AG, **t** (020) 7730 3402, *www.usitcampus.co.uk*; branches at most UK universities, including Bristol, **t** (0117) 929 2494; Manchester, **t** (0161) 833 2046; Edinburgh, **t** (0131) 668 3303; Birmingham, **t** (0121) 414 1848; Oxford, **t** (01865) 242 067; Cambridge, **t** (01223) 324 283.

USA and Canada

If you're resilient, flexible and/or youthful and prepared to shop around for budget deals on stand-bys or even courier flights (you can usually only take hand luggage on the latter), you should be able to get yourself some rock-bottom prices. Check out Airhitch (stand-by tickets), Council Travel (student discounts) or the Yellow Pages for courier companies (Now Voyager is one of the largest in the USA).

For discounted flights, try the small ads in newspaper travel pages (for example, *New York Times*, *Chicago Tribune*, and *Toronto Globe and Mail*). Numerous travel clubs and agencies also specialize in discount fares, but may require you to pay an annual membership fee.

Also see the web sites at *www.xfares. com* (carry-on luggage only) and *www. smarterliving.com*.

Airhitch, 2472 Broadway, Suite 200, New York, NY 10025, **t** (212) 864 2000, *www.airhitch.org*. Last-minute tickets to Europe from around $170.

Council Travel, 205 East 42nd St, New York, NY 10017, **t** 800 743 1823, **t** (212) 822 2700, *www.counciltravel.com*. Major specialists in student and charter flights; branches all over the USA. Can also provide Eurail and Britrail passes.

Last Minute Travel Club, 132 Brookline Av, Boston, MA 02215, **t** 800 527 8646.

Nouvelles Frontières, 6 East 46th St, New York, NY 10017, with branches on the West Coast and Canada, **t** 800 677 0720, **t** (212) 986 3343, *www.newfrontiers.com*. Discounted scheduled and charter flights on Corsair from LA, Oakland and New York to Paris (from around $400), and non-stop to some French provincial cities. Also offers hotel bookings and packages.

Now Voyager, 74 Varick St, Suite 307, New York, NY 10013, **t** (212) 431 1616.

STA, **t** 800 781 4040, *www.statravel.com*, with branches at most universities and also at 10 Downing St, New York, NY 10014, **t** (212) 627 3111, and ASUC Building, 2nd Floor, University of California, Berkeley, CA 94720, **t** (510) 642 3000.

TFI, 34 West 32nd St, New York, NY 10001, **t** 800 745 8000, **t** (212) 736 1140.

Travel Cuts, 187 College St, Toronto, Ontario M5T 1P7, **t** (416) 979 2406. Canada's largest student travel specialists; branches in most provinces.

London–Lille takes a mere 2 hours. Then change train at Lille and you can get a fast service to the main Loire Valley cities avoiding Paris completely. This means, for example, that Tours is only some 5 hours away from London-Waterloo, Angers 6 hours.

Alternatively, you can take the Eurostar service from London-Waterloo or Ashford to Paris-Gare du Nord; London–Paris takes 3 hours. But then you'll need to cross central Paris to reach Paris-Montparnasse, the station from which SNCF (the French national rail company) trains leave for the Loire Valley. For more information on SNCF services, *see* 'Getting Around' below, or start by looking at its web site, *www.sncf.fr*.

If you plan to take some long train journeys, it may be worth investing in a rail pass. The excellent-value **Euro Domino** pass entitles EU citizens to unlimited rail travel through France for three to eight days in a month for £109–204, or £80–155 for 12–25-year-olds.

There's also the **Inter-Rail** pass (for European residents of at least six months), which offers 22 days' unlimited travel in Europe (countries are grouped into zones; you pay £129/185 for one zone for under/over the age of 26), plus discounts on trains to cross-Channel ferry terminals and returns on Eurostar from £60. Inter-Rail cards are not valid on trains in the UK.

Visitors from North America have a wide choice of passes, including **Eurailpass**, **Flexipass** and **Saver Pass**, which can all be purchased in the USA. A one-month Eurailpass costs around $623/890 for those aged under/over 26 years.

Rail Europe handles bookings for all services, including Eurostar and Motorail, and sells rail passes:

UK, Rail Europe, 179 Piccadilly, London W1V 0BA, t 08705 848 848, *www.raileurope.co.uk*. Calls cost 50p a minute.

USA, Rail Europe, 226 Westchester Ave, White Plains, NY 10064, t 800 438 7245, *www.raileurope.com*.

By Bus

Eurolines offers services from London to Tours (1¾hrs), Angers (14hrs) and Nantes (15¼hrs), There are daily services and prices

are £77/87 return (under/over the age of 26). Discounts are also offered for senior citizens and children under 12.

Information and booking: t 08705 143 219, t 08705 808 080, *www.eurolines.co.uk*.

By Boat

The Channel ports of Dieppe, Le Havre, Caen-Ouistreham and Cherbourg are all within reasonable driving distance of various sections of the Loire Valley, although you'll have to take quite tricky cross-country routes rather than motorways to reach the region. St-Malo is good for the western end of the Loire Valley, although the ferry crossings from the UK take a lot longer. If you take the short crossings to Calais, Boulogne or Dunkerque, then the drive to the Loire Valley will be a fair bit longer, but you can make use of fast, if expensive, French motorways.

Brittany Ferries, The Brittany Centre, Wharf Road, Portsmouth PO2 8RU, t 08705 360 360, *www.brittany-ferries.com*. Sailings from Portsmouth to Caen (6hrs) and St-Malo (10½hrs; overnight), and from Poole to Cherbourg (4¼hrs).

Condor Ferries, The Quay, Weymouth, Dorset DT4 8DX, t (01305) 761 551, *www.condor ferries.co.uk*. Sailings from Poole to St-Malo (4½hrs).

Hoverspeed Ferries, International Hoverport, Dover CT17 9TG, t 08705 240 241, *www.hoverspeed.co.uk*. Seacats (catamarans) Dover–Calais (35mins), Folkestone–Boulogne (55mins), Newhaven–Dieppe (2hrs).

Norfolkline, t (01304) 218 410, f (01304) 218 420, *www.norfolkline.com*. An alternative option to consider between Dover and Dunkerque (for passengers with cars only).

P&O Portsmouth, Peninsular House, Wharf Rd, Portsmouth PO2 8TA, t 0870 242 4999, f (01705) 864 211, *www.poportsmouth.com*. Day and night sailings from Portsmouth to Le Havre (5½hrs) and Cherbourg (7hrs).

P&O Stena Line, Channel House, Channel View Rd, Dover CT17 9TJ, t 0870 600 0600, *www.posl.com*. Ferry and superferry from Dover to Calais (45mins).

SeaFrance, Eastern Docks, Dover, Kent CT16 1JA, t 08705 711 711, *www.seafrance.com*. Sailings from Dover to Calais (1½hrs).

Prices vary considerably according to season and demand, and, as always, it pays to shop around for the best deal.

By Car

Taking your car on a **Eurotunnel** train is the most convenient way of crossing the Channel between the UK and France. It takes only 35mins to get through the tunnel from Folkestone to Calais, and there are up to four departures an hour every day. Peak time tickets for a car and passengers should cost around £300 return in the low season, rising to £350 return in the high season. If you travel at night (10pm–6am), it is slightly cheaper. Special-offer day returns (look for them on the web site) range from £15 to £50. The price for all tickets is per car less than 6.5m in length, plus the driver and all passengers.

If you prefer a dose of bracing sea air, you've plenty of choice; see 'By Boat', above.

For information on rules and regulations when driving in France, see 'Getting Around', below.

Eurotunnel: Information and bookings t 08705 353 535, *www.eurotunnel.com*.

Entry Formalities

Passports and Visas

Holders of EU, US, Canadian, Australian and New Zealand passports do not need a visa to enter France for stays of up to three months; most other nationals do. If you intend to stay longer, the law says you need a *carte de séjour* (from the *mairie*, or town hall), a requirement EU citizens can easily get around as passports are rarely stamped. Non-EU citizens had best apply for an extended visa before leaving home, a complicated procedure requiring proof of income, etc. You can't get a *carte de séjour* without this visa.

For further information contact your nearest French consulate.

Customs

Duty-free allowances have been abolished within the EU. For travellers coming from outside the EU, the duty-free limits are 1 litre of spirits or 2 litres of liquors (port, sherry or champagne), plus 2 litres of wine and 200 cigarettes.

Much larger quantities – up to 10 litres of spirits, 90 litres of wine, 110 litres of beer and 800 cigarettes – bought locally and provided you are travelling between EU countries, can be taken through customs if you can prove that they are for private consumption only.

For more information, US citizens can telephone the US Customs Service, t (202) 354 1000, or see the pamphlet *Know Before You Go* available from *www.customs.gov*. You're not allowed to bring back absinthe or Cuban cigars.

Getting Around

By Train

The SNCF runs an efficient network of trains through all the major cities. Prices have recently gone up but are still reasonable. If you plan on making only a few long hauls the Euro Domino (*see above*) or France Railpass will save you money. Other possible discounts hinge on the exact time of your departure.

For ordinary trains (excluding TGVs and *couchettes*), SNCF has divided the year into *bleue* (blue, off-peak) and *blanche* (white, peak) periods, based on demand: white periods run from Friday noon to midnight, from Sunday 3pm to Monday 10am, and during holidays (all stations give out little calendars).

If you depart in a *période bleue* with a return ticket, travel over 200km and stay at least a Saturday night, you'll get a 25% discount (**Découverte Séjour**). Couples are eligible for a **Découverte à Deux** tariff, which gives a discount of 25% on all trains when travelling together in a blue period.

Anyone over 60 can purchase a **Carte Sénior** (€44), valid for a year and giving 25–50% off individual journeys according to availability, and 25% off train journeys from France to 25 countries in Europe. There is also a **12–25 Carte**, which offers 50% reductions in blue periods and a 25% reduction in white periods for that age group.

Anyone can save money by buying a second-class ticket at least a week to a month in advance (**Découverte J8** or **J30**), the only condition being that you must use it at the designated time on the designated train, with no chance for reimbursement if you miss it.

Tickets must be stamped in the little orange machines by the entrance to the platforms that say *Compostez votre billet* (this puts the date on the ticket, to keep you from using the same one over and over again). Any time you interrupt a journey until another day, you have to re-compost your ticket. Long-distance trains (Trains Corail) have snack trolleys and bar-cafeteria cars; some have play areas for small children.

Nearly every station has large computerized left-luggage lockers (*consignes automatiques*) that spit out a slip with the lock combination when you use them. They take about half-an-hour to puzzle out the first time you use them, so plan accordingly; also note that any recent terrorist activity in France tends to close them down across the board.

SNCF general information: t 08 36 35 35 35 (€0.5/min), *www.sncf.com*. You can book advance tickets from the USA or UK prior to departure on this web site, and pay by credit card at an SNCF machine in France.

By Bus

The bus network and extent of services varies from *département* to *département*. The timetable options for anything but travel between the major towns will not be extensive, so check carefully on times of departure and return when heading out to smaller places. Major towns normally call their bus station the *gare routière* – they're most often, but not always, by the railway station. In smaller places, stops can be in slightly surprising spots. They may not be obvious, so ask if you're in any doubt.

The timetable schedules aren't always to be trusted; the tourist office or shopkeepers near the bus stop may have a more accurate instinct for when a bus is likely to appear.

By Car

First, the requirements. A car entering France must have its registration and insurance papers. Drivers with a valid licence from an EU country, the US, Canada or Australia don't need an international licence. If you're coming from the UK or Ireland, the dip of the head-lights must be adjusted to the right. All cars in France are required to have rear seat belts and these must be worn by rear-seat passengers. Carrying a warning triangle is mandatory; if you have a breakdown the triangle should be placed 50m behind the car.

Regarding roads and driving in France, there are three particularly important points to note. First, drive on the right-hand side of the road. Second, watch out for *priorité à droite*. France used to have a rule of giving priority to the right at every intersection. This has largely disappeared, although there may still be intersections, usually in towns, where it applies – these will be marked. Third, French motorists rarely if ever respect pedestrians, even at pedestrian crossings. It's a sad fact that something like twice as many people are killed on French roads every year as are killed in Britain (and obviously a much higher percentage of the population than in the USA).

If you're involved in an **accident**, the procedure is to fill out and sign a *constat aimable*. If your French isn't sufficient to deal with this, try to find someone to translate for you so you don't accidentally incriminate yourself. The word for accident is the same in French.

Drink-driving is now being strongly campaigned against in France. From time to time you may see French police virtually blocking a road to make suspects blow into a breathalyser, particularly after Sunday lunch. Drivers can avoid worrying about this by limiting themselves to two glasses of wine only – that's what the strict limits imposed in 1995 roughly correspond to. You have been warned. Fines for drink-driving can be enormous. Fines for speeding begin at a painful €198 and are payable on the spot. Often French drivers warn others about the presence of police traps by flashing their lights.

Petrol (*essence*) is relatively expensive in France. Petrol stations can be few and far between in rural areas, shutting for the night and on Sunday afternoons. Don't get caught out. Unleaded is called *sans plomb*; diesel is often referred to as *gazole* or *gasoil*. If an attendant helps you with oil, windscreen-cleaning or checking tyre pressure they will expect a tip.

On *autoroutes*, or motorways, tolls are quite high. The network is excellent and greatly time-saving, but there are always more gentle, picturesque routes available. The N (or RN)

Car Hire

Car hire in France can be an expensive proposition. To save money, look into air and holiday package deals. Prices vary widely from firm to firm: beware the small print about service charges and taxes. It's often cheaper to book through car hire companies in your own country before you go. The minimum age for hiring a car in France is around 21 to 25, and the maximum around 70. If you decide to hire a car once there, local tourist offices can provide information on car hire agencies. Car hire firms are also listed for the larger towns in this book (*see* 'Getting There and Around' sections).

UK
Auto Europe, *www.autoeurope.com*
Avis, t 08705 900 500, f 08705 6060 100, *www.avis.co.uk*
Budget, t 08701 565 656, f (01442) 280 092, *www.budget-international.com/uk*
Europcar, t 0870 607 5000, f (01132) 429 495, *www.europcar.com*
Hertz, t 08705 996 699, f (020) 8679 0181, *www.hertz.co.uk*
Thrifty, t 08705 168 238, f (01494) 751 601, *www.thrifty.co.uk*

USA and Canada
Auto Europe, t 800 223 5555, t (207) 842 2000, *www.autoeurope.com*
Auto France, t 800 572 9655, t (201) 934 6994, f (201) 934 7501, *www.autofrance.com*
Avis Rent a Car, t 800 331 1084, t (516) 222 3000, *www.avis.com*
Europe by Car, New York, t 800 223 1516, t (212) 581 3040, f (212) 246 1458; California t 800 252 9401, t (213) 272 0424, f (310) 273 9247; *www.europebycar.com*
Europcar, t 800 800 6000, t (918) 669 2823, f (918) 669 2821, *www.europcar.com*
Hertz, t 800 654 3001, *www.hertz.com*

roads form part of the national network and when there isn't a motorway paralleling them can be very busy, for example along stretches of the Loire. D roads (*départementales*) are generally well maintained. Smaller C (or *communal*) roads can be pretty narrow at times. The speed limits are as follows: 130km/80mph on *autoroutes*; 110km/69mph on dual carriageways (divided highways); 90km/55mph on other roads; 50km/30mph in urban areas (coming into force as soon as you pass a white sign with a town's name on it and lasting until you pass another sign with the town's name barred).

The word for a **breakdown** is *une panne*; to break down is *tomber en panne*. If you break down on major roads or motorways, you can use the orange-coloured emergency telephones to contact rescue services or the police. Otherwise, if you're a member of a motoring club affiliated to the **Touring Club de France**, ring them; if not, ring the police, t 17.

By Bicycle

Getting your own bike to France is fairly easy: Air France and British Airways carry them free from Britain, for example. From the USA or Australia, most airlines will carry them as long as they're boxed and are included in your total baggage weight. In all cases, telephone ahead to the relevant airline to check on terms and conditions. On **Eurostar**, you need to pack your bag in a bicycle bag and check it in at least 24 hours before you travel, or wait 24 hours at the other end. Alternatively, Esprit Parcel Service, t 08705 850 850, can arrange for your bike to be transported on Eurostar.

The French are keen cyclists and if you haven't brought your own bike the main towns and holiday centres always seem to have at least one shop that hires out bikes – local tourist offices have lists. *Vélo* is the common colloquial word for a *bicyclette*. A *vélo tout terrain*, invariably abbreviated to VTT, is a mountain bike. Be prepared to pay a fairly hefty deposit on a good bike (from around €152). You may want to inquire about insurance against theft. You can also hire bikes from most train stations in major towns; they vary in quality, so check them. The advantage of hiring from a station is that you can drop

Special-interest Holidays

For a complete list of tour operators, *see* the Maison de France web site at *www.france guide.com* (in the US *www.francetourism.com*), or get in touch with a French government tourist office in your country. Other sources of information are The French Centre, 164–6 Westminster Bridge Rd, London SE1 7RW, t (020) 7960 2600; and the Cultural Services of the French Embassy, 23 Cromwell Rd, London SW7 2EL, t (020) 7838 2088/9, or at 972 Fifth Av, New York, NY 10021, t (212) 439 1400. Alternatively, check out the information at *www.fr-holidaystore.co.uk*.

For information on firms offering self-catering accommodation, *see* p.102.

France

Ballooning
Champagne Air Show, 9 Rue Thiers, 51100 Reims, t 03 26 87 89 12, f 03 26 87 89 14. Deluxe ballooning trips in the Loire, among other places.

Language
Eurocentres Foundation, 13 Passage Dauphine, 75006 Paris, t 01 40 46 72 00, in the USA t (703) 684 1494 or t 800 648 4809, *www.eurocentres.com*. Non-profit organization, offering intensive general and business French in a professionally equipped centre in Amboise.

Limousine
Aristo's Limousine, 12 Rue Martissot, 92110 Clichy, t 01 47 37 53 70, f 01 47 37 91 99, *aristos@infonie.fr*. Sightseeing tours of the Loire by luxury limousine.

UK and Ireland

General Interest
Abercrombie & Kent, Sloane Square House, Holbein Place, London SW1W 8NS, t (020) 7559 8500, *www.abercrombiekent.co.uk*. Quality city breaks.
American Express Europe, Destination Services, 19–20 Berners St, London W1P 4AE,

t (020) 7637 8600, f (020) 7631 4803. City breaks and fly-drives.
Page and Moy, 135–40 London Rd. Leicester LE2 1EN, t (0116) 250 7000, f (0116) 250 7123. Tours throughout France, including a tour of the Loire and Brittany.

Canal Tours and River Cruises
Abercrombie & Kent (*see* above for details). Barges and houseboats.
French Country Cruises, 54 High St East, Uppingham, Rutland, LE15 9PZ, t (01572) 821 330, f (01572) 821 072. Canal and river cruises.
Hoseasons Holidays, Sunway House, Lowestoft NR32 2LW, t (01502) 500 532, *www.hoseasons.co.uk*. Canal and river cruises.

Cooking and Wine
Arblaster & Clarke Wine Tours, Farnham Rd, West Liss, Hants GU33 6JQ, t (01730) 893 344, *www.arblasterandclarke.com*. Organizes wine trips to France, some of which take in the Loire. There's also a Loire wine and walking tour.
Inntravel, Hovingham, York YO6 4JZ, t (01653) 628 811, *www.inntravel.co.uk*. Offers the choice of a cycling holiday or a wine tour holiday in the Loire.
Tanglewood Wine Tours, Tanglewood House, Mayfield Avenue, New Haw, Weybridge, Surrey KT15 3AG, t (01932) 348 720, f (01932) 350 861. Wine breaks in the Loire.

Language
Euro Academy, 77a George St, Croydon CR0 1LD, t (020) 8686 2363, *euroacademy@btinternet.com*, *www.euroacademy.co.uk*. French courses in Tours.

Singles
Solo's Holidays, 54–8 High St, Edgware, Middx HA8 7ED, t 08700 720 700, *travel@solosholidays.co.uk*, *www.solosholidays.co.uk*. Singles holidays throughout France.

Walking and Cycling
Belle France, 15 East St, Rye, East Sussex TN31 7JY, England t (01797) 223 777, *info@belle-france.co.uk*, *www.bellefrance.co.uk*. Has the option of a Loire walking or cycling holiday in its brochure.

The Chain Gang, 4th Floor, 24 Foley St, London W1P 7LA, t (020) 7323 1730, f 7323 1731, www.thechaingang.co.uk. Guided cycling tours visiting Loire châteaux and vineyards.

Headwater Holidays, 146 London Rd, Northwich CW9 5HH, t (01606) 813 333, www.headwater-breakaway.com. Accompanied and independent cycling, walking, canoeing and rafting holidays.

Sherpa Expeditions, 131a Heston Rd, Hounslow, Middlesex TW5 0RD, t (020) 8577 2717, sales@sherpa-walking-holidays.co.uk, www.sherpaexpeditions.com. The Loire Valley walking holiday is probably one of the very easiest in their brochure.

Susi Madron's Cycling for Softies, 2 & 4 Birch Polygon, Manchester M14 5HX, t (0161) 248 8282, www.fr-holidaystore.co.uk/susimadro. Mixes a cycling itinerary in the Loire with culinary stops.

USA and Canada

General Interest

Abercrombie & Kent, 1520 Kensington Rd, Oakbrook, IL 60523, t 800 323 7308, t (630) 954 2944, www.abercrombiekent.com. Quality city and country breaks throughout France. Also river cruises and houseboats.

Europe Train Tours, 198 E. Boston Post Rd, Mamaroneck, NY 10543, t 800 551 2085, t (914) 698 9426, www.etttours.com. Escorted tours by train and car, taking in the Loire.

Maupintour, 1421 Research Park Drive, Suite 300, Lawrence, KS 66049, t 800 255 4266, t (785) 331 1000, www.maupintour.com. Barge cruises and escorted tours.

Ballooning

The Bombard Society, 333 Pershing Way, West Palm Beach, FL 33401, t 800 862 8537, t (561) 837 6610, travel@bombardsociety.com, www.bombardsociety.com. Five-day luxury ballooning 'adventures' in Burgundy and the Loire.

Canal Tours and River Cruises

Alden Yacht Charters, 1909 Alden Landing, Portsmouth, RI 02871, t 800 253 3654, t (401) 683 4200, www.aldenyachts.com. Luxury barge holidays in the upper Loire Valley.

French Country Waterways, P.O. Box 2195, Duxbury, MA 02331, t 800 222 1236, t (781) 934 2454, www.fcwl.com. Hotel barges.

Cooking and Wine

Avalon, P.O. Box 8911, Newport Beach, CA 92658, t 888 499 9463, t (949) 673 7376, www.avalon-tours.com. Wine and gastronomy tours in the Loire Valley

Gay and Lesbian

Alyson Adventures, P.O. Box 180179, Boston, MA 02118, t 800 825 9766, t (617) 542 1177, www.alysonadventures.com. Bike tours.

Language

International Studies Abroad, 817 W. 24th St, Austin, TX 78705, t 800 580 8826, t (512) 480 8522, www.studiesabroad.com. Courses in Angers.

National Registration Centre for Study Abroad, 823 N. 2nd St, Milwaukee, WI 53203, t (414) 278 0631, www.nrcsa.com. Language and culture courses in Angers, Nantes and Tours.

Walking and Cycling

Adventure Sport Holidays, 815 North Rd, Westfield, MA 01085, t 800 628 9655, t (413) 568 2855, www.advonskis.com. Biking through the Loire.

Backroads, 801 Cedar St, Berkeley, CA 94701 1800, t 800 462 2848, t 800 GO ACTIVE, www.backroads.com. Bicycling and hiking in the Loire Valley.

Brooks Country Cycling Tours, 140 W. 83rd St, New York, NY 10024, t (212) 874 5151, info@brookscountrycycling.com, www.brookscountrycycling.com. Guided cycling tours in the Loire Valley.

Cross Country International, P.O. Box 1170, Millbrook, NY 12545, t 800 828 8768, t (914) 677 6000, www.equestrianvacations.com. Organised horse-riding trails.

DuVine Adventures, 635 Boston Ave, Somerville, MA 02144, t 888 396 5383, t (781) 395 7440, www.duvine.com. Self-guided cycling tours through Loire vineyards.

Two Bicycles and a Map Ltd, PO Box 3142, Madison, WI 53704, t (608) 244 6598, info@twobicycles.com, www.twobicycles.com. Small, 'pedal at your own pace' bicycle tours.

the bike back off at another, as long as you specify where when you hire it. Rates should be around €7.5 a day, with a deposit of €45.5–61 and the yielding of a credit card number. The Loire Valley countryside offers relatively easy riding, as it is only mildly undulating. One strong recommendation – avoid the busy N roads as far as possible.

Certain French trains (with a bicycle symbol in the timetable) carry bikes for free; otherwise you have to send them as registered luggage and pay a fee of around €6, with delivery guaranteed within five days.

Maps and cycling information are available from the **Fédération Française de Cyclotourisme**, 8 Rue Jean-Marie Jégo, 75013 Paris, **t** 01 45 80 30 21, *www.ffct.org*, or in Britain from the **Cyclists Touring Club**, Cotterell House, 69 Meadrow, Godalming, Surrey GU7 3HS, **t** (01483) 417 217, *www.ctc.org.uk. See* also the list of special-interest holiday companies, above.

On Foot

A massive 40,000km network of long-distance paths, or Sentiers de Grandes Randonnées (**GRs** for short), marked by distinctive red-and-white signs, takes in some of France's most spectacular scenery. The GR3 is the main French walking path along the Loire Valley. The GR41 takes you along the Cher, the GR46 along the Indre. You can buy detailed but expensive guides to them in French (Topoguides), published by the Comité National des Sentiers de Grande Randonnée, 8 Av Marceau, 75008 Paris, **t** 01 47 23 62 32. In English, Bartholomew's, IGN and Robertson McCarta publish specialist books on walking along the Loire.

You can also find a few Loire walks recommended in books covering walking in France more generally. For information by *département*, contact the central tourist information office (*see* p.100).

Practical A–Z

08

Climate and When to Go

The first hardy cyclists tend to come out in March when the Loire roads are pretty well empty of other tourist traffic, depending on when Easter falls. In March you can see the landscape free of leaves, with large round clumps of mistletoe like winter baubles in many of the trees and the châteaux more clearly visible. Although the weather along the Loire is pretty mild, it can be quite cold, grey and wet this early in the year. Remember also that before Easter many of the sights aren't open, apart from the major châteaux and museums.

Although the French for April showers is *giboulées de mars* (March downpours), April can be cruel in the Loire too. It can also be beautiful, especially with the fruit orchards in blossom. Surprisingly, May often turns out not much warmer or more reliable than April, but then the countryside is at its freshest and greenest. June gets a fair deal warmer and you avoid the main tourist season. July and August are generally nice and hot, and very crowded around the main tourist sites. As the flow of water in the Loire dwindles, life along the river and its tributaries comes into its own, with fishermen and Loire barques enlivening the river scenes.

September is a lovely month, the weather still generally good, but with far fewer tourists, and peace and quiet returning as children go back to school. The trouble is that the noisy French shooting season starts in September, an untamed passion for many French men. October tends to have its fair share of beautiful days, with foliage changing colour, and the many wispy asparagus plants on the sandy river banks turning particularly vibrant tones of orange and yellow. This is also the time of the grape harvest, the *vendanges*.

November, December, January and February are not really tourist months. Many sites close for the winter after All Saints' Day (1 November), or Remembrance Day (11 November).

Crime and the Police

France is a safe and very policed country, but it's important to be aware that thieves target visitors, especially their holiday homes and cars – they see foreign number plates or a rental car as easy pickings. Leave anything you'd really miss at home, carry traveller's cheques, insure your property, and be especially careful in large cities. Report thefts to the nearest *gendarmerie* or *police national* – it's not a pleasant task but the reward is the bit of paper you need for an insurance claim. If your passport is stolen, contact the police and your nearest consulate for emergency travel documents. Carry photocopies of your passport, driver's licence, etc. – it makes it easier when reporting a loss.

By law, the police in France can stop anyone anywhere and demand to see ID; in practice, they tend to do it only to harass minorities, the homeless and the scruffy (the Paris police are notorious for this). The drug situation is the same in France as anywhere in western Europe: soft and hard drugs are widely available, and the police only make an issue of victimless crime when it suits them – being a foreigner may be reason enough, and there is little that your consulate can or will do about it.

Disabled Travellers

When it comes to providing access for all, France is not exactly in the vanguard of nations, but things are beginning to change. The SNCF, for instance, now publishes a pamphlet, *Guide Pratique du Voyageur à Mobilité Réduite*, covering travel by train for the disabled (all TGVs are equipped) – contact

Average Maximum Temperatures in °C/°F

	Jan	Feb	Mar	April	May	June
Centre-Val de Loire	8 / 46.5	7 / 44.5	10 / 50	16 / 61	16.5 / 62	23.5 / 74
Pays de la Loire	10 / 50	8.5 / 47	11 / 52	18 / 64.5	17 / 62.5	23 / 73.5
	July	Aug	Sept	Oct	Nov	Dec
Centre-Val de Loire	26 / 79	24.5 / 76	21 / 70	16 / 61	11 / 52	7 / 44.5
Pays de la Loire	26 / 79	24.5 / 76	22 / 71.5	17 / 62.5	12.5 / 54.5	9.5 / 49

the French Railways office in your country for details. The Channel Tunnel (*see* p.85) is a good way to travel by car since disabled passengers are allowed to stay in their vehicle, and Eurostar gives wheelchair passengers first-class travel for second-class fares. Most ferry companies will offer facilities if contacted in advance.

Vehicles fitted to accommodate wheelchairs or modified for disabled drivers pay reduced tolls on *autoroutes*. An *autoroute* guide for disabled travellers (*Guides des Autoroutes à l'Usage des Personnes à Mobilité Réduite*) is available free from **Ministère des Transports**, Direction des Routes, Service du Contrôle des Autoroutes, La Défense, 92055 Cedex, Paris, **t** 01 40 81 21 22.

The *Gîtes Accessibles aux Personnes Handicapées*, published by Gîtes de France, lists self-catering possibilities (*see* p.102, for their address).

The following organizations provide services for people with disabilities:

France
Association des Paralysés de France, t 01 40 78 69 00. A national organization with an office in each *département*, providing in-depth local information; headquarters are in Paris.

Comité National Français de Liaison pour la Réadaptation des Handicapés, 236b Rue Tolbiac, 75013 Paris, **t** 01 53 80 66 66. Provides information on access, and produces useful guides to various regions in France.

UK
Access Travel, 6 The Hillock, Astley, Lancashire M29 7GW, **t** (01942) 888 844, *info@access-travel.co.uk, www.access-travel.co.uk*. Travel agent for disabled people: special airfares, car hire and wheelchair-accessible *gîtes*.

Holiday Care Service, Imperial Building, Victoria Rd, Horley, Surrey, RH6 7PZ, **t** (01293) 774 535, **f** (01293) 784 647, Minicom **t** (01293) 776 943, *holiday.care@virgin.net, www. holidaycare.org.uk*. Publishes an information sheet on holidays in France (£1).

RADAR (Royal Association for Disability and Rehabilitation), 12 City Forum, 250 City Rd, London EC1V 8AF, **t** (020) 7250 3222, Minicom **t** (020) 7250 4119, *www.radar.org.uk*. Information and books on travel.

USA
Alternative Leisure Co, 165 Middlesex Turnpike, Suite 206, Bedford, MA 01730, **t** (718) 275 0023, *www.alctrips.com*. Organizes vacations abroad for disabled people.

Mobility International USA, PO Box 10767, Eugene, OR 97440, USA, **t/TTY** (541) 343 1284, *www.miusa.org*. Information on international educational exchange programmes and volunteer service overseas for the disabled.

SATH (Society for the Advancement of Travel for the Handicapped), 347 5th Av, Suite 610, New York, NY 10016, **t** (212) 557 0027, *www.tenonline.com/sath*. Travel and access information.

Other Useful Contacts
The Able Informer, *www.sasquatch.com/able-info*. International on-line magazine with tips for travelling abroad.

Access Ability, *www.access-ability.co.uk*. Information on travel agencies catering specifically to disabled people.

Access Tourism, *www.accesstourism.com*. Pan-European web site with information on hotels, guesthouses, travel agencies and specialist tour operators, etc.

Australian Council for Rehabilitation of the Disabled (ACRODS), PO Box 60, Curtin, ACT 2605, Australia, **t/TTY** (02) 6682 4333, *www.acrod.org.au*. Information and contact numbers for specialist travel agencies.

Disabled Persons Assembly, PO Box 27-254, Wellington 6035, New Zealand, **t** (04) 472 2626, *www.dpa.org.nz*. All-round source for travel information.

Emerging Horizons, *www.emerginghorizons. com*. International on-line travel newsletter for people with disabilities.

Global Access, *www.geocities.com*. On-line network for disabled travellers, with links, archives and information on travel guides for the disabled, etc.

Eating Out

The French tend to eat quite early, often at 12 or 12.30 for lunch, and generally between 7 and 9pm in the evening, with slightly later summer hours for dinner. Brasseries and cafés are flexible and open long hours, but

> **Restaurant Price Categories**
> In this book, recommended restaurants have prices listed for their set menus, to give a rough idea of cost. Alternatively, restaurants are split into four price categories (prices are for a three-course meal without wine per person):
>
> | | |
> |---|---|
> | luxury | over €60 |
> | expensive | €30–60 |
> | moderate | €15–30 |
> | cheap | under €15 |

restaurants don't often like serving late. Most restaurants recommended in this book offer a choice of set-price menus, and these are the prices we provide to give a rough idea of cost. Most places post their menus outside the door so you know what to expect. If service is included it will say *service compris* or s.c.; if not, *service non compris* or s.n.c.

For further information about eating in the Loire Valley, including local specialities, wines and a menu decoder, *see* the **Food and Drink** chapter, pp.69–80.

Electricity

French electricity is all 220V. British and Irish appliances will need an adapter with two round prongs; North American appliances usually need a transformer as well.

Embassies and Consulates

Foreign Embassies In France

Australia: 4 Rue Jean Rey, 75015 Paris, t 01 40 59 33 00.

Canada: 35 Av Montaigne, 75008 Paris, t 01 44 43 29 00.

Ireland: 4 Rue Rude, 75016 Paris, t 01 44 17 67 00.

New Zealand: 7 Rue Léonard de Vinci, 75116 Paris, t 01 45 01 43 43.

UK: 18 bis Rue d'Anjou, 75008 Paris, t 01 44 51 31 00, f 01 44 51 31 27.

USA: 2 Rue St-Florentin, 75001 Paris, t 01 43 12 22 22.

French Embassies Abroad

Canada: 25 Rue St Louis, Québec, QC G1R 3Y8, t (418) 688 0430.

Ireland: 36 Ailesbury Rd, Ballsbridge, Dublin 4, t (01) 260 1666.

UK: 21 Cromwell Rd, London SW7 2DQ, t (020) 7838 2000, *www.ambafrance.org.uk.*

11 Randolph Crescent, Edinburgh EH3 7TT, t (0131) 225 7954.

USA: 737 North Michigan Av, Suite 2020, Chicago, IL 60611, t (312) 787 5359/60/61.

10990 Wilshire Bd, Suite 300, Los Angeles, CA 90024, t (310) 235 3200.

934 Fifth Av, New York, NY 10021, t (212) 606 3688, *www.amb-usa.fr, citizeninfo@state.gov.*

Environment

The Parc Naturel Régional Loire-Anjou-Touraine (see pp.366–8) has been created to protect the area's heritage and traditions, and encourage both locals and visitors to take an interest in local nature and traditions.

Then there are the small Maisons de la Loire at Jargeau (*see* p.127), St-Dyé-sur-Loire (*see* pp.163–4), Montlouis (*see* p.258) and St-Mathurin (*see* p.413). They're run by people passionate about the river, and can provide further information on environmental issues.

Festivals

The Calendar of Events on the next two pages contains a fairly wide selection of festivals in the region covered in the guide. To find out about son-et-lumière shows, *see* 'Sports and Activities', below.

Each *département* publishes a booklet on the host of festivals in their area, down to the smallest events which aren't included here; contact individual CDTs (*see* p.100).

Health and Emergencies

Ambulance t 15
Fire Brigade t 18
Police t 17

France has one of the best healthcare systems in the world. Local hospitals are the place to go in an emergency (*urgence*).

If it's not an emergency, pharmacists are trained to administer first aid and dispense advice for minor problems. In rural areas there is always someone on duty if you ring the bell of a pharmacy; in cities, pharmacies are open on a rota and addresses are posted in their

Calendar of Events

Please note that dates can vary; contact local tourist offices to confirm details.

January

Jan–Feb *Rencontres Musicales de l'Est Tourangeau*. Classical music programme (contact Mairie in Montlouis-sur-Loire).

Late Jan *Festival Premiers Plans*. Festival of leading European cinema, Angers, *www.premiersplans.org*.

February

Early Feb *Festival de Danse Contemporaine*. Contemporary dance festival in Blois.

3rd week *La Quinzaine du Tourisme d'Entreprises*. A celebration of industry and entrepreneurs in Angers.

Late Feb *Fête des Vins d'Anjou*. A discovery of Anjou wines in Chalonnes-sur-Loire.

March

March *Le Printemps Musical de St-Cosme*. Classical concerts in a monastic refectory outside Tours.

1st Sat and Sun *Wine fair*, Bourgueil.

Last weekend *Fête des Plantes et des Jardins*. Brings together gardening professionals at the Château de Beauregard.

End March–late Oct *Cadre Noir*. Six horse shows and two galas at Saumur.

Easter

Easter–mid-Nov *Flower festivals* at the Parc Floral, Orléans-La Source. Events start with an Easter egg hunt on Easter Sunday.

Easter week *Festival de Paques*. series of concerts in the abbey of Fontevraud.

April

April–Sept *Rendez-vous Horticoles*. A variety of green-fingered associations, parks and gardens in Anjou throw open their doors to the public.

Early April *Fête des Plantes et des Jardins de Touraine*. Garden festival at the Château de la Bourdaisière, Montlouis-sur-Loire.

3rd week *Journees Nationales du Livre et du Vin*. Literature and wine festival in Saumur.

Last weekend *Les Musicalies de Sologne*. Music festival in Pierrefitte sur Sauldre.

Late April *Championnat d'Europe de voltige equestre*. Acrobatic riding in Saumur.

End April–early May *Carnaval* in Cholet. Parades, floats and carnival festivities.

May

Early May *Fêtes Johanniques* (normally 7–9 May). Commemorates the freeing of Orléans from the English, inspired by Joan of Arc.

3rd weekend *Festival des Animaux de la Ferme* in Pruniers en Sologne.

Late May *Aucard de Tours*. Rock festival in Tours.

Late May *Concours Complet International*. International horse competition at Saumur.

Late May–late June *Festival de Sully-sur-Loire*. A series of concerts, often with prestigious performers.

June

June (among other dates throughout the year) *Le Chore-Graphique*. Festival of contemporary dance, Tours.

Early June (Pentecost) *Journées de la Rose*. A display and sales of roses at the Prieuré de St-Cosme outside Tours.

Early June *Festival des Atipiks*. Music festival in Blois.

Early June *Concours International de Brass Band*. French and international brass bands compete at Amboise.

2nd weekend RAM DAM – *Festival de Musique et d'Animation* in Blois.

Mid-June–mid-July *Festival d'Anjou*. Theatre festival in Angers and across Anjou.

Mid-June–mid-Oct *Festival International des Jardins*. Major annual show by around 30 leading international landscape gardeners, in the grounds of the Château de Chaumont.

3rd weekend *Journées Nationales de la Chasse et de la Pêche*. Game fair around the Château de Chambord.

3rd Sun *Fête du Velo sur la Loire*. Cycling routes along the Loire, beginning at Angers and Saumur.

End June *Fêtes Musicales en Touraine*, at the Grange de Meslay north of Tours. Highly reputed festival specializing in chamber music.

End June *Festival des Geants*. Carnival of coloured floats, held on even years.

End June *Festival International de Musiques Militaires.* Military music in Saumur, held on odd years.

Late June *Solstice de Beaulieu-les-Loches.* Mix of classical, jazz and rock concerts.

Late June–early July *Festival les Orientales.* A big music festival at St-Florent-le-Vieil, combining Asian and Western music.

Late June–early July *Festival de Jazz* in Orléans.

Late June–early July *Festival Historique.* A son-et-lumière show on certain nights at the Château de Beaugency.

Late June–early July *Spectacle Théâtral 'Les Trois Mousquetaires'.* Performance of *The Three Musketeers* in the gardens of the Château de Meung-sur-Loire.

July

July *Festoyances Rabelaisiennes.* Medieval-style market in Chinon.

July and Aug *Heures Musicales de Cunault.* Music on the banks of the Loire in Cunault.

July and Aug *Angers l'Étè.* Summer festival in Angers.

2nd week *Fetival 'au Nom de la Loire'.* Street theatre and music on the banks of the Loire in Tours.

13–14 July *La Parade Tourangelle.* Dance festival at Pouzay.

Mid-July *Journées de la Rose.* Rose festival in Doué-la-Fontaine.

Mid-July *Concours d'Attelage International.* Horse and carriage competition in Saumur.

Mid-July *Fête de la Peinture.* Art festival at Montrésor.

Mid–late July *Cléry Raconte Dunois.* Evening show at Cléry-St-André.

End July *Grand Prix Retro du Vignoble.* Classic car and bike rally through the streets of Le Puy-Notre-Dame.

August

Aug *Heures musicales du Haut-Anjou.* Concerts in châteaux and churches in northern Anjou.

Early Aug *Concerts à la Corroierie du Liget.* Classical music at Chemillé-sur-Indrois.

2nd week *Festival Cosmopolite.* Contemporary and world music at Genillé.

Mid-Aug *Musique et Jardins.* Classical music concerts in the gardens of the Château de Villandry.

Last Sun *Festival de la Nature en Val de Loire* in Richelieu.

September

Early Sept *Accroche-Coeurs.* Open-air street festival in Angers.

Early Sept *Festival de Jazz* in Touraine (contact the Mairie in Montlouis, **t** 02 47 50 72 70).

Late Sept *Concours de Dressage International.* Dressage competition in Saumur.

Last weekend *Les Rendev-vous du Pain.* Bread festival in Montrichard.

End Sept *Marathon International de la Loire.* Race down the Loire in canoes and kayaks, starting from Bouchemaine.

October

Oct *Floralies du Val de l'Indre* at the Moulin de Veigné near Montbazon.

First half *Sonates d'Automne* at Loches and Beaulieu-les-Loches. Concerts, exhibitions and educational workshops.

Mid-Oct *Mondial du Lion.* International horse-riding competition in Le Lion d'Angers.

Mid-Oct *Les Rendez-vous de l'Histoire* in Blois.

End Oct *Journées Gastronomiques de Sologne.* Food festival in Romorantin-Lanthenay.

November

First half *Festival International Acteurs.* Theatre, cinema and exhibitions in Tours.

Nov–May *Orchestre Symphonique de Tours.* Programme of concerts.

All Saints' week *Festhea.* National festival of amateur theatre in Tours.

Mid-Nov *Salon International Art et Metiers du Cheval.* Gathering of artists in Saumur.

3rd weekend *Les Rendez-Vous du Touraine Primeur à Montrichard.* Celebrates the arrival of the new wine (following the third Thurs in the month).

Last weekend *Festival de BD Boum.* Comic book festival held in Blois.

December

1st weekend *Grand Marché Animé de Noel.* The Château de Brissac is transformed into a winter wonderland, attended by Father Christmas.

Christmas Eve *Midnight Mass* at the abbey of St-Benoît-sur-Loire.

windows and in the local newspaper. Tourist offices can supply lists of local English-speaking doctors.

In France, however you're insured, you pay up front for everything, unless it's an emergency, when you will be billed later. Doctors will give you a brown and white *feuille de soins* with your prescription; take both to the pharmacy and keep the *feuille*, the various medicine stickers (*vignettes*) and prescriptions for insurance purposes at home.

Citizens of the EU should bring an E111 form (available from post offices before you travel), entitling you to the same emergency health services and treatments as French citizens. This means paying up front for medical care and prescriptions, of which 75–80% of the costs are reimbursed a week to 10 days later. In the UK, see the Department of Health web site at *www.doh.gov.uk/traveladvice*. You may also wish to take out a travel insurance policy covering medical care (*see* below).

Canadians are usually covered by their provincial health insurance; Americans should check their medical insurance policies.

Insurance

Many of the larger credit card companies will also offer free travel insurance when you use them to book a package holiday or aeroplane/train tickets. Read the small print very carefully, especially if you're travelling with expensive equipment (laptops, cameras, etc.). If you're not covered on your credit card, you may want to consider taking out an insurance policy covering theft and losses and offering 100% medical refund and emergency repatriation if necessary; check to see if it covers extra expenses should you get bogged down in airport or train strikes.

Beware that accidents resulting from sports are rarely covered by ordinary insurance.

Money, Banks and the Euro

1 Jan 1999 saw the start of the transition to the euro. It became the official currency in France (and 10 other nations of the European Union) and the official exchange rate was set at 1 euro=6.56F. Shops and businesses have been indicating prices in both currencies for some time. Euro notes and coins enter into circulation in January 2002, and francs will be phased out completely by 28th February. Traveller's cheques are available in euros.

Until 2002, you'll still be using the franc (abbreviated to F), which consists of 100 centimes. Banknotes come in denominations of 500, 200, 100, 50 and 20F; coins in 20, 10, 5, 2 and 1F, and 50, 20, 10, and 5 centimes.

Euros come in denominations of €500, 200, 100, 50, 20, 10 and 5 (banknotes) and €2, €1, 50 cents, 20 cents, 10 cents, 5 cents, 2 cents and 1 cent (coins).

Traveller's cheques are the safest way of carrying money, but the wide acceptance of credit and debit cards and the presence of ATMs (*distributeurs de billets*), even in small villages, make cards a convenient alternative. Visa is the most readily accepted credit card; American Express is often not accepted, however. Smaller hotels and restaurants and bed and breakfasts may not accept cards at all. Some shops and supermarkets experience difficulties reading UK-style magnetic strips (French credit cards now contain a chip, or *puce*, containing ID information), so arm yourself with cash just in case.

Under the Cirrus system, withdrawals in francs and euros can be made from bank and post office ATMs, using your PIN. The specific cards accepted are marked on each machine, and most give instructions in English. Credit card companies charge a fee for cash advances, but rates are often better than those at banks.

In the event of **lost or stolen credit cards**, call the following emergency numbers:
American Express, Paris, t 01 47 77 72 00
Barclaycard, t (00 44) 1604 230 230 (UK number)
Mastercard, t 0800 901 387
Visa (Carte Bleue), Paris, t 01 42 77 11 90.

Exchange rates vary, and most banks and bureaux de change take a commission of varying proportions. Bureaux de change that do nothing but exchange money, hotels and train stations usually have the worst rates or take the heftiest commissions.

For bank opening hours, *see* overleaf.

Opening Hours

Shops: While many shops and supermarkets are now open continuously Tues–Sat from 9 or 10am to 7 or 7.30pm, businesses in smaller towns still close down for lunch from 12 or 12.30pm to 2 or 3pm (4pm in summer). There are local exceptions, but nearly everything shuts on Monday, except for grocers and *supermarchés* that open in the afternoon. In many towns, Sunday morning is a big shopping time. Markets (daily in the cities, weekly in villages) are usually open mornings only, although clothes, flea and antiques markets run into the afternoon.

Banks: Banks are generally open 8.30am–12.30pm and 1.30–4pm. They close on Sunday, and most close either on Saturday or Monday as well.

Post Offices: Post offices are open in the cities Monday–Friday 8am–7pm, and Saturdays 8am–noon. In villages, offices may not open until 9am, then break for lunch and close at 4.30 or 5pm.

Châteaux: The majority of châteaux are open between 10 and 12 in the morning and 2 and 5 or 6 in the evening through the spring, summer and autumn months. The more famous ones stay open all or most of the year, and have longer opening times than the rest in summer, many now even allowing you to visit through the once-sacred French lunch hours from 12 to 2. You should leave at least 1 hour to visit any château. Many can still only be seen on guided tours, which often start on the hour, so bear that in mind – really you should arrive more than an hour before closing time to be sure you can see inside a château. The term for an unguided tour is *visite libre*. The very largest châteaux may offer the occasional guided tour in English. Virtually all can provide an English text to take with you on the tour. Admission is usually €4.5–6, but can be as much as €9 or as little as €3.

Museums: Most museums close for lunch, and often all day on Mondays or Tuesdays, and sometimes for all of November or the entire winter. Hours change with the season: longer summer hours begin in May or June and last until the end of September – usually. Most museums close on national holidays. We've done our best to include opening hours in the text, but don't sue us if they're not exactly right. Most museums give discounts on admission (which ranges from €1.5–4.5) if you have a student ID card, or are an EU citizen under 18 or over 65.

Churches: Churches are usually open all day, or closed all day and only open for Mass. Sometimes notes on the door direct you to the *mairie* or priest's house (*presbytère*), where you can pick up the key. There are often admission fees for cloisters, crypts and special chapels.

National Holidays

On French national holidays, banks, shops, businesses and some museums close, but most restaurants stay open.

1 January New Year's Day
Easter Sunday March or April
Easter Monday March or April
1 May Fête du Travail (Labour Day)
8 May VE Day, Armistice 1945
Ascension Day usually end of May
Pentecost (Whitsun and Monday) beginning of June
14 July Bastille Day
15 August Assumption of the Virgin Mary
1 November All Saints' Day
11 November Remembrance Day (First World War Armistice)
25 December Christmas Day

Post Offices, Telephones and the Internet

Known as PTT or Bureaux de Poste, post offices are easily discernible by their sign of a blue bird on a yellow background. You can receive letters *poste restante* at any post office; the postal codes in this book should help your mail get there in a timely fashion. To collect it, bring ID; you may have to pay a small fee. For opening hours *see* above. You can purchase stamps in tobacconists as well as post offices.

Nearly all public telephones have switched over from coins to *télécartes*, which you can purchase at any post office or newsstand for €6 for 50 *unités* or €14.5 for 120 *unités*. The French have eliminated area codes, giving everyone a 10-digit telephone number. If ringing **France from abroad**, the international dialling code is 33, and drop the first 'o' of the number. For **international calls** from France, dial 00, wait for the change in the dial tone, then dial the country code (UK 44; US and Canada 1; Ireland 353; Australia 61; New Zealand 64), and then the local code (minus the o for UK numbers) and number. The easiest way to reverse charges is to spend a few francs ringing the number and giving your number in France, which is always posted by public phones; alternatively, ring your national operator (for the UK dial 00 33 44; for the USA 00 33 11). For directory enquiries, dial t 12, or try your luck and patience on the free, slow, inefficient Minitel electronic directory in every post office.

The old saying that it doesn't pay to be first certainly applies to France with its national computer system, the Minitel, which was distributed to every phone subscriber in the 1980s. Next to the Internet it seems a Neanderthal, but its presence considerably slowed French interest in the Internet. This is changing fast: most cities and towns now have cybercafés, and the French have some of the most remarkable web sites on the information highway.

Sports and Activities

The central tourist information centres for each *département*, the Comités Départementaux de Tourisme (or CDTs for short), can supply a great deal of thematic information depending on what you're looking for. Sometimes they have a service, Loisirs Accueil, which organizes excursions and special events. The addresses for the CDTs are given in 'Tourist Information', below. You can also contact local tourist offices for more detailed local information.

Tour operators offering special-interest holidays are listed on pp.88–9.

Bird-watching: The Loire levee on the south bank between Gien and Sully is a good spot in season, as is the Ile de Parnay, east of Saumur. The Maison de la Loire at St-Mathurin, east of Angers, can organize short trips with a local guide.

Boule de fort: Anjou's answer to English bowls, but played inside. *See* Saumur, p.391,

for a description. An initiation into the art of the game may be possible.

Canoeing and kayaking: The national centre for information is the Fédération Française de Canoë-kayak, B.P.58, Joinville Le Pont, 94340. There are a few places where you can go canoeing on the Loire itself, indicated in the touring chapters. You can also try some of the tributaries and the large lakes by the major towns.

Cycling: *See* 'Getting Around', pp.87–90. Each *département*'s CDT should be able to supply a specific guide to *circuits à bicyclette* and may organize special cycling holidays.

Deer-watching: In the autumn rutting season, the Parc de Chambord is the place to try and catch a glimpse of the beasts (*see* p.168).

Falconry: You can watch displays of falconry at the Zooparc de Beauval (*see* pp.217–18).

Fishing: A permit is required for fishing in Loire Valley rivers. Check what possibilities there are and the terms and conditions with local tourist offices.

Flying over the Loire Valley: The tourist authorities for each *département* can give you information on helicopter, plane and hot air balloon opportunities.

Gardens: The Château de Chaumont puts on the Festival International du Jardin (*see* p.237). Doué-la-Fontaine hosts a famous rose festival, as does the Prieuré de St-Cosme just outside Tours. The CDTs should be able to provide you with brochures on other gardens open to the public.

Golf: There are usually a few golf courses per *département*. For further details, contact the CDT for the relevant *département*.

Horse-riding: Local tourist offices should have lists of *centres equestres/centres hippiques*.

River boats: Blois, Saumur and Montjean-sur-Loire have old-style boats on which you can take a brief trip on Loire. You can also take more conventional river trips: in the Loiret, at Briare and at Olivet; on the Cher, from St-Aignan, Montrichard or Chenonceau; on the Sarthe and Mayenne in Anjou.

Son-et-lumière: These are popular night-time displays at some of the most famous châteaux, with illuminations and, usually, an historical commentary with actors. The most important ones are: in the Blésois, at Blois and Cheverny; and in Touraine, at Amboise, Chenonceau and Azay-le-Rideau.

Walking: See 'Getting Around', p.90, for information on the GRs and other walks.

Water sports: The big towns all have a lake near to them where a variety of water sports are usually on offer. There are a few others dotted around the countryside.

Zoos: There are two excellent zoos in the Loire Valley, one near St-Aignan, close to the Cher, and one in Doué-la-Fontaine.

Time

France is 1 hour ahead of GMT and BST, and 6 hours ahead of US Eastern Standard Time.

Tourist Information

French Government Tourist Offices

Australia: 25 Bligh St, Level 22, NSW 2000 Sydney, t (02) 9231 5244, f (02) 9221 8682.

Canada: 1981 Av McGill College, No.490, Montreal, PQ H3A 2W9, t (514) 288 4264, f (514) 845 4868, *mfrance@attcanada.net*.

Ireland: 10 Suffolk St, Dublin 1, t (01) 679 0813, f (01) 679 0814, *frenchtouristoffice@tinet.ie*.

UK: 178 Piccadilly, London W1V OAL, t 0906 824 4123 (calls charged at 60p/min), *info@mdlf.co.uk*, *www.franceguide.com*.

USA: 444 Madison Av, New York, NY 10022, t (410) 286 8310, f (212) 838 7855, *info@ francetourism.com*, *www.francetourism.com*. 676 N. Michigan Av, Chicago, IL 60611, t (312) 751 7800, f (312) 337 63 39, *fgto@mcs.net*. 9454 Wilshire Bd, Suite 715, Beverly Hills, CA 90212, t (310) 271 6665, f (310) 276 2835, *fgto@gte.net*

Comités Régionaux du Tourisme

Regional tourist authorities for the Loire are:

Comité Régional du Tourisme Centre-Val de Loire, 37 Av de Paris, 45000 Orléans, t 02 38 79 95 00, f 02 38 79 95 10, *www.loirevalley-tourism.com*

Comité Régional du Tourisme Pays de la Loire, 2 Rue de la Loire, B.P.20411, 44204 Nantes Cedex 2, t 02 40 48 24 20, f 02 40 08 07 20, *www.cr-pays-de-la-loire.fr*

Comités Départementaux de Tourisme

The following is a list of each Comité Départemental du Tourisme (CDT) relevant to this guidebook, excellent starting points for gathering information, even if their printed material is much better than their web site information for the moment. The Loisirs Accueil sections can even offer planned trips and make reservations.

Comité Départemental du Tourisme du Cher, Maison Départementale de Tourisme, 5 Rue de Séraucourt, 18000 Bourges, t 02 48 48 00 10, f 02 48 48 00 20, *tourisme.berry@ wanadoo.fr*, *www.berrylecher.com*. **Loisirs Accueil du Cher**, same address, t 02 48 48 00 18, f 02 48 48 00 28, *tourisme.berry@ wanadoo.fr*.

Comité Départemental du Tourisme du Loiret, 8 Rue d'Escures, 45000 Orléans, t 02 38 78 04 04, f 02 38 77 04 12, *tourisme.loiret@ wanadoo.fr*, *www.tourismloiret.com*. **Loisir Accueil Loiret**, same address, t 02 38 62 04 88, f 02 38 62 98 37, *tourisme.loiret@ wanadoo.fr*.

Comité Départemental du Tourisme du Loir-et-Cher, Maison du Loir-et-Cher, 5 Rue de la Voûte du Château, B.P.149, 41005 Blois Cedex, t 02 54 57 00 41, f 02 54 57 00 47, *tourisme. 41@wanadoo.fr*, *www.chambordcountry.com*.

Comité Départemental du Tourisme de Touraine, 9 Rue Buffon, B.P.3217, 37032 Tours Cedex, t 02 47 31 47 48, f 02 47 31 42 76, *tourism.touraine@wanadoo.fr*, *www. tourism-touraine.com*. **Loisirs Accueil Touraine-Val de Loire**, 38 Rue Augustin Fresnel, B.P.139, 37171 Chambray-les-Tours Cedex, t 02 47 48 37 27, f 02 47 48 13 39, *info@loire-valley-holidays.com*.

Comité Départemental du Tourisme de l'Anjou, Place Kennedy, B.P.2147, 49021 Angers Cedex 02, t 02 41 23 51 51, f 02 41 88 36 77, *anjou.cdt@wanadoo.fr*.

Comité Départemental du Tourisme de la Loire-Atlantique, 2 Allée Baco, B.P.20502, 44005 Nantes Cedex 1, t 02 51 72 95 30, f 02 40 20 44 54, *www.cdt44.com*. **Loisirs Accueil Loire-Atlantique**, same address, 44005 Nantes Cedex 1, t 02 51 72 95 32, f 02 40 20 44 54, *loisirs-accueil@cdt44.com*.

Local Tourist Offices

Local tourist offices are called *syndicat d'initiative* or *office du tourisme* in French. In smaller French villages this service is provided by the town hall (*mairie*). They distribute free maps and town plans, and hotel, camping and self-catering accommodation lists for their area, and can inform you about sporting events, leisure activities and wine estates open for visits. Addresses and phone numbers are listed in the text. Hours are generally Mon–Sat 9–12 and 3–7; closed Sun.

Where to Stay

Hotels

As in most countries, the tourist authorities grade hotels by their facilities (not by charm or location) with stars. Hotels with no stars are not necessarily dives: their owners probably never bothered filling out a form for the tourist authorities. Most hotels have a wide range of rooms and prices; a large room with antique furniture, a view and a bathroom will cost much more than a poky back room in the same hotel, with a window overlooking a car park and the WC down the hall.

Single rooms are relatively rare and usually cost two-thirds the price of a double; rarely will a hotelier give you a discount if only doubles are available (because each room has its own price). On the other hand, if there are three or four of you, triples or quads or adding extra beds to a double room is usually cheaper than staying in two rooms. **Breakfast** (usually coffee, a croissant, bread and jam) is nearly always optional. Rates rise considerable in the busy season (Easter holidays and summer), when many hotels with restaurants will require that you take half board (*demi-pension* – breakfast and a set lunch or dinner). Many hotel restaurants are superb and are listed in the text; non-residents are welcome.

Your holiday will be much sweeter if you **book ahead**, especially from May to October, when the few reasonably priced rooms are snapped up very early. Phoning a day or two ahead is always a good policy, although hotels will only confirm a room with the receipt of a cheque or a credit card number covering the

first night. Tourist offices have complete lists of accommodation in their given areas; many will call around and book a room for you on the spot for free or a nominal fee.

Umbrella organizations such as Logis et Auberges de France, Relais de Silence and the prestigious Châteaux et Hôtels de France and Relais et Châteaux promote and guarantee the quality of independently owned hotels. Many are recommended in the text. Larger tourist offices usually stock their booklets, or you can pick them up before you leave from the French National Tourist Office.

Chambres d'hôtes, bed and breakfasts, are in private homes, châteaux or farms, or may be connected to restaurants or wine estates. Local tourist offices can provide listings. Prices tend to be moderate to inexpensive. Also try **B&B France**, PO Box 66, Bell St, Henley-on-Thames, Oxon RG9 1XS, t (01491) 578 803, f (01491) 410 806, *bookings@bedbreck.demon. co.uk* (catalogue £13.99); or in France, 6 Rue d'Europe, 95470 Fosses, t 01 34 68 83 15 (catalogue €7.5).

Youth Hostels and *Gîtes d'Etape*

Most cities and resort areas have youth hostels (*auberges de jeunesse*) which offer simple dormitory accommodation and breakfast to people of any age for €6–10.5 a night. Most offer kitchen facilities as well, or inexpensive meals. They are the best deal if you're travelling on your own; for people travelling together, a one-star hotel can be just as cheap. A downside is that many are either in the suburbs where the last bus goes by at 7pm, or miles from any transport at all in the country. In the summer the only way to be sure of a room is to arrive early in the day. Most require a Hostelling International card, which you can often purchase on the spot, although regulations say you should buy them in your home country from your national YHA.

A *gîte d'étape* is a simple shelter with bunk beds and a rudimentary kitchen set up by a village along GR walking paths or a scenic bike route. Again, lists are available for each *département*. They cost around €6–7.5 a night.

Camping

Camping is very popular in France and there's at least one camp site in every town, often an inexpensive, no-frills place run by the

---

Hotel Price Ranges

Note: Prices listed here and elsewhere in this book are for a double room.

luxury €230 and over
expensive €90–230
moderate €60–90
inexpensive €30–60
cheap under €30

Self-catering Holiday Operators

France

Château de la Guillonnière, La Guillonnière, Dienne 86410, t 05 49 42 05 46, f 05 49 42 48 34, www.rent-a-castle.com. Cottages, B&B and castles in the Loire Valley.

UK

Allez France, 27 West St, Storrington, West Sussex RH20 4DZ, t (01903) 742 345, www.allezfrance.com. Wide variety of accommodation, from cottages to châteaux.

Bowhills, Mayhill Farm, Swanmore, Southampton SO32 2QW, t (01489) 877 627, www.bowhills.co.uk. Luxury villas and farmhouses, mostly with pools.

Chez Nous, Spring Mill, Earby, Barnoldswick, Lancashire BB94 0AA, t 08700 781 400, www.cheznous.com. Over 3,000 privately owned holiday cottages and B&Bs.

Dominique's Villas, 13 Park House, 140 Battersea Park Rd, London SW11 4NB, t (020) 7738 8772, www.dominiquesvillas.com. Large villas and châteaux with pools.

French Life, 26 Church Rd, Horsforth, Leeds, LS18 5LG, t (0113) 239 0077, www.cottage-holidays-france.co.uk. Selection of villages and cottages in the Loire region.

Owners In France, Harbour House, New Harbour Rd South, Poole, Dorset, BH15 4AJ, t 0870 901 3400, www.ownersinfrance.com. Privately owned properties in the area.

Vacances en Campagne, Bignor, Pulborough, West Sussex RH20 1QD, t (01798) 869 433, www.indiv-travellers.com. Farmhouses, villas and *gîtes* all over France

VFB Holidays, Normandy House, High St, Cheltenham GL50 3FB, t (01242) 240 339, www.vfbholidays.co.uk. From rustic *gîtes* to luxurious farmhouses.

USA

At Home in France, P.O. Box 643, Ashland, OR 97520, t (541) 488 9467, www.athomeinfrance.com. Apartments, cottages, farmhouses, manor houses and villas; moderate to deluxe.

Families Abroad, 194 Riverside Drive, New York, NY 10025, t (212) 787 2434, t (718) 768 6185. Sabbatical and vacation rentals, in apartments, villas and châteaux.

Hideaways International, 767 Islington St, Portsmouth, NH 03802, t 800 843 4433, t (603) 430 4433, www.hideaways.com. Villas, farmhouses and châteaux in the Loire.

Loire Tours, 158 Crosby St, Suite 3B, New York, NY 10012, t 800 755 9313. Studios, apartments and villas.

town itself (*camping municipal*). Other camp sites are graded with stars from four to one: at the top of the line you can expect lots of trees and grass, hot showers, a pool or beach, sports facilities, a grocer's, a bar and/or restaurant, for prices rather similar to one-star hotels.

Tourist offices have complete lists of camp sites in their regions. If you plan to move around a lot, pick up a *Guide Officiel Camping/Caravanning*, available in most French bookshops. A number of UK holiday firms book camping holidays and offer discounts on Channel ferries: try Canvas Holidays, t (01383) 644000; Eurocamp Travel, t (01606) 787878; or Keycamp Holidays, t 0870 700 0123.

Gîtes de France and Other Self-catering Accommodation

The Loire Valley has a range of self-catering accommodation, from inexpensive farm cottages to history-laden châteaux, fancy villas, flats or even on board canal boats. The Fédération Nationale des Gîtes de France is a French government service offering inexpensive accommodation by the week in rural areas. Lists with photos arranged by *département* are available from the Maison des Gîtes de France, 59 Rue St-Lazaire, 75009 Paris, t 01 48 70 75 75, or in the UK from their official agents, Brittany Ferries, t 08705 360360. If you want to stay in châteaux, request the *Chambres d'Hôtes et Gîtes de Prestige*. You can also book accommodation direct on their web site at www.gites-de-france.fr.

Other options are advertised in the Sunday papers, or contact one of the firms listed below. The accommodation they offer will nearly always be more costly than a *gîte*, but the discounts holiday firms can offer on ferries, plane tickets or car hire can make up for the difference.

The Loire from Sancerre to Orléans

Sancerre to Orléans

LOIRET

Pithiviers

Artenay

Vrigny

Chamerolles **5**

Beaune-la-Rolande

to km
5 miles
N

Foret

Ingrannes

Orléans

Combreux
Vitry-aux-Loges

Fay-aux-Loges

Canal d'Orléans

Montargis

Canal d'Orléans

St-Jean-de-Braye

Combleux

Chécy

Mardié

St-Denis-de-l'Hôtel

Châteauneuf-sur-Loire

Grignon

Lorris

d'Orléans

Vernisson

Nogent-sur-Vernisson

Châtillon-Coligny

Olivet

Jargeau

Germigny-des-Prés

Loiret

Neuvy-en-Sullais

St-Benoît **4**

Guilly

Bouteilles

3

Ouzouer-sur-Loire

Cuissy

Les Bézards

La Bussière

YONNE

La Source

Tigy

Sully-sur-Loire

Dampierre

Nevoy

Gien **2**

Pont-Chevron

Ouzouer-sur-Trézée

Bléneau

La Ferté-St-Aubin

Ménestreau-en-Villette

St-Brisson-sur-Loire

Briare

St-Fargeau

Lamotte-Beuvron

Châtillon-sur-Loire

LOIR-ET-CHER

Autry-le-Châtel

Neuvy-sur-Loire

St-Amand-en-Puisaye

Salbris

Aubigny

Vailly

Belleville-sur-Loire

Nançay

Cosne

Neuvy-sur-Barangeon

Henrichemont

Chavignol
Verdigny
St-Satur

Amigny
Venoise
Reigny

Sancerre **1**

Château Tracy

La Borne

Crézancy

Bué

CHER

Pouilly

Highlights

1 Sancerre's sensuous vine-covered hills

2 The Château de Gien's hunting museum

3 The Château de Sully reflected in the Loire

4 Majestic meanders in the Loire by the abbey of St-Benoît

5 The Château de Chamerolles' slick perfume museum

The sensuous vine-covered hills of Sancerre produce one of the best-known white wines along the Loire. Take the winding road to the top of Sancerre town to get a full view over the Sancerrois area and a long stretch of the Loire before heading down to explore the wine villages tucked into the folds of the area's lovely rounded hills.

After Sancerre, the landscapes become more gentle as the Loire curves slowly up towards Orléans. Most of the châteaux open to visitors in this area are built of brick rather than the bright white limestone most often associated with the Loire Valley. Of the brick beauties vying for your attention, the tattooed Château de Gien contains an impressive museum on hunting, with enough interesting material for even those opposed to the sport to be diverted by, while the Château de Chamerolles underwent a major facelift in the 1990s and is now devoted to the history of perfume. The one major white-stone château to stand out along this stretch of the Loire is that at Sully, at times magnificently reflected in the river's waters. The greying Château de St-Brisson has had a tougher time, abandoned by the Loire, but now puts on displays of medieval war machines.

You should always bear in mind that the religious legacy along the Loire is as strong as the lordly one; the Loire Valley boasts as many fine churches as fine châteaux. The major religious stop along this section of the Loire is the abbey of St-Benoît, in medieval times one of the most significant religious institutions in France, whose reputation was built on the bones of that great influence on Western monasticism, the Italian saint Benedict.

Smaller curiosities to seek out in this chapter include: the mosaics of Briare, together with that town's elegant Eiffel bridge; the appealing pottery works of Gien; and the many waterside villages which may have lost their river trade, but which have kept their atmospheric cobbled quays. The Loire and its tributaries acted for centuries as the major transport routes of the region, and this fact is well recalled at the museum dedicated to Loire mariners and river trading at Châteauneuf-sur-Loire. Since the war, the Loire has sadly seen several nuclear power stations sprout up along its length; if you follow this chapter along its course, you'll be treated to two. This hasn't stopped the river west of Sully being classified as part of the UNESCO Loire World Heritage Site; it's just odd that Sancerre has been left out, as it occupies one of the prettiest spots along the whole of the great river.

Sancerre and the Sancerrois

Such is the attention lavished on the famous white wine of Sancerre that the beauty of the town of Sancerre is often overlooked. The wine of the Sancerrois has become so successful since the war that the herds of goats that once grazed in these parts have been pushed west into the hills of the neighbouring Pays Fort as the vines have taken over almost every square inch of land. However, the area's goat's cheese, like the wines, still enjoys an international reputation.

Getting There

There's a **train** line from Paris via Melun and Montargis which passes through Cosne-Cours-sur-Loire, where you should change for the short bus link up to Sancerre. It isn't easy to reach Sancerre from west along the Loire using public transport; from Orléans, take a bus to Gien, then join the rail network.

Tourist Information

Sancerre: Office de Tourisme, Nouvelle Place, 18300 Sancerre, **t** 02 48 54 08 21, **f** 02 48 78 03 58, *ot.sancerre@wanadoo.fr*, *www.sancerre.net/otsi*.

St-Satur: Office de Tourisme, Place de la République, 18300 St-Satur, **t/f** 02 48 54 01 30, *otsi.saint.satur@wanadoo.fr*, *www.sancerre.net/saint-satur*.

Market Day

Sancerre: Saturday morning.

Where to Stay and Eat

Sancerre ✉ 18300

Le Panoramic, 18 Remparts des Augustins, **t 02 48 54 22 44, **f** 02 48 54 39 55, *panoramicotel@wanadoo.fr* (*inexpensive*). The spectacular views surpass the dullish modern architecture of this very well-located, comfortable hotel on the slopes just below Sancerre centre. The place has a good restaurant, **La Tasse d'Argent**, **t** 02 48 54 01 44 (*menus €15–43.5*).

La Tour, 31 Nouvelle Place, **t** 02 48 54 00 81, *info@la-tour-sancerre.fr*, *www.la-tour-sancerre.fr*. The swishest restaurant among the many choices on Sancerre's main square, with a smart beamed dining room. It's a good place to try regional specialities, such as goat's cheese and Berry lentils (*menus €13.5–39.5*).

Auberge La Pomme d'Or, Place de la Mairie, **t** 02 48 54 13 30. In an interesting corner of gabled houses in a quieter area by the classical town hall, a reputed restaurant with small but well-chosen menus and an excellent wine list (*menus €21–29.5*). *Closed Wed*.

St-Satur ✉ 18300

Hôtel de la Loire, 2 Quai de la Loire, **t** 02 48 78 22 22, **f** 02 48 78 22 29, *hotel_de_la_loire @hotmail.com*, *www.hotel-de-la-loire.com* (*inexpensive*). This newly reopened, lovingly restored hotel stretching along by the river offers the most characterful and appealing accommodation in the whole area (along with three-star standards). The couple who run it are part-English. Each of the 10 bedrooms has a view of the Loire waters flowing by (several also look over the eccentric little independent restaurant in front of the hotel), and has been very well decorated in individual style, with a sitting area. Georges Simenon, the famed Belgian author of the Maigret detective stories, who used to work at the Château de Tracy on the other side of the river, wrote some of his works here.

Le Jardin de St-Thibault, 7 Rue des Ponts, **t** 02 48 54 12 28. This restaurant may lie on the busy road from the Loire bridge towards Sancerre, but it has a delightful walled patio on which to savour quite gourmet local cuisine – including *couilles d'âne*, 'donkey's balls' (actually eggs in red wine!), and goat's cheese fritters (*menus €12.5–36.5*).

Verdigny-en-Sancerre ✉ 18300

L'Auberge du Vigneron, **t** 02 48 79 38 68. Simple local favourite tucked away in this winemakers' village close to Sancerre. Lots of the dishes feature ingredients cooked in wine (*menus €11.5–19*). *Closed Tues pm and Wed*.

Sancerre

The hilltop town of Sancerre dominates the Sancerrois and provides visitors with magical views down on to the Loire, the meanders to the south like a river disappearing into the background of a Gothic painting. To the north, you may be able to make out the huge chimneys of the nuclear power station of the unfortunately named Belleville-sur-Loire, churning out artificial clouds of vapour into the sky and marking the northern frontier of the old province of the Berry along the Loire.

During the Hundred Years' War, Sancerre acted as one of the important frontier posts of the shrivelled French kingdom, facing Burgundy, its enemy and poisonous ally of the English. Jean de Bueil of Sancerre became familiarly known as the Scourge of the English and was a loyal companion to Joan of Arc. What's more, in the 1460s he recorded his experiences from some of his later campaigns in *Le Jouvencel*, which has often been described as the first French historical novel.

In the 16th century Sancerre became a powerful little Protestant stronghold during the French Wars of Religion. Catholic revenge followed in a terrible siege led by the Maréchal de la Châtre in 1573. The great 19th-century French historian Michelet described this siege as one of the most dreadful events in French history; the citizens of Sancerre were reported to have been reduced to eating crushed slate in their desperation. Further show of Protestant sympathies led Henri II de Bourbon, the early 17th-century aristocratic governor of the province of the Berry, to destroy most of the town's remaining fortifications, including its castle, leaving just one flint tower. On the pinnacle of the town's hill, it still stands apart in its own clump of trees. The houses around it appear to have been shoved together on the hilltop as though they were a terrible inconvenience for the winemakers, who have otherwise colonized almost every centimetre of ground around Sancerre with vines.

Sancerre is a wonderful town to wander around. But beyond the winemakers and their shops it doesn't have any major cultural sites. The **Tour des Fiefs** of the château is rarely open (*only Sun and bank holidays pm, March–Oct*). It looks dark and forbidding above the town, like the reflection of an evil lord dominating his subjects. Anyway, you can enjoy almost as good views from many of Sancerre's streets as from the tower. **Nouvelle Place**, the main square, looks unselfconsciously charming without being over-prettified or over-restored, although its name hints at the peculiar sunken bunker of a building in the middle, housing the tourist office. Walk down some of the steep streets that lead away from this square to admire the houses provided with entrances the size of barn doors, awaiting the grape harvest. The two big winemaking names to visit in Sancerre itself are Mellot and Vacheron, with highly visible shops.

Other specialities you can find in town include goat's cheese, local biscuits known as Croquets de Sancerre, and local stoneware pottery, for instance at the Atelier d'Art de la Tour, just off one corner of Nouvelle Place, made on the spot. In the tourist season there are exhibitions by artists from further afield.

St-Satur

St-Satur is the town right by the Loire below Sancerre. Its two central grain silos the size of substantial churches may be ugly, but the riverside area of St-Thibault has plenty of appeal. On top of that, St-Satur has good sports facilities, including an outdoor swimming pool. The **Golf du Sancerrois**, **t** 02 48 54 11 22, *golf.sancerre@ wanadoo.fr, www.sancerre.net/golf*, lies just a stone's throw away. The place also has a

Sancerre's Vines of Success and Some Delicious Goats' Droppings

The lines of vines reach up and stretch around the Sancerrois like glorious patterned cloth fitted on the hillsides. Sancerre is known far and wide for the fine, crisp white wines these vines produce. Made from the Sauvignon Blanc grape variety, they frequently contain hints of gooseberry. A small amount of red wine is also produced in these parts, generally fetching a high price because of its rarity and its popularity in trendy Parisian restaurants. The reds are made from Pinot Noir grapes and can be delicately fruity.

A tour of the Sancerrois' wine villages is well worth undertaking. Verdigny and Chavignol, just northwest of town, are two highly regarded names in the Sancerrois. In very vinous **Verdigny**, one of the best wine estates to visit is that of the **André Dezat** household (**t** *02 48 79 38 82*). André Dezat was one of the locals central in bringing Sancerre it's postwar wine success, making sure that producers went for quality, although in recent years wine critics have complained that the wines of the area as a whole aren't always up to scratch.

Chavignol is the king of the *crottins* (meaning droppings), the affectionate name given to the goat's cheeses of these parts. You'll find cheese shops vying for attention with the wine cellars in the village. Among the latter, you might try **Roger Moreux** (**t** *02 48 54 05 79*). The *cave* is small and charming, the wine excellent, some of it aged in oak. On a larger scale, **Henri Bourgeois** (**t** *02 48 78 53 20*), is a big Sancerre producer who can offer a wide range of quality wines and a nice tasting.

Other particularly appealing Sancerrois wine villages to head for include the batch just west of the town of Sancerre – look out for **Amigny**, **Venoize**, **Bué**, **Reigny** and **Crézancy**, for instance, where you can seek out cellars at which to taste and buy wines. **Pouilly-Fumé**, another very popular Loire white-wine producing *appellation*, lies east just across the Loire from Sancerre, on the Burgundy rather than the Berry side of the river. The reputed, and to English-speakers rather comically named, **Château Tracy** is a very well-known, aristocratic Pouilly-Fumé estate. It's not open to passing visitors, but it stands above the Loire almost opposite Sancerre and is worth going to take a look at just for its charm, and for the nearby views back across to the Sancerrois' vine-covered hills.

boating harbour. You might be tempted to go on an **accompanied canoe trip** on the Loire – contact Loire.Nature.Découverte, Quai de la Loire, 18300 St-Satur, **t/f** 02 48 78 00 34. It can be an exhilarating way of seeing the Loire from really close quarters

The Loire Around Briare and Gien

Coming north along the Loire from Sancerre and the old province of the Berry into the Orléanais, head swiftly past the ugly brute of a power station at Belleville-sur-Loire to Briare and Gien. Although these two towns lie just outside the main Loire Valley tourist trail, they are each proud of their artistic attractions. We also suggest a few often-ignored châteaux to visit nearby.

Briare

Briare, unusually for the Loire, is marked more by the 19th century than the medieval and Renaissance periods. It's best-known for its **Pont-Canal**, a bridge built in the Belle Epoque to carry a canal over the Loire, enabling boats to avoid the danger of crossing the great river itself. The bridge was constructed by none other than Gustave Eiffel's company; it's rather surprising Briare hasn't baptized the thing the Pont Eiffel. While Eiffel's great Parisian erection sticks so vulgarly into the air, this bridge looks discreetly elegant. Spacious footpaths were thoughtfully provided either side, embellished with period lamps which give it a rather incongruous metropolitan feel in the midst of its rural town setting. The diminutive huddle of houses along the nearby levee, though, gives a typical picture of a long-established little Loire-side community.

Closer to the centre of town, you'll come to Briare's appealing **port de plaisance** (marina). At the **Maison Eclusière** (*open daily 8 July–25 Aug; certain Sundays and public hols otherwise*) you can find out about taking a boat trip along the canals of the area. The Canal de Briare on the north side of the Loire was ordered by King Henri IV's dynamic minister Sully (*see* p.118) in the first half of the 17th century; it was particularly significant as it linked the Loire with the Seine and hence Paris. The **Musée des Deux Marines** (*open June–Sept 10–12.30 and 2–6.30, March–May and Oct 2–6;*

Getting Around

There are **train** services to Briare and Gien from Paris, but don't expect a wide choice of trains each day. As for the area west of Gien along the Loire, here you'll have to rely on local bus services run by Rapides du Val de Loire (**t** 02 38 61 90 00), passing through Sully-sur-Loire and Châteauneuf-sur-Loire.

Tourist Information

Briare: 1 Place Charles de Gaulle, 45250 Briare, **t** 02 38 31 24 51, **f** 02 38 37 15 16.
Gien: Place Jean Jaurès, B.P.13, 45501 Gien, **t** 02 38 67 25 28, **f** 02 38 38 23 16.

Market Days
Briare: Friday morning.
Gien: Saturday morning; food market Wednesday morning.

Where to Stay and Eat

Briare ✉ 45250
Le Cerf, 22–24 Bd Buyser, **t 02 38 37 00 80, **f** 02 38 31 25 17 (*inexpensive*). Lies close to the sweet port, the rooms quite recently redone.

It has a restaurant (*menus €15–20; closed Christmas hols*).
Auberge du Pont-Canal, 19 Rue du Pont-Canal, **t 02 38 31 24 24, **f** 02 38 31 92 12 (*inexpensive*). You can't get closer than this to the water to eat than this inn with a pleasant waterside restaurant. *Restaurant closed Sun pm and Mon.*
Bateaux Croisières, contact at the Maison Eclusière, Port de Plaisance, B.P.58, **t** 02 38 37 12 75. You can actually eat *on* the water if you take this cruise (lunch possible every day during the tourist season; dinner Sat only). The journey lasts 3½ hours (€31). (They also offer a cruise without food; 1½ hours; €6 adults, €4 children.)

St-Brisson-sur-Loire ✉ 45500
Chez Huguette, 7 Rue du Bizoir, **t** 02 38 36 70 10 (*cheap*). Up in a peaceful village, close to the château, this traditional old-fashioned French *auberge* has been in the family for some 150 years. The cooking's cheap, featuring stocky dishes served in the dark dining room (*menus €8.5–23; closed Sun pm and Mon*). The rooms are in need of updating; you'll be woken either by the cock crowing or your neighbours whispering.

58 Boulevard Buyser, t 02 38 31 28 27), a small affair opposite the Musée de la Mosaïque (*see* below), explains well how important both the Loire and the canals were to these parts in centuries past. Briare is also a good place to hire a **river boat** for several days. For details, contact Loisirs Accueil Loiret, 8 Rue d'Escures, 45000 Orléans, t 02 38 62 04 88, *Tourisme.Loiret@wanadoo.fr, www.tourismloiret.com.*

When the industrialist Jean-Felix Bapterosses set up in Briare in the middle of the 19th century, the town became a large producer of buttons, beads and then mosaics. The **church of St-Etienne** in the centre of town, built by Bapterosses' heirs at the end of the 19th century, is crammed with mosaics. A frieze of them runs round the outside of the whole edifice, enlivening the rather dull stone. Inside, in the heady confusion of neo-Byzantine, neo-Romanesque and neo-Renaissance architecture, mosaics prolif-erate too. The aisles are covered with a swirling river carpet of little tiles, apparently symbolizing the Loire or the river of life, designed by Eugène Grasset of Larousse fame. Even the sad panels in the apse commemorating Briare's numerous war dead have been given mosaic backgrounds. The altar is decorated with beautiful Botticelli-style mosaic angels, but the results in the separate sacristy aren't as successful – two deer come to drink in what has been made to feel suspiciously like a bathroom.

Jean-Felix Bapterosses' commercial tricks and triumphs are charted in detail at the **Musée de la Mosaïque et des Emaux** (*open June–Sept 10–6.30, Feb–May and Oct–Dec*

Les Bézards ✉ 45290

****Auberge des Templiers**, entrance on the N7, t 02 38 31 80 01, f 02 38 31 84 51 (*luxury*). The height of luxury and expense in the area. The entrance may stand uncomfort-ably close to the busy road, but the rooms and luxurious facilities are dotted around in the extensive grounds beyond. The cuisine has an absurdly high reputation, for which you'll pay through the nose (*menus €59–94*). *Closed Feb.*

Autry-le-Châtel ✉ 45500

Auberge Les Trainats, south of St-Brisson, off the road from Autry to Châtillon-sur-Loire, t 02 38 36 80 64, f 02 38 36 82 91. A country inn close to the borders of the Berry and Sologne regions. You can stay at the farm, or simply eat there (you need to book either way), trying such specialities as duck with peaches, guinea fowl with cabbage, or the Berry favourite, pâté of potatoes.

Gien ✉ 45500

****La Poularde**, 13 Quai de Nice, t 02 38 67 36 05, f 02 38 38 18 78 (*inexpensive*). Overlooks the plane trees by the Loire. It has comfort-able rooms and offers fancy cooking (*menus €20.5–60*).

****Sanotel**, 21 Quai de Sully, t 02 38 67 61 46, f 02 38 67 13 01 (*inexpensive*). The best views in town if you ask for a room overlooking the Loire, as this hotel is located on the south bank, looking across to old Gien. The rooms are typical comfortable modern boxes, with decent-sized bathrooms.

You'll find a choice of basic restaurants and hotels by the busy north bank road.

Nevoy ✉ 45500

Auberge du Tranchoir, t 02 38 67 51 98, f 02 38 67 37 35 (*inexpensive*). The cow shed has been converted into a simple restaurant at this former farm on the edge of the sprawling forest of Orléans. Vegetable terrines, leek tarts and ewe's milk cheeses count among the specialities (*menu €12*). Book in advance to sleep and eat here.

Ouzouer-sur-Loire ✉ 45570

L'Abricotier, 106 Rue de Gien, t 02 38 35 07 11. A haven of good cuisine on a triangle of land just slightly off the busy north-bank D952 between Gien and Sully (*menus €20–48.5*). *Closed Sun pm, Mon and Wed pm, mid-Aug–mid-Sept, and over Christmas.*

2–6; 1 Boulevard Loreau, t 02 38 31 20 51). Only a small number of mosaics are displayed here, but the exhibits include a splendid strutting cockerel designed for the 1910 Universal Exhibition, a Grasset depiction of St Michael and, from the 1970s, a series of pieces by the artist Victor Vasarely, whose obsession with geometrical abstraction lends itself quite well to the art of mosaic-making. The story of the beads on show proves surprisingly interesting; as well as becoming fashionable with the likes of the great actress Sarah Bernhardt, they were also exported to Africa, where they were used for bartering.

Châteaux between Briare and Gien

Mosaics continue as a theme at the **Château de Pont-Chevron** (*open May–Aug Wed–Mon 2–6; t 02 38 31 92 02*), a handful of kilometres north of Briare, off the D122 between the N7 and Ouzouer-sur-Trézée. Here you get a much earlier little lesson in their decorative uses. The chic neoclassical château itself was only built in 1900 for the d'Harcourt family, but its grounds conceal two excellent, if damaged, Gallo-Roman works, dated to the 2nd century, one showing a splendid tender-faced masculine sea-god's head. On the other side of the château the lawn leads to a romantic lily-covered lake.

A few kilometres further up the N7, the brick **Château de la Bussière** (*open July–Aug daily 10–6, April–June and Sept–11 Nov Wed–Mon 10–12 and 2–6; t 02 38 35 93 35, www.coeur-de-France.com/labussiere.html*) long lay on the main route from Paris to Lyon. Enter the courtyard and you'll be struck by the superb and curious outbuilding on one side, with lozenged decorations, constructed to receive the tithe, payment in kind from vast estates. It gives a good indication of how wealthy the La Bussière lords must once have been. A walled kitchen garden has been lovingly re-created nearby.

The château proper, the oldest parts dating back to the 14th century, has been over-restored, but the first view of it standing on a lovely lake apparently planned by Le Nôtre are delightful. Inside, 19th-century comforts and tastes prevail. The present proprietors have chosen fish as the theme of the visit. The most surprising exhibit lies in Damien Hirst pose in formaldehyde, a massive primitive albino fish known as a coelacanth.

The **Château de St-Brisson** (*open Easter–15 Nov Thurs–Tues 10–12 and 2–6; the demonstration of medieval war machines takes place roughly 9 July–18 Aug Thurs–Tues at 3.30 and Sun at 3.30 and 4.30; t 02 38 36 71 29*), on the south bank of the Loire opposite Briare, once lorded it over the river. Time has sadly distanced the two; the Loire has moved many hundreds of metres due to the effects of the building of the Briare canal, combined with the Loire's natural wandering tendencies. The castle remains dramatic though, particularly seen sticking out on its rock in such flat county.

The medieval stronghold developed into a hexagonal fort, well constructed to resist bombardment with its mixture of towers and angled walls. Parties in the Wars of Religion and the Revolution took destructive swipes at the place, and the wounds had to be patched up – many of the various parts of the château you see today date from after the medieval period. The château was left to the parish at the end of the 1980s and is looked after by a team of enthusiastic local volunteers who are restoring parts of the sprawling structure bit by bit.

The interior is surprisingly old-style, the visit starting with a workaday kitchen dating back to the 16th century and an indoor well – looking down it, you can easily imagine secret passageways disappearing off into the countryside. The grand listed room in the château is the dining room. The arms of the various families who owned St-Brisson are painted on the beams and cleverly used by the guides to tell a little of the place's history. The most exciting figures to emerge are a medieval lord who became a ruthless pirate on the Loire and another who was so influenced by Rousseau's ideas that he went off to live in the woods in an attempt to convert back to the state of a noble savage – Rousseau persuaded him to come home to his château! You're taken up to see the servants' rooms and the fine roof timbers. The woodwork was apparently executed by Loire mariners, who often sought employment as carpenters in periods when the river was unnavigable.

To help compensate for the loss of its strategic position, the Château de Brisson now also flexes its little tourist muscles with demonstrations of medieval war machines, while its façades are dramatically lit up at night.

Gien

Pretty brick-patterned Gien, site of a river crossing over the Loire since ancient times, was bombed to smithereens in the Second World War, by the Germans in 1940 and by the Allies in 1944. Eighty per cent destroyed, the town was harmoniously restored after the conflict. The splendid hump-backed stone bridge was patched up. Riverside façades were recreated using traditional brick patternings of trellises and chevrons.

Meanwhile, by a stroke of good fortune, the **Château de Gien** up the hill escaped the bombs. It has witnessed a few interesting moments in its history. Joan of Arc stopped here on her way to King Charles VII's coronation in Reims in 1429. The place was then rebuilt in the 1480s for Anne de Beaujeu, daughter of King Louis XI. She would serve a short while as regent of France for her brother, the young Charles VIII (see Amboise, pp.242–3). A little later, King François I handed the regency to his mother, Louise de Savoie, here when he went off on his early 16th-century Italian campaign. And at points during the 16th-century Wars of Religion the royal family took refuge in the château, as did Louis XIV and Anne d'Autriche at the time of the Fronde uprising.

From the terrace in front of the château you can enjoy extensive views over the Loire, even taking in two nuclear power stations on a good day, Belleville to the south, Dampierre to the north. In the castle's open courtyard, surprising patterns picked out in black brick adorn some of the exterior walls like medieval masonic tattoos. The symbols include a stretched-out Star of David and, most appropriately given the modern museum inside, an arrow. A deer cast in bronze expresses its surprise at your arrival out on the lawn.

Before those of you who detest hunting dismiss the **Musée International de la Chasse** (open June–Sept 9–6, Jan–May and Oct–Dec 9–12 and 2–6; **t** 02 38 67 69 69), the museum devoted to the subject inside the château, it must be said that this place proves surprisingly interesting both historically and aesthetically. It shows extraordinarily well the excesses to which their love of the killer sport pushed the aristocracy, as it attempts to trace the history of hunting down the ages. It includes some international exhibits, including a collection of very fine German crossbows and guns encrusted with carved ivory figures of running deer and dogs chasing rabbits, some 19th-century Algerian guns, and falconry pieces from as far away as Qatar and Japan. French displays dominate though, the highlights being the paintings by Desportes, Louis XIV's specialist hunt artist. Hunting was controlled by royal order for much of French history.

Horns – one over 4.5m long – pipes, engravings, decoy ducks, powder horns, buttons from hundreds of hunts...a wealth of hunt-related objects fill the rooms, and are all very well exhibited. Among the more curious exhibits are an umbrella made of 'wood, silver and wolves' teeth' – one of the last wolves in the Berry was shot in 1900, we are informed; a shaving bowl with a deer painted in the bottom – one only hopes the owner never cut his throat in an overenthusiastic gesture thinking of the kills to come; and a hunting scene in that supremely elegant French porcelain, Biscuit de Sèvres – two beautiful women lie back with satisfaction after the killing of a deer, not the best of images for encouraging gentle masculine manners. Hunting legends recur, of the goddess Diana, of course, and of St Hubert. The story goes that the latter was so bitten by the hunting bug that he even ignored religious days to indulge his passion. Out in the forests one Good Friday, he had a vision of a deer with a crucifix between its antlers; the admonitory sign set him back on the straight and narrow and he stopped ignoring his religious duties.

Before the most impressive room displaying Desportes' canvases is one dedicated to the works of the sculptor Florentin Brigaud. His smooth, exotic, deliberately overpolished animal forms don't appear to be linked with hunting; his inspiration came instead from the Paris Colonial Exhibition of 1931 and the zoo in the capital's Jardin des Plantes. The château's great hall with its beautiful rafters contains some 80 paintings by Desportes. Some of his works are simple studies of animals, beautiful and undisturbing; others show the savagery of hunting. And then there are the beloved tranquil scenes from after the hunt, dead ducks and hares draped over aristocratic balustrades like gorgeous decorative objects.

Celebrity pieces also feature in the museum, among them three guns belonging to Napoleon. Bonaparte is also represented in an extraordinary painting of the emperor hunting in Fontainebleau, ladies looking on from carriages as the deer trapped by the chase awaits the megalomaniac's bullet. A separate series of 19th-century bronzes acts as a reminder of how cruel the animal kingdom can be too, with panthers and lions overwhelming their prey.

Beside Gien's château stands the **church of Ste-Jeanne d'Arc**. The war bombs only left the soaring narthex, or entrance tower, of the earlier 15th-century church standing. The exterior of the new edifice, by the architect André Gélis, reflects the traditional regional interest in brickwork with rich patternings, but the window tops have been given the modern twist of triangular shapes, rather than rounded or lancet arches. Red brick reigns within as well as without. A slightly sickly orange glow lights up the interior, emanating from the predominantly red and yellow stained glass by Max Ingrand. Gien potters created the striking ceramic plaques showing the Stations of the Cross and the intriguing elongated religious statues perched around the choir and transepts. Look out for the particularly tender and unusual rendering of the Virgin and Child, the baby Jesus caressing and almost kissing his mother. Behind the organ at the altar end, Joan of Arc puts in an appearance in the modern stained glass by François Bernard, her face interpreted in cubist style. Wearily trudging soldiers stand out in one panel, depicted in the vivid colours traditionally reserved for figures of devils in medieval stained glass.

It's worth wandering down into town from the upper plateau, as the centre below can be quite lively, even if the cafés and restaurants along the riverside are somewhat blighted by the noise of the traffic passing right in front of them.

The **Gien Musée de la Faïencerie and Factory** (*pottery museum open 2 May–Sept 9–6.30 (opens 9.30 on Sun), March–April and Oct–Dec 9–12 and 2–6 (opens 10 on Sun), Jan–Feb 2–6; pottery factory open Mon–Sat; 78 Place de la Victoire, t 02 38 67 00 05, www.gien.com*) lie a little west of the centre of town. It was an Englishman, Thomas Hall, who acquired a former convent here in 1821 and converted it into his pottery factory. The first room of the small museum contains a collection showing the diverse influences on the Gien factory's early production, demonstrating how derivative Gien pottery was. It became best known for its blue decorations, called, not very originally, '*bleu de Gien*'. A video explains, in English or French, how the pottery is made. Some of the exhibits likely to catch your eye in the museum are the magnificent oversized vases, over 6ft high, made for the 1900 Universal Exhibition, as was the superb Louis XIV-style clock, dripping with turquoise pendants and gymnastic putti holding the globe of the clock. Among further curious items are several *barbotines* – shiny-looking ceramic paintings; and a photo under enamel, a process developed in Gien in 1897. In the extensive factory shop you can see the range of today's output and search through seconds, including dinner services decorated with St-Exupéry drawings for his much-loved children's book, *Le Petit Prince*.

To get from Gien to Sully, consider avoiding the main road along the north bank, which passes in front of Dampierre nuclear power station. Instead, follow the south bank and branch off to Cuissy, the bumpy narrow riverside road a delight once you leave the four huge power station chimneys behind. This way you get close to the **Ile de Cuissy** in the middle of the Loire. Panels beside the road give details on the common species of birds to be found on the river and in particular on the terns that favour this spot, their eggs and their young merging with the very beige gravels here.

From Sully to the Outskirts of Orléans

The great annual gathering of Gaulish druids is supposed to have occurred in a sacred site somewhere around St-Benoît, along this stretch of the Loire, only the mysterious location (as with so many details on this culture) has been lost in the

Getting Around

Public transport seems about as unlikely in this area now as it was in the druids' days and, where it does exist, is as slow as going by boat. No trains serve the area. There is the occasional bus each day plying its way between Orléans and Gien, stopping at Sully-sur-Loire and Châteauneuf-sur-Loire – for information about times contact Rapides du Val de Loire (**t** 02 38 61 90 00).

Tourist Information

Sully-sur-Loire: Place de Gaulle, B.P.12, 45600 Sully-sur-Loire, **t** 02 38 36 23 70, **f** 02 38 36 32 21.
St-Benoît-sur-Loire: 44 Rue Orléanaise, 45110 St-Benoît-sur-Loire, **t/f** 02 38 35 79 00.
Châteauneuf-sur-Loire: 3 Place Aristide Briand, 45110 Châteauneuf-sur-Loire, **t** 02 38 58 44 79, **f** 02 38 58 52 83.
Jargeau: La Chanterie, B.P.19, 45150 Jargeau, **t** 02 38 59 83 42, **f** 02 38 59 92 62.
La Ferté-St-Aubin: Place des Cadets de la France Libre, B.P.3, **t** 02 38 64 67 93, **f** 02 38 64 61 39.
Lorris: 2 Place des Halles, 45260 Lorris, **t** 02 38 94 81 42, **f** 02 38 94 88 00.

Market Days
Sully-sur-Loire: Monday morning.
Châteauneuf-sur-Loire: Friday.
Jargeau: Wednesday afternoon.
Lorris: Thursday morning.
Fay-aux-Loges: Wednesday morning.

Where to Stay and Eat

Sully-sur-Loire ✉ 45600
Le Grand Sully, 10 Bd du Champ de Foire, **t 02 38 36 27 56, **f** 02 38 36 44 54 (*inexpensive*). Doesn't look particularly grand actually, but the cuisine here has a solid reputation (*menus €14–32; closed Sun pm and first fortnight in Jan*).
Hôtel de la Poste, 11 Rue du Faubourg St-Germain, **t 02 38 36 26 22, **f** 02 38 36 39 35 (*inexpensive*). The place is prettier approached by the shaded gravel courtyard at the back rather than by the entrance on

the busy main road. The rooms are dull, but the food again comes recommended (*menus €14.5–23*).

St-Benoît-sur-Loire ✉ 45110
Hôtel du Labrador, 7 Place de l'Abbaye, **t 02 38 35 74 38, **f** 02 38 35 72 99 (*inexpensive*). Standing calmly close to the abbey church, the Hôtel du Labrador has typical, rather dull, local architecture, with openings characterized by brick surrounds, plus a modern section. The rooms aren't bad, though, some with beams or with a view over the countryside. *Closed Jan–mid-Feb.*
Retreat at the abbey, **t** 02 38 35 72 43. For men wishing to go on a retreat for a day or more, write to the *père hôtelier de l'abbaye*, or call him, to see if he can arrange for accommodation in one of the simple cells set aside for visitors. You eat in the refectory with the monks.

Châteauneuf-sur-Loire ✉ 45110
Hostellerie du Parc and Restaurant la Capitainerie, 1 Grande Rue, **t 02 38 58 42 16, **f** 02 38 58 46 81 (*inexpensive*). An appealing small hotel, delightfully located by the gates to the château grounds, with one side overlooking the flower gardens and castle outbuildings. The little rooms are rustically furnished. Fish is the forte in the restaurant, which is not surprising given Châteauneuf's reputation, but it also offers classic French cuisine. On warm days, you can eat outside (*menus €18–41.5*).
Auberge du Port, **t** 02 38 58 43 07 (*cheap*). Also nicely located, with just four basic rooms in the quiet area beside the Loire, this inn lies just a stone's throw away from the river (*menus €10.5–26; closed Wed*).

St-Denis-de-l'Hôtel ✉ 45550
Le Cygne, 42 Grande Rue, **t 02 38 59 02 43, **f** 02 38 59 04 19 (*cheap*). A popular local address for a simple restaurant meal (*menus €8–26*). The rooms are basic.
Le Dauphin, Avenue des Fontaines, **t 02 38 46 29 29, **f** 02 38 59 07 63 (*inexpensive*). Quite comfortable, with a characterful old-style beamed restaurant (*closed Sun pm and most of Aug*).

Chécy ✉ 45430

Les Courtils B&B, Rue de l'Ave, **t** 02 38 91 32 02, **f** 02 38 91 48 20. The stocky tower of the village church peers down protectively onto this charming walled property where you can hear the church bells singing merrily through the daytime. The small, slightly awkward, but tastefully decorated rooms are under the eaves, in a specially converted barn. In the large reception room below, the owner displays some of her art. From the private garden you can appreciate a lovely, peaceful view down onto the Loire.

Combleux ✉ 45800

Restaurant La Marine, **t** 02 38 55 12 69, **f** 02 38 52 03 65. Beautifully located in a peaceful waterside hamlet by a weir where the Canal d'Orléans meets the Loire, this utterly charming restaurant looks as if it belongs to another era. It has a terrace by the water where you can make the most of the waterside in summer (*menus €16.5–23*). *Closed Tues pm and Wed out of season.*

La Ferté-St-Aubin ✉ 45240

★★★Château Les Muids, **t** 02 38 64 65 14, **f** 02 38 76 50 08, *muids@chateauxhotels.com*, *www.chateauxhotels.com/muids* (*expensive–moderate*). A splendidly patterned late 18th-century brick château 4km south of town, just off the N20. Not outrageously expensive for such an elegant stop, with swimming pool and tennis court in the grounds.

La Ferme de La Lande, northeast out of town, **t** 02 38 76 64 37, **f** 02 38 64 68 87. Very tempting, sophisticated little country restaurant in an immaculate miniature 18th-century farm, once part of the Château de La Ferté-St-Aubin's estates.

Ménestreau-en-Villette ✉ 45240

La Ferme des Foucault B&B, off the Route de Sennely (D64), **t/f** 02 38 76 94 41 (*moderate*). Lost in typical Sologne countryside some way out of the village are these splendid and spacious B&B rooms in a farmhouse restored by an enthusiastic American, Rosemary Beau, and her French husband.

You'll also find a number of good places around the Forest of Orléans:

Lorris ✉ 45260

★★Le Sauvage, 2 Place du Martroi, **t** 02 38 92 43 79, **f** 02 38 94 82 46 (*inexpensive*). This hotel is well placed on the old square (*restaurant closed Fri*).

Guillaume de Lorris, 8 Grande Rue, **t** 02 38 94 83 55. Some snazzy dishes here, where the zander may come with a *fumet de homard*, or the moules in profiteroles (*menus €17.5–26*). *Closed Tues pm and Wed, mid-Feb–mid-Mar and 10 days in July.*

Combreux ✉ 45530

★★L'Auberge de Combreux, 35 Rue du Gâtinais, **t** 02 38 46 89 89, **f** 02 38 59 36 19, *combreux@chateauxhotels.com* (*moderate*). It looks like an archetypal French village inn (some of its cosy old-styled rooms even have a fireplace), but it has modern attractions too, such as a heated swimming pool, a tennis court and a golf range. Traditional French fare served (*menus €16.5–32*). *Closed mid-Dec–mid-Jan.*

Vitry-aux-Loges ✉ 45530

Château du Plessis-Beauregard B&B, **t** 02 38 59 47 24, **f** 02 38 59 47 48 (*moderate; no smoking*). Extremely comfortable, elegant rooms in a long brick wing completed at either end by a tower. The large garden ending at the canal is delightful. Good value for this level of comfort, the rooms are provided with old furniture, *toile de Jouy* wallcoverings, crucifixes over the bed, and tasteful personal touches. You can meet the traditional French family that owns the château at the *table d'hôte*, when you can sample refined French family cooking (*table d'hôte €27.5*). *Closed Aug.*

Fay-aux-Loges ✉ 45450

Auberge A la Fortune du Pot, 2 Chemin du Hâlage, **t** 02 38 59 56 54, **f** 38 57 04 25. By the canal. End an excellent meal with a local pudding made from delicious pears and honey (*menus €20.5–32*). *Closed Sun pm, Tues pm and all Wed, plus Feb school hols and 3 weeks in Aug.*

mists of time. Traces of the seemingly vibrant Carolingian life of the late Dark Ages in these parts have survived a little better, with a small but splendid blue-and-gold mosaic from the period preserved at Germigny. The glories of this area, though, apart from the river itself, are medieval: the Romanesque abbey church of St-Benoît and the Gothic Château de Sully. It's worth also taking the trouble to discover the Loire port quays in virtually all the towns and villages along this stretch, often wonderfully atmospheric if a little neglected. Châteauneuf-sur-Loire's museum on the Loire river trading of the past will teach you a thing or two about the life of the Loire's mariners.

Château de Sully

Open April–Sept 10–6, Feb–March and Oct–Dec 10–12 and 2–5; t 02 38 36 36 86.

Enjoy, Sir, the pleasures of Paris while I am, by order of the king, in the most agreeable château and with the best company in the world.
>   Voltaire, in a letter to a friend, during his royal-imposed exile
>   at Sully from 1716 to 1719

This castle makes one of the most beautiful pictures along the whole of the Loire, even if the landscape around it is rather flat. The sparkling white-stoned château stands close enough to the Loire to be splendidly reflected in it at times, although its moats are supplied by a tributary called the Sange. Its sturdy towers with their pepper-pot tops look a model of their medieval kind, although they actually had to be rebuilt in 1908.

Three great families owned the Château de Sully. From the 10th to the 14th centuries it was the barons of Sully. Maurice Sully was from this family, the bishop who went off to order the building of Paris' famed cathedral of Notre-Dame. Then the dukes of La Trémoïlle transformed the place, living here from the end of the 14th century to the start of the 17th. The rectangular Vieux Château giving onto the Loire was commissioned by the first dukes of this family. The Hundred Years' War was raging when work began on this great keep for Marie de Sully and her husband Guy de la Trémoïlle. They had a fine architect though, the plans being by Raymond du Temple, responsible in Paris for the remodelling of the Louvre for King Charles V and for the Château de Vincennes. Joan of Arc's lightning campaign against the English was halted here after her victory at Patay, when the Lorraine upstart was kept at Sully against her will by the fractious Georges de la Trémoïlle, son of Guy and favourite of Charles VII – not all the French proved to be fans of the Maid of Orléans.

In 1602 the château became the property of Maximilien de Béthune, one of the greatest ministers in French history (*see* the box on the next page), who worked in the service of King Henri IV. He received the title of Duc de Sully, but French history prefers to refer to him simply and reverentially as '*le Grand Sully*'. His descendants lived here until they sold the château to the *département* of the Loiret in 1962. By then the massive family home lay almost empty.

Since 1962, the new administration has been progressively restoring the château and buying up pieces linked to Le Grand Sully to embellish its rooms. Some of the

France in Sully's Safe Hands

Trusted companion of Protestant Henri de Navarre, the man who would reunify France at the end of the fanatical follies of the Wars of Religion, Le Grand Sully was given a succession of important posts when his master became King Henri IV of France, and the first French Bourbon royal, in 1589. Having been made Grand Maître de l'Artillerie and Grand Voyer de France, in 1598 Sully was appointed *Surintendant des Finances*. As finance minister he became a vastly powerful man. He is commonly portrayed as a solid, reliable figure who did much to help revive the French economy after deeply troubled and divisive times, keeping a tight rein on the journey to recovery. Some of the greatest successes overseen by Sully under Henri IV's rule were the development of new roads and of the silk industry in France, the latter helping the country avoid paying for expensive foreign imports.

Henri IV was assassinated in 1610. From that period, Sully's star was in decline. Distanced from power under the new administration, he devoted himself to his estates and to expounding his theories. The very name of his oeuvre reads like the title of an accountant's diary, *Les Sages et Royales Oeconomies d'Estat*. In this work dedicated to his former boss 'Henri le Grand', he put forward his ideas on developing the economy through increased agricultural activity – probably a bedtime book for the more serious historians among you. The weighty tome was printed at Sully's expense, in one of the towers of the castle. Louis XIII did eventually confer on Sully the illustrious title of Maréchal de France in the man's old age, in recognition of his services to his father Henri IV.

chambers in the Vieux Château are on a vast scale. A splendid and much-needed focus has been given to one of these great halls by a series of tapestries illustrating the legend of Psyche, Cupid and the envious Venus. Its marbled effects are superb. The borders carry the Béthune arms. The series was bought from another of the Duc de Sully's castles, Rosny-sur-Seine, his birthplace. A room of similar dimensions above is given over to portraits of the Sully family, including one of Maximilien's brother, Philippe, governor to Henri IV's son Gaston, who became the rebellious Gaston d'Orléans. Look out for the remnants of sumptuous wall paintings around the upper room. You can also visit the Grand Sully's bedroom, while a little oratory contains a copy of the tomb made for him and his second wife; their remains were transferred here from Nogent-le-Rotrou in 1934. Climb to the top of the Vieux Château to admire 600-year-old rafters and to tread gingerly along the machicolated walkway with its views down on the Loire. The atmosphere changes in the wing where Sully had his private apartments. One ceiling is decorated with remarkable detailed images symbolizing Sully's devotion to the king, such as the eagle carrying Jupiter's bolts. Further paintings reflect major events involving Sully and Henri IV.

The Château de Sully offers a varied cultural programme through the year. The **Festival de Musique de Sully** brings classical music to the château at weekends from the end of June to mid-July; prestigious international players come to perform. Look out, too, for special theme visits round the castle – in costume, for children, or by candlelight on certain nights.

In summer, a large sandy beach stretches out indolently by the Loire in front of the château. As in so many such spots along the great river, campers set up home here during the tourist season. As for the **town of Sully** beside the château, it was heavily bombarded during the war, some 80 per cent being destroyed. It wasn't as well restored as neighbouring Gien, but is quite pleasant. Wandering around town you may spot a couple of statues honouring Sully, while the church of St-Ythier contains some interesting stained-glass windows, one showing a tree of Jesse, another illustrating the story of a pilgrim on the way to Santiago de Compostela. Down around the semi-abandoned church of St-Germain, a cluster of Loire mariners' houses remains. The Loire froze over in 1985 and the postwar suspension bridge snapped under the pressure. So now Sully has one of the most recent crossings over the Loire.

Church of the Abbey of St-Benoît-sur-Loire or Fleury

Open to visitors 8am–9pm except Sun am, the first Friday in each month, bank hols and Jan–Feb; plainchant Mass at 12 on weekdays, 11 at weekends and on special days; adm for guided tour on Sun at 3.15; t 02 38 35 72 43, www.abbaye-fleury.com.

Old saints' bones had a particularly powerful and widespread fascination for the religious-minded in the Dark Ages and Middle Ages which is hard to emphasize strongly enough today. They weren't just viewed as physical reminders of the saints' existence and exemplary lives; they were thought to work miracles and to be closely linked to divine powers.

Around 672, a band of monks who had settled into religious life at the recently founded Benedictine abbey at Fleury, by the Loire, decided to go in search of the bones of the saintly Benedict (Benoît in French). He was the Italian of the first half of the 6th century who founded the great western European monastic order named after him. His *Regula Monachorum* set down the general rule for monasticism in the West, making him an extremely important figure in the development of the Church in western Europe. He had died at his monastery of Monte Cassino near Naples around 547, but this had been destroyed by Lombards in 580.

The group from Fleury went all the way to Monte Cassino to scour the ground and recover what they could find of Benedict's remains. They carried back to their abbey on the Loire what they claimed to be Benedict's bones, discovered among the Neapolitan ruins. Outraged Italian monks protested at this action, but a papal declaration accepted that the remains should stay at Fleury. The abbey consequently became an extremely venerated site in western Christendom. The 11 July, known as the day of the *translation* of Benedict's bones, is still celebrated by the Benedictine order as a whole.

In Carolingian times, towards the end of the 8th century, Théodulfe, a renowned theologian and close adviser to Charlemagne, became abbot of Fleury, or St-Benoît as it would later become better known. The abbey blossomed as one of the centres of what has been described as the Carolingian renaissance. It was a place of great importance for teaching and learning in Charlemagne's empire, and also one that produced superb illuminated manuscripts. Nothing remains of those times at St-Benoît, the abbey of that period having disappeared, the surviving manuscripts and treasures from it dispersed in the 16th-century Wars of Religion, when the abbot, Odet de Coligny, brother of the leader of the Protestants, suddenly and treacherously converted from Catholicism and revealed the hide-outs of the abbey's riches to the Protestants. At nearby Germigny (see below), however, a mosaic from Théodulfe's private oratory can still be seen, among the oldest pieces of decorative Christian church art in France.

The abbey of St-Benoît amassed considerable territories and wealth down the centuries. The early Capetian kings were generous patrons in the 11th and 12th centuries, the period in which much of the church you can still see today was built. In return, they benefited from the international reputation of St-Benoît's network of schools and teaching, as well as from the widespread popularity of the pilgrimage to see St-Benoît's relics. King Philippe I, ruling at the end of the 11th century, even decided to be buried here. A little later, in 1130, a famous meeting took place at St-Benoît between Louis VI, Pope Innocent II and St Bernard, the latter founder of the rigorously reforming Cistercian order. By contrast, a manuscript from the end of the 12th century records 10 liturgical dramas performed here, an early flowering of French theatre! The devoutly bellicose 13th-century French king known as St Louis visited St-Benoît repeatedly to stock up on saintly support.

A relative decline in importance followed, but the monastic order, the pilgrimage and the powerful significance of the abbey remained. In 1429, Joan of Arc and Charles VII of France stopped here on the way to the latter's triumphant sacred crowning in the cathedral of Reims. After the early 16th century, when abbeys became the gift of French kings to grant as they wished, the most famous 'abbot' of St-Benoît was Cardinal Richelieu. He introduced the authoritarian reform of St-Maur here, which enabled the place to prosper for a good century more before the Revolution. The massive monastic ensemble that had grown up to the south of the church was demolished during the Revolution. The church itself was saved and for a brief period became a parish church until a monastic order was re-established in the mid-19th century.

Dominating the sweep of the Loire known as the Val d'Or, or Golden Valley, and the plain around it, today the imposing **abbey church** in its light Loire stone topped by slate looks perhaps more impressive than beautiful, the weight of its history and symbolism adding substantially to its gravity. Architectural historians consider it to be one of the most important Romanesque churches in France due to a handful of distinctive elements.

The most outstanding of these is undoubtedly the **early 11th-century narthex**, or entrance porch, with its carved Romanesque capitals. Some of them are decorated with Corinthian leaves or with animals, others with figures from the Apocalypse, others still with stories from other New Testament or early Christian texts. The most characteristic feature is the dramatic way the sculptors have made use of the curve of the capitals, so that men of stone lean forward to stare right down at you or animals rear up dramatically. As you arrive, on the right-hand central pillar, Christ appears to John of the *Book of Revelations* with the messages he is to transmit to the seven Churches, symbolized by the candelabra. On the inside of this pillar, the Lamb, symbol of Christ, opens the book of the seven seals, and the four horsemen of the Apocalypse emerge. On the outside of the pillar, the good are seen being separated from the evil. Along the right-hand row of columns, you can decipher various animal scenes including big birds lining up, seemingly to drink, and a horseman pursuing what looks like a stag. A couple of further scenes that are relatively easy to interpret are close to the church door: St Martin seen slicing his cloak to give a piece to a beggar and, opposite, the Holy Family fleeing to Egypt, Mary on a donkey.

Inside the church, past the bright nave with its Gothic arches, you can admire the second rare feature of the abbey church, the **Byzantine mosaics floor** of the choir, a many-patterned, multicoloured crazy paving. On it lies the tomb effigy of King Philippe I, with an apologetic notice on his misbehaviour; he ran off with a married woman when he was already wedded to another. In the transept close to Philippe I's figure, see if you can spot another cartoonish face carved high up in the wall opposite the Virgin, either cheek pierced by a hole; this curious stone portrait apparently represents Raynaldus, a Viking who pillaged and devastated the area before the new medieval abbey was built. The holes are said to symbolize death.

The third extraordinary feature of the church is its sombre, atmospheric **crypt**, where the bones of St Benedict still rest, according to the monks of today. Their medieval counterparts who guarded the precious bones were very wary of pilgrims who might be tempted to try to steal a piece for their personal benefit; they stood vigilantly by the relics as the visitors processed round the crypt. These relics were just visible to the pilgrims through a few slits in the protective wall of the marytrium, the inner sanctum, recreated a few decades ago. The monks nowadays run a large souvenir shop next to the church.

From the abbey you can walk down to the Loire, passing behind the Hôtel Labrador, to the site of St-Benoît's former **port**, once full of activity thanks to the vast estates of St-Benoît and the large community it sheltered. Now the village, with its little old stone mariners' houses and their well-tended miniature gardens, makes one of the most charming riverside scenes in the area. In summer, you may see fishermen wading through the shallow waters here.

It was in this village that the poet and painter Max Jacob settled for much of his life after 1921. A great friend of Picasso in his early adulthood – the two shared a Parisian room when they were setting out on their careers – Jacob was considered a brilliant mind by his generation, particularly for his poetic work *Le Cornet à dés*, a daring, mysterious prose poem once described as 'cubist poetry'. Jacob had all the makings of a troubled figure, a gay Breton Jew who converted to Christianity after a mystical experience, but he had a great sense of humour too. Leaving Paris for the peace of St-Benoît, he served as a sacristan here. In 1944, despite efforts by the abbey to intercede on his behalf, the Nazis ordered his deportation from St-Benoît for being Jewish. Already a sick man, he died in the Drancy transit camp outside Paris.

Carolingian Oratory at Germigny-des-Prés

Church open April–Sept 8.30–7, Oct–March 8.30–6; t 02 38 58 27 03.
Museum open April–Sept 9–12.30 and 2–7, Oct–Dec and Feb–March
Wed–Mon 9.30–12.30 and 2–5.30; t 02 38 58 27 97. Adm to church free;
small adm charge for the museum.

The treasured **Dark Ages mosaic** commissioned by Bishop Théodulfe may be relatively small in size, but it has its place in French art history. Théodulfe wasn't one to deprive himself, it seems. He is said to have sought out the architect of Charlemagne's great chapel at Aix-la-Chapelle to plan the delightful little building which houses the mosaic, as well as a now vanished villa nearby. The oratory was built close to the start of the 9th century. Originally it took the shape of a Greek cross, each of its arms of equal length and ending with a horseshoe-shaped apse. Only three apses remain today, while a nave was tacked on to the fourth side in the 11th century.

The interior would once have been covered with many mosaics, but only one survives. It lay hidden under paint for centuries, but now the glorious blues and golds shine once more. In the style of the Ravenna School, it represents the Ark of the Covenant, above which hover two cherubs, watched over by a couple of stern-faced, great bird-winged angels. Between their wings, the hand of God reaches down from a crack in the sky. The Latin inscription is a heady cry to prayer, with an expression of Théodulfe's vanity or his fear tacked on, which reads like a heartfelt plea coming directly to you down the centuries. Roughly translated, it reads: 'See here and contemplate the holy oracle and its cherubs. Here shines the ark of the divine testament. In front of this vision, try with your prayers to move the master of thunder, and please, do not forget to include Théodulfe in your wishes.' The church also contains some beautiful statues and sweet little foliage-decorated capitals.

The small Musée de la Grange Germignonne just next door to the church gives more details on the oratory, and you can ask there to see an exquisite Limoges enamel reliquary.

The South Bank of the Loire from Sully to Châteauneuf

The abbey of St-Benoît is perhaps most impressive seen from the south bank of the Loire. From Sully, you could follow the D951 as far as Bouteilles. From there, take the riverside road north to Guilly. Then, up on the levee, you get expansive views onto the Loire and the abbey church, as well as passing a mariners' cross, the **Croix Tibi**.

Just west of Bouteilles and Guilly lies **Neuvy-en-Sullias**, where an extraordinary collection of Celtic bronze animal statues – of a horse, bulls, deer and wild boar, among others – was found in 1861. These sophisticated and beautiful treasures, dated to the early Gallo-Roman period, are now displayed in the Hôtel Cabu museum in Orléans (*see* pp.145–6). Little is known about them or what they were doing on this land. It's no doubt coincidence that the great Celtic annual druids' meetings are known to have been held somewhere in the area.

Where the Druids of Gaul Gathered

Caesar made some fascinating observations about the druids of Gaul and their customs in his *Conquest of Gaul*. His views are particularly helpful, as the druids themselves forbade the transfer of their knowledge through writing. Caesar's account, though, should be read with reservations, precisely because the druids managed to keep their activities and beliefs so cloaked in mystery.

Caesar records how:

On a fixed date in each year they hold a session in a consecrated spot in the country of the Carnutes which is supposed to be the centre of Gaul. Those who are involved in disputes assemble here from all parts and accept the druids' judgements and awards.

Caesar then offers his insights into the druids' high standing in Celtic society and some of the druidic training, practices and beliefs:

The two privileged classes are the druids and the knights. The druids officiate at the worship of the gods, regulate public and private sacrifices, and give rulings on all religious questions. Large numbers of young men flock to them for instruction, and they are held in great honour by the people. They act as judges in practically all disputes, whether between tribes or between individuals... Any individual or tribe failing to accept their award is banned from taking part in sacrifice – the heaviest punishment that can be inflicted upon a Gaul...

...The druids are exempt from military service and do not pay taxes like other citizens. These important privileges are naturally attractive: many present themselves of their own accord to become students of druidism, and others are sent by their parents or relatives. It is said that these pupils have to memorize a great number of verses – so many, that some of them spend 20 years at their studies...

...A lesson which they take particular pains to inculcate is that the soul does not perish, but after death passes from one body to another; they think that this is the best incentive to bravery, because it teaches men to disregard the terrors of death. They also hold long discussions about the heavenly bodies and their movements, the size of the universe and of the earth, the physical constitution of the world, and the powers and properties of the gods; and they instruct the young men in all these subjects.

These observations, speculative as they may be, serve to show what a highly developed and deeply complex society the Celts of Gaul had developed.

Châteauneuf-sur-Loire

Unfortunately for the small town of Châteauneuf-sur-Loire, it lost most of its château in the Revolution and, in the course of the 19th century, virtually all of the Loire river trade on which it once thrived. During the Second World War it was badly bombed, causing it to be largely rebuilt in dull and hasty style. And yet the place still has two charming corners, its castle grounds and its riverside quays. The château's stables, which survived the Revolution, have recently been converted into an ppealing modern museum celebrating the life and work of the Loire mariners. Châteauneuf-sur-Loire also offers the unexpected delight of one of the most repellent tombs in France.

Musée de la Marine de Loire in the Château of Châteauneuf

Open April–Oct Wed–Mon 10–6, rest of year Wed–Mon except major hols 2–6.

You get a definite whiff of the grandeur of the Ancien Régime Château de Châteauneuf-sur-Loire from the stables left standing. They formed part of a lavish ensemble ordered in the late 17th century by the extravagant Louis Phélypeaux de la Vrillère, who became an important courtier under Louis XIV, serving for a time as master of ceremonies for a megalomaniac unmatched in the history of France for his love of pomp.

In the museum, just a little space is dedicated to the castle's history. In fact, a fort stood on this spot from the 11th century, certain Capetian and Valois kings even devoting it some attention through the medieval period. It was destroyed during the anti-monarchic Fronde uprising in the middle of the 17th century, leaving the way clear for Phélypeaux to erect his little Versailles. The owner after Phélypeaux, the Duc de Penthièvre, grandson of Louis XIV and Madame de Montespan, left his mark too with certain additions, including the elegant rotunda that stands out on the end of the only wing left from the Ancien Régime château.

The museum concentrates on the common people of Châteauneuf-sur-Loire rather than its lords, and more specifically on the many Loire mariners who once formed a very important part of the local community. A census of 1780 recorded this little town as having the fifth largest number of mariners along the Loire after the major ports of Orléans, Tours, Angers and Nantes. In the entrance hall, a helpful large-scale map gives visitors a clear picture of the immense size of the Bassin de la Loire, the area of France covered by the Loire and its tributaries. Read the introduction to the river in **Topics** (pp.60–62) to learn more about its great trading past, how it was used by Celts, Greeks, Romans and Vikings, and, from the Middle Ages, how its mariners formed a community to protect their interests which lasted almost to the Revolution.

All manner of goods were transported along the Loire, notably wine and salt, stones and coal, and pottery. In colonial times, much of the sugar from the French Caribbean islands was shipped up from Nantes to Orléans, while *indiennes*, patterned fabrics, were exported. The Loire mariners had a tough job, having to deal with the unpredictable conditions of an untamed river and spending a long time away from home. They gained a widespread reputation for being a troublesome lot when they weren't sufficiently occupied, regarded all too often as foul-mouthed drinkers, brawlers and *coureurs de jupons*, running after the girls. However, this museum is dedicated to honouring their memory with respect. One of their sayings went: '*Si vilains sur terre nous sommes, nous sommes seigneurs sur l'eau* (However mean we may be on dry land, we're lords on the waters).'

The museum contains models of the different types of boats they used. Some excellent film shows how the boats worked and the skill required to manoeuvre them, particularly to pass under the many bridges along the Loire. Engravings and pottery from Nevers (further upriver) depict how busy the river once was, whole caravans of boats strung together on some trips. Depending on the weather, a journey downriver from Orléans to Nantes might take five or six days, but a trip in the other direction might last three or four weeks. While the prevailing southwesterly winds normally gave a helpful push to boats travelling up against the current, when they reached Orléans boats generally had to be tugged, using manpower, not horsepower. For a big boat, up to 40 men might be required to pull.

The Loire mariners certainly formed a community apart, the profession often passed on from father to son. While the vast majority of them led a pretty basic existence, the odd one made his fortune. A big divide existed between the boat owners and the majority of poor sailors who were paid by the trip. The mariners wore distinctive clothes and jewellery, held special celebrations through the year, and their prayers and processions were devoted to particular saints, notably St Nicholas, their patron. In their houses, their furniture was marked with symbols of their profession, such as anchors and stars. While rivalry might have existed between mariners from different localities, those from the same community appear to have supported each other. At certain times of year the river wasn't navigable; many mariners then turned their hand to carpentry and woodcarving. They also played a key role in evacuating the local population when floods occurred. With their sailing skills, the mariners could even be called upon to serve on different waters in times of war; a number joined the French fleet to help the Americans in the War of Independence from Britain.

Loire river trade was still thriving in the early decades of the 19th century, as was river transport. A charmingly named firm, the Companie de Navigation Accélérée sur la Loire, even started to run the first steam boats along the Loire in the 1820s (one of them, Le Vulcain, tragically exploded at Tours in 1837; in an unsubtle publicity ploy to try and win back its customers, the company named its next model the Inexplosible!). But trains would rapidly supersede this mode of transport after railway lines along the Loire were laid in the late 1840s, and Loire river trade and transport dwindled rapidly. By the close of the century the profession of the Loire mariner had practically disappeared. Many of the men from Châteauneuf-sur-Loire families long espoused to the profession went to work for the ground-breaking bridge-maker Ferdinand Arnodin, who set up here.

Other people whose lives revolved around the river are also recalled in the museum, such as the professional Loire fishermen who, during the period of the Grande Pêche from January to June, used to erect barrages across two-thirds of the river's width in order to catch the salmon, shad and eels coming upstream from the sea. As to the passeurs, they spent their days ferrying people, cattle and goods across from one side of the river to the other. The lavendières were the women who washed clothes in the Loire's waters on specially built boats moored to land, the bateaux-lavoirs. Lastly, a few local artists inspired by the river have also been given their place in the museum.

The Loire river was the centre of attention for a place like Châteauneuf, and for the whole Loire Valley region, for so long. Now that the river has been abandoned and left to its own devices, the mariners thrown off its wild back, the memories cherished by this museum act as an important reminder of how closely men worked with the Loire in centuries past.

To Châteauneuf's Repellent Tomb and Riverside

Along Châteauneuf-sur-Loire's main street, poke your nose inside the **church of St-Martial**, split in two by war bombing. The architecture may not be particularly special, but the interior conceals the deliberately, brilliantly horrible **tomb of Louis Phélypeaux de la Vrillère**, a Baroque work attributed to the Italian Domenico Guidi. The pathetic, foppish Phélypeaux kneels between two atlantes holding up an arch in pink and black striped marble – but these figures, rather than being muscle-bound as is usually the case, are fully unfleshed, grinning skeletons. Phélypeaux wears an imploring look, hand on heart, ornamental flower on his garter. He looks like a gushing actor who knows his time is up and just hopes that the critics won't be too severe; but here the obsequious courtier's entreaties are addressed to God.

The town has a fairly good selection of shops selling local produce such as pear liqueur and forest pâtés, but you may find it excessive for such a small place to have treated itself to two covered markets. One in fact turns out to be a 19th-century shed for Loire boats, its elegant form now put to different uses.

Today the main centre of Châteauneuf's activities lie some distance from the Loire, but do go and see the **old riverside quarter**, which retains a character all of its own with its old cobbled quays. You should be able to take a look at one or two recon-structed traditional mariners' boats here, including a *gabare* called the *Gaillarde*. Or there's a lovely peaceful walk you can take to a quieter stretch of the river if you follow the track down from the château's rotunda.

The Loire Between Châteauneuf and Orléans

North Bank

Heading along the north side of the Loire from Châteauneuf-sur-Loire towards Orléans, avoid the busy N60. Stick as close as possible to the river instead, heading for **St-Denis-de-l'Hôtel**, the lofty entrance tower to its church so characteristic of the religious buildings along this stretch of the Loire and matching that of Jargeau, across the river. St-Denis's little museum, the Musée Maurice Genevoix (*open weekends and public hols 10–12 and 2–6; t 02 38 59 12 80; free*), is dedicated to a 20th-century writer of some distinction. Maurice Genevoix, once permanent secretary of that august French literary body, the Académie Française, hailed from here and loved the area. The start of his autobiographical book, *Trente Mille Jours*, reveals a mass of interesting details on Loire-side life when he was a child at the start of the 20th century, at a time when merchandise and barrels were still rolled up and down the streets to the river.

Which brings us neatly to the village of **Chécy**, which has an amusing Musée de la Tonnellerie (*open June–Sept Tues–Sun 3–6.30, early April–May and Oct weekends and public hols only 3–6.30*), devoted to coopers and vine-growers. Genevoix claimed that in the 1920s, vines still ran along the banks of the Loire practically from Sancerre to Nantes. Coopers formed an important part of the Loire-side community as well as mariners. Chécy also has the obligatory imposing church tower.

Do stop at the pretty, well-flowered former mariners' village at **Combleux**, just a bit further west; it's wedged between the Canal d'Orléans and the Loire, and well known to the people of Orléans as a picturesque place to which to escape from the big city.

The one good reason for stopping in busy, built-up St-Jean-de-Braye, effectively an eastern suburb of Orléans, is to visit the **Bollée bell foundry** (*open April–Sept 10–12 and 2–7, rest of year 2–5.30*), along the main road. Modern blocks may be going up around it, but this foundry remains firmly fixed in the 19th century, making bells in the traditional way, for instance using horse manure to aerate the earth for the hand-made moulds, and brushing on the necessary tallow with goose feathers. Enter the scruffy workshop with its earth pits where the bells are fired and you feel like you're stepping back into the pre-industrial age. Before that you're treated to a tour of the small modern museum on bell-making which Dominique Bollée set up in the early 1990s. A film explains the processes involved in making a *cloche*. You can also admire many finished pieces in the museum, including one made for the bicentenary of the French Revolution, and in memory of the 100,000 bells which apparently disappeared in that period, a telling reminder of the destruction wrought by that traumatic upheaval in French society. Dominique Bollée is the eighth generation of his family to make bells on this site. He and his colleagues produce about 100 a year, half of which are exported, mostly to churches in Africa and Asia these days, although in decades past the foundry made bells for the likes of the cathedrals of Ottawa and Buffalo.

South Bank

Following the south side of the Loire from Châteauneuf-sur-Loire towards Orléans, at **Jargeau** by the river, the Maison de Loire (*open year round exc Christmas hols Tues–Sun 9–12 and 2–6; t 02 38 59 76 60, mdl45@wanadoo.fr*) holds small temporary exhibitions on various aspects of the great river. Jargeau, apart from enjoying the distinction of having been liberated from English occupation by Joan of Arc in 1429, is known locally for its *andouillette*, or chitterling sausage.

A Dip into the Sologne via La Ferté-St-Aubin

A vast forest dotted with hundreds of lakes fills the land between the Loire's arc through the Orléanais and the Cher river to the south. This is the Sologne. Silver birch, pine and heather thrive across its flat lands. The Sologne is a hunter's paradise, teeming with rabbits and birds, ducks and fish, deer and boar. Although some find the Sologne melancholic, others respond to its mysterious, misty atmosphere. The area features in a couple of famous French works – the magical party in Alain-Fournier's *Le Grand Meaulnes* is held in the Sologne, while an even more eccentric *fête étrange* takes place here in Jean Renoir's *La Règle du Jeu*, one of the most important films in the history of French cinema.

The Sologne occupies an island of clay in the midst of the Loire Valley's limestone. As there's no stone locally, the houses are built of brick. The big difference between the dwellings of the wealthy landowners and the poor villagers stands out: while the villages consist of low, meagre cottages, large châteaux hide out in the countryside. The regional writer Maurice Genevoix wrote movingly about the social divide in the Sologne, particularly in his tale of the likable rogue of a poacher *Raboliot*. Whether modest or posh, Sologne homes are often embellished with brick patterning.

La Ferté-St-Aubin, due south of Orléans, is one of the most important gateways into the Sologne. Its pale brick château (*open April–Sept 10–7, mid-Feb–March 2–6, Oct–mid-Nov 10–6*) is one of the most appealing in the region, although it is run down. The entrance has comical bell-hatted pavilions flanking a curious classical arch. One architectural historian has compared the pavilions to deerstalkers, which seems all the more appropriate as the castle served as the setting for the tragic hunting party in *La Règle du Jeu*. The moats are fed by the Cosson river, which later flows past the Château de Chambord, one of the many famous châteaux on the western edge of the Sologne (*see* pp.165–8). The two sections of the main building went up in the 17th century, while two elegant wings providing stables and outbuildings were added later. You can visit the château's two top floors unaccompanied. The musty rooms are in a bad state of repair, but are filled with sometimes amusing bric-a-brac. A bell calls you on the guided tour through the better-preserved apartments on the ground floor, which finishes with a modest little cookery demonstration down in the basement kitchens. The owner has a lot of work on his hands in restoring this place, but a visit here proves quite entertaining, and it's good to find the stables still in use.

To appreciate something of the flora and fauna of the Sologne, visit the **Domaine Solognot du Ciran** (*open April–Sept 10–12 and 2–6, Jan–March and Oct–Dec Wed–Mon 10–12 and 2–5*), an estate set in typical Sologne woodland near the village of **Ménestreau-en-Villette**, just a short way east of La Ferté-St-Aubin. This reserve provides a haven for animals in this hunting-crazy area. You can walk through the grounds, with a fair chance of spotting deer. In the house, ask to see some of the wonderful short nature videos kept here, entries from the Festival International du Film de la Faune Sauvage (Wild Animals) held every November at Lamotte-Beuvron a little way south. (For further sights in the southern Sologne, *see* pp.211–13 in the chapter on the Cher valley.)

Through the Forêt d'Orléans

A vast swath of forest shadows the north side of the Loire from Gien to Orléans. This is the **Forêt d'Orléans**, the largest state-owned forest in France and the second largest forest in the country at around 35,000 hectares. Several place names here finish with the words 'aux-Loges', which refer to simple lodges that were built for the forest workers up until the start of the 20th century.

On the eastern edge of the forest, **Lorris** was the birthplace of Guillaume de Lorris, who wrote the first part of the great 13th-century narrative poem *Le Roman de la Rose*, a classic of chivalric literature. This beautiful but thorny piece was written by two poets born in the Orléanais region and named after their birthplaces (*see also* Meung, p.158). The poem became a medieval bestseller, not for years but for centuries. An allegorical work, loaded with symbolism, it recounts how a young man finds his way into an enchanted garden, '*Qu'il i avoit d'oisiaus trois tans/Qu'en tout le remanant de France* (Where there were three times more birds/Than in all the rest of France)', peopled by magnificent courtiers. In this entrancing place he falls in love with a rose.

The town's church of Notre-Dame, although hemmed in by houses, has several medieval features you can easily observe on the outside and, inside, one of the oldest organs in Europe. Dating from the 16th century, it perches elegantly, if somewhat precariously, high up on one side of the nave. There's a little organ museum nearby. A splendid Renaissance-windowed, black-brick patterned Hôtel de Ville and an old covered market in brown tiles sloping low towards the ground add appeal to the centre of town. A war museum in the former railway station commemorates in particular the Resistance fighters rounded up and killed here in August 1944.

The **Canal d'Orléans** passes not far from Lorris and crosses the forest. **Grignon**, **Combreux** and **Fay-aux-Loges** make up a string of quite pretty villages by the canal (Fay is a good place from which to go on a boat trip along the canal). Half-a-dozen kilometres north of Fay-aux-Loges, go to **Ingrannes** to see the Arboretum des Grandes Bruyères, only rarely open (*most Suns between April and Dec 10–8;* **t** *02 38 57 12 61*), but with atmospheric grounds inspired by the 19th-century gardener Gertrude Jekyll, full of heathers, old-fashioned roses and magnolias. The arboretum also presents a collection of trees from temperate climates around the world, arranged geographically.

Château de Chamerolles

Open July–Aug 10–6, April–June and Sept Wed–Mon 10–6, Oct–Dec Wed–Mon 10–12 and 2–5.

Midway between Orléans and Pithiviers, on the northern edge of the forest and just east of Chilleurs-aux-Bois on the N152, the Château de Chamerolles long lay forgotten and abandoned, a Sleeping Beauty of a building. It has been brought back to life in a commercial fairytale kind of way. To be honest, rather than being a Sleeping Beauty, the Château de Chamerolles had aged very badly when the *département* of the Loiret bought it from the town council of Paris for one franc, but the authorities have recently revived the place with smelling salts of a king, transforming it into a museum of perfumes and scents. The project was supported by some of the big-name perfume manufacturers, who have factories around Orléans. Every year an exhibition is devoted to a different perfumery.

The original castle on which the restoration was based was finished in 1522 under the magically named Lancelot du Lac, royal councillor and chamberlain, and one-time bailliff and governor of Orléans. Although Chamerolles is clearly something of an ersatz-château now, its effect is very pretty indeed and the restoration work has been carried out with great relish. A sturdy round tower marks each corner of the moated square. Inside the courtyard, the typical lozenge-patterned brick façades of the region dominate.

Within, local craftsmen and women made a good number of imitation period pieces, and the Orléans fine arts museum has also lent a few fine pieces to embellish the interiors. The odd original feature has survived; the chapel with its ornate entrance contains Huguenot inscriptions, apparently the oldest to be found in France. They record the Protestants' 10 commandments, and are in old French, the language, ironically, now rather Rabelaisian-sounding, comical and coarse, which isn't particularly surprising as it dates from the 16th century.

A series of rooms concentrates on *toilette* over the centuries, and in particular developments in the search for the perfect scent. The word *toilette* derives from the French word *toile*, meaning cloth – scent used to be put on a piece of linen, not on clothes or the skin; the guides admonish visitors that it is quite wrong to apply perfume directly to the skin. It came to refer to washing one's person generally, and also to one's attire and presentation. There's a representative section for each of the 16th, 17th, 18th and 19th centuries. The disappearance of the bath tub during the 17th apparently wasn't occasioned by a lack of hygiene, but because doctors began to think that bathing might be bad for the health, so people followed the fashion of the *toilette sèche*, dry washing!

Perfume bottles started to be mass-produced at the end of the 19th century, contributing their own share of glamour to scent. A sizable section of the château is devoted to the often superb design work which went into perfume bottles in the 20th century, with star contributors including the likes of Dali and Lalique. The great creators of perfumes are known rather unflatteringly as '*nez*' (noses), a name they dislike. Apparently some 80 per cent of the '*nez*' working for the big fashion names are French. In the château's attics you can amuse yourselves concocting your own perfume, or test each other on recognizing the different scents provided, a mixture of the natural and the artificial.

Chamerolles' sumptuous formal gardens were planned according to Renaissance records, the fine detail observed down to the planting and the carpentry work. Some visitors find the whole place too phoney, too Disney-like; it's certainly the slickest château you'll see along the Loire and has its own heliport awaiting its privileged seminar guests, as well as a large boutique well stocked with scents.

A few kilometres east of Chamerolles, at **Vrigny**, the more traditional little French museum of La Maison du Père Mousset (*open May–Oct weekends only 2.30–6.30*) stands in comical contrast to the Château de Chamerolles, the peasant next to the posh aristocrat. Your French needs to be good to cope with the deliberately strong provincial accent in which the guide tells of life here in the 19th century.

To the north of the Forêt d'Orléans the enormous, boring plain of the **Beauce** stretches out, Paris' great grain store.

Orléans

10

Orléans

At the crowning point of the Loire, Orléans could have been king of French cities. Under the Capetians, it was one of the French monarchs' great seats of power, vying for attention with its rival on the Seine, a little more than 100km to the north. Orléans lost out to Paris, which managed to lure the sovereign family away, while later French royalty would quite bypass the city to scamper down the Loire, its tail between its legs, with the arrival of the English armies in the second half of the Hundred Years' War. The English, however, came to lay siege to Orléans in 1428 and the town was only saved with the arrival of the maid regarded as its heroine, Joan of Arc.

Orléans has been growing apace in the last couple of decades, spreading out in all directions. It has greatly benefited recently from its proximity to Paris, picking up a lot of spill-over trade from the capital. One area outside town has been dubbed

Cosmetics Valley, as so many big-name houses (such as Dior) have set up factories here. Despite economic success, Orléans seems to lack a bit of self-confidence in its cultural riches. The centre proves very interesting, despite being badly bombed in the Second World War. Quickly constructed grey blocks were put up right at the heart of the city, around the Place du Martroi and the cathedral, but much of interest was restored.

So what can Orléans tempt you with apart from her Maid and the cathedral, the latter dominating the skyline of the centre? The Musée des Beaux-Arts is one of the finest provincial fine arts museums in France; it substantially helps fill a big chronological gap in French art history along the Loire, the Ancien Régime (that is, the 17th and 18th centuries), with its excellent collections from that period. The unpretentious Musée Archéologique et Historique de l'Orléanais in the Hôtel Cabu takes you much further back in time, its unsung highlights a fabulous array of Celtic bronze animals, the pieces of such a sophistication and beauty that they're likely to shatter many preconceptions about the culture of that period – the statue of the horse dedicated to the god Rudiobus is one of the greatest pieces of art to be seen along the Loire. Meanwhile, tributes are paid to Joan as much at the Hôtel Groslot, part of the town hall, as at the so-called Maison de Jeanne d'Arc, while the Centre Johannique keeps all manner of books and films on her. The extraordinary early Romanesque crypt of St-Aignan hides under one of Orléans' slightly outlying churches, in an eastern quarter sloping down to the Loire. Strangely though, Orléans turns its back on the river, with virtually no use made of its banks when for so long the city flourished from its quayside trade.

History

Ah! They remember me still in Orleans.
Joan of Arc in Bernard Shaw's *Saint Joan*

Remember? They're obsessed by Jeanne la Pucelle; unhealthily so, some might say. Orléans' memory is dominated by the days in 1429 when Joan of Arc so famously helped to break the English siege of the town. That week tends to be viewed rather too simplistically as a decisive moment in the Hundred Years' War, in French history and in the cementing of the French national identity. So let us widen the history of the town somewhat, as it was the setting for many other major events.

Caesar Slaughters the Carnutes

Cenabum, as Orléans was known to Caesar, was an important settlement of the Celtic Carnute tribe, lying at a strategic point on trade routes through Gaul. It had a fine bridge spanning the Loire by the time Caesar came to wreak his revenge on the place. The Celtic tribes had gathered in 52BC and decided to rise up against the recent Roman conquest of their territories. A group of Carnutes were the unfortunate foolish first to rebel. They slaughtered a number of Roman merchants who had established themselves in the city, running off with their property. Caesar came speedily to teach the Carnutes a lesson, arriving towards nightfall one day. Lacking time to attack immediately, he made camp outside the town, but reckoned that the inhabitants might try to escape in the night. This they did, falling into his trap – he had kept two legions under arms close to the bridge. He dispassionately recounts in the third person the success of his stratagem:

Shortly before midnight the people of Cenabum moved silently out of the town and began to cross the river. Apprised of this by the patrols, Caesar set the gates on fire and sent inside the legions he had kept ready for action. The town was captured and all but a very few of the enemy taken prisoner – for the narrow street and bridge were blocked by the crowd of fugitives. After plundering and burning Cenabum, and distributing among his soldiers the booty it contained and the prisoners, Caesar marched across the Loire...

Getting There and Around

By Train

Note that Orléans has two train stations, the central Orléans Gare SNCF, and Les Aubrais to the north of the centre. If you arrive at Orléans-les-Aubrais, either take a taxi, the *navette* (shuttle service) for the centre, or the new Orléans tramway. From Paris, trains for Orléans leave from Gare d'Austerlitz.

Orléans has good connections with Blois and Tours.

By Bus and Tram

Orléans has local bus and tram networks (freephone **t** 0800 012 000).

The main Gare Routière is near the central railway station.

By Car and Bicycle

Orléans is well served by motorways. From Paris, take the A10, which goes almost to the centre of town. The main non-paying road from Paris to Orléans is the N20, passing via Etampes. Historic Orléans lies on the north bank of the Loire; the town south of the river is complicated by a confusion of major roads.

Car Hire

Avis, 13 Rue des Sansonnières, **t** 02 38 62 27 04, **f** 02 38 68 01 30

Europcar, 81 Rue André Dessaux (Nord), Fleury-les-Aubrais, **t** 02 38 73 00 40, **f** 02 38 73 46 90; and 869 Rue de Bourges, Olivet, **t** 02 38 63 88 00, **f** 02 38 63 65 80

Bicycle Hire

Kit Loisirs, 1720 Rue Marcel Belot, 45160, Olivet, **t** 02 38 63 44 34

By Taxi

Taxis d'Orléans, **t** 02 38 53 11 11, runs a 24-hour service.

Tourist Information

Tourist offices: Office de Tourisme, Place Albert Ier, 45000 Orléans, **t** 02 38 24 05 05, **f** 02 38 54 49 84, *office-de-tourisme.orleans@wanadoo.fr*, *www.ville-orleans.fr*. A more central tourist office is Espace d'Accueil Touristique, 6 Rue Jeanne d'Arc, **t** 02 38 53 33 44, which can organize accommodation.

Market Days

Les Halles-Châtelet: The town's covered market, with over 30 food stalls, is open daily (morning only on Sunday).

Place du Vieux Marché and the **Rue du Cheval Rouge**: A *marché forain*, where you'll find a whole mishmash of things on sale; Saturday.

New glass Halles: A new covered building by the Loire with a big market on Tuesday.

Boulevard Alexandre Martin: Antiques market; Saturday.

Place de la République: Flower market; Tuesday, Thursday, Saturday and Sunday mornings.

Festivals

The **Fêtes Johanniques** are the week-long festivities Orléans lays on in the first week of May to celebrate Joan of Arc's part in the liberation of Orléans. These Fêtes are an enormous, cheerful, all-embracing family affair – as the Orléanais themselves say: 'Half the population comes out to watch the other half parade'! Every year a new local Joan is picked to attend ceremonies around town. Her equestrian skills are put to the test, but *mauvaises langues* (gossips) question whether the selectors test her virginity nowadays. The main Parade of Nations is the most colourful event of the week, focusing around the Place du Martroi. The illumination of the cathedral, flypasts, tanks trundling through town and a large medieval fair on the Campo Santo count among other highlights.

The Orléans **jazz festival**, end of June/start of July, has drawn big names such as Gillespie and Hancock to the Campo Santo in the past.

In November, **Les Journées Cinématographiques** film festival is devoted every second year to Japanese film; the other years are dedicated to the film of a particular country.

Shopping

Mementos of Joan of Arc abound in the souvenir shops but are probably best avoided, except as a humorous present 'in the best possible taste'.

Among the culinary specialities of the Loiret to buy in Orléans, there's **pear liqueur** – believe it or not, the pears from the Loire Valley orchards actually grow up in bottles placed on the tree!

Cotignac, a quince jelly sweet, is made at nearby St-Ay. Other Loire Valley fruits go into making the new Orléans macaroons sold in some of the city's *pâtisseries*.

Orléans was once famous for its vinegar industry. This has almost died out now, but **Martin Pouret** still produces vinegar the old-fashioned way.

You might also try out the local Orléanais **wines**, although they're no great shakes. **Goat's cheese from Olivet** may be to more people's taste.

Orléans being a big producer of perfumes, you'll find many *parfumeries* around town, for instance along Rue de la République and in the Place d'Arc shopping centre.

Sports and Activities

Although wandering by the Loire isn't very easy in Orléans, swimming, watersports and fishing are possible at the **Ile Charlemagne**, 3km southeast of Orléans (direction of St-Jean le Blanc).

At Olivet, the *bateau mouche Le Sologne* takes you along the Loiret – **t** 02 38 51 12 12 for times; the trip lasts 1½ hours.

You can also take a **cruiser** along the Canal d'Orléans, running April–Oct; call **t** 02 38 46 82 91 for times. It leaves from Mardié, a few kilometres east out of the centre of town by the north bank road towards Jargeau. With a stop at Combleux, the trip lasts 2 hours. You can eat on both boats.

Where to Stay

Orléans ☑ 45000
Central Orléans caters better for businessmen than for tourists in hotel terms, with a mass of chain hotels. The suburb of Olivet (*see* below), just south of town, has some delightful options beside the Loiret river.

Moderate
***Hôtel d'Arc**, 37 Rue de la République, **t** 02 38 53 10 94, **f** 02 38 81 77 47. In an elaborate Belle Epoque building well situated on the grand shopping street mainly dedicated to pedestrians and the tram, and linking the railway station with the main square. Modern comforts have been neatly fitted into the rooms, a few of which are very spacious.
***Les Cèdres**, 17 Rue du Maréchal Foch, **t** 02 38 62 22 92, **f** 02 38 81 76 46. 'The Cedars' lies just outside the broad, busy avenues encircling the heart of town, off Bd Rocheplatte. It's still close to the centre, but peaceful, with a little garden, the rooms spacious and decorated with personal touches.

Inexpensive
Jackotel, 18 Cloître St-Aignan, **t** 02 38 54 48 48, **f** 02 38 77 17 59. Modern, but tucked into a courtyard by the lovely tree-shaded square beside the church of St-Aignan, this place has plenty going for it, including well-kept, well-decorated rooms.
L'Abeille, 64 Rue d'Alsace Lorraine, **t** 02 38 53 54 87, **f** 02 38 62 65 84. Not only in the heart of town, right on the corner of Rue de la République; it offers nice large rooms at a reasonable price.

Olivet ☑ 45160
To reach the hotels on the north bank of the Loiret, at Olivet, head down the busy, uninspiring N20 from the centre of Orléans.
***Quatre Saisons**, 351 Rue de la Reine Blanche, **t** 02 38 66 14 30, **f** 02 38 66 78 59 (*inexpensive*). Looks more like a classic beach house than a town house, with bright clapboard, a treehouse over the river and a smart restaurant (*menus €13–48*). *Closed Sun pm and Mon, one week Nov and two weeks Feb.*
***Le Rivage**, 635 Rue de la Reine Blanche, **t** 02 38 66 02 93, **f** 02 38 56 31 11 (*moderate*). The rather dull roadside entrance to this hotel gives you no idea of the stylish-to-chic interiors that await you. The rooms are pretty swanky. On warm, sunny days you can eat seafood and game specialities on the splendid shaded terrace by the

Loiret; otherwise there's the extravaganza of the modern dining room, with big flower arrangements on pedestals watching over you (*menus €23.5–50*).

Eating Out

Moderate

Le Florian, 70 Bd Alexandre Martin, **t** 02 38 53 08 15. A wide selection of Loire wines to choose from here to accompany the fresh arrivals of fish or Sologne game. Benefits from a bright, cheerful dining room giving onto a garden (*menus €20–29*). *Closed Sun and Aug*.

La Chancellerie, 95 Rue Royale, **t** 02 38 53 57 54. Has the good fortune of being located in the noble 18th-century building on the corner of Orléans' main square and Rue Royale that survived the bombing. The food is in uncomplicated brasserie style, with such Loiret specialities as Jargeau *andouillette* (*menus €26.5*). *Closed Sun, and Feb school hols*.

La Promenade, Place du Martroi/Rue Adolphe Crespin, **t** 02 38 81 12 12. Has another of the best seats looking onto Orléans' main square and serves excellent French dishes (*menus €14.5–23*). *Closed Sun and Mon*. For a simpler option, see the sister establishment below, Le Martroi.

La Petite Marmite, 178 Rue de Bourgogne, **t** 02 38 54 23 83. Timber-framed and geranium-fronted, serving traditional local dishes in an atmospheric setting (*menus €18–29*). *Closed lunch times exc weekends and public hols*.

La Dariole, 25 Rue Etienne Dolet, **t** 02 38 77 26 67. With its cross-timbered front on this very quiet street parallel to busy Rue de Bourgogne, this is a sweet restaurant with a small but appealing menu, offering nice touches, such as saffron in the *poule au pot* (*menus €16.5–23*).

Cheap

Le Martroi, Place du Martroi/Rue Adolphe Crespin, **t** 02 38 42 15 00. Fashionable rendezvous, a colourful brasserie on one corner of the Place du Martroi, just below its posher sister, La Promenade, and with stylish cuboid chairs in which to sit outside on warmer days (*menu €13.5*). *Closed Sun*.

Les Chineurs, 253 Rue de Bourgogne, **t** 02 38 54 00 79. Very simple options of traditional French dishes made using fresh produce. The setting is appealing, with pottery on display in the entrance cabinets. *Closed Sun, and 1–15 Nov and Feb*.

Le Brin de Zinc, 62 Rue Ste-Catherine, **t** 02 38 53 38 77. An amusing little restaurant filled with all sorts of bric-a-brac, run with verve. Offers a vegetarian menu and organic choices. The place also has half a dozen simple rooms (*inexpensive*).

For **cheap** ethnic options just have a wander along Rue de Bourgogne.

Entertainment and Nightlife

Cinema

You can pick from a reasonably wide choice of films at the following cinemas:

UGC, Centre Commercial, Place d'Arc, **t** 08 36 68 68 58

Les Carmes, 7 Rue des Carmes, **t** 02 38 62 02 96

Le Sélect, Rue Jeanne d'Arc, **t** 08 36 68 69 25

L'Artistic, Bd A Martin, **t** 08 36 68 69 25

Theatre

For details on what's on at the grand main **theatre** of Orléans, call **t** 02 38 62 75 30 (*pm only*). Performances are likely to be in French only.

Bars

There are plenty of bars in and around Place du Martroi.

Le Jardin aux Dix Mille Thés. Try this discreet tea house opposite the cathedral façade for a more literary and trendy option than your normal French bar.

Le Petit Dol, 42 Rue Etienne Dolet, **t** 02 38 53 86 99 (*open to 3am*). Occasionally puts on concerts.

BBC, 15 Rue de la Bretonnerie, **t** 02 38 53 38 14 (*open to 3 am*). A central bar offering billiards and cocktails, as well as the bar (hence the name) and Internet access.

The plan of the Gallo-Roman town that grew up afterwards is still evident. The Rue de Bourgogne and Rue Parisie/Rue de la Poterne correspond to the main thoroughfares of that time. By the end of the second century the confines of the town were fixed pretty much as they would remain for a millennium. At the end of the third century the town became capital of the administrative region of the Civitatis Aurelianorum and was renamed Aurelianis, from which its modern name stems. A century later, a strong defensive wall was erected around it, a few vestiges of which can still be seen in front of the north transept of the cathedral.

The Hand of God Beats Attila the Hun

The first mention of a Christian bishop of Orléans, Diclopetus, dates from around the same time as Aurelianis. Two later bishops stand out at the end of the period of the Roman Empire. St Euverte is thought to have founded the first cathedral; legend has it that he was about to bless the building when the hand of God came down from between the clouds to do the job for him.

Orléans had another bishop as its great hero for almost a thousand years before Joan outshone him. For the 5th-century Hunnish invaders of Gaul, Orléans, more than Paris, was the centre of their attention. St Aignan is the man celebrated for having Attila removed from the city's doorstep in 451. The story goes that the terrible warlord stormed the town, his troops gathering booty, but Aignan had sounded the alarm, calling on military help from the Roman Aetius, who managed to drive the Huns out.

Orléans and Early French Royals

In 498 the Merovingian Frank Clovis took the city. The Council he assembled there in 511 importantly established the strong relationship between French royalty and the Church. On Clovis's death, Orléans became for a time capital of one of the four smaller kingdoms into which Gaul was divided. During the Carolingian period, Orléans flourished at the centre of a number of leading religious centres, with the cluster of nearby abbeys including St-Aignan and St-Benoît, or Fleury. One bishop of Orléans, Théodulfe (see Germigny-des-Prés, p.122), was one of the Emperor Charlemagne's closest councillors. Orléans' importance is further attested by the fact that Charles le Chauve (the Bald) was crowned king of the western Franks here in 848. The Viking raids along the Loire badly affected the city later in the century, but Orléans remained at the centre of French politics.

For the Capetians, Orléans was a place of enormous significance. Hugues Capet, from a line of counts of Orléans, founded the Capetian dynasty of French kings. In a vital act for the future of the French monarchy, he made Capetian kingship hereditary and indivisible with the crowning of his son Robert II le Pieux in Orléans cathedral in 987. The church of St-Aignan was consecrated in 1029. The Châtelet, the royal castle, watched over the bridge and river traffic. Robert stamped his royal and religious authority on the city on the infamous Jour des Saints Innocents in 1022, when he had a number of clerical intellectuals of the city branded heretics and burnt to death. Orléans couldn't precisely be described as the French capital at this period, but the royal retinue alternated between Paris and Orléans until Louis VI opted for the Seine rather than the Loire, even if he too was anointed in Orléans' cathedral.

Relations between Orléans and royalty became strained under Louis VII, a rebellion in 1137 leading the king to grant Orléans' merchants certain privileges. For those who may be under the false impression that classical learning was completely stifled for much of the Middle Ages, during the 12th century Arnoul d'Orléans had copious commentaries on classical authors published. An intellectual centre, the city became particularly renowned for its civil law school. This was somewhat helped by the fact that Pope Honorius III banned the teaching of the subject in Paris in 1219. Greek was also outlawed in the capital, but taught in Orléans. The majority of the 13th-century kings' lawyers were trained here. One student became Pope Clement V, elected to the papal throne thanks to King Philippe le Bel's bribes and the pope who deserted the urban dangers of Rome to become the first incumbent at Avignon in Provence. Clement V showed his gratitude to Orléans for his student days by granting the city the privilege of a university in 1306.

Joan of Arc's Finest Hour

The English brought terror to the region in the Hundred Years' War. Robert Knowles and his troops caused havoc from as early as 1358, and St-Aignan was destroyed. The town's most infamous troubles came in 1428, with the siege by Salisbury, who was killed in action and replaced by Glasdale. The English razed to the ground the churches and houses outside the city walls and erected a circle of English camps around Orléans. On 29 April 1429, Joan of Arc broke through the English defences to enter the city and give new hope to the hard-pressed population. She stayed a few days to spur on the citizens and then found another breach in enemy lines to go back out to the French army and play her part in the great attack.

The first English post was taken on 5 May. On 6 May a second was won, the Augustinian Convent. This stood in front of the main English position, the Fort des Tourelles guarding the southern end of Orléans' bridge. The fight for the fort raged all of 7 May. Joan, hit by an arrow, continued to rally the troops. She encouraged her soldiers to take to boats to help the attack from the Loire itself and, most importantly, she persuaded the troops with her to fight on rather than abandon for the day, as the French leader Dunois had proposed. Thanks to the Auld Alliance between France and Scotland, a Scottish contingent under Hugh Kennedy played an important part in the storming of the Fort des Tourelles. Late on 7 May, the French and their allies were victorious, and on 8 May the English gave up the siege of Orléans. This was to be Joan's supreme victory; it would still take a few decades for the French forces to oust the English from most of France.

Town Defences, the Wars of Religion and Explosive Protestants

In the second half of the 15th century Orléans was substantially fortified, for King Louis XI and then for Duke Louis d'Orléans, son of the famous chivalric figure Charles d'Orléans. (Despite their aristocratic family title, Blois, not Orléans, was the seat of the d'Orléans' court.) The beginning of the 16th century was a time of optimism for

Orléans, with many fine new town houses being built. This prosperity would be shattered by the Wars of Religion.

In 1560 an Estates General was assembled at Orléans in a last desperate effort to avoid war between the rival religious factions, but it failed. To add to the woes, the sickly young King François II died in the Hôtel Groslot, not in a melodramatic poisoning as fiction would have it, but from an ear infection. He left as his widow the ill-fated Mary Stuart, Queen of Scots, who was actually brought up along the Loire, at the royal château of Amboise (see pp.240–50).

Orléans became infamous in much of France for serving as a shortlived headquarters of the French Protestants during these wars. A Protestant theology college was created at the university where Calvin had previously taken his law degree, and one of the great Protestant leaders, Condé, took control of the town for a time from 1562. The powerful Catholic Duc de Guise besieged him, but was killed in front of the city. Catherine de' Medici stepped in, imposing peace, the promise of the Edict of Amboise offering the prospect of certain privileges for the Protestants. But Condé seized Orléans again in 1567 after the frictions had worsened and this time Protestants attacked the churches. Most significantly of all, they blew up the cathedral.

The backlash was inevitable. King Charles IX had taken over authority for the town, and the terrible St Bartholomew's Day Massacres of 1572 were particularly bloody in Orléans, the Protestants savagely butchered and effectively silenced. For a while Orléans stood on the ultra-Catholic side of the Ligue. The Protestant King Henri IV would have to besiege the town in 1594 and win it back. In an important gesture of religious reconciliation, Henri IV decided to have the cathedral rebuilt, and in the old Gothic style.

The Grande Mademoiselle, a granddaughter of Henri IV and obstreperous niece of Louis XIII, participated in the aristocratic Fronde uprising, which defied royal authority in the mid-17th century. Such was her power that she gathered an army which briefly occupied Orléans, taking a leaf out of Joan's book, with the aid of boats.

From Ancien Régime Success to 19th-century Decline

The new religious orders of the Counter-Reformation were established in the town in the 17th century, while Fougeu d'Escures saw to the construction of a new quarter of very grand houses which can be admired in the street named after him. Orléans experienced a time of prosperity from the mid-17th to the mid-18th centuries. The royal governor, or *intendant*, of the Orléanais became the administrator of an extensive region, which at one time stretched from Orléans to the Atlantic. In addition to well-established industries such as tanning and textiles, new ones in Orléans thrived on trade from the French possessions in the New World, especially the refining of Caribbean sugar cane. The loss of the French Caribbean and Canadian territories would bring decline, but in the meantime splendid new architectural developments such as the grand Place du Martroi and the arcaded Rue Royale went up.

Orléans had a tradition of producing prints, and many Revolutionary ones were disseminated from here. But the Revolution had a less destructive impact on the city than one architect Benoît Lebrun, so it's said. In 1793 the city was briefly outlawed because of pro-royalist intriguing. At the end of Bonaparte's Empire in 1815, the Prussian troops advanced for the first time as far as Orléans. They would come back in the Franco-Prussian War at the start of the 1870s. Meanwhile, Orléans' economy was sliding downhill. Having counted among the six richest cities in France, its sugar, textile and Loire river trade collapsed (the last due to the appearance of the railway). The Prussian troops who took over the town in October 1870 stayed until March 1871, although the Armée de la Loire gathered by General Chanzy did manage to regain it for a brief month. One of the defiant, unifying figures in Orléans during these stressful times was the bishop Monseigneur Dupanloup, a liberal religious and political figure.

Louis Pasteur, a frequent visitor to the area, became a bit of a local hero in Orléans' business circles when he found a more efficient way of making vinegar for the town's vinegar-makers. This had grown into an important industry, a rather bitter replacement for the sweet riches of Orléans' colonial days. Before the end of the century the old castle, one of the symbols of Orléans' royal past, was destroyed.

20th-century Destruction, Reconstruction and Regionalism

After economic decline came Orléans' decimation by bombs in the Second World War. Nazi attacks in June 1940 destroyed much of the historic centre. Further devastation of the area around the station was caused by American bombing in May 1943. One of the town's prominent prewar figures, Jean Zay, an important reforming Minister of Education, was imprisoned by the Vichy government and shot by its militia in 1944. The town was freed on 16 August 1944. Its liberating hero this time was General Patton. The work of reconstruction is plainly visible in many parts of the centre of Orléans, following the plans laid down by the architect Jean Royer.

When the French regions were restructured at the start of the 1960s, the creation of the unimaginatively named administrative Région Centre was one of the more bizarre bureaucratic inventions. With its birth, Orléans became the administrative capital for six *départements*, despite rivalry from Tours and despite Orléans' proximity to Paris, in whose shadow some say it lives. A new university was created for the town in 1962, to the south of the old centre, close to the Loiret, a pretty river more frequented by Orléans' inhabitants than the sadly ignored Loire, and which has also given its name to the *département* of which Orléans is the capital.

Cathédrale Ste-Croix

Open July–Aug 9.15–12 and 2.15–7; May, June and Sept 9.15–12 and 2.15–6; rest of year 9.15–12 and 2.15–5.

From a distance, central Orléans is dominated by its cathedral and the tiers of its towers. In the centre, Rue Jeanne d'Arc was specially designed in the 19th century to create a spectacular vista up to the building's great Gothic-style façade, neatly compartmentalized by simple horizontal and vertical lines. Despite the monumental scale of the work, there is something delicate about it, particularly in the tracery of the windows and arches, and in the towers. Some have accused this cathedral of being over-pretty, while Marcel Proust seemingly took a violent dislike to it, disparagingly comparing the tops of the towers not to his beloved *madeleines*, but to vulgar strawberry gâteaux instead; such a reaction may strike you as just a trifle oversensitive!

In fact, the tops of the towers resemble crowns, and crownings there were aplenty in the Cathédrale Ste-Croix under the Capetians. But the first basilica here was built way back in the Dark Ages, in the 4th century; it was for this building that the hand of God supposedly appeared to spare St Euverte the trouble of consecrating the place himself. A hand blessing the church is painted on the main boss of the apse. From the 7th century the cathedral was dedicated to the Ste-Croix, or Holy Cross. The structure grew in size as Orléans grew in importance, and Charles le Chauve (the Bald), Eudes, Robert le Pieux and King Louis VI le Gros (the Fat) were all crowned here.

Bishop Robert de Courtenay decided to commission a totally new building along the lines of Amiens cathedral late in the 13th century. This turned into a long-drawn-out affair. Work began in 1287, with the choir completed by 1329. The Hundred Years' War caused an extended pause in the building work. Thanks to the very strong links between France and Scotland through that conflict, a Scotsman, John Carmichael of Douglasdale, became a bishop of Orléans, while the great Scottish warrior John Stewart Darnley was buried in the cathedral after he was killed at the Battle of Rouvray-St-Denis, north of Orléans, in February 1429.

The transept and nave were only added at the end of the 15th century and beginning of the 16th. They didn't last long – Protestants in 1568 almost entirely ruined the previous construction which had taken so many centuries to build. Only the radiating chapels around the choir and a couple of nave bays remained standing after one of the most monumental acts of destruction of the French Wars of Religion.

The first stone of the new, present building was laid by Henri IV in 1601. This cathedral took still longer to complete than the earlier cathedral, from 1601 to 1829 (excluding the steeple), the last date handily coinciding with the fourth centenary of Joan of Arc's liberation of Orléans. The choir and transepts are 17th-century, most of the rest of the cathedral 18th. The encroachment of certain Italianate elements shows that there was some tussle between the Gothic style and the neoclassical in the rebuilding. The most comical intrusion sticks out from the transepts: Louis XIV's face, and most notably his proboscis, form the centrepiece for the rose windows, his motto 'Nec pluribus impar' (crudely translated, 'Without equal') also displayed. The cathedral steeple was only added in 1858.

In the nave, the colourful-to-gaudy 19th-century windows in the side aisles commemorate the life of Joan of Arc, a well-known triumphalist feature, the work of Galland and Gibelin. The choir stalls have superb sculpted wood panels drawn by Jacques V Gabriel and carved by Degoullons. Interesting sculptures and paintings include the tomb of Monseigneur Dupanloup, and a *Pietà* by Michel Bourdin.

The tourist office organizes regular tours of the roofs and towers of the cathedral, from which you get good views of the architecture, in particular the great timbers which support the roof. You can also admire the few monumental statues on the towers and the towers themselves – one of the bells they contain is named after Joan, inevitably. And of course you can enjoy fine views over the city from such an elevated position.

Musée des Beaux-Arts

Open Tues 11–6; Wed 10–8; Thurs, Fri and Sat 10–6; Sun 11–6.

The sober modern exterior of the imposing building next to the cathedral which hold Orléans' fine arts museum is misleading. Inside, you'll be treated to an extravagant display of the arts. In the centre of one of the largest rooms, a sculpture by Germain Pilon shows Monseigneur de Morvilliers, one-time bishop of Orléans, in sober sad reflection. It's as though he's dejected by all the outrageous opulence that surrounds him. For the rest of the vast space is decorated with works from the Cardinal de Richelieu's sumptuous collection, once held in his vast château on the Touraine-Poitou border (*see* pp.342–3). On great panels by Martin Freminet, the Evangelists and Fathers of the Church look vain as body-builders, draped in gaudy-coloured garments in the self-conscious poses of disco dancers. Below them, ornate fantasies by Claude Deruet depict the elements, aristocrats at play in the scenes: horse-drawn sleighs rush across an icy river in the snowy countryside depicting Water; a city alight with flames illustrates Fire, and so on. Such works make complaints about the vanity of today's youth culture seem pretty petty by comparison. These paintings reveal the vanity of the leaders of France's Counter-Reformation.

The collections gathered together here from the churches and monasteries of the Orléans region during the Revolution scarcely give you a different impression. The works from the Monastère Notre-Dame de Bonne Nouvelle, the Couvent des Capucins and the Chapelle du Collège des Jésuites, among others, share the general characteristic of being outrageously extravagant. Typical works include Claude Vignon's *Le Triomphe de Saint Ignace* and Jean Senelle's *Saint François donnant le cordon du Tiers-ordre à Louis XIII*. A host of famous artistic names of the period are represented. All told, to severer Catholics and good puritan Protestants, the 17th- and 18th-century treasures of this museum might be regarded as a fair exhibition of the degenerate nature of French Ancien Régime art.

As with the cathedral, so here Louis XIV puts in an appearance or two. Another Deruet painting in the museum portrays the future Sun King as a child; so much lace can't have been good for the boy, you can't help thinking, while his girlish locks are decorated with what look like a panoply of AIDS ribbons. A later portrait of the megalomaniac by Rigaud and his studio shows the king decadently aged, mouth puckered, baggy-eyed, weighed down by furs. With rather worrying undertones for European unity, in another room a picture by Jean-Baptiste Martin (alias 'Martin des Batailles') shows the 1673 siege of a Dutch town by Louis XIV's troops, the smoke of war rising in puffs around Maastricht.

Other classic French works include the *St Sébastien soigné par Irène* from the Georges de la Tour studio, in the immediately recognizable candle-lit atmosphere of that painter. Irène's eyes appear to be disconcertingly distracted from the arrow wound to the lightly covered groin of the beautiful young man she's tending. The more understandably raunchy Le Nain brothers' *Bacchus découvrant Ariane à Naxos* uses almost cloisonné colour painting. From an artist born in Pithiviers in the Orléanais, look out for Lubin Baugin's *La Déposition de Croix*, Christ's body painted in extraordinary white soft focus. Among some fine sculptures, a series of trials in terracotta by Jean-Antoine Houdon represents famous men of letters of the 17th and 18th centuries.

The 19th-century collections include some typical Orientalist paintings and some notable Romantic ones. As for more experimental 19th-century artists, Gauguin went no further than Brittany, then considered foreign and exotic, for his *Fête Gloanec*. Alfred Johannot, meanwhile, tried a rendering of the Grande Mademoiselle's entrance into Orléans. Alexandre Antigna's depiction of women in *Les Baigneuses* caused a scandal in his day. Of course the museum wouldn't be complete without its collection of works on Joan of Arc, and many a 19th-century French artist went quite potty about her.

The more provocative early 20th-century Orléans sculptors Henri Gaudier-Brezska and Charles Malfray are also devoted space. Gaudier-Brezska was viewed as a precursor of much modern sculpture, a member of the Vorticist movement and friend of Ezra Pound. Another collection concentrates on Max Jacob (*see* St-Benoît-sur-Loire, p.121, for his connection with the area).

There are five floors of exhibits to visit in this purpose-built museum. The lighting is exemplary and useful texts on the works are provided in many rooms. While we've focused on some of the best French paintings above, the place also contains a fair collection of works by foreign schools and artists, Flemish, Dutch and Italian, most famous among them the *Saint Thomas* by Velasquez.

Hôtel Groslot

Open daily 9–6 except during weddings and official receptions.

The Hôtel Groslot lies almost opposite the Musée des Beaux Arts. Its elegant patterned brick façades serve as the backdrop for many an Orléans wedding photo, the civil ceremonies taking place within. The *hôtel* was originally built for a *bailli* called Groslot, a high-ranking official under King François I. The renowned French Renaissance architect Du Cerceau probably played a part in its design. It was decorated with typically indecorous Mannerist-style statues, including a naked-breasted woman. After 1790 it served as Orléans' town hall. The extremities of the two wings were a mid-19th century addition, but harmoniously designed by the architect Albert Delton.

A double stairway sweeps up to the main entrance, in front of which stands a sculpture of Joan of Arc, clad in copper, conceived by Princess Marie d'Orléans, daughter of the mid-19th-century King Louis-Philippe. The other sculptures in the niches are by Jouffroy, depicting famous figures in Orléans' history. The interior is in 19th-century neo-Renaissance style, sumptuously exaggerated. Joan dominates inside; clearly an inspiration if not an obsession for Marie d'Orléans;

another sculpture by the princess shows the Maid on horseback, directing her steed to avoid a wounded soldier. There's no historical evidence, however, that Joan was particularly gentle in war, although she said at her trial that she had never killed a man. A painting of Joan in the style of Ingres is also displayed. Yet another work depicts her wearing a gown, 19th-century decorum trying to dress her up as a woman. This is historically perverse once more; one of the main reasons for Joan's condemnation was her supposed 'unnaturalness' in refusing to revert to wearing women's clothing. And there's an Aubusson tapestry interpretation of the warrior woman.

The room for wedding ceremonies is slightly disconcertingly the one in which King François II, short-lived husband of Mary Stuart, died. A painting hanging in the room morbidly recalls the event. It can scarcely be uplifting to be reminded of such a tragic, brief marriage, you'd have thought.

Hôtel Cabu and Musée Archéologique et Historique de l'Orléanais

Open July–Aug Tues–Sun 10–6; May, June and Sept Tues–Sun 2–6;
rest of year Wed and weekends 2–6.

The Hôtel Cabu may also have been planned by Du Cerceau. Mainly built of brick, some decorative Renaissance details are picked out on its façades. Second World War bombing badly damaged the building, which was restored under the watchful eye of Paul Gélis. The interior houses the city's small archaeological and historical museum, which holds a fabulous surprise.

The horse dedicated to the Celtic god Rudiobus, sometimes compared with the Roman god of war Mars, poses majestically as the centrepiece in a wonderful little collection on the ground floor, part of a cache unearthed east along the Loire at Neuvy-en-Sullias. The proud beast is thought to date from the 2nd century. Its dressage dignity, its flaming mane, its muscular tautness convey great power and poise. The wild boar, beautifully ugly brutes from the same find, were a great symbol for the Gauls, their ardent fighting spirit most admired by the Celtic warriors. The animal was also associated for the Celts with the world of the dead. The splendid deer was made in molten bronze, the breast patterned with detail, its antlers removable. Deer antlers, which in the natural cycle fall in winter and grow again in spring, symbolized the cycle of death and rebirth, and the Celtic god Cernunos was traditionally represented crowned with them.

The Gauls' great spring carnival apparently began with a deer hunt and the ritual death of a deer. After the chase the hunters would don the skins of the dead animals and dance in them, before stripping to dance naked. These so-called 'Gaulish bacchanalia' were supposed to reflect the rebirth of nature. Human figures, too, are portrayed in the ground-floor room, a naked man running and women dancing, arms raised and full of movement. They appear much more primitive representations than those of the animals, but still make very powerful images. The site of Neuvy has thus far offered no clues as to the provenance of this cache. It may be that the pieces were hidden there at a time of barbarian invasions.

The other collection of objects found at Neuvy are from the classical tradition. Among them stands a typical Gallo-Roman goddess mother figure, suckling a child on either breast.

On the first floor, carved fragments from vanished or damaged churches around the Loiret constitute the main feature, including bits of floral-patterned stuccowork from the Carolingian oratory at Germigny and five capitals originally from the abbey of St-Benoît, one featuring mermaids holding on to a fish. Joan of Arc is represented in yet more travesties of historical fact. Among old depictions of Orléans, one from the 17th century clearly shows the strong city walls that were built after the Hundred Years' War. Other rooms display local ephemera, including delicate Loire mariners' brooches and local pottery.

Maison de Jeanne d'Arc and Centre Jeanne d'Arc

The **Maison de Jeanne d'Arc** (*open 2 May–Oct Tues–Sun 10–12 and 2–6, Nov–April 2–6*) is a museum which retells Joan of Arc's short, dashing visit to Orléans and her role in its liberation (*see* 'History', above). It occupies a substantial brick-and-timber-frame house on Place du Général de Gaulle. The building had to be totally re-created after the war. Despite the name it's been given, the place actually belonged to Jacques Boucher, the duke of Orléans' treasurer, and Joan only stayed a handful of days in the house before the great attack.

You can follow the events in Joan's campaign in front of a large model of the town, the excited commentary provided in French or English. The video on the floor above, presenting the more general history of the times, is only in French, although further little models recreate scenes in the important towns through which Joan passed during her short military career. Otherwise, the museum contains a curious collection of memorabilia on Joan, such as commemorative plates. You may leave with the feeling that so many models and little mementoes don't do justice to one of the most extraordinary women in European history (*see* the box).

You can study Joan more seriously in Orléans at the **Centre Jeanne d'Arc** (*open Mon–Thurs 9–12 and 2–6, Fri 9–12 and 2–4.30; t 02 38 79 24 92*), near the cathedral at 24 Rue Jeanne d'Arc. This research centre, open to all, has its home in a very grandly fronted school, and its rooms resemble a school library. All visitors are free to consult the very large number of volumes and papers written on Joan, classified by theme. If you telephone in advance, you might even consider spending a rainy afternoon in Orléans watching one or two of the many films about Joan which the centre keeps.

A Walk Around Orléans

The obvious place to start a walking tour of Orléans is at Joan of Arc's feet, paying homage to her statue at the centre of the **Place du Martroi**, heart of the modern Orléans, but once a market place on its edge. The bronze piece representing a standard-bearing Joan in formidable armour on her war horse was executed by

Jeanne la Pucelle

O astonishing virgin!...Thou art the honour of the reign, thou art the light of the lily, thou art the splendour, the glory, not only of Gaul but of all Christians.

Alain Chartier, 15th-century writer

After Mary, mother of Jesus, Joan of Arc is no doubt the most famous virgin in Christian history. Joan too received messengers from God, she said. Her voices were rather more modest than Mary's, and simply told her that she was to save the dignity of the French king and remove the English, who had taken over so much of the French royal territories in the Hundred Years' War. After persuading the Crown and French representatives of the Catholic Church to listen to her own persistent voice (they were all pretty desperate at the time, it must be remembered – *see* Chinon, pp.349–50), Joan was given the royal and religious seals of approval and the troops to allow her to play her part in booting the English off the continent. Her whirlwind campaign lasted from May 1429 to May 1430.

Joan was only a teenager, but she can hardly be claimed to have been an innocent one. She had a plan, she had pigheaded ideas on how to execute it, and she had an unquestioning, strongheaded belief in her own calling. She was, it appears, a born leader, a captivatingly strong character for the war-weakened French, unhesitating and persuasive at a time when the French monarchy was in desperate straits, and in need of positive thinkers, if not miracles. Uneducated and unabashed, Joan spoke her mind and managed to get her way to an almost incredible extent. Not that she always had it as she wanted it, mind you. Dunois led the French troops to Orléans, choosing a route which cantankerous Joan complained went against the advice of her voices.

Her part in the relief of Orléans, though, was her greatest moment. With this *tour de force* her credibility as a military leader was established, and she went on to play a crucial role in French victories across the Orléanais, bringing triumph at Jargeau, Meung, Beaugency and Patay. The English positions on the Loire were captured within weeks of Orléans' liberation. The details of Joan's precise military contribution are unclear. She claimed never to have killed a man, but as Marina Warner in her excellent book on Joan makes clear: 'whether or not Joan played a key part in the military manoeuvres fades into insignificance beside the historical truth that her contemporaries, on both sides, thought that she had.' Hers was in good part a victory in psychological warfare.

Joan became a legend in her own lifetime and has remained one for centuries. For the French side, she was a miracle worker. For the English she was inspired by the devil. But Joan's downfall was swift and no one in the French camp came to her rescue when she was captured by Burgundian troops, allies of the English, at Compiègne northeast of Paris on 23 May 1430. The Burgundians handed their

Foyatier and dates from 1855. The Maid actually appears to point her sword rather tentatively down at the ground, as though unsure about the idea of violence. The bas-reliefs below the statue depict scenes from Joan's life.

precious prisoner to the English authorities in France, but people don't always realize that it was University of Paris theologians who put forward the request for her trial as a heretic. This complex event, of which the records remain, began in January 1431 in Rouen in Normandy; at the end of May she was found guilty of heresy and condemned to death. She briefly recanted, only to show her stubbornness one final, fatal time. She was burnt at the stake on 30 May 1431. The French Crown she had helped save hadn't lifted a finger to try and save her. It took some time until her rehabilitation trial was held by the French, in 1456, once the English had been driven out of most of France. This retrial, which took place in Orléans, cleared Joan's name, but was also exploited in good part to reassert the French king's legitimate position.

Joan was a deeply controversial figure from the beginning. Her claims of contact with the divine made her extremely suspicious to the Church on both sides of the war divide. The Church in the French camp rigorously tested her religious views and virginity before accepting her. The assertion of her individual will and her claim to be able to execute the wishes of God directly, bypassing the Lord's bureaucratic institution on earth, have been seen by some as a kind of Protestantism before its day. She managed to assume a position of military authority despite being of lowly birth (although not as peasantish a shepherdess as romantics would believe). She wore men's clothes, which was very shocking. All round, she was a disturbing figure, 'unnatural' in so many ways. She was also utterly extraordinary, managing to gain so much power in such a rigid society and acting as such an inspiration. Her claims were certainly not a unique occurrence in the medieval world (and wouldn't be in today's world, for that matter), but Joan got concrete results.

All sorts of causes have adopted Joan in a terrible confusion of ways. First and foremost, she's been seen as the symbol of a glorious France, a reunified country under a divinely ordained king. For many French people she's been *the* symbol of national pride. It matters little that in her day the leaders of many regions of what is now France wanted to remain independent of French royalty rather than become subservient to such an acquisitive and exploitative central power. Many tend to forget, too, the fact that it took a good many years after Joan's triumphs to get the English out of France. Confusingly, while the inhabitants of Orléans somewhat understandably recall and celebrate every year the town's liberation after the terrible siege, the right-wing Front National party organizes an alternative annual Joan of Arc march with more sinister undertones. As to the modern Catholic Church, it took a long time to recognize the supposed sanctity of this young military leader – Joan was after all condemned to death by one of its own most powerful branches – and she was not canonized until 1920. More recently, some have searched for the schizophrenic in Joan, while others have seen definite signs in her of a combative lesbian or bulimic, among a plethora of speculative theories.

The large scale of the Place du Martroi gives some impression of the former Ancien Régime splendour of the city. It's very easy to tell the few prewar remnants from the newly built. The façade of the **Chancellerie du duc d'Orléans** remains typical of mid-18th-century grandeur. A good number of brasseries and restaurants spill out onto the square in summer and some of the town's liveliest streets lead off in various directions.

The two main shopping arteries head respectively north and south from Place du Martroi. **Rue de la République**, the grand thoroughfare leading north straight to the central railway station, exudes Belle Epoque elegance and has an array of shops, including several specializing in perfume. **Rue Royale**, sloping south towards the Loire, recreates the soberly sophisticated arcaded Ancien Régime street destroyed by war bombing; some very smart clothes shops and culinary stops are protected by its arches.

Rue Royale acts as something of a dividing line in the centre of Orléans. The quarter west of Rue Royale suffered terribly from war bombing and doesn't have the same atmospheric appeal as the area to the east of it. For example, **Place du Général de Gaulle** is a chaotically rebuilt big triangle of a square. One one side of it you'll find the misleadingly named **Maison de Jeanne d'Arc** (*see* above), standing out with its brick and beam patterning.

Along **Rue du Tabour**, taking you back to Rue Royale, the substantial French Renaissance **Maison d'Euverte Hatte**, built for a wealthy 16th-century merchant, now houses the **Centre Charles Péguy** (*open Mon–Fri 8.45–12 and 1.30–6 ; free*). A portrait of this angry Belle Epoque intellectual looking like a monk with a monocle, his books protected under glass, period posters, photos and caricatures on the walls don't quite add up to enough elements to give a clear picture of one of Orléans' most intelligent and combative sons. You'd really need to read him or about him to learn more. An impassioned socialist and prolific writer, among other massive labours Péguy rewrote Joan of Arc's life in a huge three-volume dramatic work, *Jeanne d'Arc*, interpreting his native town's heroine according to his own ideals; the bigoted, mule-headed, unstoppable nationalist was turned into a warrior for the oppressed against a leadership indifferent to suffering. After Péguy had been converted to mystical Christianity in 1909, he redrafted the drama of the Maid as *Le Mystère de la charité de Jeanne d'Arc*. As the threat of war grew, his idealistic hopes for a universal society had to yield to the realities of the tense and fragmented situation in Europe and he became increasingly patriotic. He died fighting in the First World War.

Continue from Rue du Tabour down Rue Royale to the **Pont George V**, Orléans' elegant central bridge across the Loire. Rebaptized in honour of an English king, it was in fact built under Louis XV; it's known to the locals as the Pont Royal. The modern quarters on the south bank of the Loire may look uninspiring, but it's worth crossing the Pont George V as you get fine views back across the river to the historic town, its roofs and its churches, including those soaring strawberry gâteaux placed so delicately on top of the cathedral towers.

On the south bank, set back from the Quai Fort des Tourelles, stands another **bronze statue of Joan of Arc**, from Napoleonic times, by Gois *fils*. This originally stood in Place du Martroi, but Joan's plumed standard-bearing pose didn't go down well among the Orléanais (she does look rather combatively prissy in this version), so she was removed and replaced by Foyatier's Joan. The site of this statue is significant, though; it was here that the epic struggle to free Orléans of the English centred on 7 May 1429.

Crossing back over to the north side of the river, the area immediately east of the Rue Royale has several very charming and lively streets. In their midst, the large modern shopping centre-cum-covered market known as **Les Halles-Châtelet** looks rather dull architecturally, but its stands and boutiques may draw you in. Several French Renaissance houses have been preserved in the streets around it, for instance the **Maison du Cerceau** on the street of the same name, attributed to one of the best-known French architects of that period.

Rue de Bourgogne, one of old Orléans' liveliest streets, is packed with restaurants. Certain timberframe houses stand out along its length, as well as the round **Temple**, a 19th-century Protestant church. Take some time to explore the streets and little squares between Rue de Bourgogne and Rue Jeanne d'Arc as they are the most atmospheric in the city, containing several fine Renaissance mansions and overseen by the belfry commissioned by the town's councillors in the 15th century.

From **Rue Jeanne d'Arc** you can enjoy the most splendid vista onto the cathedral. On the north side of this broad, busy, very straight street you can seek out the **Centre Jeanne d'Arc** (*see* above). Rue Jeanne d'Arc leads to the big square in front of the cathedral, **Place Ste-Croix**. Head north from here, past the **Musée des Beaux-Arts** and the **Hôtel Groslot** (*see* above), to take a look along **Rue d'Escures**, which contains some of the smartest, largest houses in town, including the grandiose Pavilions d'Escures. These were commissioned by a dynamic mayor of Orléans who became a close friend of King Henri IV and they reflect the period taste for mixing brick and slate, as in the Place des Vosges in Paris. The imposing **church of St-Pierre-du-Martroi**, just off Rue d'Escures not far from Place du Martroi, was also rebuilt in brick after the 16th-century Wars of Religion.

Back at the cathedral end of Rue d'Escures stands the curiously vacuous **Campo Santo**. This site served for many centuries as Orléans' main cemetery. Arcades resembling cloisters were built around it from the 15th century, but by the 18th century the place was declared a danger to public health and closed. The large arcades have been restored, and although the large space looks empty for much of the year, it regularly serves as a useful venue for all manner of cultural events.

Do walk all the way round the **cathedral**. On the north side you can see just a few vestiges of Orléans' 4th-century Gallo-Roman wall, while from the walled garden of the Ancien Régime **bishop's palace** you can appreciate the flying buttresses around the cathedral's choir end particularly well. Off the south side of the cathedral, Rue Pothier leads to the **Préfecture**, the smart administrative seat of the Loiret *département*.

East of the Préfecture, you enter a quieter old district, with atmospheric streets sloping down towards the Loire from Rue de Bourgogne. Down one, you'll be drawn by the slightly neglected medieval forms of the **church and cloister of St-Pierre-le-Puellier**, now converted into a venue for exhibitions and concerts. Down another, the

Tour Blanche stands out, a medieval tower built on Gallo-Roman foundations. Down a third, seek out the **Fonds Régional d'Art Contemporain du Centre** or **FRAC** (*12 Rue de la Tour Neuve*, *t 02 38 62 52 00, www.frac-centre.asso.fr*), where new modern art pieces acquired by the region are put on display.

The big new glass building close to the Loire is a **covered Halles**, with a big market on Tuesday. But the most appealing attraction in this quarter is the sunken, tree-lined Square du Cloître St-Aignan with the **church of St-Aignan** looming over one side of it. This Gothic church has suffered from much mutilation and isn't open to the public for the moment, but its large, atmospheric crypt is (*contact tourist office for tours; open July–Aug 2–6*).

Already in Carolingian times, St-Aignan was a collegiate church, but it was rebuilt in the 11th century for King Robert le Pieux. The crypt is all that has survived from Robert's time. However, it constitutes an impressively large remnant, built on a grand scale (the same apparently as that made to protect the great St Martin's very precious remains in Tours) and housing not just bones belonging to St Aignan but also those of half-a-dozen other saints. The remarkable carved capitals were only rediscovered in 1953. They're cleverly presented, still encased within the supporting pillars added at a later date. Some feature plant decoration, with superbly carved acanthus leaves; others depict violent scenes – monsters spit fire, while a man with a sword is seen fighting, no doubt against evil, on one side of a capital, but running away on the other side!

The *martyrium* was the inner sanctum reserved for the venerated relics. It was provided with small slits in the wall through which the pilgrims could look or pass objects such as a piece of cloth on a stick to benefit from the miraculous touch of the reliquary.

South of Orléans: Olivet, Orléans-La Source and the Loiret

The road south out of the centre of Orléans across the Pont George V takes you down to **Olivet** and the pretty banks of the Loiret. To reach its bourgeois-housed and restaurant-flanked sides you need to look out for a vast Auchan supermarket on the western side of the road and turn right *before* the supermarket. Go past the hotels and restaurants to find the public car parks by the Loiret. From here you can go walking along the tow path, a delightful narrow way taking you past old watermills and along the backs of the houses and gardens – their terraces and lawns are turned to the river, with its boathouses and landing jetties, rowers and ducks. Weeping willows are particularly numerous among the magnificent trees. You can take a boat trip down the Loiret from here.

The other place to visit in the vicinity is **Orléans-La Source**, next to Olivet. La Source refers to the fact that the Loiret river emerges here, in what is now the Parc Floral (*open April–mid-Nov 9–6, rest of year 2–5*). This is a beautifully tended public garden. The river source itself isn't particularly spectacular, although the Loiret does come fully formed out of the ground; the roses, irises and dahlias are the real stars, according to the season. The park has a butterfly greenhouse and an aviary, as well as its innumerable flowerbeds.

South, opposite the Parc Floral, lies the university campus. For those interested in modern architecture there are some interesting buildings to be seen in its 100 hectares, particularly around the artificial lake.

The Loire from Orléans to Blois

11

Orléans to Blois

N

10 km
5 miles

Orléans

157

St Jean le Blanc

St Ay

Les Muids

Olivet

Meung-sur-Loire

La Source

Marchenoir

LOIR-ET-

Cléry-St André

LOIRET

924

Talcy

❶ Beaugency

Tavers

E09/A71

20

921

La Ferté-St-Aubin

CHER

St-Laurent-Nouan

957

152

Muides-sur-Loire

Montlivault

St-Dyé-sur-Loire

Maslives

20

Blois

Nozieux

❷ Chambord

Huisseau-sur-Cosson

Château de Beauregard

Mont-près-Chambord

Châilles

Villesavin

Bracieux

Neung

Cellettes

Cour-Cheverny

Fontaines-en-Sologne

922

St-Viâtre

Chitenay

Troussay

❸ Cheverny

Ouchamps

La Gaucherie

956

102

Marcilly-en-Gault

Fougères-sur-Bièvre

Contres

Mur-de-Sologne

Millançay

Veilleins

Highlights

1 Beaugency's beautiful squares sloping down to the Loire
2 Chambord, a city of a royal château
3 The Château de Cheverny, the most elegant of all Loire castles

The Loire begins its determined, slow marathon of a descent southwestwards to the Atlantic once past Orléans. In this chapter we cover the river between Orléans and Blois. On the north bank, the little towns of Meung-sur-Loire and Beaugency now offer delightful Loire-side havens off the commercially scarred N152. Their protected slopes made them sought-after sites in the early medieval period, hence their legacy of châteaux and vast churches. On the south bank, opposite these two hillside towns, the fertile land is flat as a pancake, making the huge church of Notre-Dame de Cléry, chosen burial place of King Louis XI, stand out all the better.

At the massive nuclear power station at St-Laurent-Nouan you leave the Orléanais (now the *département* of Loiret) for the Blésois (the *département* of Loir-et-Cher). Passing swiftly along the south bank you arrive at St-Dyé-sur-Loire, the port which served the building site of that mammoth among Loire Renaissance châteaux, Chambord. The château, surrounded by the thickest of forests, was commissioned in part as a hunting fantasy by that outsized 16th-century French king, François I. It's a mesmerizing fairytale palace to visit. A handful of much more modest but very appealing châteaux nearby are also open to the public: Villesavin, Beauregard, Troussay, Fougères-sur-Bièvre and Cheverny – Loire châteaux don't come any more refined than the last.

The Loire from Orléans to Beaugency

Beaugency, with its clutch of impressive medieval monuments, is the highlight of this stretch of the Loire river, although Meung-sur-Loire also has its moments. The Basilique de Cléry-St-André and the Château de Talcy offer less well-known surprises.

Meung-sur-Loire

The bishops of Orléans chose Meung-sur-Loire for their out-of-town residence in medieval times and 'The Bishops' Castle' might be a suitable nickname for the château at Meung. They weren't ones to deprive themselves, clearly. The town also boasts a vast ancient abbey church quite out of keeping with its present scale.

The **Château de Meung** (*open July–Aug 9–12.30 and 1.30–6.30, April–June and 5 Sept–6 Nov 10–12 and 2–5, rest of year weekends only 10–12 and 2–5*) has a run-down, ramshackle charm from the outside. Peeling wallpaper and damp counted among the most noticeable features on the tour within until recently; the château has just changed hands, so things may change. The guides used to take you round from the severe medieval-looking entrance, the towers and walls in irregular small stone and roughcast, to the back façade, coated a startling pink and giving onto a wild garden. After visiting a series of sparse rooms, you would then be taken underground into creepy corridors, part of a network that once ran under the town. Inevitably the atmosphere brought out the nastiest kinds of tales, of imprisonment and torture and, worst of all, of the unwanted being walled up alive. Out in the garden, the *oubliette*, or dungeon, looks very much like the ice houses it was once fashionable to

Getting Around

Meung-sur-Loire and Beaugency are well served by regular **trains** between Orléans and Blois.

For **bus** times, contact Rapides du Val de Loire (t 02 38 61 90 00, t 02 38 86 26 12), or Transports du Loir-et-Cher (t 02 54 58 55 55).

Tourist Information

Meung-sur-Loire: 42 Rue Jehan de Meung, 45130 Meung-sur-Loire, t 02 38 44 32 28, f 02 38 44 72 22.
Cléry-St-André: Place de l'Eglise, 45370 Cléry-St-André, t/f 02 38 45 94 33.
Beaugency: 3 Place de l'Hôtel de Ville, B.P.44, 45190 Beaugency, t 02 38 44 54 42, f 02 38 46 45 31.

Market Days

Meung-sur-Loire: Thursday afternoon and Sunday morning.
Cléry-St-André: Thursday and Saturday mornings.
Beaugency: Saturday, all day.
Tavers: Sunday morning.

Where to Stay and Eat

Meung-sur-Loire ✉ **45130**
Auberge St-Jacques, 60 Rue du Général de Gaulle (N152), t 02 38 44 30 39, f 02 38 45 17 02 (*inexpensive*). Well regarded locally for its cuisine (*menus €13.5–39.5*), this traditional, basic French inn is where d'Artagnan was wounded in a skirmish in 1625, after which he was tended by the beautiful Milady, so the story would have it. Situated along the unattractively busy main road.
L'Olivier, 15 Rue du Général de Gaulle, t 02 38 45 13 41. This ivy-clad restaurant has a certain charm within and serves good fish dishes (*menus €12–39.5*).
Café du Commerce, t 02 38 44 32 35. On an historic square, with generous awnings above the green terrace chairs, a delightfully unpretentious place at which to try simple menus (*menus €11–21*). *Closed Mon pm, and first fortnight Jan.*

Les Muids/Mareau-aux-Prés ✉ **45370**
Le Clos des Muids B&B, 1045 Rue des Muids, t/f 02 38 45 63 16 (*inexpensive*). An energetic couple have been restoring the farm buildings around their courtyard in the village of

dig in one's château's grounds. Two famously sharp-witted medieval French poets are associated with Meung's history, and one, Villon, is said to have been locked up here for a time.

Villon led a wild life in Paris, being found guilty of theft and murder on a couple of occasions. His charm and his poetry, the latter full of pathos, pain and puns, helped get him out of many a sticky situation. He's most famous for his mock wills written in verse, in which, as he had so few possessions, he would ironically distribute all he owned with great pomp, down to old egg shells and his hair clippings, reserved for the people he most detested. His wit may have helped Villon get away with murder, literally. But he was imprisoned on several occasions. If he did spend a stint in the Château de Meung's *oubliette*, it's a terrifying thought, and a miracle that he made it out alive, as the sheer walls and lack of light or ventilation make this place even more disturbing than the grisly corridors underneath the castle.

Below Meung's château, the **church of St-Liphard** stands out like a cathedral in a village. Much of it was built in small irregular stone rather than tidy big blocks, but it mainly dates from the Gothic period, with its originally shaped trefoil choir end and its flying buttresses. The place does contain the odd older Romanesque feature; the base of the stone rocket of a steeple goes back to the 11th century, for example, while the north transept is distinctly from the earlier period.

Les Muids, close to orchards a handful of kilometres north of Cléry-St-André, off the D951. They've introduced a few high-tech features into the comfortable rooms, such as electronic shutters. Not only are the bathrooms excellent here, there's even a lovely heated indoor pool you can use below the rooms (*table d'hôte €17*).

Beaugency ✉ 45190

***Hôtel de l'Abbaye**, 2 Quai de l'Abbaye, t 02 38 44 67 35, f 02 38 44 87 92, *abbaye@ chateauxhotels.com* (*moderate*). Set in former abbey buildings dating back to the Ancien Régime and superbly located by the Loire, this large hotel offers many characterful rooms with views of the river. The fine restaurant serves traditional Loire cuisine (*menu €29*).

**Hôtel de la Sologne, 6 Place Saint-Firmin, t 02 38 44 50 27, f 02 38 44 90 19 (*inexpensive*). A charming little labyrinth of a hotel, surrounded by the best monuments in town. The rooms are lovingly looked after and a bargain.

**Le Relais des Templiers, 68 Rue du Pont, t 02 38 44 53 78 (*inexpensive*). Makes a pretty picture, with a private garden and terrace.

**L'Ecu de Bretagne, Place du Martroir, t 02 38 44 67 60, f 02 38 44 68 07 (*inexpensive*). Not quite as charming to look at as the ones above, with a modern annexe as well as the old posting inn, but its rooms are generally comfortable. The menus aren't cheap, but then the chef experiments with rich dishes such as rabbit with gingerbread and pork in honey (*menus €19.5–30*). *Closed Sun pm and Mon in low season and in Feb.*

Le P'tit Bateau, 54 Rue du Pont, t 02 38 44 56 38. In a typical Beaugency light white stone house, with a beamed dining room where you can try fish specialities (*menus €12.5–22*). *Closed Sun pm, Tues pm and Wed, and 15 Aug–10 Sept as well as Feb school hols.*

Tavers ✉ 45190

****La Tonnellerie, 12 Rue des Eaux-Bleues, t 02 38 44 68 15, f 02 38 44 10 01, *tonnellerie@ chateauxhotels.com* (*expensive*). A quite luxurious hotel, but it keeps its pleasures well hidden behind its unassuming façade in this peaceful village just southwest of Beaugency. Within, elegant rooms, a pretty terrace, a walled garden and a swimming pool await; the cuisine is stylish too (*menus €22–40*). *Closed Jan and Feb.*

Inside, huge lancet arches hold up the nave, while the side-aisles are flanked by side chapels, in a couple of which ornate reliquary boxes have been perched high on brackets. The temple-reliquary boxes in St Theresa's chapel are adorned with gruesome scenes of martyrdoms. Cast iron gates with angels mark the entrance to the side-chapel containing St-Liphard's relics.

The pretty shape of the church's trefoil end is emphasized by the splendid vaulting in the apse and transepts, the ribs falling down like so many spider's legs. Look out for the stained glass in one end chapel, representing not St Liphard, but St Joan, shown celebrating Mass after another of her Loire-side victories here in this very Meung church – adoring, kneeling onlookers are distracted from thoughts of God to stare entranced at the Maid in her armour. Once again Joan is represented sweeping all before her, here stealing the limelight from St Liphard and the Lord.

Leaving Meung's old main square by the choir end of the church, go past the covered market, the splashing modern fountain and the mill stream to come out close to the riverside. Much of Meung's north bank lies in the shade of five splendid lines of plane trees (although the scene is slightly marred by the municipal camp site). There's no old stone bridge here, only a relatively modest, modernish crossing. You may notice a couple of rather bad statues down here. One of them represents Gaston Couté, a local boy who hit the big time as a Montmartre crooner at the beginning of the 20th century, here interpreted in the Chinese workers' school of sculpture.

The other figure is the other great poet associated with Meung: Jean de Meun has been made to look like a straight-backed, tight-waisted, prim spinster of a man here, holding a rose in one hand. The flower makes reference to his famous work; he was the main author of that medieval bestseller *Le Roman de la Rose*, taking over where Guillaume de Lorris (*see* p.128–9) left off, writing the bulk of the composition and adding a much sharper, more prickly twist to it, turning the allegory into a critique of contemporary society and mores. However, Christine de Pisan, one of the great female writers of the medieval period in France, attacked the poem for being obscene and degrading to women, and a debate long raged on the work and the various ways of interpreting it. Chaucer, Dante and Petrarch were all familiar with the poem. It's written in beautiful old French, which looks harder to read than it sounds when read out loud, but you need a firm grasp of the language to tackle it.

One other prickly thing that shouldn't go unmentioned in Meung is the fine collection of holly bushes planted at the **Arboretum des Prés des Culands** (*open April–Oct, but only by reservation and you are taken round by a guide;* **t** *02 38 63 10 49*), a national *conservatoire* of the species, set in the charming watery scenery of Les Mauves, the name given to the streams that congregate at Meung, in a quarter where the mills used to grind the corn from the Beauce plain to the north.

Basilique de Cléry-St-André

Cross to the very flat south bank of the Loire from Meung to reach the grand late medieval Basilique de Cléry-St-André, which stands out like a great vessel in a desert. It's thanks to a large dose of medieval superstition that the diminutive place was donated such a disproportionately vast church. In 1280 a local farmer ploughing his field supposedly dug up a statue of a woman and child. They were claimed to be the Virgin and baby Jesus, of course, and were said to have begun to work miracles. Such was the impact that royal Capetian patronage was quickly in on the act. King Philippe IV's generous sponsorship allowed for the building of a splendid church which became an important stop on the pilgrimage route from Paris to Santiago de Compostela. The English army passing this way in the second half of the Hundred Years' War showed absolutely no respect for the Holy mother and child or their achievements and destroyed Philippe le Bel's church. Miracle of miracles, the Virgin and child survived, and the local Count Dunois, aided by King Charles VII, supported a rebuilding programme. The reputed architects Pierre Le Paige and Pierre Chauvin worked on it, but progress was slow until the supremely superstitious King Louis XI spurred on the work after what he reckoned was an act of divine intervention by the Virgin of Cléry. As dauphin, or heir to the French throne, in 1443 Louis had been fighting the English up in Dieppe with Dunois. The battle was going against the French. The story goes that Louis asked his companion in which direction he should pray to the Virgin of Cléry to call on her aid. She apparently heard him and interceded, so the future king believed, reversing the tide of the battle and bringing the French victory. In repayment of the Virgin's largesse, Louis became personally involved in the rebuilding of her church at Cléry-St-André and showered money on the project. Most significantly, the king of paranoia decided to be buried here. So anxious was he to see the place completed before his death that he even spent a couple of months at Cléry in 1482 as the site was nearing completion but his health was failing. In the end, the church wasn't quite ready by the time of his death in 1483; but he was able to decompose here in peace, even though Protestants in the 16th century Wars of Religion destroyed his tomb effigy.

The basilica's nave is a huge, airy, light Gothic space. Louis XI's effigy was replaced in the 17th century, the fine new sculpture of him executed by the Orléans artist Michel Bourdin in 1622. It was placed at a curious angle in the nave. The king kneels soberly in prayer, looking severe and ascetic despite his robes decorated with fleurs-de-lys and in contrast to the putti holding up a coat of arms on each corner. Nearby, steps lead down to a crypt holding the sarcophagi of the king and his wife. The original statue of the Virgin and child still graces the church, sitting perched high up in an overelaborate 19th-century neo-Byzantine structure. The brown-robed Mary looks distinctly surprised by all the attention and the elevation. Only a few stained-glass windows remain in the church, high up in the choir. On the left-hand side, you can see a representation of the lifting of the siege of Dieppe. The king in the central panel under the Virgin isn't Louis XI, but Henri III, easily distinguished by his distinctive *barbichette*, or goatee beard; this 16th-century work depicts him creating the knightly Order of the Holy Spirit. Back at ground level, grotesques stare out from the choir stalls.

Two important side chapels lie off the south aisle. The Chapelle de Longueville, in Flamboyant Gothic style, was the burial place of Dunois and his wife Marie d'Harcourt. The Chapelle Saint-Jacques has typical elements of decoration from the time of the transition from Gothic to Renaissance in France, at the start of the 16th century (*see* pp.51–4). The walls have been showered with symbols representing the men for whom it was built, Gilles and François de Pontbriant (Shining Bridge), close to King François I. Also off the south side of the main church, look out for a secretive winding staircase leading up to a comfortable chamber with a big fireplace and a little peep hole, made for Louis XI to observe Mass in private from up high; he could peer down onto the choir and follow the service unobserved.

Beaugency

A patched-up, bumpy medieval bridge, cobbled quays, vast plane trees shielding the low waterfront houses, and behind them, soaring medieval monuments... Seen from the south side of its bumbling old bridge, the oldest one on the Loire, Beaugency is one of the most beautiful towns along the river. Head up the slope and you'll discover a surprising number of interesting old buildings packed close together around a series of interconnecting triangular-shaped squares.

In medieval times Beaugency lay on the limits of the Blésois, the territory of the extremely powerful counts of Blois. It was long a particularly important place because of its bridge, for centuries the only crossing point on the Loire between Orléans and Blois. Such strategic importance meant that it was bound to suffer badly in times of conflict. A few traces of the town's medieval ramparts and gates do remain. In fact, such was the importance of Beaugency in that period, and such its decline after it, that it only started to grow beyond its historic walls in the mid-20th century.

Start a visit of Beaugency down by the Loire. Close to the bridge you can appreciate the extent of the gently sloping **quays** and imagine the busy trading activity that must once have enlivened this area. Beaugency's **medieval bridge** looks particularly magnificent from here, with its variety of arches and the visible hiccups in its construction. Behind the line of quayside plane trees, the long façade of a substantial 17th-century **abbey building** (now a hotel) looks out to the water.

The most imposing evidence of Beaugency's medieval importance is the massive keep known as the **Tour de César**. There are a couple of other keeps like this along the Loire, for example at Montbazon and at Loches, which show the formidable nature of this type of early stone feudal military architecture. This one dates from the last quarter of the 11th century and still looks frighteningly severe – it rises to around 100ft – despite the beautiful colour of the blocks of stone in which it was built and the mullion windows added in the 16th century to give it more light. Originally it had five levels of chambers within. A fire started by Protestants during the Wars of Religion caused the roof to burn; it was never replaced and the keep gradually fell into ruin. The place can't be visited as it's now dangerous, having been abandoned for so long; plants have sprouted on it and crows are now lords of the manor. But it still makes an impressive sight. So, too, does the **Tour St-Firmin** beside it, a remnant of a church that has otherwise disappeared. On the shaded square below these massive towers stands the obligatory Loire statue of Joan of Arc, put up by a grateful populace – only in 1896, it turns out!

Not far down from the keep, and dating from the same Romanesque period, is the **church of Notre-Dame**. It too was badly damaged by religious fire in 1567, but was restored in 1642. Back in medieval times, this church served as the setting for the discussion of a couple of extremely difficult royal marital crises. The first major council at Beaugency was held to consider King Philippe I's excommunication from the Catholic Church – in 1092 he had repudiated his wife Berthe and taken off with Bertrade de Montfort, unfortunately already married to the count of Anjou.

The second council, in 1152, was more serious still, deciding on the annulment of King Louis VII of France's marriage to Eleanor of Aquitaine. The reason given was consanguinity, but this was an excuse. The irrepressible Eleanor and pious Louis were incompatible; furthermore they had not produced a male heir, and there were even rumours of Eleanor committing adultery in Antioch when the couple had gone off on a Crusade. As a result of the annulment of the marriage at Beaugency, Eleanor took back the vast inheritance of southwest France she had brought to the French Crown, and promptly married Henri Plantagenêt, count of Anjou (west along the Loire) and the future King Henry II of England. In a way, it could be argued that the decision taken at Beaugency led to the years of war between France and England that ensued.

Inside the church, massive Romanesque columns hold up the nave and aisles, with bold capital designs, some representing primitive foliage, others fighting or humorous figures. One capital has been cleverly turned to form a man's magnificently large nose! You can walk round the lovely open ambulatory at the choir end and back up to the organ at the entrance, finely carved wood panels adorning the front of it.

A gateway to one side of the church leads into the small, urban Château Dunois, housing a cluttered museum, the **Musée Régional de l'Orléanais** (*open April–Sept Wed–Mon 10–12 and 2–6, Mar and Oct–Dec Wed–Mon 10–12 and 2–5*). This château was the seat of Jean, Bastard of Orléans, illegitimate son of Louis I Duc de Orléans (brother of King Charles VI) and Marguerite d'Enghien. Being a bastard in those times didn't mean social ostracism, and on the tour you can see fleurs-de-lys proudly displayed on Jean's coat of arms, only with a prominent diagonal bar across it, symbolizing the illegitimacy. Jean had the principal parts of his château built from 1440 and lived here for 17 years. He most famously fought alongside Joan of Arc – in fact, it was he who led the French troops to free Orléans with Joan. After her death he continued the successful fight against the English, beating them at Montargis, Chartres and St-Denis, and playing his part in the recapturing of Paris.

The architecture within the partly arcaded courtyard looks slightly disappointing. Cement has been spread about in seemingly slapdash manner in the modern restoration work. You're herded through the museum rooms without much time to linger in front of the 8,000 or so objects apparently on display, of which a small number prove interesting. Special collections include representations of the Loire in the region and items on life on the river; religious robes and statuary; and most cosmopolitan, works of sculpture by the American John Storrs. Many of the rooms illustrate old local ways of life and local traditions. Of course the museum wouldn't be complete without a set of plates telling the life of Joan of Arc.

The **town hall** (*open 10–12 and 2–5, except Sat pm, Sun and public hols*), on a higher square, boasts an unmissable over-decorated, over-restored French Renaissance façade – the building was badly damaged in the Revolution and had to be substantially repaired; the excess of decoration is quite mesmerizing. The outstanding feature is the fleurs-de-lys scattered on the front, *semées à pleine main*, sown by the handful, as the delightful and accurate French phrase has it.

Inside, eight exquisitely executed embroideries are displayed, their original provenance and precise symbolism a mystery, although they were brought here from the abbey and are reckoned to date from the 17th century. Four of them appear to illustrate curious scenes of Celtic sacrifice, richly coloured and distinctly disturbing. The others show allegories of the continents, each rather approximately symbolized by a different woman and by exotic animals. Although some of the creatures look absurd, the human faces are beautifully depicted.

Further up the slope still, you come out on the bright and often bustling **Place du Martroi**. The stumpy little medieval **church of St-Etienne** stands timidly to one side. It once formed part of a a priory dedicated to the Holy Sepulchre and dates back to the 11th century. The pleasing sunken interior now serves for exhibitions.

The Death of Two Poets' Passions

Two great French literary figures of the 16th century became closely associated with Talcy. Pierre de Ronsard and Agrippa d'Aubigné, both to become acclaimed poets, fell madly in love with Salviati girls. Bernardo Salviati had a daughter, Cassandre, who quite turned the tonsured head of the young Pierre. He met her at a Blois ball in 1545, when he was a stripling of 21, she a mere 15. *Les Amours de Cassandre* are the only certain fruits of Ronsard's passion, 183 sonnets to the Salviati girl from the most lyrical of all French poets. Cassandre, unfortunately, was married to someone else the year after they met. The rumours claim that Ronsard and Cassandre continued to see each other and that one of her children was in fact fathered by the poet.

It was Cassandre's brother Jean who inherited the Château de Talcy. His daughter Diane was called upon to tend a soldier wounded in fighting in the Wars of Religion. The warrior she cared for was none other than the hot-headed Huguenot, Agrippa d'Aubigné. He in his turn was driven to poetry when hit by amour's *coup de foudre*: 'My love for Diana turned my mind to poetry,' he wrote. Unfortunately, the passion these lovers shared was destroyed by family religious differences. Diane's relatives were strictly Catholic and strongly disapproved of Protestant d'Aubigné. It was the man who went off to be married this time, breaking Diane's heart.

A Detour to the Château de Talcy

The north bank of the Loire from Beaugency to Blois is best avoided, as the A10 motorway and the unattractive N152 hardly make it possible to appreciate the valley. However, one detour worth considering due west of Beaugency is to the Château de Talcy (*open April–Sept 9.30–12 and 2–6, rest of year 10–12 and 2–4.30*), a stern-looking castle standing guard over an isolated village on the edge of the huge flat cereal plains of the Beauce.

The Florentine banker Bernardo Salviati bought the place in 1517, to be close to the French court, still largely based at Blois at the time. There's nothing Italianate about the château though; the stocky 15th-century keep looming over the village pavement looks severely medieval, although slightly mellowed by subsequent embellishments. The delicately decorated interiors, dating from a later period, prove much more charming than the grey façades. Wood panelling in light greys and greens, family portraits, embroidered chairs, games tables, *objets* from the French colonies, bureaux with secret drawers all conjure up the refined Ancien Régime good living enjoyed here by the Burjects. This Protestant family held on to the castle until 1932, when it was sold, fully furnished, to the state.

Châteaux Around Blois

Between Beaugency and Blois, it's much more rewarding to follow the south bank of the Loire. The riverside becomes prettier the nearer you get to the city, but the main tourist attractions hide out in the woods south of the river. Chambord, a magical

Getting Around

It's not easy to get to the clutch of châteaux in this section if you're relying on public transport – try Transports du Loir-et-Cher for local bus services (**t** 02 54 58 55 55), or look for excursions operated from Blois.

Tourist Information

St-Dyé-sur-Loire: 75 Rue Nationale, 41500 St-Dyé-sur-Loire, **t** 02 54 81 65 45, **f** 02 54 81 68 07.
Bracieux: Mairie, **t** 02 54 46 42 37.
Cour-Cheverny: Cedex 403, 41700 Cour-Cheverny, **t** 02 54 79 95 63, **f** 02 54 79 23 90.
Cellettes: 2 Rue de Rozelle, **t** 02 54 70 30 46.

Market Days

Bracieux: Thursday afternoon.
Cours-Cheverny: Tuesday afternoon.
Contres: Friday.

Where to Stay and Eat

Here we've moved into major Loire château and tourist country, which means lodgings don't come quite so cheap, but good places proliferate.

Muides-sur-Loire ✉ 41500
Château de Colliers B&B, **t** 02 54 87 50 75, **f** 02 54 87 03 64 (*expensive*). Low curving wings greet you like open arms at this very charming but modest château right by the Loire just west of Muides. The rooms are

delightful, the hosts charmingly professional, the painted dining room memorable (*table d'hôte €38*).
La Chanterelle, 21 Av de la Loire, **t** 02 54 87 50 19. By the banks of the Loire beside Muides' bridge and camp site, this is an obvious place to try Loire fish specialities (*menus €13–19*).

St-Dyé-sur-Loire ✉ 41500
Manoir de Bel Air, **t 02 54 81 60 10, **f** 02 54 81 65 34 (*moderate*). Spectacularly located, renovated old manor above the Loire, many rooms with views down onto the river. There's a large dining room with views as well (*menus €21–39*).
La Bourriche aux Appétits, 65 Rue Nationale, **t** 02 54 81 65 25. There's a good selection of river fish specialities to sample in this pleasing, simple new restaurant in the centre of St-Dyé, the dining room rustically decorated with old pots and pans. Try such tasty recipes as *sandre* with chives, pike in chervil, carp with saffron, shad with sorrel, or lamprey or eel stew (*menus €17–21*). The delightful adjoining shop offers a wide selection of river fish terrines and specialities, as well as a kind of casual exhibition on Loire fishing and more general gifts.

Chambord ✉ 41250
Hôtel St-Michel, 103 Place Saint-Michel, **t 02 54 20 31 31, **f** 02 54 20 36 40 (*inexpensive*). You'll need to book ages in advance to get a room at this hotel as it's in the exclusive position of having many rooms looking out onto the château – don't forget to ask

mammoth in stone, stands in the midst of its enormous forest south of the Loire-side village of St-Dyé. South of Chambord, a handful of other delightful but much more discreet castles lie low in the woods: Cheverny, Beauregard, Villesavin, Troussay, Fougères. Track them down – they're well worth it.

Along the South Bank of the Loire via St-Dyé

St-Dyé-sur-Loire once thrived as the port which served the massive building site of the Château de Chambord. Today, as you wander along its abandoned river front, you can only imagine the bustle and excitement that once gave life to the place. St-Dyé has a Maison de la Loire (*open June–Sept Mon–Sat 3–6, Sun 3–7;*

for a room with a view. The restaurant has a solid reputation. The hotel's terraces may be crammed with tourists during the day, but early or late in the day you can enjoy the pleasure of relative peace by the magnificent palace. The strangely artificial street on which this hotel stands is filled with a choice of simpler restaurants (*menus €20–33*). *Closed mid-Nov–mid-Dec.*

Le Chambourdin, Route de Bracieux, t 02 54 20 32 64. Not far from the château, this restaurant takes you a bit away from the hubbub (*menus from €10.5*).

Maslives ✉ 41250

★★L'Orée de Chambord, 14 Route de Chambord, t 02 54 81 61 62, f 02 54 81 66 76 (*inexpensive*). A cheap and cheerful address at which to stay and eat, just a few kilometres northwest of Chambord (*menus €11.5–38*).

Huisseau-sur-Cosson ✉ 41350

Château de Nanteuil, t 02 54 42 61 98, f 02 54 42 37 23 (*inexpensive*). Lies prettily on the Cosson just a few kilometres west of Chambord (*menus €13.5–29*). *Closed Mon and, for restaurant, Tues lunch also; annual closure last fortnight of Nov and first fortnight of Jan.*

Bracieux ✉ 41250

★★La Bonnheure, 9 Rue René Masson, t 02 54 46 41 57, f 02 54 46 05 90 (*inexpensive; also a couple of more expensive apartments*). Modern, unpretentious, well-flowered place to stay.

Bernard Robin/Le Relais de Bracieux, 1 Av de Chambord, t 02 54 46 41 22. Highly reputed if rather overpriced restaurant run by an illustrious chef. From the roadside the place looks deceptively normal, even old fashioned; however, the dining room is modern and bathed with light from the garden. The cooking is classic stuff, but with interesting touches such as the use of flambéed Loire *marc* (*menus €46.5–81.5*). *Closed Tues evening and Wed (except in Jul and Aug) and 20 Dec–Jan.*

Mont-près-Chambord ✉ 41250

★★Le Saint Florent, 14 Rue de la Chabardière, t 02 54 70 81 00, f 02 54 70 78 53 (*inexpensive*). This place makes a pleasant stop, with light bedrooms and two dining rooms which serve up reasonably priced regional cuisine (*menus €14.5–31*). *Restaurant closed Mon lunch, whole hotel closed Jan.*

Manoir de Clénord B&B, Route de Clénord, t 02 54 70 41 62, f 02 54 70 33 99 (*moderate*). Highly regarded, very pretty and very well-established B&B, in an 18th-century manor (*table d'hôte possible if booked in advance, €21–29*).

Cellettes ✉ 41120

Château de la Roselle, 15 Rue de la Rozelle, t 02 54 70 31 27. Rich, delicious French cuisine served in a big, bright conservatory elegantly fitted onto the end of an 18th-century manor. It's set in its own grounds just above this village on the D956 south of Blois (*menus €23.5–36.5*).

rest of the year Mon–Sat 2–5, Sun 2–6) which puts on little exhibitions on river themes, changing regularly.

A few kilometres after St-Dyé towards Blois, just past Montlivault, the view opens onto the **Château de Ménars**, a superb riverside château on the north bank, remodelled in good part for Louis XV's celebrated mistress, the Marquise de Pompadour. In 1760 she had the king's architect Jacques-Ange Gabriel, genius of Versailles' Petit Trianon, reshape the château. She died in 1764, but her brother, the Marquis de Marigny, carried on with the château's expansion, notably calling on the architect Soufflot for embellishments. Tantalizingly inaccessible to visitors, the château presents a wonderful perspective from the south bank. Magical Chambord lies just half-a-dozen kilometres southeast of here, hidden in its massive oak forest.

Cheverny and Cour-Cheverny ✉ 41700

★★★**Château du Breuil**, Route de Fougères-sur-Bièvre, outside Cheverny, t 02 54 44 20 20, f 02 54 44 30 40, breuil@chateauxhotels.com (*expensive*). The driveway through the densely wooded park to this delightful little château puts you into a dreamlike state. It is set in a glade-cum-garden; the reception rooms, in Louis XVI style, are superbly refined, the bedrooms extremely comfortable.

Ferme des Saules B&B, south of Cheverny, just off the road to Contres, t 02 54 79 26 95, f 02 54 79 97 54, merlin.cheverny@infonie.fr (*inexpensive*). With a little white tower attached to the sweet house, a little well in front of it, and a little swimming pool beyond, this is a cute B&B option close to a camp site (*table d'hôte €13.5–19*).

★★**Hôtel des Trois Marchands**, Place de l'Eglise, Cour-Cheverny, t 02 54 79 96 44, f 02 54 79 25 60 (*inexpensive*). In a sprawling mass (or mess) of buildings around the church, this place is a bit of an institution, with functional rooms and naff paintings, but a comfortable large dining room serving reliably good meals (*menus €16.5–47*). *Closed Mon and Feb–mid-Mar*.

★★**Le Saint-Hubert**, Rue Nationale, Cour-Cheverny, t 02 54 79 96 60, f 02 54 79 21 17 (*inexpensive*). Rather similar to the above, but on a smaller, more family scale (*menus €14.5–42.5*). *Closed Wed and mid-Jan–mid-Feb*.

Le Grand Chancelier, 11 Av Chênes des Dames, Cheverny, t 02 54 79 22 57. Close to the château, a traditional French restaurant offering some tasty options, the chef generous with fine vegetables to accompany well-cooked meat dishes (*menus €15–27*).

Chitenay ✉ 41120

★★**Auberge du Centre**, Place de l'Eglise, t 02 54 70 42 11, f 02 54 70 35 03 (*inexpensive*). Some nicely done rooms and a garden in which you can eat in summer, just west of Troussay (*menus €14–51.5*). *Closed Sun pm and Mon, and last fortnight Feb*.

Contres ✉ 41700

★★★**Hôtel de France**, 37–39 Rue Pierre-Henri Mauger, Route de Blois, t 02 54 79 50 14, f 02 54 79 02 95 (*moderate–inexpensive*). If you're seeking modern luxuries such as a heated pool, a sauna and a gym, then this might be the place for you. The practical rooms are set in a typical local building (*menus €17.5–41*). *Restaurant closed Feb–early Mar*.

La Botte d'Asperges, 52 Rue Pierre-Henri Mauger, Route de Blois, t 02 54 79 50 49. Rustic restaurant, whose name is a good indicator that serving seasonal local produce is the chef's main concern here (*menus €12-29.5*). *Closed Mon out of season*.

Ouchamps ✉ 41120

★★★**Relais des Landes**, t 02 54 44 03 33, f 02 54 44 03 89 (*expensive*). An old converted manor. You could work off a sumptuous lunch here (*menus €26.5–45*) by hiring bikes, playing tennis, or taking a siesta in your spacious room. *Closed mid-Nov–Mar*.

Château de Chambord

Open July–Aug 9.30–5.45, 2 Nov–June 9.30–11.45 and 2–4.45, Sept–Oct 9.30–11.45 and 2–5.45; t 02 54 50 40 00, www.chambord.org.

King François I's 'hunting lodge' is a palace, rather than the traditional cottage, in a glade. The Château de Chambord is one of the great European symbols of royal megalomania, a truly glorious and absurd monster of French architecture. From whichever way you approach Chambord through the long alleys of the mysterious walled forest that encircles it, it makes a staggering sight, looking like a riotously exuberant yet self-contained royal city. On first seeing it you immediately realize you're in front of one of the greatest buildings in France.

Work began on Chambord in 1519, but it's something of a mystery as to whom the original architect was. The name of Leonardo da Vinci, who spent the last few years of his life at Amboise, down the Loire (*see* pp.251–2), is tantalizingly associated with Chambord, without firm evidence. A name more concretely linked with it is that of another extremely talented Italian, Domenico da Cortona. He had come to France in King Charles VIII's retinue and made models of various constructions for François I certainly as early as 1517. One model was a version of Chambord. This included the extraordinary Greek cross plan (a Greek cross has four arms of the same length extending out symmetrically from a central crossing), which was incorporated into the main building. The overall basic structure was fixed. Important details would prove quite different from the model, but much of the credit for Chambord seems to be due to Domenico da Cortona.

François I wasn't a man afraid of advancing his own ideas, so it's quite possible that he too had a major influence on the planning, for instance maybe insisting on some of the features which have a traditional French feel. For although Chambord contains a panoply of Italianate Renaissance features, its general forms actually harp back a lot to medieval architecture. The formidably solid round towers at the corners, in

Chambord, a Fantasy Château Where the Living Was Hard

A very substantial portion of Chambord was completed by 1547, the year in which François I died. But the palace was virtually never lived in; as it was a building site for almost the entire span of François' reign, he was scarcely able to spend much time here beyond the odd extravagant reception. And then there were the disasters of the mid-1520s which kept him away, notably his capture by the Holy Roman enemy at the Battle of Pavia in Italy, which forced him to remain a pampered prisoner of Charles V's in Madrid for some time. On top of all this, he had lost his first wife. During his imprisonment, it was agreed between François and Charles V that he should marry Charles' sister, Eleanore of Austria, and he organized a sumptuous reception for her at Chambord in 1530. In 1532 and 1534 he stayed in the palace for hunting parties. Then in 1539 he laid on the most dazzling show for Charles V, who was travelling through France from Spain to his northern territories, Flanders. This was no doubt Chambord's finest evening.

It took until the pomp of Louis XIV's court to bring a further spark of royal life to the château. Not surprisingly, Chambord appealed to the Sun King, who felt at home with its preposterously vain scale, and came with his massive court retinue to hunt and play. He was also amused here; Molière staged the first performances of his plays *Monsieur de Pourceaugnac* and *Le Bourgeois Gentilhomme* at Chambord, in 1669 and 1670 respectively, converting one of the arms of the Greek cross into a theatre. Louis XV, however, proved uninterested in the château. In 1725, in an act of dubious generosity, he gave the place to his father-in-law, the exiled king of Poland, Stanislas I Leszcynski. Such were the insanitary conditions that one summer 50 of his servants were put out of action! After Leszcynski's death Louis XV offered the Maréchal de Saxe the honour of Chambord in recognition of his services to the crown. This eccentric military man had splendid delusions of grandeur and kept the place in particular, with their roofs like great upturned funnels, could come from a textbook image of a chivalric castle. But Chambord is also an obsessively ordered building, neo-classical Renaissance ideas imposing symmetry and precise proportions on the façades. Chambord has virtually none of the idiosyncratic crooked and comic quirks of medieval castles, instead being a rigorous mathematician's delight.

Why build so magnificently in the marshy middle of a vast forest? 'Chambord was like a great royal advertising campaign,' the guides wittily explain. It certainly wasn't built simply for royal hunting. You should bear in mind what an important royal seat the nearby town of Blois was at the time. Chambord was also a deliberate demonstration of royal magnificence and power at a time when western Europe witnessed a clash of titanic leaders; François I came to the throne not long after the young King Henry VIII had started ruling England, and soon Charles I of Spain would outbid them both (thanks to the massive financial backing of the German banker Jacob Fugger) in the stakes to become Holy Roman Emperor. (Charles from then on was better known as the Emperor Charles V.) These three monumental kings continued to compete with each other in their outrageously expensive games of power politics and prestige.

flamboyant style. A bodyguard of negroes from Martinique accompanied him round it on white horses. Parties would visit him from court and he would hold dinners for a modest 150. But the marshal reflected on the insalubrious living conditions which continued to blight those who tried to settle in this château in its marshy forest: 'Chambord is a hospital,' he wrote once. 'I have more than 300 sick, several dead, and others have the look of exhumed corpses.' Royal governors then appointed to look after the dilapidated vastness could do little to stop Chambord's decay.

The Revolution saw most of the interiors stripped of their contents, including the wood panelling that had been added for Louis XIV, but Napoleon's era had preten-sions to the absurd grandeur needed to revive the place. In 1809 the emperor donated Chambord to Maréchal Berthier, for whom the title of Prince of Wagram was created. It was symbolic of the times that one of this man's ambitions was to replace the innumerable F motifs at Chambord, referring to François I, with Ws, to stamp the honour of his newly acquired title on the place! He was dead by 1815, leaving his widow with a simply impossible house to run. Louis XVIII permitted her to sell the estate, and it was bought by public subscription to be donated to King Charles X's heir. This was his grandson, Henri, Duc de Bordeaux, whom it was hoped would become King Henri V of France. He took on the title of Comte de Chambord. First though, his mother, the endlessly intriguing Duchesse de Berry, had to fight for Chambord's survival, stopping the dismantling of the building to sell its stone. But with the 1830 revolution the Orléans royal family had to flee, and the Comte de Chambord stayed in Austria for the next 41 years, returning to spend his one and only night in Chambord in July 1871. His nephews, the Duc de Parme and the Comte de Bardi, tried to stem some of the damage to Chambord after 1883. Finally the French state bought the property in 1930. Someone has calculated that the château, in all its existence, has only been lived in for 20 years.

As tends to be the case with all outsized buildings, Chambord is less perfect than it looks at the outset. Inside, what you see and visit the guides like to describe as one of the first apartment blocks in modern Europe; in the fillings between Chambord's Greek cross arms, hundreds of rooms repeat the same patterns, the vast majority having kept their original volumes. Chambord has a staggering 85 staircases: 70 lesser ones, 14 major ones, and one considered a work of genius, a monument in itself, its intriguing double ramps possibly designed by Leonardo. This masterpiece of a central staircase takes you up to the amazing **roofs**, where you can wander around the fabulous chimneyscape. (Be aware that on the way up or down you may be swept aside by packs of schoolchildren racing round the castle.) The roofs, which may at first appear like a triumphant medieval riot, are actually meticulously ordered behind the wild visual fireworks. Similes have rained down on these wonderful roofs: they've been compared to an overcrowded chessboard, an exotic Eastern palace and even, by the rather excessive French Romantic Chateaubriand, to a woman's locks dishevelled by the wind! Our favourite description, which seems in fact to sum up the whole of Chambord best, is that of 'un gigantesque bouquet de pierres (a gigantic bouquet of stones)'.

Chambord is so vast that most of its interiors have stood empty for ages. But in recent times, more and more has been done to fill the voids. On the first floor you can visit a series of sumptuously furnished **royal apartments**, where you'll learn more about the various owners of the castle and see paintings of them, as well as personal items. On the second floor, the **Musée de la Chasse**, focusing on hunting, was redone in 1997. Hunting objects, tapestries and paintings bring the drama of the hunt inside, including one particularly startling scene where a fleeing deer comes racing into a dining room. In 2001 the castle also started to put on exhibitions on architecture.

All sorts of special tours of the castle and its grounds are organized at various times of year. The main one is **Les Métamorphoses de Chambord** (July and Aug Mon–Sat night except the last two days in Aug; April–June and Sept normally Fri and Sat nights), when you can wander freely round the castle at night, swept along by sound-and-light shows. To check out other possibilities, such as **boating** on the Cosson river, **cycling** round the grounds, **riding** in a horse and carriage, or going to see the **deer rut** in autumn, call **t** 02 54 50 40 00; it's highly recommended to organize such special trips in advance, given the crowds.

Château de Villesavin

Open March–Sept 10–12 and 2–7, Oct–20 Dec 2–5.

Construisez bien, construisez beau, mais construisez modestement (Build well, build beautifully, but build modestly).
        François I to his friend Jean le Breton

The delightfully modest Château de Villesavin lies discreetly on the southern edge of Chambord's forest, near Bracieux. A chip off the old block of Chambord is the way the château is frequently described – it would be more apt to compare it to a little piece of the monster's roof that might have miraculously blown off in the wind and landed in the middle of these charming woods close to the Beuvron river. Some say that it was no miracle, but that the man for whom Villesavin was built, Jean le Breton, diverted funds and workers from the king's building site to construct himself a nice little château on the side.

King and courtier were very close. Jean le Breton fought for François I at the Battle of Pavia. Both men were captured and shared a period of captivity for around 14 months. François I greatly appreciated Le Breton's company, and once they were released he made him administrator of the County of Blois, among other positions. His tasks included overseeing the works at Chambord. During the king's imprisonment, work had stopped on the great château, so the project, involving hundreds of employees (maybe around 1,800 of them), had to be set in motion again.

It is clear that Jean le Breton made the most of the fine workmanship so close at hand to help build his relatively modest shack. Construction of Villesavin began at the end of 1526 or beginning of 1527 and was finished within 10 years. The place may seem something of a half measure of a château in size, but it is full of charm, even if it does looks rather top heavy – the single storey is only 9m high, the roof over 11m.

The château's features are refined and enchanting. Two stand out in the **central courtyard**. First, the almost pyramidal tops to the pavilions on the corners of the *cour d'honneur* which give the place its delightfully idiosyncratic character. These roofs were early precursors of an architectural fashion which grew enormously in popularity under Louis XIII. The second outstanding feature is the Loire *lucarnes*, or dormers, superb examples of their kind. The ones on the right are carved with symbols of the arts, with an Italian mandoline symbolizing music, comedy depicted with three lilies, and tragedy, typically, stabbing herself. Worn by time, these sculptures are the originals. Six Renaissance terracotta medallions representing Roman emperors decorate the plain wall on the opposite side of the courtyard.

In the centre of the *cour d'honneur* stands a beautiful Renaissance fountain. It has been claimed that this superbly carved work in Carrara marble may have been destined for Chambord but diverted here. Villesavin's guides loyally describe it as a gift from the Florentine craftsmen of Chambord to Jean le Breton, and it certainly fits in elegantly here. It's covered with typical Renaissance devices and faces, the bottom of the bowl simulating fish scales, with lion's heads protruding discreetly from among them.

The tour inside the château is relatively short but sweet. You see three out of the four pavilions and a few other rooms. The diminutive **chapel** is covered with frescoes badly worn by time, but still evocative. The style of the major wall paintings is strikingly 16th-century Italian, and have been attributed to the reputed court artist Niccolo dell'Abate. He's known to have lived in France from 1552, assisting Primaticcio in the decoration of Fontainebleau. The depiction of the Flagellation of Christ is particularly moving, not wincing at the cruelty of the scene. The 17th-century putti on the vaults rather clash with the sobriety of style below. They were ordered by Jean Phelypeaux (*see also* Châteauneuf-sur-Loire, p.126), a later owner of Villesavin and counsellor to Louis XIII, and may be the work of Jean Mosnier, who decorated so much of Cheverny's interior. Among the interesting details, St Veronica is depicted in putti guise, the shroud showing the vague outline not so much of an imagined Christ's face, but more, apparently, that of Phelypeaux himself, with his goatee beard.

Entering the main building, the hall and recently restored pavilion room on the south façade are elegant rooms. The first includes a Chardin and a study for the Comédie Française's statue of Poquelin, alias Molière. The second has niches for statues and oval portraits. Moving to the two **kitchen** chambers, one described temptingly as the pâtisserie room, these have a rich rustic feel, with thick beams, sloping stone floors, vast fireplaces and an extensive collection of pewter ware. It is rather ironic to find in a château a fine Revolutionary mirror capped by a *bonnet phrygien*, that symbol of peasant revolt.

A substantial collection of wedding garments and accoutrements, mainly dating from the 19th century, has recently been acquired by the château to try and add a distraction to please large groups of visitors. But Villesavin will always remain on an intimate scale. Beyond the wedding collection you're shown the dovecote, with its hundreds of holes for pigeons, and the long back façade of the castle with its 19th-century inscription and rather neglected air – the unpretentious but devoted young couple who've inherited this place clearly need the aid of more tourists.

The Renaissance gardens have disappeared but the château's setting is delightfully wooded. Villesavin proved a little too modest, however, for King François I's humble servant Jean le Breton. He didn't limit himself to this one château, and passed away at another, much more famous and rather larger one which he had built in the Touraine west along the Loire, the Château de Villandry (*see* pp.322–4). Le Breton was something of a rarity in François I's service, a councillor who died without being disgraced and who held on to his châteaux until the end, rather than having them confiscated by the Crown.

Château de Beauregard

Open July–Aug 9.30–6.30, April–Sept 9.30–12 and 2–6.30, Oct–mid-Jan and mid-Feb–Mar Thurs–Tues 9.30–12 and 2–5.

This shy château hides down a long, dark, deeply wooded alley off the busy D765 linking Blois with Romorantin-Lanthenay – it's less than 10km from Blois. Its sober, almost dull exterior gives no clue as to the highly decorated series of rooms that await you within. Beauregard's outward sobriety stems from the fact that it's a château of what's termed the second French Renaissance, dating from around the middle of the 16th century. Any lingering playful influences of Gothic were wiped out by this time.

Although the lordship of Beauregard was granted by François I to his uncle René de Savoie, the building you see now was ordered by the owner who succeeded René's widow in 1545, one Jean du Thier, Seigneur de Ménars. This man served as secretary of state to the treasury under King Henri II. A patron of the arts, he was the sponsor of two of the famous Pléiade poets, Pierre de Ronsard (*see* Tours, pp.285–6, and Talcy, p.162) and Joachim du Bellay (*see* Liré, p.461). The outside of his château is disappointingly covered in roughcast for the most part, rather than being in seductive blocks of Loire limestone. At least the decoration of the pilasters and the medallions stands out pleasantly on the main façade, while the slate encrusted on the dormer windows and certain chimneys imitates certain decorative features from Chambord.

Florimond Robertet came by the château in 1566. He held some of the same political posts as his predecessor. But as he also owned the much grander Château de Bury, west of Blois, he paid little attention to Beauregard. The family which wrought the biggest changes on the interiors of Beauregard after Du Thier were the Ardiers. Paul Ardier, one-time controller-general of wars and treasurer of the royal savings bank, retired to Beauregard having served three French kings – Henri III, Henri IV and Louis XIII. It was he who ordered the **Galerie des Illustres**, the highlight of the interior, in the 1620s. This gallery offers a wonderful lesson on the leading figures in western European history across several centuries, as well as on the looks and fashions of those times. It is covered with rank upon rank of portraits of famous people, a staggering 327 in total, going from the reign of the first Valois, Philippe VI, through to Louis XIII.

Beauregard is unique along the Loire, but at one time it wasn't unique in France. There was in fact something of a vogue for such galleries in the 17th century. Not surprisingly, it's an Italian, Paulo Jove, who's credited with launching the fashion in his villa near Lake Como. This humanist bishop wrote a book on the great deeds of the famous men featured in his gallery. He donated one manuscript on his collection to the future Henri II of France, which contained miniature reproductions of the portraits in his house. An edition of his book was printed in 1577, spreading the style. The Uffizi in Florence has a famous set of portraits of great men running through its galleries and many of those at Beauregard look recognizably similar.

Faced with such a daunting number of historical figures, it can be hard to know where to focus your attention at first. But the groupings are chronologically displayed for the most part (proceed round left from the fireplace) and well ordered, by series of 12 portraits according to each reign, the monarch featuring last in each cycle, except in the cases of Henri IV and Louis XIII, each given special prominence. The equestrian portrait of Henri IV framed by double portraits above the fireplace was where the painting began. From here it spread to cover the centuries, completed over three generations of the Ardier family. The artists aren't known, although Jean Mosnier of Cheverny fame (*see* below) is associated with the project. It's probable that most of the panels were painted in Paris and are copies (or no doubt copies of copies) of original portraits. All the faces are painted against a black background, full on, in semi-profile or in profile. The collection of ruffs alone impresses. The reds of the cardinals and popes also stand out prominently. Among the hats you may remark a Turkish one, a reminder of the alliance made by François I with Suleyman II which so shocked Christian Europe at that time. These may not be great works of art in themselves, and through time they've been more or less badly restored, but the general effect is wonderful.

The guides sometimes use the room to give you a very long and elaborate history lesson, darting from one figure to another, so the advice is to study hard the section on the Valois and early Bourbons in the History chapter at the beginning of this book if you want to keep pace with their commentary. As well as the French kings, English monarchs are well represented here, from Edward III – claimant against Philippe VI to the French throne and thus instigator of the Hundred Years' War – to Charles I, via the easily recognizable likes of Henry VII (1457–1509), first Tudor king; Henry VIII, who died the same year as the equally monumental François I; and Elizabeth I, as severe as ever. Among infamous enemies of the English, you can observe the French heroes of the Hundred Years' War, the pale, evil-looking Du Guesclin and the armour-clad Joan of Arc. From the English ranks come the Black Prince and Talbot, the man who lost the final battle of the Hundred Years' War, at Castillon in southwest France in 1453.

You can also see many of the main figures in France's Wars of Religion of the second half of the 16th century. The Loire was one of the main battlegrounds and Catherine de' Medici one of the major royal figures caught in the bloody chaos, here looking innocent and nun-like. Twenty-one women feature in all, including Catherine's rival in her husband's affections, Diane de Poitiers. Americans should have little difficulty spotting Amerigo Vespucci, the Florentine explorer who gave his name to their continent – he features in the Louis XII section.

Underneath the triple ranks of portraits, allegories and arms symbolize the mottoes of the French kings. The most relevant to English visitors is that under Louis XIII, showing a snail pierced by an arrow with the inscription 'Esto domi' ('Stay at home'), a dig at the English navy, whose fleet was too slow to come to the rescue of Huguenot La Rochelle. Not only are the room's walls plastered with hundreds of figures and paintings, the floor is covered with an army on the march, painted on Delft tiles from the 17th century, 17 different military corps depicted.

Carefully avoiding stepping on the precious soldiers, you're taken through the library, or south gallery, whose beams are embellished with the painted busts of Pléiade poets. Among the notable objects here are a late 16th-century Brussels tapestry showing the marriage of King Henri IV, in the guise of Solomon and his 1,000 wives; 17th-century Spanish chairs inlaid with ivory depicting hunting scenes; and a grotesquely decorated Lyon Mannerist cupboard, whose doors are opened by placing a finger up a lady's skirts.

The **Cabinet des Grelots** next to the south gallery is another splendidly decorated room, this time small in scale. It dates back to the days of Du Thier, who commissioned the finely carved gilt oak panelling from the Italian Scibec de Carpi. The three golden *grelots*, or bells, featured on the Du Thier family arms are here repeated in much greater number. Along with the sumptuous details of the carving and the glowing colours of the wood, painted panels depict the artistic and scientific pursuits of the day, including of course the art of war. The tour finishes by bringing you down to earth with a copious display of copper kitchenware in the servants' quarters.

Beauregard's grounds were given added appeal by the creation of a sunken garden in the mid-1990s, the **Jardin des Portraits**. The forms here play on the famous portrait gallery within, the garden divided up into 12 boxes containing a wealth of plants.

Château de Cheverny

*Open July–Aug 9.15–6.45, April–June and Sept 9.15–6.15, rest of year
9.30–12 and 2.15–5; self-guided tour.*

The Château de Cheverny is the most refined Loire château of the lot, a lesson in French architectural and aristocratic good taste. Ironically, this splendid, pristine-looking 17th-century masterpiece was built following a terrible family scandal (*see* below).

The château (which lies just south of Cour-Cheverny, close to the D765 road from Blois to Romorantin) was commissioned by Henri Hurault, count of Cheverny, and his second wife, Marguerite Gaillard. Henri was descended from an illustrious line of aristocrats close to the French Renaissance kings of France. His ancestor Raoul Hurault, a minister of finances under François I, had in fact had an earlier castle built on the site at Cheverny at the start of the 16th century, but this was entirely wiped away by his descendant. As for Henri's father, Philippe Hurault, he served as chancellor to both kings Henri III and Henri IV. Henri Hurault himself was close to the dapper Vert Galant (Henri IV).

It's sometimes said that Henri Hurault destroyed the family home that already stood at Cheverny to try and forget the past. But it was over 20 years after the infamous events that work began on the new Cheverny. The main building work lasted from 1626 to 1648, the year in which Henri Hurault died. His best-loved daughter Elisabeth, Marquise de Montglas, oversaw completion of the château.

The main architect associated with the château is Boyer, or Jacques Bougier, of Blois, who worked with the likes of the eminent Salomon de Brosse, best-known for his royal Palais du Luxembourg in Paris. Although the Château de Cheverny was built on a relatively small scale, the architecture was at the forefront of its time, adopting the

Cuckoldry at Cheverny

King Henri IV was inadvertently the cause of the scandal which shook the Hurault household to its core. The story goes that one day when Henri Hurault was at court, he spotted the king in a mirror poking fun at him, making the sign of the cuckold behind his back. The proud and fiery Hurault left that instant, riding through the night to reach Cheverny, arriving at five in the morning, his anger at boiling point. The Burgundian gentleman in bed with his wife Françoise Chabot was quick enough to jump from a window into the garden, but broke his leg and lay there injured; Henri Hurault put a definitive end to his amorous misconduct by running him through on the spot. Having summoned the local priest, Henri then offered his wife the choice of ending her days by poison or the sword. Parish records note that she died 'poisoned, as the common rumour has it, for her adultery'. She was apparently carrying a baby boy in her womb. Such was the hierarchy of justice in that period that Henri Hurault was simply exiled to Cheverny for a time by way of punishment. In 1604 he was remarried to Marguerite Gaillard, and the two had many children together, as well as creating the Château de Cheverny.

so-called Louis XIII style – classicism mixed with extravagant roofing and decoration that became typical of Ancien Régime France. Boyer died in 1632. It isn't certain who continued his work, but it's thought that his successor stuck to his plans. The exterior has scarcely been altered since it was built. Some of the interiors, notably on the ground floor, were modified in the 19th century. A descendant of the Huraults, the count of Vibraye, still owns and lives in the château.

A generous smooth lawn leads to the Château de Cheverny's immaculate front. The main façade looks so white and clean, and the stones are laid in such a seamless manner, that many have mistaken the effect for whitewashed clapboard. You might feel it a weakness that such an expensive cut-stone façade should resemble a less noble material. Some critics have complained, too, that the central section and the two adjoining pavilions stand uncomfortably squashed in by the two great curving-roofed end pavilions, with their mansard windows like bulging frogs' eyes. However that may be, this is a great piece of Loire architecture. The building is slimly elegant, the whole château only one room thick, light pouring through it. The ensemble is also pleasingly symmetrical. On the main façade, a pediment tops each window like a stylized eyebrow. Along the first floor, a series of busts of 12 Roman emperors runs across the whole façade.

Cheverny isn't a vast château, so there aren't endless rooms to see inside. It is very sumptuously furnished, though. Cheverny is the Loire château which probably boasts the finest collection of paintings and tapestries. In this respect it resembles a fine arts gallery, but it is also still clearly lived in and very lovingly maintained. On the self-guided tour round the château you visit much of the ground and first floors.

Among the outstanding features of the interiors are the allegorical classical wall paintings by Jean Mosnier. This accomplished artist haled from Blois, like the architect Boyer, and was also involved in preparing the Palais du Luxembourg in Paris. Much of the decorative ensemble he and his team executed at Cheverny has been well preserved. For example, in the dining room on the ground floor, Mosnier panels illustrate the tales of Don Quichotte (Quixote). This Spanish comic masterpiece was the height of fashion at the time. The embossed Cordoba leather covering the walls of the dining room is stamped with the Hurault family coat of arms.

Still on the ground floor, the western rooms contain some splendid works of art. In the antechamber hangs an exquisite 17th-century Flemish tapestry showing a fishing scene after Téniers. Alongside royal portraits, several fine depictions of Hurault family members are displayed in the great drawing room, including those of Philippe Hurault and his wife Anne de Thou, as well as a rendering of a later countess of Cheverny by Mignard. But these works are eclipsed by a portrait of Cosimo de' Medici attributed to Titian and one of Jeanne d'Aragon by the school of Raphael.

Don't miss the splendid portraits in the more cramped vestibule. Three by the most renowned French court painter of the mid-16th century, François Clouet, represent Philippe Hurault and his wife again, while the last represents Jacques Hurault, his brother. The château also displays four portraits by that great portraitist under Louis XIV, Hyacinthe Rigaud. American visitors may also spot the small equestrian statue of George Washington by Baron Carlo Marochetti; the château also owns a document signed by the great president witnessing the membership of Charles de Loménie de Brienne, an ancestor of the Vibrayes, in the Order of Cincinnati, founded to celebrate the role of high-ranking French officers who played a part in the American War of Independence. On the ground floor you may notice one portrait of the infamous Henri Hurault, although to date he hasn't been given much prominence.

Take the steps up the main staircase slowly to admire the finesse of the carved work around it, seemingly executed by a mysterious F.L., who signed his oeuvre in 1634. Then enter the substantial **Salle des Gardes**, the largest room in the château, and your eyes will be drawn to the extravagant fireplace flanked by gilded wooden statues, the caryatids surmounted by figures of Mars and Venus. The central painting, by Mosnier, represents the death of Adonis. Old armour hangs on the walls around the room, but below, along the wainscoting, the anachronistic images depict flowers, with pithy Latin sayings associated with them: 'Self-love was my downfall', reads that by the narcissus. Mosnier supposedly sent his assistants into the surrounding countryside to pick many of the plants from which the illustrations were painted.

Beyond the Salle des Gardes lies the most sumptuous room of all, the **Chambre du Roi**, made in preparation for a royal visit, although none was ever received at Cheverny. Here several decorative features vie for your attention: the dazzling main wall paintings by Mosnier illustrate the classical legend of Perseus and Andromeda, the smaller ones depict episodes from the tale of Chariclea and Theogenes (made popular by a period bestseller), while the amazingly fine tapestries from Paris show the labours of Ulysses after cartoons by Simon Vouet. On the bed, the most exquisite Persian silk cover is embroidered with flowers and figures. After such a lavish artistic feast, the simple and charming private rooms you can also visit on the first floor make for a pleasant, intimate few minutes of relaxation to help you digest what you've seen.

Cheverny's park is best known for it pack of **hunting dogs**, which are to be seen chasing across the lawn in most clichés of the place. Ordinarily you can go and watch the doleful mutts lazing around in their cages. They're a mix of English fox hounds and French Poitevins dogs, and are tattooed with the V for Vibraye. Between September and March they go out hunting twice a week. Otherwise, you can watch them being fed in the afternoon, their trainers keeping the scrum under control. Near to the dog pens, a room is dedicated to the hunt, hung with hundreds of trophies and given colour by a large stained-glass window. Between April and November you can also hire little **buggies** and **boats** to go round enjoying the extensive grounds and their shade.

On an amusing last note, readers of Tintin may feel that the Château de Cheverny looks rather familiar – that's because it served as Hergé's model for Captain Haddock's home!

There's an international 18-hole **golf course** (*t 02 54 79 24 70*) hidden away down a track just south of the château. The course, set around a typical Solognot lake, takes you round delightful countryside. You can eat at the clubhouse.

The Wines of Cheverny

A friend whom I introduced to a red Cheverny wine looked up with surprise from her wine glass and said: 'It tastes like the dust from moths' wings.' Somewhat alarmed by the comparison, I asked whether it was unpleasant. 'No, but distinctly unusual.' I'd agree with that. I've noted on the occasions that I've drunk Cheverny red that I've found it 'musty'. Is this, I wonder, roughly the taste that one wine critic famously described as 'wet foxes in the undergrowth'? You can imagine foxes running around the rather flat lands of the Cheverny *appellation*, on the edge of the Sologne forest; this wine area is even known unofficially as the Sologne *viticole*. The red Cheverny wines aren't really powerful enough to go with game and strong sauces, however. They're very pale in colour, distinctly light and quite transparent, with orange tints, but in the best ones the fruit flavours, even dried fruit tastes, emerge young. Gamay combines with Pinot Noir to make these reds, just a touch of Cabernet Franc or Côt sometimes added. The major white grape variety in the area is Sauvignon, which can be pleasantly aromatic, complemented by Chardonnay and sometimes also a hint of Menu Pineau. This white wine could make a crisp accompaniment to the ubiquitous *sandre*.

The Cour-Cheverny wine area is a curiosity, awarded AOC status in the 1990s. The white wine which can carry the AOC label is made from Romorantin, a rarity of a grape variety if ever there was one. Its origins aren't local, but they are royal. François I, whose family held the castle of Romorantin in the Sologne, had 80,000 vines brought over from Burgundy to plant in this region in 1519. The special Burgundian variety favoured by the king's household adapted well to the move, while in time it dwindled in importance in its homeland. The grape variety then took on the name of the place to which it had been transplanted. The Romorantin wines, dry whites, tend to have a lively start and a long, lingering flavour.

The name to cite for a visit is Christian Tessier at the **Domaine de la Desoucherie** (*t 02 54 79 90 08*), between Cour-Cheverny and Fontaine-en-Sologne. Not only does he produce the range of local still wines, he has also made a sparkling white, a *crémant* which won a medal at one of the prestigious annual wine competitions in Paris.

Troussay

Open June–Aug 10–7, Sept 10–1 and 2–6, French school holidays at Easter and All Saints' 10.30–12.30 and 2–6, other periods between Easter and All Saints' Sun and public hols 10.30–12.30 and 2–6.

Troussay, just a few kilometres west of Cheverny, is in fact a *gentilhommière*, or manor house, rather than a château. It provides a good example of the architecture and living arrangements of the minor nobility of its period. But its comparatively modest frame contains some rather grand pieces of decorative art taken from other, larger Loire châteaux and houses that fell into disrepair or disappeared off the map.

The pretty house was built in the 15th century. Alterations were made to it in the 16th. The fine quality of the decorative display within is due to historian Louis de

Saussaye, who inherited the property in 1828 and called upon Jules de la Morandière to help restore it. The idea was not just to help the house but also to find a home for some of the works of art from châteaux in danger of falling into ruin. Several of the most important pieces came from the very sorry remnants of the Château de Bury, one of the first great Renaissance châteaux in France, situated west of Blois. The carved wooden door to Bury's oratory is the finest piece on display, but there are also excellent fragments of stone carving from there. The porcupine, on the back of the house, symbol of Louis XII, was taken off the Hôtel Hurault de Cheverny in Blois. The stained-glass windows, from the early 16th century, come from the so-called Hôtel Sardini in Blois. The Louis XII tiling in the manor is one remaining original interior feature, though.

The other collection at Troussay is connected with the peasant Sologne rather than courtly Blois; everyday household and farming implements are displayed in the outbuildings, and there is a small exhibition on traditions of witchcraft in the region.

Château de Fougères-sur-Bièvre

Open April–Sept 9.30–12 and 2–6, Oct–Mar 10–12 and 2–4.30; visits can be made with or without a guide.

The Château de Fougères-sur-Bièvre is a bit of an odd man out in this area. Most of the other châteaux open to the public around these parts are characterized by open-ness, generally constructed of sparkling clean-cut blocks of white stone, the towers roomy and decorative. Fougères looks defensively medieval with its massed turrets, its small irregular stones and its inner courtyard paranoiacally enclosed on all four sides. Despite this stern exterior, the château you see was built in the last quarter of the 15th century.

Fougères was constructed on the foundations of an earlier fort for Pierre Refuge, a financier who built his fortune serving the royal family and who obtained permission from King Louis XI, a few years before the latter died, to re-establish Fougères 'as a *château-fort*'. Some additions were perhaps made to the castle for his grandson Jean de Villebresme, who inherited the place in 1497.

Through the imposing north wing of the château you come into the wonderfully atmospheric courtyard. Here a mixture of different styles – Gothic, Renaissance and plain idiosyncratic – is much more obvious. Fougères hasn't survived intact down the centuries, however. The moat was filled in and for most of the 19th century a spinning mill was installed here, the course of the Bièvre stream even being diverted under the château to help in the work. In the 20th century the place became a poor house for a while before the state acquired it in 1932. During the Second World War, Fougères served as a depot for some of the country's great art collections.

Through time, therefore, the interiors have been stripped and converted. You can see this immediately on entering the chapel, where nothing much remains apart from a couple of *culs-de-lampe* and a mill wheel, which was placed in here in the château's spinning days. Many of the rooms stand empty, with just their volumes to please the visitor. Climb right to the top; the most enjoyable part of the tour is under the roofs, with fine rafters to admire and interesting displays on the various building trades involved in château construction changing annually.

Blois

12

Blois

250 metres
250 yards

N

Musée de l'Objet

RUE FRANCLADE

RUE DU BOURG NEUF

RUE C. ROBIN

RUE BRETONNERIE

RAMP CHAMBOURDIN

RUE GALLOIS

RUE DES MINIMES

RUE J. MOULIN

RUE DU P. MONSABRE

RUE CHEMONTON

RUE PORTE CHARTRAINE

Préfecture

POL

RUE D'ANGLETERRE

PLACE DE LA RÉPUBLIQUE

Halle aux Grains

University

RUE DU PRECHE

RUE DES TOURNEAUX

MAIL CLOUSEAU

Palais de Justice

RUE TROUESSARD

RUE DU PERE BROTTIER

PLACE FLANDRES DUNKERQUE 1940

RUE DES

ROUILLIS

PLACE J. JAURES

AV MAUNOURY

RUE DU 18 JUIN 1940

RUE DES CORDELIERS

PLACE GUERY

RUE A. FRANCE

Jardin de l'Evêché

Hôtel d'Alluye

RUE ST-HONORE

BEAUVOIR RUE DU PALAIS

Maison des Acrobates

Cathédrale St-Louis

PLACE ST-LOUIS

RUE DU PORTE CLOS

IMPASSE ST-JEAN

Hôtel de Ville

St-Vincent-de-Paul

RUE DENIS PAPIN

RUE P. COTE

RUE DU COMMERCE

RUE PARDESSUS

RUE BASSE

RUE R. PENIL

RUE HAUTE

RUE DES CLEFS

RUE P. DE BLOIS

RUE DES JUIFS

RUE DES SAPEGAULTS

RUE DU PUITS CHATEL

RUE VAUVERT

RUE FOULERIE

RUE A. SAVEUSE

Pavillon Anne de Bretagne

PLACE V. HUGO

AV J. LAIGRET

To Train Station

RUE DES

RUE DENIS PAPIN

RUE D. POIDS DU ROI

PLACE AVE MARIA

RUE H. DRUSSY

RUE DU MAL DE LATTRE DE TASSIGNY

Maison de la Magie

RUE DE LA VOUTE DU CHATEAU

PLACE DU CHATEAU

Château de Blois

BLD DES F. DU CHATEAU

RAMPE F. DU CHATEAU

PLACE E. GAUDET

RUE ST-MARTIN

RUE DES VIOLETTES

RUE ST-LUBIN

RUE DES ORFEVRES

RUE DU COMMERCE

PLACE LOUIS XII

RUE E COLAURENS

PLACE DE LA RESISTANCE

RUE J. D'ARC

PONT J. GABRIEL

RUE ANNE DE BRETAGNE

RUE DES JACOBINS

RUE ROBERT HOUDIN

SQUARE V. DE LA VAISSIERE

QUAI DE LA SAUSSAYE

St-Laumer

St-Nicolas

RUE DES 3 MARCHANDS

QUAI DE L'ABBE GREGOIRE

Loire

AV WILSON

PLACE DE LA GREVE

King Charles VIII bumped his head on a door at the Château d'Amboise, down the Loire, and died. So it was that in 1498 Charles' cousin, Louis, duke of Orléans but based at Blois, became the new king, Louis XII, and his town the centre of French politics – a big role for what now seems like a modest provincial town. Blois had been a place of great importance through medieval times, though. In the early Middle Ages, the powerful counts of Blois had their headquarters for their substantial territories here and built a large castle. Louis XII commissioned a new one to his tastes, to which his successor, François I, added a grandiose new Renaissance wing. After François, in the Wars of Religion, the château became the setting for one of the most memorable bloody murders in French history, instigated by King Henri III. In fact, several important ghosts of France's past wander round the Château de Blois.

For years, the château was the only thing that was easy to visit in town, and contained most of Blois' museums, though its layers of grime were hardly appealing. A magic wand was waved over the place in the 1980s. Blois' fairy godmother took the flamboyant form of the high-profile mayor, Jack Lang, for many years France's trendy graffiti-art-friendly socialist Minister for Culture, now Minister for Education. The château's contrasting façades were scrubbed clean and the interiors completely reorganized to house a whole array of new museums. As a mark of gratitude, a likeness of Jack Lang replaced one of the medieval carvings on the castle. Still more surprisingly, a museum of magic suddenly appeared on the château's esplanade in the late 1990s, although its start has been somewhat shaky. Another startling recent apparition in Blois is the Musée de l'Objet, dedicated to the object as work of art.

A handful of the town's churches made it through the Revolution, most noticeably that dedicated to St Nicholas, which punctures the Blois skyline with its very sharp slate towers. The cathedral has recently received controversial modern glass. In between these two main churches, up the steep Loire-side slopes of the town, the sumptuous houses of many royal courtiers have survived the centuries, giving an indication of just how grand Blois was at its height.

History

The name of Blois apparently stems from the Celtic word for a wolf, *bleiz*, conjuring up the picture of a thickly forested area around the early settlement. Indeed, forests still surround Blois to this day. The emergence of a powerful dynasty of counts of Blois dates back to the time of the Norman invasions of the mid-9th century. A century later, it was the Thibaud family, first viscounts of Tours, then of Blois, which asserted its supremacy. This became an extremely important aristocratic dynasty in the Loire region and in France in the early Middle Ages. At the start of the 11th century the line was pitted against the ambitious Foulques Nerra of Anjou, who pushed east and managed to take much of the Blois counts' territories in Touraine. Count Eudes II of Blois made up for these losses by inheriting the region of Champagne, east of Paris. With their two centres of power, the subsequent counts were often absent from Blois, but a *prévôt* was left in charge of the administration of the town. Trade prospered and the main Blois fair at the end of August became one of the most important on the Loire, its date marking the time when vassals had to pay their dues to their lords.

By the time of Thibaud IV, in the first half of the 12th century, the counts of Blois were very much figures to be reckoned with – Thibaud IV's territories effectively surrounded the southern boundaries of the very small holdings of the kings of France in the Ile de France. Thibaud IV's brother, Etienne de Blois, like him a grandson of William the Conqueror, became King Stephen of England (unfortunately, he proved a disastrous monarch). The power games between the great families of the Loire continued across the Channel; Henri Plantagenêt of Anjou made Stephen declare him as his rightful successor to the English throne, and as a result became as King Henry II. Meanwhile, Adèle de Champagne, daughter of Thibaud IV, was the woman who married the French King Louis VII after he had divorced Eleanor of Aquitaine.

Getting There and Around

By Train

Trains from Paris to Blois leave the capital from Gare d'Austerlitz. Blois SNCF train station (t 02 47 20 50 50) is fairly central, to the west of the château. It has regular connections along the Loire to Orléans, and to Tours and towns further west.

By Bus

For information and tickets for local buses, the Point Bus office is at 2 Place Victor Hugo (t 02 54 78 15 66).

By Car

The A10 Paris–Bordeaux motorway passes Blois. The main non-toll road route from Paris to Blois is the N20 to Orléans, then the N152 along the northern bank of the Loire.

By Taxi

Taxi-Radio Blois, Place de la Gare (t 02 54 78 32 80); they will also do private excursions. Other taxis are also available from the station (t 02 54 78 07 65).

Car and Bicycle Hire

Car hire companies include:
ADA Location de Véhicules, 108 Av Maunoury, t 02 54 74 02 47, f 02 54 74 02 97.
Avis, 6 Rue Jean Moulin, t 02 54 74 48 15, f 02 54 78 66 61.
Europcar, 105 Av de Vendôme, t 02 54 43 22 20, f 02 54 43 23 24.
Ligérienne de Location, Route Nationale, La Chaussée St-Victor, t 02 54 78 25 45, f 02 54 78 86 62.
For bicycles try:
Bucquet S.A., 33 Av Wilson, t 02 54 78 12 94.
Cycles Leblond, 44 Levée des Tuileries, t 02 54 74 30 13.

Carriages and Helicopters

Old Blois is small enough to explore by foot, but it is full of steep and awkward stairways. To take the pressure off your feet, you could always take a ride in a **horse and carriage** from the château entrance (*every day July and Aug, weekends and public hols May, June and September*). For those of you on a *châtelain's* budget, contact the tourist office for informa-tion on **helicopter rides** above the châteaux (*June–Sept*).

Tourist Information

Tourist office: Pavillon Anne de Bretagne, 3 Av Jean Laigret, 41000 Blois, t 02 54 90 41 41, f 02 54 90 41 49, *resa@loiredeschateaux.com*.
Maison du Loir-et-Cher: Bureau d'Information Touristique Départementale, 5 Rue de la Voûte du Château, B.P.149, 41005 Blois Cedex, t 02 54 78 55 50, f 02 54 74 81 71, *tourisme.41@wanadoo.fr*, *www.chambordcountry.com*. Provides information on the whole *département* of Loir-et-Cher.

Market Days

Rue Pierre et Marie Curie: Wednesday morning.
Parc des Expositions, south of the river: Wednesday afternoon.
Rue Chateaubriand: Thursday morning.
Place Louis XII: Monday, Thursday and Saturday mornings.
Quartier Croix Chevallier: Saturday morning.
Mail and **rue Jeanne d'Arc**: Flea market; every second Sunday in the month.
Marché de Chez Nous, Place du Château: Market for regional specialities, local farmers and craftsmen coming into town to sell their wares; Thursday afternoon (*July and Aug*).

Festivals

The town shows its support for French-Canadian culture with an annual **Festival du Cinéma Québecois** in mid-October.

On a funnier note, the end of November sees the **Festival de la Bande Dessinée** (cartoons) at the Halle aux Grains and Bibliothèque Abbé Grégoire.

Le Festival Paroles Plurielles at the end of March revolves around storytelling. Blois holds a **carnival** every year one Sunday in mid-May.

Sports and Activities

If you're tempted to go **canoeing** on the Loire here, call t 02 54 78 65 90 or t 02 54 78 67 48.

At the Lac de Loire (very close to the river off the D951 south bank road towards Orléans), you can try out a whole range of **watersports**, from water-skiing to pedaloes (t 02 54 78 65 90).

ULMs are **microlights**, and if you feel that wafting above the châteaux of the Blésois might be the best way to tempt you into trying such means of flight, the Lac de Loire base (t 02 54 20 68 51) is the place to ask.

Where to Stay

Blois ✉ 41000
The choice of characterful places to stay in Blois is a bit disappointing; you may find more exciting places outside the city.

Expensive–Moderate
***Mercure**, 28 Quai St-Jean, t 02 54 56 66 66, f 02 54 56 67 00. A big chain hotel, but here done with some style and located close to the château. Some parts have views onto the Loire. A swimming pool and *espace fitness* count among the extras. The restaurant is well regarded (*menus €15–35*).
***Holiday Inn Garden Court**, 26 Av Maunoury, t 02 54 55 44 88, f 02 54 74 57 97, *holibloi@imaginet.fr*. Another high-standard chain hotel with a solid reputation, even if it looks like a shopping mall from the outside. Inside, it offers such little luxuries as a pool and sauna, along with well-equipped rooms. Reasonable food served (*menus 14.5–23*).
***Le Médicis**, 2 Allée François Ier/Route d'Angers, t 02 54 43 94 04, f 02 54 42 04 05, *medicis@chateauxhotels.com*. It overlooks an uninspiring roundabout west of the train station, but has some quite elaborately decorated rooms and some nice touches. High-quality traditional French cuisine is served in the smart dining room (*menus €18–68.5*). *Closed Jan*.

Inexpensive
Le Jardin Secret Maison d'Hôtes, 2 Place du Château, t 02 54 56 06 82. Michelle and Michel are the charming hosts at this house set in a splendid location on the esplanade beside Blois castle. The two interconnecting B&B rooms under the eaves have a comfortable, family feel. One has the advantage of a view down onto the Loire. For details on eating here, *see below*.
****Hôtel Anne de Bretagne**, 31 Av Jean Laigret, t 02 54 78 05 38, f 02 54 74 37 79. Only a few hundred metres from the château, with pleasant enough though somewhat noisy rooms. *Closed late Feb–late Mar*.
****Le Savoie**, 6–8 Rue Ducoux, t 02 54 74 32 21, f 02 54 74 29 58. An unpretentious family-run hotel. *Closed second half of Dec*.
****Le Monarque**, 61 Rue Porte Chartraine, t 02 54 78 02 35, f 02 54 74 82 76. Awkwardly situated on a busy hillside junction; the rooms and restaurant are rather dull, but the place has some good-value rooms and food (*menus €1.5–27.5*). *Closed mid-Dec–mid-Feb*.

Cheap
*Hôtel du Bellay**, 12 Rue des Minimes, t 02 54 78 23 62, f 02 54 78 52 04. A pleasant little surprise, a miniature 18th-century cottage with bright rooms that are a complete bargain.
A la Ville de Tours, 2 Place de la Grève, t 02 54 78 07 86, f 02 54 56 87 33. Another surprisingly characterful cheap address, close to the river and the centre of town, with the quirky kind of bathroom facilities you should expect in French hotels of this category.
Auberge de Jeunesse, t 02 54 78 27 21 (*open March–mid-Nov*). A youth hostel 4km from Blois at Les Grouëts, in the direction of Tours.

Eating Out

The choice of appealing restaurants in town is much more extensive than that of hotels, but beware: some of the best are curiously closed at the height of the season, in mid-August.

Expensive–Moderate
L'Orangerie du Château, 1 Av Jean Laigret, t 02 54 78 05 36. Formerly in the castle grounds, now set back from a main road by a

spacious courtyard, this restaurant in a swish building offers an elegant setting for a meal, facing the façade of the château (*menus €21–53*). *Closed Mon exc public hols and Sun pm out of season.*

Au Rendez-Vous des Pêcheurs, 27 Rue du Foix, **t** 02 54 74 67 48. The restaurant with the best reputation in town. Set in a small town house close to the river, it is crammed, even slightly cramped, with good things. The food is extremely refined and rich without being heavy, the speciality being river fish and seafood (*menu €23*). *Closed Sun, Mon lunch, public hols, Feb school hols and, please note, 1–22 Aug.*

L'Espérance, 189 Quai Ulysse Besnard (west along the river out of town), **t** 02 54 78 09 01. Although it's fronted by a terribly quirky and messy façade, inside you can appreciate much more harmonious, inventive cuisine in a bright, raised dining room overlooking the Loire, perhaps contemplating herons and other river birds as you eat. Fish is the appropriate savoury speciality, but the chef also pays tribute to Poulain's legacy with delicious chocolate puddings (*menus €19–37*). *Closed Sun evening and Mon, Feb school hols and 2nd fortnight in Aug.*

Moderate–Cheap

Le Jardin Secret, 2 Place du Château, **t** 02 54 56 06 82. There's more of an atmosphere of an informal house party than of a restaurant here. The dining room, decorated with old-fashioned good taste, has an intimate feel and just a few tables, while on sunny days a few more are set out outside. You don't get a choice of menus; Michel just prepares delicious, beautifully seasoned home-made terrines, dishes and desserts. The pear and chocolate pudding he offered us melted divinely in the mouth. You must book (*table d'hôte €18*). *Open for lunch Tues–Fri, for dinner Thurs and Fri.*

Le Bistrot du Cuisinier, 20 Quai Villebois-Mareuil, **t** 02 54 78 06 70. It's worth finding a little extra energy to cross Blois' old bridge to enjoy the appealing combination of good food and good setting here. A dash of alcohol enlivens many of the sauces, while the historic town across the river forms the best of backdrops (*menus €16–22*).

Le Castelet, 40 Rue St-Lubin, **t** 02 54 74 66 09. With its beamed dining room, this boasts a wide choice of menus, including local specialities in Les Gourmandises du Val de Loire, and even that French provincial rarity, a *formule végétarienne* (*menus €14.5–30.5*).

L'Embarcadère, 18 Quai Ulysse Besnard, **t** 02 54 78 31 41. A lively, popular address right by the river, west along the nothern quays, serving simple food such as mussels and chips.

Entertainment and Nightlife

Son-et-Lumière

Blois' main summer night-time attraction is the son-et-lumière at the château, called '*Ainsi Blois vous est conté*' – mug up on your history of Blois and the Loire to understand what's going on. For information and bookings, call **t** 02 54 78 72 76. The show takes place virtually every night from June to the 1st week in Sept, and on a couple of weekends in May, with the rare English night.

Film, Theatre, etc.

Blois' main **theatre, dance and music** activities take place at the Scène Nationale, La Halle aux Grains, **t** 02 54 56 19 79.

You can choose from three **cinemas** in town: **Les Lobis**, 12 Av Maunoury. **Les Trois Clefs**, 12 Rue des Juifs. **Les Césars**, 23 Av Wilson.

Bars and Clubs

Les Boucaniers, Quai St-Jean, **t** 02 54 55 07 84. Fun place, set on a barge on the Loire.
Pub Mancini, 1 Rue du Puits Chatel, **t** 02 54 55 07 84. For late-night owls (*open to 4am daily*).

A couple of others you might try are:
The River Side, 3 Rue Henri Drussy, **t** 02 54 78 33 79.
The Loch Ness, 7 Rue des Juifs, **t** 02 54 56 08 67. Discos include:
L'Avenue Foch, 3 Rue du Puits Chatel, **t** 02 54 90 00 00.
Z64, 4 Rue du Maréchal de Lattre de Tassigny, **t** 02 54 74 27 76.

In the second half of the 12th century, Blois' Jewish community was subjected to a terrifying persecution, apparently due to the jealousy of a countess who suspected her husband of having an affair with a Jewish woman. The Jews were accused of ritually murdering children, and some 30 were burnt in Blois on trumped-up charges in 1171.

The Thibaud line came to an end in 1235 and the Châtillons took over. This family retained power until 1392, when, strapped for cash, the last in the line sold the Blésois to Louis d'Orléans, brother of King Charles VI. It was from this time, and for several centuries to come, that the town of Blois confusingly served as the seat of power for a string of men of royal blood carrying the title of Duc d'Orléans. This royal connection caused Blois to grow rapidly in political importance in the 15th century. Louis d'Orléans was infamously assassinated in 1407 by the men of Jean sans Peur (the Fearless), duke of Burgundy. Louis' wife, Valentine Visconti, from Milan, took refuge in Blois. Her Italian blood would later prove crucial to French royal claims across the Alps, leading to the Italian campaigns which brought Renaissance ideas across to France.

One of Valentine's sons was the famous Duke Charles d'Orléans, captured by the English at Agincourt in 1415 and held prisoner in England until 1440. Joan of Arc showed a particular attachment to the cause of this cultivated, chivalric poet-knight, and stopped at Blois on the way to liberate Orléans in 1429. On his release from prison, Charles d'Orléans settled back in Blois, and made changes to the medieval château. The court he gathered round him brought both prosperity and culture to the town. Charles became a patron of the arts and was greatly acclaimed as a versifier himself. The merchants of Blois catered to aristocratic tastes, many becoming wealthy from trade on the Loire and some changing career to serve Charles as financiers and advisers. As early as 1462, Florentine ambassadors visiting the Blois court praised the beauty of the town, its bridge and its fountains. When Duke Charles was nearly 70, his wife bore him a son, named Louis, like his kingly cousin Louis XI.

Louis XI was succeeded by his son Charles VIII. The male heirs produced by Charles and his wife, Anne de Bretagne, didn't survive early childhood, and when Charles met his fate with a door at Amboise, the young Louis d'Orléans became the new king of France as Charles VIII's closest cousin. The new king immediately divorced his crippled wife on the grounds that the marriage hadn't been consummated and married Charles VIII's widow. Blois became the centre of the royal court in place of Amboise and Louis XII, with Anne, decided to make the Château de Blois grander. The builders who had been employed at the Château d'Amboise were transferred here. The glorious days of royal Blois followed, wealth pouring into the town. Many of the main acts of Louis XII's reign were signed at the château.

Louis wished to claim his Italian inheritance, through his grandmother Valentine Visconti, in the region of Milan, and followed the example of the forays Charles VIII had led into Italy in the late 1490s. Charles had brought back Italian booty and artists from his campaigns, but Italian influences were only just beginning to show at the end of his reign. Under Louis XII and at Blois they were to affect ways of living and building more profoundly, although late Gothic French style and new Italianate forms coexisted for a period. The powerful men under Louis XII would commission new town houses and new country seats near Blois. Florimond Robertet, one of the king's closest advisers, for example ordered both the Hôtel Alluye in Renaissance style in Blois itself and the sumptuous Château de Bury (sadly vanished) a little west of the city. The population of Blois grew by a massive 20,000 during Louis XII's reign. Purveyors of luxury goods thrived in the town, notably goldsmiths and clockmakers.

Louis XII and Anne had a daughter, Claude, who married François d'Angoulême. As Anne there was no male heir, on Louis XII's death in 1515 François d'Angoulême became king of France, the outsized François I. François had been brought up largely at the Château d'Amboise, and on his enthronement he and the queen decided to share their time between the respective châteaux of their youths. At Blois, they commissioned one of the most famous examples of early French Renaissance building, although the most monumental of François's self-glorifying building projects, the Château de Chambord, was only a few miles east across the Loire from the city (see pp.165–8).

Through the first half of the 16th century, many influential figures in Blois were won over to the Protestant, Church-reforming cause. When François I's son, King Henri II, began to persecute Protestants, or Huguenots, they began to leave for Geneva and other more tolerant havens. Crisis came with the rule of Henri's sons François II, Charles IX and Henri III, and the outbreak of the vicious Wars of Religion. A terrible massacre of Protestants in 1562 led to the first uprising and Blois was among the towns taken by the Huguenots for several weeks. Catherine de' Medici, Henri II's widow and the hugely influential Queen Mother, came to the town in 1563 to nego-tiate with the Protestant leaders, Condé (held prisoner for a time at the château) and Coligny. But dialogue couldn't stop the second outbreak of war. This time, in 1568, Blois was ravaged. The town was the setting for talks gathering together the Estates General at the end of 1576.

In the meantime, the extremist Catholic Ligue was asserting its power in many parts of the country, especially in Paris, and its leaders, the Duc and Cardinal de Guise, had amassed enough power to threaten royal authority. Henri III's desperate action to remedy this situation would bring notoriety to the name of Blois in French history. Forced to flee Paris in the face of his formidable adversaries, Henri III repaired to the castle of Blois in 1588. His bloody solution to the problem was to call a meeting of the Estates General to which his opponents were invited; he then proceeded to have the De Guises assassinated in the castle. While Paris, in the grip of the Ligue, went wild on hearing news of the king's actions, Blois remained on his side. It would also support his successor, France's reunifying King Henri IV.

Henri IV's trouble-making widow, Marie de' Medici, was exiled to the castle for a time by her son Louis XIII. A still more troublesome royal figure closely associated with Blois was Louis XIII's brother Gaston, a rogue of a royal. In 1626 he received the duchy of Orléans as an appanage. For some time, Louis XIII and his wife didn't produce male offspring, making Gaston the heir presumptive. He wasn't content to wait in the wings. Gaston plotted against the king and was exiled to his Blésois capital. Here the fractious man set about planning the destruction of the former royal château in favour of a grand new scheme to his greater glory, designed by the most famous of 17th-century French architects, François Mansart. One wing was built, but Gaston's funds ran out quickly, leaving much of the 16th-century royal palace standing. Gaston was an active patron of the arts in Blois, however, and also saw to the founding of new religious communities and a hospital.

Blois finally became a cathedral city under Louis XIV. But the latter's Revocation of the Edict of Nantes made life intolerable for the Protestant contingent in town. One of those who left for England was the renowned scientist, Denis Papin, after whom the main street and great stairway of Blois are now named. He has the distinction in the world of French *haute cuisine* of being considered the inventor of the pressure cooker, but his experiments with the use of steam power were much more widely influential. In the early 18th century, a couple of notable architectural features were added to the cityscape by Jacques V Gabriel, notably the archbishop's palace and the town's beautiful central bridge.

Blois has sometimes been described as 'moderately revolutionary'; some of its inhabitants were revolutionary enough to destroy virtually all the parish churches. However, a certain Abbot Henri Grégoire of Blois distinguished himself during the Revolution as a strong advocate of the rights of man; he also became member of parliament for the region and president of the National Assembly in 1791. Blois became the capital of the Loir-et-Cher, one of the new *départements* into which France was divided at the Revolution. Notable 19th-century commercial successes in town included Auguste Poulain's chocolate-making business – Poulain is a household name in France, but the company was acquired by Cadbury not long ago – while Blois potters successfully specialized in mock-Renaissance ware. Blois also developed as a centre with an increasingly large working class in an essentially rural *département*.

In the Second World War, Blois was badly bombed, both in 1940 and in 1944. Much in the historic quarter between the foot of the château and the river was destroyed. The architect Nicod was put in charge of the reconstruction of the town. Since then, Blois has developed into a city with an unusually high proportion of social housing, but culturally it has become much richer in recent decades. In the 2001 elections, Jack Lang finally lost his grip on the town when a young upstart from the centre-right, 34-year-old Nicolas Perruchot, beat him to become mayor, ousting Blois' fairy godmother.

Château de Blois

*Open July–Aug daily 9–7.30, 15 Mar–June and Sept daily 9–6, Oct–Mar daily 9–12 and 2–5. You can go round the château by yourself or on a 1-hour guided tour. The special **Visite Insolite** tour takes you on a different circuit, to the cellars and attics, July–Aug daily at 10.30 and 3, rest of year weekends only at 3. For further information, call t 02 54 90 33 32.*

The mismatched wings of the Château de Blois resemble an architectural game of Misfits, pieces of four clashing styles shoved next to each other. The effect is by no means unattractive; it's even rather amusing, and certainly extravagant. Each piece offers a sumptuous example of its period's style, and some of France's finest builders and craftsmen worked on the different wings.

The château has been meticulously restored and its museums all reorganized in a massive-scale house-cleaning operation. The place now contains: an archaeological museum; a Musée Lapidaire, or museum of old stones; the François I wing with its collections of furniture and objects; and Blois' fine arts museum, in the Louis XII wing. All these elements combine to make this one of the richest buildings in provincial France, a major royal château once properly lived in by a king and princes (unlike that other Blésois giant, Chambord), and one still left standing in far greater part than royal Amboise downriver.

The legacy of historic tales at the Château de Blois is weighty as well. All told, the place crams rather too much in. The museum of fine arts, for instance, would merit a separate visit to appreciate it fully, rather than being treated as an impossibly rich dessert at the end of a banquet. This description begins with the architecture of the château, mixed with some of the historic tales associated with the place, and ends with the museums.

The Architecture of the Château de Blois

Before plunging into a chaos of architecture and anecdote, pause for a breath of fresh air in front of the château entrance on the open esplanade, a high platform above the Loire. The main remnant of the medieval structures is the **Salle des Etats**, one end clearly visible from the esplanade, its pale stone attached to the splendid brick-patterned Louis XII wing.

Although begun in 1499, this **Louis XII wing** is essentially late Gothic in character, not Renaissance. Just the odd Italianate element managed to creep in. Work on this wing started very shortly after Louis had ascended to the throne. Symmetry was clearly not a major consideration; even the entrance gateway lies off centre. The windows, generous in size and showing the greater openness of late Gothic, were decorated with the typical exuberant motifs of that period and topped by characteristically extravagant Loire *lucarnes*, or dormers. The trellis patterning in brick, with only trimmings in stone, follows the architectural fashion of the time. But there are notable elements of French Gothic missing here; no sturdy corner towers, no battlements, no fortified gateway, no drawbridge. Colin Biart, who had worked for Charles VIII at Amboise, may have been the master builder here. The 19th-century equestrian statue in the niche represents a young king riding a splendidly dressed horse with formidable armour-plated headgear, as though ready to charge to war; and charge to Italy Louis XII would.

Once you've passed through the entrance to the castle, it comes as quite a shock to emerge in the **inner courtyard**; the Château de Blois is just such an architectural hotchpotch. On the right, the salamander-strewn François I wing, with its twisting outer staircase, vies for attention with the powerful classical bulk of Mansart's building straight ahead. Turn your back on these for a while to continue concentrating on the already familiar Louis XII wing first. On this inner side it has an arcaded gallery; peer closely at its columns and you'll notice the subtle inclusion of Italian Renaissance motifs here, such as candelabra, vases and long-beaked birds appearing in among the bravura of the late Gothic detail. Look up to see the crowned porcupines on the end tower – they're the main emblem associated with Louis XII. The notion was that porcupines could use their quills both for immediate protection from close up, and in long-range ripostes, by firing them, although in truth they're not able to do so. Among the figures carved high up, see if you can spot the one representing Jack Lang, shown baring his backside to visitors!

Before going on to contemplate the two flashiest inner wings, don't entirely ignore the most neglected side of the courtyard. Beyond the remnant of a gallery topped curiously by a Flemish gable stands the **Chapelle St-Calais**. Royal emblems decorate the rooftop, while the little spire is suitably gilded. This so-called 'chapel' is in fact only a choir end which survived from a much larger church built under Louis XII and consecrated in 1508. During Louis and Anne's reign it was apparently filled with the most magnificent paintings of the time. With Gaston d'Orléans' ambitions to totally transform the château in the 17th century, the nave was destroyed in preparation for Mansart's work to start along this side too, but the masons never got this far. The choir has lost much of its interest. The entrance façade is a 19th-century invention, while the stained-glass windows date from even later, commissioned from Max Ingrand in the 1950s. These windows do, however, usefully illustrate some of the major figures in Blois' history.

Opposite the chapel rises the **François I wing**, with its extraordinarily decorated stair tower. The François I inner façade makes a lavish display of Gothic style fusing with that of the Renaissance. It was begun in 1515, almost immediately after François had inherited the throne. Symmetry is still not especially sought. The salamanders, François I's favourite emblem, plastered over the walls may present a Gothic-looking flourish, but many other details are very much Italianate. A grid of horizontal lines, an Italian influence, breaks the traditional vertical movement of French Gothic architecture. The shape of the steep roof may remain traditionally French, with the proud *lucarnes* a feature not to be found in Italy, but the niches added in these dormer windows, a putti placed in each, are a typical device of classical fashions.

The **François I stair tower** is a celebrated Loire monument in its own right, although the staircase at Chambord runs away with first prize in the category. The protruding spiral stair tower was a well-established feature of French Gothic architecture, not of the Italian Renaissance, the latter preferring straight ramps more discreetly incorporated into the main building. The openwork sides, though, impart an Italianate touch, allowing for fine courtly display – just try to resist any temptation to practise your own royal wave when you walk up the ramp. The openings and balustrades, rather than concealing the angle of the stair ramps, reflect it with their sloping shapes and friezes. The procession of sculpted salamanders add to the great sense of movement. The swans shot through by an arrow were the melodramatic symbol of Louise de Savoie, François I's influential mother. During grand ceremonies, the loggias at the top of the stair tower could be used to observe events below.

No one is sure who conceived the plans for this famous façade, nor for the **outer façade of the François I wing**, which has a totally different character, facing the town. It consists of a series of arcaded storeys much more Italian Renaissance in style. Curiously, the architect didn't make the balconies interconnect, giving the feel of some snooty Renaissance hotel, each window given its separate, exclusive terrace. Henry James, visiting the château towards the end of the 19th century, wrote of them being 'repainted with red and blue, relieved with gold figures; and each of them looks more like the royal box at a theatre than like the aperture of a palace dark with memories'. Elaborately sculpted panels also adorn this outer façade, but they're very hard to decipher from a distance; the Musée Lapidaire can help you appreciate such fine detail.

Actually, the so-called François I wing might just as well be known as the Queen Claude wing, as François I's wife was personally involved with the plans, the king being frequently absent. When she died in 1524, the same year as François was captured at the disastrous Battle of Pavia in Italy, work at Blois was halted. On his eventual return, François moved his attentions elsewhere. His heart, it seems, had gone out of the project.

In the 1630s, Gaston d'Orléans decided to knock down the whole Château de Blois which he found outmoded and disordered. He wanted to replace it with a magnificent, coherent, fashionable classical model to rival the Palais du Luxembourg in Paris, the latter conceived for Marie de' Medicis by Salomon de Brosse in 1615. Gaston's architect was the most famous of the French classical period, François Mansart. The one **Mansart wing** that was completed before funds ran out stands in stark, ordered contrast to the delightfully eccentric, slightly chaotic other wings. Symmetry and the classical orders triumph in the bright light-grey stone. Gone are the joyously individualistic elements of Gothic decoration. Gone are the elevating, exuberant Loire *lucarnes* which stretch the gaze skywards. There is playfulness to Mansart's design, but here the joviality comes in the subtle use of the double pilaster and other such humorous classical copybook elements. Henry James wrote of the Mansart wing that 'taken in contrast to its flowering, laughing, living neighbour, it marks the difference between inspiration and calculation'. This wing reflects the triumph of classicism in France, but also how inventively certain French architects treated it.

The Museums and Collections in the François I Wing

On the ground floor of the François I wing you'll find the **Musée Lapidaire**, displaying the old stones of the château. When Félix Duban set about restoring the decayed castle in the mid-19th century, he was confronted by crumbling masonry and beautiful sculptural details eaten away by time. He had the good sense to make detailed records on the state of the architecture and, in particular, the fine stonework. He kept the very worn originals as well as plastercasts of the replacements, enabling us now to observe some of the fine details of decoration from close up, such as monk gargoyles from Louis XII's time, and the fat salamanders and the labours of Hercules from the François I wing. Duban is devoted a special room up in the royal apartments. Down in the basement, there's an **Archaeological Museum** in the former castle kitchens, with displays on the history of Blois, concentrating on medieval finds.

You enter the **royal apartments** of the François I wing via the great staircase, which sweeps you up to the first floor. Just as the exteriors of the château have been

An Evil Queen Mother, Scarface Guises, and the End of the Valois Line

To appreciate a tour round the Château de Blois, and the François I wing in particular, it's important to understand something about Catherine de' Medici, the three sons of hers who became the last three kings of the Valois dynasty, and the formidable dukes and cardinals of the aristocratic De Guise family who threatened the stability of the French monarchy.

Catherine de' Medici is a figure who continues to fascinate the French, and is generally thought of as the most evil of queen mothers. At the outset of the Wars of Religion in the 1560s she did in fact attempt to bring together the feuding parties and sue for peace. But the forces were far beyond her control and she and her sons became caught up in the violent maelstrom. Most infamously, she is held in large part responsible for giving the go-ahead to her son King Charles IX for the St Bartholomew's Day massacres of 1572, when leading Protestants were brutally murdered in the night in several major French cities.

On a more playful note, looking at the decoration in the royal apartments at Blois you may notice Catherine's royal initials painted here and there. The pretty interlinking initials H and C refer to her and her husband King Henri II. It's rather unfortunate that the Cs laid back to back within the initials also form Ds, the initial of Henri II's mistress, Diane de Poitiers. Long said to have been intentional, the ambiguity in this device is now thought to have been accidental. What is sure is that the lives of Catherine de' Medici and Diane de Poitiers were all too closely linked. Diane helped bring up the royal children at the Château d'Amboise. She was most famously given the Château de Chenonceau as a gift by Henri II. But after the king's death, Catherine de' Medici made her swap Chenonceau for the only slightly less glamorous Château de Chaumont. Catherine de' Medici was forced by the circumstances of the turbulent Wars of Religion to stay at the Château de Blois from time to time. In fact she died here on 5 January 1589, very soon after the infamous assassinations arranged by her son King Henri III here in the royal apartments.

Who were the dangerous De Guises whom the king felt he had to do away with so dramatically? Henri de Guise came from a line of formidable De Guise dukes of Lorraine who amassed extraordinary power in the course of the 16th century – to such an extent that they had become a threat to royal power during the Wars of Religion in the second half of that century. The Maréchale de Retz is said to have written of them in the late 16th century: 'These Lorraines had such an air of distinction that alongside them the other Princes looked plebeian.'

Henri's grandfather, Claude de Lorraine, had been a staunch supporter of François I, and was conferred some of the powers of regent during the king's captivity after the Battle of Pavia. Claude was ennobled with the title of duke in honour of his crushing of a peasants' revolt in Lorraine in 1527. His daughter Marie would marry James V of

scrubbed clean, the interiors have been given a thorough going-over. The striking, swirling dark patterns splurged all over the walls and beams were commissioned by Duban, the big leaves and flowers inspired by forms he'd found on illuminated

Scotland, by whom she gave birth to the ill-fated Mary Queen of Scots. Claude's son François de Guise was the second duke in the line, and the first family member to be called Le Balafré – Scarface. The contemporary writer Brantôme described him as towering above the other officers of the realm 'as a great and sturdy oak has pride of place in a plantation'. A brilliant military man, he it was who successfully wrested Calais from the English in 1558. The following year, the French king, Henri II, died. His and Catherine de' Medici's eldest but very sickly young son became King François II.

The Queen Mother and the De Guises struggled for dominance. The De Guises were supremely well placed; François de Guise's niece, Mary Queen of Scots, was queen of France. François de Guise and his brother, Cardinal Charles de Guise, became the most influential figures in French politics along with Catherine de' Medici.

Persecution of the French Huguenots, or Protestants, had increased under Henri II. Ardently anti-Protestant, the De Guises led the Catholic side in the persecution of their enemy, beginning in earnest with the bloody repression of the Huguenot conspiracy of the Conjuration d'Amboise in 1560 (see pp.248–9). Full-scale civil war in the form of the first War of Religion broke out two years later, in 1562. By this time, the minor Charles IX was on the throne, Catherine de' Medici was acting as regent, and the rival factions were out of all control. François de Guise died, murdered at the hands of a Huguenot while besieging Protestant-held Orléans in 1563.

François's son Henri became the second family Scarface and the third in the line of dukes. He pursued his father's anti-Protestant hatred with even greater zeal, not only fighting the Huguenots in battle, but also acting as one of the main instigators of the St Bartholomew's Day massacres in 1572. He went on to command the Ligue, the Catholic league founded in 1576 against the Huguenots, the latter headed by Henri de Bourbon, king of Navarre. Henri de Guise, whose power cannot be underestimated, was closely supported by his brother, the cardinal Louis de Guise.

After Charles IX's death in 1574, a third son of Henri II and Catherine de' Medici took the crown as Henri III. Married but childless, Henri III was left with no Valois heirs on the death of his brother, the Duc d'Anjou, in 1584, but he had promised the crown to Protestant Henri de Navarre. Henri de Guise, though, appeared to have aspirations to find a new Catholic monarch, if not to become king himself. By 1588, Henri III was in desperate straits. He called the Estates General of the realm, with representatives of the nobles, the clergy and the people, to meet at the Château de Blois to try and work out the terrible national crisis. But while they were gathered there he resorted to the most cowardly and vicious of means to do away with Henri de Guise and his cardinal brother Louis. Three months after the gory events of the 23 and 24 December 1588 in which they died, the widowed Duchesse de Guise was granted her request that formal statements by witnesses be recorded by the Court of Parliament. The events have been pieced together by historians from those reports.

manuscripts and old cloth. The apartments were recently provided with new tile floorings; they may look brash and overbright, as much fit for a modern bathroom as an old royal castle, but apparently they do follow the spirit of the original

On the bitterly cold morning of 23 December 1588, during the gathering of the Estates General at Blois, the king called Henri de Guise to his chambers. Henri III had prepared his trap meticulously, disposing the men he had picked for the mission (a bunch subsequently known as the notorious 'Quarante-Cinq') around the royal apartments. Two priests were ordered to repair to the royal oratory and told in vague terms to pray for the successful outcome of a project the king had embarked upon to ensure peace in his realm. As Henri de Guise passed through the king's bedroom he was savagely attacked. He put up a strong resistance, but set upon by a pack of murderers he was mercilessly stabbed by them. Such was his phenomenal strength that the apocryphal story has it that he managed to drag himself across the room, to fall accusingly by the king's bed.

Immediately after the murder, the royal side declared that an attempt had been made on the king's life. They spread the rumour that a purse had been found on Henri de Guise containing a treacherous note revealing his collusion with France's enemy Spain and declaring that to keep the civil war going in France it was necessary to raise 700,000 livres a year with Spanish aid. Several men were arrested, including the merchants' provost of the town of Blois. He reported being taken to the place of the assassination and seeing two pools of blood still so hot that they were steaming.

Louis de Guise was among those arrested. Henri III wanted to do away with him as well, but it's said that no one from Henri III's personal guard would accept the order to kill a religious man, especially one of such high rank. Other soldiers had to be found to carry out that dirty deed. The following day Louis de Guise was assassinated. The same provost of Blois doubtless didn't need a keen nose to smell the horrific stench of burnt flesh in one staircase up which he was taken – he reported that he was told by a guard that the bodies of the murdered De Guises had been burnt there.

In Paris, which was in the hands of the Ligue, hysteria followed the news of the murders. The De Guises were conferred an almost saintly status by many supporters around the land. Henri III had had his archrivals butchered in his very own royal apartments, by what some French history books call 'Florentine means', supposedly passed on to him by his Medici mother, as though this were another of the features exported to France from Renaissance Italy. Henri would very soon get his comeuppance; he was assassinated in his turn the following year, in Paris, by a fanatical Catholic monk. So the Valois dynasty, which had ruled France since 1328, came to its bloody end, and the head of the Bourbon family, Henri de Navarre, the pro-Protestant leader, became the reconciling King Henri IV, although the Wars of Religion raged on until 1598. The newly hung **Salle des Guises** in the François I wing displays paintings illustrating imagined scenes of the notorious murders.

decorations. The fine pieces of furniture displayed don't date from the French Renaissance, but are mainly extravagant 19th-century interpretations of the style of that period.

One or two original elements have remained in some of the royal apartments, including some panelling and parts of certain fireplaces, and, most engrossingly, the **Cabinet de Travail**, an Italianate studiolo, the finest room in the wing. It has retained its rich array of original carved wood panels. Don't bother trying to count the overwhelming number of Renaissance motifs depicted, as someone has done the job already – apparently there are 237 in all. This room has been described as a kind of Renaissance copybook of designs: masks, dolphins, cornucopia and many other familiar emblems abound. Cabinets lie discreetly behind certain of the panels. As to their uses, the 19th-century novelist Alexandre Dumas spread the notion that they were caches for poison. This idea delighted the popular imagination, such was the poisonous reputation of Catherine de' Medici and her final Valois sons. But the cabinets were probably used more prosaically for storing and displaying curios and the most beautiful objects of the royal collection; some exquisite pieces are now on show in them.

Through the Other Wings of the Château de Blois

The **Salle des Etats Généraux** is the name given to the early 13th-century medieval hall, although the Estates Generals referred to are those of 1576 and 1588. Somewhat squashed into a corner between the Louis XII and François I wings, it's hard to appreciate the hall's architecture from the outside, but you can visit its enormous, if now vacuous, interior after the apartments of the François I wing. The place gives an indication of the power of the medieval counts of Blois and Champagne. A row of alarmingly slender columns divides the massive space into two. The ceiling is of painted wood. Again, the polychrome designs you see now are 19th century, Duban's work in the 1860s, handed on to Jules de la Morandière.

Blois' **fine arts museum** takes up the first floor of the Louis XII wing. It doesn't contain the collections of royals – the Loire Renaissance kings transported their movable items (their *mobilier*, as the French call furniture) as they went from château to château (the architecture being what French estate agents would call *immobilier*), and then the monarchy went off to Paris, taking many of its riches to its châteaux there.

There is amusing tale about the way the Blois fine arts museum was founded. The story goes that Napoleon III had fallen for an actress from the Comédie Française. Called away on imperial business, he was overcome by the desire to see her again and wrote to her telling her to meet him at the museum of Blois. He then sent word to the town to expect him for a visit to the museum. The Blois authorities were mighty embarrassed, however, because of one important detail – the town had no museum! The wealthy citizens are supposed to have gathered round and generously donated some of the finest pieces of their private collections, hung within 48 hours, in time for the royal visit and assignation. All supposedly went off smoothly.

The speed of the museum's creation is only mildly exaggerated in this comic tale. Early in the 19th century, the château was serving as a barracks. In middle of the century a town mayor managed to persuade the French army to cede at least the François I wing for the town to start a fine arts collection. In 1850, the local council called for donations of works. Pieces flowed in, the town acquired more, and it put in a few successful requests to the state for additional paintings. New barracks were built in town so that by 1867 the army had a new home in Blois, leaving the authorities free to use all the château's interiors as they wished. The Louis XII wing was chosen as the best setting for the collections.

Among the 16th-century pieces, two typically bizarre Mannerist works stand out: *L'Enlèvement d'Europe* by Jean Cousin Le Fils, Europa holding on tight to the garlanded bull-god's horns in this strange rush of love, putti escorting the odd couple on the back of sad-eyed sea monsters; and Martin de Vos's Flemish Mannerist *La Mort d'Adonis*, dogs posing here with swans. English visitors will no doubt be moved by the French painting depicting Thomas More being taken to the Tower, his distraught daughter trying to embrace him. Of particular interest given the Blois royals' connections with and designs on northern Italy, Lombard early 16th-century art is represented by the *Vierge à l'enfant et anges musiciens* by Marco d'Oggiono, a pupil of Leonardo da Vinci – the latter spent the last years of his life just down the Loire at Amboise.

The museum possesses a couple of engrossing series of portrait panels, famous figures painted in rows, removed from châteaux in the wider region. Such series are quite rare now, but there was something of an aristocratic fashion for them at one time. One is still in place in the Château de Beauregard a short way south of Blois (see p.171). The art work may not be of the highest order, but what a fine way of giving one's children a history lesson at home.

Another striking donation from a château, this time Cheverny (see pp.173–5), close to Blois, is *La Force, la Fortune et le Temps*, a richly composed work by Jean Mosnier, the mid-17th-century artist who substantially helped create the most refined château interior along the Loire. Among other 17th-century pieces, look out for the pouting Grande Mademoiselle, Gaston d'Orléans' difficult daughter, in her blue décolleté dress, with her curls, pearls, and slightly manly nose...she certainly looks like she'd be a terrible handful. Among other notable Ancien Régime pieces, seek out Sébastien Bourdon's Poussin-like, bustling *Eliézer et Rébecca*, Claude Vignon's tenderly melodramatic *La Mort de Lucrèce*, dagger deep in Lucretia's breast, and François Boucher's *Psyché recevant les honneurs divins*.

Three 17th-century tapestry cycles also feature. The most impressive, woven in Paris in the tapestry workshops Henri IV set up with Flemish experts, represents scenes from the life of the Emperor Constantine, after cartoons by Reubens. The events interpreted are the discovery of the True Cross, Constantine entering Rome, and Constantine's wedding. The *Histoire d'Artémis*, from the same workshops, were executed after cartoons by Antoine Caron. Finally, the third series has a French royal theme, the life of Louis XIV, produced between 1663 and 1675 at the recently created Gobelins works, following Charles Lebrun's cartoons (the scenes are of the taking of Dunkerque and the surrender of Marsal).

Some splendid clocks and watches recall a skilled craft for which Blois was long famous. Portrait medallions feature prominently in one room. One of the museum's curators acquired almost 60 medallions by the 18th-century artist Jean-Baptiste Nini, closely associated with the Château de Chaumont (see pp.233–7). Among them you can see Benjamin Franklin represented wearing his glasses and Voltaire looking like a smug Roman emperor. The interesting 19th-century French Romantic sculptor Auguste Préault gave some of his own works to the Blois museum, including *Lélia*, a rendering of a character in one of George Sand's novels, and a Gaulish soldier, his face full of grim determination. Daniel Dupuis, another 19th-century sculptor, donated around 500 works of his to his town museum, including medallions illustrating many famous figures of his day. There are also a few sculptures of famous Blésois figures by that rare phenomenon, an 18th-century female sculptor, Julie Charpentier.

Among the 19th-century paintings, famous French historical figures are delivered into the hands of the 19th-century troubadour stylists, for example Hippolyte Lecomte's *Jeanne d'Arc et Charles VII*; of course the artist couldn't resist giving the Maid an overfeathered hat and a prominent bust line. King François I, too, sports an absurdly overdone helmet plumage, fit for a transvestite show, in Louis Ducis' *François I armé chevalier par Bayard*.

Finally, moving to the other side of the castle's courtyard, don't miss the sensational interior of the **Mansart wing**. Baroque has swept into the building here, creating a heady feeling of melodrama in the magnificent lobby – just look up to the splendid oval cupola, framed through the shape of a cross. Ornate sculptures were meant to add still more to the wondrous effects, but the work was never completed, although in certain spots you can see drawings on the ceiling indicating where the pieces were to go. Blois' town library was housed in this wing until quite recently, but it has moved to modern premises and the rooms here are now given over to temporary exhibitions relating to the castle; go and see what's on if you're not too exhausted by the marathon tour round the castle.

A Walk Around Blois

Historic Blois spreads over two hills, the western one crowned by the castle, the eastern one by the cathedral. We start this walking tour on the upper esplanade outside the castle, known as the **Place du Château**. This triangular, gravel-covered square is full of wealthy-looking houses and has a couple of clusters of restaurants and tourist shops. The **Maison de la Magie** (*open July–Aug 10–12.30 and 2–6.30; April–June daily except certain Mons 10–12 and 2–6; Sept Wed, Thurs and weekends 10–12 and 2–6; t 02 54 55 26 26*) occupies a splendid renovated brick mansion opposite the castle. Unfortunately, this ambitious new magic museum and centre has got off to a faltering start financially since it opened in the late 1990s, but under new management its fortunes may improve.

The museum was inspired by and pays particular homage to the 19th-century Blois-born magician Jean-Eugène Robert-Houdin, the name almost as complicated as some of his tricks. So far did his fame spread that Robert-Houdin even gave a private performance at Buckingham Palace in 1849, showing off his Cabalistic Clock,

The Wonderful Orange Tree and The Ladies' Favourite (whatever that might have been), among other tricks. In his colonializing century, Robert-Houdin apparently felt a calling to add his powers to those of the French military, which had recently conquered Algeria, and went off there to show some of the North African religious leaders just how weak they were in the face of his magic tricks. As impressive as the modern presentation of this centre are the regular magic shows.

Among the other façades on the Place du Château, look out for the **Maison du Vin** if buying Loire wine appeals. On the esplanade's open side, views stretch out over the town roofs, but beyond the formal flowerbeds and row of clipped trees the Loire is barely visible from up here. The church of St-Sauveur, where Joan of Arc had her banner blessed in April 1429, stood on this terrace until the church was destroyed at the Revolution.

Close to the Musée de la Magie, you can look down the grand stairway leading to Blois' main shopping quarter, but if you can avoid being tempted in that direction, turn back and descend from the esplanade via the **Rue de la Voûte du Château**, next to the Salle des Etats Généraux. Along this sloping street you might care to stop for tourist information on the whole of the Blésois (known nowadays as the *département* of the Loir-et-Cher) at the swish **Maison du Loir-et-Cher**. You might also cast an eye over the temporary art exhibitions which are held in the smart galleries downstairs.

The Rue de la Voûte du Château will take you down past the layers of loggias of the outer façade of the château's François I wing and into **Place Victor Hugo**, round which cars race. In the square, with its great sequoia and cedar, the Fontaine Corbigny is decorated with a bas-relief by Julie Charpentier depicting the Loire, although by now you have completely turned your back on the river.

Across the square stands the **church of St-Vincent-de-Paul** (*under restoration at the time of writing*), a grandiose 17th-century building, the central classical façade with its rose window bordered by sides finished with lavish scrolls, the lantern topped by a fleur-de-lys. The scent of royalty hangs over this church. Henri III founded the Collège de Blois in 1581, served by the Chapelle St-Louis on this site. The Jesuits were given control of this institution in 1622 and their most celebrated architect, Père Martellange, drew up a plan for a new church in 1624. But it was his successor in over-seeing much Jesuit architecture, Frère Turmel, whose design was used, building work beginning in 1634. Both Gaston d'Orléans and his obstreperous daughter gave gener-ously for the construction, which continued slowly through the century. Their arms and initials can be made out on the front. You can also make out signs of how the church was re-dedicated to St Vincent de Paul after the Revolution.

The interior was restored by La Morandière in the 19th century and was largely daubed in paint mimicking marble. The architectural style within remains predomi-nantly 17th-century classical, although a hideously vulgar Virgin over the altar will distract your attention from everything else at first. The venerated medieval French King Louis IX, or Saint Louis, is represented by initials placed here and there and by a carving in the choir; the sculpture in this section is by Gaspard Imbert. The monu-ment to the left representing Faith, Hope and Charity once held Gaston d'Orléans' heart. That to the right depicting Religion, Pity and Generosity was a modest memorial to his daughter La Grande Mademoiselle.

Some may find the **Musée de l'Objet** (*6 Rue Franciade; open June and July Wed–Sun 2–7*), the other new museum opened in Blois in the 1990s apart from the Musée de la Magie, even more esoteric than its counterpart. Established in the town's school of fine arts, it is reached by taking the Rampe Chambourdin, just north of Place Victor Hugo. The museum concentrates on, well, objects. But objects turned into art. Ordinary-seeming chairs, for example, feature prominently, but placed in a different context from the everyday, so that you don't just contemplate them as desirable objects to sit on or for their craftsmanship. With its roots in surrealism, this is provocatively modern art, often ironic, conceptual, commenting on contemporary life. While many of the titles of the pieces may seem facile or silly (*De la chaise occidentale considérée comme un monument tibétain* is a typical example), their deliberate placing or misplacing, manipulation or metamorphosis gives them new, often more profound or surprising, meanings. Much is absurdist to be sure, but there are other messages too, political, playful, poetic.

Back at Place Victor Hugo, Avenue Jean Laigret leads you past the castle's former **orangerie**, a greatly altered 16th-century building turned restaurant. It once lay in the splendid château gardens, which covered a wide area here until they were pitifully abandoned upon the death of Gaston d'Orléans. The **pavillon Anne de Bretagne**, a little further up, is another fragmentary remnant from the château's once-glorious grounds; now it houses the town's tourist office. With its heavily restored brick façade and balustrade, and the symbols of Louis XII and Anne de Bretagne, it retains its Gothic outlines, but the interior shows the fusion of Gothic and Italianate styles.

Avenue Jean Laigret leads up to the train station; instead, cross south into the **Jardin des Simples et des Fleurs Royales**, behind the ugly institutional façade of the former Ecole des Garçons opposite the tourist office. This public garden is a successful conversion of the school gardens, now planted on the theme of royal and medicinal plants. But its feel is more late 20th-century civic than Renaissance regal; it was designed by a leading French landscape architect, Gilles Clément.

Next, head for the sharp soaring spires of the **church of St-Nicolas**. The church's spiky twin entrance towers with their defensive look, and the crossing with its sharp needle of a spire to match, are the easiest landmarks to spot in town, puncturing the Blois skyline. To reach the church from the Jardin des Simples you pass below the imposing outer façade of the Gaston d'Orléans wing. This way leads you down into what used to be the old commercial riverside part of Blois, the **Quartier St-Nicolas**. It was badly bombed in the war, but luckily the church survived relatively unharmed. Cross **Rue des Trois Marchands** and **Rue St-Lubin**, two fine streets that were restored with care after the war, although other ones in the neighbourhood weren't so easily patched up. Still, the Quartier St-Nicolas has atmosphere, especially close to the looming church. A good number of restaurants hide out in this area.

St Nicholas' church has retained its medieval grandeur, even if it looks a bit grim in parts. You can get a good view of it along Rue St-Laumer, named after the previous saint to whom the edifice was dedicated. Impressive Romanesque and early Gothic features give the church fine credentials. The first church was erected around 924, but burned down in 1114. The building you now see was begun in 1138, construction going from east to west. Most of the nave was constructed in the 13th century. From Rue St-Laumer you can make out the break in style on the outside. The name of the church was changed in 1791 in memory of a church dedicated to St Nicholas which didn't make it through the Revolution.

St-Nicolas' choir end is a harmonious demonstration of Romanesque geometry, with its radiating chapels in 12th-century Benedictine style. The choir is supported by very early examples of flying buttresses, probably from the end of the 12th century. Double flying buttresses hold up the later nave. The façade contains remnants of 14th-century sculpture, including the angels, prophets and saints of the central doorway. The west rose window was redone in Gothic style in the 17th century. As to the soaring spires, they actually only date from the 19th century.

Inside the dankness of this vast vessel, the eastern end has a rare Romanesque grandeur, with its impressive rib vaults and its series of chapels. This part also demonstrates very graphically how, in medieval times, the church authorities weren't averse to masons depicting the sinful ways of man; among the capitals are a few extremely bawdy carvings. Prudes avert your eyes. The wall paintings in the Chapelle des Fonts were an abortive 19th-century attempt to revive period decoration. The sculpture in the end chapel by the Blésois Gaspard Imbert represents the Assumption of the Virgin. The upper windows of the choir were decorated with stained glass by the postwar specialist Max Ingrand. The western section of the church shows how quickly the influence of the great cathedral building of Chartres reached Blois and the Loire. The style is of course more elevating and sober than the Romanesque part – no naughty sculptures here to deflect attention from the glorification of God.

The Rue des Trois Marchands leads down to the river. At Place de la Grève, the small **Musée de la Résistance, de la Déportation et de la Libération** (*open Tues–Sun 2.30–5.30; free*) is devoted to the memory of the Second World War anti-Nazi struggle in the Loir-et-Cher. South of here lie the quays, with views onto the old bridge. Head east along **Quai de l'Abbé Grégoire**, then turn up Rue Robert-Houdin. Attached to the southern side of St-Nicolas you'll see the remains of the **Ancien Couvent des Jacobins**. Once a large abbey complex, it was destroyed in the Wars of Religion, rebuilt in the 17th and 18th centuries by the Benedictines of St-Maur, and converted into a hospital after the Revolution. Only vestiges of the convent and the cloister were left standing.

Reached via Rue Anne de Bretagne off Rue Robert-Houdin, the **Musée Diocésain d'Art Religieux** (*open Tues–Sat 2–6, closed public hols; free*) contains religious artefacts, including statuary, robes, paintings and goldsmiths' work. Head north from here to rejoin **Rue St-Lubin**, with its collection of fine old houses, No. 41 displaying a statue of the bishop of Chartres, No. 31 boasting an unusual slate sundial.

Rue St-Lubin leads east into busy **Place Louis XII**, at the foot of grandiose stairs up to the château. The square was laid out in the 19th century, but had to be remodelled after the war, its principal feature the Louis XII fountain, a copy of the medieval one embellished by Louis XII, with its fleur-de-lys balustrade and spouting dolphins. By the stairs to the château you can also see the ruins of another of Blois' churches, St-Martin-des-Choux.

The shopping quarters start in earnest here. It's a good area to pause at one of the many cafés or pâtisseries. Some of the liveliest **shopping streets**, the Rue du Commerce and Rue Denis Papin, lie just northeast of the square. Rue Denis Papin, on the former route between Chartres and Bourges, is the town's main thoroughfare, with a 19th-century Parisian air. The perspective along it ends to the north with the dramatic flight of stairs up to the 19th-century statue of that steamy scientist Papin. The way south leads to busy **Rond Point de la Resistance**, with its big town feel and bustling cafes next to the bridge.

The **Pont Jacques V Gabriel** is surely the most refined bridge over the Loire. It replaced the medieval one swept away in 1716 and its famous architect is honoured in its name. An Egyptian-style needle adds grandeur and ornament to the central point. Blois **south of the river** doesn't have many interesting sites, but cross the river to appreciate the splendid views of the historic town from the cobbled southern quays and to visit the church and cemetery of St-Saturnin; these are set in a pleasantly quiet corner down off the Quai Villebois-Mareuil.

The **church of St-Saturnin** was a popular place of pilgrimage in the Middle Ages. Visitors came to pray to Notre Dame des Aydes, Blois' patron. The church was commissioned in late Gothic, Flamboyant style by Anne de Bretagne to replace an earlier medieval one. The *ex votos* to Notre Dame des Aydes and the mariners' chapel count among the curiosities inside. The cemetery of St-Saturnin is often described as a cloister and its form makes it easy to mistake it for one, especially as the graves have disappeared and the space is now used to display fragments of local sculpture from across the centuries. Built from 1516 to 1520, the architecture took Renaissance forms. Rue du Poinçon Renversé, just north of the cemetery, contains several low old Loire mariners' houses.

Taking the bridge back over to the north side of the Loire, on the hillside to the east of Rue Denis Papin you can explore many of Blois' most atmospheric, smart old **residential streets** leading up towards the cathedral. They contain a good number of fine old town houses with appealing features: intimate courtyards with wells, stair towers, galleries and Gothic sculptures; sometimes Renaissance decoration; even the odd royalist symbol from Louis XII's period that survived the Revolution. Many royal courtiers took up home in this quarter. Seek out such streets as Rue du Puits Châtel and Rue Pierre de Blois.

Place Ave Maria forms the charming meeting point of a handful of tracks up the hillside. The **Maison des Acrobates**, further north on Place St-Louis, is the most appealing of all Loire town houses, full of late Gothic humour, comically covered with wooden beams carved with figures of playful jesters.

A hurricane in 1678 destroyed much of the church on what is now the site of the **Cathédrale St-Louis**. So this is essentially a late 17th-century building, funded by the Colberts – the wife of Louis XIV's famous minister, Marie Charron, hailed from the Blésois. A church to St Peter may have stood on the spot as early as the 6th century. At the end of the 10th, a religious edifice was definitely in existence – the tomb of a 9th-century Tourangeau hermit, St Solennis, was transferred here at that time. This figure became confused with the more widely recognized Solenne, 6th-century bishop of Chartres, supporter of the Frankish Clovis. The story, hijacked for Blois' greater glory, has it that Solenne's body was discovered in the Poitou. The intention was to carry it back to Chartres, but after a halt at Blois, the tomb became impossibly heavy to transport. This was taken as a divine sign that the saint was destined to remain in Blois. Pilgrims flocked to the church, which Thibaut le Tricheur's widow had built in the saint's honour. Greatly transformed in François I's reign, the place remained part of a priory from 1132 to 1672, when it was elevated to become Blois' cathedral.

The cathedral's great bell tower acts as the old town's eastern landmark. The façade actually remains mostly 16th century, a survivor of the inclement weather. Its classical motifs once again show the Italianate style mixed with the traditional French. But Gothic designs dominate elsewhere, evidence of that style persisting in religious architectural aesthetics; as at Orléans cathedral, this church demonstrates that classicism didn't take over completely in Ancien Régime France. Inside, several of the side chapels contain obtrusive tombs from the 17th and 18th centuries. The 19th-century stained glass by Lobin of Tours throws a rather sickly light over some of the interior, while the very recent additions of stained glass by the Dutch artist Jan Dibetts, although controversial, prove fairly anodyne, with Christian phrases in Latin placed at strange angles like colourful transfer lettering. The descent into the crypt is a sobering experience.

East of the cathedral lies the **Jardin de l'Evêché**, a very pleasant 18th-century garden, ending with a belvedere and containing a 1921 statue of Joan of Arc by the American artist Anna Huntington Hyatt. The garden gives good views over the town and onto the Pont Jacques Gabriel. That architect also designed the bishop's palace by the cathedral. It briefly became the headquarters of the newly created *département* of the Loir-et-Cher after the Revolution, then a museum at the start of the last century, but since the Second World War has housed the town hall after the previous one was destroyed. Rose enthusiasts may appreciate the lower terrace in season, planted as it is with hundreds of rare varieties.

A detour up via the Mail Clouseau northeast of the cathedral leads you up to the plateau of the **Place de la République** and the **Place Jean-Jaurès**, surrounded by their mix of 19th- and 20th-century civic buildings. The 1850 **Halle aux Grains**, or corn exchange, has been converted into the main town theatre. The old water towers date from roughly the same time. Among the recent buildings are the conference centre, the 1990s university buildings and Blois' ultra-modern public library. The Loir-et-Cher administrative buildings and law courts are also up here.

So too, curiously, is the **Haras National de Blois** (*open May–Sept Thurs pm – contact the tourist office for details*), Blois' national stud farm, on Avenue Maunoury heading northeast off these squares. In the vast, specially built 19th-century buildings, bordered with brick, some 50 stallions, thoroughbreds, draught horses and ponies are pampered for breeding.

Bourges and the Cher Valley

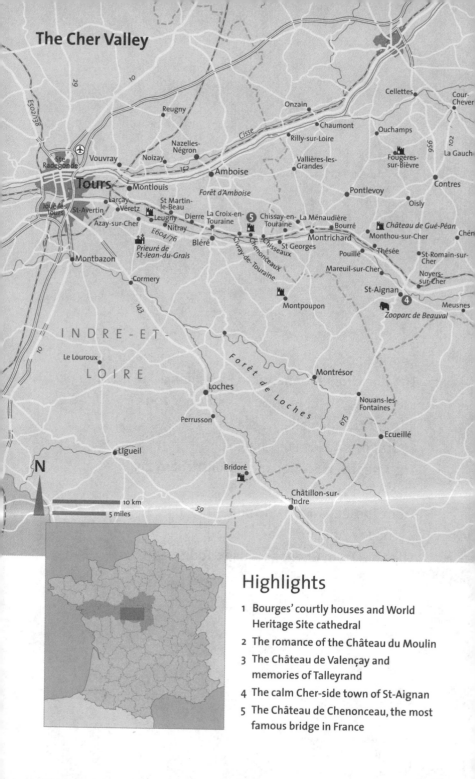

The Cher Valley

29
10
E502/138

Reugny
Onzain
Cellettes
Cour-
Chever

Cisse
Chaumont
Ouchamps
La Gauch

Nazelles-
Négron
Rilly-sur-Loire
Fougères-
sur-Bièvre
702
956

Ste-
Radegonde
Vouvray
Noizay
Vallières-les-
Grandes
Contres

Amboise
Pontlevoy
Oisly

Tours
Montlouis
Forêt d'Amboise
152

Joué-lès-
Tours
St-Avertin
Larçay
Véretz
St Martin-
le-Beau
La Croix-en-
Touraine
Chissay-en-
Touraine
La Ménaudière
Château de Gué-Péan

Leugny
Nitray
Dierre
5
Bourré
Monthou-sur-Cher
Chên

Azay-sur-Cher
E604/76
Bléré
Chenonceaux
Chisseaux
St Georges
Montrichard
Thésée
St-Romain-sur-
Cher

Prieuré de
St-Jean-du-Grais
Civray-de-Touraine
Pouillé
Mareuil-sur-Cher
Noyers-
sur-Cher

Montbazon
Cormery
St-Aignan
4
Meusnes

143
Montpoupon
Zooparc de Beauval

INDRE-ET-

10
Le Louroux

LOIRE
Forêt
de
Loches
Montrésor

Loches
Nouans-les-
Fontaines
675

Perrusson
Ecueillé

N
Ligueil
Bridoré

10 km
Châtillon-sur-
Indre

5 miles
59

Highlights

1 Bourges' courtly houses and World
   Heritage Site cathedral

2 The romance of the Château du Moulin

3 The Château de Valençay and
   memories of Talleyrand

4 The calm Cher-side town of St-Aignan

5 The Château de Chenonceau, the most
   famous bridge in France

Rising out of the Berry plains like a great spiritual silo, the cathedral of Bourges rivals that of Chartres in greatness. It dominates an exceptionally beautiful, compact, historic city, built by tributary rivers a little east of the Cher. This chapter starts with the splendours of the Berry's capital. It ends with an even greater highlight, in Touraine: the most famous Loire Valley château of them all. Chenonceau's famous gallery actually spans the Cher a little east of Tours.

In between these two magnificent places you can seek out restful, rustic little towns such as Selles, St-Aignan and Montrichard, and surprisingly delightful châteaux such as Valençay, Bouges or Du Moulin. Wine and goat's cheese add further tasty attractions to this stretch of the Cher river.

Bourges

'The huge, rugged vessel of the church overhung me in very much the same way as the black hull of a ship at sea would overhang a solitary swimmer,' wrote Henry James of Bourges cathedral. 'It seemed colossal, stupendous, a dark leviathan.' UNESCO was just as impressed and made Bourges cathedral a World Heritage Site in 1992. The rest of the city is packed with fine historic streets and museums.

History

Avaricum, capital of the Bituriges tribe, was one of the glories of Gaul. Caesar destroyed it after a siege in 52 BC and chillingly described how his troops dealt with the Celts: 'None of our soldiers thought about making money by taking prisoners. They were exasperated by the massacre of Romans at Cenabum [Orléans] and the labour of the siege and spared neither old men, nor women, nor children. Of the whole population – about forty thousand – a bare eight hundred...got safely through to Vercingetorix.' Under the Romans, the town became for a time the capital of the vast Gallo-Roman province of Aquitania.

The French Crown took possession of the viscounty of Bourges in 1101, when Philippe I bought it, making eastern Berry one of the earliest possessions of the Capetian kings. Work began on the Cathedral of St-Etienne in 1195. In 1360, Jean, a son of King Jean le Bon, was made Duc de Berry and would later also control the Auvergne and the Poitou. He was a ruthless ruler, and fleeced his subjects to support his refined taste in the arts. In 1412 he tried to negotiate with the English, causing the French to besiege Bourges. The duke submitted.

After his death, the future King Charles VII inherited the territories and Bourges became one of the bases of his peripatetic court. Charles was a weak, indecisive figure, often mockingly referred to as 'le petit roi de Bourges' while Paris lay in English hands. Two vital figures came to his rescue. One was Joan of Arc. The other was Jacques Coeur, one of the most successful merchants in French history, who had one of his main bases in Bourges and grew fabulously wealthy from trade with the Orient and supplying the court with luxuries. As Charles VII's finance minister, Coeur worked the miracles economically which Joan of Arc had inspired militarily. However, his influence earned him many enemies and in 1451 he was arrested on false charges of having poisoned the king's mistress. Just as Charles VII had done nothing to aid Joan of Arc, so he did nothing for Coeur. Coeur escaped to work for the pope while his money helped to finance the expulsion of the English from France.

Charles VII's son, Louis XI, was born in Bourges and saw to the founding of Bourges University in 1463. It became known for law and theology; German students brought with them the seeds of Luther's preaching and planted them in the brain of Jean Calvin, a student here in 1530. By the 17th century, following the Wars of Religion, Catholicism was ascendant again, although more friction was inevitable, with the rebellious Condé family based at Bourges. When Louis XIV came to Bourges, he destroyed the Grosse Tour – a symbol of Condé power – and authority passed to the monarchy. Bourges declined, and would only really pick up with what might be

Getting There and Around

There are **trains** to Bourges from Paris via Orléans and Vierzon; also from Bourges to and from Tours and the southern Berry.

Tourist Information

Tourist office: 21 Rue Victor Hugo, 18000, Bourges, t 02 48 23 02 60, f 02 48 23 02 69, tourisme@ville-bourges.fr, www.ville-bourges.fr.

Where to Stay and Eat

Bourges ✉ 18000

Expensive
★★★**Hôtel de Bourbon**, Bd de la République, t 02 48 70 70 00, f 02 48 70 21 22. The smartest hotel in Bourges, set in a converted 16th-century abbey, with a fine restaurant, **L'Abbaye St-Ambroix**, in a former chapel (*menus €38–64*).

Moderate
★★★**Hôtel d'Angleterre**, 1 Place des Quatre Piliers, t 02 48 24 68 51, f 02 48 65 21 41. Excellent location and elegant exterior, but the comfortable rooms turn out to be unimaginatively decorated. It has a stylish restaurant, **Le Windsor** (*menus €14.5–20.5*).

Inexpensive
★★**Le Christina**, 5 Rue de la Halle, t 02 48 70 56 50, f 02 48 70 58 13. In a dull modern block, but in a pretty good central location with a few rooms furnished with character, and views on to old Bourges rooftops.
Philippe Larmat, 62 bis Bd Gambetta, t 02 48 70 79 00. Little restaurant named after its star of a chef, with some surprisingly good-value options for such sophisticated cuisine (*menus €19.8–38*).
Jacques Cœur, 3 Place Jacques Cœur, t 02 48 70 12 72. Reasonably priced traditional French fare, in a grand neo-Gothic dining room (*menus €23–29*).

described as an explosion in its arms industry under the Second Empire, which, by the First World War, employed more than 20,000. It has remained the centre of the French arms industry, yet its population has been strongly left wing since the war.

Cathédrale St-Etienne

The roughly almond-shaped old town boasts the first French Gothic cathedral built south of the Loire, begun in 1195 under Archbishop Henri de Sully. His brother was archbishop of Paris, and Bourges cathedral is just as large and grand as Notre-Dame. Consecrated in 1324, its five-portalled façade is unique. Below the arches stands a wealth of sculpture – almost all from the 13th century – depicting the Last Judgement, the lives of St Etienne, St Just, St Ursin, the Virgin and St William, a Bourges archbishop. Between the portals, at the level of the niches, a series of bas-reliefs represents scenes from the life of Christ and from Genesis. The magnificent rose window above was added at the end of the 14th century by order of Jean Duc de Berry.

Unfortunately the ground wasn't strong enough to support the weight of the cathedral towers. On the south side, the Tour Sourde (Mute Tower – it has no bells) is propped up by an enormous pillar which was once a church prison. To the north, the Tour de Beurre (financed by patrons in return for a dispensation to eat butter and milk during Lent) fell down in 1506 and had to be restored. Like Chartres, St-Etienne spectacularly demonstrates the engineering and visual possibilities of the flying buttress, which allow for much glass, and hence light, for the interior. The north and south side portals have Romanesque sculptures from an earlier cathedral. The north presents the story of the Virgin but was badly damaged by Protestants. Owls and monkeys add a lighter note. The south portal shows Old and New Testament figures.

Inside, the rows of Gothic lancet arches to the apse reach higher than the arches of Notre-Dame. Don't miss the complex astronomical clock from 1424. Originally, nave and choir would have been separated by a *jubé*, or rood screen. The famed 13th-century stained-glass windows in the ambulatory feature a whole array of geometrically patterned settings.

You can only visit the crypt on a guided tour which allows you to see vestiges of the 13th-century rood screen, the Duc de Berry's tomb, a magnificent work by Jean de Cambrai, and several tall statues from the towers. After visiting the crypt, the ticket allows you to climb the Tour de Beurre for views of the old city.

Palais Jacques Cœur and the Bourges Museums

Although first impressions are that the **Palais Jacques Cœur** (*open Jul–Aug 9–1 and 2–7, April–June and Sept–Oct 9–12 and 2–6, Nov–March 9–12 and 2–5; 10 bis Rue Jacques Cœur, t 02 48 24 06 87*) needs a good clean, this palatial town house is full of delights. Gothic sculpture adorns much of the building and above the entrance doorway look out for the false windows with stone people who – as Henry James wrote – 'appear to be watching for the return of their master, who left his beautiful house one morning and never came back'. Cœur had a finger in every pie: real estate, mining, banks and the arms trade. Appointed Charles VII's Minister of Finance in 1439 and ennobled in 1441, he became the king's councillor in 1442 and began this house in 1443. The bitter tale of Cœur's demise (legend has it that he was killed by the Turks, with a weapon he had sold to them) contrasts with the lightheartedness of the sculpture in his homes. Entertainingly carved fireplaces are highlights of the interiors, while in the magnificent little chapel Jacques Cœur and his wife each had a private oratory.

The Hôtel Cujas housing the **Musée du Berry** (*open 10–12 and 2–6, closed Sun am and Tues; 4 Rue des Arènes, t 02 48 57 81 15*) was built around 1515 for Durand Salvi, a Florentine trader. It contains two extraordinary exhibits: a re-created Gallo-Roman necropolis and some extremely moving marble *pleurants* (mourners) from Jean Duc de Berry's splendid tomb. Other rooms are given over to artefacts of Berrichon life in the 18th and 19th centuries.

A rich merchant family of German origin built the fine Hôtel Lallemant (1490–1518), now the elegant **Musée des Arts Décoratifs** (*open 10–12 and 2–6, closed Sun am and Mon; 6 Rue Bourbonnoux, t 02 48 57 81 17*). Its fine Renaissance features include a loggia, frescoes and an oratory with an engrossing coffered stone ceiling, each square decorated with an angel or symbol. Another joyous late Gothic house, the Hôtel des Echevins, built as a new town hall in 1487, contains the riot of 20th-century colour of the **Musée Estève** (*open 10–12 and 2–6, closed Sun am and Tues; 13 Rue Edouard Branly, t 02 48 24 75 38*), with the abstract works of Maurice Estève, a native of the Berry. The **Musée des Meilleurs Ouvriers de France** (*open July–Aug 10–6.30, Sept–June 10–12 and 2–6, closed Sun am and Mon; Place Étienne Dolet, t 02 48 57 82 45*), in the 17th-century classical archbishops' palace, encourages modern craftsmanship.

Between Bourges and Vierzon

Northwest of Bourges, between the Berry's capital and Vierzon, a few little stops might appeal to you. Quiet **Mehun-sur-Yèvre** contains the meagre but appealing ruins of one of the great vanished medieval castles of France, built for Jean Duc de Berry. Cross the Cher, and you can discover the tiny but intriguing wine territories of **Quincy** and **Reuilly**.

By the Cher, just before Vierzon, **Brinay**'s church of St-Aignan stands by the village green. The choir contains some of the most moving Romanesque wall paintings in France. The east wall – normally the location for a Christ in Majesty – is occupied by a harrowing Massacre of the Innocents here. On the south wall, Christ is shown overcoming the devil's temptations and turning water into wine at the feast of Cana.

The Cher from Mennetou to St-Aignan

This is a quiet stretch of the Cher, offering the calm provincial pleasures of Mennetou, with its crafts shops, and Selles, best known for its goat's cheese. Some quite delightful but often overlooked châteaux lie to north and south of Selles. To the north, heading into the Sologne, the Château du Moulin has the prettiest brick façade of all the châteaux in that peculiarly atmospheric forest. It lies a dozen kilometres west of Romorantin-Lanthenay, quiet capital of the Sologne.

To the south of Selles, the Château de Valençay is a typical Loire hulk in blonde limestone, with a vineyard running down from it. Head some way further south for the jewel-box Château de Bouges.

Mennetou-sur-Cher to Selles-sur-Cher

Mennetou-sur-Cher, some way west of untouristy Vierzon, is a meagre slice of a medieval town, its crooked houses and cobbled streets encircled by run-down ramparts now sadly sandwiched between a railway line and a main road. In the Middle Ages the Cher ran just past the gateway known as the Porte d'En Bas, roughly along what is now the *camion*-clattering N76, but the river has shifted a good way south since then and now it's the Canal du Berry that's more central. Bridges over this canal lead to the pretty riverbanks, where locals seek the shade of the weeping willows in summer. Craftspeople have been tempted to settle in Mennetou – have a look at the Galerie ACT, with its some 30 *créateurs*. And visit the Gothic church of St-Urbain.

On the south side of the Cher from Mennetou, the Romanesque church at **St-Loup** contains some worn frescoes which you'll need to strain your eyes to decipher. They probably date from the end of the 12th century or early 13th. A particularly spectacular Catherine wheel of doves, gifts of the Holy Spirit, radiates out from the Virgin's heart.

The name of **Selles-sur-Cher** is more widely associated with goat's cheese than with a château, but when reflected in the river, the central castle forms a pretty picture.

Getting Around

A railway line runs along the Cher valley from Vierzon to Tours, with stations at Gièvres and Selles-sur-Cher. To reach Valençay by train you need to change at Gièvres.

Different bus lines from Blois serve Romorantin-Lanthenay, Selles-sur-Cher, St-Aignan and Valençay.

Tourist Information

Mennetou-sur-Cher: 21 Grande Rue, 41320 Mennetou-sur-Cher, t/f 02 54 98 12 29.

Selles-sur-Cher: Place du Général de Gaulle, 41130 Selles-sur-Cher, t 02 54 95 25 44, f 02 54 95 25 50.

Romorantin-Lanthenay: 32 Place de la Paix, 41200 Romorantin-Lanthenay, t 02 54 76 43 89, f 02 54 76 96 24, *romorantin-lanthenay@fnotsi.net, www.members.aol.com/otsiromo*.

Valençay: 2 Av de la Résistance, t 02 54 00 04 42.

Market Days

Mennetou-sur-Cher: Thursday morning.
Selles-sur-Cher: Thursday morning.
Romorantin-Lanthenay: Wednesday all day and Saturday morning.
Valençay: Tuesday morning.

Where to Stay and Eat

Selles-sur-Cher ✉ 41130

★★Hôtel du Lion d'Or, 14 Place de la Paix, t 02 54 97 40 83, f 02 54 97 72 36 (*inexpensive*). This old house benefits from the historical bonus that Joan of Arc is said to have stayed here. Inside it's quite bright and cheerful, with clean, reasonably priced rooms and both traditional regional Berrichon-Solognot cuisine and more original dishes combining meat with shellfish (*menus €13–20*). *Closed Sun evening and Mon (except in Jul and Aug) and late Jan–early Feb*.

The following are a few suggestions close to the Château du Moulin, taking you into the Sologne:

La Gaucherie ✉ 41250

La Fontaine aux Muses, La Gaucherie (*on the D765 between Cheverny and Romorantin-Lanthenay*), t 02 54 79 98 80. Dip into the Sologne and Sologne cuisine here (*menus €23–44*). *Closed Tues pm and Wed*.

Mur-de-Sologne ✉ 41230

★★★Domaine de Fondjouan, Route de Lassay, t 02 54 95 50 00, f 02 54 83 91 77 (*moderate*). Recently restored 19th-century château offering simple accommodation and relaxation, and a restaurant that even caters for vegetarians (*menus €12–36.5*).

Veilleins ✉ 41230

La Chèvrière, Domaine de Tréfontaines, t 02 54 83 86 27. A little east of Mur-de-Sologne, at this *ferme-auberge* the stables have been converted into a dining room where the proprietors, who rear goats, prepare satisfying country cooking, with goat's cheese featuring in a variety of guises (*menus €10.5–16.5*). *Book in advance*.

Chémery

Château de Chémery, t 02 54 71 82 77, f 02 54 71 71 34 (*inexpensive*). At this picturesque run-down château some of the rooms have been converted into *chambres d'hôtes*. The price is a bargain for an eccentric night in a château. The kind hosts can offer *table d'hôte* for around €18 on request. *Closed Dec–Feb*.

Romorantin-Lanthenay ✉ 41200

★★★★Grand Hôtel du Lion d'Or, 69 Rue Georges Clemenceau, t 02 54 94 15 15, f 02 54 88 24 87, *liondor@relaischateaux.fr, www.relaischateaux.fr/liondor* (*luxury*). The soberly smart façade in the centre of town conceals a fabulously luxurious restaurant run by Didier Clément and some truly delightful luxury rooms (*menus €68.5–99*).

★★Le Colombier, 18 Place du Vieux Marché, t 02 54 76 12 76, f 02 54 76 39 40 (*inexpensive*). Down-to-earth central option (*menus €17–26.5*).

In fact the Château de Selles-sur-Cher (*open mid-June–Sept Wed–Sun 10–12 and 2–6, Tues 2–6; April–mid-June and Oct weekends and public hols only 10–12 and 2–6*) is more like two châteaux rolled into one. The remnants of a 13th-century fortress, which replaced an earlier one destroyed by Richard the Lionheart's men, were added to in the early 17th century. These grand extensions, mainly built in brick, were ordered by Pierre-Philippe de Béthune, brother of Maximilien, the famed Duc de Sully, grand minister to Henri IV (*see* Sully, pp.117–19). The Pavilion Doré, the main 17th-century wing, is sumptuously decorated with painted coffered ceilings, frescoed walls and gilded fireplaces. Pierre-Philippe, like his brother, was a man of standing, an ambassador for King Henri IV who travelled to Italy. In the 18th century the château became the home of the Polish queen in exile, Marie Sobieska.

In the centre of Selles, the former abbey of St-Eusice has been roughly handled through time. The foundation may date back to the Frankish period, but Normans destroyed the first abbey and Protestants wrought much damage on the Romanesque architecture that replaced it. Heavy 19th-century restoration has exacted its own toll, in the choir in particular. Fragments of Romanesque decoration do survive, including a rare sculptural feature, the imaginative and amusing late 11th-century friezes carved in stone on the outside of the apse. One series tells the life of the hermit Eusice and another depicts scenes from the New Testament, all in the raw Romanesque style. The best time to see Selles-sur-Cher is at the spring goat's cheese festival. The little Musée du Val de Cher (*open June–Aug Tues–Sat 3–6, Sun 10–12 and 3–6*), with the church cloister attached, explains how the cheeses are made and other local traditions.

To reach St-Aignan from Selles via the Cher valley you can either follow the north bank or take the route on the south side, passing through **Meusnes**, with its very early Romanesque church of St-Pierre housing lovely statues from the 16th and 17th centuries. Meusnes also has a small museum on gunflint; this whole little area was devoted to production of the stuff in Napoleonic times to serve the vast armaments needs of the emperor's troops.

Into the Sologne

Château du Moulin

Open April–Sept Thurs–Tues 9–11.30 and 2–6.30, Oct–15 Nov Thurs–Tues 9–11.30 and 2–nightfall, March weekends only 9–11.30 and 2–5.30; t 02 54 83 83 51.

The Château du Moulin, lost in Sologne woods 12 kilometres west of Romorantin-Lanthenay, is the romantic star of the brick châteaux of the Sologne. It's a dreamy place, hidden in the countryside, reached by an alley of oaks you have to walk down, and surrounded by trees dipping their branches into the moat. Swans swim elegantly in its waters. The buildings that remain are fragments of a once more solid ensemble. The brick changes colour here and there, going from orange to purple. The typical

Sologne lozenge patterns in the brick give way at one point to an intriguing pattern of squares within squares. The slim cylinders of the entrance towers convey elegance, despite the horizontal crossbow slits, mean eyes of defence. The little chapel has twisting Gothic tracery windows, while Renaissance decoration encroaches in other parts, with shells above certain windows.

As the mix of architectural elements indicates, this is one of those Loire Valley châteaux built at the time of the transition from Gothic to Renaissance styles, at the turn of the 15th to the 16th century. The name Moulin here refers not to a mill, but to the man who commissioned it, Philippe du Moulin, a loyal servant of Charles VIII. Charles VIII was the first French king to go campaigning in Renaissance Italy; Du Moulin rescued him on the disastrous return journey when the French came close to complete humiliation at the Battle of Fornova in 1495.

The main *logis* is still very much lived in as you'll discover on the guided tour – the *châtelaine* has to vacate her room every morning to let the visitors through! It was restored at the start of the 20th century for M. de Marcheville, ancestor of the present owner, who turned it into an extremely liveable country retreat. The interiors are very light and agreeable. It seems only appropriate in this hunting forest that several pieces of furniture should depict animals being chased. The chapel contains some lovely period stained glass. Among the more unusual objects on display in the side buildings are a formidable crossbow – the arrows apparently shot off at 200 kilometres an hour – and an enormous, curious spit, apparently worked by a dog running round in the wheel!

If you go to the village church of St-Hilaire at **Lassay-sur-Croisne**, just north of the château, you can see an early depiction of the castle as it looked originally in one of the wall paintings in Philippe du Moulin's chapel, his monument desecrated during the Revolution.

Some way west of the Château du Moulin, the much put-upon **Château de Chémery** (*open daily 10–nightfall*; **t** 02 54 71 82 77) has become very dilapidated and is now under attack from the nondescript modern village of Chémery. But the courageous owners have taken on the battle to try and save some of this little castle's dignity, patching it up as best as they can, organizing cultural events in the courtyard in summer and taking in B&B guests (*see* p.210).

Romorantin-Lanthenay and Aliotis

If Leonardo da Vinci's outrageously ambitious plans had gone ahead to transform Romorantin-Lanthenay for King François I, the town would no doubt have become one of the most famous in France. François had spent some of his childhood at Romorantin, and once crowned king decided to have a sumptuous new castle built here in his beloved hunting Sologne. Leonardo, who had come to France at François' behest, began drawing up ideas for this wonderful palace in 1517. Among other magnificent Renaissance features, the château was to have a series of arcaded galleries looking over the Sauldre river.

As it happened, unfortunately, in 1518 an outbreak of the plague struck the town and the king decided to have his fabulous new hunting lodge built a bit to the north, in the forests of Chambord (*see* pp.165–8). Romorantin-Lanthenay was left to play a rather minor part as isolated capital of the Sologne, hardly a very exciting role considering what might have been. Although the fair number of mills built along the Sauldre and its islands brought economic activity to the place, Romorantin came to be viewed as something of a symbol of *la France profonde*, backward, provincial France. Things have changed somewhat in recent times. The centre has been spruced up, and the townspeople have enjoyed a certain prosperity since Matra cars set up a factory here in 1968; the Renault Espace model is made here and you can visit the **Espace Matra Automobile** (*open Wed–Mon 9–12 and 2–6, Sun from 10;* **t** *02 54 94 55 55*).

A new museum, the **Musée de Sologne** (*open April–Oct Wed–Mon 10–6, Sun am only; rest of year Wed–Mon 10–12 and 2–6, Sun 10–12;* **t** *02 54 95 33 66*), has been created in some of the renovated Sauldre mills and pays its respects to the area. A wall painting gives you a picture of Leonardo's dreams for Romorantin, while a Renault Espace counts among the museum exhibits. In addition, Romorantin has its ambitious Pyramide, rural rival to that of the Louvre in Paris; at Romorantin, this Espace François I is used for cultural events.

Aliotis (*open early Feb–Oct daily 10–early evening; rest of year school hols, Wed and Sun same times;* **t** *02 54 95 26 26*), the Sologne aquarium, lies near Villeherviers, just a few kilometres east of Romorantin. The complex is protected by a curious funky permanent tent-like structure. The development of soggy Sologne for fishing dates back at least to early medieval times, when monks began regulating the waters with a whole network of lakes. A Sologne lake stopper made out of oak and reckoned to be 800 years old counts among the most ancient of objects on display. Now the Sologne has a staggering 3,000 lakes in all, covering some 12,000 hectares. In the aquarium's tanks you can see the fish that thrive in these lakes, and in the rivers of the Loire Valley more generally.

You might head north from here via the likes of **Millançay** or **Marcilly-en-Gault** to explore the major area of lakes, although most are in private hands and are difficult to appreciate close up. A bit further northeast, the village of **St-Viâtre** has more displays devoted to this lakeland at the Maison des Etangs (*open 15 June–15 Sept 10–12 and 2–6;* **t** *02 54 88 23 00*), along with panels suggesting walks in the area.

South from Selles-sur-Cher

Château de Valençay

Open 9–12 and 2–6; grounds open until nightfall.

'Shit in a silk stocking' was the not entirely flattering way in which Napoleon apparently once referred to Talleyrand, the most significant historical figure associated with the splendid Château de Valençay. But this massive castle, which stands aloof to one side of a pretty little town due south of Selles-sur-Cher, is once again the typical Loire Valley mix of late Gothic and French Renaissance forms, dating mainly from the

16th century. The two main features which immediately stand out when you arrive are the château's ornate keep and the great pepper-pot towers on one side, the latter the hallmark of Valençay. The keep, really something of a redundant military element left over from medieval architectural design, was here embellished with Renaissance features. It would almost be worth using binoculars to admire the wealth of sculptural details on the frieze placed high up around it.

Walk into the inner courtyard and the scene changes somewhat. The most imposing wing within was built at the start of the 18th century. To the south, views open onto the little Nahon valley, while to the east lie the château's vineyard and the town.

The entertaining guided visit around the grand interiors focuses on Talleyrand. Napoleon also said of this brilliant man: 'He was the most capable of all my ministers.' He became the emperor's massively powerful foreign minister, and was allowed to entertain foreign dignitaries at Valençay. Talleyrand married Catherine Worlée, whose beauty is clearly shown in a famous portrait of her at the château, painted by the reputed female artist Vigée Le Brun. But Catherine's stupidity was as great as her looks. She was said to have had '*pas plus d'esprit qu'une rose* (no more intellect than a rose)'. Although she became Princesse de Talleyrand, she was easily supplanted in her husband's affections by the wife of Talleyrand's nephew, his '*chère nièce*', as she was euphemistically known. She was an intelligent, driven woman who eventually came to reign with Talleyrand at Valençay. They entertained royally and liberally, the famous cook Carême cooking up sumptuous dishes for their guests.

After taking in the pompous Napoleonic interiors, wander round Valençay's grounds, which are populated with a whole menagerie of animals, while a makeshift outbuilding also holds an extensive collection of old cars.

Château de Bouges

Open July–Aug 10–1 and 2–7, April–June and Sept Wed–Mon 10–12 and 2–6, March and Nov weekends only 10–12 and 2–5.

You'll find pure elegance at the Château de Bouges, east off the D956 between Valençay and Levroux. A simple classical rectangle, it is sometimes compared with Versailles' Petit Trianon. The château built in 1762 for Count Charles Le Blanc de Marnaval, an owner of ironworks. His family didn't benefit from it long, and it too fell into Talleyrand's grasping hands for a time.

It is furnished the elegant accoutrements of noble life from the 18th and 19th centuries: a man's dressing table for powdering his wig; a *voyeuse* chair for women in vast crinolines to watch the society games comfortably; a *table à ouvrages* around which a family could sit, each member carrying out its own occupation, a locking drawer in front of every seat; a library ladder which folds away impeccably into a leather-covered stool; and a rent-farmer's table, with a turning drawer to avoid the vulgarity of passing money from hand to hand.

In season, beautifully arranged cut flowers from the garden adorn many rooms, while the generous grounds visible out of the windows beckon for a stroll.

The Cher from St-Aignan to Montrichard

St-Aignan is the nicest spot on the Cher after Chenonceaux. It's a very appealing little town, although its major tourist attraction is a well-run zoo well to the south. Montrichard, dominated by modern tower blocks as well as its medieval keep, makes an interesting historical stop too.

Between St-Aignan and Montrichard lie Cher valley vineyards and discreet attractions such as the Château du Gué-Péan, lost in its woods, the Gallo-Roman finds of Thésée, and the quarries of Bourré, reputed to have provided the purest stone in the Loire Valley. The mangled remnants of the abbey of Pontlevoy come as a big surprise rising out of the plain north of the Cher valley.

Tourist Information

St-Aignan: Maison du Tourisme, 26 Av Wilson, B.P.41, t 02 54 75 22 85, f 02 54 75 20 26.
Thésée-la-Romaine: Mairie, 41140 Thésée-la-Romaine, t/f 02 54 71 45 45.
Montrichard: 1 Rue du Pont, 41400 Montrichard, t 02 54 32 05 10, f 02 54 32 28 80.

Market Days

Montrichard: Monday afternoon and Friday morning.

Where to Stay and Eat

Noyers-sur-Cher ✉ 41140
★★★**Clos du Cher**, Route de St-Aignan, t 02 54 75 00 03, f 02 54 75 03 79, closcher@ chateauxhotels.com (*moderate*). This very pleasant hotel hides coquettishly on the north bank of the Cher outside St-Aignan, in a private park off the main road. It has characterful rooms furnished with antiques. The cuisine has style too (*menus €15–53.5*). *Hotel closed Jan–mid-Feb, restaurant closed Wed pm and Thurs out of season.*

St-Aignan ✉ 41110
★★**Grand Hôtel St-Aignan**, 7–9 Quai J-J Delorme, t 02 54 75 18 04, f 02 54 75 12 59 (*inexpensive*). With large windows looking onto the Cher, this ivy-clad building is the archetypal old-fashioned French hotel (*menus €13.5–31.5*). *Hotel closed last 2 weeks Nov and mid-Feb–mid-Mar, restaurant closed Sun eve and Mon out of season.*

Hôtel-Restaurant du Moulin, 7 Rue de Novilliers, t 02 54 75 15 54 (*cheap*). A miniature *auberge* for bargain hunters, with a jumble of corridors, a peaceful inner courtyard and clean rooms right by the river (*menu €8*). *Closed Sun evenings in season and all Sun out of season.*
Chez Constant, Place de la Paix, t 02 54 75 10 75. With its old painted beams and its bright red plush seats, this is a lively new restaurant in a rather splendid old setting, professionally run and offering good local dishes (*menus €10–15*).

Mareuil-sur-Cher ✉ 41110
Ferme Auberge La Lionnière/Bouland B&B, t 02 54 75 24 99, f 02 54 75 44 74, *fa-lionnière @wanadoo.fr* (*inexpensive*). Lost in the countryside (follow the signs carefully from Mareuil's *boulangerie*) is this charming little country farm B&B with restaurant attached. The good-value rooms, neatly set under the eaves, are bright and fresh, with the rural pleasure of the farmyard just outside. It helps to like goat in all its forms if you come and eat, as it predominates on the very filling menus. Lamb, duck, guinea fowl and freshwater fish can also be on the menu – check when you ring. On sunny days you can eat out on benches in the delightfully unkempt garden (*menus €15–20.5*). *You must book in advance; closed Mon out of season.*

Thésée ✉ 41140
★★**Moulin de la Renne**, 15 Impasse des Varennes, t 02 54 71 41 56, f 02 54 71 75 09 (*inexpensive*). This place's setting is its main

St-Aignan

Like a decadent parody of a Jacob's ladder, a magnificent monumental staircase climbs from St-Aignan's church not up to heaven but up to the **château of St-Aignan**. The interiors aren't open to the public, but you can appreciate its grand exterior, and from the splendid terrace you can enjoy good views down onto this delightful town. One side of the town tumbles down the slope to the Cher. On the other side, the old town roofs, a mix of brown tiles and slate, are crammed together in the cramped valley of a tributary of the Cher.

Aignan, after whom the town is named, was the bishop of Orléans who saved that city from Attila the Hun. An island in the middle of the Cher here is known as **L'Île aux**

charm, with possibilities for fishing and walking. The rooms are rather bare, but the cooking's good value (*menus €13–33.5*). *Closed Sun evening and Mon out of season, and mid-Jan–mid-March.*

Oisly ✉ 41700

Le Saint Vincent, southwest of Contres (via the D675 and the D21), t 02 54 79 50 04, f 02 54 79 64 19. This may not look anything special on the village square, but inside the chef is devoted to his cuisine. Original dishes include the likes of guinea fowl served in aromatic wine and pork confit with rhubarb cream (*menus €13.5–32*). *Closed Sun pm and Mon, and end Oct.*

Pontlevoy ✉ 41400

**Hôtel de l'Ecole, 12 Route de Montrichard, t 02 54 32 50 30, f 02 54 32 33 58 (*inexpensive*). The flower- and ivy-covered façades have an immediate charm, set back just off the main street in this calm little town. There's a pleasant garden where you can eat in summer – the food is well executed (*menus €15.5–43.5*). *Hotel closed Feb–mid-March and Tues rest of year.*

Montrichard ✉ 41400

***Le Bellevue, 24 Quai de la République, t 02 54 32 06 17, f 02 54 32 48 06 (*inexpensive*). Big and modern, it has some comfortable rooms with good views of the river. The restaurant serves filling fare (*menus €13.5–44*).

***La Tête Noire, 24 Rue de Tours, B.P.03, t 02 54 32 05 55, f 02 54 32 78 37 (*inexpensive*).

Offers slightly cheaper but good quality rooms, while the annexe has a shaded garden leading down to the Cher (*menus €15–40.5*). *Closed Jan.*

Chissay-en-Touraine ✉ 41400

***Château de Chissay, Chissay-en-Touraine, t 02 54 32 32 01, f 02 54 32 43 80, chateau-chissay@wanadoo.fr (*expensive*). A pure white château that stands out proudly among the woods above the Cher valley road. Its architecture has been mutilated in parts for visitors' comfort and commercial expansion, but it has many attractions, in particular characterful, bedrooms furnished with antiques, a tiny chapel and fine vaulted reception rooms. In the superb dining room try imaginative avant-garde cuisine on curiously shaped plates. The swimming pool lies down the slope, the railway line close by a slight irritation amid such luxuries (*menus €28–45*). *Closed mid-Nov–mid-Mar.*

La Ménaudière ✉ 41401

***Château de la Ménaudière, B.P.15, t 02 54 71 23 45, f 02 54 71 34 58, menauderie@chateauxhotels.com (*expensive*). Another luxurious choice, on the D115, this dates back to the 16th century, like nearby Chenonceau. The château's rooms are spacious and stylish, the setting peaceful. There is a heated swimming pool and a tennis court, and the restaurant is of a high quality (*menus €18.5–49*). *Hotel closed early Jan–early March; restaurant closed Sun pm and Mon out of season.*

Trois Evêques, 'the island of the three bishops', indicating the ancient divide between the territories of the dioceses of Orléans, Tours and Bourges that lay here. The hillside above became a site of strategic importance in the territorial struggles between the counts of Blois and of Anjou at the start of the second millennium. A southern fort for the Blois family, the place was attacked by the dreaded Foulques Nerra of Anjou, who extended his vast domains down the Cher valley in the early 11th century.

Descending the château staircase, you're led straight into the great narthex of the **church of St-Aignan** below. The soaring tower is a 19th-century addition to the large Romanesque building beyond. (You can climb the tower in summer for a small fee.) On the front of the church, note the words '*République française*', left from the time the holy place was forcibly converted to secular use at the Revolution. Inside, 19th-century restorers have had their cleansing way, giving the spaces an almost hospital-like whiteness. The capitals in the choir look absurdly sparkling and new, although the figures are in the entertaining Romanesque tradition. For a recorded commentary on the church, on the left as you enter there's a button which activates a 15-minute recorded guided tour.

The high point of the church interior is the **crypt**. This was an older church upon which the larger one above was later plonked. The dark, dank place contains some fine vestiges of Romanesque wall paintings and capitals; it also offered excellent conditions for a local wine merchant to keep his stock in the last century, saving this level from the clinical restoration work carried out above. The most original painting depicts events not from the life of St Aignan but from that of St Gilles; here he performs acts of charity and miracles, clothing a beggar, healing a man bitten by a snake bite and even praying powerfully enough to rescue a ship from being wrecked. A grandiose Christ in Majesty was painted in the inner chapel. He is flanked by St Peter and St James Minor, who appear to bow before his glory thanks to the curve of the ceiling. At the feet of their robes, cripples grovel, one with a stick holding out a coin, another moving along on walking irons. The frescoes to the side of this scene are much later, from the 15th century, but also show penitent, frail mortals, the lord of St-Aignan, Louis II de Chalon, and his second wife, Jeanne de Perellos. They caused a terrible scandal in 1420 when they eloped from the Burgundian court – Louis was unfortunately already married to Marie de la Trémoïlle. Look out too for a 16th-century interpretation of the Last Judgement, illustrating what Louis and Jeanne might well have lived in fear of.

The cobbled streets and squares in the little town below the church are full of old houses, a few with crooked medieval frames and carved beams, others in more controlled 16th- or 17th-century styles. You can take a **boat trip** down the Cher from St-Aignan with Le Val de Cher, **t** 02 54 71 40 38, or hire canoes or pedaloes.

Zooparc de Beauval

Open April–Nov 9–nightfall, Nov–March 10–nightfall.

This top-class zoo (clearly marked south from St-Aignan) started with an innocent-sounding request which should act as a cautionary tale to all parents. Madame

Delord was asked by her three-year-old daughter whether they could keep a couple of birds in their Paris apartment. Now she runs this large zoo with her children – fortunately still impassioned about animals now that they've grown up. Some of the species kept and bred here and some of the pens built for them in this quiet, well-tended little valley make Beauval compare favourably with the most respected zoos in the world. More than a dozen of the animals are part of the European Endangered Species Programme (EEP).

One of the strengths of the park is its sizeable **aviary** full of tropical birds. Outside, the vultures, owls and parrots are limited to more conventional little pens. The parrots tend to come from Parisian owners who got sick of their pets, as do a few of the more dangerous animals – Beauval doubles as something of an animal sanctuary. Parrots were prized as possessions rarer than many a fabulous jewel by the Loire Valley kings of France. Along with the booty and artists which Charles VIII brought back with him from his Italian foray at the end of the 15th century was a Moor from Naples, recruited to serve as royal parrot-keeper!

In the mammals section of the zoo, the **wild cats** are particularly impressive. The most famous inmates are the white tigers, their shaggy coats striped with brown lines. The mature ones reach the size of small bulls and are infinitely more awe-inspiring. White lions, snow panthers, black panthers, pumas and jaguars – in all a collection of around 30 types of big cats – also laze in their enclosures. In the house for apes and monkeys, the gorillas and the mournful-faced orang-utangs don't look as though they would hurt a flea, but the chimpanzees are generally completely out of order, the males outrageously aggressive. A major investment of recent years has been in the large **seal pool**, a clear commercial venture to increase the number of visitors. In season there are displays of seal acrobatics, as well as of falconry. The 'savannah' beyond, a largish section of hillside cut out in the shape of Africa, has also been developed to hold a selection of animals from south of the Sahara, such as giraffes, zebras, antelopes and rhinos. Panels throughout the park impart educational information about the animals.

From Thésée-la-Romaine to the Château du Gué-Péan and the Abbey of Pontlevoy

Vineyards begin to hold their own on the Cher's southern slopes west of St-Aignan. The D17 leads to Pouillé, where you can cross north to **Thésée-la-Romaine**. This place has a rather grand name to indicate the small Gallo-Roman finds made here. The town hall, a tall, sparkling white building in a pleasant park, has a small Musée Archéologique (*open July–Aug Wed–Mon 2.30–6.30, Easter–June and Sept–mid-Oct weekends and public hols only 3–6*) on the top floor. The Gallo-Roman objects on display include some pieces of quite ornate pottery. These fragments came from the ancient settlement of the ruined **Tasciaca**, or **Les Maselles** as it's now known, 1km west of the village (*open July–Aug Wed–Mon 2.30–6.30*). Small vestiges of Gallo-Roman walls still stand here.

The **Château du Gué-Péan** (*open July–Aug 10.30–12.30 and 2–6.30; t 02 54 71 37 10*) is a Sleeping Beauty of a castle, not quite cut off by impenetrable woods and brambles, but lost down dark tracks beyond the village of Monthou-sur-Cher and its undulating vineyards. Gué-Péan means 'paying ford', but it's hard to imagine anyone forking out money to pass via such obscure back roads in centuries past.

A joy to look at as you arrive, the château seems somewhat dejected when you get closer, even badly run down at the back. It is full of charm though. Each corner is marked by a solid tower, one standing out from the rest – comparisons with a bell, a pepper-pot or even a German military helmet don't seem wholly absurd. The front sections of the buildings beyond date from the middle of the 16th century. These parts were built for François Alaman, a high-ranking royal taxman. He amassed enough of a fortune to transform the previous château on the spot, which his family had owned for over a century. Further back still, the two main wings were redone in the 17th century, in plain but noble style. Decayed elegance has been the main feature of the *cour d'honneur* until recently, especially with its disused pool in the centre. And inside, the string of *salons* wore an air of jaded beauty. But the castle has been acquired by new owners who may bring the place the new lease of life it needs.

Oisly, northeast of Gué-Péan, is known for its wine cooperative (*see box on p.221*). Northwest of Gué-Péan is the **Abbaye de Pontlevoy** (*open July–Aug daily 10–12 and 2–6, Easter–June and Sept daily exc for Mon public hols 10–12 and 2.30–5.30; t 02 54 32 60 80*), an extraordinarily large and imposing religious complex seemingly set in the middle of nowhere. Approached from the south, the top of the abbey church looks like a lovely little Gothic chapel tossed into the air. The structure in front of it, by contrast, has the sturdy neoclassical appearance of a military school. It turns out that the abbey did serve for a short time as a military school, during the reign of Louis XVI.

The guided tour around the curious array of grand buildings is bizarre indeed, mixing a history of the abbey with a trawl through a series of strange museum collections. It tour takes some time, so be prepared. The abbey's history goes back almost 1,000 years. The guides maintain that its tradition of excellence in education has continued virtually uninterrupted through that time – you have to count recent stints as an apprentices' school and as a heavy goods vehicle training centre! Certainly the abbey has had a typically rough ride for a French religious foundation, devastated on several occasions.

The oldest part you visit is the Gothic church, where the nave has gone AWOL. That's why the choir seems to soar so strangely by itself into the air when you see the abbey from a distance. However, the choir alone is the size of a decent church. Its architecture dates from the end of 13th century to the beginning of 15th, with heavily restored Gothic tracery windows and side chapels radiating out from the centre. Inside, the decoration is 17th century, an indication of the establishment's revival after Cardinal Richelieu (*see pp.342–4*) became its abbot. Look out for the splendid choir stalls and a couple of superb, excessive Baroque altarpieces. A very worn older fresco of St Martin was also uncovered relatively recently.

Richelieu established a Benedictine order at the abbey, which then gained a reputation for the excellence of its teaching. In the course of the 18th century, military education triumphed at Pontlevoy though. With its religious and conservative army connections, the institution was scarcely likely to be popular at the Revolution, but a dynamic abbot restored the place's fortunes at the start of the 19th century, training many students for the elite military *grandes écoles*, encouraging that heady worship of God and country. An awful number of teachers and students died serving in the First World War.

After visiting the church, you're taken along past the 18th-century façade of the abbey, a massive length of white Loire masonry. It's no surprise to learn that this wing has room enough to house a theatre, but on the tour inside you see very little apart from the empty refectory, which contains a fine Delft stove removed from the Château de Chambord, and the grand staircase with its magnificent trapezoid stair-well. You're then taken through the remains of the cloister in the vast inner courtyard.

The guided tour becomes increasingly daft and disjointed from this point on as disparate collections are lovingly commented on by the all-too-enthusiastic and rigor-ously trained guides. After the old heavy goods vehicle collection come Poulain drinking chocolate posters and then photographs of early aviation. The connection? Up until recently the abbey was used a training school for road haulage studies; the founder of the Poulain chocolate company was born in Pontlevoy; and the very early airfield here was used as a halt on the 1910 Paris to Madrid race.

Troglodyte Bourré

Bourré sits back on the Cher's north bank, just east of the town of Montrichard. Its name is synonymous with some of the finest-quality stone in the Loire. Across the region, château guides will cite the name of Bourré with pride if it's been used in the construction of their particular architectural treasure. It's astonishing to hear that in the course of four centuries, some 400 kilometres of quarries were carved out in the area around Montrichard. The best tufa in these parts lay around 20–30m under the earth, and was known as *le blanc royal*, royal white – the stone of Bourré apparently whitens with age as the water in the stone evaporates. The most famous buildings to use Bourré blocks include some of the most illustrious Loire châteaux, notably Chambord, for which some 450,000 pieces were required.

To appreciate Bourré's picturesque cliffside setting, it's worth taking a look at it from the south, in the valley. No longer exploited for stone, the former quarries have been converted to other uses. Mushrooms are cultivated in vast caverns you can visit – follow the signs for the **Caves Champignonnières des Roches** (*open Easter to All Saints', guided tours at 10 and 11, and on the hour 2–5; t 02 54 32 35 15*). The newest troglodyte site in Bourré has been created by the young and dynamic Maurice de Lalande, whose family own the mushroom farm, some of whose ancestors were stone quarriers.

On a tour of the **Carrière de Tuffeau and Ville Souterraine** (*open April–Nov 10–6, tours on the hour; t 02 54 32 35 15*) you can not only learn about the centuries of quar-rying that went on in these parts, but also see the work of a couple of present-day sculptors who have created a fake village in stone in a corner of the quarry. The main artist, Christian Lhermite, working with an assistant, Luc Bodin, has spent an enor-

Goat's Cheese and Wine in the Cher Valley

It's not just wine that can get an *appellation d'origine contrôlée* label along the Cher valley: the goat's cheese has a very strong reputation. Good places to try it or buy it include the *fromagerie*, or cheese shop, on the church square at Selles-sur-Cher, the *ferme-auberge* at Mareuil-sur-Cher, where you can go and visit the goats before tasting their produce (*see* p.215), or the Ferme de Bellevue at Pontlevoy, with a choice of *appellation* cheeses on offer, which you can taste at a small charge with some Touraine wine.

From around St-Aignan and west to the Touraine border, vineyards prettify the banks of the Cher valley. A large percentage of the grapes go for vinification to the Oisly et Thésée *confrérie* (rebaptized Wally and Teazy by some in the British wine trade). This cooperative, based at Oisly, has established a solid reputation for improving the quality of the local wines since it was founded at the start of the 1960s.

Slightly confusingly, the best wine produced in this part of the Loir-et-Cher is categorized as AOC Touraine. A small number of vinegrowers vinify and bottle their own production, reds, rosés and whites, and very occasionally sparkling wine too. The characteristic Loire grape varieties feature and are most often stated on the label to differentiate the types. Gamay dominates in the reds, with Cabernet France and Côt added in varying amounts. Sauvignon wins out in the whites, possibly supplemented by Chenin Blanc or Pineau de Loire.

A fine address to start tasting at would be the **Clos Roche Blanche** (*t 02 54 75 17 03*) at Mareuil-sur-Cher, splendidly located overlooking the valley, with a cellar in the cliff face where they sell their organic wine. Slightly northeast of St-Aignan, the **Domaine du Chapitre** (*t 02 54 71 71 22*) at St-Romain-sur-Cher has been run by the same family for a couple of centuries. The **Domaine Joel Delaunay** (*t 02 54 71 45 69*) at Pouillé, on the south bank opposite Thésée, benefits from magnificent views. Here you can appreciate the recently installed modern vat house for vinification. At Pontlevoy, you could try **Michel Roy** (*t 02 54 32 51 07*), who welcomes you in an unpretentious little reception room.

In Montrichard, the **Caves de Monmousseau** (*t 02 54 71 66 66*) is the well-known name (*see* Montrichard, p.222). Also in Montrichard, Paul Buisse, a former professional cook turned winemaker and merchant, will enthuse to you in his cliffside cellars on Route de Vierzon, the **Caves de la Boule Blanche** (*t 02 54 32 00 01*).

Finally, there are a couple of vineyards you might visit at St-Georges-sur-Cher close to Chenonceaux. At the panoramically sited **Domaine Guenault** (*t 02 54 32 31 36*), Noël Bougrier is a vinegrower and wine merchant who sells a wide variety of Touraine wines. The substantial **Domaine de la Rablais** (*t 02 54 71 36 14*) is also well used to receiving tourists.

mous amount of time shaping façades, human figures and animals. There are even vines in stone down here. It's a slightly curious enterprise, to have carved out such a static place in rock when there are so many pretty, living (or at least semi-living) villages above ground in these parts.

At **La Magnanerie** (*open April–Oct Wed–Mon; visits at 11, 2, 3, 4 and 5*) the guided tour teaches you about further uses to which the caves were converted, both for human habitation and for silk worm production.

Montrichard

The authorities at Montrichard clearly decided to place housing above tourism at one time in the town's not-too-distant past. The result is the provocative siting of an army of modern apartment blocks on the hillside beyond Montrichard's splendid remnant of a medieval keep. Judge for yourselves how successful the decision was. The keep still manages to hold its own on the skyline, though. It has stood the test of time rather better than the ruined fortifications around it. The whole medieval complex recalls the period when Montrichard was fought over by the great regional counts and by English and French royalty. Yes, Foulques Nerra of Anjou raises his ugly head again. He only had a wooden fortification built here, however; the stone keep you can still see went up a century after Foulques Nerra. The keep itself is now too structurally unsafe to enter. A narrow, cramped tower among the fortifications manages though to squeeze in the **local museum** on its different levels. Displays on archaeology, history and local explorers who headed for wider horizons (the Sahara) are neatly fitted into the tiny spaces.

Popular legend has it that the town's name, Mount Richard, derives from Richard the Lionheart's connection with the place (he was apparently responsible for ordering the fortifications surrounding the foot of the keep, as well as the town walls, late in the 12th century) – but in fact the name of Montrichard preceded his arrival. The town experienced a further flurry of royal activity in the 15th century, under King Louis XI, who brought the fief into the French royal possessions the year of his accession, 1461. Superstitious to a fault, he couldn't resist getting control of the **church of Notre-Dame de Nantheuil**, whose statue of the Virgin and Child was said to work miracles and attracted a large number of pilgrims. As with the Notre-Dame de Cléry (*see* pp.158–9), Louis lavished money on this building to his beloved Virgin. The pilgrimage church still draws Catholics devoted to the Virgin on Whit Monday. Louis XI had it restored, but the old Romanesque forms were respected, with the addition of elaborate Flamboyant doors, whose admirable decoration includes Louis' arms.

Beyond fortifications and church, Montrichard boasts quite a fine legacy of medieval buildings. It's worth going to the tourist office just to take in its grand brick façade. The other houses worth a look at stand close by. A fair amount of the life of the town is concentrated down by the river, with its little cobbled quay leading to the water. On the eastern edge of town, the **Caves de Monmousseau** (*t 02 54 32 35 15*) are impressive quarries on several levels turned into wine cellars for a firm which produces Loire bubbly wine on a grand scale. The guided tour through an impressive labyrinth of limestone corridors takes you to the Musée des Confréries Européennes, devoted to the mass of wine fraternities across France, and ends with a tasting. West of Montrichard, in the village of **Chissay-en-Touraine**, the alcoholic curiosity is a strawberry liqueur distillery. From Montrichard, you can take to the Cher on the *Leonard de Vinci*, a grandiosely named little boat (*t 02 54 75 41 53*).

The Cher from Chenonceaux to Tours

The Château de Chenonceau (without an 'x') by the village of Chenonceaux (with an 'x') is the star of this stretch of the Cher, of course. Lost in woods to the south of it, the Château de Montpoupon has recently opened a museum on hunting. A few splendid little villages lie along the Cher valley west of Chenonceau before the suburbs of Tours.

Château de Chenonceau

Open mid-March–mid-Sept 9–7, rest of Sept 9–6.30, early March and first half of Oct 9–6, rest of Oct and mid–end Feb 9–5.30, first half Feb and first half Nov 9–5, mid-Nov–Jan 9–4.30; t 02 47 23 90 07.

As the royal party passed by, trees burst into cascades of fireworks and fountains gushed with wine. The later fêtes were more licentious; in 1573 women dressed as men and Henri III and his acolytes were gorgeously dressed as girls.

Marcus Binney on parties at Chenonceau, in *Châteaux of the Loire*

Most glamorous of all the Loire Valley châteaux, with its galleries spanning the Cher, the Château de Chenonceau almost incites decadence, it's so irresistibly gorgeous. It's also said to be the most visited castle in France after Versailles. You can well believe it when you see the crowds crammed into its relatively small space. Those of you who feel put off by the chattering, cluttering groups might try using your imaginations to re-create the atmosphere of those 16th-century royal parties.

You approach the château through a dramatic alley of vast plane trees, at the end of which you can make out the entrance façade romantically filling the view at the end of a tunnel of branches. There are two distinct parts to the château itself. The square block you get a glimpse of from afar is the earlier part. With its splendid corner turrets and windows, it was built for Thomas Bohier, an inspector of finances for kings Louis XII and François I. He had bought the property in 1512 from the bankrupt Marques family. who had been the owners of the estate here from the 13th century, in 1423 replacing a manor house with their château. Thomas Bohier had this medieval castle destroyed, save one sturdy tower, the Tour des Marques. It still stands, on your right as you arrive in front of the castle.

Bohier decided to build his château on the Cher itself, using the foundations of a mill built on the river. Construction began in 1515, the year of François I's accession. A regional builder, Pierre Nepveu, known as Le Trinqueau, directed the work. He would also play an important part in the building of Chambord (*see* pp.165–8) for François I. As Thomas Bohier accompanied the king on his expeditions, including to Italy, it was his wife Katherine (née Briçonnet) who oversaw many of the developments. The initials TB and TK to be seen in numerous locations around the château refer to Thomas Bohier and Thomas and Katherine. The Bohiers' magical residence was completed by 1521, the year in which Thomas' brother Antoine, archbishop of Bourges, came to consecrate the chapel.

Bohier's 'keep', as this first château is sometimes rather misleadingly called, has
splendidly elegant proportions and rooms. On the eastern side built over the river,
two prows of stone protrude, the first containing the chapel, the second two rooms,
including a delightful library. The pillars of the arch under Bohier's building were
ingeniously fitted with kitchens, a little stairway leading down to a platform at which
boats could dock to unload deliveries.

The king had granted the Bohiers permission to construct a bridge over the Cher,
but they both died in the mid-1520s, before any work on one could be started.
Financial scandal ruined the families of many of François I's financiers and the
builders of many of the Loire's most famous châteaux. After Thomas Bohier's death,
he was found guilty of embezzlement and his son was forced to hand over the
château to the crown in 1535 by way of repayment. So the extravagant François I
gained possession of yet another beautiful Loire Valley castle, and Chenonceau was
temporarily reduced to serving for the occasional hunt. The Holy Roman Emperor
Charles V, during his visit to France in 1539, was brought to see Chenonceau on the
tour of royal properties François I organized to impress him.

François I's successor, his son Henri II, gave away Chenonceau as a token of his love –
unfortunately not to his wife, Catherine de' Medici, but to his mistress, Diane de
Poitiers, instead. The deeds described the donation as one of gratitude towards
Diane's late husband, Louis de Brézé, for his services to the king. It's perhaps not
surprising that this unsubtle ruse might have galled the formidable Catherine. Diane
had many ideas for Chenonceau and had her architect, the famous Philibert de
l'Orme, draw up plans. Arches were built over the Cher to reach the other bank and
the intention appears to have been to build a gallery on top of them, but this wasn't
done. Some of the garden designs Diane approved were carried out at vast expense.
Diane herself virtually never came to Chenonceau, preferring her stunning château at
Anet, much closer to Paris.

Catherine de' Medici had her revenge on her husband's death in 1559. Henry
James called it 'the most pardonable of all the revenges with which the name of

Catherine de' Medici is associated'. She forced Diane to give up Chenonceau and accept in exchange the only slightly less gorgeous Château de Chaumont on the Loire (*see* pp.233–7). Under Catherine, Chenonceau underwent its most important transformation. It was Catherine who ordered the second wing of Chenonceau to be built, with its beautiful galleries over the Cher. The name of the architect remains uncertain, but it seems most likely that Jean Bullant was responsible for the work. The construction is extremely graceful. Dating from the 1570s, it's much more soberly classical in design than the square 'keep'. There is, though, a wonderful rhythm to the galleries' bays and details, for example the *œil de bœuf* windows in the roof. And the ceaseless swirling of water in the Cher beneath it adds movement and excitement.

Catherine also greatly altered the appearance of the earlier Bohier château, some say rather grossly, adding great caryatid figures in the grotesque Mannerist style favoured at the time and redoing many windows. These changes were got removed at a much later date. Most extravagantly, Catherine had plans for two great wings fanning out from the Bohiers' building. These wings would have dwarfed the château as we know it today, but were never constructed. Outbuildings were added in the outer courtyard, though.

Getting Around

Chenonceaux is on the slow Tours–Romorantin **train** route, which also stops occasionally at some of the towns and villages along the way, notably Bléré.

By **road**, the south-bank N76 is slightly prettier than the north-bank D140 between Tours and Chenonceaux.

There are a couple of **buses** a day between the Château de Chenonceau and Tours (Touraine Fil Vert ligne C). Bléré, Athée-sur-Cher and Azay-sur-Cher lie on Touraine Fil Vert Ligne D.

Boat trips are possible from Bléré and Chisseaux.

Tourist Information

Chenonceaux: B.P.1, 1 Rue Dr Bretonneau, 37150 Chenonceaux, t 02 47 23 94 45.
Bléré: B.P.43, 8 Rue J-J Rousseau, 37150 Bléré, t 02 47 57 93 00, f 02 47 30 81 88, *tourisme@blere-touraine.com*.

Market Days

Bléré: Tuesday morning and Friday afternoon.

Where to Stay and Eat

Chenonceaux ✉ 37150

★★★Le Bon Laboureur, 6 Rue du Dr Bretonneau, t 02 47 23 90 02, f 02 47 23 82 01, *laboureur@chateauxhotels.com* (*expensive*). An 18th-century coaching inn, now the closest place to stay to the château in this village packed out with hotels and restaurants. The rooms are actually spread out in four different buildings, and are comfortable. On sunny days you can eat out on the terrace (*menus €26–50.5*). Hotel closed mid-Nov–mid-Dec and early Jan–early Feb; *restaurant closed Wed pm and Thurs Nov–March*.

★★★La Roseraie, 7 Rue du Dr Bretonneau, t 02 47 23 90 09, f 02 47 23 91 59, *lfiorito@aol.com* (*moderate*). This wasn't as well looked after as its neighbour, but new owners have recently taken over and have been giving the place a face-lift. The rooms are simpler. The cooking is hearty and generous (*menus €15–26*). Closed mid-Nov–mid-Feb.

★★La Renaudière, 24 Rue du Dr Bretonneau, t 02 47 23 90 04, f 02 47 23 90 51, *gerhotel@club-internet.fr* (*inexpensive*). Furthest of the bunch from the château, but it isn't far, and it has a chic brick

So often portrayed as a totally wicked witch of a Queen Mother, Catherine de' Medici held sumptuous festivals here, the *'triomphes de Chenonceau'*. Henry James isn't sparing in his estimation of her selfish capacity to enjoy parties, writing of 'the terrible daughter of the Medici, whose appreciation of the good things in life was perfectly consistent with a failure to perceive why others should live to enjoy them'. Like so many other writers, he got a bit carried away by his own rhetoric of vilification. But the parties were outrageous.

The first of Catherine's Chenonceau *triomphes*, described in the opening quote, was held for her sickly son King François II and his wife, Mary, to go down in history as the unfortunate Queen of Scots. The artist Primaticcio masterminded the ceremony, which stood in such ironic contrast to the recent bloody repression of the Protestants involved in the Amboise Conspiracy (*see* pp.248–9). Cannon salvos greeted the young royals, while black banners recalled the Queen Mother's mourning for her recently dead husband. The courtyards and gardens were decked out with follies – a triumphal arch, obelisks, false altars and statues – and poets had prepared adulatory texts. Spectacular entertainments were laid on. Actors appeared as classical figures declaiming in grandiose fashion. One fountain splashed out claret. All in all, the entertainment was outrageously lavish.

façade and a pretty garden. One of its menus recreates old recipes (*menus €15– 39.5*). *Closed mid-Nov–mid-Dec and early Jan–mid-Feb.*

★★Hostel du Roy, 9 Rue du Dr Bretonneau, **t** 02 47 23 90 17, **f** 02 47 23 89 81 (*inexpensive*). A pleasing little turret marks the façade of this cheaper option. The rustic touches have been laid on a bit heavy-handedly here, but the food is copious, fitting the setting (*menus €10.5–28*). *Closed early Jan–mid-Feb.*

Au Gâteau Breton, 16 Rue du Dr Bretonneau, **t** 02 47 23 90 14. The small dining room expands in summer to the larger terrace outside. You can try Touraine specialities here for a good price (*menus c.€16.5*).

Civray-de-Touraine ✉ 37150

★★Château de l'Isle, 1 Rue de l'Ecluse, **t** 02 47 23 63 60, **f** 02 47 23 63 62, isle@chateauxhotels. com (*expensive*). This modest 18th-century manor set in private grounds which go down to the Cher river takes you well away from Chenonceaux's bustle, even though it lies just a little west of the château. Each room has its own character and the cuisine is well prepared (*menus €25.5–28.5*). *Hotel closed mid-Nov–mid-Jan.*

Bléré ✉ 37150

★★Le Cheval Blanc, 5 Place Charles Bidault, **t** 02 47 30 30 14, **f** 02 47 23 52 80 (*inexpensive*). Has a good reputation locally for its inventive cuisine, and cosy rooms are in an 18th-century house (*menus €14.9–38*). *Closed Feb, and Sun pm and Mon outside high season.*

★Hôtel du Cher, 9 Rue du Pont, **t** 02 47 57 95 15, **f** 02 47 30 26 35 (*inexpensive*). By the bridge, a basic, unpretentious address (*menus c.€13*).

Maison Pommé, 21 Rue Paul-Louis Courier. For a special tasting of Touraine charcuterie specialities, which are something of a local institution. Try *rillons*, *rillettes* and *andouillettes* washed down with local wine.

St-Martin-le-Beau ✉ 37270

★★Auberge de la Treille, 2 Rue d'Amboise, **t** 02 47 50 67 17, **f** 02 47 50 20 14 (*inexpensive*). Serves good traditional French dishes in its beamed interior (*menus €10.5–39.5*). *Closed mid-Feb–early March and Sun pm and Mon out of season.*

Larçay ✉ 37270

La Planchette, 46 Rue Nationale, **t** 02 47 50 54 73. Set in a 17th-century barn, this restaurant serves copious portions of barbecued meats and local wines at bargain prices.

On François II's early death, King Henri III's gay abandon enlivened the place. Some have speculated that his mother tried to tempt him with wild parties here into making love to his wife and thus making more of an effort to continue the Valois line. Apparently more successful were the seductresses of Catherine de' Medici's 'flying squadron' of beautiful and intelligent aristocratic young women, trained to entice the leading nobles of the realm, all the better to spy on them for the Queen Mother! Henri III's wife, Louise de Lorraine, was devout and devoted. It was to her that Catherine de' Medici would in fact leave Chenonceau. After Henri III's assassination in 1589, Louise became a recluse, mourning in white, as was the royal tradition. When she passed away, the château was pretty well neglected for a century and more.

It was an ancestor of the writer George Sand, a tax gatherer by the name of Dupin, who restored some dignity to Chenonceau after he bought it in 1730. His wife gathered together many figures of the Enlightenment in parties at the château. Jean-Jacques Rousseau even served for a while at Chenonceau as teacher to the Dupins' son. At the Revolution, an attempt to dismantle this once-royal home is said to have been averted by the subtle reasoning of a local priest; he advanced the purely utilitarian argument that it would be a disservice to the community to get rid of the only river crossing between Montrichard and Bléré! So Chenonceau survived unscathed.

Another in a line of important woman in Chenonceau's history, one Madame Pelouze, bought the château in 1863. She asked the architect Felix Roguet to follow as closely as possible the engravings of Chenonceau drawn by the architect Du Cerceau at the end of the 16th century, in order to try to restore the château to its Renaissance appearance, and the original forms re-emerged.

The Interiors of the Château de Chenonceau

Within, evocative 19th-century decoration was made to complement what was left from the 16th century. This has since been added to by the private owners since 1913, the Menier family, who built their fat fortune on chocolate bars. The interior of the château holds many delights, particularly on sunny days, when the sparkling light reflecting off the Cher's waters jumps around the rooms. The tour is easy to follow off the single central corridor.

On the ground floor, an eccentric ceiling has highly decorated key stones. The first room, the so-called **Salle des Gardes**, sets the tone for the chambers that follow, decked out with 16th-century tapestries and chests. Off it lies the little **chapel**, retaining its original door and graffiti scratched by the Scots guards who protected the French royal family. It was a captain of the Scots guard, Gabriel Montgomery, who accidentally killed King Henri II in a jousting tournament. The next room is described as **Diane's bedroom** and has an extraordinary fireplace by Jean Goujon, decorated with lions and putti on balls and flanked by caryatids. A modern portrait of Catherine de' Medici is framed in the centre of it. Is it a joke that one of the tapestries depicts *The Triumph of Charity* and another *The Triumph of Power*? The *Virgin and Child* is attributed to Murillo. Off this room, the interlaced Cs of the magnificent ceiling make clear who made the green cabinet her own. Powerful paintings also decorate the room. The **library** jutting out over the river has a coffered ceiling which recalls the Bohiers with their initials. It's a perfect little room, even if there are no books in it.

Heading on to the **gallery** over the Loire, despite its magical light, it's slightly disappointing to find the long, elegant room empty. The place is so patently made for celebration that nothing short of candles, moonlight and dancing would make the atmosphere live up to the imagination. In the First World War, the gallery served as a makeshift hospital. During the Second World War, once France had capitulated and up until the end of 1942, Chenonceau lay on the frontier between German-occupied France and Vichy France, formed by the Cher at this point. The gallery is said to have been used at the time by members of the Resistance. The place was then occupied by the Germans and targeted by Allied bombs in 1944.

The so-called **François I room** has a fireplace covered with Bohier's motto 'S'il vient à point me souviendra', roughly interpreted as meaning that if he completed his work (the château) he would be remembered. Diane de Poitiers is recalled here in a painting by Primaticcio, said to have been executed at Chenonceau when Diane was proprietor. The *Three Graces* by Van Loo depict the Des Nesles sisters, favourites of Louis XV. Signs of royalty decorate the place, the salamander and full ermine on the fireplace referring to François I and Claude de France, while Louis XIV, always generous about donating paintings of himself to the provinces, left a Rigaud work surrounded by an overelaborate gilded frame. Rubens' *Baby Jesus with St John* contrasts with it.

The finely wrought stonework of the staircase leads to the simpler corridor on the first floor, lined with exquisite 17th-century Audenaarde tapestry scenes of a hunt. Fine furnishings abound on this upper level. The names given to the four main chambers recall royal figures and events: one is named after Catherine de' Medici; another, that of the Five Queens, after her five well-married girls (her two queenly daughters and three queenly daughters-in-law); yet another after Henri IV's favourite, Gabrielle d'Estrées, whose son by the king, César de Vendôme, would be married to a niece of Henri III's widow. A morbid room on the top floor re-creates the tearful surrounds in which the White Queen, as Louise de Lorraine became known because of her attachment to white mourning clothes, lived her last 11 years.

You can wander along the river banks and through the relatively small but well-tended **formal gardens**. The **Bâtiment des Dômes** outbuildings contain a waxworks museum, recreating some of Chenonceau's historic moments, and a tea house. The château's **son-et-lumière** (**t** *02 47 23 90 97 for information and bookings*) recalls in particular the importance of the women in Chenonceau's history.

From **Chisseaux**, east of Chenonceaux, you might consider joining a boat trip or gourmet cruise on board the *Bélandre* (**t** *02 47 23 98 64*), which takes you along the river and under Chenonceau's arches. When Henry James came to visit Cheonceau, he was most surprised to encounter a gondolier he had met in Venice, and who had been brought to the château, gondola in tow, to paddle prettily in the Cher.

Château de Montpoupon

Open July and Aug 10–6; April, June and Sept 10–12 and 2–6; May and Oct weekends and public hols only 10–12 and 2–6; t 02 47 94 21 15.

Montpoupon feels far from the madding crowds of Chenonceau, although it lies only a little way south. The château looks quite picturesque on its charming rise above three diminutive valleys. A pleasant Gothic-to-Renaissance gateway stands in front of the much restored main building. Montpoupon once lay on the royal road to Spain. Owned by the De Prie family from the early 14th to the mid-17th centuries, the place thrived on hunting. It is still devoted to the sport, with a smart hunt museum, the Musée du Veneur, set up in the outhouses. As at the Gien hunt museum (*see* pp.112–13), the exhibits are good enough to be of interest even to visitors unsure about hunting. Inscribed antlers, costumes, buttons, weapons, a generous collection of topical scarves from Hermès, prints and memorabilia give a full picture of the long-established aristocratic pastime.

From Chenonceaux to Tours

Before you reach the sprawling outer suburbs of Tours, the Cher valley reserves a few further picturesque little spots along its banks. **Bléré** comes to life in the summer, with activities on the river. On the north bank, **La Croix-en-Touraine** and **Dierre** each have charming village churches, the latter's restored partly thanks to a donation from the British Queen Mother, who must have been moved by her visit to the place. **St-Martin-le-Beau**, with its mixture of brown and slate-tiled roofs like its bigger wine cousin Montlouis, to the west, also produces wine under Montlouis' *appellation* (*see* p.259). Five extraordinary layers of foliage and geometric Romanesque decoration surround the doorway to the village church. Inside, the refined white marble Virgin is attributed to the great Tours Renaissance sculptor Michel Colombe.

Cross back south over the river here to appreciate the Cher's climbing bank. A string of châteaux line the way, best seen from the GR41 national walking route. After the château in **Nitray**, whose park you can visit and whose wines you can taste, you carry on west past the châteaux of Beauvais (neo-Gothic), Leugny (late 18th century, copying Versailles' Petit Trianon) and Coteau. **Azay-sur-Cher**, by the latter, is yet another pretty riverside village.

Do seek out the **Prieuré de Saint-Jean-du-Grais** (*open late April–mid-June weekends and public hols 10–7*) if you're around these parts at the weekend. It's the most delightful ensemble of disused religious buildings, set in the quiet countryside just a few kilometres south of Azay-sur-Cher. An enormous forest covered this area in early medieval times, and two hermits, Renaud Fremaud and Geoffroy Paissonnel, chose to settle in it in 1120. They were on the vast territories of Count Foulques V of Anjou. The count was away crusading at the time, but his forest guards were busily enforcing his rights and insisted that the two hermits pay their taxes.

When Foulques V returned to France, he lifted these taxes and even donated land to the hermits in 1127. The official document registering this act was signed by other notable regional figures of the day, including Pétronille de Chemillé, abbess of Fontevraud abbey (*see* pp.368–75), and Hugues de Payens, founder and Grand Master of the Knights Templars, who became bankers to the Crusades. In 1129, Foulques V left with Hugues on another campaign against the so-called infidel. He never returned, becoming King of Jerusalem and dying in the Middle East.

From 1163, the little religious community that had grown up at Grais began to construct priory buildings in stone. Now the prior was given powers over the local area, and was able to dispense justice in these parts, but soon the powerful heads of the nearby abbey of Cormery (*see* pp.290–91) and the deanery of St-Martin in Tours wrangled over who should have control over the priory. The papacy was asked to intervene, and decided to resolve the situation by putting the priory under its direct control, following which the history of the priory was relatively uneventful for centuries.

At the Revolution, the buildings were sold off to wealthy farmers, who turned the priory to agricultural uses. Inevitably the place was badly damaged. Although a stone rocket of a church tower still stands out from the ensemble, the rest of the church was brought down, its stone sold off. Around the opened-out courtyard, you're now shown a few empty but evocative chambers, including the lovely chapterhouse, the dormitory above, with traces of intriguing medieval graffiti, and the refectory with its beautiful oak timbers, its protruding pulpit and a fragment of badly damaged fresco representing Christ surrounded by the Evangelists. You're also shown round the separate 15th-century prior's lodgings, which the owners, the Darrasse family, plan to restore. It was Raymond Darrasse who did much to rescue the priory from total neglect from 1927, and added on some outbuildings, built in keeping with the style of the place. Although there isn't much to see at the priory at the moment, the passion of the owners for the place and its history, as well as the beauty of the setting, really make this a very appealing stop. There's a tea shop to incite you to linger a little longer.

Back by the Cher, the Eglise Notre-Dame at **Véretz** contains fine Renaissance art, with 16th- and 17th-century murals, and Christ and the Disciples depicted in terra-cotta medallions. **Larçay** plunges you right back into Gallo-Roman times; the ruins of a *castrum*, with its eight defensive towers is among the best in France of this kind of typical fortification, dating from the 3rd century when barbarian hordes were invading from the east. The name of the Château de Cangé at **St-Avertin** recalls the desperate straits of the French government in 1940 as the Germans swept through the country at the start of the Second World War. Winston Churchill dashed over to the meeting here, where the French decided on their terrible, humiliating armistice.

The Loire from Blois to Tours via Amboise

14

Blois to Tours

10 km
5 miles

N

Highlights

1 The Château de Chaumont, plus its cutting-edge Festival International des Jardins

2 Amboise, with all its courtly and touristy attractions

3 The Cisse valley, for its secretive side and its Vouvray vineyards

Châteaux abound in this area. Many, like Mick Jagger's, are in private hands or have been turned into posh hotels. But two very mighty ones which are open to the public survey the Loire majestically from their heights: first Chaumont, then Amboise. The town of Amboise is the major attraction along this stretch of the Loire, the royal castle dominating the riverside while the Clos Lucé, a manor house on the outskirts of town, was where Leonardo da Vinci spent the last few years of his life. Funnily enough, though, it's the modern aquarium at Lussault, a little west of town, which gets the largest number of tourists in these parts. Amboise is surrounded by further surprising attractions, including the Parc des Mini-Châteaux, presenting miniature versions of the most famous Loire Valley châteaux. You can get a rather more authentic feel for the former aristocratic grandeur of the area from a visit to the forlorn clown of the Pagode de Chanteloup, sole remnant of a vast 18th-century palace.

Shadowing the north bank of the Loire between Blois and Tours, the river Cisse is lined with delectable little villages as well as castles. A few châteaux here, such as Valmer and Jallanges, have opened their grounds to the public. Follow the Cisse and the Loire westwards and you come into major Touraine wine and troglodyte territory around Vouvray. Vouvray is renowned in France for its range of Chenin Blanc white wines, going from dry and sparkling to the super-sweet. Montlouis, opposite on the south bank of the Loire, also produces good Chenin Blanc wines. The Château de la Bourdaisière on Montlouis' outskirts is devoted to stranger fruit for the Loire, the tomato.

The Loire from Blois to Amboise

The splendidly located Château de Chaumont is the first major stop along this stretch of the Loire. We also introduce you to the Cisse valley here.

Château de Chaumont

Open 15 Mar–Sept 9.30–6, Oct–14 Mar 10–4.30 – doors close 30mins after last times indicated; closed 1 Jan, 1 May, 1 and 11 Nov and 25 Dec. You can visit the château with or without a guide; you can only visit the stables with a guide. The park closes at nightfall.

The Château de Chaumont boasts one of the best locations of all the châteaux along the Loire, looking dramatically down onto the river. You can best appreciate the place, standing proudly on its hillside, from the north bank. 'Hot mount' appears at first glance to be the translation for 'Chaumont'. There is certainly quite an invigorating walk up the slope to reach the castle, but it turns out that the name derives from the Latin for 'bald hill'. Today the château is surrounded by woods.

The counts of Blois had a fortress here around the year 1000, at a time when they were in direct conflict with the counts of Anjou to the west. That keep has vanished, but Chaumont does have a medieval chivalric feel to it, even if it is in fact another of those transitional Loire châteaux, built in the period when Italian Renaissance features were merging with French late Gothic forms. Construction began at the start of the 1470s, after the previous castle had been destroyed on King Louis XI's orders as punishment for the owner Pierre d'Amboise's part in a rebellion. Pierre was subsequently pardoned and allowed to build a new château on the spot. The north and west wings went up before his death in 1473. His grandson Charles II d'Amboise inherited Chaumont in 1481. Charles II was an enormously influential figure in French politics in his day, serving as governor of Milan for a period, and being appointed marshal and admiral of France under King Louis XII. Thanks to his money, from 1498 to

Getting There and Around

Occasional **trains** on the Blois–Tours line stop at Chouzy, Onzain and Limeray. There's a **bus** service between Amboise and Tours.

Tourist Information

Chaumont-sur-Loire: 28 Rue du Maréchal Leclerc, t 02 54 20 91 73, f 02 54 20 90 34.

Where to Stay and Eat

On the south bank of the Loire between Blois and Amboise:

Candé-sur-Beuvron ✉ 41120

**La Caillière, 36 Route des Montils, t 02 54 44 03 08, f 02 54 44 00 95 (*inexpensive*). Looks a picture, with cosy rooms in the old inn and parasols in the garden. And it serves interesting dishes; for example you might be able to try *sandre* served with an original citrus and ginger sauce to pep it up (*menus €15–41*). *Closed Wed, and Jan and Feb*.

Chaumont-sur-Loire ✉ 41150

La Chancelière, 1 Rue de Bellevue, t 02 54 20 96 95. Restaurant tucked under the Loire cliffside, offering quite refined, good-value cuisine in its two cosy dining rooms (*menus €12–30*). *Closed Thurs in season, plus Wed pm out of season, and Nov and Feb hols*.

Vallières-les-Grandes ✉ 41400

Ferme de la Quantinière B&B, t/f 02 54 20 99 53, *fermequantiniere@minitel.net*, *www.france-bonjour.com/la-quantiniere/* (*inexpensive*). A B&B run by a wonderfully welcoming couple, Annie and Daniel Doyer.

They play their roles with relish if you book to eat with them *table d'hôte* (*€15*); Madame cooks up a storm, while Monsieur entertains with anecdotes. The former farm buildings are set in peaceful, flat countryside south of Rilly-sur-Loire. The comfortable handful of rooms have been very tastefully decorated.

On the north bank of the Loire between Blois and Amboise:

Molineuf ✉ 41190

La Poste, 11 Av de Blois, t 02 54 70 03 25. Up the picturesque little Cisse valley, serving experimental as well as traditional cuisine (*menus €13–32*). *Closed Sun pm and Wed, and Feb*.

Herbault/Landes-le-Gaulois ✉ 41190

***Château de Moulins, t 02 54 20 17 93, f 02 54 20 17 99, *moulins@chateauxhotels. com* (*expensive*) Still further up the Cisse, a little south of the D957 from Blois to Vendôme by the D138, this posh and very appealing little ivy-clad château sits nobly in its vast grounds. Inside, you should be delighted with the grand salons, coffered ceilings and antique furniture.

Chouzy-sur-Cisse ✉ 41150

***Hostellerie les Couronnes, by the N152, t 02 54 20 49 00, f 02 54 20 43 78 (*moderate*). An old farm converted to offer comfortable modern rooms set in a golf course, with tennis court and swimming pool. The dining room is charming. The food is better value than the rooms (*menus €14.5–21*). *Closed Dec–mid-Mar*.

Onzain ✉ 41150

****Domaine des Hauts de Loire, Route de Herbault, t 02 54 20 72 57 or t 02 54 20 70 43, f 02 54 20 77 32, *hauts-loire@relais*

1510, a vital period in the change in French architectural style, the rest of the château was completed.

Two massive but charming towers flank the main gateway, which cuts diagonally across the southeast corner of the castle. The frieze running along the outside sports interlacing Cs, referring to Charles d'Amboise, while the motifs between them represent burning hills, an amusing if slightly silly pun on the words 'hot mount'. The symbols of a cardinal's hat pay their respects to Charles II d'Amboise's uncle, the vastly powerful Georges d'Amboise. He oversaw much of the work at Chaumont, as well as chateaux.fr, www.relaischateaux.fr/hauts-loire (luxury). Another hunting pavilion disguised as a château, this one 19th century and full of luxuries, situated well above the rather ugly little town below. It has beautiful rooms with painted beams. In the restaurant, sample refined regional cuisine, such as crispy eel salad and beef poached in Montlouis wine. Tennis court, swimming pool and, of course, helicopter landing pad in the grounds. You could splash out on a trip over the Loire by helicopter or hot-air balloon from here – just ask at reception (menus €48–60). Closed Dec–Feb; restaurant closed Mon and Tues lunch in winter months.

***Château des Tertres**, Route de Monteaux, t 02 54 20 83 88, f 02 54 20 89 21 (moderate). For a much more reasonably priced stay in another 19th-century château, try this place, set on the wooded hillside a couple of kilometres west of Onzain, its grounds providing a very peaceful setting. Closed mid-Nov–late Mar.

Seillac ✉ 41150
Domaine de Seillac, at Seillac, north of Onzain on the D131, t 02 54 20 72 11, f 02 54 20 82 88, seillac@chateauxhotels.com (moderate). Reflected in its lake, this smart Ancien Régime and 19th-century manor house makes a pretty picture. But note that only a small number of the Domaine's rooms are in the manor; most are in bungalows set around the large grounds, which also include the luxury of three tennis courts and a heated swimming pool (menus €20–44). Hotel closed mid-Dec–early Jan.

Cangey ✉ 37530
Le Fleuray, Route Dame Marie-les-Bois (along the D74), t 02 47 56 09 25, f 02 47 56 93 97, lefleuray@wanadoo.fr (moderate). Run by an enthusiastic British couple who have put a great deal of effort into turning this Touraine farm into a tasteful country hotel; they also prepare and serve the food, on a terrace in summer, by a log fire in winter (menus €23.5–40.5). Closed pre-Christmas–early Jan, and most of Feb.

Limeray ✉ 37530
***Auberge de Launay**, Le Haut Chantier, t 02 47 30 16 82, f 02 47 30 15 16 (inexpensive). With reasonable rooms, this place serves tasty popular local dishes such as Tourangeau kid with Gratin Dauphinois, or eel pie marinated in white wine and cognac. In summer you can eat out in the garden (menus c.€30.5). Closed mid-Dec–early Feb, restaurant weekly closure Mon pm and Tues lunch out of season.

Pocé-sur-Cisse ✉ 37530
La Croix Verte, Route d'Amboise, t 02 47 57 03 65. Closed mid-Jan–end Jan. A pleasant restaurant just outside Pocé-sur-Cisse, with a good choice of menus (menus €13–28).

Nazelles ✉ 37530
Château des Ormeaux B&B, Route de Noizay, t 02 47 23 26 51, f 02 47 23 19 31, chateaudesormeaux@wanadoo.fr, www.pro.wanadoo.fr/chateaudesormeaux (moderate). A very posh B&B, this gorgeous hillside property is a square-sided little château with cute slender corner turrets. The rooms were all redone in 1998 in grand style and have lovely views and excellent bathrooms. There's a swimming pool in the grounds. The place doubles as an antiques shop (table d'hôte dinner €38, all included).

at his sumptuous early Renaissance Château de Gaillon in Normandy. He was clearly a cardinal with a taste for the temporal in his spare time. A powerful figure in his day, he was a one-time contender for the papacy, and effectively served as King Louis XII's top minister for a period. Further symbolic lettering on the building apparently refers to Diane de Poitiers, the mistress of King Henri II, who beat his wife, Catherine de' Medici, in the battle for the king's affections. Diane is represented not just by 'D's, but also by a Greek delta and by depictions of the accoutrements of the goddess Diana the Huntress.

The tale of how the beautiful Diane came to receive Chaumont isn't a particularly pretty one – Henri II died in 1559 and she was forced by his jealous widow to exchange the romantic Chenonceau (*see* pp.223–8) for the colder Chaumont. Some say that Catherine de' Medici bought Chaumont expressly to arrange this exchange and organized the swap even before she had paid for the place. In fact she had acquired this lucrative château with its large estate back in 1550. She appears barely to have stayed here at all, despite the legend (*see* box opposite). Nor did Diane, once she became the owner, although she had work carried out on the château in the 1560s.

In 1739 the proprietor knocked down the north wing of Chaumont, opening up the courtyard as you now see it, so that it looks out onto the Loire. Unfortunately, the views from here don't match those up to the château, as they take in the village's ugly modern bridge over the Loire and the dull flat plain to the north. Around the middle of the 18th century, Jacques-Donatien Le Ray bought Chaumont and turned it into something of a centre of artistic production. A glassworks in the outbuildings attracted the English glass painter Robert Scott Godfrey, and the pottery brought the Italian J. B. Nini. Among the latter's terracotta medallions, one represents a famous American visitor to France of the time, Benjamin Franklin. This period of artistic activity at Chaumont was followed by one of abandonment at the start of the 19th century. But wealthy new owners came to the rescue. The Comte d'Aramon, who bought the château in 1833, ordered the first restorations. His widow married the Vicomte de Walsh from Anjou, who called upon Jules de la Morandière, the well-known restorer, to help here.

However, the look of the place was most altered inside and out by another 19th-century architect-cum-restorer, Paul-Ernest Sanson. His work was commissioned for a spoilt young woman who supposedly spotted Chaumont when out on a day trip and asked her daddy to buy it for her. Monsieur Say duly did, in 1875. He was almost literally a sugar daddy, his massive fortune coming from the sugar-refining industry. His daughter Marie married Prince Amadée de Broglie, who had just as extravagant tastes as she. They apparently acquired two hamlets just to knock them down to improve the view and extend Chaumont's park. They didn't like the village church either, so they changed that too. In addition, they had electricity installed in the village below, making it one of the first in France to boast street lamps. Back up in the château, the entertainment was lavish. One very enthusiastic maharajah, to thank the couple for his stay, gave them an elephant, Miss Pungi, which Marie loved. The Say girl's story all ended in tears of course, the family sugar beet business going bankrupt. The château was sold to the state in 1938.

The interiors still bear the marks of 19th-century good living, however, with under-floor heating added at that time, along with the collection of fine art pillaged from a pot-pourri of places. You get a Victorian view of chivalric centuries past here, grand Gothic turned neo-Gothic. But there are some sumptuous pieces of art to admire on the tour, like the late 16th-century tapestries depicting classical gods representing days of the week, hanging in the **Salle de Conseil**. Look out too for the Nini terracotta medallions in the library. The dining room is on a grand scale, while weapons set out in the shape of fans decorate the Salle des Gardes, making a formidable display of

A Bad Heir Day

The story goes that, soon after her husband's death, Catherine de' Medici came to Chaumont with one of the famous astrologers of the day, either Ruggieri or Nostradamus. Contemporary writers allude to the horrifying vision of the future with which she was confronted in a magic mirror. Catherine's male children appeared one after the other, followed by Henri de Navarre, of Bourbon blood. The princes were said to have walked in a circle for as many times as they had years to reign. Thus the untimely death of Catherine de' Medici's sons and the downfall of the Valois dynasty were supposedly foretold to the Queen Mother at Chaumont. Henri de Navarre would become the first French Bourbon king after Henri III was assassinated. However dubious the legend may be, it is true that, just as with certain members of the British royal family today, many of the kings and queens of France set great store by their astrologers.

warring fashions. In the last rooms, Renaissance superstition and historical legend take over (*see* box). You pass through the chamber known as Catherine de' Medici's room, the chapel and the Chambre de l'Astrologue, all heavily restored, the brooding bedrooms heavily furnished.

The château visit also includes a separate guided tour of the extravagant 19th-century **stables** built by Sanson. Do go for a walk around the château grounds as well. The Princesse de Broglie called in the landscape architect Achille Duchêne to design the *parc à l'anglaise*, with its sweeping lawns and meandering paths through beautiful trees. Part of these grounds now serve as the setting for the prestigious annual **Festival International des Jardins** (*open 15 June–20 October 9–nightfall; separate admission fee*); in the summer months, modern garden designers are given the chance to experiment with compact contemporary creations in this excellent, thought-provoking gardening extravaganza.

Along the Cisse Valley between Blois and Amboise

The north bank of the Loire west of Blois sees the appearance of vineyards producing a sub-*appellation* of Touraine wines, allowed to carry the title AOC Touraine-Mesland, after the village of **Mesland**. Most of the vines grow on the sandy and gravel plateau above the river; maybe it's the good south-facing position of the vines that gives the local wines a certain durability. Gamay grapes dominate the red production; for the whites, Chardonnay and Sauvignon are blended with Chenin Blanc, while the Vin Gris is a quite enjoyable rosé. To get a taste of these wines, try visiting the Clos de la Briderie at **Monteaux**, west of Chaumont, where a characterful barn has been converted into a tasting and reception room, or the Domaine de Lusqueneau up in Mesland, where modern equipment dominates in the vat house, although some of the buildings date back to the 11th century.

As to the Cisse river north of the Loire, it 'slithers like a silvery snake through the meadow grasses', as Balzac poetically put it. The Cisse is so diminutive that you'd think it might have an inferiority complex when compared with its majestic neighbour, but in fact has developed a delightful character all of its own. While the N152 road offers grand views of the Loire along its way, the D58 and D1 along the Cisse are calmer and more charming. The pocket-sized French country vegetable plots of yesteryear still thrive here, flowers too, grown in rows. The hillsides are peppered with caves. Past the concentration camp for poultry at Cangey (well known for rearing the fowl), **Limeray**'s peeling-whitewashed church interior is lined with an impressive array of statues, collected together by a priest in the 19th century. **Pocé-sur-Cisse** and **Nazelles-Négron** have characterful village churches, and then you reach Amboise.

Amboise, Cradle of French Renaissance Royalty

French towns don't come more royal than Amboise (its dominating château remains in French royal hands today). The place makes a splendid sight seen from the north bank of the Loire. Along with Saumur, in Anjou, Amboise is the most typical old limestone town to lie on the very banks of the great river. A row of riverside houses runs along the foot of the massive château ramparts. These defences look austere to say the least, protecting a plateau of land above the town on which the remnants of the château stand, with a line of typical Loire *lucarnes* ornamenting the roof over-looking the river. A large proportion of this once-vast royal castle has disappeared, but it still makes a fine impression, flags flying from the battlements.

Few French towns have received more Italian tourists than Amboise, either. This is in good part because Leonardo da Vinci spent the last three years of his life here. But Amboise is also where King Charles VIII, the first French king to invade Renaissance Italy, brought home his booty, even if these riches have long since been carted off elsewhere. After Charles VIII, the Château d'Amboise served as one of the principal residences of a string of French Renaissance kings and princes. It was that collector extraordinaire, King François I, who paid for Leonardo to come to Amboise and sit in attendance. Leonardo lived in the manor of the Clos Lucé, and was buried in the château's collegiate church. The church has disappeared, but Amboise retains the genius' bones.

Pre-Royal Amboise

Early man occupied the well-located, easily defended plateau above the Loire at Amboise. It seems that there was a Neolithic settlement here. Later, some of the Celtic Turones tribe made their home on the spot. Then a Gallo-Roman community devel-oped. The plateau overlooks l'Ile d'Or, the Golden Isle, in the middle of the river. This is where, in 503, the Frankish King Clovis is supposed to have met with the Visigoth leader Alaric II to sign a peace 'for all time'. The story goes that they shook each other by the goatee beard, seemingly settling the disputes between them. A couple of years later Clovis slew Alaric near Poitiers.

Viking drakkars travelled up up the Loire in the second half of the 9th century, terrifying the locals, the Norsemen pillaging Amboise several times. French counts

Getting There and Around

Amboise is easy to reach, an important stop on the **train** line between Tours and Paris-Austerlitz passing via Orléans and Blois. You can also get **buses** from Tours to Amboise.

Tourist Information

Tourist Office: Bureau de Tourisme, B.P.233, Quai du Général de Gaulle, 37402 Amboise, t 02 47 57 09 28, f 02 47 57 14 35, *tourisme. amboise@wanadoo.fr*.

Market Days

Friday and Sunday morning.

Where to Stay

Amboise ✉ 37400

Expensive

★★★★Le Choiseul, 36 Quai Charles Guinot, t 02 47 30 45 45, f 02 47 30 46 10, *choiseul@ wanadoo.fr*. This luxury hotel and restaurant by the Loire roadside, just east of the centre, is packed with interesting things. Its well-maintained gardens back onto the limestone hillside which contains superb former grain stores, the so-called **Greniers de César**, a tourist sight in themselves; contemporary art exhibitions are held in them April–Oct. The rooms in the neat 18th-century building are extremely comfortable and intimate. You can watch the Loire flow by from the restaurant and the cuisine is highly regarded – lunch menus are more reasonable than evening ones (*menus c.€45.5*). There's a pool in the grounds. *Closed mid-Dec–Jan*.

★★★★Le Manoir Les Minimes, 34 Quai Charles Guinot, t 02 47 30 40 40, f 02 47 30 40 77, *manoir-les-minimes@wanadoo.fr*. Le Choiseul's immediate neighbour and rival, this beautiful, recently opened hotel occupies an 18th-century house built on the site of a convent founded by King Charles VIII just below the château. The hotel is set back in its own spacious courtyard. The first floor has superb suites, the second floor smaller but still very smart rooms under the eaves (*no restaurant*).

Inexpensive

★★★Le Bellevue, 12 Quai Charles Guinot, t 02 47 57 02 26, f 02 47 30 50 51 23. Together with a view of the Loire from its terrace and some of its rooms, inside, the hotel has nicely furnished rooms which are well maintained. *Closed mid-Nov–mid-March*.

★★Hôtel du Lion d'Or, 17 Quai Charles Guinot, t 02 47 57 00 23, f 02 47 23 22 49. Yet another option looking out over the river, with cheaper rooms. Avoid the cafeteria and go for the old-fashioned dining room, although you pay more for your meal here (*menus c.€23*). *Closed mid-Nov–mid-Jan; restaurant closed Sun and Mon out of season*.

then established their supremacy over the region, and for a time the fiefdom fell to Ingelger, count of Anjou. Amboise became a divided town, however, when château and plateau came into the hands of the Amboise family, while the town became the property of the Buzançais.

The most successfully bellicose of the early medieval Loire feudal lords, Foulques Nerra of Anjou, then swept in to take control. Around 1030 he built one keep here in his great ring of Touraine fortifications, as well as a collegiate church dedicated to St Florentin. Direct Angevin control came to an end in 1107, however, when Hugues I of Amboise and Chaumont became master of château and town, his descendants maintaining their dominance until 1422. It then fell to a viscount of Thouars, who became Louis d'Amboise and fought against the English in the Hundred Years' War, notably supporting Joan of Arc. Unfortunately for him, he was also implicated in a plot against La Trémoïlle, favourite of King Charles VII. His life was spared but he was forced to hand over Amboise to the Crown in 1431 as a forfeit.

★★Le Blason, 11 Place Richelieu, **t** 02 47 23 22 41, **f** 02 47 57 56 18 (*inexpensive*). A pretty timberframe and limestone building overlooking a large square south of the centre, but some of the rooms could do with renovation. The menus are fairly good (*menus €14–34*). *Closed Tues and Wed.*

Hôtel La Pergola, 33 bis Av de Tours, **t** 02 47 57 24 79. Has the advantage not just of Loire views but also a pool, while the rooms are quite simple.

Chargé ✉ 37400

★★★★Château de Pray, **t** 02 47 57 23 67, **f** 02 47 57 32 50, *pray@chateauxhotels.com* (*expensive*). A thoroughly delightful and intriguing little château just east along the Loire from Amboise, with a wonderful garden laid out on terraces over the Loire. The interior decoration is stylish, both in the rooms and in the splendid dining room. Pigeon in acacia honey sounds the appropriate kind of speciality for such a setting (*menus €23.5–46.5*). The place has a heated swimming pool. *Closed 2 Jan–mid-Feb.*

Lussault-sur-Loire ✉ 37400

Château de Pintray B&B, **t** 02 47 23 22 84, **f** 02 47 57 64 27, *marius.rault@wanadoo.fr* (*moderate*). This is a distinguished centuries-old winemakers' property south of Lussault along the D751. It makes for a peaceful stop, and has woods as well as vineyards.

Eating Out

Expensive

Manoir St-Thomas, 1 Mail St-Thomas, **t** 02 47 57 22 52, **f** 02 47 30 44 71. The splendid house with its private grounds in the middle of town dates from the Renaissance and provides a fine setting for a highly regarded restaurant. *Closed Sun pm and Mon, and Feb–mid-Mar.*

Moderate

L'Epicerie, 18 Rue Victor Hugo, **t** 02 47 57 08 94. Set in a lovely timberframe house close to the intimidating ramp up the side of the château, this restaurant serves classic, reliably good and relatively good-value dishes. *Outside 15 Jun–15 Sept closed Mon pm and Tues.*

La Closerie, 2 Rue Paul-Louis Courier, **t** 02 47 23 10 76. A quiet little setting for more traditional cooking, black pudding with apples, rabbit with prunes and oysters with a Vouvray *sabaglione* on the menu. *Closed Sun pm and Mon.*

Pâtisserie Bigot/Le Fournil, Place du Château. Elegant, old-fashioned, proudly family-run pâtisserie which tempts you inside with its chocolate and cake displays, but you can also sit down to enjoy a savoury tart, a cake or a home-made ice cream. The cocoa specialities include the *ambroisines*, filled with Touraine grape liqueur.

This is how the place acquired its royal owners. For the next century and a half, its château developed into an important centre for the peripatetic French royal family, and for lines of French royal children in particular. Amboise's centre switched to the château, off which the town thrived.

Château d'Amboise

*Open July–Aug 9–7.30, April–June 9–6.30, Sept–Oct 9–6, Feb–March and Nov 9–12 and 2–5.30, Dec and Jan 9–12 and 2–5; **t** 02 47 57 00 98.*

French would-be royalty is still just about alive and it owns the Château d'Amboise, under the guise of the Fondation St-Louis. Its head is the new Comte de Paris, who took over after his ancient father died in 1999, leaving something of an inheritance scandal behind him. The line descends from the Orléans branch of the Bourbon royal family; Louis Philippe, their ancestor, was the last king of France, playing the part from 1830 until 1848, the latter being another French revolutionary year, one in which the

the Amboise plateau. For instance, a new Logis Royal on the southwestern side was completed by 1465, although it has now completely disappeared.

In 1469, Louis retired to Amboise to work out the terms of peace after his humiliating defeat by the formidably independent duchy of Burgundy, then ruled by his relative and enemy Charles le Téméraire (the Fearless). That same year, in a much more positive act for the French monarchy, Louis established the knightly order of St-Michel in Amboise's chapel of St-Florentin.

Louis XI chose the Château d'Amboise as a place of safety for Queen Charlotte, his wife, to bring up the royal children. She stayed here pretty well permanently to look after them, while Louis travelled around on affairs of state and warring campaigns. The Château d'Amboise was the secure childhood home of his heir, the future King Charles VIII, born in the palace in 1470. Louis would become increasingly paranoid through his reign and was immensely protective towards his son and heir. Those permitted to visit the castle and even the town were carefully vetted. Devoted servants of the king were put in charge of Charles' education, notably Jean Bourré, Seigneur du Plessis (*see* pp.443–6), who sent Louis regular reports on his progress.

Louis occasionally returned to the family home, in 1476 accompanied by a royal mistress on each arm, La Passe-Fillon and La Gigonne, two conquests from a visit to Lyon. They were set up in apartments in the château; it was quite normal for French kings to have mistresses. The queen didn't entertain greatly in the king's absence, but it can hardly be said that she lived frugally, having an enormous budget of 37,000 livres for her housekeeping in one typical year, a huge amount. Rich materials and tapestries on classical themes embellished the castle's chambers. As well as having an extravagant penchant for shoes, Queen Charlotte liked her books, gathering together a rare collection of more than 100 manuscripts, including not only pious works, but also ones debating the role of women in society, such as Alain Chartier's *Débat de quatre dames* and Christine de Pisan's *Cité des dames*.

Louis reared his son carefully for kingship. Meanwhile, he paired off his daughters in politically arranged marriages, as was the way in those time. The eldest, Anne, was wedded to the influential figure Pierre de Beaujeu, a mere 21 years her senior. Another daughter, Jeanne, bright but severely crippled, was early betrothed to her royal cousin Louis d'Orléans, her father thereby hoping to put an end to a potentially fractious rival line, imagining that Jeanne and Louis would never be able to have children.

King Charles VIII Rebuilds Amboise and Takes On Brittany and Italy

In 1482, important lords of the land gathered at Amboise to hear Louis XI lecture his heir Charles on his duties towards the realm and his subjects. The following year, the boy was formally engaged here to Marguerite d'Autriche, daughter of the Holy Roman Emperor Maximilian. If Charles was young, Marguerite was barely out of infancy. At three and a half years of age, she was known as '*la petite reine*' and was brought up at Amboise. Such early arrangements and preparations for royal marriages were commonplace at the time.

Louis XI died in 1483 and Anne de Beaujeu assumed the regency until the following year, when Charles turned 14, the age at which French kings were allowed to assume power. Charles wouldn't marry Marguerite, however. Brittany, an important independent duchy west of Anjou, had long been a thorn in the side of the French realm. The councillors of Anne de Bretagne, the young, ugly, but very desirable heir to the duchy, were organizing her marriage to the Holy Roman Emperor. Charles VIII's side, pursuing his father's campaigns to unify a greater France, saw the opportunity for bringing Brittany under royal control by getting Charles to marry Anne de Bretagne himself. Charles and his men went fully armed into her province to persuade her party to change her marriage arrangements, and Anne was in effect forced to accept Charles' hand. As to the young Marguerite d'Autriche, still not in her teens, she was sent tearfully packing back to Flanders with a heavy gold chain as consolation from the French king.

Work began on altering the Château d'Amboise as the 15th century came to a close. Having spend his childhood there, Charles VIII was deeply attached to Amboise, and under him it was to become *the* favoured French royal residence. It was Charles who ordered the bulk of the building work above the massive ramparts. He wanted something grandiose, and the plans were inevitably expensive. The building was financed by raising an additional levy on the existing hated salt tax, the *gabelle*, and started in 1492. The two first wings to be completed were the one you still see overlooking the Loire, flanked on one side by the enormous Tour des Minimes, and the wing on the opposite side of the courtyard, overlooking the Amasse valley, the arcaded Logis des Sept Vertus. This wing was named after statues adorning its façades – it has disappeared, save the massive Tour Heurtault matching the Tour des Minimes.

Hundreds of workers, especially stonemasons, were employed on the site and the accounts show that they even worked by candlelight through the winter, sometimes needing to make fires to unfreeze the building blocks. Charles VIII went on a great shopping spree for his new château, buying vast tapestry cycles which depicted Old Testament, classical and traditional French chivalric scenes. Also on display inside the château were magnificent arms and armour, including Joan of Arc's suit, the swords of several French kings, a dagger of Charlemagne, a weapon belonging to King Dagobert, Clovis' axe and Lancelot's sword, history becoming somewhat confused with legend in the typical medieval way! It's just a shame that all these precious objects have vanished from Amboise.

On the self-guided visit round the château, you can admire the two enormous towers still standing from Charles VIII's time, the **Tour des Minimes** and the **Tour Heurtault**. Rather than being purely defensive, these were in fact extravagant entrances, with wide spiralling ramps leading up from the valley to the plateau. Horses and even carriages could comfortably ascend this way.

The beautiful **chapelle St-Hubert**, another building from Charles VIII's time, has also survived. This jewel box of a chapel sits precariously on the edge of the fortifications. It's a delightful work from the late Gothic period, topped by a needle of a spire visible from far and wide. The lintel above the entrance depicts the legends of St Anthony, St Christopher and St Hubert (*see* Château de Gien, p.113, for an explanation of the last). The beautiful carving was executed by Flemish sculptors. Above, the tympanum was filled in in the 19th century with sculptures representing Charles VIII and Anne de

Charles VIII, His Italian Adventures, His Courtly Life at Amboise, and his Banal Death There

Very few signs of Renaissance architecture and decoration made it into Charles VIII's building programme at Amboise. But as it was underway, he set out on the first in a line of hot-headed French royal forays into Italy, which changed the course of French history, architecture and the arts, as successive monarchs tried to assert their inheritance claims there. Charles may have been seduced by Italy, but he didn't exactly woo it; he ravished it. In Charles' first Italian campaign of 1494–5, he and his troops may have captured the kingdom of Naples, but they were lucky to escape with their lives after being trapped at Fornova on the way back. Some of the loot they had amassed, including castle gates and stained glass, was stopped from leaving the peninsula, but another load which did get through from Naples to Amboise in 1496 included 130 tapestries, 172 carpets, sculptures in marble and porphyry, and over 1,000 manuscripts from the king of Aragon's collection. Much of the art was destined to decorate the Château d'Amboise's Logis des Sept Vertus.

Charles didn't come back with booty alone. He also imported men. Among the group of around 20 Italians to come to France in his train were the famous architects Domenico da Cortona and Fra Giocondo, a scholar of Greek and a sculptor, along with couturiers, a gardener and a Moor to pamper the king's parrots! And so the refinements of the Italian Renaissance entered France. The history books have ascribed huge cultural significance to this first French royal adventure in Italy, which transformed the ways of the French monarchy and aristocracy, creating the French Renaissance of the 16th century. But these Renaissance influences arrived too late to much affect the Château d'Amboise's expansion under Charles VIII.

Records give a taste of what the royal daily life here was like under Charles VIII. After the serious attendance of Mass and the council on state affairs, much of the rest of an ordinary day would be given over to games. Dice, cards and chess were very

Bretagne kneeling before the Virgin and Child. Inside, among the wealth of curling tracery, if you look hard you can make out little carved animals, such as serpents, toads and bats, concealed in the stone. The dinky fireplaces in the minute transepts show the comforts royalty allowed themselves even in prayer. The stained glass is by that prolific 20th-century artist Max Ingrand, made busy after the shocks from Second World War bombs destroyed so much of the older decoration. The life of St Louis, alias pious, crusading King Louis IX, is recounted in these windows. A simple plaque in the chapel commemorates Leonardo da Vinci, whose bones were transferred here after the chapel of St-Florent was destroyed in the 19th century.

In fact, curiously, it was in Napoleonic times that much of the Château d'Amboise was destroyed. But the remaining **Charles VIII wing** has been beautifully restored and embellished in recent years, even if the feeling is rather over-scrubbed for some tastes. You visit the guards' quarters first, with a sober vaulted room furnished with Gothic-style furniture and late 16th-century Aubusson tapestries. The walkway from here gives onto the Loire, an excellent viewing post. The palm vaulting of the Salle des much the fashion among the courtiers, although the king disliked these pastimes, apparently beaten too many times by his sister Anne when he was a boy. The *jeu de paume*, or real (as in royal) tennis was more to his taste, along with falconry. Hunting was a great favourite, but it seems that the kings would be led astray by more than the wild animals they were out to capture. Anne de Bretagne is supposed to have accompanied Charles on long hunts even when she was pregnant, to check that if the party had to stay away from home the king shouldn't be tempted by a hostess's overgenerous hospitality. Animals of all sorts fascinated French royalty in this period. Pets were doted on. Rare animals were cherished, and lions were kept in the ditch on the château's plateau. Meanwhile, the fashion for monkeys was just taking off.

The king had two personal confessors and the same astrologer as his father, consulted for all important events as to the most propitious day on which to hold them. In painting, Jean Perréal and Jean Bourdichon continued to prepare royal portraits after Jean Fouquet. Poetry and reading were also pastimes, often singing the praises of noble princes, but sometimes being more bawdy in tone. Easter and May were the times for the colourful jousts.

A couple of Italians were commissioned to write the official chronicles of Charles VIII's reign, while Philippe de Commynes (or Comines) kept his diaries in secret. He records the bathos of Charles VIII's death. After all the care that had been taken to protect the king as a young man, after all the foolhardiness of his Italian campaigns, one day in 1498 in the midst of all the frivolous court entertainment, Charles bumped his head in Amboise castle's Haquelebac gallery overlooking the real tennis court, in a passageway where '*tout le monde pissait*' (we don't think you require a translation for that). The king got up and continued to talk on religious subjects, having recently entered something of a pious phase in his life. But he quickly collapsed again and lay on the ground in the same spot for some nine hours, only regaining consciousness three times to call upon God and his beloved saints before dying from a final stroke.

Gardes Nobles is striking, while two 16th-century Milanese coats of armour stand empty guard. Above, the flooring in the Salle des Tambourineurs is stamped with fleurs-de-lys and leads to the superb **council chamber** with its double row of vaulted bays. The light central columns are flecked with fleurs-de-lys and ermine tails, the latter the symbol of Charles VIII's wife Anne. Try deciphering the amusing restored Gothic sculpture in the room. The four seasons are depicted down the central capitals of the chamber. Some of the stone sculpting illustrates proverbs, the big ears in one corner reminding courtiers of the fact that walls have ears! One Renaissance detail at least has crept in here, the marble medallion of Alexander the Great over one of the room's chimneys.

Louis d'Orléans, married to Charles VIII's crippled sister Jeanne de France, succeeded to the throne as Louis XII after Charles' fatal accident at Amboise (*see* box), as Charles and Anne de Bretagne had no heir. He immediately rid himself of the handicap that his wife represented to his ambitions. This was made relatively easy by the fact that Louis' marriage to Jeanne was unconsummated, and that Charles VIII, in his marriage contract with Anne, had stipulated that, in the case of their having no heir, she should be obliged to marry his successor. Louis took Anne to Blois – he was deeply attached to the château there, the place where his father had held court, and scarcely wanted to live in Charles VIII's shadow.

King François I at Amboise

The Château d'Amboise wasn't entirely neglected, though, and the second half of the château tour takes you into what's known as the **Louis XII-François I wing**, although it would be more appropriate to call it the Louise de Savoie wing. Louis XII gave Amboise to her and her children, François and Marguerite d'Angoulême, important figures in the royal circle. Louise herself had been brought up in part at the Château d'Amboise by her aunt Anne de Beaujeu. In 1488 she had married Charles d'Angoulême of the Orléans royal branch. Much older than her, he died in 1496. But, vitally, by then she had had children by him. So long as Louis XII and Anne de Bretagne remained without male heir, Louise's son François stood first in line to inherit the French throne. A new wing was built on to the Château d'Amboise for Louise and her children.

From the outside, you can see how the upper part of its façade, heavily restored, bears the influences of the Renaissance. Compare, for example, the window decoration of this wing with that on the Charles VIII wing, this one with its Italianate columns, stylized capitals and pilasters. Within, many excellent pieces of furniture decorate the rooms, now beamed rather than vaulted.

The first chamber, the Salle de l'Echanson, contains pieces of furniture on which food would be placed and tasted, and extendable tables in the newly imported Italian fashion. The sumptuous tapestries are 17th-century Aubusson works, the bold biblical and classical scenes made after cartoons by Le Brun. The Henri II chamber plunges you further into the Renaissance, with its very ornate bed sporting channeled columns and pilasters and all manner of Renaissance carved detail. Two great chairs show early examples of trompe-l'oeil low relief perspective carving. More symbols of royalty and Brittany have been added around the window, as well as a symbolic pilgrim's staff and purse. The last period room is the Passage de la Cordelière. The fireplace is ornately decorated with looping Franciscan chords, symbols of Anne de Bretagne's piety. Around the shield, the shell necklace is that of the Order of St Michel (*see* p.241). The salamander on the wood panel above refers to François I, who came back to the Château d'Amboise for some very grand celebrations once he had become king.

The French Wars of Religion and the Decline of Amboise

Monumental events were occurring in Germany at the start of François I's reign. Luther's devastating criticisms of the Catholic Church, its traditions and corruption, were rocking religious stability in Europe. Then the Holy Roman Emperor Maximilian I died in 1519, leaving the competition open for his succession. Massive amounts of money were spent in promoting their causes by Charles I of Spain, Henry VIII of England and François I of France. Charles won the contest. From this time on,

François I spent less and less time at Amboise, almost always on the move. But he would occasionally stay here. On the morning of 18 October 1534, while staying at Amboise, he woke up to find a pamphlet stuck to his door. It contained a stinging attack on the meaning of the Mass. The troubles of the Reformation had been spreading through France. The French king, defender of the Catholic faith, had remained moderate in his views towards the Protestants up until now. But such irreverent gall in an episode which became known as the Affaire des Placards (*placards* here meaning pamphlets, not cupboards) enraged him, and he decided to take action against the Huguenots. The persecution of the French Protestants was underway. This led to the terrible Wars of Religion which split the country in two during the second half of the 16th century. In the turmoil, the Château d'Amboise became a safe haven for bringing up the French royal children.

As was the productive way in those times, Catherine de' Medici (who married François I's second son and successor, Henri) gave birth to 10 children between 1544 and 1556. Although all of them were born outside the Loire, they all spent time being educated at the Château d'Amboise, where the air was considered particularly healthy and the surroundings safe. Their parents, even when they came to visit them, had little time to spare for them, what with the councils, diplomatic receptions and balls that followed in quick succession. The children were hardly neglected though. An army of attendants looked after them; and a small fortune was spent on their pills alone.

Diane de Poitiers, King Henri II's most famous mistress, played a significant role in overseeing the royal children. It wasn't just Henri II's legitimate children who were brought up at the château. Another Diane, a bastard royal daughter by Filippa Duci, six years older than the dauphin, also received her education here. Then in 1548 the six-year-old Mary Stuart arrived from Scotland, her hand promised to the future king of France. Her beautiful governess set Henri II alight again; the son they had, Henri d'Angoulême, had soon joined the numbers in this warren of a château. Sketches of some of the Amboise royal children drawn by a governess have survived, and the great court painter of the period, François Clouet, was also occasionally sent down to Amboise to prepare royal portraits.

Beyond this innocent Amboise of pampered royal childhood, as Henri II's reign progressed, the troubles with the Protestant factions were growing out of hand, as was their persecution. By the end of his rule France was ready to slide into civil war. The bloody precursor, the Conjuration d'Amboise, occurred in and around the town.

After the appalling period around the Amboise Conspiracy, the Château d'Amboise was more or less abandoned by royalty. For a time under the control of Louis XIII's brother Gaston d'Orléans, it was confiscated from him. As with many other Loire châteaux, it then served as a gaol – Louis XIV's finance minister Fouquet was briefly imprisoned here after he was accused of corruption on a massive scale. In the 18th century, attention switched to the grand new Château de Chanteloup which the Duc de Choiseul, a figure of prime importance under Louis XV, had built a short way outside of town. The Château de Chanteloup all but disappeared in the early 19th century. So too did most of the buildings of the Château d'Amboise, when Napoleon's friend Pierre-Roger Ducos had most of the place dismantled.

In 1821 the future King Louis-Philippe regained royal possession of the château and some work was carried out to make this into a royal summer residence. The style changes completely in the **Louis-Philippe rooms** you visit on the first floor of the Louis XII wing. Rich red walls and drapery serve as the backdrop to royal family portraits, executed with the crisp stylization of Winterhalter, among others. Extremely elegant

The Amboise Conspiracy

By 1558, the dauphin François and Mary Queen of Scots were married. A year later the boy became King François II, after his father had died from a wound accidentally inflicted on him by one of his Scots guards in a jousting tournament. François II's reign was to be a short-lived, and ill-fated for Mary too. Mary's overbearing uncles, the De Guises (see Blois, pp.191–3) had amassed considerable power for the Catholic cause. Through Mary, a much more powerful character than her sickly husband, they had become the controlling force in French politics. There were many Protestant sympathizers in high places, however. The most powerful were the Bourbons: Antoine, king of the little region of Navarre near Spain, and his brother Louis, Prince de Condé. They were outraged at the influence the De Guises had acquired at court. On their side stood Gaspard de Coligny, admiral of France. A major plot was hatched by Condé in 1559. The aim was to capture the De Guises from the royal court and put an end to their stranglehold on affairs of state. The main backing for this plot came from the disgruntled lesser nobles, the *gentilshommes*, led by Jean du Barry, lord of La Renaudie, from the Perigord. He soon gathered a large number of supporters.

The Conjuration d'Amboise might be described as France's foreshadowing of England's Gunpowder Plot, but played out in reverse. In this case, Huguenots aimed to overthrow the controlling ultra-Catholic De Guises, it's said with the support of Protestant England. Arms depots for the rebels were set up at Tours, Orléans and Châteaudun. Initially, the plan was to capture the De Guises at the Château de Blois, some time between 6 and 10 March. But the De Guises were on the look out for trouble. And La Renaudie was too indiscreet. He confided the dates to Des Avenelles, a Paris lawyer then on the Protestant side, but who switched allegiance. Des Avenelles informed the De Guise party of the plot and an extraordinary period of paranoia ensued.

The king had been out hunting with the court around the Loire. It was decided to retreat to the stronghold of the Château d'Amboise. The De Guises told François to summon Condé and Coligny to the château to persuade them to disassociate themselves from the conspirators. Only Coligny came. Already a little earlier in the decade he had met with Catherine de' Medici at Blois to work on an edict of pacification between the rival factions. This was now worked on again, and a declaration was issued that Protestants who peacefully agreed to live on Catholic terms would go unharmed.

Restoration or Louis-Philippe furniture enriches the rooms still further, with a notable Récamier-style bed, its mahogany front decorated with delicate bronze work. From these apartments you can go out onto the roof of the Tour des Minimes for one of the most memorable views onto the Loire.

After Louis-Philippe fled into exile, the château served as a prison for a period, for example housing the Algerian chief Abd El-Kadr, who had tried to resist the French colonialists. Later in the century, what remained of the great royal castle was restored

---

But the atmosphere of fear mounted as 6 March approached. Light relief was sought in a *bal travesti* in the gardens of the Château d'Amboise. But when the dreaded day arrived, a Spanish ambassador at court described the trepidation at Amboise being 'as great as though there were an army at the gates'. The whole household was armed to the teeth.

Nothing happened, and a few days later the king went out hunting again. However, a further rebel defected from the Protestant side, and disclosed that a new date for the attack had been set for 15 March. He also revealed that many of the conspirators were gathering at the Château de Noizay, on the north bank of the Loire close to Amboise. This time the De Guise faction wouldn't wait any longer. The Duc de Nemours sent out a reconnaissance party, which immediately captured a couple of the Protestant leaders at Noizay. Then all able-bodied men in the royal retinue at Amboise were called upon to form a 500-strong cavalry which rode out to the little château just north of the Loire. It was surrounded and the conspirators there captured.

On news of this blow, La Renaudie acted rashly. He ordered the scattered rebel troops to converge on Amboise, but without giving them a coherent plan of action. Arriving in dribs and drabs, they were easily captured by the De Guise side. Condé, sensing trouble, had responded to the king's invitation and arrived at Amboise on 16 March. But the very next day an attack was launched on the town by the Huguenots. Rumour did its worst and the court thought that thousands of Protestants were at the gates. They didn't know that there were in fact only a couple of hundred Huguenots outside, mounting a rather pathetic attack. Once they had been eradicated, the king's response was to name François de Guise lieutentant-general of France and to hand over to him the task of the suppression and punishment of the rebels.

Executions followed in nauseating waves at Amboise. It was written that the De Guises planned executions after dinner 'to give some entertainment to the ladies whom they saw getting bored having to stay for so long in this place'. La Renaudie was early captured and killed. His body was prominently displayed in town, hanging for a day before being chopped into five parts, one placed over each town gate. Other conspirators were tied up in sacks and thrown into the Loire to drown. The most famous image from the suppression of the Huguenots at Amboise is of bodies being left to hang from the château's battlements. The end of the Amboise Conspiracy was a very gory preface to the dreadful decades of the French Wars of Religion.

by Victor and Gabriel Ruprich-Robert. So much of the Château d'Amboise's architecture has disappeared, but you can muse on the significance of this royal castle while wandering around the gardens, or descending the monumental but finely decorated Tour Heurtault, offering the irreverent among you some crude late Gothic imagery as light relief after so much talk of royal goings-on, including one figure scratching its backside.

A Walk Around Amboise

Amboise grew fat at the château's feet. The town supplied the court with its vast needs and picked up the crumbs from its elevated table. Courtiers settled here, as did fine craftsmen, and some splendid town houses remain. Those along **Rue Victor Hugo**, running parallel to the formidable ramp you have to take up to visit the château, are now crammed with cafés, restaurants and shops; tourists have replaced the courtiers as the source of Amboise's revenue. Burrowed into the walls under the ramp, **Les Vignerons d'Amboise** offers a cave of a space where local winemakers are allowed to present their production on a rota basis.

At the northern end of Rue Victor Hugo, you can join Amboise's main shopping street, the **Rue Nationale**, by turning left turn and walking under the impressive 14th-century **Porte de l'Horloge** topped by a late medieval belfry. If you don't turn into Rue Nationale, you come to the **Hôtel de Ville**, or town hall, looking out over the river. This grand town house of the very early 16th-century went up for the then mayor of Tours, Pierre Morin, but it has been rather altered through time. Now it contains a handful of beautiful works of art, some Aubusson tapestries from the Château de Chanteloup and the statue of the Virgin which used to grace the Tour de l'Horloge. On the other side of the street from the Hôtel de Ville, rises the late medieval **church of St-Florentin**. Commissioned by Louis XI, it was formerly known as Notre-Dame-en-Grève (on-the-riverbank). Inside, it has been rendered unrecognisable by 19th-century restoration work, while it was given modern glass after the war.

If you cross the bridge over the Loire opposite the town hall, you get onto the **Île d'Or**, from which you can appreciate splendid views up to the château, particularly from beside the bronze statue of a naked, recumbent Leonardo. Perhaps it's best that the artist who executed this figure, generously donated by Paris in the 1970s, should remain anonymous.

Back on the town side of the Loire, the walk along the river bank is a favourite with the people of Amboise at weekends. Head west and you'll pass the **Max Ernst fountain**, a comical piece by the celebrated surrealist artist featuring many turtles and frogs. Ernst was helped to become a French citizen in 1958 by the then mayor of Amboise and leading politician Michel Debré – the Debré family political dynasty is still strongly associated with the town. By the post office and theatre, a road leads down towards the **Collégiale St-Denis**, another heavily restored old church, with elaborately carved capitals and a shockingly realistic 16th-century recumbent figure, said by some to be a representation of Marie Babou, a mistress of François I, who drowned in the Loire.

It's quite a long walk from the centre of town to Leonardo's last home, the Clos Lucé. Signs indicate the shortest way. But heading southwards, you could meander through the quiet old streets admiring ancient mansions, but not feeling too guilty about missing the rather modest and bizarre further little tourist attractions in the area. These include: the **Musée de la Poste** (open July–Aug Mon–Fri 2–6, or by appointment; t 02 47 23 47 23), in a fine mansion, recalling the history of the French postal service and King Louis XI's important role in getting it organized; the **Théâtre Illustré** (generally open Tues–Sun 10–12.30 and 2–6.30; t 02 47 57 20 81), presenting garish interpretations of Gustave Doré's famed engravings for Rabelais' Gargantua tales in a theatre-fronted building; and the **Maison Enchantée**, featuring automated figures in the setting of a scruffy courtyard opposite the Théâtre Illustré. The large **Place Richelieu** beyond is presided over not only by a pompous statue of the interfering 17th-century cardinal, but also by a bad rendering of the royal painter Jean Fouquet.

Château du Clos Lucé

Open July–Aug 9am–8pm, late March–June and Sept–Oct 9–7, Feb–late March and Nov–Dec 9–6, Jan 10–5; t 02 47 57 62 88.

Don't expect too much great art at the Clos Lucé. The house is rather fine, though. Originally constructed in 1477 for a royal forest warden, Etienne Le Loup, it was bought by King Charles VIII for his wife Anne de Bretagne to have a quiet retreat to which she could retire to pray in peace; a pretty oratory was added to the place for her. François I then donated the house to Leonardo da Vinci as one of his perks for agreeing to come to work for the French king at Amboise.

Rampant tourist commercialization has taken over today. Not that Leonardo wasn't commercially minded himself; he was more than handsomely paid by François I to come to France, so perhaps it isn't so outrageous that the Clos Lucé owners should be profiting by him in turn. But what Leonardo came up with was just a little higher class than this. Before experiencing Leonardo the Arms Maker, you're treated to Leonardo the Aphorist. You don't get any of Leonardo the Artist. Or rather, you get cheap copies, although it's thought that in one of these rooms Leonardo completed his famous painting of St John the Baptist.

The owners have tried to re-create a 16th-century atmosphere in many of the chambers. Others have an 18th-century feel; in that period, the Clos Lucé belonged to the d'Amboise family, who left their mark. One room contains some magnificent furniture saved from the Château de Chanteloup, with gilded wood and marquetry. Rich tapestries further adorn the rooms.

Among Leonardo's many creative talents, he proved a wizard at imagining new, ever more destructive weapons for his day. This is the side of his work brought out most clearly in this museum. The basement displays concentrate on models of many of his war machines, kindly recreated by IBM. Not all of Leonardo's drawings reproduced here are on the art of war, and they do show what a visionary engineer he was. He was also a great architect, who certainly drew up plans for a château for François I at

Romorantin-Lanthenay in the nearby Sologne area. This was never executed, but it is widely believed that Leonardo played some part in the design of François I's great Château de Chambord before his death. He certainly helped plan great entertainments for the court here at Amboise. He also delighted the king with his enlightened conversation and the breadth of his erudition. With his insatiable desire for knowledge he wrote down all manner of his thoughts in his notebooks – in mirror writing. Legend has it that Leonardo died in King François I's arms.

Justice doesn't appear to have been done to Leonardo's memory at the Clos Lucé, but you may leave here hungry to know more – the shop can provide not just T-shirts declaring 'Je suis un génie' but also some more substantial material in the form of good publications, including Leonardo's notebooks.

Pagode de Chanteloup

Open July–Aug 9–7.30, May–June and Sept 10–6, April and Oct 10–12 and 2–5.30, March 10–12 and 2–5, first half of Nov and second half of Feb 2–5; t 02 47 57 20 97.

The Pagode de Chanteloup (2.5km south of Amboise via the D31) is the charming, comical, but also slightly melancholy remnant of the great Château de Chanteloup. The pagoda's seven decreasing circles end with a clownish hat of lead topped by a golden ball. An architectural Pierrot, the form is reflected in a half-moon of a pool. Beyond this, a great channel of water once led up to the château. The surroundings are now somewhat subdued, the arrival at the car park not particularly encouraging, but the place itself has an enchanting quality. One of the entrance pavilions before the pagoda houses a little museum on the history of the once vast palace that stood here.

The Château de Chanteloup, had it been left standing, would have been one of those relative rarities for the Loire, a great 18th-century castle. Although the name most often associated with the place is that of Louis XV's powerful minister the Duc de Choiseul, the building was begun earlier, in 1711, for the Princesse des Ursins. Robert de Cotte, Mansart's brother-in-law and famous in his own right for such work as the dome on Les Invalides in Paris, was the architect. On his death in 1722, D'Aubigny continued the work. The Duc de Choiseul only bought the property in 1761 and ordered further work from Lecamus de Mezières, which included the colonnades, extensive outbuildings and the pagoda, constructed in the 1770s. Counting the colonnades to either side of the main block, the main building extended to a staggering 350ft in length.

Choiseul held many of the most important political posts of his day, serving as Minister of Foreign Affairs, of War and of the Navy. In 1768 he organized the securing of Corsica for France. By 1770 he had fallen out of favour, though, ousted by the king's controlling mistress, Madame Du Barry. Choiseul retired to Chanteloup, where he established something of an alternative court, attracting many influential European figures. Some claim that it inspired the dramatist Beaumarchais' famous pre-Revolutionary play, *Le Mariage de Figaro*.

Eighteenth-century visitors raved about the place. Animals were apparently held in high regard at Chanteloup, and Choiseul often toured the property with his guests to look at them. Among the exclusive menagerie was a monkey dressed as a grenadier and prize sheep, sometimes admitted to the salon. On one memorable social occasion the most splendid of the estate's rams, named Cathédrale, was lured inside with food to be presented to the archbishop of Tours. The excitement of the honour must have been too great for the sheep, who disgraced himself in front of the prelate causing such a commotion that he ran amok, his hooves leaving their mark on the parquet floor. The Choiseuls were well loved by the local people as well as by the courtiers who came here. Financial ruin eventually caught up with the exile, despite the devotion and money of his extremely rich wife, who would die in destitution in Paris having retired to a convent.

The next owner brought a direct royal connection to the place. Louis-Jean-Marie de Bourbon-Penthièvre bought the property in 1786. He was the grandson of Louis XIV and the latter's longtime favourite, Madame de Montespan. He was seemingly not resented by the people of Touraine and died in 1793, not by the guillotine, but indirectly by it, from the pain of hearing of the death at its sharp edge of his cousin, King Louis XVI. Bourbon-Penthièvre's daughter married the Duc d'Orléans who, although he had voted for the king's death, didn't escape the guillotine himself.

Under Napoleon, one of the emperor's greatly intelligent councillors, the chemist Jean-Antoine Chaptal, bought the château in 1802. Here he developed the production of sugar beet, which helped the French in the face of the enemy blockade of France. Chaptal ran up huge debts, however, and was forced to sell the château – to demolition men. The forest and pagoda were then acquired by the future King Louis-Philippe.

The pagoda and grounds are now run by an association. You can climb to the top of the pagoda. First, though, you might take the time to take in the discreet Chinese elements of its decoration: the oriental curve of the small sections of roof, the geometric patterns, and the inscriptions. The stairs snail up inside the building, the rooms at each level having smaller and smaller domes. The increasingly vertiginous little circular walks outside are definitely not for you if you suffer from vertigo. The views from the top are quite exhilarating, paths radiating out into the forest of Amboise. In summer you can picnic in the grounds around the pagoda, hire out a croquet set, or even take a trip in a hot air balloon.

Other Tourist Attractions Around Amboise

A new attraction near Chanteloup inflates you to Rabelaisian giant proportions. The **Parc des Mini-Châteaux** (*open June–Aug 9–7, April–May and Sept 10–6, Oct–11 Nov 10.30–5;* **t** *02 47 57 09 28, www.amboise-valdeloire.com*) displays miniature versions of the most famous châteaux of the Loire Valley. Here you can get bird's-eye views of over 20 Loire castles – the selection could perhaps help you choose which châteaux most take your fancy to then visit properly. (Remember also that the Château de

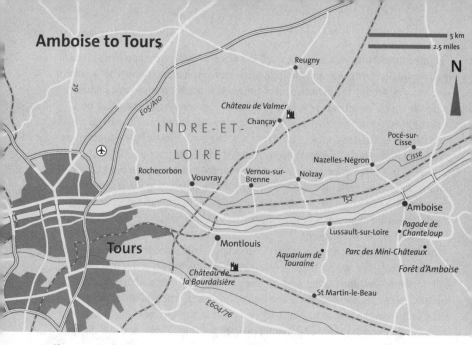

5 km
2.5 miles

N

Reugny

Château de Valmer
Chançay

INDRE-ET-
LOIRE

Pocé-sur-
Cisse
Cisse

Nazelles-Négron

Rochecorbon
Vouvray
Vernou-sur-
Brenne
Noizay

T52

Amboise

Pagode de
Chanteloup

Lussault-sur-Loire

Tours
Montlouis
Aquarium de
Touraine
Parc des Mini-Châteaux

Forêt d'Amboise

Château de
la Bourdaisière

St Martin-le-Beau

E604/76

Chenonceau lies only a short distance south from here, on the Cher river – *see* pp.223–8.)

For those mad about donkeys, a new donkey park, **Le Fou de l'Ane** (*open June–Aug 9–7, April–May and Sept 10–6, Oct–mid-Nov 10.30–5*), near the Parc des Mini-Châteax, is an added bonus in the area, with more than 60 braying beauties and the possibility of donkey-carriage rides.

Continuing along the south bank of the Loire river from Amboise to Tours, you come to what is surprisingly the most popular of all the tourist attractions along this stretch of river, not a château, but an aquarium, apparently the largest for fresh water fish in Europe. The **Aquarium de Touraine** (*open July–Aug 10–7, April–June and Sept 10–6, rest of year 10.30–5; t 0825 0825 22, www.alize.parc.com*) takes the form of a massive complex of tanks. It looks like a modern conference centre on the outside, but within a lovely light filters down into the very clean tanks on sunny days. You can see here all the fish you can eat along the Loire, plus many more, but they have the advantage of still being alive. Some tanks have been made to stretch right over the ceiling at certain points. Details are given on the fish presented.

The Loire and Cisse from Amboise to Tours

The delightful little Cisse river cheekily steals a ribbon of territory in the Loire's valley between Amboise and Tours. It's well worth following it through a string of pretty villages and past numerous cliff-side châteaux. West along the Cisse, you come into primary Touraine wine and troglodyte territory. The vineyards of Vouvray stretch up the north bank of the Loire, while those of Montlouis slope down from the south side.

From Amboise to Vouvray

The village of **Noizay** boasts two châteaux on its slope; the darker Château de Noizay is the one where the Huguenot conspirators of the Amboise Conspiracy gathered before they were butchered. This little castle was transformed after a fire in the 17th century. This is also the village where the complex 20th-century French composer Francis Poulenc lived much of his life. **Vernou-sur-Brenne** is a rather larger but still attractive village, former country seat of the bishops of Tours.

Getting Around

Noizay and Montlouis are both served by **train** from Tours, Blois and Orléans. There are regular **bus** services between Amboise and Tours, and occasional stops at Rochecorbon, Vouvray, Vernou and Noizay on the north bank, and Montlouis and the aquarium of Lussault near the south bank; contact Touraine Fil Vert for times, t 02 47 47 17 18.

Tourist Information

Vouvray: N152 or Mairie, 37210 Vouvray, t 02 47 52 68 73 or t 02 47 52 70 48, f 02 47 52 67 76.
Rochecorbon: Place du Croissant, 37120 Rochecorbon, t/f 02 47 52 80 22.
Montlouis-sur-Loire: Place de la Mairie, 37270 Montlouis-sur-Loire, t 02 47 45 00 16.

Market Days

Vouvray: Friday morning.
Montlouis-sur-Loire: Thursday morning.

Where to Stay and Eat

Noizay ✉ 37210

★★★★Château de Noizay, t 02 47 52 11 01, f 02 47 52 04 64, *noizay@relaischateaux.fr* (*expensive*). A splendid little château. What with its private park, cliff caves, a tennis court, swimming pool and walks in the wood, Noizay has all the ingredients to help you relax in style, plus a fascinating history (*see* Amboise, p.249). The chef cooks up memorable Loire dishes (*menus €23.5–54.5*). *Closed 20 Nov–18 Mar*.

Vernou-sur-Brenne ✉ 37210

★★Les Perce-Neige, 13 Rue Anatole France, t 02 47 52 10 04, f 02 47 52 19 08, *brigitte@ perceneige.com, www.perceneige.com* (*inexpensive*). This place is charming and characterful, a village house with pretensions, its cramped entrance courtyard trying desperately to imitate big-town grandeur. Most of the rooms are simple but pleasant and extremely good value. There's a lovingly tended garden to one side where you can appreciate the local cuisine on sunny days (*menus €15–29*). *Closed Sun pm and Mon out of season, mid-Nov–mid-Dec and early Jan–mid-March*.

Château de Jallanges B&B, t 02 47 52 06 66, f 02 47 52 11 18, *info@chateaudejallanges.fr, www.chateaudejallanges.fr* (*expensive*). This splendid brick château full of architectural interest is set in grand grounds up from the village of Vernou, in the winding valley of Vaugondy. You can stay in the grand rooms as a B&B guest. The *table d'hôte* at around €39.5 isn't unreasonable for the lavish surrounds; perhaps finish the evening with a game of billiards. The place has a heated pool and the proprietors can organize all sorts of luxury trips for you.

Vouvray ✉ 37210

Domaine des Bidaudières B&B, Rue du Peu Morier, t 02 47 52 66 85, f 02 47 52 62 17, *info@bandb-loire-valley.com, www.bandb-loire-valley.com* (*expensive*). This is an Italianate dream of a place built on terraces along the Loire cliffside a little east of Vouvray. This is an utterly gorgeous 18th-century wine property, restored in the mid-1990s. The place actually feels more like a luxury little hotel than a B&B address, the owners very discreet. The rooms have been beautifully decorated with designer furnishings and tasteful fabrics. There's a wonderful conservatory by the swimming pool.

Take the D46 north for Reugny and follow the signs for the **Château de Valmer**, near troglodyte Chançay. This is one of the few châteaux that you can visit along this stretch, but only for its gardens, only in high summer, and only in the afternoon (*open July and Aug Tues–Sun 2–6; also open afternoons on Sat, Sun and public hols in June and Sept*). It does, though, occupy one of those memorably picturesque corners of Touraine that is well worth seeking out. The château was built in the mid-17th century, but the main buildings have been sadly reduced. Three graceful matching

★★Le Grand Vatel, 8 Rue Brûlée, t 02 47 52 70 32, f 02 47 52 74 52 (*inexpensive*). This has a choice of dining rooms, one daubed with bawdy 1950s wall paintings, the other modern and bright. River fish and seafood are mixed on the one plate, with *sandre* served with a seafood coulis, and you may find more exotic touches such as lobster with mango (*menus €19–38*). *Closed Sun pm and Mon out of season, first fortnight in Dec and first fortnight in Mar*.

Rochecorbon ✉ 37210

★★★★Les Hautes Roches, 86 Quai de la Loire, t 02 47 52 88 88, f 02 47 52 81 30, *hautes roches@relaischateaux.fr* (*expensive*). This unique and magical cliffside hotel has some of the most extraordinary rooms along the Loire, luxuriously fitted in troglodyte hillside caves, with light window openings, fireplaces and canopied beds! The dining room (fish and seafood the speciality) and reception rooms lie in the neat square-angled 18th-century pavilion alongside the caves. The only slight negative is the busy road separating the hotel from the Loire (*menus €25–56*). *Closed Feb–mid-Mar*.

Château de Montgouverne B&B, at St-Georges, just west of Rochecorbon, t 02 47 52 84 59, f 02 47 52 84 61, *montgouverne@ chateauxhotels.com, www.chateauxhotels .com/montgouverne* (*expensive*). This delightful 18th-century home is set in splendid grounds in the Vouvray vineyards, with swimming, riding and cycling possible.

L'Oubliette, 34 Rue des Clouets, t 02 47 52 50 49. Also in a cave, and another address where attention is paid to detail. The menu is tempting and regional, with *croustillant de petits gris des Pays de la Loire* served with *rillons* and sweet garlic purée and *pommes de terre au Chinon*, while even the lobster

comes in a sweet Vouvray sauce (*menus €15–44*). *Closed Sun pm and Mon*.

Hostellerie de la Lanterne, 48 Quai de la Loire, t 02 47 52 50 02, f 02 47 52 54 46. This has the refreshing attraction of a garden by the whiter-than-white 18th-century posting inn. You can eat a grill outside in summer, take the three-course menu which includes a carafe of wine, or opt for such classic dishes as snails with mushrooms or duck à l'orange (*menus €15–35*). *Closed Sun pm and Mon, and mid-Jan–mid-Feb*.

Montlouis-sur-Loire ✉ 37270

Château de la Bourdaisière, 25 Rue de la Bourdaisière, t 02 47 45 16 31, f 02 47 45 09 11, *labourd@club-internet.fr, www.chateaux-france.com/-bourdaisière* (*expensive*). For a description of this grand Loire Valley château *see* pp.258–60. The suites and rooms are very spacious and luxurious. Twenty are in the château itself, while a further six have recently been created in the eaves of the stables – these last are darker, but extremely well kitted out. You can seek out a tennis court and swimming pool in the lovely grounds.

★★Hôtel de la Ville, Place de la Mairie, t 02 47 50 84 84, f 02 47 45 08 43 (*inexpensive*). Neat, cheap rooms, plus a terrace and garden in the centre of the town (*menus €12–33.5*). *Closed 20 Dec–10 Jan*.

Relais de Belle Roche, 14 Rue de la Vallée, t 02 47 50 82 43, f 02 47 45 01 66. The dining room here is cut into the Loire rockface, and a good choice of typical Touraine dishes is offered (*menus €16.5–35*). *Closed Tues pm and Wed pm*.

La Cave, t 02 47 45 05 05. Truly cavernous; a very popular, sometimes loud former stone quarry along the riverside in which to eat meats cooked over a wood fire, as well as the usual Loire fare (*menus from €19*).

Vouvray Wines

A tingling taste on the tongue, even with a dry, still Vouvray served as an apéritif, gives away this wine's natural leanings towards bubbles. The other great character- istic of Vouvray, apart from its very slight natural effervesence, is the Chenin Blanc grape variety. In fact, it's virtually the exclusive grape variety here, although a tiny percentage of Arbois may be found. Vouvray produces some of the finest Chenin Blanc wines. In fact Vouvray is the largest producer of Chenin Blanc in France, made from 1,750 hectares planted with the variety.

The Vouvray vineyards extend across eight parishes (Vouvray, Rochecorbon, Ste- Radegonde, Parçay-Meslay, Vernou, Noizay, Chançay and Reugny), and importantly lots of them slope down the well-sheltered creases of five litte valleys coming down to the Loire. In many places the steep exposed tufa hillsides were quarried in ages past and provide some wonderful cellars in which the wine can be made and kept.

Some people can find the tingle and the tastes of Vouvray Chenin Blanc startling. It definitely has bite. Too much acidity is the enemy in bad years or bad wine- making here. The aroma can jump out at you as well, what with its touches of exotic fruits and fragrant flowers. With age, you can often detect hints of roasting or slight burning, either of nuts or of raisins. Honey, too, is often used to describe Vouvrays.

It's interesting to distinguish the different characteristics of the various types of wine produced here. The dry white makes for a powerful-tasting apéritif. In Touraine it could easily be served with fish and seafood. The demi-sec is the kind of sweet wine the French used to think the English loved best, but its flowery honey flavour is less popular these days – some suggest trying it with Touraine goat's cheese! The Chenin Blanc character often comes out to good effect when transformed into sparkling wines, Vouvray *mousseux*, its flavours strong enough to cope with the distraction of the bubbles, the honeyish aroma still present. The very liquorous sweet *moelleux* will only be made in good years, that is ones where noble rot sets in; these sweet wines are a completely different matter and can age for decades, even up to a century in rare vintages. They can have a mouth-filling richness and develop a variety of complex flavours.

A couple of estates have the irresistible appeal of a superb château along with their wine. The **Château de Valmer** (*t 02 47 52 93 12; closed Dec–April*) at Chançay is mentioned elsewhere for its gardens, but also produces good wine. The **Château de Moncontour** (*t 02 47 52 60 77; check if there's a charge for the visit*) stands proudly above the valley road outside Vouvray. A highly respected name among producers in Vouvray is that of Huet – **Domaine Huet** (*Le Haut-Lieu, t 02 47 52 78 87*). A wider selection of the wines can be tasted at the **Cave des Producteurs des Grands Vins de Vouvray** (*38 La Vallée Coquette, t 02 47 52 75 03*), which has hundreds of metres of galleries in the rock. At Rochecorbon, the **Etablissements Brédif** (*87 Quai de la Loire, t 02 47 52 50 07; closed Aug; small fee for the visit*) are well known for the quality of their wines, produced in superb caves, some dating back to the 10th century.

outbuildings trip gaily down the slope to greet you. Above them lie balustraded formal gardens, an archetypal picture of their period, with statues and urns scattered elegantly around. A 16th-century chapel is hidden in the rock face. The wine cellars are worth a visit as you're now in Vouvray country.

Reaching the town of **Vouvray** itself, the lower part looks a bit of a mess down in the valley. Signs signal potential wine tastings, *dégustations*, at every turn. There's also a renowned charcuterie down here, Hardouin, with one shop in the centre of Vouvray and one on the N152. These specialist *charcutiers* add a dash of Vouvray wine to their array of specialities. Their products are sold not just in the village, but also in some of the most prestigious grocery shops in Paris, notably Fauchon.

Seek out the Ecomusée du Pays de Vouvray (*open 15 March–11 Nov 10–7*) up in the elegant upper village. The place is dedicated to the viticulture and viniculture which have made this little corner prosper. You can also do some serious studying of the wines of Vouvray here with a comparative tasting.

Rochecorbon, towards Tours from Vouvray, also conceals a wealth of extraordinary troglodyte homes. You can occasionally get the chance to visit an elegant 18th-century troglodyte home, the Manoir des Basses Rivières (*open July and Aug Wed–Mon 2–7; also open Sat, Sun and public hols from Easter to June and in Sept*). One room is actually thought to date from the 11th century, while a great staircase dug into the tufa links together the various levels. Just west of Rochecorbon is the cliff side where St Martin of Tours founded his famous monastery in the 4th century, **Marmoutier**, the second to be founded in France. The sacred place isn't open to visitors as it lies in the grounds of a religious establishment turned into a private school.

Montlouis and Around

The **Maison de la Loire** (*open April–mid-Oct Wed–Mon 2–7*) in Montlouis-sur-Loire has information and puts on regular little exhibitions on the flora, fauna and geology of the Loire valley. There are observation posts and the possibility of hiring binoculars.

Château de la Bourdaisière

Salacious stories of royal mistresses hang around the Château de la Bourdaisière, an impressive, typical-looking Loire Valley château which has just about managed to keep aloof from the suburbs stretching into southern Montlouis. Although the castle looks the very image of an early 16th-century French palace, it is in fact a 19th-century reinvention; the Baron d'Angelier, a massively wealthy mayor of Montouis in that period, had his fantasy built on a site with many historical resonances. In medieval times a fortress stood here. The first traceable lord was a great warrior figure, Jean le Meingre, better-known as Boucicaut. Then in 1520, Philibert Babou, a finance minster to François I, commissioned his fine château. François I appreciated not just Babou's housekeeping for the nation, but also the women in his household. The lusty royal visited on many occasions to enjoy the delightful company of Philibert's wife Marie

Montlouis-sur-Loire and its Wines

Former stone quarries have been converted into dramatic wine cellars by many wine producers in Montlouis. Most of Montlouis' vines grow on slopes facing south towards the Cher river rather than the Loire, in the parishes of Montlouis, Lussault and St-Martin-le-Beau. As with more famous Vouvray, only white wines are produced here, exclusively from the Chenin Blanc variety, also known in these parts as Pineau de Loire. The soils across the small 250 hectare *appellation* territory are lighter than on the north side of the Loire, a sign that the wines should reach maturity more quickly. The same range of whites is made, with some dry, some demi-sec, and in years when the noble rot allows it, some *moelleux*, which then needs to be aged for the acidity to melt. As at Vouvray, the Chenin Blanc comes out quite well, in the sparkling *mousseux*.

The **Chidaine** family (*t 02 47 45 19 14*), along Montlouis' Grande Rue, is very well respected for its wines. For a larger-scale introduction to the *appellation*, you could try the **Cave des producteurs des vins de Montlouis** (*2 Route de St-Aignan, t 02 47 50 80 98; best to visit between Mon and Thurs when there's more activity*).

The **Domaine Deletang** (*t 02 47 50 29 77; closed Sun pm*) gives you a good reason to visit the attractive little village of St-Martin-le-Beau. Close to the church, the family cellars have a good reputation. *Perruches*, flinty clays, are recognized for their part in producing good quality wines here. The presence of these flints probably explains why experts often describe Montlouis wines as more mineral than Vouvrays. See if you can spot nutty flavours too, almonds and hazelnuts regularly cropping up in tasting notes.

Gaudin, and of her daughters. Moving on a few generations, Gabrielle, a great-grand-daughter of Philibert's, may have been born at La Bourdaisière in 1565. She went down in history as King Henri IV's famed mistress, Gabrielle d'Estrées.

In the 18th century, when the Duc de Choiseul had been exiled to Amboise by Louis XV, he decided to expand his Château de Chanteloup (*see pp.252–3*). He had most of the Château de la Bourdaisière demolished to use the stone in the new building work. The story goes that he did this in part to spite his rival the Duc d'Aiguillon, who had an eye on La Bourdaisière, wanting to add it to his nearby estates at Veretz on the Cher.

The De Broglie family which now owns the château has put a great deal of effort into sprucing up the castle in recent years. As well as developing the buildings as a hotel, they have had much work carried out on the gardens, open to the general public. The château forms the photogenic centrepiece. An Italianate gateway in the grounds has been attributed to Leonardo da Vinci. Up above the château, the walled kitchen garden has been transformed into a beautifully designed vegetable garden, the hundreds of varieties of tomato cultivated here the pride of the collection. Down in the sumptuous stables by the castle (one original feature to have survived from Babou's 16th-century château), the De Broglies have created the Conservatoire de la Tomate where you can learn about the history of tomatoes, and the great number of varieties that exist today around the world. The euphemistic term for tomatoes in

French is *pommes d'amour*, apples of love, which seems suitable enough given La Bourdaisière's history. A very tasty boutique allows you to buy all sorts of tomato products, while in season you can also sit down to a light tomato lunch. The castle's estates also produce a respectable Montlouis wine.

Tours

Tours

Bienheureux qui comme la Loire suit son cours dans son lit. (Happy those who, like the Loire, follow their course in their bed.)

graffiti at the University of Tours

Tours is the kind of glamorous French town where it's easy to enjoy a very laid-back French time, wandering idly through historic streets, browsing in tempting shops, sitting in cafés, watching the world go by. Certainly the courses must seem a distraction to the large number of students who pose a great deal around the centre. Back in the mid-19th century, Balzac wickedly wrote of complacent Touraine contentment in *Le Curé de Tours*, describing the place as 'an area where no one wants to be disturbed for any reason whatsoever, not even for a pleasure'. Nowadays, innumerable foreign students deliberately descend upon the town, coming here to learn what's considered the purest French in France. So the feeling is cosmopolitan and distinctly lively. Occasionally Mick Jagger pops in from his château not far off for a drink at his favourite bar on the Place Plumereau, the social hub. Tours has a great buzz to it.

Tours is an excellent central spot from which to visit the very famous châteaux to east, west and south in the Touraine. It's also very much worth a stay in its own right, a vibrant cultural centre with numerous attractions and attractive quarters, despite the terrible damage inflicted on it in the Second World War, particularly by the river and down its main drag. The heart of the historic part of town is divided in two by the latter, the long, straight north–south Rue Nationale, and is located north of Place Jean-Jaurès with its grandiose Hôtel de Ville. On the western side of the centre lie the frantically pumping Place Plumereau and the pedestrian streets around it, as well as the Quartier St-Martin, recalling one of France's greatest saint's extremely close connection with the city. On the eastern side, the streets lead to the quieter yet characterful cathedral and *préfecture* district. Both parts are bordered to the north by the Loire, and you can wander along the high quays where ships once moored.

While fellow travellers are rushing out to do their daily handful of châteaux, you might enjoy a couple of days just discovering Tours. It has its own handful of interesting museums. The Musée des Beaux-Arts has taken over the former archbishop's palace next to the cathedral and offers the peculiarity in the Loire of predominantly 18th-century art. The Hôtel Gouin holds a typically rich archaeological collection and beautiful fragments from some of the grand Tours buildings which have disappeared. The Musée du Compagonnage, by contrast, proves distinctly bizarre and amusing, dedicated to the *chefs-d'œuvre* of master craftsmen, including old cake preserved for posterity.

Another unusual museum is the Musée du Gemmail, where 20th-century works of art are interpreted in glowing shards and layers of stained glass. The other museums in town are quite small affairs, a couple dedicated to Tours' history, another to wine, and yet another to St Martin.

St Martin's 4th-century legacy meant that Tours became a important spiritual centre in France, with numerous religious orders and churches established here, early drawing pilgrims. Of the religious buildings that remain, the Cathédrale St-Gatien, the church of St-Julien and the ruins of the church of St-Martin, with the 19th-century St-Martin's basilica close by, are the most significant. On the outskirts of town, the ruins of the Prieuré de St-Cosme are seasonally filled with the scent of roses, the beauty of which also pervades the poetry of Ronsard, the great French Renaissance versifier who ran this priory for a time.

Tours' material attractions will probably retain most visitors' attention now more than its spiritual legacy. It has long thrived as a trading centre, going back to Roman times at least. One new attraction for visitors is a silk-making factory still using old-fashioned techniques and acting as a reminder of the fact that Tours specialized in silk-making for centuries. Today the city has some splendid shopping quarters. As well as appealing to tourists, they cater to the doctors, lawyers and university teachers settled here in large number, not forgetting the innumerable château owners coming in from the surrounding region to furnish their *salons* and stock up on *froufrous*, *foie gras* and *petits fours*.

History

The Gallo-Roman history of the town pales into insignificance compared with what's known of its early Christian history. However, the Gallo-Roman settlement, called Ceasarodunum, founded in the first half of the 1st century AD, became an

Getting There and Around

By Air
Tours has a small airport, Tours Val de Loire (t 02 47 49 37 00), 6km northeast of town. Rumour has it that one of the providers of cheap flights from Britain will soon be running a regular service from one of the London airports to Tours.

By Train
Be warned that Tours has two main stations, the central one and St-Pierre-des-Corps. The central train station is a tourist sight in itself, the work of Victor Laloux, architect of the Gare d'Orsay in Paris (now the Musée d'Orsay). The amazing TGV fast train service means that central Paris is only 1 hour away from central Tours. Slower, slightly cheaper trains are also available.

By Car and Bicycle
The A10 motorway, the main route from Paris to Bordeaux and Spain, cuts through the eastern side of the city centre. If you arrive early in the day you may find a space on the free parking bays down on the Loire quays right by the centre, otherwise there are plenty of paying car parks.

Car Hire
Avis, Place Général Leclerc, t 02 47 20 53 27.
Europcar, 76 Rue B Palissy, t 02 47 64 4 76.
Hertz, 57 Rue Marcel Tribut, t 02 47 75 50 00.

Bicycle Hire
Amstercycles, 5 Rue du Rempart, t 02 47 61 22 23.
Vélomania, 109 Rue Colbert, t 02 47 05 10 11.

By Bus
The intercity bus station is in front of the train station. The local bus station is on the nearby Place Jean-Jaurès, where Avenue Grammont enters the square from the south. There's a Kiosque Information, Rue de la Dolve, or telephone Allo Fil Bleu, t 02 47 66 70 70.

By Taxi
Allo Taxi, t 02 47 20 30 40.

Tourist Information

Tourist office: Office de Tourisme, 78–82 Rue Bernard Palissy, B.P.4201, 37042 Tours Cedex, t 02 47 70 37 37, f 02 47 61 14 22, *info@ligeris.com*, *www.ligeris.com*. The Carte Multi-Visites allows you to visit the town's six municipal museums for a mere €7.5. The tourist office organizes a whole programme of *visites à thèmes*; these tours in French concentrate on particular topics, such as ancient Tours, St Martin, Renaissance Tours, the cathedral, Victor Laloux, and the silk-making works.

Market Days
There are traditional French markets in different parts of town every morning of the week except Monday – the tourist office can supply listings. Other regular specialist markets include:
Place de la Résistance: the *Marché gourmand*, first Friday in each month, 4–10am.
Place de la Victoire: second-hand junk markets; Wednesday and Saturday.
Boulevard Béranger: fourth Sunday in month.
Rue de Bordeaux: first and third Friday of month.
Place des Halles: craft market; Saturday.
Boulevard Béranger: flower market; Wednesday and Saturday.

Where to Stay

Tours ✉ 37000

Expensive
★★★★**Château Belmont Jean Bardet**, 57 Rue Groison, t 02 47 41 41 11, f 02 47 51 68 72, *sophie@jeanbardet.com*. A name known across France for the highest standards of cuisine, but recently rocked by a scandal over

important city. It was one of the 50-odd towns created as heads of the districts of Gaul under the Roman Emperor Augustus, roughly following the territorial divides of the Celtic tribes. The region around Ceasarodunum had been the land of the Turones and the Roman region was named the Civitas Turonorum.

misleading customers about wines. However, this is still a chi-chi restaurant and hotel. The substantial town house stands in the posh part of the suburbs on the north bank of the Loire, east off Av de la Tranchée. The rooms are charming. The garden is lovingly tended, and has a pool. If you don't want to spend too much on a meal, there's a quite reasonable value menu. The one jarring note is the boutique – avert your eyes; here bad taste reigns.

***Hôtel de l'Univers, 5 Bd Heurteloup, **t** 02 47 05 37 12, **f** 02 47 61 51 80. At the heart of the town, a grand Belle Epoque building where the famous automatically used to stay in Tours, as the portrait gallery on the ground floor flaunts. Churchill counted among the number to grace one of its 89 relatively luxurious rooms. The restaurant isn't bad, the prices quite reasonable (*menus €17–33.5*).

Moderate

***Le Grand Hôtel, 9 Place du Général Leclerc, **t** 02 47 05 35 31, **f** 02 47 64 10 77. Large and by the railway station, but has a certain charm and is quite reasonably priced. *Closed mid-Dec–early Jan*.

***Le Royal Clarine, 65 Av de Grammont, **t** 02 47 64 71 78, **f** 02 47 05 84 62. On the big bustling artery south of Av Jean-Jaurès. It has a peculiar mix of contemporary and old-fashioned rooms, again at reasonable price.

Inexpensive

Hôtel du Cygne, 6 Rue du Cygne, **t 02 47 66 66 41, **f** 02 47 66 05 13, *hotelcygne.tours@wanadoo.fr*. There's a lovely old-fashioned character to this very centrally located, very good-value little hotel.

Le Moderne, 1–3 Rue Victor Laloux, **t 02 47 05 32 81, **f** 02 47 05 71 50, *hotelmoderne@minitel.net*. On a quiet, central street corner with well-kept rooms and an owner who doubles as a good cook in the evenings.

Le Balzac, 47 Rue de la Scellerie, **t 02 47 05 40 87, **f** 02 47 05 67 93. Another well-located

small hotel with some charm, including a little inner courtyard where you can have breakfast in summer.

Châteaux de la Loire, 12 Rue Gambetta, **t 02 47 05 10 05, **f** 02 47 20 20 14, *hoteldes chateaux.tours@wanadoo.fr*. West of the Rue Nationale, this has some relatively spacious rooms and a bar.

Cheap

*Mon Hôtel, 40 Rue de la Préfecture, **t** 02 47 05 67 53, **f** 02 47 05 21 88. Well located for such bargain prices, in one of the chicest parts of Tours, close to the railway station, but with most of the rooms you have to share the toilet and washing facilities.

*Le St-Eloi, 79 Bd Béranger, **t** 02 47 37 67 34, **f** 02 47 39 34 67. A small town house further out on one of the main thoroughfares cutting through town, but set back from the road with its front garden and parking.

Eating Out

Expensive

Jean Bardet, *see* 'Where to Stay', above. The crème de la crème for cuisine in Tours.

Charles Barrier, 101 Av de la Tranchée, **t** 02 47 54 20 39. The other really exceptional restaurant north of the Loire, in the same part of town as Jean Bardet. This place too is named after the chef who made its name, although he has gone to pastures new and the place has been stylishly redecorated.

Moderate

Les Tuffeaux, 21 Rue Lavoisier, **t** 02 47 47 19 89. Opposite Tours' now quite meagre château, this address has beams as well as tufa walls, and offers warm traditional Touraine cooking, several dishes usually including Touraine wine sauces.

La Rôtisserie Tourangelle, 23 Rue du Commerce, **t** 02 47 05 71 21. This is a well-established restaurant with impeccable manners.

It seems strange that the town should have been built on the flat south bank of the Loire, liable to floods, rather than on the hillside of the north bank. But with the Cher river to the south, perhaps this gave the location something of the protection of an island. A few vestiges of the Gallo-Roman town have been discovered in the course of

L'Atlantic, 59 Rue du Commerce, t 02 47 64 78 41. High-quality seafood, but also regional fish specialities such as eels in a Touraine wine sauce with prunes.

Cheap

Le Petit Patrimoine, 58 Rue Colbert, t 02 47 66 05 81. Lively narrow little restaurant down a very pleasant shopping street, serving traditional Tourangeau dishes (*menus €10.5–23.5*).

Chez Jean-Michel – Le Charolais, 123 Rue Colbert, t 02 47 20 80 20. Wine bar specializing in Loire *appellations*, and also offering a simple selection of Touraine dishes.

Brasserie Buré, Place de la Résistance, t 02 47 05 67 74. Big Belle Epoque-style brasserie.

Le Singe Vert, 5 Rue Marceau, t 02 47 61 50 10. A madly cluttered brasserie named after what was once a house of low repute. A place to go if you like your charcuterie and grilled meats.

Au Bistrot des Halles, 31 Place Gaston Pailhou, t 02 47 61 54 93. By the covered market, busy brasserie serving traditional French fare.

Entertainment and Nightlife

Look out for *Tours Cultures*, the quarterly cultural magazine for the town, listing events, or email *vie-culturelle@ville-tours.fr*, or look at the cultural pages at *www.ville-tours.fr*.

Cinema

Cinémas Studio, 2 Rue des Ursulines, t 02 47 20 27 00. Shows an extensive programme of classic and contemporary films in original versions, behind the cathedral.

CGR Rex, 45 Rue National, t 08 36 68 04 45. Has disabled seating.

CGR Mega, Av Marcel-Merieux, t 08 36 68 04 45.

Events

Centre de Congrès Vinci, 26 Bd Heurteloup, t 02 47 70 70 70. Major contemporary centre for cultural events, as well as conferences.

Theatre

Grand Théâtre, 34 Rue de la Scellerie, t 02 47 60 20 20. Theatre venue in 19th-century grandeur, where concerts, dance and other events are also staged.

Théâtre Louis Jouvet, 12 Rue Léonard de Vinci, t 02 47 64 50 50. Specializes in contemporary theatre.

Dance

Centre Chorégraphique National de Tours, 47 Rue du Sergent Leclerc, t 02 47 36 46 00.

Classical Music

Salle Jean de Ockeghem, 15 Place de Châteauneuf, t 02 47 20 71 95. Main stage for classical concerts, although several churches in Tours put on interesting classical concerts.

Contemporary Music

Le Petit Faucheux, 23 Rue des Cerisiers, t 02 47 38 29 34. Main jazz venue.

Le Bateau Ivre, 146 Rue Edouard Vaillant, t 02 47 44 77 22. Another well-known jazz address.

Les 3 Orfèvres, 6 Rue des 3 Orfèvres, off Place Plumereau, t 02 47 64 02 73. Rock, reggae, blues, jazz, etc.

Bars and Clubs

For bars and clubs, the area around Place Plumereau is very lively and quite chic. Down Av Grammont are bigger, more popular places.

Music Festivals

Aucard is a rock festival held on the main island in the Loire in central Tours. It was recently held in late May, but check dates.

Florilège Vocal is a choral singing festival in late May or early June. For info, call t 02 47 21 65 26. **Fêtes Musicales en Touraine**, at the Grange de Meslay, t 02 47 21 65 08, is a highly reputed chamber music festival held late June in a splendid former fortified farm standing on drab isolated flatland above the Loire valley some way north of town, and within sight and hearing distance of the A10 motorway.

digging foundations for new buildings around the cathedral area. The clearest trace of Gallo-Roman times is seen in the straight line of the former main street, or *decumanus*, now the Rue Colbert. A curving street behind the cathedral apparently follows the line of a Gallo-Roman arena. Invasions from the east led to the building of the town's first fortifications – a few vestiges can be seen by the remnants of the medieval château.

Tours had an important Christian community early on by French standards. Gatien is the first recorded bishop, at work before the Roman Emperor Constantine, who would proclaim Christianity as the Empire's religion from 324, came to power. A first cathedral was begun in 337 under Bishop Lidoire, but the present Tours cathedral is named after Gatien. The most important bishop of Tours, Martin, was appointed in the 370s. He stands out as one of the most important figures in French Christianity (*see* box on next page).

With the popularity of the cult of St Martin and the magnetic magnificence of the early basilica, a whole new quarter of town grew up slightly to the west of the older city and the place was transformed, in time becoming known as Martinopolis. Tours formed an early strong royal connection when Clovis, king of the Franks, stopped at the shrine in 496 and said that he would convert to Christianity if he beat the Alamanni. This he managed and he went on to be baptized at Reims, a decisive step in the establishing of the divine right of the French kings. Clovis went on to defeat the Visigoths under Alaric II in 507. St Martin was considered to have played his part in these victories and he became a particularly cherished figure for the Merovingian dynasty.

Pilgrims flocked to the new town, including Gregory, a nobleman from distant Auvergne. He stayed in the place and was nominated bishop of Tours in 573. His great historical work, the *Historia Francorum* (*The History of the Franks*), is one of the most important texts of the Dark Ages in Europe, a riveting read about those centuries of turmoil, crammed with details of the events, superstitions and prejudices of the period, and depicting the ruthlessness of the period. Tours' Benedictine abbey of St-Julien was founded at this time, between the new quarter of St-Martin and the old town, an area which was given over to vines then! Both main centres were granted the right to mint money, a considerable privilege. The distinctive division of two parts of town is still perceptible today.

The Carolingian dynasty maintained strong links with Tours. Charlemagne's third wife, Luitgarde, died here in 800. The so-called Tour Charlemagne close to St-Martin's basilica is really named thus because of her. The great Carolingian scholar Alcuin of York was named abbot in Tours in 796. He founded a brilliant school. The curriculum centred on grammar, rhetoric and dialectics, and its method of teaching set the way for the great medieval centres of learning. Alcuin also established a centre for producing manuscripts which became one of the finest schools for Carolingian illuminated works. For some time Tours was one of the major intellectual centres of the West.

The abbey of St-Julien survived the Viking raids in the mid-9th century, but the St Martin's quarter of the city was devastated. The abbey of St Martin had to be reconstructed and a timber fortification was replaced by stone, while the whole area was given defences and became known as Châteauneuf. With the breakdown of the Carolingian empire, the regional feudal counts became the important figures. Under Count Eudes of Blois in the first part of the 11th century, a new bridge was built over

St Martin

Here ends the first book, which covers five thousand, five hundred and ninety-six years from the beginning of the world down to the death of Saint Martin.
Gregory of Tours, *The History of the Franks*, written in the 590s

The line ending Gregory of Tours' first book on the history of the Franks makes clear the massive importance ascribed to St Martin in the Dark Ages. Martin came originally from Hungary and fought as a soldier for the Roman Empire, although he was to abandon his military ways. He's most famously represented as a fighter on horseback, putting his sword to charitable use. Travelling through Amiens in Picardy, in northern France, he came across a wretched, naked beggar; he was moved to divide his cloak in half to give protection to the suffering man. The oft-reproduced image makes a touching scene, even if Martin isn't depicted getting down from his mount and may seem a little less magnanimous than St Francis of Assisi, by half a coat at least. But St Martin is said to have been a great inspiration for the famous medieval Italian, as well as for innumerable Christians through the Dark Ages.

Martin, in the night after the incident of the cloak, is said to have seen Christ appear to him, holding the other half of his mantle. The mercenary was converted to the Christian faith, his mission clear to him. With Hilary, bishop of Poitiers, Martin created the first monastery in France, at Ligugé in the Poitou, in 360. He then travelled up to Tours, where he founded a second monastery, Marmoutier, its present incarnation now on the eastern outskirts of town, just north of the river. Martin was made bishop of the city around 371. Throughout the time after his conversion and from Tours, St Martin organized missionary activities said to have had a profound impact in converting many parts of France to the new faith. Patrick, who became the patron saint of Ireland, may have received spiritual guidance from Martin.

The extraordinary circumstances of Martin's death, related in Gregory of Tours' history, occurred in Candes, a village to the west of Tours (*see* pp.362–5). His body was boated back along the Loire to Tours and a cult to St Martin began to grow in town. Miracles were said to have taken place at the cemetery where he was buried. His tomb was moved to a specially constructed chapel by St Brice, which was replaced by a grand basilica by Bishop Perpet and became an important place of pilgrimage.

Gregory of Tours had good reason for regarding St Martin so highly – he believed that he himself had been cured from sickness by his visit to the holy man's shrine in the 560s. Miracles continue to occur. The power of his relics is even supposed to have repulsed one Viking invasion in the 9th century. The Norsemen had made a breach in the city walls and were about to enter to ravage the place when St Martin's bones were held up in front of them. They immediately turned back. With such incredible powers ascribed to Martin, it's no surprise that Tours pays homage to its greatest historical figure; a special basilica, a museum and a set of stained-glass windows in the cathedral stand out as the most important Martinian legacy in the city. The power of his life and miracles drew the pope to Tours in 1996. In countless churches not just across the Loire Valley but also throughout France and Europe, you will see representations of St-Martin on his charge, dividing his cloak in two for the pauper.

the Loire and to the south of it the Bourg des Arcis grew up between the two fortified areas of town. The neighbouring counts of Anjou, however, overran Touraine in the first half of the 11th century and the region fell totally under their control in 1044. The Bourg des Arcis continued to expand until it was merged when old city with the new walls went up in the mid-12th century.

Touraine had been absorbed into the so-called Plantagenet empire, but would be won by the French king Philippe Auguste early in the 13th century. In that century, further expansion of the town occurred with the establishment of the mendicant orders of the Franciscans and the Dominicans, while the port thrived. The distinct urban areas and activities had gradually come closer together. With the start of the Hundred Years' War, the two main parts of Tours were finally joined behind a new defensive wall. The fact that Tours had become such a fortified town no doubt helped paranoid King Louis XI decide to choose it as his capital after the Hundred Years' War ended in 1453. Son of Charles VII, Louis had been brought up in the Berry and in Touraine, after his father was hounded out of Paris by the English. He became king in 1461. His centre of power was the Château de Plessis-lès-Tours, which he developed into a regal residence; a sad remnant of it now lies choked by Tours' western suburbs. With the court's presence, trade and culture flourished in the city. Jean Fouquet of Tours continued as the great 15th-century court painter. The musician Ockeghem was appointed treasurer of the cathedral; of Flemish origin, he would serve as court composer to three successive French kings, Charles VI, Charles VII and Louis XI. Luxury crafts, such as goldsmiths' work, took off in Tours. So too did printing, while Louis XI particularly encouraged the development of the silk industry, having mulberry bushes planted around the town.

When Louis XI died in 1483, the court under Charles VIII moved to Amboise, but Tours continued to enjoy a time of great prosperity and administrative and trading importance, the royal court frequently châteaued nearby for a century to come. Fine town houses were built. Although this period was on the cusp of the final glorious Gothic extravaganza and the sobering symmetry of the Renaissance, most of the Tours town houses of the turn of the century were Gothic in style. The odd grand Renaissance façade stands out, in particular those of the Hôtel Gouin and the Hôtel de Beaune-Semblançay.

In the second half of the 16th century, Protestantism had many converts among the merchant class of which Tours was full and the town was inevitably shaken by the bloody Wars of Religion. King Henri III took refuge in Tours after he had had the over-powerful De Guise brothers murdered in his castle at Blois in 1588 (*see* pp.191–3). He called a meeting of the Estates General here and importantly held talks with the Protestant leader who was to become his successor, Henri de Navarre, seeking reconciliation with him.

After the new Bourbon French royal family had abandoned the Loire Valley of the Valois, the 17th and 18th centuries were quieter for the city which had previously played such a central role in the kingdom's history. The ministers Richelieu and Colbert tried to revive the silk industry and tapestry-making. The Revocation of the Edict of Nantes in 1685, though, caused many of the successful Protestant merchants to pack up shop and emigrate, draining the town of much wealth. One Catholic to emigrate from Tours was Marie de l'Incarnation, leaving the Ursuline convent to go and heavy-handedly help convert the natives of Quebec. With its port on the Loire, Tours still remained a significant trading town through this period.

In the Ancien Régime, the French provinces were administered by centrally appointed *intendants*. In the second half of the 18th century the royal administrator of Touraine, the *intendant* Du Cluzel, controlled the vast Généralité de Tours, extending over several modern-day *départements*. He was supported by the powerful minister, the Duc de Choiseul, and raised the finances to build the magnificent Rue Royale (now the much duller postwar Rue Nationale), cutting north to south through Tours' centre, part of the grand new royal route from Paris to Spain.

By the Revolution, the citizens of Tours appear for the most part to have been a tame lot. The tendencies of this potentially prosperous region were towards conservatism and deep-rooted Catholicism. In 1790 the town became the capital of the new *département* of the Indre-et-Loire, the new name for Touraine. The stately architecture of Du Cluzel's projects continued to be developed through the 19th century.

'Balzac invented the 19th century,' Oscar Wilde wrote of the stupendously ambitious Tourangeau writer born along Rue Royale in 1799, just as the turmoil of the French Revolution was being replaced by the lunatic dictatorship of the Napoleonic Empire. Several of Balzac's works, including *Le Lys dans la vallée* and *Le Curé de Tours*, expose the petty-minded shenanigans of the citizens of the city in the early 19th century. With the end of Napoleon, the Prussians came as far as Tours and French royalty was re-established. Steam ships were now paddling their way up and down the Loire, but the arrival of the railway in 1845 changed France's transport and trade practically over-night, the stations at Tours helping a little to stimulate the town's economy. Terrible floods in the second half of the century caused passing difficulties for the town.

In the Second Empire of the mid-19th century, a new town centre began to emerge slightly further from the river and closer to railway transport, around what's now the Place Jean-Jaurès. Grand new public buildings went up. They briefly received the French government fleeing the Prussians, who had advanced on Paris in 1870. Léon Gambetta famously got round the blockade by leaving Paris for Tours by hot air balloon, going on to act as distanced dictator in southwest France for five months, the Prussians having pushed as far as Tours again. The Belle Epoque from the close of the 19th century to the start of the 20th left a happier mark on the city, best seen in the grandiose architecture of the town hall.

Given a long period of political passivity, it comes as a surprise to learn that Tours was the birthplace of the French Communist party. In December 1920, the Congrès de Tours, the 18th conference of the Section Française de l'Internationale Ouvrière, was being held in the city. Delegates had to decide whether or not to adhere to the Komintern founded by Lenin in Moscow in March 1919. Léon Cachin, who ran the newspaper *L'Humanité*, led those in favour of joining, Léon Blum those against. The latter went off to found the French Socialist Party, Cachin to lead the Communists. Thus the divide in French left-wing politics of the 20th century was decided.

At the start of the Second World War, Tours once again became the capital for a French government on the run. On 10 June 1940 the ministers arrived. On 13 June Churchill flew over for a final meeting with the French. The Germans were heading apace towards Tours for a third time in such a short period and the French government fled to Bordeaux, in a move which was becoming something of a recurring pattern. Fighting broke out along the Loire in Touraine. Thousands upon thousands of refugees flocked to Tours to try and escape by rail, but bombing was beginning and the line was cut. On 18 June an artillery battle caused the outbreak of a terrible fire and 12 hectares in the historic centre burned to the ground. A small band of some 300 North African snipers kept the Germans at bay for a couple more days, but then the town fell into enemy hands and remained in occupied France throughout the war. Further bombing in 1944, this time by the Allies, wrought yet more catastrophic damage before the area was liberated in September.

Virtually nothing remained of Tours' old riverside quarters. But the city was one of the first places in France to benefit from concerted attempts at careful postwar renovation promoted by the Loi Malraux of 1965. The reconstruction programme had many successes, as well as some inevitably hasty and shoddier results. After the war, Tours' image may have remained a predominantly conservative one to outsiders, despite those early Communists in its midst. But from 1959 to 1995 it was run by the energetic Jean Royer, an independent mayor, if basically to the right. He helped make Tours the vibrant, lively city it undoubtedly is today. Things moved a liberal stage further with the 1995 elections, when a left-wing mayor won Tours, although in 2001 the city swung again to the right.

One important development in the 1990s was the arrival of the TGV fast train line as far as Tours. Paris is now just an hour away, and although it makes their critics laugh, those proud of Tours now like to say that it's just a month behind the French capital's fashions.

Cathédrale St-Gatien

Open 9–7; Mass at 10 and 6.30 on Sunday, and at 7pm on weekdays.

There are many grander cathedrals, but there are probably few more pleasing; and this effect of delicacy and grace is at its best toward the close of a quiet afternoon, when the densely decorated towers, rising above the little place de l'Archevêché, lift their curious lanterns into the slanting light...

Henry James, *A Little Tour in France*

The lantern tops of St-Gatien stand out gracefully on the Tours skyline still today. The façade below contains a mass of Flamboyant Gothic detail, with a rose window from the early 16th century. A little later in the century, during the Wars of Religion, the statuary in the Gothic niches was destroyed by Protestants, and was replaced in the 19th century.

Behind the façade, the rest of the cathedral offers a lesson in the evolution of the Gothic style, working west from the choir to this Flamboyant front. So as you walk into the cathedral and through to the choir, you go progressively back in time. While the façade is mainly 15th-century, the nave and north transept are 14th century. The choir goes back one century more and contains some superb 13th-century stained glass. Just small portions of an earlier Romanesque building remain visible here and there.

The splendid choir was built under the mason Etienne de Mortagne. The tracery and the richness of the glass have led some art historians to make connections between this choir and Paris's celebrated Sainte Chapelle, dating from slightly earlier. King Louis IX, for whom the Paris Sainte Chapelle was built, apparently followed the development of Tours cathedral choir with interest. The oldest glass, from the 1240s, stands in the three radiating chapels at the end of the apse. In the central one, scenes depict Christ's life. The stained glass in the neighbouring chapels, though of the same period, wasn't in fact made for this building; on the south side, the pieces come from the abbey of St-Julien and illustrate the life of St Férréol. To the north, the life of St James originally appeared in the abbey of St-Martin, and serves as a reminder that Tours lay on a major pilgrimage trail from Paris to Santiago de Compostela. The upper, clerestory windows, mainly from the 1260s, depict the lives of a number of other saints, including Martin, Julian and Maurice; in fact, until 1498, the cathedral was named after St Maurice, whose remains were brought here in 1267. The cathedral was later rededicated to underline the see's long history. Some of the glass here is painted in grisaille, alternating with the coloured glass.

The transept rose windows contrast tellingly with each other, the southern one a perfect picture, the outer circle displaying the arms of St Louis and his mother Blanche de Castile. In the northern one a bulky column passes right through it, quite spoiling its effect – this whole section was in danger of collapsing and had to be propped up when it was rebuilt in the 14th century.

The most beautiful and moving work of art in St-Gatien is a tomb, ordered for two royal children. Commissioned in 1499, it displays the effigies of Charles-Orland and Charles, the two sons the ill-fated Anne de Bretagne had by King Charles VIII, whom she had married in 1491. Because Anne failed to produce a male heir who made it to adulthood, she was forced, by contract, to marry Charles' successor, his cousin Louis XII. The sculptures around the tomb are thought to be from the work-shop of the famous Tours sculptor, Michel de Colombe. The sarcophagus sculptures, still more accomplished, are attributed to the Florentine, Girolamo da Fiesole. Henry James described the monument rather unfeelingly as 'really a lesson in good taste', when the sad truth behind its commission is that of an historic tragedy movingly commemorated.

You can visit the **Cloître de la Psalette** (*small fee*) from within the cathedral. This cloister may have lost one side, but the 15th- and 16th-century remains are quite beautiful. The former library still shelters some earlier wall paintings. You can also climb the cathedral's south tower on special tours, while thanks to restoration work being carried out on the choir end, you can at present join tours up onto the scaffolding to get a close look at the Gothic exterior from among the flying buttresses (*contact the tourist office for details*).

Musée des Beaux-Arts

Open Wed–Mon 9–12.45 and 2–6, closed Tues; t 02 47 05 68 73.

A beautiful concave triumphal arch leads into the grounds of the former archbishop's palace next to the cathedral, where a vast and splendid cedar spreads
out its arms to greet you inside the courtyard. Fritz the elephant is kept in the former
stables to the right; he was a circus animal who went on the rampage in Tours at the
start of the 20th century. Shot dead, his body was sent to Nantes to be stuffed and
was then brought back up to Tours by boat. Formal French gardens lie on the far side
of the courtyard.

The main Ancien Régime buildings inside the grounds house the Tours fine
arts museum. The big gate and wall to protect this splendid archbishop's residence
were put up just before the Revolution, but didn't stop the place from being taken
over for the benefit of the people. In 1792, Charles-Antoine Rougeot, who had
founded the town's art school, was given the task of gathering together works
from abandoned Touraine abbeys, churches and the homes of aristocrats who had
emigrated. Paintings were brought in from such august Touraine religious institutions as Marmoutier, Bourgueil and La Roche, while works from the Château de
Chanteloup outside Amboise (*see* pp.252–3) also arrived here after the Duc de
Penthièvre's death.

To add to this sudden influx of fine art from the region, in the Consulate period (just
before Napoleon became emperor) the museum became one of 15 across the country
to benefit from donations from France's central national depot of art. Tours received
30 works, among which are the most famous international pieces in the collection.
The magnificent Mantegna panels, *Christ in the Olive Grove* and *The Resurrection*,
made for the church of San Zeno in Verona, came as booty from Bonaparte's Italian
campaign. The gorgeous scenery, the static poses of the sleeping bodies and the
drama of the events are movingly depicted, in soft colours. In *The Resurrection* Christ
emerges from an extravagantly decorated sarcophagus, surrounded by a peacock's
wheel of red and white angels and radiating light. In the middle of these two panels
should be a scene of the Crucifixion, actually in the Louvre, although a later room in
the Tours museum contains Degas' approximate reworking and homage to the
missing piece; some may find it a poor substitute, but it is fascinating.

Rubens' *Ex-Voto of the Virgin Presenting the Child to the Donor Alexander Goubeau
and his wife Anne Antoni* of 1615, another 'gift' to Tours from the nation, was commissioned by an Antwerp family. The artist depicts an extraordinarily intimate meeting,
the picture dominated by the Virgin's red dress whose colour seems to be reflected in
the donors' faces. The other very famous name in the museum's collection is
Rembrandt, represented by a small early painting of his, *The Flight into Egypt*, with a
rather doe-eyed donkey, the human figures with even smudgier eyes, but the whole
conveying a dreadful feeling of darkness and gloom in its dramatic chiaroscuro
effects, the infant Jesus's head glowing like a bright beacon in the night.

The collection's first stay in the archbishop's palace was short-lived, as the bishops
regained their seat. It was only in 1910 that the town once more became the owner of

the palace, its peripatetic collection hung here again. In the meantime, though, further important donations had been made during the 19th century by leading families, and further ones in the 20th century considerably augmented what was on show. Octave Linet left a collection of early Italian and Flemish paintings. State help and exchanges with other museums allowed the museum to acquire a very fair representation of 19th-century French art examples of neoclassicism, Romanticism, Orientalism (notably Delacroix's *Bouffons arabes*) and realism all on display. The 20th-century collection includes challenging works by the likes of Olivier Debré, Michael Haas and Joe Davidson.

The main emphasis of the museum, however, remains very much on the 17th and 18th centuries. And it isn't simply painting which is represented. Fine statues and furniture feature, for example the pieces from the Château de Chanteloup, including lacquer-work from the East. The overall atmosphere in the rooms is one of spacious elegance and calm, at many times affording an extremely refined yet much more private experience than a visit to a Loire château. The Galerie de Diane has particularly splendid decoration to frame Jean-Antoine Houdon's 1776 bronze of the hunting goddess.

Views of Tours and the Loire are one interesting theme to follow in the museum. Again from Chanteloup, two interesting landscapes by Jean-Pierre Houel, painted in 1769, show a *View of the Loire Between Amboise and Lussault* and *Paradise View near Chanteloup*. One room is given over to Touraine in the 17th and 18th centuries, with an absorbing panorama by Charles-Antoine Demachy, who has somewhat exaggerated the hills south of the Cher, turning them into the foothills of mountains!

Among Touraine literary figures to be seen in portraits are Descartes, Racan, Destouches and Bouilly. The *intendant* François-Pierre de Cluzel is also well represented thanks to generous donations from the family. Most famous perhaps of all the great figures Touraine has produced, Balzac is shown in thoughtful pose in a study by Louis Boulanger for the painting commissioned by Balzac's great love, Madame Hanska. Balzac is also to be seen in a copy of Rodin's famous sculpture of him, bound in a swirl of draped stone; the piece appeared merely unfinished to many when it was shown at the Salon de la Société des Beaux-Arts in 1898, but it has since been viewed as a revolutionary work. Look out too for works by the Tourangeau François Sicard, an important French sculptor of the Second Empire, commissioned to produce a great number of monuments in Touraine. Here it is his wife and the wife of the architect Laloux who are represented.

Other Tourangeau artists whose work is well represented include Jean-Charles Cazin, who served as curator of the museum from 1869 to 1872; his best known work is *Hagar and Ishmael in the Desert*. The works of the 19th-century ceramicist, Charles-Jean Avisseau, and the school that formed around him are numerous, distinguished by a bright mix of colours and a delight in botanical and small animal forms. But without a doubt the most fascinating Tourangeau artist represented in the museum is Abraham Bosse. An engraver of the 17th century, he depicted all walks of society and all manner of trades, offering enlightening details on life under the reign of

Louis XIII. A room in the basement displays a frequently changing series of his etchings, showing his eye for detail and satire. His series on the five senses, dating from around 1635, was interpreted in paint by an unknown artist and is also on show in the museum, the delightful works crammed full of symbolism.

Château de Tours

The truncated remnants of the Château de Tours lie not far north of the cathedral, close to the Loire, in a slightly ignored corner of town. All that remains of Philippe le Hardi's late 13th-century fort are two towers, the northern one known as the Tour de Guise, named after the mighty Catholic family. Charles de Guise, son of the duke of Lorraine murdered on King Henri III's orders in Blois castle (*see* pp.191–3), remained imprisoned here for several years after the bloody death of his father, to stop him continuing the family struggle for power. He would eventually escape. Other more illustrious events had taken place in this château before that time, including two French royal weddings. In 1413, Marie d'Anjou was married to the future King Charles VII here, and later in the century Margaret of Scotland's union with the future King Louis XI was celebrated at the château. The Logis du Gouverneur is the separate late 15th-century wing parallel to the Loire. Under it, you can make out remains of the Gallo-Roman town wall, used as foundations.

The Musée Grévin is France's answer to Madame Tussaud's in London, and it has a branch here, the **Historial de Touraine** (*open July–Aug 9–6.30, mid-March–June and Sept–Oct 9–12 and 2–6, rest of year 2–5.30;* **t** *02 47 61 02 95, www.historialtouraine. com*). This distils the history of Touraine into 31 set-piece scenes. The waxworks look, well, like waxworks, rather fake and extremely static. To liven the place up a bit, music accompanies the scenes – it's just slightly unfortunate that the tapes for the different tableaux tend to overlap, causing occasional cacophony. Some of the major events in Touraine's history are very clearly presented, however, simple explanations supplied on the tour leaflet or panels. Among the more entertaining scenes, St Martin blesses Patrick on his way to convert the Irish; the Frankish King Clovis I and the Visigoth King Alaric II pull each other's goatee beard as a sign of their short-lived friendship; while Joan of Arc is reminiscent of pop singer Lisa Stansfield and looks as though she's about to break into a 1970s disco dance. In addition, the château holds an aquarium with exotic fish.

In the Logis du Gouverneur the history of Tours is treated in rather more serious fashion by the **Atelier Histoire de Tours** (*open Wed and Sat only 3–6.30;* **t** *02 47 64 90 52; free*). The archaeological and pictorial evidence, as well as models and videos, give some idea of how the town developed through history and in scale.

Saint-Julien Abbey and its Museums

The entrance to the large, grubby **Eglise Saint-Julien** is tucked away behind the post-war precinct of the Rue Nationale, close to Tours' historic bridge, the Pont Wilson. The church seems somewhat contemptuously treated in such surrounds. Yet for centuries this was one of Tours' great monastic institutions, founded by

Gregory of Tours. Gregory was from the Auvergne and Auvergne monks first settled here, having brought with them the relics of St Julien de Brioude, a revered saint of their region.

The Vikings destroyed the first monastery, and a new one was built in the 10th century. The towering porch dates from this time, although it was so heavily restored in the 19th century that only the form remains original. A violent storm brought down the Romanesque building, which was replaced between 1243 and 1260 by the Gothic construction you see today. Inside, you can appreciate its pure, uplifting Gothic style. The beautiful tracery of the east window stands out. The stained glass didn't survive the war, but was replaced by modern work by Le Chevallier. Two strange museums are to be found in the other remaining buildings from the monastic foundation.

Old cake preserved for posterity counts among the most curious exhibits in the **Musée du Compagnonnage** (*open mid-June–mid-Sept daily 9–12.30 and 2–6, rest of year Wed–Mon 9–12.30 and 2–6;* **t** *02 47 61 07 93*), housed in the former 16th-century dormitory of St-Julien, above the cloister. This museum is surely one of the very strangest in France. It's crammed with craftsmen's *chef-d'oeuvres*, made with all the pride of their various professions. As you enter you're faced with a chaos of information on the history of *compagnonnage*. The whole notion is made to sound most strange, but basically it involved different trade guilds encouraging their crafts and supporting their brothers, including through ritual and masonic-type ceremony. Mysterious, legendary roots are cited, with Solomon, Jacques de Molay – the last persecuted leader of the Knights Templars, burned to death in Paris in 1314 – and Père Soubise mentioned as formative figures.

Following the mass, or rather mess, of pieces on the history of *compagnonnage*, the displays beyond are clearly divided by craft. The tools and works on display date from the 18th century to the present, a whole host of crafts represented. Many of the craftsmen represented won the prestigious prize of *meilleur ouvrier de France* (best work in France). The staggering number of hours many of the pieces took to make is stated in many cases. Most of the masterpieces are miniature examples of their profession, for example, intricate, perfectly executed small-scale timber roofs or wrought iron gates. Some of the exhibits are not so miniature for their trade, though, for instance the works by the *pâtissiers*, the bizzarest among the bizarre. 'Let them not eat my cake!' would be the all too appropriate motto for these proud fellows, their pastry works protected behind glass. In the food section, it's perhaps the culinary model of the Hospices de Beaune in Dijon which takes the biscuit. Made from 20kg of pasta, with 22,000 coloured tiles and leaves of gelatine (for the stained glass), it took 800 hours to complete and won the first prize at the cooking olympics of 1976 in Frankfurt. You can see why.

Down in the former cellars of St-Julien abbey lurks the **Musée des Vins de Touraine** (*open same times as Musée du Compagnonnage*). Many excellent quotes on the wonders of wine scattered around the massive, vaulted room are the best thing about the place. Otherwise, the very old-fashioned look is desperately in need of modernization.

Hôtel Gouin (Musée Archéologique)

Open 9.30–12.30 and 2–6.30; t 02 47 66 22 32.

A riot of Renaissance detail has proliferated like brambles across the extraordinary façade of the Hôtel Gouin, just west of the Rue Nationale and Pont Wilson. The front was the only part of the building to survive the war bombs, and was itself added on in the 16th century to a previous Gothic mansion for René Gardette, a merchant who made his fortune in silk. The façade shows the extent to which Italian fashion had caught on in France at that period. The name of Gouin refers to a Breton banking family which later owned the house, making it the headquarters of its operations from around 1738 to 1940. After the war the family left the very badly damaged remnants of the house to the town on the understanding that it would be turned into a museum.

Once you've taken in the startling façade, the Touraine archaeological museum within takes you from the prehistoric and Gallo-Roman finds displayed in the basement, via the fine collection of medieval and Renaissance pieces, up to the 18th-century Enlightenment science cabinet from the Château de Chenonceau and a display of 18th-century pottery.

The basement is packed with both prehistoric fragments and everyday objects from Gallo-Roman life, including amphoras, childrens' toys and votive offerings, while marble from that period shows that trade was of course being carried on with Italy in those days. Many of the fine pieces of medieval sculpture in the museum were saved from Touraine religious buildings that have been destroyed, several coming from the church of St-Clément, which stood on the Place des Halles but was demolished at the end of the last century. The museum contains a whole array of beautiful sculptures of saints, including some from the Prieuré St-Cosme (*see* pp.285–6) depicting the persecuted Syrian doctors St Cosme and St Damien, who came west only to be decapitated.

The medieval trades are also represented in sculpture, but in much more humorous ways. The different professions tended to chose a patron saint whose agonies in martyrdom reflected their work to some extent, and how they too suffered for it. St Laurent was grilled to death, and yes, in sick reverence, the *rôtisseurs* – sellers of roast meats – adopted him as their mascot, as did cooks more generally. Ste Apolline, who had all her teeth wrenched out, and who looks the painful part holding her jaw, was the dentists' saint. Among some highly amusing medieval carvings, one post carries the sign of a *hongreur*, a castrator of horses; two women are depicted carrying out an operation on some poor creature who turns out to be a figure half-man, half-chicken.

Engravings show interesting details of Tours in centuries past, with the Ile Simon (previously known as the Ile St-Jacques) a veritable village in its own right, sat in the middle of the Loire. You can also admire the grandiose 19th-century aspect of the area which once stood around Tours' main bridge before the Second World War devastation. The Cabinet de Physique et de Chimie from Chenonceau reflects the fashion among the 18th-century aristocracy and enlightened for carrying out scientific experiments at home. Tours, a town where the liberal professions flourished, was quite an intellectual centre in centuries past, and learned societies became fashionable in the Ancien Régime.

Musée du Gemmail

Open weekends and public hols only 10–12 and 2–6.30; t 02 47 61 01 19.

The Musée du Gemmail, tucked away in its own courtyard in an early 19th-century house on Rue du Mûrier, close to glorious Place Plumereau (*see* p.282, below), is another of Tours' more unusual museums. It celebrates a radiant 20th-century development in the art of stained glass. The word *'gemmail'* was coined by Jean Cocteau, one of the many notable artists to rave about this stained-glass art form; it derives from the amalgamation of the words *gemme* and *émail* (enamel). Of course gems aren't used, just coloured glass that's made to take on gem-like qualities.

In the 1930s, the artist Jean Crottie had the idea of superimposing thick bold layers of coloured glass on top of each other to create luminous works of art. The man who developed the soldering technique necessary for this unique art form was a Touranageau called Roger Malherbe-Navarre. No leading is used and only very rarely any paint to add finishing touches. Rather, layer upon layer of glass, coloured in the mass, is cut and soldered together with enamel to compose a vivid and complex, textured picture. Each *gemmail* is executed by two people, the *maître d'œuvre* guiding the *gemmiste*; they work to a model on an easel, the former literally overseeing the latter from on high, the *gemmiste* placing the pieces of glass according to precise instructions. Roger Malherbe-Navarre can be seen directing a work in progress in the short explanatory video shown at the museum.

The museum contains an extraordinary collection of interpretations of works of art in this medium. Of several of Picasso's works transformed into stained glass, *Les Adolescents* and *La Tête Noire* stand out. Rouault is another modern master whose works have been well interpreted. Pollet's magnificent *Dinde* (Turkey) presents a riot of changing coloured plumage as you pass by. Jean Cocteau and Roger Malherbe-Navarre set up an annual international prize in 1957, the object being to select one contemporary work to be newly interpreted as a *gemmail*; the town has now taken over the prize-giving. Some of the more recent pieces may seem rather vulgar, but there have been notable successes, such as Margotton's Greek-inspired *L'Amphore*, lending itself wonderful to the luminosity of the form.

The museum has the added curiosity of an **underground chapel** dating from the 12th century, which makes for a particularly atmospheric setting for some of the displays.

A Walk Around Tours

We start this tour in front of the cathedral. After admiring its façade, wander all the way round the outside. The area just behind the cathedral provided the backdrop for

Balzac's tale of vicious petty religious rivalry leading to the persecution of an all-too-innocent priest in *Le Curé de Tours*.

The pretty, shaded **Place François Sicard** lies just to the south of the cathedral outside the archbishop's palace. This square typifies Tours' civic elegance. It's named after a Tourangeau sculptor. Several other sculptors' works here honour other local figures. The **Rue Bernard Palissy** off the southwest corner of the square leads down to the tourist office and train station. Two of France's greatest 16th-century artists, the painter François Clouet and the sculptor Michel Colombe, once had their studios along this street.

The quarter behind the cathedral is full of atmosphere. You could take the curving **Rue des Ursulines**, leading off the southeastern corner of Place François Sicard (by the entrance to the archbishop's palace), to get there. The garden of Touraine's archives building contains some Gallo-Roman ruins and the Brèche des Normands, where in June 903 the marauding Vikings supposedly turned back and fled in reaction to the holy flashing of St Martin's relics. The Rue des Ursulines is also the site of the 17th-century **Chapelle St-Michel**, where Marie de l'Incarnation took her vows in 1633 before she set out to spread the Gospel in Canada. She and her sisters spent a great deal of time in Quebec not just trying to wash off the native children's pagan 'sins', but also to wash them clean of the practical protective grease they traditionally wore to protect their skin. The chapel was restored by the Association Tours-Canada.

Nearby, down Rue du Petit Pré, the **Centre Marie de l'Incarnation** (*open mid-June–mid-Sept 3–6, rest of year Wed only 3–5; t 02 47 66 65 95*) is a small museum devoted to the religious figure.

North of Rue des Ursulines, curving **Rue du Général Meunier**, with its high walls on either side, breathes the air of a different age. The curve is attributed to the former site of a huge Gallo-Roman amphitheatre, said to have been bigger than the one in Nîmes, possibly built from the time when the Emperor Hadrian passed through Tours in the 120s. Many religious orders established themselves on this street just behind the cathedral, and a few are still based here, hidden from public gaze by their high walls. You're forced to do a loop back to Place Grégoire de Tours behind the cathedral. From here head up Rue Racine to Place des Petites Boucheries. Then head west along Rue Albert Thomas and Rue Colbert. The long straight line they form follows the track of the main street back in Gallo-Roman times. Where Rue Thomas and Rue Colbert meet, Rue Lavoisier leads up to the remnants of the Château de Tours and the river.

Rue Colbert, with a fair number of restored timber-framed fronts from the 15th and 16th centuries, is a fine street. Look out for the occasional beams and doorways carved with figures and animals. **Place Foire-le-Roi**, crammed with grand old town houses, was a market square back in medieval times. It was also here that public executions often took place. The most famous house on the square is No.8, the **Hôtel Babou de la Bourdaisière**. Philibert Babou was for some time treasurer to the young King François I at the start of the 16th century who had several fine homes erected for himself, including the Château de la Bourdaisière (*see pp.258–60*). His fine town house was much added to in subsequent centuries. Another remarkable house has slate-covered sides, a style you'll see in one or two other spots in Tours. Continuing along Rue Colbert, at No.66, look out for the little alleyway which gives you an inkling of what the medieval maze of the city must have felt like. No.39 is where Colas de Montbazon is supposed to have bashed out Joan of Arc's armour.

As you approach the abbey of St-Julien the old houses give way to the makeshift ones put up after the bombing of this quarter in the Second World War. Head south down **Rue Jules Favre**. The splendid mid-18th century Hôtel du Commerce was built for an association of Tours merchants. The most striking architecture here, though, is the ruins opposite, the shell of the façade of the great Renaissance **Hôtel de Beaune-Semblançay**, left standing like a theatrical backdrop after the bombardments. The place was built for Jacques de Beaune-Semblançay, treasurer to Louise de Savoie and then to her kingly son, François I. The madly ambitious François spent a fortune on his projects and wars in Italy. Jacques de Beaune-Semblançay tried all the tricks in the accountant's book to try and shift the debt from one place to another. But finally the precarious financial edifice fell and in 1523 the king was left bankrupt. Semblançay was accused of embezzling vast sums. In fact he had taken money from the Queen Mother's accounts to help finance the king. But François I saw in him someone to blame for the dreadful mess in which he found himself. He had Semblançay executed, at the ripe old age of 80, although his good name was rehabilitated not long after. On the square, the magnificently carved fountain, the work of Martin and Bastien François, and the perched Sainte-Chapelle were also ordered by Jacques de Beaune-Semblançay.

Rue de la Scellerie, stretching between Rue Nationale and Place François Sicard, where we started the walk, is lined with fine buildings. The most imposing is the 19th-century **theatre**. Beyond it, off the side streets, you'll find the town's best antiques shops. **Rue Corneille** leads down from the theatre to the square with the **Préfecture**, the administrative centre of Touraine, its offices installed in Napoleonic times in the buildings of a former convent. Busts of Roman emperors from Richelieu's great vanished château in southern Touraine have been placed here.

Rue de Buffon leads south from Place de la Préfecture down towards the central train station; take it and at the end you can't miss Jean Nouvel's 1990s creation, the **Centre de Congrès Vinci**, with a vizor at the front like the peak of a baseball cap. Jean Nouvel is best known for the Institut du Monde Arabe building in Paris, but this is a really striking building too. Opposite it, across the major boulevard of Heurteloup and a large car park, stands the splendid old train station, designed by Victor Laloux, the builder of the original Musée d'Orsay in Paris, itself originally a railway station of course. The **Centre de Création Contemporaine**, at 55 Rue Marcel Tribut offers a generous space for contemporary art exhibitions.

Victor Laloux also designed the grandiose façade of the Hôtel de Ville on **Place Jean-Jaurès**, the bustling heart of Tours. The colossal atlantes shouldering the weight of the town hall's balcony were sculpted by François Sicard. Two figures of river gods recline on either side of the great clock, symbols of the Loire and the Cher which embrace the centre of Tours. Other grand buildings on the square include the law courts and the Hôtel de l'Univers. The major arteries serving Tours head off from here,

Boulevard Heurteloup and Boulevard Béranger going east and west respectively, and
Rue Nationale and Avenue de Grammont north and south. The wide, tree-lined
Avenue de Grammont heads straight as an arrow down to the Cher river.

Rue Nationale, the largest shopping street in Tours, leads up to the Loire. Although
the big stores along it attract large numbers, the street itself isn't beautiful, as it all
had to be rebuilt after the war. However, the chic shops may tempt you into the prettier streets off its length. At the northern end of Rue Nationale, Place Anatole France
looks rather soulless, despite statues of Rabelais and Descartes. It's surprising not to
find a statue of Balzac, who was actually born along Rue Nationale. By the river, the
intriguing copper-roofed building in Moroccan style is Tours' Bibliothèque (municipal
library), a gilded statue beside it recalling American links and French gratitude.

You can get down to the lovely **Loire-side quays** here and go for a walk along the
river. Tours' main historic bridge, the **Pont Wilson**, is of beautiful white stone and is
also known as the *pont de pierre* by the townspeople; but it's collapsed so often in its
history that it might almost be built of sand. The last time part of it fell down was in
1978. Walk westwards along the cobbled riverside and you pass below the arts facul-
ties of the university. The steep riverside walls cut with narrow stairs and the mooring
rings are a reminder of the river trading that once took place in Tours. It now seems
unbelievable that large ships once stopped here. In the middle of the Loire lies the Ile
Simon, an uninhabited island on which you can go for a walk by crossing the Pont
Napoléon, west of Pont Wilson.

Back at the Rue Nationale, now head into the western half of Tours' historic centre.
The Rue du Commerce leads into an area packed with bars and restaurants heralding
the superbly restored **Place Plumereau**. The network of streets around it is filled with
remarkable beamed houses, the woodwork sometimes carved with figures, the courtyards embellished with splendid stair towers. This was the quarter where many of
Louis XI's courtiers lived in the second half of the 15th century (there are many later
additions of course). It's not only the mixture of architecture and small squares that
makes the place so appealing. The place is full of life. Restaurant and café tables stand
at the ready on the pavements for the waves of arts students leaving their lecture
halls. The liveliness doesn't abate in the summer holidays, when foreigners take the
students' places.

The Place Plumereau quarter is the most famous area of post-war restoration in
Tours, and the most successful, although immediately after the war it still wasn't
considered a desirable corner of town, many immigrants living in poverty here. Some
say the area was then practically cleansed. Today the square and its surrounds are
extremely sought after, full of chic and chichi apartments. Place Plumereau was the
hat-makers' domain in medieval times, but its plumed name derives from a Tours
councillor who had a mansion in the middle of the square. A particularly fine row of
15th-century houses lines Place Plumereau's south side. In summer passers-by are
only allowed a narrow strip of pavement to walk along; virtually every centimetre of
the square is taken up by café chairs and tables.

For a satisfying tour of the quarter, go for a walk through the streets towards the
river via the breach in the north side of the square. You come out first at the **Jardin de**

St-Pierre-le-Puellier, where the ruins of a medieval church have either been left showing in the ground or incorporated into a variety of idiosyncratic buildings. This is a spot with an extremely distinguished Christian history, as Clothilde had a convent founded here in the Dark Ages. Clothilde was the wife of Clovis, the first Frankish king to convert to Christianity, in good part thanks to her powers of persuasion. To the west of this curious and charming garden, **Rue Briçonnet** contains some particularly fine houses at its northern end.

Just south from Place Plumereau lies the once strongly religious quarter of **Châteauneuf**, with its links with St Martin. Make for the Place Châteauneuf via Rue du Change and Rue de Châteauneuf. On the north side of the square you can peer at the remnants of a 14th-century château, once the residence of the counts of Touraine, now given over to the Conservatoire de Musique. The château gave its name to a whole walled quarter of Tours before that time known as Martinopolis, which had sprung up around the tomb of St Martin.

Many churches have succeeded each other on St Martin's burial site. Gregory of Tours described Perpet's basilica, built between 466 and 470, as the finest in Gaul. Several centuries on, Charlemagne appointed Alcuin as abbot of St-Martin and he set up his famed school here. A couple of 10th-century fires destroyed the church of that time. In 1014 an immense structure was consecrated. Two towers still standing along Rue des Halles, the **Tour Charlemagne** and the **Tour de l'Horloge** (off Place du Châteauneuf), give a very good impression of the vastness of the edifice, one of the most significant early Romanesque buildings in France. One 12th-century writer, Aimery Picaud, compared it to the great pilgrimage church of Santiago da Compostela in northern Spain. Through the medieval period this mammoth building suffered from numerous fires. By the time of the Revolution the place was already badly run down and most of it was subsequently destroyed. The Tour Charlemagne is the mightier of the two towers left, the remnant of the north transept of the great church. At its foot you can see a plan of the whole ensemble as it once stood. The Tour de l'Horloge was one of the two towers on the main west front, added at the end of the 12th century.

Although these soaring towers are extremely impressive, it's hard for them to convey the spiritual significance of the site below them now, as the area around is given over to tempting shops. It's worth trying to remember though that the old church of St-Martin was, with Notre-Dame de Paris, Reims and Chartres, one of *the* most important Christian sites in medieval France. The **Musée St-Martin** (*open mid-March–mid-Nov Wed–Sun 9.30–12.30 and 2–5.30; t 02 47 05 68 73*) occupies the former Chapelle St-Jean on Rue Rapin and gives historical details both on St Martin and on the previous churches on the site. It's a small museum, but contains some fragments of sculpture and even one or two remnants of murals. Off it lie the beautiful remnants of the **cloister of St-Martin's**. There are traces of Gothic work on the west side, but the 16th-century Renaissance east gallery is the real attraction.

The tomb of St Martin was rediscovered in the course of an archaeological dig in 1860. This gave cause to celebrate with the creation of the **Nouvelle Basilique**

St-Martin, a self-important white whale of a building from the outside, with a large dome. The plan was by Victor Laloux, and it was built between 1887 and the start of the 20th century. The interior glistens with polished Vosges granite columns, topped by capitals in neo-Byzantine style. A bronze statue of St Martin decorates the interior of the dome, while at the back of the crypt below, François Sicard's sculpture of Cardinal Meignant pays tribute to the man who ordered the building of this new basilica. The crypt contains St Martin's tomb. The cult of St Martin is very much alive and well, to go by the number of people who come to pray here.

Just west along Rue des Halles or Rue Rapin, you come to the modern covered market and the end of Tours' major historic quarter.

North of the Loire: Les Trois Tours Silk Factory

One good reason to cross to the north bank of the Loire from the centre of Tours is to visit the fascinating old-fashioned silk-making factory known as Les Trois Tours, recently opened to the public (*you can only visit it on special tours organized by the tourist office*). To take this step back in time, you will be taken across the Loire to the Quai Paul Bert via the foot bridge known as the Pont de Fil, which serves the Ile Aucard, this island given over to sports grounds, but in summer the venue for a lively rock music festival.

Lyon may be the French city most closely associated with fine silk production, but Tours also became a specialist centre in the late 15th century, spurred on by King Louis XI and his courtiers. The tradition in Tours has continued quietly to this day, with two companies still making high-quality silk fabric. Roze in St-Avertin, in southern Tours, is the older of the two, dating back to the 17th century, but now mainly using modern, mechanized machines. It isn't open to the public. Les Trois Tours, by contrast, although only set up in 1829, has continued to use old-fashioned techniques and machines in the main, and is now open to visitors. The tour offers an extraordinary insight into traditional silk-making.

Walking through the entrance into the courtyard, you're confronted by a striking image of 19th-century industry. An array of old looms is lined up in the building at the back of the courtyard. The company owns almost 80 old models, almost all in working order, and listed. Many are famous Jacquard looms, named after the Lyon silk-weaver who invented an ingenious system of punch cards to facilitate the copying of patterns in the early 19th century. Les Trois Tours has kept its records, including over 4,000 designs, and the vast majority of its work is now taken up reproducing its old silk patterns, to old-fashioned methods and standards.

A video in English lasting 15 minutes explains the various stages in traditional silk-making, which is useful as you're unlikely to see all the processes going on on the same day – after all, Les Trois Tours is working to commercial orders. But it does do virtually all the processes in silk-making, apart from the dyeing, in-house. On the tour, you'll learn about the great variety of qualities of silk that can be produced, and how the likes of velvet are made with the help of razor blade cuts. Seeing the expert silk-weavers in action is both impressive and deafening. It takes some five years or more for workers to become skilled and at ease in the craft. Using the old-fashioned machines, they can create around 2m of silk a day. In the 19th century, some 150 people worked at the factory. They must have made a hellish noise. Now there are around 20 workers bashing out their materials. At the end of the tour you can admire an exhibition of silks; there are also pieces to buy, such as cushions and bags, or, more simply, framed silks.

Prieuré de St-Cosme

Open June–mid-Sept 9–7, mid-March–May and mid-Sept–Oct 9–12.30 and 1.30–6, Feb–mid-March and Nov 9.30–12.30 and 2–5.

Go west out of the centre of Tours following the south bank of the Loire and the route to the Prieuré de St-Cosme is well signposted. The confusion of roads surrounding this ruined priory may be unprepossessing, but once in the grounds you find yourself in a delightful spot, beautiful gardens planted around the sides of the buildings that remain.

The figure most closely associated with the place is the great 16th-century French Renaissance Pléiade poet Pierre de Ronsard. But the priory dates back to well before that period. A little chapel dedicated to saints Cosme and Damien already existed in the 10th century. At the end of the 11th century the chapter of St-Martin in Tours took control and established a priory with five canons following the Augustinian rule. Many of the vestiges left today are from the 11th and 12th centuries. King Louis XI had his favourite château of Plessis-lès-Tours very close by – unfortunately only a sad wing of that palace remains. Louis paid for the restoration of the priory church in the 15th century, but that has been demolished since.

Charles de Ronsard became prior in the mid-16th century. But his poetic brother was apparently so taken with the place that in 1565 Charles agreed to swap it with one of Pierre's benefices. The first main building you come to, the Logis du Prieur, has been turned into a museum in Pierre de Ronsard's memory, with details of his life and loves (four major ones). Ronsard is mainly thought of as a lyrical versifier on the human passions and nature these days. But in his time he was also a political poet. He composed much of his *Franciade* here, an epic work singing the praises of France. The supreme lyricist of the French language, whose verse flows like water, is buried in the priory grounds, a tombstone to him lying in the remnants of the church.

The refectory and guesthouse have survived much better than the church. The former, which you enter through a doorway patterned with triangular teeth of stone, appears totally out of proportion for the needs of the dozen religious men who made up the core of the religious community here. But the place also served as a stop for pilgrims heading down to Santiago de Compostela. The refectory pulpit, with its geometric designs, its bearded prophets and its sirens, draws the attention.

The gardens will tempt you out for a wander. The best collection is of roses, appropriately enough, as Ronsard is famed for his descriptions of these flowers, which serve as symbols of the transience of love and life – the lines in *A Cassandre* count among the most famous in the French language:

Mignonne allons voir si la rose
Qui ce matin avait declose
Sa robe pourpre au soleil
A point perdu ceste vesprée
Les plis de sa robe pourprée,
Et son teint au vostre pareil.

(Darling, let us go and see if the rose/Which this morning had disclosed/Its scarlet robe to the sun/Might not this eventide/Have lost its folds so crimson-dyed/And its hue so similar to you.)

The Indre South of Tours

16

The Indre South of Tours

Highlights

1 The sweet Indre-side villages between Tours and Loches

2 Loches, for its citadel, its lower town and its underground caves

3 The D760 country road to the magnificent village of Montrésor

4 Le Grand-Pressigny's fossil of a château

This chapter leads you into some of the quietest and most enchanting little valleys not just in Touraine, but in the whole region covered by this guidebook. The main cultural centre is magnificent little Loches, briefly a courtly town under King Charles VII in the 15th century. It had fallen back into sleepy rural life by the time Descartes spent his childhood around these parts in the early 17th century; he went off elsewhere to wake up the European mind to modern thinking. Now Loches and the Lochois are utterly charming backwaters, the countryside strung with the prettiest of quiet villages and the most picturesque remnants of religious establishments, showing how monks once sought out the inspiring tranquillity of the area. Beyond Loches, the area's highlights are Montrésor, with its stuffy old château, and Le Grand-Pressigny, its castle converted into a museum of prehistory – Neolithic man loved this corner too.

The Indre and Indrois Valleys from Tours to Loches

Travelling down from Tours to Loches, avoid the busy N143 rushing through flat and uneventful cereal land and follow a much quieter, prettier, winding route along the Indre's intimate, enclosed valley. It's recently been nicknamed the Vallée Verte, the Green Valley, and offers a delightful mix of pretty villages, châteaux, water mills, pastures and copses, shimmering plantations of poplars standing out.

Between Montbazon and Loches

We start at **Montbazon**, on the Indre river due south of Tours. The A10 motorway and N10 pass through. In fact, this quite pretty place is rather spoilt by being split in two by the very busy N10, once the royal road to Spain. The centre of Montbazon is overseen by the ruins of a substantial keep, one of the many built for that indefatigable Loire campaigner, Foulques Nerra of Anjou. This may even be the first stone castle he had erected, and Montbazon keep fights it out with that in Langeais (west along the Loire) for the title of the oldest stone keep built in France. Montbazon's is certainly much more impressive than the one in Langeais; parts of its cracked, herring-bone patterned walls still reach almost 100ft in height. Eleanor of Aquitaine and Richard the Lionheart apparently counted among its owners.

The building is capped by a spectacular sour-looking copper Virgin carrying the baby Jesus. Weighing in at 20 tonnes, she was put up here on the insistence of a mid-19th-century priest. It's thanks in good part to William Dudley, a US soldier who came over to France to fight in the First World War, that the keep has stayed standing. He settled here after the war and carried out vital reparation work. Now an enthusiastic British Canadian and his French wife have bought the ruin. They have ambitious plans to transform it into a tourist sight, bringing out its important history and using it as a dramatic backdrop for events.

Getting There

Many of the villages along the Indre between Tours and Loches are served both by local **bus** and **train** services.

Tourist Information

Montbazon: B.P.2, Pavillon du Tourisme, 37250 Montbazon, t 02 47 26 97 87, f 02 47 34 01 78, *office-tourisme-montbazon@ wanadoo.fr*.

Veigné: Le Moulin, 37250 Veigné, t/f 02 47 26 98 37.

Cormery: 13 Rue Nationale, 37320 Cormery, t 02 47 43 30 84, f 02 47 43 18 73.

Genillé: 17 Place Agnès Sorel, 37460 Genillé, t 02 47 59 57 85, f 02 47 59 59 78.

Chemillé-sur-Indrois: Mairie, 37460 Chemillé-sur-Indrois, t 02 47 92 60 75, f 02 47 92 67 98.

Market Days

Montbazon: Friday afternoon and Tuesday morning.
Cormery: Thursday morning.

Where to Stay and Eat

Montbazon ✉ 37250

****Château d'Artigny, Route de Monts, along the D17, t 02 47 34 30 30, f 02 47 34 30 39, *contact@artigny.com* (*expensive*). This outrageously sumptuous castle west of Montbazon looks out over the Indre valley. The image of an elegant French château of the Ancien Régime, it was actually built at the start of the 20th century. The rooms, divided between the château and a number of outhouses, are immaculately decorated and there are enough of them to receive fairly large parties of American and Japanese tourists. It's all very chichi. The frescoes on the central dome may repel sensitive tastes, but the cuisine is extremely elegant, the wine list vast. In the gardens *à la française* are a swimming pool, two tennis courts and a helipad (*menus €33.5–74.5*). *Closed early Dec–mid-Jan*.

La Chancelière and **Le Jeu de Cartes**, 1 Place des Marronniers, t 02 47 26 00 67. La Chancelière is a highly regarded, exclusive, refined little restaurant in the centre of Montbazon, Le Jeu de Cartes its simpler, cheaper little brother (*menus from €25*). *Closed Sun pm and Mon, late Aug and most of Feb*.

Veigné, just east along the Indre from Montbazon, stands in a picturesque riverside setting. A handful of wine producers in neighbouring **Esvres** make one of the least known of Touraine wines, Noble-Joué, an intriguing *vin gris*, or rosé to you and me. It once graced the French royal court, Louis XI having a particular liking for it. The Noble-Joué of Touraine has the distinction of being the only wine in France made from three varieties of Pinot grape, the Pinot Noir, the Pinot Meunier and the Pinot Gris. It can accompany light meats and fish.

The Benedictine **abbey of Cormery**, a step further east, was once an important French religious institution, founded with the blessing of Pope Leo I and Alcuin of York, its constitution dating back to 800. The Vikings laid waste to the place in 853. Fragments of later buildings spanning the medieval centuries remain, although much was destroyed after the Revolution. Parts of the abbey were transformed to personal use by some village families. For example, the 15th-century Lady Chapel has long served as a barn! The main vestige of the abbey is the Tour St-Paul, while the Rue de l'Abbaye follows the line of the former nave. To get an overall understanding of the place and to appreciate its quirkiness, follow a tour organized by the Syndicat d'Initiative, the local tourist office. The monks may have left Cormery long ago, but

Auberge de la Courtille, 13 Av de la Gare, **t** 02 47 26 28 26. A good option for traditional Tourangeau food (*menus €15–29.5*). *Closed Sun pm, Wed, and most of Aug.*

Veigné ☒ 37250

★★★Domaine de la Tortinière, Les Gués-de-Veigné, Route de Ballan-Miré, **t** 02 47 34 35 00, **f** 02 47 65 95 70, *domaine.tortiniere@wanadoo.fr* (*expensive*). A sparkling-white little Second Empire château with grounds sloping down to the Indre. The delightful rooms have lovely views onto the valley. You can go boating on the river, or swimming in the heated pool. The chef does stunning things with goat's cheese, using it to stuff Touraine pigeon or to add to his sorrel soup (*menus €35–64*). *Closed Sun pm and Mon, and 20 Dec–Feb.*

★★Le Moulin Fleuri, Route du Ripault, **t** 02 47 26 01 12, **f** 02 47 34 04 71, *fleuri@chateaux hotels.com, www.chateauxhotels.com/fleuri* (*inexpensive*). If any place were appropriate for eating frogs' legs, this hotel's modern dining room right by the river would be it. The cuisine is of a high order. The rooms in this mill, which dates in part from the 16th century, are more ordinary, but it's quite fun being so close to the water (*menus €26.5–47*). *Closed Mon, and Feb–early March.*

Reignac-sur-Indre ☒ 37310

Château de Reignac B&B, Rue Louis de Barberin, **t** 02 47 94 14 10, **f** 02 47 94 12 67, *reignac@chateauxhotels.com, www.chateauxhotels.com/reignac* (*expensive*). A handful of stylish B&B rooms in this grand little restored Loire castle (*table d'hôte €30.5*).

Azay-sur-Indre ☒ 37310

Le Moulin de la Follaine B&B, **t** 02 47 92 57 91, *www.multimania.com/moulinde follaine* (*inexpensive*). Set on an island in the Indrois just before it joins the Indre and just below a little medieval castle, this delightful watermill has been converted into a romantic B&B, some of the decorative details perhaps a touch over-romantic for some tastes. The owners are passionate about this lovely property which they have done up; the main waterwheel is beautifully displayed.

L'Auberge des Deux Rives, **t/f** 02 47 92 58 11. In the centre of the village, a provincial restaurant with a really bright dining room, but also a terrace at which you can eat on sunny days. The chef pays attention to detail, although the cooking is fairly simple and inexpensive (*menus €12–19*).

their macaroons remain, their shape said jokingly to resemble the religious brothers' belly-buttons!

Courçay makes the pretty next little stop, with an extraordinary rough-stone 12th-century spire to its church and a picturesque windmill. Only the monstrous old watermill on the river spoils one corner of the picture. Along the south bank here, at the Rocher de la Pinone, Rabelais would have us believe that the first-ever rainbow was witnessed here when Gargantua stopped to pee! **Reignac**, with its château and mill, has a very old church tower and, within the church, the peculiarity of a choir at the west end instead of the traditional east. A major summer attraction up by the N143 is the **Labyrinthus** (*open mid-July–end Aug 10–7.30*). Each year a portion of the dull agricultural plain by this main road is turned into a vast maze, to the delight of children in particular. It makes for an extremely enjoyable game to work your way round it. There's a viewing tower too.

Two châteaux dominate the well-located village of **Azay-sur-Indre**, neither open to the public. At Azay-sur-Indre the Indrois joins the Indre, having travelled west from Montrésor via a string of picturesque villages, Chemillé, Genillé, St-Quentin and Chédigny.

Loches and the Lochois

...elle fait vivre mille ans en un jour (it brings to life a thousand years in one day)
Onésime Reclus, 19th-century traveller, on Loches

Loches is a splendidly imposing model of medieval defence named rather sweetly after the little fish found in the Indre river. Now viewed as an extremely picturesque tourist spot, Loches must have made a formidable sight for centuries, its walls and keep standing proud above the plains that surround it. Loches is in fact one of the most important medieval strongholds left standing in France. As you'll see, rather than there being one single château, the place has a whole upper city, entered via the steep Rue du Château and Porte Royale. The citadel includes a variety of inter-esting buildings from different centuries, not just a castle, but also a separate, soaring keep. The four towers in a row on the medieval church of St-Ours also cut an extraordinary figure. The elegant houses within the ramparts date from the 17th and 18th centuries in the main; one contains a museum devoted to a 19th-century landscape painter from Loches, Emmanuel Lansyer. The hill below the citadel contains a warren of caves from which stone was quarried for centuries; you can go on an extraordinary visit through some of them at the Carrière Troglodytique de Vignemont.

Getting There

The **bus** service between Loches and Tours is more regular than the train service. Both bus and train stations at Loches are extremely central.

Tourist Information

Loches: Place de la Marne, B.P.112, 37600 Loches, **t** 02 47 91 82 82, **f** 02 47 91 61 50, *loches.en.touraine@wanadoo.fr*.
Montrésor: Place de la Mairie, 37460 Montrésor, **t** 02 47 91 43 07, **f** 02 47 92 71 11, *otsi.montresor@wanadoo.fr*.

Market Days

Loches: Wednesday all day and Saturday morning.
Montrésor: Saturday morning.

Festivals

Loches' **son-et-lumière** at the château takes place on Friday and Saturday nights through the summer. Opera is staged in the splendid setting of the *'théâtre de verdure'* up among the fortifications in the **Festival de Théâtre Musical** in July.

Where to Stay and Eat

Loches ✉ 37600
***Hôtel George Sand**, 37 Rue Quintefol, **t** 02 47 59 39 74, **f** 02 47 91 55 75 (*moderate*). In a house once used by ground-breaking 19th-century female novelist George Sand as stables, sandwiched between the river Indre and a narrow busy road. The Fortins have converted it into an extremely attractive, well-kept hotel. It's a lovely place for sunny lunch or summer dinner, as it has a terrace overhanging the river, as well as good food (*menus €14.5–44*).
Hôtel de France, 6 Rue Picois, **t** 02 47 59 00 32, **f** 02 47 59 28 66 (*inexpensive*). Smart old town house, some rooms with views onto the medieval city. It does quite good food too, at quite a good price (*average meal price c.€18*). Outside July and Aug, closed Sun pm and Mon, and mid-Jan–mid-Feb.

Beaulieu-lès-Loches ✉ 37600
Hôtel de Beaulieu, 3 Rue Foulques Nerra, **t** 02 47 91 60 80 (*cheap*). Accommodation in convent buildings dating back to the 12th century, with a simple brasserie next door. *Closed Oct–March.*

East of Loches the beautiful route along the D760 is strung with as many fragments of religious buildings as there are beads on a rosary. These important foundations must once have brought a good deal of life to this area, now so calm. There are medieval fortifications too, particularly in the perfectly picturesque village of Montrésor. Head for Nouans-les-Fontaines for an artistic surprise.

Southeast from Loches, the little-known Château de Bridoré boasts a defensive speciality of its own, the *caponnière*.

Loches

Logis Royal et Donjon de Loches

Opening hours vary slightly for the logis and the keep: July–Aug 9–7 for both; mid-March–June and Sept 9.30–6 for the logis, to 7 for the keep; rest of year 9.30–12 and 2–5 for the logis, 10–1 and 2.30–6 for the keep. You can buy a combined ticket. Logis t 02 47 59 01 32, keep t 02 47 59 07 86.

The counts of Anjou won Loches through marriage, not war, in the 10th century. Given Loches' easterly position in relation to their main territories, it became an important outpost for them in their protracted conflict with the counts of Blois. Its hill was an obvious place for fortifications and the first remaining ones probably date from the great Foulques Nerra of Anjou, built possibly as early as the 1030s.

Royal connections came with Henri Plantagenêt of Anjou, later King Henry II of England. He added greatly to the earlier defences, in particular with the building of ramparts and the digging of a great ditch, still to be seen. His rebellious son Richard the Lionheart rose against him, in collusion with the French King Philippe Auguste. Richard took Loches from his father's troops in 1189, but when Richard was later trapped in prison, Philippe Auguste decided to add the place to his possessions. Richard, on his angry return, is said to have recaptured the citadel in three hours, at which the Chronicler of Anjou expressed his wonder, 'since Loches is the strongest and most heavily defended place, both by nature and by artifice'; the probable explanation for the ease of Richard's victory was that the gates were opened to him.

Philippe Auguste's men won Loches back from King John and the English Crown in 1205 after a terrible one-year siege – the citadel did at least have its own well to help its defenders. The end of the siege brought to a close Plantagenet control in the region, and Philippe Auguste donated Loches to Dreux de Mello, the son of his victorious captain. In 1249, King Louis IX bought the place back to form part of the French royal domain.

Through the 13th century, Loches' fortifications were reinforced by *tours à bec*, beak-pointed towers, and further military architecture was added in the course of the 14th and 15th centuries. The royal lodgings, at the other end of the outcrop, date from this time. Expansion also continued around the keep. The great Tour Neuve is something of a second keep in its own right, added in the 15th century. Nearby, the

Martelet, from Charles VII's reign, burrows underground into former quarries to provide three levels of dungeons. These towers have a very dark reputation in history, associated with Louis XI's cruelty. A further surround of 16th-century positions completed the defences of the hilltop.

The Donjon or Keep, the Tour Ronde and the Martelet

It makes sense in historical terms to start the tour with the 11th-century **keep**. With black jackdaws circling round its sheer walls, the place looks forbidding and impregnable. It's considered the finest example of a keep in France. The holes puckering the outer walls were apparently used for beams to hold up the scaffolding. You get inside the keep passing via an arrow-head-shaped barbacane and a draw-bridge. This keep was of course lived in in medieval times. The entrance stairway in an abutting tower leads to the first floor of the main structure, which was the headquarters of the building. The space below was used for cooking and storage. The second floor was reserved for sleeping and the top level for the guards. Originally this keep would have been roofed, with a walkway on the outside of the top floor. A small chapel was squeezed into the side tower along with the stairs.

Loches' keep and adjoining towers have been converted into something of a museum on torture and imprisonment. Louis IX formalized the use of torture, considered an improvement on the otherwise unregulated practice. Medieval procedure for the euphemistically named *question* (for *question* read torture) was quite painstakingly codified. If a suspect refused to confess, the judge could proceed to the *question préparatoire*, divided into an 'ordinary' and an 'extraordinary' torture. Its form varied according to region. The *question ordinaire* might involve 9 litres of water being forced down the prisoner's throat by funnel, the *question extraordinaire* 18 litres. Another common method of torture was stretching. For the guilty, there were also various methods of death. At the end of the 15th century, one Louis Secretin was sentenced to burn to death in boiling water in Tours, having been found guilty of counterfeiting. The executioner failed to heat the water sufficiently and Secretin got out relatively unscathed; the executioner was beaten and Secretin went on to marry and have five children.

After the death of King Charles VII, who had held court at Loches, his son King Louis XI, clearly harbouring bad memories of the place, converted it in good part into a prison, which it remained for centuries. One of the terrible iron and wood cages Louis XI ordered for the prison has been recreated in the keep. Their bizarre euphemistic nickname was *fillettes*, little girls. One of the figures supposed to have languished in such a cage was Cardinal La Bahue, servant of Louis XI, punished for treacherously supporting the king's great enemy, Duke Charles the Bold of Burgundy.

Terrible tales survive of men holed up in Loches' *oubliettes* (from the French *oublier*, to forget). Numerous tunnels disappear under the citadel. A governor of Loches a little after Louis XI's reign is said to have explored these and to have come across a seated man holding his head in his hands; as the governor approached, the man disintegrated where he had rotted. A researcher of more recent times has revealed that a lot of the supposed haunted *oubliettes* were probably dug for sanitation purposes.

The prisoners' graffiti to be found on the walls of the keep and the great round tower nearby, the **Tour Ronde**, are being carefully preserved for posterity. Some date back to the 12th and 13th centuries, although deciphering them and dating them is pretty difficult. Among the crude engravings, religious symbols, a hunting scene and a flat-bottomed riverboat stand out. The Tour Ronde has great machicolations with gargoyles and superb views onto the the citadel and the lower town.

Next you come to the **Martelet**, with its three levels of cells. It isn't as grim inside as might be expected. Its most famous prisoner was Ludovico Sforza, duke of Milan and patron of Leonardo da Vinci. Sforza was a pragmatic, ruthless politician and man of culture who amassed great power in Italy at the end of the 15th century. Ruler of Naples, which he defended against King Charles VIII of France's attack, he came by his position as ruler of Milan through usurping power from his young nephew. He surrounded himself with the most brilliant of courts. In 1500, during Louis XII's Italian campaign to claim his rights over Milan, Sforza was captured and brought to France. After four years imprisoned at Lys-St-Georges in the Berry he was transferred to the Martelet at Loches.

Sforza was apparently well treated as an aristocratic prisoner and used the resources of his culture in what must have been dark days. His cells were decorated with insignia and inscriptions. You can clearly make out the murals on the wall of the larger chamber, with its fireplace, which apparently carried his portrait. Even the latrines were decorated, with cannons, deer and hearts. Sforza was later transferred to the top of the Tour Ronde, but the legend of terrible treatment doggedly survived. The old story went that after years and years deprived of seeing any daylight, he died from the shock of seeing the sun on finally being taken outside. Even if conditions were relatively good for him, he never left the region again, however, and the circumstances of his death are uncertain.

Loches' defences continued to serve their purpose as a prison, for Huguenots after Louis XIV's Revocation of the Edict of Nantes and for local lords at the Revolution. In the 20th century, an enthusiastic prison director even got his inmates involved in archaeological excavation of the site. Ironically, the continued if degrading use of these medieval buildings as a gaol probably stopped them from falling into ruin.

The Logis Royal

To appreciate the easier side of life in the citadel, go to the other end of the promontory from the keep, to the Logis Royal. The amusing statues of dogs greeting you at the entrance are 19th century. The lodgings were much restored in that period, and consist of two adjoining wings of different style, the first originally built at the end of the 14th century, the other at the end of the 15th to the beginning of the 16th.

The main section was the celebrated home of King Charles VII's powerful mistress, Agnès Sorel (*see* box on next page), she of the single bared breast memorably immortalized in pictures by France's greatest known 15th-century painter, Jean Fouquet.

Agnès Sorel wasn't the only influential woman to leave her mark on Loches. Two more of the most memorable women in French history are associated with the castle. Before Agnès, Joan of Arc came to Loches after the French victory freeing Orléans

Agnès Sorel, King Charles VII's Scandalous Mistress

Agnès was a woman who stirred the passions. She was both greatly loved and profoundly hated in her time. She had been in the service of Isabelle de Lorraine, wife of René d'Anjou (*see* Angers, p.425), when in 1444 she entered the royal court retinue as a lady-in-waiting to the queen. Soon it was the queen, Marie d'Anjou, who would have to wait to see the king as she continued to devote her life to producing offspring for Charles – she gave birth to 14 royal children in all, many of whom died in infancy.

Agnès' beauty was famed, even if the oft-copied depiction of her by Jean Fouquet may not match our present notions of aesthetics. For instance, the fashion of her day was to pull the hair harshly up to display the forehead prominently, plucked of excess strands, in a style known as *le front épilé*. Breaking with traditional etiquette, the king had Agnès served like a princess, allowing her a retinue of her own. One chronicler remarked that the trains of her dresses were longer than those of any other woman at court, which probably says a great deal about her position and her extravagance. Agnès' nickname of La Dame de Beauté, while playing on her looks, came from one of the many expensive gifts the king lavished upon her, the estate of Beauté-sur-Marne. Agnès also gave prominence to the extremely influential courtiers and patrons Jacques Cœur and Etienne Chevalier; she was one the best clients of the former, the greatest merchant in France. Winning the king's affections, Agnès exercised political as well as emotional power over him. And she bore Charles three daughters.

Royal scandal is nothing new. Agnès Sorel shocked many in her day with her extravagant and unabashed ways and fashions. The future Louis XI, son of Charles VII, detested her. He wasn't the only one. The pope railed against her; she made the Church see red, and many others complained about the outrageous expense of her circle and the manner in which she distracted the king's attention from the queen. The weakness of Charles VII seems more to blame than anything. He it was who decided on the fortune to be spent dressing the court ladies, the money coming from taxes raised from the common people. Agnès tried to deflect some of the venom directed at her by making numerous generous charitable donations to the poor and to religious institutions. That is why she was allowed to be buried in Loches' church of St-Ours. However, for three centuries following her death, the canons of the church pressed for the removal of her tomb, permission being granted during Louis XVI's reign. The beautiful alabaster work now rests in the Logis Royal. Agnès died as a result of a miscarriage in 1450. Once again dark rumour steps in and says that she was poisoned. All three of her daughters were publicly recognized by Charles VII.

from the English siege, and spurred Charles VII to go through English-occupied territory to be crowned in the sacred French royal ceremony at Reims cathedral. Anne de Bretagne, the third great 15th-century woman connected with Loches, was the pious wife of two French kings, Charles VIII and Louis XII. Her **oratory** is the best preserved of the rooms in a quite disappointingly bare series in the Logis Royal, several containing rather uninspiring copies of famous paintings. Henry James described the oratory in a typically American way as being 'hardly larger than a closet'. So it may be – but it is a sumptuously decorated one. The splendid **Grande Salle** is the hall where Joan of Arc was received after her triumphs in the Orléanais and is now embellished with fine 17th-century Flemish tapestries. Beyond Agnès Sorel's tomb, its two lambs playing on her Christian name, look out for a beautiful late 15th-century triptych, brought here from the nearby Chartreuse du Liget. It appears to be the work of the great period artist Bourdichon.

Church of St-Ours

Even if you don't buy a ticket to visit Loches' keep and castle, you can wander around parts of the citadel and see inside the church of St-Ours. This is a really curious and charming building, much commented on by architectural historians. Between the quite normal entrance tower and crossing tower, the bays of the nave have also been covered with a quirky tower each, upturned cones dubbed *dubes*. These unique features date from the middle of the 12th century, like the rest of the church. Under the entrance porch, you can admire some fine Angevin vaulting. Imaginative sculptures, on the usual themes of Romanesque carving, with monsters and semi-human creatures, draw attention to themselves. Somehow packed in under the vault is a further collection of early Gothic sculptures. The church was the proud owner of a supposed piece of the Virgin's girdle, a relic donated by Geoffroy Grisegonelle, the count of Anjou who founded the place in the late 10th century. The relic encouraged pregnant women to come here to pray for an easy childbirth, a custom that continued into the 20th century.

La Maison Lansyer

Open July–Aug daily 10–7, June and Sept Wed–Mon 10–7, April–May and Oct–early Nov Wed–Mon 10–12 and 1.30–6; t 02 47 59 05 45.

On the main street leading out from the citadel down into the centre of town, this pretty house was once owned by the 19th-century landscape painter Emmanuel Lansyer (1835–93), a prolific artist. Brought up in the Vendée, south of the Loire estuary, he went up to Paris to try and make a career in the arts. He first studied briefly under the architect Viollet-le-Duc and then under the fiery painter Courbet, who promised that he would teach his fervent followers of realism to paint faster than you could take a photograph! But Courbet's skill didn't live up to the rhetoric, and Lansyer found a better teacher in lesser-known Harpignies. He went on to be represented at the famous alternative Salon des Refusés of 1863. Lansyer then headed off on trips to Brittany and other provinces, where he found inspiration for his rather sweet interpretations of the French countryside. He won a first prize for his work in 1865.

Lansyer was no starving artist, as you can tell from his comfortable house. He became close to the likes of Princess Mathilde, a cousin of Napoleon III. His works were even sold to the emperor himself as well as to many aristocrats. He lived along Quai Bourbon on the Ile St-Louis, in the centre of Paris. Lansyer spent some time, too, in his picture-pretty family home in Loches. He painted some delightful canvases of the town and the area around it. He died childless and a large number of paintings were left to Loches. His house has recently been restored. Inside, you can watch a slide show on Lansyer's life and times, featuring early photographs he took, before wandering round the picturesque 19th-century-style salons filled with paintings by the artist, including a good collection of Lochois and Breton scenes. Lansyer emerges as a kind of bright-skied Boudin. He was also a collector of engravings, from works by Piranesi and Canaletto to pieces by the likes of Gustave Doré and Victor Hugo. An exotic touch is added to the house by his Japanese collection.

A Tour of Loches

Wandering down through the curving old streets of the town is a real pleasure. The feel is mainly 15th and 16th century. The Rue du Château turns into the **Grande Rue**, off which lies the town hall square, a wonderfully atmospheric corner. The **Porte Picois** is the very image of a late Gothic town gate. It formed part of another line of Loches fortifications, built to protect the lower town. Further pieces of these ramparts still survive. The splendid house tucked into the corner next to this gateway is the **Hôtel de Ville**, built in 1535 in the then still young Renaissance style.

If you venture out of the gateway, turning left into the Place des Blés and then right down the Rue Descartes, you come out at the **Place de Verdun**. The church of St-Antoine stands on the site of the former Ursuline convent. Opposite it lies the neoclassical 19th-century Palais de Justice, or law courts. In the centre of the square, the statue by respected regional sculptor François Sicard honours a famous son of Loches, the great Romantic writer Alfred de Vigny, born here in 1797 (though he actually spent little time in the town).

Alternatively, take the Rue St-Antoine out of the town hall square to reach the **Tour St-Antoine**, an imposing mid-16th-century belfry, one of Loches' landmarks. It was once attached to a church, but that was destroyed. Continuing round, cross the river and you come to the pretty public garden, the Indre flowing gently past the houses. From here you get lovely views onto the château's Logis Royal.

La Carrière Troglodytique de Vignemont

Open Easter–All Saints' Day daily; call t 02 47 91 54 54 to book a time for the 1-hour guided tour. They normally leave at 10, 11, 2, 3, 4 and 5.

These former quarries below the citadel, count among the most spectacular you can visit in the Loire Valley region. The owners lead you on a didactic tour round the place. The quarries themselves only date back to the 18th century, but on the visit you're taken through the history not just of quarrying in France, but also of the geology of these parts. The 80m of tufa limestone stacked up under the earth in these parts of Touraine took 4 million years to form, during a time when the whole region lay under sea. Crushed shells are the main constituent of this sedimentary rock and it took billions of them to form just 1m of limestone.

On from shells to men. In these quarries, separate corners are dedicated to the ways the stone was extracted in different periods, and the uses to which it was put. The

Gallo-Romans employed a lot of limestone blocks, but they extracted them from open-air quarries. It seems that it was the Merovingians who started quarrying underground. They had a particular penchant for making stone sarcophagi or tombs. Although the medieval period is sometimes regarded as backwards, it was during this age that there was an explosion in building in stone, for the construction of forts, churches and all manner of houses, such as those in Loches. On the tour, the owners go into some detail about the methods of extraction and the tricks of the traditional quarriers' trade; these men worked underground mainly from November to March; many would have agricultural land to look after the rest of the year.

The quarries of the Loire Valley weren't only used for stone extraction. They could also serve as refuges in times of war. Not only would the population go down to hide in the underground tunnels, they would also bring their cattle down. The refuges generally had at least two entrances, one large one which might be found around the churchyard, one much more secretive, which might for example be hidden down a well. All sorts of defensive tricks were incorporated into the architecture of the refuges. Some 150 of them have been identified in Touraine. A portion of one has been recreated in the Carrière de Vignemont. But as we've said, this quarry was only opened in the 18th century. After a time, it served for a period as a troglodyte home, as you'll see at the entrance, with its domestic features still clear, including a wine press and even a dog's kennel. In the mid-19th century quarrying took up again for a short time, until from the 1870s the cavernous place was turned into a mushroom-growing centre.

The present owners have cleaned up the place and present it with passion. Although the whole network here extends for some 15km, on the guided tour you're treated to 600m.

Religious Forests East of Loches

Beaulieu-les-Loches is Loches' near neighbour and once-important rival down in the plain. Its Abbaye de la Sainte-Trinité, of which only dislocated fragments remain, was founded by that fearsome warring Angevin count, Foulques Nerra. Foulques Nerra was a man of extreme passions, often exceedingly cruel and destructive, but also clearly concerned about the state of his soul, as was quite typical of his age. He ordered Beaulieu's abbey so that monks could pray night and day for his salvation, and donated the precious relic of a supposed piece of Christ's tomb to the place. Some might ask whether it was divine punishment that the abbey's great nave burnt down the day after its consecration in 1007. Foulques Nerra was buried here in 1040. Destruction by fire was to return as a theme, but only after the abbey had enjoyed several centuries of prosperity, the town around growing large enough to have three parish churches, the markets providing thriving trade. The Hundred Years' War brought disaster in the form of a couple of further major conflagrations. It was decided to move the market from Beaulieu to better-protected Loches, effectively sounding the death knell for commercial life in the town.

A few kilometres outside Beaulieu on the D760 you enter what was once the ancient royal forest of Loches. You may spot a surprising obelisk along the way, one in a line set up across the forest as elegant markers for the hunt in the 18th century. Signs point to **L'Etang du Pas d'Ane**, a lake in the forest around which you can go walking. Before you reach the Chartreuse du Liget, at **Couroirie**, the gorgeous mellow medieval buildings opposite a waterlily-covered lake are now privately owned, but can be visited (*June–mid-Aug 2–6*). They were once the monastic dwellings for the lay brothers of the charterhouse, and separated by quite some distance from the monks' quarters. This division was traditional in the very strict Carthusian order. The buildings date from the 12th century (for example the church) to the 15th.

The main monastery or **Chartreuse du Liget** (*also private property now, but it is generally easy to visit by asking permission at one of the houses above the remnants of the monastery*) is still protected by great lengths of walls marked by the occasional little turret. The sophistication of the entrance gateway seems particularly out of place in the quiet wooded surrounds, but it looks so enticing that it tempts you to stop. Up close, it's very strange to be confronted by the elaborate artificiality of Baroque in this landscape. On the front of the gateway the monk flying to the altar is St Bruno, founder of the Carthusian order. On the other side, John the Baptist (patron saint of the monastery) looks rather self-consciously desperate, a dove descending towards him through a cascading cloud.

King Henry II Plantagenet is said to have founded the original institution in 1178 as part of his penance for the murder of Thomas à Becket in Canterbury Cathedral in 1170. But the entrance gate is pure 18th century and the bulk of the collection of buildings descending the slope date from the Ancien Régime. At the bottom of the valley, at an angle to the other architecture, though, the substantial remains of a late 12th-century church still stand, close to the vestiges of a vast 17th-century cloister.

At the Chartreuse you can ask for the key to a tiny circular chapel, **St-Jean du Liget**, set in the midst of a field among the woods a kilometre back west, signposted off the D760. It looks almost as though someone has deposited this little round box of a building here for safekeeping. It has been scrubbed clean on the outside. Within, murals depict six scenes from the New Testament, from the tree of Jesse to the Dormition of the Virgin, saints and bishops depicted in the intervals.

The **Ermitage Ste-Trinité de Grandmont-Villiers** is a tattier yet charming vestige of yet another religious establishment which settled these parts. It lies a bit east of the Chartreuse du Liget off the D760, and is still occupied by a few religious men. An old track takes you to the peaceful spot, the delapidated buildings, including the truncated, heavily restored chapel, set around a grassy courtyard. The Grandmont order, founded in the Limousin region of southwestern France by Etienne Muret in the early Middle Ages, emphasised absolute poverty and charity, together with humble manual labour. The father at Grandmont-Villiers today, Père Philippe Etienne, is appropriately enough a bright-eyed, bellicose former trade-unionist. Unlike in other orders, the father isn't divided from the brothers, but leads the same religious life as them.

Montrésor

Montrésor exudes charm from every stone. A delightful village of brown-tiled houses, it's located in a curve in the Indrois, a tributary of the Indre. The village is overseen by a fortified castle and thoroughly deserves its membership of the association of Les Plus Beaux Villages de France. The feel is late medieval, although the village was much developed in the early 16th century, when Imbert de Bastarnay gave it its imposing church and had the château enlarged. A legend ascribes the name of the town, Mount Treasure, to the unlikely emergence from the local rock of a lizard covered in gold. Today at the château you'll find rather unexpected treasures from Eastern Europe; the many Polish street names in the village are explained by the family of Polish origin that has long owned the castle.

You pass through the early medieval fortifications of the **Château de Montrésor** (*open April–Oct 10–12 and 2–6; t 02 47 92 60 04*) via an impressive, partly ruined Gothic gateway which gives you a feel for the age of the place. One of Foulques Nerra's associates, the disturbingly named Robert le Petit Diable (Little Devil), built an early medieval keep here around the turn of the first Christian millennium, but this was dismantled in the 19th century. After Robert le Petit Diable, Henri Plantagenêt added his fortifications, sturdy remnants of which are also to be seen down below in the village. The place was taken from the Plantagenets in 1198 by the French King Philippe Auguste. The buildings within the curtain walls date from much later and were ordered in the main by Imbert de Bastarnay after he came by the castle in 1493. He served several French kings and was the grandfather of King Henri II of France's great lover, Diane de Poitiers. At the Revolution, much of the castle was burnt down.

Count Xavier Branicki, whose name gives away his origins, was a Polish émigré who fled from the Russians and bought the castle in 1849, as the French Second Empire was getting under way with Napoleon III. The count was a friend of the new emperor and a leading financier of the time. His descendants still own and live in the château, which has been preserved in 19th-century Polish aspic inside. It's crammed with mementoes of Poland, including, apparently, the stuffed wolf, one of the most startling of innumerable trophies hanging on the dining room walls. Some of the Polish objets d'art are magnificent, a plate showing Warsaw particularly memorable. Trophies from war with Turkey add a further note of surprise. Family portraits and busts look at you from all around, stamping the family character on the place. Further interesting paintings adorn the refined interiors, showing that the family were collectors of taste, with works from Italian schools and by Elisabeth Vigée-Lebrun. Finely wrought furniture also features, with a particularly remarkable Renaissance piece from Amboise.

The **Collegiate Church of St John the Baptist** stands a little outside the castle precinct. It looks disproportionately splendid for such a small village. Built in neat white stone, it was completed in 1541. The main restored tomb is that of the lordly Bastarnay family, with fine effigies of the lord, his wife and his son. They look rather like a family tucked up in bed, their heads deep in their stone pillows. The sculptures have been attributed to the famous master Jean Goujon. The choir contains amusing contemporary misericordes, figures with their tongues hanging out. Two early French Renaissance stained-glass windows have also survived. The aisleless nave is hung with four Italian paintings donated by the Branickis, who also gave the 17th-century work in the north choir chapel, the *Annunciation* painted by Philippe de Champaigne, artist to the French royal family in his time. It comes as a surprise to find such artistic riches hidden away in such a quiet corner of Touraine.

Nouans-les-Fontaines

Still more surprising is the great work at Nouans-les-Fontaines, a one-painting village a little east of Montrésor. But the picture is breathtaking, dominating the perspective as you enter the otherwise unremarkable old **church of St Martin** (*open 9–8; a small contribution will allow you to see the panel lit up and to listen to a sensible commentary in English while you survey the painting*). Known as the **Nouans *Pietà***, the work ranks among the finest masterpieces of late medieval French art, its rediscovery an exciting event not just for the village, but also for French art historians.

In 1931 the painting was sent to be cleaned. As the restorer removed the grime of ages it suddenly became apparent what a great work it was. Its history remains something of a mystery. The extremely large panel is generally agreed to be the work of the 15th-century royal court painter Jean Fouquet, intended as the central part of an altarpiece. Jean Fouquet, born in Tours around 1420, died there probably at the start of the 1480s. He's generally considered the first known great French artist to be remembered in history. He probably trained in Paris. He had gained such a fine reputation by his 20s that he was commissioned by King Charles VII and Pope Eugenius IV to paint their portraits. Best remembered for his depiction of Agnès Sorel as the Virgin (*see* Loches, above), he also executed a miniature self-portrait, a rare early portrait of an artist.

A consummate manuscript illuminator, whose most famous work was the Book of Hours for Etienne Chevalier (friend of Agnès and a greatly influential man in those times), Jean Fouquet combined the delicacy of the northern International style of painting with more monumental and classical influences from Renaissance Italy. Fouquet may be referred to in French as a *primitif*, which doesn't sound too complimentary (in French art history, it simply means that his work dates from before the Renaissance period), but he had travelled to Italy and absorbed lessons there. His example demonstrates how painting was ahead of architecture in its adoption of Italianate forms in 15th-century France, but also how French artists could find a style of their own.

As soon as you open the church door, you perceive the body of Christ ghostly white in the distance, stretched out, pale from death, his body just brought down from the cross. The figures are superbly characterized. Christ, his eyes closed, looks calm in death, youthful, smooth-skinned, with elegant hands, while the Virgin resembles an exhausted Meryl Streep, drained by emotion, hands clenched, feelings of suffering so evident. Nicodemus and Joseph of Aramathea are lowering Christ's body on to a shroud in front of her, his bent form stretching diagonally across the panel. All the accompanying figures look down or across to his body, concentrating the attention on the sombre event, conveying the power and pain of the moment.

The identity of the donor, who's depicted kneeling on the right-hand side, represented on the same large scale as the religious figures in the painting, remains a mystery. The mass of his white robe, seen from afar, rather disconcertingly connects him to the white Christ. One theory is that the painting was made for the chapel in the palace in Bourges of the fabulously wealthy merchant Jacques Cœur. However, Jacques Cœur died in 1456 and most scholars date the painting to the 1470s. What makes the Jacques Cœur theory tempting still, apart from the vast wealth and power this councillor-cum-merchant commanded until his disgrace, and the fact that he was known as a patron of the arts, is that the donor is overseen by St James the Pilgrim (St Jacques in French). Scholars continue to search for another suitably rich patron by that name to link to this superb work.

West and South of Loches

Head northwest from Loches for **Chanceaux-près-Loches**, a delightful place with the ruins of a medieval fortress, a Second Empire château built for the hugely wealthy ironworks industrialists, the Schneiders, and main street protected by vast plane trees. From Chanceaux continue via Dolus-le-Sec and St-Bauld to reach **Le Louroux**. This fortified village has preserved its medieval character and is exceptionally unspoilt by 20th-century encroachments. The village was owned from the end of the 10th century to the 18th by the wealthy abbey of Marmoutier outside Tours. An impressively large 15th-century barn divides the place in two. The church tower is the oldest remaining building, from the 12th century. To the east lie the lord's lodgings. The great 19th-century artistic prodigy Eugène Delacroix came to stay in the village as his brother had a house here, and he started his fascinating journal here in 1822, as he records, collecting his first recorded thoughts by the moonlight of Louroux.

Heading south from Loches, the village church of **Perrusson** is one of the most ancient in Touraine, with portions of 10th-century walls still standing and a couple of Merovingian sarcophagi in the choir. **Verneuil-sur-Indre**, off the N143, has a restored Romanesque church and two contrasting private châteaux.

The little-known **Château de Bridoré** (open Aug–mid-Sept 2–6), on Touraine's border with the medieval province of Berry, is impressively fortified. To reach it turn southwest off the N143 after Oizay Cerçay. The soaring keep separates two courtyards. In the main, the buildings date from the 14th century, supplemented by Renaissance window openings and defensive elements added in the Wars of Religion. The visit is short but reasonably interesting. The originality of the château lies in its *caponnières* in the dry moat. These are so rare that you're unlikely to find the word in your dictionary. Bridoré claims to possess four out of the eight that exist in France. You may have spotted one at Loches. Nantes has another. These 16th-century defences, mean and low, attached to the corners of the main building, protrude like outsized armoured feet from the building. The château also boasts a sauna from the 14th century, the idea for it imported from the Middle East during the Crusades. You can climb the keep – latrines at all levels – to reach the top, where you'll get superb views over the landscape the château dominates.

The Southern Tip of Touraine

Ce coin de terre ignoré et exquis (This unknown, exquisite corner of land).
André Theuriet

Touraine is shaped like a vine leaf. Its sharp southern tip below Loches and Ste-Maure is extremely attractive. Not many tourists come down this way, but the area has profound charm thanks to the numerous deep little wooded valleys that carve their way through it. Along the Claise river you come to the most substantial sight in these parts, the Château du Grand-Pressigny, housing Touraine's museum of prehistory. But there are also plenty of very attractive rural villages to potter round in these parts, with their Romanesque churches, little local museums and their own châteaux, as well as the odd dolmen, proof of a much earlier thriving human presence.

The Villages of Southern Touraine

Ferrière-Larçon, some way southwest of Loches, plunges you into the mood of this deeply rural little region. For such a quiet village, you may well wonder why it has such a substantial rocketing spire shooting out over the rustic brown-tiled roofs of the houses. It's said that the church of St-Mandet and St-Jean was built with proceeds from the Crusades by wealthy Knights Templars. Typical Romanesque carving decorates the west end. The tower dates from the second half of the 12th century, quite out of proportion with the place, while in the nave a 13th-century Gothic section dwarfs the early 12th-century one. The outsized, splendidly vaulted choir wasn't completed, possibly because funds ran out. In the village, the Rue des Caves contains rather more modest buildings, with some semi-troglodyte houses where numerous weavers once worked.

From Ferrière-Larçon, one option is to follow the Brignon river along the D100 towards Descartes, seeking out the dramatically defensive site of the **Fortresse du Châtelier** on its steep spur, the dolmen known as **Pierre Chaude** (Hot Rock) and the beautiful mill of Aunay at **Neuilly-sur-Brignon**. Then you're almost at Le Grand-Pressigny.

Alternatively, head down from Ferrière-Larçon for **La Celle-Guénand**, tucked into another typical southern Touraine valley, with a charming church and château. The church is late Romanesque, its doorway decorated with bearded heads, the château late Gothic, with bold towers. You may be able to walk into the grounds, which include a picturesque ensemble of early 17th-century houses and barns known as La Juiverie; it's said that Jews were protected by the lord here in times past. The village

Getting Around

Trains don't come this far. Just a couple of **buses** a day link Le Grand-Pressigny with Tours. Strangely, there are a few more connections a day between the villages of Preuilly, Le Petit-Pressigny, La Celle-Guénand and Ferrière-Larçon. Descartes, La Guerche and Yzeures are served by a separate line.

Tourist Information

Le Grand-Pressigny: Mairie, 37350 Le Grand-Pressigny, t/f 02 47 94 96 82, *tlc.ot@ wanadoo.fr*.
Descartes: Mairie, 37160 Descartes, t 02 47 92 42 20, f 02 47 59 72 20.

Market Days

Le Grand-Pressigny: Thursday morning.
Descartes: Sunday morning.

Where to Stay and Eat

Le Petit-Pressigny ✉ 37350
Dallais-La Promenade, 11 Rue du Savoureux, t 02 47 94 93 52. This place is reason in itself for many Tourangeaux to come and discover southern Touraine, as you can taste gourmet cuisine at a bargain price in this

former inn (*menus €21.5–64*). *Closed Sun pm and Mon, 2 weeks end Sept–start Oct and 3 weeks in Jan.*

Preuilly-sur-Claise ✉ 37290
**Auberge St-Nicolas, 6 Grande Rue, t 02 47 94 50 80, f 02 47 94 41 77 (*inexpensive*). Basic but welcoming stop (*menus €17.5–36*). *Closed Sun pm and Mon out of season, and 3 weeks Sept.*

Yzeures-sur-Creuse ✉ 37290
***La Promenade, 1 Place du 11 Novembre, t 02 47 91 49 00, f 02 47 94 46 12 (*inexpensive*). Quite stylishly decorated rooms in a former posting inn. The proprietor also cooks up a good meal (*average price for meals c.€30.5*). *Closed Tues lunch, and Jan.*

Chambon ✉ 37290
Le Vieux Fournil, Place de la Mairie, t 02 47 91 02 23. The old village bakery has been transformed into a cheerful restaurant, offering local cuisine (*menus €14.5–25*).

La Guerche ✉ 37350
La Tour d'Ardoise, 2 Rue du Four Banal, t 02 47 94 92 68 (*cheap*). Set pleasantly close to the bridge and the château, this is a rustic little place that tempts you inside (*menus €7.5–26*).

museum, the Musée de l'Outil et des Vieux Métiers (*open July–Aug 9.30–12 and 2–6.30, second half June and first half Sept 2–6, rest of period mid-March–mid-Nov weekends and public hols only 2–6*), celebrates old trades, with thousands of objects on display.

The D50 leads southeast to **Le Petit-Pressigny**, down in another valley, that of the Aigronne, with wash houses by the stream and a Romanesque church. A detour east along the D103 takes you to **Charnizay**, whose Ancien Régime château belonged at the start of the 20th century to Comte Robert de Montesquiou-Fezensac, a Paris society figure and poet, model for the Baron de Charlus in Proust's *A La Recherche du temps perdu* and for some time an extremely influential friend-cum-patron of the great author. On a height a couple of kilometres northeast of the village seek out the **dolmen de Charnizay**, also known as **Les Palets de Gargantua**, the Rabelaisian story having it that giants threw these massive Neolithic stones down here.

Preuilly-sur-Claise lies a little further south. The main, startling monument in this slightly larger place is the abbey church of St-Pierre, a once-grand Romanesque structure very heavy-handedly restored in the 19th century. The restoration included rerooting a bell tower with coloured tiles in the Dijon style, surprising in Touraine, but you can still admire the skill of the Romanesque builders of the choir with its many apses. Inside, the place is decorated with carved capitals, but the Cleveland museum in the USA bought another set from a second Romanesque church in Preuilly, that of Ste-Melanie, attached to the Château du Lion and partly destroyed by the ruling 16th-century Protestant family here. The early fortress ruins remain next to a 19th-century château. The Musée de la Poterne (*open July–Aug Tues–Sun 2.30–6.30*), in the medieval gatehouse, contains archaeological and traditional regional displays, including of Touraine lace and embroidery.

The forest of Preuilly stretches eastwards. Taking the D725 through it you reach **Azay-le-Ferron**, just in the Berry, but its heavily restored château owned and run by the Tours town authorities. North from here in the forest, the **Parc Zoologique de la Haute Touche** protects a splendid and varied collection of deer in its substantial grounds. Many other animals from around the world are also to be seen in the spacious runs.

Back at Preuilly, cross the Claise and then head immediately west for a pretty detour past the beautifully framed **Château de Boussay**. A couple more turns south bring you to **Yzeures-sur-Creuse**, where the Musée de Minerve (*open 9–12 and 2–5; free*) presents interesting fragments of Gallo-Roman art from the 2nd century in the form of carvings of classical mythological figures and other archaeological pieces. This isn't the only museum in this little spot. The other consists of a dressing room dedicated to Mado Robin, an opera singer who died in 1960; she was particularly famed for her interpretation of Delibes's Lakmé, and a sublime piece of music hijacked by British Airways advertising. Stage costumes she wore accompany recordings of her singing at the Musée Mado Robin (*open 8–6; free*). A statue of the singer stands in the village.

If you've come this far south, we'd thoroughly recommend that you cross the regional border into Poitou to visit the gorgeous village of **Angles-sur-l'Anglin**, another dozen kilometres south. Its name is supposed to derive from 5th-century Angles who settled here. The ruins of the medieval château (*open July–Aug Wed–Mon 10–12 and 2.30–6.30*) present romantically crumbling towers and lodges rising out of the limestone cliff above the river. Steps hewn into the rock help in the slightly precarious walk up to a Romanesque chapel above the castle, converted into a showroom for local embroidery and cutlery. The embroidery is known as Les Jours d'Angles because of its openwork effects.

Heading north from Yzeures along the Creuse valley, the D750 road is a joy, as the countryside opens up generously in unspoilt agricultural gentleness. While most of the châteaux in this corner of Touraine are private and not open to visitors, the **Château de la Guerche** (*open late June–mid-Sept Mon–Sat 10–1 and 2–7, Sun 1–7*), overlooking the Creuse, is a rare exception, and occupies a marvellous riverbank spot. Go onto the bridge across the Creuse to get the best view of the château on this beautiful stretch of river. The building dates from the very end of the 15th century, most probably built for Arthus de Villequier, son of Charles VII's favourites, André de Villequier and Antoinette de Maignelais. Originally it had four wings surrounded by moats.

From the bridge you can see the Gothic aspect of the building, which was constructed at a time when comforts were beginning to be thought of as well as defence. The upper floors were for the lord's apartments – few of these are included in the visit. Instead the tour concentrates on the castle's defensive elements. You're shown the two lower floors of the river wing. The bottom one contains the artillery rooms, finely built, with strong vaults and sturdy towers, as were the interconnecting store rooms of the level above. On sunny days the shifting light reflected off the Creuse fills these chambers with brightness. The château prison was also on this level. It contains several touching pieces of graffiti.

Château du Grand-Pressigny

Open June–Sept 9.30–6.30, mid-March–May 9.30–12.30 and 2–6, Feb–mid-March and Oct–Dec 9.30–12.30 and 2.30–5.30; t 02 47 94 90 20.

The Château du Grand-Pressigny, a dozen kilometres southeast of the little town of Descartes, is a pure delight of typically impure Loire architecture. The site was chosen for its defensive potential at the close of the 12th century. From this position on top of a plateau, the valleys of the Aigronne and the Claise could be surveyed and the countryside around controlled. The local lord took the French king's side against the Plantagenets of Anjou. The fortifications were made more elaborate through time, with the addition during the 15th century of a barbican and, in certain parts, machicolations and a *chemin de ronde*. In the second half of the Hundred Years' War, the troops of Jean sans Peur, duke of Burgundy and ally of the English, took the castle in 1417, although the French dauphin, the future King Charles VII, won it back the following year.

In 1523, René de Savoie, half-brother of Louise de Savoie (mother of King François I), became owner of the château. His son Honorat de Savoie-Villars was the one to order the classical gallery, built some time between 1550 and 1580. The classical block splits the medieval buildings neatly in two. It isn't in the tentative style of the first French Renaissance, but much more assuredly Italian in influence and order. Its stone looks somewhat grey and coarse, however, which gives the whole a rather heavier appearance than the Renaissance châteaux to the north. This classical gallery contains the main section of the **Musée de la Préhistoire**.

Starting in the first courtyard, the Salle de Paléontologie contains a massive collection of marine, plant and animal fossils, showing the geological and natural prehistory of the area. The exhibits are extremely neatly and clearly laid out. You can climb the stairs in this large room; they lead out onto the *chemin de ronde*, an amusingly crooked outer walkway. In another corner of the courtyard you can climb the thin stick of a tower known as the Tour Vironne for an even better panorama of the surrounding area and the brown-tiled village houses tucked into the valley below.

The rooms of the **Renaissance wing** house thousands of artefacts demonstrating the substantial presence of prehistoric man in the area. Important communities settled here from the Stone Age; they churned out flint instruments on a massive scale. The flint blades could be employed for all manner of agricultural uses. Such was the quality of the implements produced here that they were exported across Europe; finds of Pressigny flints have been unearthed in Belgium and Switzerland. From a much later period relatively speaking, but still very ancient, a few other objects complement these collections, including swords and jewellery and a fine ancient Gaulish religious statue with a necklace.

Through the central arch of the Renaissance building, the second courtyard has a charming little Renaissance pavilion dwarfed by an early medieval keep. The keep hasn't kept so well recently, as two walls fell down one day in 1988, but it is the oldest part of the fortifications remaining, dating from the late 12th century. What you now see does give you a fine cross-section of this type of building, while the spiral stair-case open to the winds looks, rather fittingly, fossil-like.

To get some impression of a prehistoric flint works in action, take the D42 from Le Grand-Pressigny for Descartes. Along the way, at **Abilly**, is the Archéolabe (*open mid-June–mid-Sept 2.30–6.30*). An archaeologist will explain the site, which was exploited between 2800 BC and 2400 BC.

Descartes

René Descartes didn't live for long in the small Touraine town that's taken his name, and his childhood years here were his least significant, intellectually speaking. But the place has done him and itself the honour of setting up a small museum, the **Musée Descartes** (*open June–Sept Wed–Mon 2–6*), dedicated to this towering genius of mathematics and philosophy. The town was known in Descartes' day as La Haye and lay just in the Poitou region. Although born in Châtellerault, the prodigy was baptized here and spent his early years in La Haye. Probably around the age of 10 Descartes left the town to go and study at the prestigious Jesuit college just founded by Henri IV at La Flèche, north of Anjou. Later, it was to Holland that he would go to produce his famous works.

Descartes is generally regarded as the founder of modern philosophy. His best-known work, his *Discours de la Méthode* of 1637, proves a highly entertaining read. In it he describes how he tried to overcome the terrible doubts of the self and the problems of people's differing opinions and faiths. Among his most important notions were '*cogito ergo sum* (I think therefore I am)', the dualism of mind and matter, and the idea that God equalled absolute perfection. The museum also contains memories of another writer of a rather different complexion, who tackled issues of a rather less profound and mysterious nature. René Boylesve (real name Tardiveau, 1867–1926) offered insights in his novels into the pettiness of provincial life. His best-remembered work is *L'Enfant à la balustrade*. Who could possibly be cruel enough to look for a reflection of his themes in the donkey-like, attractively dopey old town of Descartes?

The Cher, Indre and Vienne Join the Loire

17

Western Touraine

Courcelles-de-Touraine
959
Rillé
Savigné-sur-Lathon
Parçay les Pins
Château de Champchevrier
Hommes
Cléré-les-Pins
Vernoil
Gizeux
Tours
St-Etienne-de-Chigny
Luynes
Cinq-Mars-la-Pile
Berthenay
Savonnières
Langeais
Grottes Pétrifiantes
St Michel-sur-Loire
Villandry
St Nicolas-de-Bourgueil
Chevrette
Planchoury
Restigné
St Patrice
Bréhémont
Château de Candé
Bourgueil
Ingrandes-de-Touraine
Marnay
Montbazon
Château des Réaux
Rivarennes
Azay-le-Rideau
Monts
Chouzé-sur-Loire
Rigny-Ussé
Saché
Candes St-Martin
Avoine
Château d'Ussé
La Chapelle-Ste-Blaise
INDRE-ET-
St Germain
Beaumont-en-Véron
Parc Naturel Regional
Villaines-les-Roches
LOIRE
Loire-Anjou-Touraine
Chinon
La Devinière
Cinais
Cravant-les-Côteaux
Avon-les-Roches
Lerné
Rivière
Crissay-sur-Manse
Ste-Catherine-de-Fierbois
Seuilly
Vienne
Panzoult
St-Epain
La Roche Clermault
Tavant
Crouzilles
Noyant-de-Touraine
Marçay
Veude
L'Ile Bouchard
Parçay
Ste-Maure
Château du Rivau
Pouzay
Manse
Champigny-sur-Veude
N
Loudun
Richelieu
Luzé
Braslou
Abbaye de Bois-Aubry
10 km
5 miles
Razines
Descartes
Faye-la-Vineuse
Château de Grillère

Highlights

1 The finest kitchen garden in France at the Château de Villandry
2 The narcissistic Château d'Azay-le-Rideau
3 Sleeping Beauty's Château d'Ussé
4 The gorgeous D21 vineyard route east from Chinon to the Manse valley
5 Chinon, a courtly town with a hint of glamour

The châteaux of Villandry, Azay-le-Rideau and Ussé count among the most famous castles not just in this chapter, not just in this guidebook, but in all of France. The three don't stand by the Loire, but by the great tributaries of the Cher and the Indre. These two rivers and that of the Vienne further south reach the Loire in western Touraine. Beyond being rich in châteaux and churches, their valleys are particularly beautiful and fruitful. As you head west, the fruit orchards give way to dense vineyards, Bourgeuil north of the Loire, Chinon south of it, along the Vienne.

Much of splendid western Touraine now forms part of the Parc Naturel Régional Loire-Anjou-Touraine created in the 1990s (*see* pp.366–8). Touraine's neighbour Anjou was the original territory of the Plantagenets, who went on to form a dynasty of English kings. But one of King Henry II Plantagenet's favoured royal residences was the Château de Chinon, now an impressive ship of a ruin stranded above a splendid courtly town. Several other of France's best-known national figures have close links with western Touraine, notably Joan of Arc, Rabelais, Richelieu and Balzac, all with museums recalling them.

We've mentioned the famous things about western Touraine in this introduction, but the whole area is full of delightful villages and smaller sights. And if most of our attention focuses south of the Loire, we would also encourage you to consider visiting the posse of intriguing lesser-known castles just to the north of it.

The North Bank of the Loire West of Tours

While the châteaux south of the Loire from Tours to the Anjou border are famously light and bright and gay, those you can visit just to the north of the mighty river look much more severe on the outside. However, Luynes, Langeais, Champchevrier and Gizeux all prove surprisingly fresh within. West beyond them you come into the wine-making territory of Bourgueil.

Château de Luynes

Open April–Sept 10–6; t *02 47 55 67 55.*

Standing guard high above the Loire in the first town west of Tours along the river's north bank, the formidable medieval Château de Luynes first opened its gates to the public in the mid-1990s. From the outside it looks forbidding rather than inviting. The grey medieval armour of its exterior dates back to the 13th century in the main. Large stone pimples protrude from several of its towers. Under King Louis XI, in the second half of the 15th century, one of the lords of the local Maillé family brought a great deal more light to the château with the addition of an array of windows.

Charles d'Albret bought the Maillés' château in 1619. He had been brought up with King Henri IV's son, the future Louis XIII, and the two had become particularly firm pals through their love of falconry. Their friendship would become less innocent as they grew up: in 1617, when Louis XIII came of age, the two of them conspired to have Concini, the powerful Italian adviser-cum-lover to the Queen Mother Marie de' Medici, assassinated. Charles took on the title of Duc de Luynes, after a place in

Getting Around

Cinq-Mars-la-Pile and Langeais lie on the **train** line from Tours to Saumur, but don't expect a wide choice of trains. A very limited **bus** service from Tours passes through Cinq-Mars, Langeais, Planchoury, St-Patrice, Ingrandes, Restigné to Bourgueil. Another line serves Luynes, Cléré-les-Pins, Savigné-sur-Lathan, Rillé, Hommes, Gizeux and Parçay-les-Pins.

Tourist Information

Luynes: 9 Rue Baugé, B.P.1, 37230 Luynes, **t** 02 47 55 77 14, **f** 02 47 55 52 56, *luynes@wanadoo.fr*.
Cinq-Mars-La-Pile: Mairie, 37130 Cinq-Mars-la-Pile, **t** 02 47 96 43 43 or **t** 02 47 96 20 30, **f** 02 47 96 38 52.
Langeais: Place du 14 Juillet, B.P.47, 37130 Langeais, **t** 02 47 96 58 22, **f** 02 47 96 83 41, *otsi@neuronnexion.fr*.
Bourgueil: 16 Place de l'Eglise, 37140 Bourgueil, **t/f** 02 47 97 91 39, *otsi-bourgueil@wanadoo.fr*.

Market Days
Luynes: Saturday morning.
Langeais: Sunday morning.
Bourgueil: Tuesday and Saturday mornings.

Where to Stay and Eat

Luynes ✉ 37230
****Domaine de Beauvois, Route de Cléré, **t** 02 47 55 50 11, **f** 02 47 55 59 62, *beauvois@wanadoo.fr* (*expensive*). Very elegant manor set in a pretty wooded valley. The rooms are excellently furnished. The large Louis XIII-style dining room gives onto the smart front garden. A lake and a swimming pool lie down below, and there's a tennis court in the grounds (*menus €30.5–61*). Closed Feb–mid-Mar.

Courcelles-de-Touraine ✉ 37330
***Château des Sept Tours, **t** 02 47 24 69 75, **f** 02 47 24 23 74, *info@7tours.com* (*expensive*). A castle which cuts quite a dash northwest of the Château de Champchevrier, its grounds turned into a golf course. It all looks very grand; just the odd bit of tasteless decoration lets it down.

Langeais ✉ 37130
***Errard Hosten, 2 Rue Gambetta, **t** 02 47 96 82 12, **f** 02 47 96 56 72 (*moderate*). The exterior isn't unpleasant, but it isn't harmonious either, and doesn't do justice to what awaits you inside. The rooms are smartly and tastefully decorated, while you can sample very fine cuisine in the elegant

Provence, and the name of the Touraine château and town changed to reflect his new appellation. He went on to become Connétable de France and the most important minister in the land – Richelieu would take his place soon after he died. Descendants of the duke still live in the château. Modifications to the château were made through the 17th century, and again in the 19th.

Once across the dry moat, which has been planted as an enchanting garden, you enter a surprisingly sophisticated courtyard, its elegance in such contrast to the stern exteriors of the castle. Inside, you visit a series of grand rooms, finely furnished, some with absolutely splendid views onto the Loire. The rooms are unexpectedly light. Particularly memorable is the vast sunken Salle des Jeux, with its traditional ochre walls, and above it the Grand Salon, with an elaborate fireplace thought to be the work of Jean Goujon. Look out for some splendid portraits, sumptuous furniture and very well-preserved tapestries.

Maillé had a Gallo-Roman ancestor, Malliacum. Archaeological digs on the plateau above the town have brought to light remnants of the early civilization here, including an isolated piece of aqueduct east of town to which a pretty pink house has attached itself like an outlandish barnacle. Fine medieval houses and a 15th-century

dining room (menus €22–37.5). Closed
Sun pm and Mon out of season, and mid-
Feb–mid-March.
**La Duchesse Anne, 10 Rue de Tours, t 02 47
96 82 03, f 02 47 96 68 60 (moderate). A
notch less expensive, with clean rooms and
a delightful town garden, as well as solid
traditional French fare (menus €13.5–33).
Closed Fri pm and Sat out of season, and
most Feb).

Hommes ✉ 37340
Vieux Château d'Hommes B&B, near Savigné
up the D57 from Langeais, t 02 47 24 95 13,
f 02 47 24 68 67 (moderate). A 15th-century
barn converted to give five high-standard
chambre d'hôte rooms. Swimming pool
(table d'hôte €25).

St-Michel-sur-Loire ✉ 37130
Château de Montbrun B&B, 47 Route du
Coteau, Domaine de la Riboisière, t 02 47
96 57 13, f 02 47 96 01 28, montbrun@
chateauxhotels.com, www.chateauxhotels.
com/montbrun (expensive). A delightful
19th-century Loire-style little château
with lovely views over the Loire valley.
You're likely to have an entertaining time
here, with swimming and archery possible
in the grounds and a host who's sung
at the London Palladium. The swimming

pool is heated and table d'hôte is offered
(€29). Closed Jan–Feb.

St-Patrice ✉ 37130
****Château de Rochecotte, t 02 47 96 16 16,
f 02 47 96 90 59, rochecotte@chateaux
hotels.com, www.chateauxhotels.com/
rochecotte (expensive). Absolutely splendid
18th-century aristocratic country house with
formal French gardens hidden on the
wooded Loire bank. This became one of the
homes of Talleyrand, close associate of
Napoleon. The spacious rooms are decorated
in period style, and the elaborate cuisine is
served in the colonnaded dining room.
Heated swimming pool (menus €34.5–53.5).
Closed first fortnight Dec and Feb.

Chouzé-sur-Loire ✉ 37140
Château des Réaux B&B, Le Port-Boulet, t 02 47
95 14 40, f 02 47 95 18 34, reaux@chateaux
hotels.com, www.chateauxhotels.com/reaux
(expensive). Utterly enchanting historic
castle described in the touring section
below. The woman who runs it is a bit of a
character, and together with her husband
she has lovingly restored the château and
turned it into a B&B. The rooms are full of
individual character and many are rather
romantic. The place is a real delight (table
d'hôtes €38).

covered market are the main attractions down in the town itself. A short way west,
the village church of **St-Etienne-de-Chigny** contains a richly decorated 16th-century
interior, much of the work commemorating Jean Binet, a mayor of Tours, and his wife,
their family arms plastered all over the walls.

Cinq-Mars-la-Pile
A brick pile, or tower, rises slightly east of the village of **Cinq-Mars-la-Pile**. For a long
time its original purpose remained a mystery. Some speculated that it had been
constructed as a lighthouse for boats on the Loire, others as a marking point for
pilgrims travelling along the great river, others as some grandiose milestone. It's now
reckoned to have been erected as a mausoleum for a rich 2nd-century merchant. It's
an impressive 100 Roman feet high.
The ruined medieval **Château de Cinq-Mars-la-Pile** (open March–Oct Wed–Mon
9–nightfall, rest of year Wed–Mon 11–nightfall) was famously decapitated in the
1640s along with its young owner, Henri Coiffier de Ruzé d'Effiat, Marquis de
Cinq-Mars. Power went to the head of this political prodigy. A protégé of Cardinal
Richelieu, he quickly rose to high rank and became a favourite of Louis XIII, possibly

even sexually intimate with him as the rumour had it. The seductive young upstart amassed such influence that he then conspired with Gaston d'Orléans, the king's brother, to get rid of Richelieu. The plot was discovered and Cinq-Mars was executed at the age of 22. The château was partially revived during the 19th-century. Today, you can visit a couple of semi-ruined 12th–13th century towers and admire the 16th-century moat.

Château de Champchevrier

Open July–Sept daily 11–6, May–June weekends and public hols only 11–6.

A pack of hounds barks wildly as you arrive at this stocky grey château (*take the D34 from Cinq-Mars-la-Pile for Château-la-Vallière; it's just after Cléré-les-Pins*) surrounded by alleys of towering plane trees that line up in ranks like giant guardsmen. The place is rather forbidding, if atmospheric. The hounds indicate how important hunting is in the history of Champchevrier. The very name of the place reflects this, *chevrier* apparently derived from *chevreuil*, the French word for roe deer. The first castle went up in the forests here back in the 11th century. In late medieval times, Louis XI, one of the keenest among the hunting-mad Loire kings, stopped to indulge in his pleasure here.

In the 16th century the estates came by marriage into the De Daillon family, which already owned the mighty Le Lude castle a bit further north, on the Loir (without an 'e'). Jean de Daillon had much of the medieval castle demolished and new Renaissance façades built. If the architecture looks distinctly messy on the side facing the road, you'll find a much greater harmony to the main façade giving onto the large grass-covered courtyard. A boxy chapel was added off one corner. An extremely long line of outbuildings was later attached to the main wing in the 17th century, when the château was in the hands of the De Roquelaure family, one of whom became a leading military figure of his day, elevated to the ultimate height of marshal of France.

But the De Roquelaures soon sold the place to one Jean-Baptiste de La Rüe du Can, in 1728. This man served as Secretary of Buildings to Louis XV and was honoured with the title of baron of Champchevrier in 1741. At the Revolution, the drawbridge was destroyed and some of the architectural refinements hacked off, including the dormer windows. But otherwise the château remained relatively untouched, even if some of the family had to flee or face imprisonment. The present owners, the Bizards, are descendants of the baron of Champchevrier, and very much devoted to their château.

Through the 1990s they opened up an increasing number of rooms in the château. On the guided tour inside, after the old hunting trophies and old carriages, you're treated to an array of family portraits and, above all, a splendid display of tapestries. These have been superbly preserved. Some were made in Flanders, others in Picardy, in Amiens and Beauvais. The oldest shows a hare hunt in naive 16th-century style. The most famous are a series made from cartoons by Simon Vouet. This superlative French 17th-century artist was greatly influenced by his classical training in Italy and worked for Louis XIII. He was commissioned to make cartoons for a series of magnificent classical cycles; the one at Champchevrier illustrates the mythological Loves of the Gods, some with exceptional movement and energy. Adonis fleeing from Venus, Neptune and Ceres, Bacchus and Ariadne and the rape of Prosperina by Pluto are the main scenes. Mars, Jupiter and Hercules are also represented in further tapestries.

A few minor events in Champchevrier's war history may interest British and American visitors. At the outbreak of the Second World War in France in June 1940, the castle was chosen as the place to which the British embassy should retreat, though they only stayed a week before having to flee. And at the end of the conflict, an American bomber accidentally dropped a bomb somewhere on the estate; the crater it caused has become a drinking hole for deer!

If you don't want to go on the guided tour inside, you can buy a cheaper ticket just to wander round the outbuildings on your own, and look in at the old-fashioned rustic kitchens and laundry. A video of about an hour concentrates on hunting and hunting horns. Visitors can also go and admire the pack of mutts lounging around. They have a fine pedigree, their history going back to 1804 – they are apparently one of the oldest packs in Europe.

Château de Langeais

Open mid-July–Aug 9–9, April–mid-July and Sept 9–6.30,
Oct 9–12.30 and 2–6.30, rest of year 9–12 and 2–5.

A kitsch 1950s neo-Gothic bridge spans the Loire at Langeais. The town's formidable château is the real thing, however. In fact there are two castles or forts here, the grey Gothic monster's walls concealing the ruins of one of the very oldest stone keeps in France. If the main Château de Langeais looks a villain of a Loire château, then it comes as no surprise to learn that the severe King Louis XI ordered its building after the end of the Hundred Years' War. There's none of the usual exuberance of so much late Gothic architecture here.

Langeais' sternness does impress, though, from the outside, and as you gaze up at the towering mass, the machicolations and double layer of *chemins de ronde* look defensively down on you. The castle's tall walls and stern towers cast their sinister shadows over the town houses around them. Yet inside the picture is entirely different, the warmth of the rooms utterly contrasting with the coldness of the exterior. The château turns out to have one of the richest interiors along the Loire, full of fine furnishings and, in particular, glorious tapestries.

First, cross the sturdy 19th-century reconstruction of a drawbridge and enter the castle via its imposing gateway. The earlier keep comes into view on the hillock beyond the open courtyard whose formal garden has suffered badly from an overdose of cement. The ceaselessly combative and constructing Foulques Nerra, count of Anjou, had the old hillside stronghold built, possibly as early as the very end of the 10th century. This may well be the oldest stone keep in France (*see* Montbazon's claim on p.289). What remains is a truncated shell. You need to imagine a structure that would have towered above the trees with sheer cliff-faces of masonry for walls. The Plantagenets added to the fortifications before they lost their lands to the French King Philippe Auguste, but during the Hundred Years' War many of these defences disappeared.

Louis XI asked his trusted servant Jean Bourré (he for whom the Château du Plessis-Bourré was built in Anjou, *see* pp.443–6) to oversee the building of a new château here in 1465, guarding the Loire at the western entrance to Touraine. It should be recalled that Louis had moved the centre of the kingdom to his main castle at Le Plessis-lès-Tours, not far off on the western outskirts of Tours. The original plan at Langeais was doubtless for a four-sided château, but only two were built. In fact, Bourré seems to have handed over charge to Jean Briçonnet, a mayor of Tours and another close confident of Louis XI, soon after 1465. At roughly the same time the king gave the castle under construction to his cousin François Dunois d'Orléans (son of the Dunois who fought with Joan of Arc), who had married the king's sister. Building work continued under Dunois and was practically complete by 1490. It was in this castle that the fate of Brittany's independence was effectively sealed when the French King Charles VIII forced Anne de Bretagne to marry him here in 1491. Dunois helped organize the celebrations, but died before the event took place in December.

The interior like the exterior was heavily restored in the 19th century. In 1886 the wealthy entrepreneur and banker Jacques Siegfried bought the place from a friend, and with his wife devoted himself to recreating a Gothic warmth. Although the pieces aren't originally from Langeais, the Siegfrieds' good taste gave harmony to the rooms. The Petit Salon sets the tone, panelled with polychrome carved wood taken from a Normandy church, an exquisite Flemish triptych adding to the strong Gothic feel. The main artistic theme of the interiors, fine tapestries, starts in the millefleurs drawing room. The walls of the rooms that follow have often been embellished with stylized 19th-century neo-Gothic painting, the floors decorated with elaborate tiles, while splendid coffers and pieces of furniture line up along the sides. The Salle des Jeux offers a good example of this neo-Gothic decoration, with linenfold panelling added. The initials A and K refer to Anne and Karolus (Charles), the cords to Anne's pious attachment to the Franciscan order. Some of the tapestries are particularly entertaining in the Guards' Room with its monumental fireplace, one scene showing Louis XII consulting with his astronomer, another floppy-eared, but vicious-eyed, hunting dogs, several congregating around the drooping intestines of a deer that's being skinned.

The first room on the first floor has a beautiful Flemish tapestry depicting Christ's crucifixion. Next door, the Salle des Aristoloches has the most curious tapestry of the château's whole collection, with Oriental-style birds set against a background of bizarre large curling vegetal leaves after which the room is named. The Blue Room continues with the rich variety of tapestries. Here the millefleurs are almost over-whelmingly dense with petals, of which there must indeed be many thousands. Another great hunting scene continues the collection on that theme.

The Salle Anne de Bretagne is on a different scale. Huge tapestries celebrating heroes from antiquity, the Bible and the Dark Ages are hung around the walls. Joshua,

David, Hector, Alexander, Caesar, Arthur and Godefroy de Bouillon (11th-century crusader elected ruler of Jerusalem after the holy city was taken in the First Crusade) feature, but Judas Maccabaeus and Charlemagne are missing from the cycle. These large scale tapestry panels rather eclipse the slightly repellent waxwork models commemorating the marriage of Anne to Charles VIII on 6 December 1491, a moment of monumental significance in French regional history.

A barge brought Anne de Bretagne's dearest personal possessions up the Loire from the Château de Nantes, her home in the then capital of Brittany. Among the items were her two beds and sumptuous dresses. She was about to give away her virginity and the independence of Brittany in style. All these acts were rather forced upon her. Her father, François II Duc de Bretagne, had intrigued until his death in 1488 to try and protect Brittany's independence from the French Crown. Not that the Breton ducal family was overconcerned about its people. Although Brittany had been run down by warring, the pious Anne loved her luxuries and she found the money to pay for what is surely one of the most famous wedding dresses in French history. True, the weather was likely to be cold, but to pay 58,000 livres, as some estimated! The attendants wore silk and velvet dresses. Even the horses were decked out in black and crimson. It must have been a sumptuous ceremony, belittled by today's small waxworks display.

Up above, the Salle de la Chapelle (only so-called since the last century) has a splendid wooden ceiling in the form of an upside-down ship's hull, while a superb reliquary chest also draws the attention. After a breather walking round part of the castle's *chemins de ronde*, only a couple more furnished rooms await you. Once again fine tapestries feature. Fittingly enough, the visit ends with a room where tapestries are exhibited and sold, so if you've developed a taste for them on the marathon tour and feel flush, this may be a good place to look for one.

To Bourgueil

From Langeais the N152 runs close to the Loire up to the Anjou border. However, you can also follow the D35 high road to Bourgueil if you turn off at **Planchoury**. The Château de Planchoury has the bizarre attraction in its outbuildings of an extensive collection of Cadillacs in the Musée du Cadillac (*open May–Aug 10–6, rest of year Wed–Mon 10–6, also closed Jan*). The road along the valley ridge via St-Michel to St-Patrice offers some wonderful views across to the other bank of the Loire. Ingrandes-de-Touraine used to stand on the border with Anjou before the Revolution. You're now entering the wine territory of Bourgueil.

Bourgueil itself is a pretty little market town. Its abbey is its most significant historic building. Its origins date back to the days when the counts of Blois ruled this far west, at the end of the 9th century. Count Thibaud le Tricheur's daughter Emma founded the institution in 990, and it prospered more or less until the Revolution, when most of it was done away with. Much of what's left is still occupied by nuns and old people. Tourists can go via the vestiges of a late-medieval cloister and an 18th-century refectory up a magnificent staircase to the cluttered displays of the Musée Arts et Traditions Populaires (*open July–Aug Thurs–Mon 2–6, April–June and Sept–Oct weekends and public hols only 2–6*).

The Wines of Bourgueil and St-Nicolas-de-Bourgueil

The *appellations d'origine contrôlée* areas of Bourgueil and St-Nicolas-de-Bourgueil lie just north of the Loire, pretty well opposite the Chinon vine-growing area. The two *appellations* produce red wine, almost exclusively from the Cabernet Franc variety (a tiny amount of Cabernet Sauvignon has crept in). Around 1,200 hectares are planted in the Bourgueil territory; St-Nicolas-de-Bourgueil forms an enclave within it of some 800 hectares. The vines here mainly extend over a plateau of more or less sandy, gravelly and limestone ground.

What tells the Bourgueils apart from Chinon reds and from each other? Some Bourgueils may be more tannic, the ones stemming from limestone ground giving meatier aromas; some from the gravelly terrain may have a more distinctive aroma of raspberries (although violets, as at Chinon, are also traditionally associated with the Bourgueil bouquet). In successful years they could be left to age a bit longer than they are, but as ever along the Loire, reds tend to be drunk very young. The St-Nicolas-de-Bourgueils are generally lighter wines from lighter soils and can be pleasantly fruity.

The name of Bourgueil is well known to the average French drinker. The wine became trendy in Paris in the 1980s, but has never been as well recognized as Chinon abroad. To get to know some good Bourgueils you could try **Lamé Delille Boucaud** at Ingrandes-de-Touraine or **Joël and Clarisse Taluau** (*t 02 47 97 78 79; open weekdays*) at Chevrette. Also in Chevrette, at the **Cave Touristique de la Dive Bouteille** (*t 02 47 97 72 01; open every day in season, weekends only out of season*) for a small fee you get a museum display on the local wines as well as a tasting. An up-and-coming producer at Restigné, Jean-François Demont's wines from the **Domaine des Mailloches** (*t 02 47 97 33 10; telephone in advance if you want to visit in the week; open Sat, closed Sun*) are highly regarded.

Heading from Bourgueil to the Loire, make a small detour to marvel at the most extraordinary geometric patterns adorning the façades of the **Château des Réaux** (*you can wander around the outside for a small fee*). Past the pea-soup moat, the chequered brick and tufa walls make this one of the most astonishing of Loire châteaux. From the front, it looks a bit like a building that's caught a dose of well-ordered measles. At the back, chevron decorations on the square tower make that part resemble an absurd precursor of a road traffic sign. In all, several buildings of different ages and styles have been joined together to form a wholly eccentric but charming ensemble. The original château was built for a Touraine notable in the first half of the 16th century. The name of the place was changed in the mid-17th century from Le Plessis-Rideau to Les Réaux, after the excellent but all too little-known memorialist and moralist who lived here.

Arriving back at the great river, **Chouzé-sur-Loire** once thrived as a river port. Some handsome tufa houses remain as evidence of profitable trading times, as do the quays, and the place wistfully remembers its lucrative past with a little Musée des Mariniers (*open June–Aug weekends and public hols 3–5*).

Château de Gizeux

Open May–Sept Mon–Sat 10–6.30, Sun 2–6.

Fifteen kilometres north of Bourgueil along the D749 is another massive but isolated Loire castle. The long driveway up to the Château de Gizeux befits such a massive home, which was probably built in the 16th century for René du Bellay. But the main building is almost eclipsed by the extent and beauty of the stables, added in 1741, with their picturesque dormer windows. The round tower you see as you come to the courtyards is a restored remnant of an earlier Du Bellay castle finished in 1415.

Inside the château, on the ground floor you're taken through an enfilade of rooms with grey-painted woodwork and an 18th-century feel. The first salon contains a portrait of the Marquis de la Contade, proprietor at the time of the Revolution. He didn't die by the guillotine, but apparently from a fit brought on when he thought one of his servants had supported the uprising. Although he looks as though he must have been a difficult character, he is much appreciated in the culinary world for making foie gras fashionable in France. One bastard son of his, Héros de Seychelles, became something of a Revolutionary hero, but he did end up going to the guillotine for his relatively moderate stance. Here he's represented as a sweet-faced youth. The Salon des Dames has a more intimate feel, with embroideries executed by the present owner's grandmother. Two dining rooms follow, one chic, the other for *la chasse* – this one often smells of cooking, showing how lived in the château still is.

On the first floor you're even sometimes allowed to poke your head into the owners' bedroom! But your attention will be drawn away by splendid views down two long galleries at right angles to each other. Both are elaborately painted. One contains a vast number of bouquets, each different, and scenes of courtly life. The walls of the other, the **Galerie des Fresques**, were used as practice space by a school of painters. It seems totally incongruous in the midst of the region of great Loire châteaux that the panels should depict royal châteaux of the Ile de France around Paris. Art historians reckon that pupils from the Ecole de Fontainebleau were given free reign to hone their skills here. Among the scenes, the one of Fontainebleau leaves the most delightful impression, with ships sailing in the moat. One Loire château does make it into the gallery, royal Chambord.

Go to the village church to admire the splendid kneeling effigies of two couples of Du Bellays, cut from white marble. The **Sentier d'Interprétation** walk marked out in Gizeux by the Parc Régional Naturel Loire-Anjou-Touraine draws your attention to the variety of trees around the château, including the alleys of planes absolutely teeming with woodpeckers' nests.

The Cher and the Indre West of Tours

The staggering vegetable garden of the Château de Villandry is the mouth-watering *pièce de résistance* along the final stretch of the Cher west of Tours. But do go exploring the atmospheric, ignored isthmus between the Loire and the Cher

Getting Around

Azay-le-Rideau lies on the **train** line between Tours and Chinon. From the A10 **motorway** take the exit south of Tours between St-Avertin and Montbazon. Coming along main roads from the centre of Tours, follow signs either for Montbazon or for Joué-les-Tours, and then continue on to Monts.

Tourist Information

Villandry-Savonnières: Le Potager, 37510 Villandry, **t** 02 47 50 12 66, **f** 02 47 43 59 16, *otsivillandry@aol.com.*

Azay-le-Rideau: B.P.5, Place de l'Europe, **t** 02 47 45 44 40, **f** 02 47 45 31 46.

Where to Stay and Eat

Berthenay ✉ 37510
La Grange aux Moines B&B, t 02 47 50 06 91 (*inexpensive*). A traditional Touraine farmhouse on the delightful spit of land between the Loire and Cher west of Tours, very nicely converted to offer extremely comfortable chambre d'hôtes rooms. Pool in the back garden (*table d'hôtes possible*).

Savonnières ✉ 37510
Prieuré des Granges B&B, t 02 47 50 09 67, **f** 02 47 50 06 43, *salmon.eric@wanadoo.fr* (*moderate*). Very nice, private rooms and a pool.

Villandry ✉ 37510
Domaine de la Giraudière, t 02 47 50 08 60. For the ultimate goat meal experience, head southwards out of Villandry towards Druye to this goat farm.

Bréhémont ✉ 37130
Le Castel de Bray et Monts, t 02 47 96 70 47, **f 02 47 96 57 36, *cooking-class-infrance@wanadoo.fr* (*moderate*). A discreetly charming hotel set in a typical wealthy Loire house from the 18th century. There are spacious grounds and a tennis court. It's a lovely place to try Loire fish and other specialities (*menus €19–42*).
La Clé d'Or, t 02 47 96 70 26, **f** 02 47 96 73 13 (*inexpensive*). Totally unpretentious, clean and recently restored, a bargain hotel

on the way from Touraine's capital to the château. Savonnières to the east of Villandry, and Bréhémont to the west, count among the most gorgeous villages in western Touraine.

The last stretch of the Indre river from Montbazon south of Tours to the Loire is packed with fairytale châteaux. The most famous are the romantic Azay-le-Rideau and Ussé, but others have strong stories to attract you: the Château de Candé, where the Duke and Duchess of Windsor got married, and the Château de Saché, where that stupendous 19th-century Touraine writer Balzac wrote his greatest romance, *Le Lys dans la vallée*, are set along this section of the Indre with its many mills and castles.

To the Château de Villandry from Tours

The land between the Loire and the Cher west of Tours narrows into a thin, flat peninsula. It's a rarely explored, but wonderful spit of sandy land. There are no châteaux to visit, although these territories once formed part of the estates of the **Château de Plessis-lès-Tours**, the centre of King Louis XI's world, its sad remnants now swallowed up by the western outskirts of Tours.

A number of Italian visitors continue to visit the little chapel housing the tomb of St François de Paule near the Château de Plessis-lès-Tours. The great Italian hermit in a wonderful position close to the village church and the outsized Loire quays, with a brilliant little raised wooden terrace which allows you to eat almost on the Loire (*cheap menus*).

Monts ✉ 37260
L'Auberge du Moulin, Au Vieux Bourg, **t** 02 47 26 76 86. Traditional seasonal cooking in a pleasant modern interior (*menus c.€15–30*).

Azay-le-Rideau and La Chapelle-Ste-Blaise ✉ 37190
★★★Le Grand Monarque, 3 Place de la République, **t** 02 47 45 40 08, **f** 02 47 45 46 25 (*moderate*). Set in a former posting inn, offering good food and accommodation. Every day the restaurant serves a different regional dish (*menus €25–45*). *Hotel closed mid-Dec–Jan.*

★★Biencourt, 7 Rue Balzac, **t** 02 47 45 20 75, **f** 02 47 45 91 73 (*inexpensive*). Charming rooms divided between an 18th-century town house and a 19th-century school, with a patio. *Closed mid-Nov–Feb.*

★Le Balzac, 4–6 Rue Adélaïde Riché, **t** 02 47 45 42 08, **f** 02 47 45 29 87 (*inexpensive*). A

simpler, cheaper address in another old town house (*menus €10.5–21*). *Closed Mon out of season, and Jan.*

L'Aigle d'Or, 10 Av Adélaïde Riché, **t** 02 47 45 24 58. A good place to eat out in summer. Local Azay wines make it into some of the sauces (*menus €16–38*).

Les Grottes, 23 ter Rue Pineau, **t** 02 47 45 21 04. Atmospheric troglodyte restaurant which also has a walled terrace where you can try the refined cuisine in summer (*menus €15–30.5*).

Manoir de la Rémonière B&B, La Chapelle-Ste-Blaise, **t** 02 47 45 24 88, **f** 02 47 45 45 69 (*expensive*). A joy for fishermen as it borders a good stretch of the Indre; a renovated 15th-century manor with a handful of high-standard rooms. There's a pool in the grounds.

Saché ✉ 37190
Auberge du XIIe Siècle, Rue Principale, **t** 02 47 26 88 77, **f** 02 47 26 88 77. Splendid old beamed house, a very inviting place with its great fireplace. The chef is inventive rather than rooted in tradition, despite the ancient setting (*menus €21–53*).

and spiritual leader came to Louis XI's bedside in 1483, called upon by the king as he lay dying in his château. François de Paule stayed on to offer spiritual guidance to several French royal figures, as well as establishing the Ordre des Minimes in France at Plessis-lès-Tours. He died here in 1507.

Continue on the D88 road along the **south bank of the Loire**. From the quiet, patched-up levee road raised along here you get an excellent chance to observe the Loire flowing by. The river looks at its most typical along this stretch, the sandbanks and different varieties of trees easy to observe. Instead of encountering thundering traffic, as you do on the Loire's north bank opposite, you may meet men going out fishing or, in season, hunting, or farmers picking their asparagus.

The Loire and the Cher then converge and you can turn back in the direction of Tours' southern suburbs, now following the **north bank of the Cher**. The first bridge you come to following this itinerary takes you over to the very pretty riverside village of **Savonnières**, its church covered with typical Romanesque carvings.

The road west from Savonnières leads to the **Grottes Pétrifiantes** (*open April–Sept daily 9–7, early Feb–March and Oct–mid-Dec Fri–Wed 9.30–12 and 2–6*). The streams trickling through the former stone quarries are particularly rich in limestone, which will quickly coat objects left in the water. The sparkling sugary look is definitely an acquired taste, which you can take or leave in the shop, but the tour of the caves is quite amusing.

Château de Villandry

Château open July–Aug 9–6.30, April–June and Sept–mid-Oct 9–6, Feb 9.30–5, March 9–5.30, mid-Oct–mid-Nov 9–5. Garden open May–mid-Sept 9–7.30, April and mid-Sept–mid-Oct 9–7, March 9–6, rest of year 9–5.30.

Vegetables are transformed into art at the Château de Villandry. They're the enticing main attraction of the place. But in truth it isn't simply the vegetables, but also the complex geometrical and symbolic calculation of the whole ensemble of gardens that create a sense of wonder and delight. The château itself shouldn't be overlooked, a fine piece of French Renaissance architecture.

Villandry's Gardens

Villandry's gardens only date from the start of the 20th century, but they follow the spirit of formal Renaissance design. They were conceived by a Spanish-American couple, Dr Joachim Carvallo and Anne Coleman (the latter from Pennsylvania), who bought Villandry in 1906. The late 16th-century bird's-eye plans of noble French estates made by Du Cerceau in his *Les Plus Excellents Bastiments de France* served as a particular source of inspiration. These showed clearly the almost architectural qualities of the gardens at that time, concentrating on carefully constructed patterns. This formal French style had developed out of two traditions: the French medieval monastic garden and the Italian noble estate, ideas on the latter brought over by the likes of Dom Pacello da Mercogliano, one of the gifted Italians to come back with Charles VII from the latter's daredevil adventure there at the close of the 15th century. However, several important elements in Villandry's gardens date from the 18th century, such as the formal pools used for irrigation.

The gardens are laid out on various levels. The famous **potager**, or vegetable garden, on the lowest level, must surely be the most enviable kitchen garden in the world. Flowers and fruit trees have for once to bow to the beauty of the beet, the charm of the comely cabbages, the perfection of the peppers. Some of the vegetable visions at Villandry are unforgettable: a dense bed of leeks sprouting among rose bushes, or an intense crowd of celery against a backdrop of pruned pear trees. Of course the range of vegetables and colours on show depends on the season, but apart from in winter there's almost always a dense and colourful patterning of plants to admire.

An hilarious little booklet, *The Gardens of Villandry – Techniques and Plants*, will give you some understanding of the seven gardeners' tasks through the year. It also relates some wonderful, sometimes absurd little tales told in a comically poor translation which sometimes descends into gibberish. The sinister solanine-poisoned aubergine 'is, in a manner of speaking, the loose, smooth-thighed woman of the plant world... A Turkish legend refers to it as being responsible for the constant fainting of one of their imams when he ate it in the presence of his naked concubines.' The carrot is 'inclining towards the phallic inwardness of its root, its regenerative power, source and channel of the active principle of the seed. In this it is the reverse of the standing stone (a reversed acupuncture of the soil)...

The Gaulois made it their national plant.' On the cabbage, the booklet will inform you that: 'The bundled bouquet that it resembles in maturity is the very image of a group united in collective action with the same thought in mind... However, the cabbage is also associated with the concept of self-centred egotism because of its high sulphur content...cabbage makes the intestinal functions regular. Cato the Censor said that, because of cabbages, the Romans were able to do without doctors for more than ten centuries.' The most extraordinary revelation in the booklet is as to why so many Greek philosophers forbad the eating of broad beans: 'According to Pliny, the broad bean contains the souls of the dead. This is why the interdictions of Orpheus and Pythagoras stated that to eat broad beans was the equivalent of sharing the food of the dead.'

The little booklet also tackles the small *jardin des simples*, or **medicinal herb garden**, on the next level up from the *potager*.

On the opposite side of the vegetable gardens, below the hillside, you come to the **ornamental gardens**. Here, box hedges have been carefully cut into splendid symbols of the different forms of chivalric love. You'll need to climb up past the *jardin d'eau*, or **water garden**, swans gliding on the mirrored pools, to get a good view down onto the chivalric designs. Tender love is reassuringly represented by complete hearts encasing the romantic allusions of a masked ball. Fickle love takes the form of fans, objects of dissimulation, interspersed with the horns of the cuckold, while the love letters remind of the potential deception of words and a lover's absence. Daggers and swords evoke the duels of tragic love, red flowers symbolising spilt blood. In the last square, the hearts have been broken by the disruptive dance of mad, passionate love. To the left of these four interpretations of love, various crosses and fleurs-de-lys have been cut out in further box hedges. Beyond, you can make out musical topiary, with stylized lyres, harps, notes, and even candelabra to light the sheet music. The whole thing is quite magical.

The Château

A château already stood here in the 12th century. It was at the medieval Villandry, on 4 July 1189, that Henri Plantagenêt, alias Henry II of England, signed a peace with the French Capetian King Philippe Auguste, with whom Henri's own son Richard the Lionheart had entered into an alliance. Philippe Auguste gained the Berry and the Auvergne through this treaty. It went down in history as the Paix de Colombiers, as Villandry was then known. King Henry died two days later in Chinon, and was buried at the abbey of Fontevraud in Anjou close by.

In the 16th century, Jean le Breton, a minister of King François I, used the remains of the medieval castle to start off his Renaissance château. Its three wings were set on the slightly irregular base inherited from the previous fort, with a water-filled moat on a couple of sides, while the southwest tower was actually left from the earlier castle. A close friend of the king, Le Breton shared time in captivity with the monarch in Spain, and afterwards was given charge of the construction of Chambord. Near that monster in the Blésois he built a delightful little château for himself, Villesavin (*see* pp.168–70). While Villesavin is charming, Villandry is much more glamorous. Villandry went up through the 1530s, and its architecture displays many of the features of the elegant new Renaissance style derived from Italy – regular window openings, these windows framed by pilasters, strong horizontal bands dividing up the façades, elegant colonnades on the ground floor. Certain French tastes remain evident, such as the splendid array of Loire *lucarnes* in the slate roofs – one carries Le Breton's arms.

Descendants of Le Breton held on to the château until the 1750s, when it fell into the hands of the Castellane family. French nobles of the neoclassical period frequently wanted to modernize Renaissance châteaux. The new marquis decided on numerous changes, including changing the windows, embellishing the oldest tower, filling in the moat and adding neoclassical outbuildings. The latter still exist, but when Dr Carvallo bought the place, he set about restoring many of the original Renaissance features. You cross the watery moats that Carvallo reopened to come into the enchanting cobbled courtyard of the *cour d'honneur* for a tour of the interiors.

Inside, first you might watch the slide show presenting the gardens through the four seasons. Many of the rooms that follow were remodelled during the 18th century for the Castellane family. Two other striking features characterize the interiors: instead of freshly cut flowers, there are beautiful displays of vegetables in bowls; and Spanish art is very much in evidence, brought in by the Carvallos. Several disturbing works from the school of Goya count among this Spanish collection. In the Petit Salon, the *Décapité pendu par les cheveux* is a disturbing reminder of the terrible massacres by the French army of Spanish civilians in 1807.

The Grand Salon looks as though the *châtelains* have just left it before you. Two typical Spanish 17th-century still lifes stand out here, as does the *Temptation of St-Anthony* by the school of Tintoretto. The portrait of *Isabella de Bourbon* is interesting in terms of French royal genealogy, as this daughter of King Henri IV and Marie de' Medici married Philip IV of Spain, giving birth to Marie-Thérèse, future wife of Louis XIV. In the Salle à Manger, the Castellanes added a touch from their native Provence with the cooling fountain.

Further interesting Spanish works adorn the staircase and the first floor. The gallery is given over to temporary exhibitions and leads to a curious room with a Moorish ceiling, taken from a 13th-century Spanish mosque.

Climb the tower, with its exhibition of old photos of Villandry revealing just how much the Carvallos changed the place. From the top you get splendid views down on to the five hectares of château gardens and right across to the north bank of the Loire.

West of Villandry, turn at Le Moulinet to follow the wonderful Loire riverside road, a beautiful route little-known to most tourists. The village of **Bréhémont**, with its great quays, makes a magical sight. The 19th-century church seems ready to slip into the river for a bathe. You can continue along this delightful little Loire-side road to reach the Château d'Ussé (*see* pp.331–3).

Along the Indre from the Château de Candé to the Château de Saché

To join this section of the Indre, head towards Montbazon, due south of Tours along the N10, turning west off onto D87 a little north of Montbazon to reach the Château de Candé.

Château de Candé

Open June–mid-Sept weekends only, for guided tours only, leaving at 1.30.
To book, contact the Service des Monuments du Conseil Régional,
t 02 47 31 43 27.

Wallis Simpson's 28 pieces of luggage containing 66 dresses (among other things) arrived a few weeks after she did at the Château de Candé in May 1937. She had come here to be married for the third time, to the man who had abdicated as King Edward VIII of Britain the year before because of his love for her. The wedding of the Duke and Duchess of Windsor, as they became known, took place at the Château de Candé on 3 June 1937. The property served as the backdrop in the famous photographs of what many called the marriage of the 20th century.

This was the high point in the Château de Candé's history. Otherwise the story of the castle is a fairly modest one, even if St Martin, the great evangelizing bishop of Tours in the Dark Ages, is supposed to have wandered this way converting the local peasants. A first fortification was built in the 10th century on this high spot overlooking the Indre valley. The name Candé derives from an old word for a confluence, the St-Laurent stream joining the Indre at this point. The medieval lords of Candé were vassals of the lords of Montbazon close by.

In 1499, François Briçonnet, a powerful courtier and one-time mayor of Tours, bought the property and transformed the fort into a charming country hunting pavilion. This new building was on quite a small scale by Touraine standards. Numerous families then owned the property, including, very briefly, a Huguenot Guillaume Bertrand, one of the many victims of the terrible St Bartholomew's Day massacres of Protestants of 1572. In the 18th century, a gunpowder-making factory was built by the Indre river below the castle, and still mars the valley. Several further proprietors owned the castle after the Revolution, until in the middle of the 19th century a flamboyant and very wealthy Cuban by the name of Drake del Castillo bought the property and decided to substantially enlarge the château. The Tours architect Jacques-Aimé Meffre drew up the plans, tripling the size of the place. It became a pastiche of a Loire Valley castle, but on an impressive scale. Drake's son Jacques served as a much-loved mayor of nearby Monts, but his son in turn sold the castle, this time to a Frenchman who had gone off to make his fortune in America.

Charles-Eugènes Bedaux made a mint with his model for labour efficiency in industry. He became a US citizen, although in the First World War he enlisted for foreign service. In 1927 he bought Candé and installed all manner of modern comforts that he had come to enjoy in America: efficient heating, luxurious bathrooms, the latest telephone systems. A wheeler-dealer on an international scale, he courted the powerful of all persuasions, including the likes of Citroën in France and, much more notoriously, Hitler and Mussolini in fascist Europe.

In the meantime, Edward, heir to the British throne, had met Wallis Simpson in 1931 and fallen under her charm. After his father died, he became King Edward VIII in January 1936. But his love for Wallis was too strong, and he decided that in order to marry her (she was a divorcee, and as head of the Church of England he was forbidden to marry her) he would abdicate. He had to leave Britain and the couple wanted to find a place in which to get married in France. They had recently met Bedaux, who suggested his castle. So arrangements were quickly made. Some sumptuous evenings were held here before the wedding, the chef Legros preparing dishes in the grand Ancien Régime style, the great organist Marcel Dupré playing for the guests. One sad moment came when the couple's favourite dog Slippy was bitten by an adder and died; the Duke of Windsor buried him in the grounds of Candé.

Bedaux made sure that the wedding day was carefully planned, and managed to arrange for the ceremony to take place at the château itself rather than at the local town hall, as is the normal legal requirement in France. Madame Bedaux roped in the locals to play their parts as servants and lackeys, dressed in elaborate uniforms. Tales of the event still thrill many of the nearby families involved. A certain number of press people attended, but many were thrown off the scent by heading for the Château de Candé in neighbouring Anjou. A priest from Britain defied the Archbishop of Canterbury's orders, and came and presided over the religious ceremony.

As you arrive for the short tour inside the château, you may recognize some of the architectural details from the celebrated wedding photos. Above the doorway, the ceramic scene represents St Martin dividing his cloak in two, somehow a symbol fraught with ambiguities with regards to the duke and duchess. Within, the look is predominantly neo-Gothic, with heavy wood panelling and big painted beams. Bedaux's library with its organ was where the wedding ceremony took place. The fireplace carries graffiti supposedly scratched into the wood by the duke and duchess to record their romantic day. You can also see a few other grand rooms, now used by the county council of Touraine. The council has owned the place since 1974, Madame Bedaux having left the château to the French state after her husband had killed himself in gaol awaiting trial on charges of collaborating with the Nazis. For the moment, the guided visit concentrates on a walk around the grounds, but there are plans for the council to develop the château as a more significant tourist centre, possibly opening more rooms and presenting a video on the famed Windsor wedding.

Keep to the north bank of the Indre beyond Monts to appreciate the beauty of the valley to the full along this stretch. Balzac sang its praises in one of his most famous novels, *Le Lys dans la vallée*. He portrayed it there as a '*vallée riante* (a laughing valley)', where '*la sensibilité coule à torrents* (sensitivity runs in torrents)'. While the Indre here offers an enchanting picture of bucolic delight, with its mills on the water and its châteaux on the slopes, the Balzac tale is a deadly white water rafting adventure of the emotions. You can learn more about Balzac at the Château de Saché, by a very pretty village just south of the Indre.

Saché and Villaines-les-Roches

The restful village of **Saché** has an amusing Alexander Calder sculpture. The American took to this area and one of Calder's metal mobile monsters incongruously surveys the old village square. Southwest of Saché the village of **Villaines-les-Rochers** had some wacky sculptures of its own too, made by local basket-weavers. The place

Balzac, Slave to Words

Balzac was by turns a saint, a criminal, an honest judge, a corrupt judge, a minister, a fop, a harlot, a duchess, and always a genius.
André Maurois in *Prometheus: The Life of Balzac*, 1966

His mother's infidelity led Honoré de Balzac to Saché. She had a liaison with the owner, Monsieur de Margonne, and a child by him, Balzac's half-brother Henri. Balzac was always very well received by De Margonne and came to stay here, seeking refuge to write and to avoid his creditors in more or less brief stays in the 1820s and 30s.

Honoré himself had been born along Tours' main street in 1799. His father, of peasant origin, managed to climb the social ladder to become a civil servant, got a post in Tours and married an 18 year old when he was 50. Balzac's mother was particularly fascinated by the occult, but not especially interested in her first son. He was sent off to boarding school and saw little of her. He took solace in literature from an early age. A large amount of childhood autobiographical detail creeps into the start of *Le Lys dans la vallée*.

The Balzacs moved to Paris in 1814. Honoré trained there to become a lawyer, but wished to be a writer. He deliberately avoided finding a job in the law and devoted himself to more imaginative word play, starting out with several pieces that he himself admitted were literary filth. The coarse Rabelais was a great influence on the exuberant young man. So too were several older women, guiding spirits-cum-lovers. One of his first important liaisons was with Laure de Berny, whose mother had served Marie Antoinette as a lady-in-waiting before her royal mistress got the chop.

Balzac embarked on a business venture in printing in the mid-1820s which soon ended in bankruptcy. He was left with huge debts, in particular to members of his family. But his writing rapidly began to earn him literary success. At the age of 30, *Les Chouans* brought him critical acclaim. From this time on a flood of novels poured from his pen; he is one of the most prolific writers in French letters. The advances on his books couldn't keep up with the debts he continued to accumulate, however, and that his life reads like a race to dash off more and more novels to meet deadlines and stem financial crises. Although this inevitably meant that his writing was rushed, he cared deeply for the detail. Just look at the extent of the corrections he made to his proofs, on display at Saché.

Between times Balzac carried on torrid love affairs and burning correspondences, in particular with 'L'Etrangère', as a mysterious correspondent from Eastern Europe signed herself in her first letter to him. It was the start of a passionate friendship. A Balzac enthusiast has calculated that the author's lifetime of letters to Mme Hanska add up to a quarter of the *Comédie Humaine*!

has a long tradition in this craft, with a cooperative, the Vannerie de Villaines, which dates back to 1849. This cooperative is well worth a visit as you can see how the basket-weavers handle the willow wicker. The shop has an excellent collection of wicker objects for sale. The village itself is typically Tourangeau and attractive, stretching along the narrow valley, caves dug into the rock.

This *Comédie Humaine* was Balzac's grandiose scheme, from the early 1830s, to make the bulk of his works into a coherent whole, giving a full picture of early 19th-century French society. The works in *La Comédie Humaine* bring to life almost 2,500 characters, the more important ones cropping up in several books, be it only in cameo parts or by reference.

Readers who enjoy Balzac do tend to get addicted to him, although there are several different styles to his writing. The *Contes drolatiques*, for example, are a collection of bawdy tales set in the Touraine, 'the chronicle of the old manors and abbeys of this region' as Henry James described them, inspired by Rabelais, but sub-Rabelaisian in seriousness, lacking the same substance. Balzac also wrote several books in which the supernatural plays an important role, such as *La Peau de Chagrin*, *Louis Lambert* and the daring *Séraphita*.

But Balzac is generally considered as a writer whose stories were rooted in 19th-century reality – to such an extent that in French editions of his works, the academics tend to put in a good number of footnotes explaining that such and such an event occurred in reality on this day in May, not that one given by Balzac. Balzac was interested in the broader issues behind different types and individuals and behind French society in his period. The breadth of his coverage is phenomenal. That giant of American literature, Henry James, summed it up when he wrote admiringly of him that 'Balzac, in the maturity of his vision, took in more human life than any one since Shakespeare.'

It's not a pretty picture that Balzac paints. France had just emerged shaken to the core and deeply scarred by the massive upheaval of the Revolution followed by the Napoleonic Empire. While Rabelais covers up the complexities and horrors of his 16th-century times beneath a thick surface of absurd humour, the barbs stick out of Balzac's works. His humour is ironic, cruel, pitiless. He kicks his characters when they're down, and in the world he creates, fate shows no pity for the weak. Time and again in his plots, those who are tender and emotionally vulnerable are punished and trampled on for their weakness.

Touraine appears as a prominent background in several of Balzac's works, most notably the *Contes drolatiques*, *Le Lys dans la vallée* and *Eugénie Grandet*, the last set just across in Saumur in Anjou. A fair number of his shorter stories also take place in Touraine, such as that of the persecuted Birotteau in *Le Curé de Tours*, or *La Grenadière*, named after a house which Balzac once rented for Mme de Berny.

Some say Balzac was killed by the coffee he drank in such quantities to keep him going, although the complications of gangrene seem a more plausible explanation of what, in 1850, put an end to this '*galérien de la plume et de l'encre* (galley slave of pen and ink)', as he once described himself.

Château de Saché and Musée Balzac

*Open July–Sept 10–6.30, mid-May–June 10–6, mid-March–mid-May
9.30–12.30 and 2–6, Feb–mid-March and Oct–Nov 9.30–12.30 and 2–5;
t 02 47 26 86 50.*

Behind the intriguing long walls of its estate, the Château de Saché proves a rough, rugged 16th-century manor rather than a pretty castle. What gives the house its fame is that Balzac stayed here frequently. In 1952 it was converted by the owner into a museum to commemorate Balzac, or as the guide puts it, 'to pay homage to his excesses'. It should be said that while the interiors and grounds are charming, those who aren't already experts on the rampant writer might appreciate some simplifying introduction (*see* box on preceding pages) before facing the mass of books and information on Balzac provided at the museum.

Although Balzac didn't spend substantial periods at Saché, they proved to be particularly productive times. This place provided an oasis of tranquillity in his storm of a life. He worked like a maniac, at the bizarrest of hours, often getting up between 2 and 5am and working through to 5pm. Coffee, toast, fruit and more coffee was his basic diet. He would occasionally come down to give a reading. The results were large portions of *Le Lys dans la vallée*, *César Birotteau* and *Le Père Goriot*. The house is full of memorabilia about the man and his works, not just focusing on what Balzac wrote at Saché, but also collecting items to give glimpses of his chequered life and loves and his multitude of other works, although giving special prominence to those incorporating recognizably local detail. Visitors who've worked in publishing may particularly appreciate Balzac's agonies over copy and be horrified by the number of amendments and additions he scribbled on in brown ink, sometimes on as many as nine sets of proofs! The museum also attempts to recreate the early 19th-century atmosphere which would have surrounded Balzac. Of course, adulatory pieces have been added, such as the bronze of the author by the Tourangeau sculptor Sicard and details of other memorials to him. On the top floor, Balzac's little guest bedroom has been done up as he might have known it. Caricatures of the literary giant and his characters help lighten the tone.

Château d'Azay-le-Rideau

*Open July–Aug 9.30–7, April–June and Sept–Oct 9.30–6, rest of year
9.30–12.30; t 02 47 45 42 04.*

...almost a rival of Chenonceaux
Henry James, *A Little Tour in France*, 1884

The beauty of Azay-le-Rideau's château reflected in its moat encourages extravagant comparisons. Balzac likened it to a 'diamond with is multiple facets set in the Indre'. Like that other supremely romantic image of the Loire, Chenonceau, Azay-le-Rideau is built on the water. Although the word Rideau (the French for curtain) in the name in fact refers back to the name of a medieval lord, a curtain of trees does separate the château fairly well from the delightful village outside.

The site by the Indre was important in medieval times as a crossing point over the river. An earlier construction was burnt to the ground on the orders of the future French King Charles VII who, passing through here in 1418, apparently took ruthless revenge on the Burgundian troops manning the place who insulted him. The town was known for a long time as Azay-le-Brûlé (the burnt).

The château you see now was started in 1518 for Gilles Berthelot, a treasurer of France for King François I. Only the large tower as you arrive in the courtyard is a throwback to the earlier medieval building. Gilles being so often away on business, his wife Philippe or Philippa, née Lesbahy, oversaw much of the work. The man in charge of the architecture appears to have been one Etienne Rousseau.

Azay is so often cited as the example par excellence of French Renaissance architecture, but in fact it dates from that transitional early 16th-century period during which Gothic elements lingered on. The pepper-pot towers, the walkway, the steepness of the roof, its finial tips, all give a Gothic twist to the whole. The Italian influence can be seen particularly in the move towards symmetry, in the pilaster-framed, standardized windows, and in many typical carved Italianate decorative details, such as medallions and candelabra. The famous staircase too was built in the Italian manner, with straight ramps allowing for a noble procession up as opposed to a cramped French stair tower.

The emblems of the salamander and the ermine on the building pay tribute to the royal couple François I and Claude de France. This is somewhat ironic, as building work wasn't entirely completed in 1527 when Berthelot had to flee to avoid being caught up in the financial scandal caused by the inculpation of his cousin by marriage, Jacques de Beaune-Semblançay, François I's treasurer. (Semblançay was later cleared of the charge, but it came rather late, as he had already lost his head.) François I grasped Berthelot's possessions and so yet another Loire château fell under his control. He handed it to his captain of the guards, Antoine Raffin. A number of refinements would only be made as late as the 19th century. Standing in the courtyard, the ensemble still may not feel quite complete to you. Unusually, there are only two wings to the château, in an L-shape. A third wing may have been planned originally.

Before going inside, it's worth wandering round the château to enjoy the splendid view of it across the Indre. The château isn't reflected in this river moat at all times of the year. Sometimes the water is too fast-flowing, at others it may be covered with plant life, but when the calm mirror of the water does reflect its form, it makes a delightful sight, elegant, light and sparkling. While the traditional dried-blood colour of the top floor shutters does jar slightly, the chimneys in brick, stone and slate give an elegant finishing touch to the château's exterior.

Within, the rooms are somewhat empty and unexciting, but you start the visit down in the kitchen, which has some hilarious Gothic touches in the culs-de-lampe, a dog chewing on a bone, a man mooning at visitors. After that it's the usual round of tapestries, chests and, generally speaking, bad copies of paintings. A few 16th-century royal and noble portraits are the exception. The tapestries are particularly atmospheric in the Grande Salle, bathed in shimmering reflected light on sunny days.

You can wander round the gardens, which in the past few years have been used as the setting for an idiosyncratic *son-et-lumière* show, **Les Imaginaires d'Azay-le-Rideau**, where visitors walk round to see and experience the effects at their own pace (*daily June–Sept, plus Ascension and Whitsun weekends; contact the château, t 02 47 45 42 04, or the tourist office for further details*).

Leaving the château through the elegant 17th-century outbuildings with their gilded tops, it's only a short walk to the village **church of Saint-Symphorien** with its extraordinary Romanesque façade. Three sets of diminutive statues stand in niches like worn stone dolls. No one knows exactly when these figures were made or whether they were meant to be part of this church. Around them, crisscrossed and diagonal stonework adds to the curiosity of the church front.

Azay-le-Rideau to Rigny-Ussé

After Azay-le-Rideau, the Indre draws closer and closer to the Loire. A few curiosities stand out between Azay-le-Rideau and Ussé. After passing the splendid private Château de l'Islette on the Indre, look out for signs to the **Château de la Chatonnière**, much more discreetly hidden at the bottom of its own little valley. This intimate castle presents an enviable picture of Touraine comfort. A half-dozen small, charming themed gardens have recently been created around it. While you can't enter the defensive walled building itself, wandering around the sloping gardens you can enjoy prying on the castle and its enclosed courtyard below.

At **Marnay**, the Musée Maurice Dufresne (*open March–Nov 9.15–6, rest of year 9.15–5*) contains a massive collection of old agricultural machines and the tools of many other trades (including a guillotine for your professional executioner). The place reflects the passion of a zany collector. All the pieces are immaculately presented in massive buildings on an estate with a mill on the Indre. At **Rivarennes**, the Musée de la Poire Tapée (*open June–Aug 3–6*) revives the traditional craft of pear-drying and bashing – the British Navy used to be a customer for this practical, nutritious food.

Château d'Ussé at Rigny-Ussé

Open July–Aug 9–6.30, Easter–mid-June and first 3 weeks of Sept 9–12 and 2–6.45, mid-Feb–Easter and end Sept–11 Nov 10–12 and 2–5.30; t 02 47 95 54 05.

To the French, the Château d'Ussé is a symbol of romance. This is the castle said to have inspired the tale of Sleeping Beauty. The picture-book château nestles on the wooded bank of the Indre leading up to the forest of Chinon. The architecture combines a series of elements from different periods. Any trace of the Viking Gelduin I, who settled here in Foulques Nerra's time, has disappeared. So too has the 12th-century fortress that then went up. The De Bueil family, supporters of kings Charles VII and Louis XI in the second half of the 15th century, ordered a third construction. The substantial southwest tower is the oldest part. The south wing and some of the west wing had gone up by the time the château was sold to Jacques d'Espinay, servant of Louis XII. By the 1520s the D'Espinay family had completed the east, west and north wings, some Italianate details creeping into the overall Gothic design. In the course of the 17th century, the Marquis de Valentinay ordered profound changes, especially adding to the lightness of the interiors. Off came the north wing, while the south wing was given much more generous windows. A whole new section to the west brought a completely different style into the picture, without towers. The slope down to the water was beautifully transformed into formal terraces, where oranges trees were shipped in to add an exotic touch. The garden terraces are still immaculately manicured.

One story links the Château d'Ussé with Sleeping Beauty. This tale of the writing of *Sleeping Beauty* goes that Charles Perrault, the 17th-century author of the romance, stopped in this area on his way back to Paris and was offered hospitality by the count of Saumur. Put up in the château, Perrault was moved to pen notes here for this most famous of children's (and castles') fairytales. If you can't remember the story exactly, before the tour of the apartments you can try to piece it together from the scenes recreated with waxwork models at the top of the greatest of the château's towers. They seem to be quite out of sequence. As this version would have it, the princess is first revived and rescued by a handsome prince from her century of sleep, even before the evil witch has had time to cast her spell on her or the princess to prick her finger on an old woman's spinning wheel. To leave your head reeling further, walk around the towers' *chemin de ronde* (outside walkway), which looks rather daunting, with chunks of stone missing, although these gaps do provide splendid views over the village of Rigny-Ussé.

Before the guided tour inside the castle, you can also visit the separate chapel. This is a gem of early French Renaissance building. High relief carvings of the Apostles in medallions frame the entrance. Worn memento mori add to the effect, only slightly spoilt by some unfortunate graffiti. The interlaced initials C and L refer to the couple for whom the chapel was built, Charles d'Espinay and Lucrèce de Pons. The interior has an almost marble-like whiteness. Nuns, men with a barrel, and a reptilean man with a beaded backbone count among the fine carvings on the pews, said to have come from Jean Goujon's atelier. The beautifully sweet faïence Virgin was produced by the Italian Della Robbia family.

Two impressive great cedars of Lebanon stand next to the many towers and turrets of the château itself. They were a gift from the Romantic writer René de Chateaubriand to the owner of Ussé in his day, the Duchesse de Duras. Inside the castle, the Duchesse de Duras' daughter contributed her own modifications to the many 17th-century alterations made for the Marquis de Valentinay. A pot-pourri of styles and objects fills the rooms, reflecting the changing tastes and increasingly exotic travels of the line of Ussé's aristocratic owners. The costumes on the waxwork models in several of the rooms change periodically, adding to the historical confusion. Extravagant trompe-l'oeil false marble painting covers the ceiling of the Salle des Gardes, with its collection of arms and Oriental pieces brought back in the 19th century by Count Stanislas de Blacas, ancestor of the present owner.

In what was the original chapel, among the 16th-century Flemish tapestries and the Ancien Régime furniture, lie mementoes of French Romanticism, including a portrait of Chateaubriand, the greatest of French Romantic writers. His friend the Duchesse de Duras was a novelist herself, her works *Edouard* and *Ourika* little known now, despite her award from Louis XVIII of a Sèvres vase depicting a scene from one of the novels. Such was the intensity of the duchess's and Chateaubriand's relationship that when she heard of his death abroad she had all the clocks in the château stopped. Secret passageways dug into the rock disappear off from the kitchen. One tapestry hides a passageway. A great series of further tapestries adorns the long gallery. These fine 18th-century Flemish works were made after cartoons by David Teniers, and ironically depict peasant scenes. The architecture of the grand staircase is all refinement, planned by François Mansart, the most illustrious French architect of the first half of the 17th century. The little steps were made taking into consideration the great big clumsy dresses that were the fashion for ladies back then. The vast mudguard postilion boots make a comic contrast.

On the tour inside, the best is saved until last. During Louis XIV's reign, leading aristocrats had to decorate one room of their château in sumptuous style in case of a visit from the king. Ussé's Chambre du Roi has been splendidly rejuvenated recently, with new gold-leaf detailing and rich reds framing exquisite pieces of furniture such as the Boulle bureau in red tortoiseshell and copper. Royal portraits of Louis XIV and of Mademoiselle de Blois, Princesse de Conti, the daughter of the Sun King and Louise de la Vallière, add to the wealth of the room. Unfortunately the king never came.

The Pays du Véron

West of Ussé you come into the Pays du Véron, as the arrowhead of land between the Loire and the Vienne is known. It's a curious spit, with sandy terrain and pine landscapes which at times make you think you might be approaching the coast. Typically pretty old Touraine houses embellish the vine-growing countryside. But the clouds of the nuclear power station above Avoine (yes, you can visit it) on the Loire hang over the place, somewhat spoiling the tranquillity of the picture. The little town of **Avoine** has grown mighty rich on the money that the French government has poured into it to sweeten the pill against nuclear fear and the place has sporting facilities worthy of a large town – such is the subtlety of French government bribery to persuade workers of the joys of nuclear power. The vines of Chinon extend this far.

The Manse, Vienne and Veude Valleys between Ste-Maure and Chinon

The Vienne river enters Touraine south of Ste-Maure on its plateau. The name of Ste-Maure is synonymous for French people with goat's cheese, the town's main claim to fame. West of Ste-Maure, the Manse valley is a well-kept secret, offering a

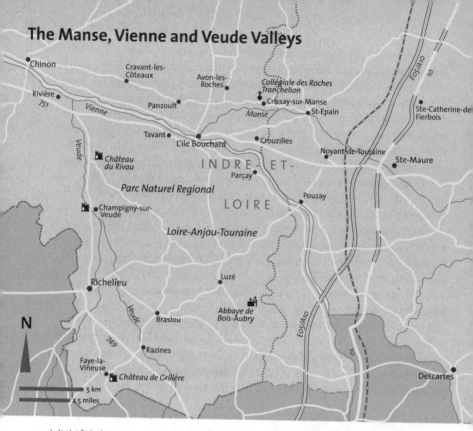

The Manse, Vienne and Veude Valleys

Chinon
Cravant-les-Côteaux
Avon-les-Roches
Collégiale des Roches Tranchelion
Ste-Catherine-de-Fierbois
Rivière
751
Vienne
Panzoult
Crissay-sur-Manse
St-Epain
Manse
Tavant
L'Ile Bouchard
Crouzilles
Noyant-de-Touraine
Ste-Maure
Château du Rivau
INDRE-ET-
Parçay
Veude
Parc Naturel Regional
LOIRE
Pouzay
Champigny-sur-Veude
Loire-Anjou-Touraine
N
Richelieu
Luzé
Veude
Braslou
Abbaye de Bois-Aubry
EOS/A10
749
Razines
Faye-la-Vineuse
Château de Grillère
Descartes
5 km
2.5 miles

delightful alternative route to Chinon from the better-known Vienne valley. The Vienne's banks are so dotted with Romanesque churches that you have to conclude that this area was much more popular and populated in medieval times than now. Vines appear on the gentle Vienne valley slopes as you approach Chinon.

South of the river and the great Plantagenet town, you can follow the Veude and Mable valleys further south for a detour past some startling castles to the model 17th-century town of Richelieu. The whole area covered in this section is well worth discovering.

Ste-Maure-de-Touraine

Ste-Maure simply means **goat's cheese** to your average Frenchman; the long cylindrical type with a piece of straw sticking through the middle, so highly regarded that it's been awarded its own *appellation d'origine contrôlée* status to protect its exclusivity. What remains of the 14th- and 15th-century château in town has been converted into a local museum, the **Musée de la Ville** (*open April–mid-Sept 10–11.30 and 2.30–5.15*), which sings the praises of the cheese (tasting included, of course), as well as presenting local history and ways. Perhaps the greatest attraction of the town is the Friday morning market, the place to buy the local speciality. The market spreads over two squares divided by the splendid **Halles**, or covered market, built in 1672 for the powerful Rohan family, the latter's coat of arms visible over a couple of the entrances. You might also like to visit the vast 11th–12th-century crypts under the church, but they're only open on Thursday mornings.

Ste-Catherine-de-Fierbois

A few kilometres north of Ste-Maure, Ste-Catherine-de-Fierbois is the village famed for providing Joan of Arc with her sword. Her trusted weapon with its five crosses came from here, as she herself said in her trial. A legend which pleased French nationalists who took Joan as their symbol was that this was the sword of Charles Martel, the 8th-century king who so significantly in French history beat the Moors on a site between Tours and Poitiers in 732, putting a stop to the Arabs' great northern advance. Some maintain that the battle took place on the plateau of Ste-Maure. Legend has it that a chapel to Catherine of Alexandria stood in a forest clearing in the vicinity and that Charles Martel gave his sword to the saint in thanks for his great victory.

Ste-Catherine certainly lay on a pilgrims' route from Chartres to Santiago de Compostela. Before Joan's day, a blind paralytic who visited the dilapidated chapel in 1375 was cured here and had the place restored by way of thanks. Apparently, a tradition then arose for passing knights to leave a sword in the chapel in thanksgiving to St Catherine. This could explain the presence of a spare sword lying in the chapel when Joan came by. The lord Boucicault payed for the creation of a hospice to St James here in 1415 and this is where Joan stayed nearing the end of her journey from Lorraine to seek out the Dauphin Charles at Chinon. The present **church** was built

Getting Around

There's an A10 motorway exit at Ste-Maure. Coming by **bus** from Tours, two lines serve the area; one goes to Ste-Maure and Ste-Catherine, the other, very limited indeed, goes through St-Epain, Crouzilles, l'Ile Bouchard, Champigny and Richelieu.

Tourist Information

Ste-Maure-de-Touraine: Rue du Château, 37800 Ste-Maure-de-Touraine, t 02 47 65 66 20, f 02 47 34 04 28.
Ste-Catherine-de-Fierbois: Mairie, 37800 Ste-Catherine-de-Fierbois, t 02 47 65 43 46.
St-Epain: Maison de Pays d'Accueil, 33 Grande-Rue, 37800 St-Epain, t 02 47 65 84 63.
Richelieu: 6 Grande Rue, 37120 Richelieu, t 02 47 58 13 62 or 02 47 58 10 13, f 02 47 58 29 86, *otsi.richelieu@wanadoo.fr*.

Market Day

Ste-Maure-de-Touraine: Friday morning.

Where to Stay and Eat

Ste-Maure-de-Touraine ✉ 37800
***Les Hauts de Ste-Maure**, 2 Avenue Charles de Gaulle, t 02 47 65 50 65, f 02 47 65 60 24, *saintemaure@chateauxhotels.com*, *www.chateauxhotels.com/saintemaure* (*moderate*). The town's 16th-century posting inn, with comfortable rooms with beams and old furniture, traditional French fare served in the restaurant, a shady garden with a heated pool, and a collection of old cars (*menus €16.5–38*).

Noyant-de-Touraine ✉ 37800
***Château de Brou**, t 02 47 65 80 80, f 02 47 65 82 92, *brou@chateauxhotels.com*, *www.chateauxhotels.com/brou* (*expensive*). A 15th-century castle with a full range of turrets set on a large estate west of Ste-Maure towards the Vienne.
La Ciboulette, 78 Route de Chinon, t 02 47 65 84 64, f 02 47 65 89 29 (*menus c.€15–45.5*). May be rather close to the motorway, but it

after her rehabilitation in the 1450s by order of Hélie de Bourdeilles, the Franciscan whom Charles VII appointed to re-examine her condemnation for heresy so long after her death. The village also has a **Musée de Traditions Populaires** full of local bric-a-brac (*open mid-June–mid-Sept Mon, Tues Thurs and Fri 10.30–12.30 and 4.30–6.30; Wed and Sat 10.30–12.30*).

The Manse Valley

The Manse valley west of Ste-Maure makes for a memorable little half-day trip. **St-Epain**, with its collection of 15th- and 16th-century houses and earlier medieval church, this one with Angevin vaults and 16th-century misericordes, sets the tone. The Maison du Pays sells regional produce from one of the fine houses. The next stop, **Crissay-sur-Manse**, gently descends the valley slope. An early medieval keep and a church spire topped by a Renaissance dome stick out above another fine collection of 15th- and 16th-century houses with mullion windows, rounded stair towers and old wells. Most of the church dates from the 15th century, and has Flamboyant Gothic decoration. It was built for a member of the powerful local family, the Turpin-de-Crissé, lords here from 1120 to 1632. Lancelot and Antoine Turpin, both of whom served as royal chamberlains, erected the château in the 15th century. Vestiges remain, including some of the dependencies built into the rock. The whole village is lovingly cared for. Art exhibitions, antiques displays and a theatre company bring life to this little place in summer.

has a terrace which gives onto vines and the forest and serves tasty Loire specialities.

Pouzay ✉ 37800
Le Gardon Frit, t 02 47 65 21 81. Close to a bridge over the Vienne, well known for its fish and seafood dishes (*menus c.€10.5–27.5*).

L'Ile-Bouchard ✉ 37220
Auberge de l'Ile, 3 Place Bouchard, t 02 47 58 51 07. Bathing in the Vienne, a restaurant done up in elaborate Louis XVI style. The cuisine is refined (*menus c.€15–45.5*).

Panzoult ✉ 37220
Domaine de Beauséjour B&B, t 02 47 58 64 64, f 02 47 95 27 13 (*moderate*). Rooms in a lovely winemakers' property on a hillside covered with vines. The rooms are charming and there's a pool you can use.

Cravant-les-Coteaux ✉ 37500
Le Domaine de Pallus B&B, t 02 47 93 08 94, f 02 47 98 43 00 (*moderate*). A very refined address. The rooms, which are stylishly

decorated, have melting vineyard views and there's a swimming pool in the garden.

Champigny-sur-Veude ✉ 37120
Domaine de la Pataudière B&B, t 02 47 58 12 15 (*inexpensive*). Your hosts can offer an afternoon's introduction to truffle hunting in winter, otherwise simply a pleasant rural retreat.

Richelieu ✉ 37120
La Maison B&B, 6 Rue Henri Proust, t/f 02 47 58 29 40 (*moderate*). Very smart early 19th-century town house with a lovely garden.
Madame Leplâtre's B&B, 1 Rue Jarry, t 02 47 58 10 42. Another town house with a garden, and the owner can tell you a lot about the history of Richelieu.

Razines ✉ 37120
Château de Chargé B&B, t 02 47 95 60 57, f 02 47 94 67 25 (*moderate*). Once the country château of the governors of Chinon and Richelieu, now with three splendid *chambre d'hôtes* rooms and a pool.

Take a very small detour from here to see the **Collégiale des Roches Tranchelion**, a dramatically perched and picturesque ruin of a church, originally built at the start of the 16th century, as is clear from the predominantly Renaissance features of the entrance façade, although a statue of the Holy Father as a blessing bishop seated on high shows Gothic influence. Very much in a state of romantic abandonment, the skeletal remains of the choir vault cast black shadows in the sunshine, which may bring out guardian hornets. The château that once stood here has all but disappeared. However, in 1449 King Charles VII and his councillors met here and decided on a further campaign against the English which would lead to the final French victory in the Hundred Years' War. The name of Tranchelion apparently refers back to a cruel crusading legend, the local lord supposedly returning from the Holy Land with a lion to whom he served serfs who displeased him. Continue on to the next village, **Avon-les-Roches**, its village church embellished with ornate Romanesque portals.

Leaving the Manse, which heads down to join the Vienne, and following the D21 through Panzoult to Cravant-les-Coteaux you enter utterly enchanting vine territory. This is arguably the prettiest wine route in Touraine. In **Cravant**'s Vieux Bourg, the disused church with its remarkable chequerboard exterior decorations said to date back to Carolingian times, has been converted into a Musée Lapidaire (*open 9–12 and 1.30–7*; **t** *02 47 93 12 40*), a curious little thing. Among the fragments of sculpture inside, a collection of old carved pillars stand out. Charles VII's favourite, George de la Trémoille, added on a southern side chapel in which he is represented with his daughters kneeling in prayer to the Virgin, the period fashion in evidence. From Cravant, vines accompany you to Chinon's outskirts.

The Vienne Valley Through Touraine

Parçay has one of a whole string of charming Romanesque churches along the Vienne river banks as it arrives in Touraine, this one rich in sculpture inside and out and reflecting the strong influence of the Poitou region on the valley.

The island which gives the small town of **L'Ile-Bouchard** its name proves slightly disappointing. It could be charming, with many weeping willows lining the riverside, but the bald square where a château once stood isn't pretty. However, on the south side of the river, the truncated priory church of St-Léonard comes as a delightful surprise. Only the choir end has survived through time. Its ambulatory, with its wings and its little roof, looks like a diminutive semicircular theatre. The columns are decorated with superb Romanesque carvings of New Testament stories. The wave-like long hair and finger-pointing of the human characters is typical of mid 12th-century carving, executed with a feeling for drama. The church of St-Maurice, also south of the river, is a much more substantial affair, standing out with its hexagonal belfry and spire dating from 1480. Although St-Gilles, on the north bank, is the oldest church in town, thought to date from the late 10th century possibly, the stone of its vegetal decorated entrance eaten away, the interior presents a naff 19th-century restoration.

Close to L'Ile-Bouchard, the village of **Tavant** is reputed for an extraordinary Romanesque fresco cycle in the crypt of the **church of St-Nicolas** (*open by appointment only March–Nov Wed–Mon 10–12 and 2.30–6; t 02 47 58 58 06 in advance*). The church doesn't look particularly impressive from the outside, nor is its site very remarkable. And you enter via the cemetery. However, the frescoes in the crypt are outstanding. They may lie buried in a restricted little columned coffer of a space, but the figures spring full of life from the walls.

Art historians have waxed lyrical about these paintings, which are considered by many to be the most refined frescoes of Romanesque Europe. Instead of the normally rather static poses of Romanesque art, here the highly expressive gestures of outstretched arms and hands and the curves of many of the bodies convey great movement. It's as though characters in a medieval passion play had been caught in their poses. The chronology of the stories moves from Old Testament scenes in the west to New Testament ones in the east, but the variety of people represented between the scenes breaks up any notion of a coherent narrative. Several typical medieval characters feature: a knight in armour who fights with a devil; a pilgrim; and a woman piercing her own breast, one of the Middle Ages's most favoured and most disturbing visions of sin, Luxuria or lust. These were the kind of visual images which you can well imagine kept the medieval mind in fear of Christian teaching and morality, and their powerful expressions may well remain with you.

The frescoes in the church above, which include a Christ in Majesty (occupying the apse dome as was the tradition in Romanesque churches) and pieces from the New Testament, are later than the work down below.

St-Nicolas was one of two churches built in the village, both attached to the powerful abbey of Marmoutier near Tours. St-Nicolas was the parish church, while **Ste-Marie** served the priory. Ste-Marie was built earlier than 12th-century St-Nicolas, from around 1070. It hasn't been neglected so much as swallowed up by village houses, along with vestiges of other priory buildings. Virtually all its sculptural decoration has been stripped away, the portals sold to an American woman in 1927. The belfry was rebuilt in the 15th century, with one of two carved 11th-century stone slabs incorporated into the building, which once went down to the river.

Rivière is a another sweet, tranquil spot along the Vienne. Head down to the water's edge in summer and you may well see locals fishing from their traditional brightly coloured little boats. Wander round the outside of the Romanesque church of Notre-Dame to appreciate its 11th-century exterior decoration, including its chequerboard work and bas-reliefs. Within, you'll be startled by the gaudy mock-medieval decoration, the 19th-century work of the Comte de Galembert; it's worth remembering that medieval churches were filled with colour. The sculpted capitals of the choir have been painted too, as is virtually every millimetre of wall. River scenes feature, among others.

Down in the dark crypt-like lower chapel the atmosphere is much more intense, sobering and moving, a small arch framing the tomb of the lords of Basché, their 16th-century effigies decapitated.

Down the Veude and Mable to Richelieu

Chinon lies only a few kilometres away, but consider a wonderful detour south along the D749 to the Château du Rivau, Champigny-sur-Veude, Richelieu and Faye-la-Vineuse. This road offers a typical view of southern Touraine's delights, châteaux and manors scattered prettily about the undulating countryside, which is peaceful, open and bright, the whiteness of the stone quite blinding.

Château du Rivau

Open July–Aug Tues–Sun 2–7, May–June and Sept weekends and hols 2–7.

The Château du Rivau makes a fantastic picture of a medieval fort, a white castle rising out of the wide, rolling Touraine fields just off the D749 from Chinon to Richelieu. It was built in the mid-15th century for the Beauvaus, an ancient aristocratic family from Anjou, closely linked to French royalty of the period. Pierre de Beauvau served as Grand Chamberlain to King Charles VII. Several descendants also worked for French kings, one François Beauvau acting as Grand Ecuyer to King François I. The Beauvaus were a warrior family and their castle was provided with magnificent royal stables where war horses were reared. Many horses from here went into battle in François I's campaigns. Le Rivau's fortified stables, built in surprisingly sumptuous Italianate style, have been classified an historic monument in their own right, along with the château. The place played a significant part in the 16th-century Wars of Religion.

The Beauvaus stayed at Le Rivau up to the very end of the 17th century. Then from 1695 to the Revolution, the Castellane family of the Château de Villandry owned the fort and its massive estates. At the Revolution the lands were broken up and sold. The buildings weren't demolished, but they did fall into a state of neglect. From 1960 to 1990, Brenot, a well-known poster artist, lived in the rather crumbling castle. At the start of the 1990s, the Laigneaus, a wealthy and dynamic couple, bought Le Rivau to restore it. They've poured an impressive amount of money into the work. Monsieur is an architectural expert, while Madame is a designer who has recreated the gardens. Our guide described the place as 'in effect a big farm'. What a farm! The whole ensemble is surrounded by tall, thick white stone walls. The place looks impressively solid from afar, but get up close and you can see how it has been battered by time. The white stone blocks have become chipped and stained like old teeth. A vast amount of dental work has already had to be carried out at Le Rivau to give it a new, self-confident look; a little more time is needed for the place to look polished again.

Pass through the imposing walls and you come into the spacious outer, farm court-yard surrounded by agricultural buildings still in the process of being restored. They're on a very grand scale. The outstanding portion is the stables. One story has it that Joan of Arc came this way to collect horses on her famed Loire campaign in 1429. But she wouldn't have seen these refined 16th-century buildings. The only classified stables in France, they may have been designed by the great Italianate architect

Philibert de l'Orme. The details are cleverly conceived. For example, look at the keystones over the windows; they've been given the stylized form of horse's heads. Several massive barns also surround this farm courtyard. In one corner you can see the grape-pressing area, held up on wooden pillars, where the fruit from 45 hectares of vines are once turned into wine. In the centre of the courtyard, the sunken pool is a *pédiluve*, where the horses were washed. A kitchen garden has now been created around it, the vegetables protected by wicker sides.

A huge white keep stands guard at the entrance to the main turreted castle. Although very imposing, look closely and you can see how the stone has been eaten away at the base. A drawbridge takes you over the dry moat into the castle's court-yard. The *logis* here dates from the mid-15th century and has typical Gothic features. All the rooms were provided with fireplaces, showing the desire for comfortable living inside. When the Laigneaus bought the property, all lay empty. The big chambers with their stone floors and massive beams have been restored in the last few years. The most interesting, the **Salle du Festin de Balthazar**, contains a fresco showing the biblical scene, the feast depicted as a Rabelaisian event of excess. Rabelais himself knew the château.

To give you an idea of the scale of restoration carried out at Le Rivau recently, the Laigneaus had to organize for 140 windows to be replaced and for two hectares of roofing to be redone. Despite all this work on the buildings, the main focus for visitors at present is on the gardens. They've been divided into 10 sections and play on medieval and Renaissance themes and on the senses. Beyond the chequerboard of roses and old-fashioned fruit trees stands a little wood with alleys lined with ewes and new plantations of truffle oaks – the lucrative fungus grows successfully in these parts. Homage is of course paid to Rabelais, comical giant sculptures by the artist Basserode suspended from certain trees.

The area around the Château du Rivau, although now deeply rural, is peppered with white-stoned châteaux, many still in private hands. Not far east of Le Rivau, for example, stands the impressive Château de Brizay, protected behind substantial walls. Head south from Le Rivau and you come to the village of Champigny-sur-Veude, with a castle that could boast even finer stables than Le Rivau.

Champigny-sur-Veude

The honours are evenly divided between the Almighty and the family of Bourbon-Montpensier.

> Ian Dunlop on Champigny-sur-Veude's Sainte-Chapelle, *Châteaux of the Loire.*

You can be forgiven for mistaking the dazzling outbuildings in the centre of Champigny-sur-Veude for a château. They're just so grand; and with their particularly distinctive corner towers, they certainly look the part. It's somewhat disingenuous to describe these aristocratic remnants as outbuildings, as they in fact formed part of the outer court of a much larger ensemble that was built here in the 16th century.

Louis I de Bourbon inherited the estate, which included an old castle, in the 1470s. Having accompanied King Charles VIII on his mad dash to Italy, and once married to Louise de Montpensier in 1504, he decided to build a sumptuous new château, including, of course, a princely chapel. Work progressed slowly on the vast project, much of it completed under Louis' son, Louis II de Bourbon, and his wife, Jacquette de Longwy.

So what happened to the main portion of the splendid, vast edifice? Gaston d'Orléans, King Louis XIII's awkward brother, inherited it through his marriage in 1626 to Marie de Montpensier. His enemy, the king's political servant Richelieu, whose family seat lay so close by, wanted to put Gaston d'Orléans down a peg or two. Historically, the lords of Richelieu had owed allegiance to the lords of Champigny. In typical fashion, in the 1630s Richelieu ordered both that Gaston d'Orléans swap this château for another and that Champigny-sur-Veude be destroyed. What a waste. Richelieu had at least embarked on his own vast new château just a few kilometres south, and some of the stone from Champigny may well have gone that way. The outbuildings and the chapel survived, the latter, it's said, through the intervention of Pope Urban VIII. He had once celebrated Mass there and in response to Richelieu's request for a demolition order, sent an envoy (the future Pope Innocent X) to check out the place. The chapel was declared to be magnificent and in good repair, and not to be destroyed.

Go round to the entrance front of the outbuildings and you'll see that these are no stables. The entrance pavilion, or Pavillon de Jupiter, a triumphal arch of a gateway, proudly presents the decorative elements of the classical Renaissance. These outbuildings are not open to the public, apparently owned and guarded by a secretive Japanese company.

The freestanding **Chapelle St-Louis** remains open (*open April–Sept Wed–Mon 2–6*). This clean, neat, little white building transforms into a jewel-box inside. Carried away by the vision within, it would only be exaggerating a little to say that the stained glass in here represents Renaissance France's answer to the Gothic stained glass of the Ste-Chapelle in Paris. Mind you, here it's the precision of the artistry more than the vivacity of the colours that stands out.

Most of the exterior of this little chapel, begun in 1508, in fact clings to late Gothic outlines, although the details are interpreted in unusual shapes signalling an original inventiveness. The porch, tacked on later, has totally assumed Renaissance features, which have also crept inside the building. The stained glass was commissioned later too, by the Cardinal de Givry, as a staggering wedding gift for Louis II and Jacquette in 1538. It is thought to have been executed through the 1540s, perhaps by Robert Pinaigrier. This glass counts as one of the great Renaissance works of the Loire. The scenes have a brilliant clarity. The bottom strip depicts figures from the Bourbon and Valois families, as well as Jacquette and the Cardinal de Givry. The main sections concentrate on the life of St-Louis, the ultra-pious and crusading Louis IX. For viewers unclear about what's going on, French inscriptions in the windows give explanations. The lozenge shapes at the top of the windows follow Christ's Passion and Resurrection, except for the Crucifixion, where his suffering takes on grander proportions.

Richelieu

King Louis XIII's great political fixer, Cardinal Richelieu, has the disgraceful reputation of having acted as a vandal of major proportions in the French regions. Stamping on provincial independence, he had many a powerful piece of provincial architecture pulled down, asserting the central authority of the royal State and his own will with ruthless purpose. But he also commissioned two outrageously ambitious architectural plans to his greater glory here, in an out-of-the-way corner of France. Ironically enough, one of the two achievements, his château, has been almost entirely demolished, whereas the other – a whole new town built from scratch to provide courtiers and merchants to kowtow to the châtelain – survives as a fairly unspoilt 17th-century utopian vision, albeit with a somewhat neglected air today. The plans for both came to fruition in the 1630s.

Why build such grand designs in so distant a corner on the Touraine-Poitou border (old engravings refer to Richelieu as being in the Poitou) by a meagre river called the Mâble? The principal reason was that this had been the Richelieu family seat and that a château belonging to the cardinal's ancestors already stood here. The family had fallen on hard times, but the cardinal bought the château and lordship back for himself in 1621. He was born into a family of impoverished aristocracy, and regaining the family honour and leaving his stamp on posterity surely contributed to the scale of his ambitions. Local rivalry with royalty also possibly played its part – just north of Richelieu lay the massive Château de Champigny-sur-Veude, which became the property of Gaston d'Orléans, Louis XIII's obstreperous brother and one of Richelieu's greatest bêtes noires in 1626. The old family château remained standing on the other bank of the Mâble until the cardinal's new château was well on the way to completion, but it was then eradicated.

Park of the Former Château de Richelieu

Open April–Sept 10–7, rest of year Wed–Mon 10–7.

We begin with Richelieu's none-too-modest house, embarked upon before the town. Richelieu started dreaming up the château in 1624, and the following year the architect Jacques Lemercier came up with plans. The château's splendour would more or less eclipse just about every previous château of the Loire, maybe even rivalling Chambord. Building continued through the 1630s and 40s, with Jacques Lemercier's brothers Pierre and Nicolas taking over from him.

The Château de Richelieu was without doubt one of the most ostentatious buildings of 17th-century France, adorned with a fabulous art collection, now dispersed. So too are the stones which housed it. A pavilion, of doll's house proportions compared with the château when it was complete, is all that remains. This humiliatingly small remnant consists merely of a tower from the south wing of the middle of three great courtyards. But as sole survivor from such vastness, it still manages to impress a little. Inside, past a lonely polychrome ceramic parrot, the models and engravings which recall the full architectural event should make you gasp. The place was clearly staggering.

Cardinal Richelieu's ghost hangs over the place. He didn't see his work completed, as he died in 1642. But to furnish the place he had acquired one of the most eye-watering collections of art ever amassed in France. Many of the divided spoils have ended up in the Louvre or at Versailles. The Louvre, for example, received the two statues by Michelangelo known as the *Dying Slaves*, made for the tomb of Pope Julius II and bought by Richelieu on his home-building spree. A fair number of other pieces can be seen in the fine arts museums at Orléans and Tours. The little museum in the remaining pavilion contains just a few copies of some of the château's treasures.

The destructive utopian reforms of the Revolution didn't put an end to the château, but the temporarily dispossessed Richelieu family was forced to hasten it to its death soon afterwards. The family, having battled to regain possession of the place after the turmoil, briefly won it back only to have to sell it in 1805 to a certain Bourton. This entrepreneur then took it to pieces. In 1930 the last so-called duke of Richelieu, Odet-Armand de Jumilhace, donated the property to the Rectorat de Paris, alias the Sorbonne. The Richelais complain that it has sadly not shown much interest in the place. You pay a small entrance fee to wander in the park, with its towering shaded plane tree alleys, its fine perspectives and its lingering scent of grandeur. Apart from the isolated pavilion, you can visit the wine cellar and the orangery to the east, which stood at the arching garden end, completing the perspective of the property to the east and mirroring the great concave semi-circular entrance to the west, part of which can be seen on the road to Faye-la-Vineuse.

Richelieu's Model Town

To accompany his château, Richelieu wished for a model town, where courtiers would buy a retreat and gather to enjoy cultivated, exclusive society. Jacques Lemercier planned an ideal classical town. Maths dominates. So close to all the idio-syncracies of most Loire architecture, the rectangle is god here. It's all too precise for words. The plan employed the measure of the *toise*, roughly 2m in length. Just look down the principal street, the **Grande Rue**, and you'll appreciate the symmetry imposed. Each property here occupies a 10-*toise* plot. The obsession with order can perhaps be seen to reflect the cardinal's obsession with imposing order on every-thing, trying to control courtiers, country, life, etc.

You might think that there would be something lifeless about a plan so coldly mathematical, that it wouldn't leave much leeway for quirks of the imagination, for eccentricity or for whimsical humour. But it's hard not to find something pleasing about the order of the place. The symmetry gives a rhythm to the streets, and also a certain playfulness. There's pleasure in playing with numbers in this way, and a perverse pleasure too in looking for spots where the the maths doesn't quite add up.

Not all the buildings are alike. The two outstanding ones stand on Place du Marché, with the **Halles**, or covered market, on one side, its splendid timber frame covering a sizable space, the **church of Notre-Dame** on the other. Pierre Lemercier planned the latter building, also rectangular of course. Statues pose in the niches of the church's classical façade. Curiously though, the façade is on the east, rather than the traditional west end. The interior appears disproportionately large for such a small town church, but a fair congregation still packs the boxed stalls on a Sunday. The small **Musée de l'Hôtel de Ville** (*open July–Aug Wed–Mon 10–12 and 2–6; rest of year Mon, Tues, Thurs and Fri 10–12 and 2–4*) in the town hall contains further details and drawings on the construction of the town and the château.

None of the courtiers at the time of Richelieu bought into his dream. But by the start of the 18th century, 3,000-plus people were installed, which is more than there are nowadays. Today there's a desolation to the place, the grand social ideals behind its construction undermined by an air of apathy. It feels like a grand town that has become a backwater in this rather remote corner of the Touraine. Individuality has managed to find a place through time. Within the walled town, spot the house fronts and roofs which have modified a detail here or a detail there! But generally speaking little has been altered, even if the place looks a little neglected, the streets somewhat deserted. Outside the main grand gateway, little allotments and shacks have rather charmingly taken over the moat.

Around Richelieu

Faye-la-Vineuse stands prettily atop its gentle hill south of Richelieu, a typical old-fashioned styled French village, church spire rising above the roofs. It looks undisturbed by modern development, except for the water tower, which rather distractingly reaches higher to the heavens than the church. The place seems virtually lifeless now, but is was more important in local history than it appears, fortified by none other than Foulques Nerra of Anjou and, much later, twice the scene of terrors in the Wars of Religion. Its church, the Collégiale Saint-Georges, survived the harassment of the Huguenots, but suffered at the hands of a restoring priest of the 19th century. It boasts the largest crypt in the Indre-et-Loire. This has the appearance of a Romanesque church (admittedly with modern cement flooring), with typical capitals.

The feel of the landscape is more like southwestern France than the Loire Valley, with scattered big farms on their rises, their large, gently sloping open fields baked by the sun in summer. The local white crystalline stone is known as *galuche* and rings if you knock pieces of it together. You can visit the elegant **Château de la Grillère** (*open mid-June–mid-Sept 9–12 and 2–7*) on its height. One of the family of Lemercier architects responsible for Richelieu made it out this far, converting the medieval forms to 17th-century fashions. From the château, which has been lavishly furnished, you get fine views of the countryside around.

East of Richelieu you can follow little roads through scarcely inhabited lands via Braslou and Luzé to **Bois-Aubry** for a brief look at the ruins of the abbey there. Dating back to the 12th century, the place appears bombarded by time. In 1978 a number of Orthodox monks reinhabited the buildings that remained. The top of the great octagonal spire dates from the 15th century. Within lies a remarkable 12th-century effigy thought to be that of Clement, the abbot who had much of the abbey built. The restored chapter house contains Romanesque capitals.

Chinon and the Chinonais

The Plantagenets, Joan of Arc, Rabelais and red wine have brought this irresistible part of Touraine more than its fair share of fame.

Chinon

With fine medieval houses as close knit as chain mail fighting for space down between the hillside and the Vienne river, Chinon is dominated by the secure walls of one of the great ruined castles of the Plantagenet kingdom. The town may appear distinctly provincial today, but Chinon is a place that retains more than a spark of old courtly glory. It's a magnificent little spot, with charming streets behind the busy riverside road and its pruned trees. For the most dramatic views of the town lorded over by its hilltop fortifications, take in the scene from the south bank of the Vienne.

Arriving through the Chinonais vineyards from the plateau to the north, by contrast, the sturdy curtain walls of the castle remain concealed – you just get a

Getting There and Around

With a combination of **train** and **bus** services, Chinon can be said to have a regular service with Tours. Trains and buses arrive at the train station, about 1km east of the centre.

Tourist Information

Chinon: Office du Tourisme du Pays de Chinon, B.P.141, Place Hofheim, 37501 Chinon, t 02 47 93 17 85, f 02 47 93 93 05, www.chinon.com.

Market Day

Chinon: Thursday.

Where to Stay and Eat

Chinon ✉ 37500

You can choose from a lovely selection of mid-range hotels in town, even if there's nowhere particularly grand to stay.

★★★**Hôtel de France**, 47 Place du Général de Gaulle, t 02 47 93 33 91, f 02 47 98 37 03, www.bestwestern.com/fr/hotelde-francechinon (moderate). Set back in the leafy, calm northern corner of this central square, the rooms neat and comfortable (menus €17.5–49). Closed second half Nov.

★★**La Boule d'Or**, 66 Quai Jeanne d'Arc, t 02 47 93 03 13, f 02 47 93 24 25 (moderate). This former posting inn has some nicely decorated rooms overlooking the river and an interior courtyard where food is served in summer. The menu Gargantua is huge, interesting and relatively heavy, given the old-style dishes it recreates (menus €15–28). Closed Sun pm and Mon out of season, and mid-Dec–Jan.

★★**Hostellerie Gargantua**, 73 Rue Voltaire, t 02 47 93 04 71, f 02 47 93 08 02 (moderate). Occupies one of Chinon's most famous historic houses. It has some very comfortable rooms, a medieval-style dining room serving quite modern cuisine, and a pretty courtyard where you can eat on warm days (menus c.€23). Closed Wed and Thurs lunch out of season.

★★**Hôtel Diderot**, 4 Rue Buffon, t 02 47 93 18 87, f 02 47 93 37 10 (inexpensive). The rooms are set around a delightful courtyard, in buildings which include a lovely 18th-century ivy-covered house. This place offers peace and quiet in the centre of town, except for early-morning footsteps across the gravel. Closed mid-Dec–mid-Jan.

Agnès Sorel, 4 Quai Pasteur, t 02 47 93 04 37, f 02 47 93 06 37 (inexpensive). Another hotel looking onto the river, with just six delightful rooms in varying styles. It's run by a wonderfully hospitable young couple.

sudden view of the risibly thin Tour de l'Horloge rising above the edge of the plateau. This tower is now devoted to the memory of *the* greatest visitor to Chinon, who came here to find Charles VII who had run off from the English in the Hundred Years' War. But the person who most marks the tourist town today, more even than Joan of Arc, is a brilliant and bawdy 16th-century monk, doctor and writer born in the Chinonais, François Rabelais, one of the outstanding figures of the French Renaissance period.

History

Way before the glitter of the medieval courts and Renaissance times, the protective white cliff and the shimmering waters of the Vienne were reasons enough for Gallo-Romans to settle here. The place was then known as Caïno. Despite building a *castrum* for walled protection against the descending barbarian hordes, their town was taken by Visigoths around 400 AD.

But Christianity also established a firm foothold. St Martin came to preach in the neighbourhood, while Brice, his successor as bishop of Tours, established a church in

Hôtel de la Treille, 4 Place Jeanne d'Arc, t/f 02 47 93 07 71 (*cheap*). For cheaper options, a basic hotel with six rooms in what was once a medieval episcopal house. You can also eat well here (*menus €10–20.5*).

Au Plaisir Gourmand, Quai Charles VII, t 02 47 93 20 48, f 02 47 93 05 66. The outstanding restaurant in town, reputed far and wide, discreetly set back from the river and with its own little garden. Jean-Claude Rigollet mainly prepares traditional French cuisine to perfection, such as oxtail in a deep, dark Chinon sauce, but also the odd newer dish, for example snail-filled ravioli with garlic cream (*menus €26.5–37*). *Closed Sun pm and Mon, and Feb.*

L'Océanic, 13 Rue Rabelais, t 02 47 93 44 55, f 02 47 93 38 68. Excellent seafood (*menus c.€30.5*).

La Maison Rouge, 38 Rue Voltaire, t 02 47 98 43 65, f 02 47 95 78 33. Serves both as a fine foods store and as a restaurant where you can sample regional specialities. For €12 you can try the platter of six cold dishes or one speciality plus a hot dish (*menus €12–29*).

Beaumont-en-Véron ✉ 37420

**Hôtel La Giraudière, off D749 on the way from Chinon to Avoine, along the Route to Savigny, t 02 47 58 40 36, f 02 47 58 46 06, *giraudiere@hotels-france.com* (*moderate*). A slightly unkempt, eccentric manor house, but it offers charming rooms within its 17th-century architecture. The atmosphere is very calm. It's a nice place to linger over a long lunch (*menus c.€24.5*).

Château de Coulaine B&B, t 02 47 93 01 27 (*inexpensive*). Still more eccentric, a wonderful-looking restored 16th-century château with bathrooms in the round towers. The rooms may not be sophisticated, but the place is great fun. This is also an excellent winemaking property.

Manoir de Montour B&B, 176 Rue du Véron, t 02 47 58 43 76 (*inexpensive*). Much more elegant, beautifully decorated rooms in a lovely manor. *Closed All Saints' to Easter.*

Marçay ✉ 37500

****Château de Marçay, t 02 47 93 03 47, f 02 47 93 45 33, *marcay@relaischateaux.fr*, *www.relaischateaux.fr/marcay* (*luxury*). A perfect picture of a Loire castle of the late medieval period, set in undramatic but restful countryside due south of Chinon along the D116. Rooms are split between those in the château itself, some a bit jaded, and the ones around the courtyard, freshly decorated and with private little gardens. Make the most of the delightful terraces or salons for an apéritif before going in to dinner. Heated swimming pool and tennis court (*menus €23.5–58*). *Closed mid-Jan–mid-March.*

honour of him in the middle of the 5th century. Visigoths and locals were united in their efforts to repel the Roman governor of Gaul, Aegidius, when he lay siege to the town. Lacking water, Chinon's defenders were reduced to desperation. When the rains came with a thunder storm, the miracle was attributed to another follower of St Martin, Maxime, also known by the abbreviated name Mexme. He founded a second church and a monastery at Chinon. A third religious institution was established in honour of a Breton hermit, Jean, who was consulted by Queen Radegonde about her troubled marriage to Clotaire. Such an early concentration of religious activity helped make Chinon an attractive, active trading town and in the 6th century a Merovingian mint was producing coins here. The Norman invasions of the 9th century put paid to the town of the Dark Ages.

Provincial power then became concentrated in the hands of formidable counts. First the counts of Blois occupied the site and erected a keep as early as the middle of the 10th century. Their Anjou rivals were pushing to expand their territories eastwards, however, and in 1044 Geoffrey Martel of Anjou took Chinon and proceeded to add to its defences. The town's first great courtly age came with Henri Plantagenêt of Anjou. Actually the town didn't form part of his inheritance, but that of his brother Geoffroy, from whom Henri seized the place. He decided that Chinon was excellently situated to administer the vast territories he had acquired, known as the Plantagenet or Angevin empire. These possessions included not just Anjou, Maine and Normandy, but Aquitaine and, let's not forget it, England. The château was enlarged to become the largest fortress of its time in Europe. Henri loved the place and spent a great deal in it. This was the principal stopping point for his peripatetic court.

Henri died at Chinon in 1189 and a struggle then raged between his sons – Richard the Lionheart, followed by John – and the Capetian French King Philippe Auguste. Richard the Lionheart may have died in one of Chinon's town houses after being mortally wounded at the Battle of Châlus in Poitou, to the south. As for John, he was married to Isabelle d'Angoulême at Chinon. Philippe Auguste's forces triumphed over John's in a one-year siege of the town, and the ill-fated English king had subsequently to relinquish virtually all his Plantagenet lands in France in the first few years of the 13th century. Chinon lost the importance it had briefly acquired in these early Middle Ages, although further building work on the château was carried out by the French Crown. Philippe Auguste, Louis IX (alias St-Louis) and Philippe III would stay at the château from time to time.

A couple of particularly gruesome incidents stain the history of Chinon in the first half of the 14th century. The Knights Templars had acquired massive power in France through their role as bankers for the Crusades and the special privileges accorded them. King Philippe IV le Bel decided to wipe them out, and the Templars were rounded up in 1308, many being sent to Poitiers. On the way there, several of the leading figures of the order, including its Grand Master, Jacques Molay, fell ill and were kept prisoner at Chinon instead. Cardinals came to the town to hear them confess. The commonly held belief is that they were tortured by the Inquisition, or threatened with torture, and admitted to heresy, idolatry, witchcraft, profanity and

Joan of Arc Won't be Fobbed Off by a Blue Beard and Persuades the Gentil Dauphin to Listen to Her Voices

La Trémouille: I wonder will she pick him out!
The Archbishop: Of course she will.
La Trémouille: Why? How is she to know?
The Archbishop: She will know what everybody in Chinon knows: that the Dauphin is the meanest-looking and worst-dressed figure in the Court, and that the man with the blue beard is Gilles de Rais... [Joan appears.]
The Duchess [to the nearest lady-in-waiting]: My dear! Her hair! [All the ladies explode in uncontrollable laughter.]

From *Saint Joan* by George Bernard Shaw, 1923

Joan came to Chinon in late winter 1429, the reputation of her divine messages preceding her. She said that the voices of several saints were transmitting orders from God which declared that with her help Charles would be fittingly crowned king in the sacred royal ceremony at Reims and that the English would be expelled from France. The French leaders were in desperate straits, in terrible need of divine intervention. Although sceptical about Joan's claims, they were willing to put them to the test.

Once Joan appeared in town, where she took up lodgings and set to praying, she was quickly granted an audience. But a trap was set for her. Charles VII's courtier Gilles de Rais (later to be infamously condemned to death for paedophilia and killing children on a massive scale) was made to pretend to be the king. Joan of Arc is said to have seen through this ruse immediately – perhaps not as difficult as it may sound if Gilles really did sport 'the extravagance of a little curled beard dyed blue at a clean-shaven court' as Shaw has it. She picked out the dauphin (the French

Back outside in the **Château du Milieu**, head west for the main hall and royal apartments, past the well through which stone for the château was quarried and raised. The great hall was added for Charles VII and it's in this building that Joan of Arc recognized the dauphin in the crowd.

The history of the place is much more remarkable than the contemporary displays. The visit of the interiors is certainly not particularly taxing, with only a few pieces of sculpture, including a Gallo-Roman funerary stone, a polychrome wooden statue of St Martin (where the beard of the pauper he's supposed to have helped appears very unfortunately stuck to the horse's bottom) and some classical busts from Richelieu's castle (*see* pp.342–3). A few tapestries, some tacky copies of works of art, a video on the genealogy of the kings of France and the interesting model of the Château de Chinon as it once stood add to the meagre tour through this part of the castle.

So the interiors aren't the Château de Chinon's strongest point. But back out in the leafy courtyard of the Château du Milieu, it is a pleasure to walk to the ramparts on the other side, which include the **Tour des Chiens** (the Dogs' Tower), a 12th-century construction where the royal dogs were once pampered, and the **Tour d'Argenton**, heir to the throne) without any difficulty and soon persuaded him of the importance of her mission.

'The recognition scene at Chinon has been depicted, in paint and in words, as a secular equivalent of the Annunciation to Mary, with Joan as Gabriel announcing to Charles that he is himself France's Messiah,' writes Marina Warner in her meticulous analysis of Joan in *Joan of Arc: The Image of Female Heroism*. It's a meeting that has acquired mythical, and for many who wish to look no further, supernatural significance in French history. Joan herself at first didn't admit during her trial to seeing an angel picking out Charles. But as she became more confused, she elaborated on this tale. Then the fictionalizers of history took up the case, not content with Joan's elaboration, or simply ignoring the trial transcripts. Extraordinary explanations have been advanced for why Joan was so readily accepted by Charles. A whole series turn on the wild notion that Joan was an illegitimate royal child sent away from court but later able to return and impart secret family information to Charles. These theories ignore the evidence about Joan's past from the many witnesses at the rehabilitation trial after her death.

The medieval French leaders weren't as superficial as you may have been led to think. Joan wasn't immediately allowed to assume a position of power and a military post unquestioned and unchallenged. She had first to be thoroughly examined, not just theologically, but physically too. She was sent to Poitiers to undergo these tests to check that she wasn't an impostor and came out with flying colours, her reputation intact, confirmed as the French virgin sent by God to restore the integrity of the French kingdom.

Once back at Chinon she was supported by the royal figure of Yolande d'Aragon, given her own band of men to lead into battle and, donning men's armour, set out for Orléans (*see* p.139).

added for the château's governor at the end of the 15th century, Philippe de Commines, the famed chronicler of Louis XI's reign.

The two further forts are separated by large ditches from the Château du Milieu. The eastern ditch spanned by the entrance bridge was dug by order of Henri Plantagenêt, providing further internal defences to the vast complex. As you entered the castle you may have spotted the reconstructions of medieval siege machines displayed in the eastern ditch. The **Fort St-Georges** across this ditch was also built at this time, but the little that remains of it isn't open to the public.

You can visit the better-preserved **Fort du Coudray** to the west. Philippe Auguste ordered these mighty defences. The Tour du Moulin marking the westernmost point was the original keep here, but the most daunting of the many towers is the Coudray keep, a splendid piece of architecture. Inside, you can admire a fantastic fan of arrow slits and intriguing medieval graffiti. From this end of the fortifications, Charles VII would apparently later keep discreetly in touch with his mistress. He saw to it that Agnès Sorel (*see* p.296) had a house close to the château easily accessible via underground tunnels.

After Charles VII's reign, the château was used mainly as a base for military operations and as a state prison. Governors of Chinon lived up in the fort. At the very end of the 15th century, following Charles VIII's untimely death, it was at Chinon that the new king, Louis XII, received the news of Pope Alexander VI's official granting of the annulment of his marriage to the infertile Jeanne de France. Great celebrations were held by the king for this event.

On a couple of occasions during the 16th-century Wars of Religion the fort was used by royal forces, but the château was gradually falling into a state of disrepair, patchily restored during the short time the Prince de Condé owned the place early in the 17th century. Cardinal Richelieu acquired the property in 1633, when King Louis XIII sold it to him. Richelieu added this territory to that he had amassed close to his family home to the south. In his usual manner, his first thought was to demolish the place. Instead it was simply left to fall further into ruin by him and his descendants.

When Prosper Mérimée, the writer-cum-influential inspector of historical monuments, visited the castle in 1855, he realized the importance of saving what remained of the fortifications. A local architect from Saumur, Joly-Leterme, was called upon to consolidate what he could, so that many of the towers and ramparts were spruced up in the 19th century. It's a joy that they were saved.

A Tour of Chinon

The thin wedge of land below the castle between cliff and river is crammed with splendid architecture. The most striking element of the buildings is the variety of stair towers, some round, some square, some in timberframe and brick, others in local limestone. Several of the buildings house hotels, restaurants or museums, notably in the main string of streets.

But first, on the western end of the quays, the very clean-looking former abattoir has been turned into the new Chinon riverboat museum, the **Maison de la Rivière** (*open July–Aug Tues–Sun 10.30–12.30 and 2–6.30; April–June and Sept Tues–Fri 10–12 and 2–5, weekends 3–6; Feb–March and Oct Thurs–Sun 2–5;* **t** *02 47 93 21 34*). The displays give you some notion of what daily life must once have been like by the Vienne, with its mariners, ferrymen and fishermen. An interesting range of models of the different sorts of boats that were used on the river is displayed in cabinets and the use of each explained. Old postcards of Chinon show it in the days when *bateaux-lavoirs*, washing boats, were moored to the river bank. Now in the tourist season, you can book to go on a river boat from the quays outside the museum, while the gift shop offers river-related gifts.

It isn't a long walk through the old town. Start at the western end of the **Rue Haute St-Maurice**. The **church of St-Maurice**, with its soaring spire, looks as though it's been squeezed in between the narrow side streets here. Both the belfry and the north aisle date back to the 12th century, when Henri Plantagenêt donated money for the building. Typically, 19th-century restorers insensitively renovated the place. The north aisle used to be the nave and is covered with Angevin vaulting and little sculptures. The south aisle is of much later date, mid-16th century, paid for by prosperous Chinon merchants.

Just east of the church, the **Hostellerie Gargantua** may have a real connection with Rabelais, as this was once the Palais de Baillage, where Rabelais' father may have carried out some of his legal business.

A little further east you come to the **Musée du Vieux Chinon** in the Maison des Etats Généraux (*open mid-April–mid-Oct 11–1 and 3–8*). This local history museum is situated in one of the most significant historic houses in town. Richard the Lionheart may have died here from his battle wounds in 1199. It's also the house where King Charles VII called the Estates General of France to meet in 1428, after the English had begun to lay siege to Orléans. The local archaeological and historical society has turned it into a small museum.

Undoubtedly, the most moving piece of sculpture within is a mould of the Crucifixion taken from Chinon's 11th-century church of St-Mexme, closed for many years for restoration, but devoted a section here. The Crucifixion scene is one of the most painfully emotional depictions of Christ's suffering from French medieval art, his face that of an exhausted old man, stretchmarked by agony. Older fragments of civilization have been unearthed in Chinon, including a find of Merovingian coins from the town's mint in the Dark Ages, the museum displays some of the oldest *deniers* in France; this silver coin was adopted in 675 and was to last six centuries as the basis of the French monetary system.

Chinon Wines

'*A boire! A boire! A boire!* (A drink! A drink! A drink!)', rang the immortal first screeches of the giant baby Gargantua as he was born through his monster of a mother's left ear, in a field in the Chinonais. And the baby wanted wine from the start, thirsting for a stiff drink, not your namby-pamby milk. The quest for the '*Dive Bouteille* (the Divine Bottle)' becomes the great objective of the spoof quest in Rabelais' giant cycle.

Wine tasters most frequently discover violets and rubies hidden in Chinon wines, grown and produced along the final stretch of the Vienne river as it approaches the Loire. Chinon wines are almost exclusively red. Cabernet Franc (the soft, 'feminine' grape variety that makes up the most important ingredient in the great wines of Pomerol and St-Emilion in the Bordelais) makes up the major grape variety here. It's rather confusingly known as 'Breton' locally. Chinon's *appellation d'origine contrôlée* wine territory spreads over some 1,850 hectares in 19 parishes, going from around L'Ile Bouchard to the Vienne's confluence with the Loire.

The different soils along the valley produce different characteristics. The low gravels by the river give lighter, fruity wines with aromas that emerge very young. The vines on the slopes and the plateaux above, with siliceous-clay or limestone-clay ground, yield more powerful wines, some of which have a surprisingly good ability to age in fine years. But as with all but the great sweet Loire wines, they tend to be drunk young.

In wine terms a 'château' often refers simply to an individual wine-producing property, which usually just has an ordinary house attached. With several of the best-known Chinon vineyards, however, you get a proper little Loire château thrown in.

The big hall where the Estates General met has some further interesting religious sculpture, contrasting with some tacky copies of works of art, including a notably hideous rendering of Joan of Arc. The portrait of Rabelais was the work of Eugène Delacroix for the 1834 salon. Bought by the State, it was fittingly donated to the town, although it isn't a great work by the artist. Among a further eclectic range of objects, the most famous is the **chape de St Mexme**, or St Mexme's cope. This turns out in fact to be a piece of Arab, possibly Egyptian, silk from the 11th century, thought now to have been made for a horse! It's decorated with an eye-catching pattern of chained wild cats. Other displays include a particularly tortured *Pietà* in polychrome wood and 19th-century Loire pottery from Langeais, a 19th-century taste, with pieces first made in brown or reddish-brown and later embellished with gold leaf, some displayed at the Great Exhibition in London in 1851.

The road down from this museum leads to the start of the main shopping street of the **Rue du Commerce** (later turning into the Rue Rabelais), and off that to the bridge. Keeping on the higher streets, though, at the start of the Rue Voltaire stands the brick façade of the **Maison Rouge**, the original building constructed around 1400. Joan of Arc should therefore have seen it it, as she stayed in a house that then stood next door, called the Hostellerie du Grand-Carroi, when she first arrived at Chinon. As she recounted with such innocent conviction at her trial: 'I was almost always in prayer in

Among the most spectacular vineyards to visit for a wine tasting are: the **Château de la Grille**, a little north of Chinon, splendidly visible on the road to Ussé (*t 02 47 93 01 95; open every day, but Sunday and public holidays only by reservation*), and the **Château de Coulaine** (*t 02 47 98 44 51*), on the way to Beaumont-en-Véron from Chinon. The Château de la Grille is a long-established wine-producing property; the Château de Coulaine is an up-and-coming one. Both châteaux have a fascinating history and at Coulaine they also produce *confiture de vin*, wine jam. In Chinon itself, the house of **Couly-Dutheil** (*12 Rue Diderot, t 02 47 93 05 84; small fee*) has a high reputation for the quality of its wines, the Clos de l'Echo even mentioned in Rabelais. It has very modern winemaking equipment combined with ancient cellars.

East of Chinon, Cravant-les-Coteaux and Panzoult are highly-regarded Chinon wine parishes, and exceptionally picturesque. At Cravant, **Domaine Gouron** (*t 02 47 93 15 33*), on the heights, with a modern-cut rock cellar, and **Domaine du Morilly** (*t 02 47 93 38 25; closed last week of August*), with an older troglodyte feel, including a tasting room with a troglodyte fireplace, are well used to receiving visitors. At Panzoult, the **Domaine de Beauséjour** (*t 02 47 58 64 64*) and the **Domaine du Roncée** (*t 02 47 58 53 01*) make for extremely pleasant visits. When you're looking on wine lists in a restaurant, **Olga Raffault** and **Charles Joguet** are names of top-class Chinon producers that feature regularly.

Not actually in the Chinon *appellation*, but nearby at St-Germain-sur-Vienne, down river towards Candes-St-Martin, the **Château du Petit Thouars** (*t 02 47 95 96 40; closed Sun and Mon*) is another estate that combines good winemaking – here of AOC Touraine red and rosé – with a spectacular house and cave cellars. The family has been making wine here for 350 years.

order that God should send the sign of the king; and I was staying at my lodgings at a good woman's house close to the castle of Chinon when he [the archangel] came; and then we went together to the king; and he was well accompanied by other angels with him, which other people could not see.' Once Joan had convinced Charles and then the Church authorities in Poitiers, when she returned to Chinon she was upgraded, given the honour of being put up in the castle itself.

A little east along the **Rue Voltaire** you come to a cul-de-sac with the **Musée Animé du Vin et de la Tonnellerie** (*open April–Sept 10.30–12.30 and 2–7*), a display on wine-making in the Chinonais set in a former stone quarry. The Chinonais vines grow almost up to the château walls on the plateau beyond the castle (*see* the box on the preceding pages). Life-sized models slowly enact the laborious work involved in wine-making. To reward you for your attention, you're treated to a wine tasting at the end. An impasse next to this one contains the **Cave Peincte**, a painted cave mentioned by Rabelais and generally reserved for the meetings of Chinon's wine fraternity; but ask at the tourist office and a visit may be possible in July and August.

The Rue Voltaire ends in the very pleasant 19th-century square of **Place du Général de Gaulle**, with the town hall on the north end and a crowd of cafés at the southern end, by the proud statue of Rabelais. Continuing along from the northern end of the square, the **Rue Jean-Jacques Rousseau** takes you on to several important Chinon churches. The west front of the **church of St-Etienne** carries the arms of Chinon, an archbishop of Tours and the late 15th-century governor Philippe de Commines. The last saw to the completion of the church's rebuilding. The interior is simple, without side aisles. Joan of Arc crops up twice; once in a white marble statue of 1900 by the Tourangeau François Sicard, and again in the 19th-century stained glass in the choir, by Léopold Lobin. Two further important religious figures for Chinon, St Mexme and Ste Radegonde, also feature in glass.

The **church of St-Mexme** (*contact the tourist office to join a guided tour inside*) lies just down the street from St-Etienne. Its sturdy slate-capped towers dominate this part of town, but below them the building hasn't fared well. It was quite obviously once a fine piece of Romanesque architecture, however, with what must once have been an awe-inspiring front full of sculptured stone panels, hacked off in turbulent times. Mexme founded a monastery here in the 5th century. Archaeological evidence has shown seven periods of building on the site, from early Christian times through to the 15th century, but the bulk of the work left standing was carried out in the 11th and 12th centuries. The church will never recover from the neglect it suffered after the Revolution. Briefly serving as an arms depot, its crossing tower fell in 1817, destroying most of the choir. The town authorities bought the remnants to open a school in the nave! One side of the north aisle was simply done away with to extend the school buildings. The last pupils only left in 1983. It's worth joining a guided tour of the town if you're interested in seeing the now bare but atmospheric interior, with a few evocative traces of stone carving and wall paintings left in the impressive entrance tower.

South of St-Mexme lies the big **Place Jeanne d'Arc**, with its bellicose statue of Joan of Arc on horseback pelting over bodies, sword and flag triumphantly outstretched.

It's a rather frightening vision of the maid who isn't supposed to have killed a single soul in battle. It was made in the late 19th century by Jules Roulleau.

The path up the hillside east of St-Mexme takes you to the very curious **Chapelle Ste-Radegonde** (*contact the tourist office to join a guided tour inside*), built partly into the rock. Walking along the Vienne cliffside to the chapel you get rather too good a view down on to the modern quarters of Chinon. The chapel itself is a curious ruin standing in front of a warren of caves, some of which were inhabited by very poor families up until the 1950s. The religious origins of the site go back to the early Christian era. This is the place to which Queen Radegonde fled from her violent husband Clotaire to find sanctuary with the hermit Jean le Reclus around 550. She went on to found the nunnery of Ste-Croix near Poitiers, while the hermit was buried in his cave. The hermitage became a place of pilgrimage, and to accommodate the Christian visitors a larger chapel was excavated and decorated. The semi-ruined place contains a significant little segment of wall paintings from around 1200. The courtly figures seen riding along on horseback are thought to be members of the royal Angevin Plantagenet family. One of the figures is thought to be a rare representation of Eleanor of Aquitaine, King Henry II's extraordinarily powerful wife. If the figures are unclear, the horses on which they ride look splendid with their flowing manes.

The set of caves around the chapel now contains an atmospherically neglected museum of local traditions. After negotiating the narrow labyrinth of this troglodyte collection, you come to the most startling surprise in Chinon, the **underground well**, possibly dug in the 6th century. You peer down into it through a triangle of a hole in the rock, dug at a strange angle that somehow draws you in and makes you lose your sense of orientation. You can imagine pilgrims feeling awed by the sight. The waters were supposed to cure eye ailments. The place still feels magical, one of the most mesmerizing visions in the Loire Valley.

La Devinière and the Musée Rabelais

Open May–mid-Sept 10–7, mid-Mar–April 9.30–12.30 and 2–6, Feb–mid-March and mid-Sept–Nov 9.30–12.30 and 2–5, Dec–Jan 10–12.30 and 2–5; t 02 47 95 91 18.

Southwest from Chinon, via the troglodyte village of **Cinais**, La Devinière commemorates the Chinonais' favourite, most intelligent and most cleverly frivolous son, François Rabelais. Rabelais was born here around 1494. If Rabelais has become even more of a popular marketing tool than Henri Plantagenêt or Joan of Arc in the Chinonais, let's face it, he was funnier than either of those two great historical figures. But the museum paying homage to him is a relatively sober affair.

What a quiet spot for the big mouth of French letters to have been born. François Rabelais' mother was specially driven to this family farmhouse to give birth; such was often the custom for well-to-do women in that period, to be sent packing to the fresh air of the country. Her baby may well have come into the world in a field, rather than in the house itself. Readers of *Gargantua* may remember the way that

Rabelais and His Raunchy Romps through Early French Renaissance Ideas

Beuveurs tres illustres, et vous, Verolez, tres precieux...à vous, non à aultres, sont dediez mes escriptz... (Very illustrious drinkers, and you most precious people poxed with venereal disease, it's to you, not to others, that my writings are dedicated...)
Rabelais, prologue to *Gargantua*, 1530s

Rabelais' writing isn't all fornicating friars, gross feasting, belching and farting, endless inebriation and smutty word play worthy of today's sleaziest tabloids – although it does contain plenty of all that. His books are also crammed with classical, theological, medical and legal allusions and comment. Beneath the absurd bullshit lies serious philosophical enquiry.

The telling of bawdy tales of giants who might, for example, accidentally eat pilgrims in their salad or discover with delight that a live goose is the softest way to wipe their bum, Rabelais took from a well-established popular medieval tradition. It sounds very drily academic to interpret his uproarious fictional giant cycle as an intellectual investigation into forms of contemporary education and learning and the way to make sense of life more generally. Rabelais mixes low culture with high culture in an increasingly masterful manner through his books. He has a go at all the serious professions of his time, subjecting them to debasing ridicule. He was extremely well placed to comment; the son of a lawyer, in his lifetime he tried his hand at being a monk, a doctor and a teacher. He also had to be careful of the powerful censors and of being too blatantly critical of the established Church at a time when the spread of Protestantism and the questioning of the grip of Catholicism were beginning to split French society apart. Rabelais was daring, but he also used his comedy as a clever defence.

Rabelais wrote four, possibly five, books in his cycle on giants. *Pantagruel* was the first, *Gargantua* the second, although it tells the tale of the upbringing of Pantagruel's father. Many of the scenes in these two works are set in the Chinonais, the little place names referred to still existing, but blown out of all proportion into mock-epic sites. The other books in the giant cycle – known by the really unimaginative titles of the *Tiers Livre*, the *Quart Livre* and the *Cinquiesme Livre* – take the adventures further afield into more obscure realms of the imagination and of language. They become increasingly experimental and philosophical. The protagonists travelling from isolated island to isolated island encounter one potty lot after another, rendered barmy by their fanatically blinkered views.

Nowadays, Rabelais' endless word play, absurdism and intellectual stabs can be a struggle to fathom out, and his contemporary love of puns a big pain, but reading his books in an edition with serious explanatory notes can be an engrossing pleasure.

Rabelais' fictional hero's mother, Gargamelle, gives birth to her giant of a son, first eating too much tripe, then vilely cursing her husband (wishing in particular that he had had his male member cut off) before the vast baby Gargantua squeezes

out through her left ear. Rabelais, for most of the first six years of his life, was left
in the hands of the tenants who brought him up, again a traditional practice.
From the ages of six to eleven he was educated at the nearby village of Seuilly, by
Benedictine monks.

The pretty, late-medieval farmhouse of La Devinière is fronted by a fine *fuye*,
or dovecote, from the 17th century, with numerous pigeon holes on its low gable.
The Rabelais-related collections in the house concentrate on depictions of
the man and of his characters, as well as touching on legends more widely in France.
Jean du Bellay left a contemporary description of Rabelais; he apparently had a
wide forehead, a beard along the line of his jaw, a short-sighted look and, not
surprisingly, a sarcastic smile. Matisse made a famous sketch of the writer for La
Devinière in 1951, which appears an accurate version of the description. The other
best-known drawings associated with Rabelais are Daumier's cluttered grotesque
interpretations of Gargantuan episodes. The museum has also pursued country
and medicinal themes, with displays on the great variety of plants Rabelais mentions
in his writing.

The Battlegrounds of the Picrocholine Wars in the Rabelaisie

A terrible war ravaged the area immediately around La Devinière, referred to in the
tourist jargon as **La Rabelaisie**. It's scarcely believable that this quiet corner witnessed
the megalomaniac ambitions of a terrible general. We are of course referring to
Picrochole of the Picrocholine wars in Rabelais' *Gargantua*.

The shepherds of Gargantua's country were out at harvest time chasing the star-
lings from the vines when they saw the *fouaciers* (makers of a kind of unleavened
bread) of Lerné passing by. The shepherds asked if they could buy some *fouaces*, but
their request wasn't just turned down by the men of Lerné; the latter also threw a
torrent of unrepeatable abuse on the shepherds. These responded, with their nut-
picking allies nearby, in the only way they saw fit, beating the men of Lerné with their
sticks '*comme sus seigle verd* (as on green rye)' and took some of the *fouaces*. Thus are
wars started. Picrochole, irascible leader of the men of Lerné, wanted vengeance,
refused reconciliation, and his bellicose ambitions took on proportions foreshadowing Napoleon's as he decided he could take on and conquer the world. At La
Devinière you can buy a card which marks the various locations of the campaigns in
this major European war.

Rabelais' birthplace is overseen in the distance by the magnificent silhouette of the
Château de Coudray-Montpensier, the archetypal late-Gothic Loire castle, now
housing a school for children with learning difficulties.

The little village of **Seuilly** is charming, with a few 16th-century houses remaining
between the church and the abbey, just like the one from which Rabelais' fictional
hero of a monk, Frère Jean, emerged to defend his beloved vines against the louts of
Lerné, making a rousing speech to his fellow monks on the importance of wine.

La Roche Clermault to the east of Seuilly and **Lerné** to the west of Seuilly continue the war trail, the latter entering troglodyte country.

The glorious pilgrimage village of Candes-St-Martin, at the confluence of the Loire and the Vienne, although marking Touraine's western boundary, is covered at the beginning of the next chapter as it's so closely tied to its Angevin neighbour Montsoreau.

The Loire from Saumur to Angers

18

Eastern Anjou

Le Lion d'Angers
Cheffes
Ecuillé
Tiercé
770
162
Briollay
Marcé
23
E60/A85
766
Baugé
Pontigné
Le Lude
Genneteil
306
307
La Boissié
Br
76
Noyant
Le Vieil-Baugé
766
Mo.liherne
761
Avrillé
Angers
Trélazé
Château de Montgeoffroy
La Fontaine-
Guérin
Bocé
Bouchemaine
Beaufort-en-Vallée
Brion
St-Georges-
sur-Loire
Mürs-Erigné
St-Sulpice
Loire
St-Mathurin-sur-Loire
23
Savennières
St-Saturnin
sur-Loire
St Rémy-
la-Varenne
Le Thoureil
Longué
Vernoil
Chalonnes-
sur-Loire
Rochefort-sur-Loire
Coutures
St-Aubin-de-Luigné
Chaume
Brissac-Quincé
Aubance
Les Rosiers
Gennes
St-Clément-des-Levées
Brain-sur-Allonnes
Beaulieu
MAINE-ET-
LOIRE
Grézillé
Cunault
St-Lambert-du-Lattay
Rablay
Faye d'Anjou
Louerre
Chênehutte-les-Tuffeaux
Bourgueil
Chanzeaux
Bonnezeaux
Parc Naturel Regional
Loire-Anjou-Touraine
St-Hilaire-St-Florent
485
160
Le-Champ-
sur-Layon
Thouarcé
Layon
761
Saumur
Faveraye-
Mâchelles
Matigné-Briand
Rou-Marson
Chemillé
Rochemenier
La Fosse
Aubigne-sur-Layon
St-Georges-sur-Layon
Doué-la-Fontaine
960
Varrains
Montsoreau
Champigny
Candes St-Martin
Vihiers
Mestré
St-Germain
960
Le Coudray-
Macouard
St Cyr-en-
Bourg
Fontevraud
Neuil-
sur-Layon
Les Verchers-
sur-Layon
Montreuil-Bellay
Lerné
751
Les Cerqueux-sous-
Passavant
Passavant
sur Layon
Le Puy-Notre-Dame
938

N

10 km
5 miles

Highlights

1 The pilgrimage village of Candes-St-Martin

2 Fontevraud, the best-preserved abbey
  in France

3 Saumur, a gem of a winemaking, horsey
  country town with a famous château

4 Layon and Aubance valley vineyards,
  including the Château de Brissac

5 The splendid stretches of the Loire between
  Saumur and Angers

Plus me plaist le sejour qu'ont basty mes ayeux
Que des palais romains le front audacieux,
Plus que le marbre dur me plaist l'ardoise fine,
Plus mon Loyre gaulois, que le Tybre latin,
Plus mon petit Lyré que le mont Palatin:
Et plus que l'air marin la douceur angevine.

(The house which my ancestors built deligts me more/Than Roman palaces which put pride to the fore/I find fine slate more pleasing than a marble frieze/More pleasing my Gallic Loire than the Latin Tiber/More pleasing than the Palatine my little Lyré/And more pleasing than the seas my Angevin peace.)

Joachim du Bellay, 16th-century Angevin and Pléiade poet

No wonder poor Du Bellay yearned for his Angevin Loire when stuck in Rome – the Loire is at its most splendid and seductive in Anjou. East of the region's capital, Angers, the great sweeps of the river and its strands could mislead you into feeling that you're approaching the sea via a great estuary, while in fact the Loire still has a reasonably long course to run. It has a mesmerizing, exotic beauty here.

The stunning Loire-side town of Saumur is the main cultural centre of eastern Anjou. Known as the *perle de l'Anjou* because of its whiteness, and the *ville du cheval* because of its cavalry school and horse-riding traditions, it can claim to be one of the most interesting small provincial towns in France. It has a fairytale château, churches hung with extravagant tapestries and streets through which you can still easily imagine the carriages trundling by.

In the Saumurois, the area around and south of Saumur, the riches continue. The abbey of Fontevraud is one of the best-preserved medieval abbeys in Europe, where the famed Angevin kings of England Henry II and Richard the Lionheart lie buried along with Eleanor of Aquitaine. The Loire cliff face between Saumur and Montsoreau to the east consists of an almost unbroken succession of extraordinary villages, not just built against the rock but actually into it. On the plateau above grow the vines of Saumur, producing excellent reds and sparkling wines.

The locals make the distinction between *troglodytisme de coteau*, hillside troglodyte dwellings, and *troglodytisme de plaine*, where the caves have been dug down into the ground, as they have in vast number in and around Doué-la-Fontaine, west of Saumur. Here you'll find underground farms, underground houses, even an underground zoo. In a couple of spots artists have gone underground to create startling galleries.

Beyond these unusual and fascinating subterranean attractions, back above ground the Saumurois has more than its fair share of traditional Loire attractions. Fine churches abound, from major ones like Cunault, to delightful little rural ones. And along with the château at Saumur, there are other splendid white-stoned castles to visit, notably those of Brézé, Montreuil-Bellay and Montsoreau, the latter by the headquarters of the Parc Régional Naturel Loire-Anjou-Touraine, which incorporates the vast majority of eastern Anjou, both sides of the Loire.

Eastern Anjou to the north of the Loire presents a very different picture. The river's broad flat flood plain stretches into the distance, wide enough for the Authion river to steal a strip of land from the Loire. The sandy plain, sometimes termed the Vallée d'Anjou, is ideal for the intensive growing of fruit, flowers and vegetables. It was also susceptible to massive floods until Henri Plantagenêt (King Henry II of England) decided to control the waters by ordering a long artificial bank to be built right to the outskirts of Angers. This *grande levée*, as well as serving a crucial practical purpose, makes one of the most picturesque of all Loire-side roads. Romanesque churches are one cultural feature northeastern Anjou shares with the richer southeast, several standing out because of their alarming twisted spires. And one convent in these parts claims still to possess a piece of Christ's cross, sumptuously mounted. Almost as extravagant, seek out the exceptionally well-preserved Ancien Régime Château de Montgeoffroy on the north bank of the Authion. But the star of this chapter remains the Loire, absolutely magnificent seen from both banks between Saumur and Angers.

The Loire East of Saumur

Along the Loire, the change from Touraine to Anjou, and from the modern regions of Centre-Val de Loire to the Pays de la Loire, is seamless. Candes-St-Martin and Montsoreau, two stunningly beautiful villages by the Loire, may be in separate *départements*, but they're stuck together like Siamese twins. We've kept the two together by putting Candes-St-Martin in this chapter. From Montsoreau westwards to Saumur, some of the Loire Valley's most spectacular troglodyte houses have been dug into the sharp limestone cliff. The abbey of Fontevraud, one of the finest abbeys left standing in the Western world, with one of the most interesting histories, is the major cultural sight in this section.

Candes-St-Martin

This riverside village steeped in the memory of the great 4th-century missionary and monastic St Martin has one of the prettiest locations along the whole of the Loire Valley. It's particularly lovely viewed from the north, across the Loire or the Vienne, for it lies at the point where the last great Touraine tributary pours into the Loire, forming a very wide mass of water and announcing the start of the splendid Angevin Loire. The name Candes derives from the Latin for confluence, and Gallo-Romans settled here. If you climb the steep path to the top of the village, you can get spectacular views of the confluence and of the two rivers forking away from each other into the distance. The village below is only slightly troubled nowadays by the busy road to Saumur which tries to squeeze through its narrow main street.

Church of St-Martin

St Martin had a particular affection for this spot. He had a church built here, dedicated to the memory of St Maurice, another converted Roman cavalier, who refused

Getting Around

Reasonably regular **buses** link Fontevraud, Montsoreau, Turquant, Parnay, Souzay-Champigny and Dampierre with Saumur, except on Sundays.

Tourist Information

Montsoreau: Av de la Loire, 49730 Montsoreau, t 02 41 51 70 22, f 02 41 51 75 66.
Fontevraud-l'Abbaye: Chapelle Ste-Catherine, 49590 Fontevraud-l'Abbaye, t 02 41 51 79 45, f 02 41 51 79 01.

Market Days

Montsoreau: Flea market; every second Sunday in the month.
Fontevraud l'Abbaye: Wednesday.

Where to Stay and Eat

Candes-St-Martin ✉ 37500

Auberge de la Route d'Or, 2 Place de l'Eglise, t/f 02 47 95 81 10. Definitely worth a pilgrimage to, a tiny restaurant tucked into the lovely square by the the great village church. The dining area is almost as much a grotto as a dining room, with a comfortable feel, gentle service and interesting dishes such as eel in Roquefort sauce (menus €13–29).

Montsoreau ✉ 49730

**Hostellerie Le Bussy, 4 Rue Jeanne d'Arc, t 02 41 38 11 11, f 02 41 38 18 10 (*inexpensive*). Utterly charming hotel in a wonderful old house in the village street just above the château. Many of the rooms have been done up to three-star standard, so they're a real bargain. *Closed Dec–Feb; no restaurant.*
Diane de Méridor, 12 Quai Philippe de Commines, t 02 41 51 71 76, f 02 41 38 15 93. Standing close to the château, a warm place to eat (*menus €18–32.5*).
Le Saut aux Loups, Route de Saumur, t 02 41 51 70 30, f 02 41 38 15 30. In its sensational troglodyte setting above the Loire, a simple restaurant specializing in *galipettes*, monster mushrooms filled with goat's cheese, and *rillettes*, among other choices (*menu €9.5*). *Ring to check when it's open.*

Fontevraud-l'Abbaye ✉ 49590

**Prieuré Saint-Lazare, Rue St-Jean-de-l'Habit, t 02 41 51 73 16, f 02 41 51 75 50, *prieure@abbeyhotelfontevraud.com* (*moderate*). Actually part of the old abbey, a slick adaptation of the lepers' monastery, the cells turned into comfortable rooms, although a friend claimed she smelt a

---

to fight a band of Gaulish Christians and was punished for his insubordination with death. At the beginning of November 397, St Martin came to sort out a quarrel between clerks here, he fell ill and died. The story of the undignified argument over possession of his body is memorably told by Gregory of Tours, graphically revealing the importance attached to the securing of relics of holy men in early Christian times:

As soon as the holy man was taken ill in the village of Candes, as I have said already, the people of Poitiers and Tours began to assemble at his death-bed. When he was dead, a great altercation arose between the two groups. The men of Poitiers said: 'As a monk he is ours. He became an abbot in our town. We entrusted him to you, but we demand him back. It is sufficient for you that, while he was a Bishop on this earth, you enjoyed his company, you shared his table, you were strengthened by his blessing and above all you were cheered by his miracles. Let all these things suffice for you, and permit us at least to carry away his dead body.' To this the men of Tours replied: 'If you say that we should be satisfied with the miracles which he performed for us, then admit that while he was with you he did more than in our town. If all his other lingering odour of nuns in her room. The cloister and church have been transformed into delightful dining areas. The tranquillity can often be broken, however, as the place is large enough to act as a conference centre (*menus €15–47*).

La Croix Blanche, 7 Place des Plantagenêts, t 02 41 51 71 11, f 02 41 38 15 38 (*inexpensive*). Well-established hotel in the village, almost at the entrance to the abbey, It's built around a very pleasant old-fashioned looking courtyard with gallery. The rooms are in old-fashioned style too, but well maintained. The restaurant looks rather functional, but the food is fine (*menus €16–35*). *Closed early Jan–early Feb and mid-Nov.*

La Licorne, Allée Ste-Catherine, t 02 41 51 72 49. Set in an 18th-century house close to the church, with a private garden, this restaurant is highly reputed for its cuisine. Try such dishes as guinea fowl in Layon wine sauce (*menus €21–35*). *Closed Sun pm and Mon out of season.*

Le Domaine de Mestré, at Mestré between Fontevraud and Montsoreau, t 02 41 51 75 87 or t 02 41 51 72 32, f 02 41 51 71 90, *domaine-de-mestre@wanadoo.fr* (*moderate*). Once part of the abbey's estates, a fine stone property where pilgrims were put up (*table d'hôte €22*).

Turquant ✉ 49730

Demeure de la Vignole, 3 Impasse Marguerite d'Anjou, t 02 41 53 67 00, f 02 41 53 67 09, *demeure@vignole.com, www.demeure-vignole.com* (*moderate*). Exquisite little new hotel between the cliffside and vines. The rooms and sitting rooms in the 15th- and 17th-century lodgings are beautifully decorated with tiles. There's a big troglodyte cave in which meals can be served on request. Just one or two jarring notes which the owners can't do much about: the nearby electricity pylons and the occasional gassy smell from the mushrooming caves nearby. But this place is utterly gorgeous.

Saumur (western outskirts) ✉ 49400

Château de Beaulieu B&B, Route de Montsoreau, t 02 41 67 69 51, f 02 41 67 63 64, *chbeaul@club-internet.fr* (*moderate*). A charming young couple have recently taken over this delightful 17th-century manor neighbouring the large Gratien et Meyer sparkling wine centre. They've redone most of the rooms, but also invite their guests to make the most of the *enfilade* of salons down below, decorated with wood panelling. The place is a listed building, but there is a swimming pool in the sloping garden.

miracles are left out of the count, he raised two dead men for you and only one for us; and, as he himself used often to say, his miraculous power was greater before he was made Bishop than it was afterwards. It is therefore necessary that what he did not achieve with us when he was alive he should complete now that he is dead...'

Ruse rather than reason settled this unseemly squabble:

When the men of Tours saw that all the Poitevins had fallen asleep, they took the mortal clay of that most holy body and some passed it out through the window while others stood outside to receive it. They placed it in a boat and all those present rowed down the River Vienne. As soon as they reached the River Loire, they set their course for the city of Tours, praising God and chanting psalms.

So much for high ideals. During the journey carrying St Martin's body back up the Loire to Tours, a further is miracle supposed to have occurred, the trees and shrubs on the banks coming into leaf or flower. A mild late autumn is known in French as an *été de la St-Martin*.

Many of the most famous early French saints made it here to pay their respects to St Martin, including St Geneviève, who helped protect Paris from the Huns; Clotilde,

Clovis' wife, who persuaded the Frankish leader to become the first French Christian king; and St Radegonde, the put-upon wife of the violent Clotaire.

The present solid, dominating, squat church in the village, dedicated to St Martin, was built from 1175. It looks, from a distance, rather like a great hall topped by a small helmet of a Romanesque tower. The defensive appearance becomes still more apparent when you see the west front, which has crenellations and two square towers stuck to the front. There are also crenellations above the north porch. These 15th-century additions were deliberately made to impress and put off potential attackers.

The church was an important place of medieval pilgrimage. Many French kings stopped here. Pilgrims would arrive from the river bank and this may explain why the north porch was given such prominence, facing the river. A little sloping square leads up to it, the eye attracted by the wealth of sculpture decorating it and by a single, improbably slender column which stands in the centre of it. It looks far too fragile to support the weight of the Angevin vaults above. The outer statues are full-size figures, a mixture of the Apostles and later saints. The tympanum represents the intercession of the Virgin and St John. Human faces and fabulous monsters congregate at the door, the most remarkable lot of sculptures. The statuary dates from the first half of the 13th century, some in a reasonable state of repair, some mutilated in religious wars.

Inside, the church appears somewhat unstable, with sloping floor and irregular bays. The feeling of a spacious hall comes from the fact that the aisles are the same height as the nave. This plan was started from 1215, after a pause in the building programme due to warring between the French and the English. The choir end is the earliest part of the building. Before you reach it, peer up at the extraordinary painted sculptures at the tops of the columns, notably along the gathered shafts. Among them, armoured knights and angels fight it out with monkeyish devils (the distance up makes it hard to make out these details clearly). The ceiling is covered by Angevin vaults. The northern side chapel commemorating St Martin probably occupies the site of the original chapel to St Maurice. One 19th-century stained-glass window here depicts St Martin's body being taken upriver by boat.

Montsoreau

Entre Candes et Montsoreau, il n'y paît ni vaches, ni veaux (Between Candes and Montsoreau neither cows nor calves can graze).

As the old saying so poetically puts it, it's hard to see where the buildings of Candes-St-Martin stop and those of Montsoreau begin. Montsoreau has, like its neighbour, become a member of the association of Les Plus Beaux Villages de France. Passing into it from Candes, it's said that you cross a very ancient frontier between Touraine and Anjou, the point apparently once marking the division between the Gaulish tribes of the Turoni and the Andes.

A first medieval fort of some kind went up in the 9th century. The medieval lords of Montsoreau built their castle to oversee a thriving Loire port here; they could make a good living exacting tolls from those on the river crossing the regional border. Jean II de Chambes was the local lord in the middle of the 15th century and became an important adviser to King Charles VII, given numerous titles, including Master of the Royal Hunt. He had a new château built right by the Loire. The walls of his castle virtually bathed in the river itself, the Loire supplying the moat. Now the castle is separated from the river by the main road, the D947 to Saumur, which virtually touches its tufa walls.

Château de Montsoreau

Open May–mid-Sept 9.30–7.30, mid-Sept–mid-Nov 10–6, mid-Feb–April 10–6.

What remains of the medieval Château de Montsoreau has recently been renovated and turned into a slick new museum, **Les Imaginaires de Loire**. Actually, just one wing is left of Jean de Chambes' castle, but it's still a beautiful piece. The exterior looks sober and simple for the period, with big square end towers and a lack of decoration on the outside, even in the curious split-level dormer windows. But there is an openness to the building which shows the period's changing approach to lordly architecture, increasingly taking into consideration good living as well as strategic location and defence. Entering the courtyard with its garden on the cliff side, though, you'll see how the Renaissance has been tacked on here in the form of an ornate stair tower of the 1520s, given typical Renaissance motifs. The stonemasons kept a medieval sense of humour, though – one scene depicts two monkeys at work, with the motto '*Je le feray (I'll do it)*'. This extravagant stair tower was built to celebrate a family wedding.

From inside the castle you can enjoy splendid views onto the Loire, with little boats and an island visible below. The stylish contemporary exhibition helps you focus on the Loire and its many facets more generally in a presentation that's part museological, part show. With its light and visual effects, it's been organized by past-masters in the art of entertainment, the Grévin company. Nature along the Loire, the history and economy of the river, the château's past and the legendary Dame de Montsoreau (*see* opposite page) are all covered.

To get an even better view onto both château and Loire, take some of the steep streets up through the village, which has become the headquarters of the new Parc Naturel Régional Loire-Anjou-Touraine.

Parc Naturel Régional Loire-Anjou-Touraine

Address for correspondence: Maison du Parc, 49730 Montsoreau,
t 02 41 53 66 00, f 02 41 53 66 09.

This specially protected area covers the lands between Tours and Angers, surely the richest culturally along the Loire, and arguably the most beautiful. It was almost turned into a separate *département* at the Revolution. and would have

La Dame de Montsoreau

The De Chambes family produced a number of dramatic characters in the 15th and 16th centuries. One of Jean II's daughters married the famous 15th-century French chronicler, Philippe de Commines, in 1472. Another became the mistress of Louis XI's brother, Charles de Berry, but just missed her sister's wedding as she died from poisoning. More sinister still was the case of the great-grandson of Jean de Chambes who, in the course of the civil war of the Wars of Religion, led the slaughter of Protestants in Anjou during the St Bartholomew's Day massacres. Elevated to the rank of count for his services, he was in turn assassinated. His brother Charles took on the family title and married Françoise de Maridor.

She is the famed Dame de Montsoreau, the one fictionalized by Alexandre Dumas in his typically heavy-handed manner in the novel of the same name, the sequel to the book which produced the extremely popular and utterly historically misleading recent film, *La Reine Margot*. Françoise de Maridor was subtly rechristened as Diane de Maridor in Dumas' book. His story has it that Diane was forced to marry Count Charles de Chambes. The young Bussy d'Amboise tried to come to her rescue and fell madly for her. The two become lovers in the tale, but eventually Bussy is killed in cowardly manner.

In reality it seems that Bussy was a terrible scoundrel, a violent participant in the murder of Protestants in the St Bartholomew's Day massacre too, a ruthless ruler as governor of Anjou, and a major womanizer. He did seemingly attempt to seduce Françoise de Maridor, even writing to a friend at court that he 'had captured the grand huntsman's doe in his net'. A tender trap was set for him, though, in Anjou, and he fell into it. He went to meet Françoise, only to be assassinated. Dumas once again altered the facts and had his murder take place in the Château de Montsoreau, while the event actually took place at the family Château de la Coutancière, across from here on the north bank of the Loire.

incorporated the wonderful towns of Saumur, Chinon, Richelieu and Bourgueil. This didn't come about, but in 1996 the area was turned into a French regional nature park. The Parc Naturel Régional Loire-Anjou-Touraine also covers the areas around Azay-le-Rideau, L'Ile-Bouchard, Montreuil-Bellay, Doué-la-Fontaine and Beaufort-en-Vallée.

The park authorities' aim isn't to try to preserve the area in aspic; indeed the new A85 motorway linking Tours and Angers is still being built through it, despite protests. But their mission does include protecting the area's heritage and traditions and bringing them to the fore, encouraging the continuation of traditional life and ways as far as possible.

While navigation along the Loire died out long ago, the park's staff maintains its stretch of river and works to make people appreciate it more. For example, the atmospheric quays at Candes-St-Martin and Chouzé-sur-Loire have already been restored and are now illuminated at night. At Candes-St-Martin, one of the finest viewing points along the Loire, the park authorities have put up a big orientation table, while at St-Michel-sur-Loire they have erected a belvedere from which to appreciate the river better. Also, a Circuit de la Confluence has been prepared by the artist Denis Clavreuil to guide you round certain particularly picturesque spots.

Another aim of the park is to make not just the local people, but also visitors, take note of more discreet local nature and local traditions. Already, some five **Sentiers d'Interprétation** have been laid out, walks of between 3 and 7km with panels along the way to get you to look more closely at the typical elements of the countryside. You can follow such Sentiers at **Gizeux** (near the château), **St-Rémy-la-Varenne** (passing by a Loire island), **Le Puy-Notre-Dame** (going through Loire vineyards), **Brain-sur-Allonnes** (concentrating on a forest) and **Andard** (leading you through the fertile flat plain north of the Loire). The brochures and panels cater to English-speaking visitors. A programme of special nature walks and events is also organized from May to October – look out for Les Carnet de Sorties for details, but to appreciate these you really need good French. Keep an eye out too for the Escapades, events organized around one specific place in the park each year. In addition, you can stay at special environmentally friendly *gîtes* chosen by the park authorities, the Gîtes Panda.

Plans for the future include the opening of a Maison du Parc for the public, as an introductory centre; Maisons à Thèmes, little museums each featuring a particular tradition; and a Circuit Patrimoine, a more substantial cultural trail. The one tradition which the park authorities have already tried to bring to the fore is the surprisingly inventive basket-weaving at Villaines-les-Rochers (*see* pp.327–8).

The Abbey of Fontevraud

Open June–3rd Sun in Sept 9–6.30, rest of year 9.30–12 and 2–5.30; for the abbey's cultural and concert programme contact the Centre Culturel de l'Ouest, t 02 41 51 73 52, f 02 41 38 15 44.

The burial place of the Angevin Plantagenet kings of England; the greatest vestiges of a monastic establishment left standing in France; the first in a special order of monasteries founded from the early 12th century; originally set up as an ascetic community but to become one of the richest royal religious retreats in the realm; under Napoleon demoted to serve as a prison which saw one of the worst of France's literary *enfants terribles* locked up here. Only in 1963 was the abbey of Fontevraud acquired by France's State Heritage Department. It became the largest site of restoration of an historic monument in France, and the prisoners were replaced by tourists. Today, the emptiness of most of Fontevraud's great spaces gives little idea of the busy communities which once brought life to it, but the architecture will impress you with its grandeur, including the largest cloister in France and the unique 12th-century fish-scale-roofed kitchen.

Fontevraud's most surprising claim to fame alongside the Plantagenet royal tombs and the architectural legacy is the fact that, quite exceptionally, especially for the Middle Ages, for virtually all the abbey's history women ruled the roost.

The History of Fontevraud

Robert d'Arbrissel, the Abbey's Charismatic Founder

The name of Fontevraud derives from the fountain of Evraud. Evraud wasn't the founder of the abbey; in fact nothing is known of him, although a story long did the rounds that he was a local bandit who changed his ways under the influence of the great founding figure of the abbey at the end of the 11th century, Robert d'Arbrissel. Monasticism was in a state of crisis at that time. The best-known reforming influence of the period was Bernard de Clairvaux, the influential early Cistercian monk who adopted and advocated a very strict form of the Benedictine order. At the same time Robert d'Arbrissel began his own branch of this order.

Brought up in Arbrissel in Brittany, Robert was the son of a priest who lived unmarried with a woman. Well educated, Robert followed in his father's footsteps as a priest and helped Sylvestre de la Guerche, a soldier who hadn't received any training in the priesthood, to become bishop of Rennes. It seems Robert left Brittany because of complications caused by Sylvestre's dubious promotion. Continuing his studies in Paris at a time when the Church was undergoing major moral changes, Robert learnt that in the eyes of the reformers he came from a doubly sinful situation, the son of a priest who lived in sin with a woman, and benefiting from corrupt Church practices.

Both Robert and Sylvestre underwent a conversion to the reformers' ways of thinking. Robert was called upon by Sylvestre to help reform the Breton clergy in about 1085 'in order to liberate the Church from its shameful servitude to the secular and to stamp out the incestuous copulation between priests and lay people'. This heady conversion, with Robert given the title of 'archipriest', didn't go down well with other Breton clergy. Such was the opposition to him that on Sylvestre's death Robert had again to leave the region. He went to teach theology in Angers, but then decided to become a hermit in the region of Maine, north of Anjou. By this time, however, he had won many supporters, and his reputation as a charismatic preacher had spread far and wide. He apparently attracted women in particularly large numbers. Followers quickly forced him out of his solitude and Robert founded a first community at Notre-Dame de la Roë, in Maine.

Pope Urban II travelled to western France in 1096, drumming up support for the First Crusade. He used the opportunity of his visit to put Robert's preaching to the test and was so impressed by what he heard that he declared D'Arbrissel 'sower of the divine word', ordering him to extend his work. While the pope continued madly recruiting knights to go fighting abroad, Robert was left to spread Christian fervour at home. He attracted further followers in droves. More and more women were mesmerized by his preaching and their presence would lead to numerous rumours. Many felt scandalized by the Breton's heady powers. Accusations were flung at D'Arbrissel, wild-haired and wildly popular ascetic that the sources make him out to have been, most notably that he slept with many of his women followers. He reportedly retorted in bold terms that if the women in his following excited his sexual desires, it was all the better for him to reject these.

His ragbag of followers were massed together in hovels at first. Lepers counted among the numbers living in ramshackle huts or in grottoes. Some order was soon established with the founding of the abbey of Fontevraud in 1101; the land was offered by the lord of Montsoreau and placed under the protection of the bishop of Poitiers.

Significantly and exceptionally for the times, from the beginning Robert insisted that women should be given an important position in the establishment, and very soon this would become a predominant one. Women and men were placed in the same abbey, but in separate priories. Mixed orders had existed since the 5th century, although they were unusual, but the more exceptional aspect of Fontevraud was that overall control should have been given to women.

Robert d'Arbrissel was, however, in charge of the new community at Fontevraud at first. But he was intent on converting others and setting up new priories. It also seems that some of the women of noble birth who joined the order exerted their influence from a very early stage, for example objecting to some of the ambiguities of Robert's rule. They certainly contacted Geoffroy de Vendôme, a powerful Benedictine abbot and relative of one nun, Pétronille de Chemillé. Geoffroy wrote a stinging letter to Robert, euphemistically accusing him of wanting to crucify himself in a new form of martyrdom...in some of the women's beds. For whatever reasons, Robert left the abbey of Fontevraud in the hands of a woman, Hersende de Montsoreau, to be assisted by Pétronille de Chemillé, and went off to found further priories, setting up a whole separate Fontevrist order of monasteries before he died in 1116.

From as early as 1106, the community at the mother establishement was divided into four groups, a separation which then dictated the architecture of the abbey. The principal section, the Grand Moûtier, was the convent for young women of noble birth and widows of good virtue, dedicated to a contemplative life. Repentant women and women who had been married several times, as well as lay sisters, were settled in the convent of La Madeleine, devoting their attentions to manual labour. Lepers, meanwhile, were tended by sisters in the Prieuré St-Lazare, set a little distance away from the other buildings. The men were given the monastery of St-Jean-de-l'Habit (short for *habitation*).

Women Less Sinful Than Elsewhere in the Christian World?

After Hersende de Montsoreau's death in 1115, D'Arbrissel appointed Pétronille de Chemillé abbess of Fontevraud. At the same time, the statutes confirmed in writing that women should be placed before men in the establishment. This female leadership caused some tensions. It has been suggested that D'Arbrissel may have been particularly exceptional in his times for arguing against the deeply rooted notion that women were to be regarded as more sinful than men, because one of their number had led Adam, and hence mankind, astray. D'Arbrissel may also have given women authority by way of thanks to the noble women who had joined his order and through whose wealthy connections the establishment had received generous donations of land. The cult of the Virgin had also grown strong in this period. D'Arbrissel advised that it might be best to appoint widows as abbesses, with their knowledge of the wider world, although for a long period the power of the cult meant that it was virgins who were selected to rule the abbey. It seems that D'Arbrissel placated many of the men by pointing out that being subservient to women was an act of humility on their part and therefore could help them in their quest to attain paradise!

When D'Arbrissel died at his priory of Orsan in the Berry, Pétronille went to fight over his body with the monks there and won, transporting his remains back to Fontevraud. He was buried in the church choir, but unusually for medieval times, after his death no cult grew up around any relics. It may be that he had been too controversial a figure – certainly he was never canonized. Pétronille de Chemillé continued overseeing his wider work, ruling over all the Fontevrist establishments, with 50 priories set up by the time she passed away in 1150.

It was the next abbess, Mathilde d'Anjou, sister of Geoffroy Plantangenêt, who established the strong link between the famous Angevin dynasty and Fontevraud. Henri Plantagenêt even stayed at Fontevraud before he set off for England to be crowned King Henry II in Westminster Abbey in 1154. Two of his children, Joan and John, were educated for several years at the Angevin abbey. And, most famously, Henri was buried at Fontevraud in 1189. This wasn't as he had wished, but as his son Richard the Lionheart dictated. Such was the displeasure that this difficult son of his had caused Henri through his lifetime that one chronicler claimed that at the funeral blood began to flow from the dead king's corpse in protest at this final act of insubordination.

Henri's widow, Eleanor of Aquitaine, chose to live at Fontevraud from 1194 until her death in 1204. She even took the veil just before she passed away. She it was who deliberately decided to maintain Fontevraud as the royal Plantagenet resting place. Her children Richard the Lionheart and Joan died in 1199 and she ordered a necropolis for them. She in turn was buried here. Isabelle d'Angoulême, the wife of King John, was also interred on the site, as was Raymond VII, son of Joan and a member of the powerful dynasty of Toulouse counts.

By 1189, 129 Fontevrist monasteries had been created. In all, 149 would come into existence, four in England, the most well known at Amesbury in Wiltshire. After its initial illustrious period, however, the abbey of Fontevraud and the Fontevrist order declined in importance for a long time. Financial crises followed one after another, while the rules were flouted. The moral order changed completely, with the different sexes even said to have shared parts of the abbey.

A strict religious hand came to take back the reins in the mid-15th century. Mind you, the new abbess, Marie de Bretagne, had her position bought for her by her uncle, Duke Arthur III of Brittany. She spearheaded a thorough reform of the order. Then in 1491 the reign of Bourbon abbesses of royal blood began at Fontevraud. The job would be handed down from aunt to niece. Money poured in to maintain and add to the buildings. The 16th century saw the second great period of building work at Fontevraud, with many of the earlier constructions, including the vast Grand Moûtier cloister, being replaced. Even with the powerful Bourbon abbesses, protests by the brothers arose periodically.

Medieval Men Getting a Taste of Their Own Medicine

Throughout the abbey's history, monks periodically protested against the rule of the abbesses. In the 17th century there are some particularly interesting examples of actions taken by the male inmates. Memorable struggles occurred with Jeanne-Baptiste de Bourbon after she imposed her strict leadership as abbess from 1639. One group of monks, sent away for a time to a Parisian priory, took the opportunity to run off to a different abbey in another order. The abbess was swift to take legal action, going straight to the king's Grand Council – she did have the slight advantage that the king happened to be her brother. The argument centred on who held superiority of spiritual jurisdiction and many subtle arguments were constructed around questions of biblical interpretation. The abbess, needless to say, won the case. During the same troubled period, other monks still at Fontevraud drew up a text with the unhappy title 'Reasons for which the brothers of St-Jean-de-l'Habit argue that they should not be forced to leave their problems in the hands of Madame'. Among their demands were that they should be treated as priests 'ordained by the Church and not as slaves'! For once, historical examples of power politics between the sexes working the other way.

The noble Rochechouarts took on the title of abbess from the late 17th century. Mademoiselle de Montespan, a close family relation who was to become famous as Louis XIV's lover, came to visit the abbey on several occasions. The naivety of the nuns amused her, but she was apparently most interested in being allowed to see some of their number who had gone mad in the institution. The ideals of convent life didn't suit all. Later, Mademoiselle de Montespan came to stay for a year. She brought her interest in culture to Fontevraud. Although the abbess of the time had reinstigated strict rules for the nuns and monks, she couldn't resist her wordly leanings herself. The Racine play *Esther* was put on at the abbey, a new abbess's palace was built during this period and the gardens were well tended.

In 1738, Louis XV entrusted the education of his four daughters to Louise de Rochechouart. The royal princesses remained at Fontevraud until 1750. Louis XV was distressed to have so many daughters. That Fontevraud was chosen for them shows the importance of the abbey, but also how distanced the girls were from their royal parents. They took to calling the abbess '*maman*', as distinct from their mother whom they referred to more formally as '*maman reine*'.

Come the Revolution, the nuns and monks were expelled and the abbey was put up for sale in lots. St-Jean-de-l'Habit and La Madeleine found buyers, who dismantled many buildings for their stone. The furniture of the whole abbey disappeared. But the larger buildings were simply left in a state of neglect. Napoleon's administration had the utilitarian idea of transforming the place into a vast penitentiary, the architect in charge of this unedifying conversion, Charles-Marie Normand, destroying old elements which interferred with his greater plans.

Fontevraud continued to serve as a prison even well after the Second World War. The outcast criminal and homosexual author Jean Genet spent time imprisoned here and revealed the chilling side to Fontevraud during that period in *Le Miracle de la Rose*: 'Of all the prisons in France, Fontevrault is the most disturbing. It is the one which gave me the strongest impression of distress and desolation, and I know that the inmates who were familiar with other prisons experienced comparable feelings of emotion and suffering as I did, just in hearing the mention of its name.' This part of the abbey's history is all too often forgotten. It's a shock to consider that the last inmates only left in 1985, although the Grand Moûtier began to be cleared in 1963. The traces of this ugly past are being wiped away. Meanwhile, Fontevraud had already been selected as the site for a more edifying project, the Centre Culturel de l'Ouest, a cultural centre serving several *départements*, as Fontevraud is well positioned close to Anjou's borders with Touraine and Poitou.

Visiting Fontevraud

You enter the abbey grounds via an impressive neoclassical gateway. The first court-yard, cobbled and of curious shape, is lined with the Bourbon abbesses' house and stables, noble Ancien Régime architecture. This makes rather a wordly introduction to an ancient abbey. Only once through the ticket office and extensive shop does the more contemplative side of the place emerge.

Of the sections into which medieval Fontevraud abbey was divided, you principally see the Grand Moûtier. The Prieuré St-Lazare has been converted into a hotel-cum-conference centre. The other two priories practically disappeared, but the St-Benoît infirmary has survived. The **abbey church** is grand and relatively plain, dating back to close to the abbey's founding. Inside, it's one of those staggering church spaces which seems to gain in grandeur for being stripped of virtually all decoration now. The church was a massive project for its time, proof of what the Romanesque architects were capable of. The apse, choir and transepts were built first, Pope Calixtus II coming to consecrate the high altar in 1119. The choir rises jubilantly skywards. The nave, from later in the 12th century, is less restrained in detail. Its bulk is held up by massive pillars with carved capitals, its ceiling by a row of beautifully fully-shaped domes in the Angoulême style. When the church was turned to prison uses in the 19th century, the nave was divided into four floors, traces of which can be made out up the walls.

Dwarfed by the size of the great edifice, the four **Plantagenet tombs** lie on the church's floor like carefully arranged matchsticks. They haven't stayed here through history, but have been moved from cloisters to kitchen, to a hiding place during the Revolution. With the entente cordiale, the idea was even advanced to dispatch them to England. They got as far as Versailles to be painted; the pale polychrome colours of blues, reds and pinks date from that time. All four royal figures have great nobility. Each lies on a bed, three in stone, Isabelle's of wood, with false drapery carved below the body. Henri's fine-featured head rests, crowned, on a plump pillow. One hand holds tightly onto his sceptre. Eleanor of Aquitaine is portrayed rather primly reading a book, a less restful picture, her raised hands giving her effigy more life. She had already seen her son Richard the Lionheart die. His effigy lies next to hers, a tough young bearded figure asleep. Isabelle's tomb is of slighter proportions. She lies on her narrower bed, her hands rather anxiously clasped on her chest. Visitors sometimes leave roses at the feet of these tombs.

The **cloisters** off the abbey church are monumental. They reflect the scale on which they were planned in the 12th century, but were rebuilt in the mid-16th century, as were the surrounding buildings. The style is therefore French Renaissance. The cloisters are claimed to be the best example of that period's conventual architecture to survive in France. The double columns employed around them have been said to symbolize the two sexes of the mixed order. While most of the buildings were relatively soberly decorated, the **chapterhouse** stands apart, held up by exquisite vaulting. Reforming the Bourbon abbesses may have been, shy and retiring they certainly weren't – humility doesn't seem to have be a strong point, to go by the initials left marked in the stone carving here, referring to Renée de Bourbon and Louise de Bourbon. The temporal initials are complemented by symbols of vanity, memento mori. Even more surprisingly, the semicircles beneath the arches have been painted with sumptuous New Testament scenes, concentrating in particular on stories of the Virgin; only Mary's glory has been added to by that of the abbesses. They pop up in the corners of the paintings, praying. Actually most of their portraits were added after the artist Thomas Pot had completed his work, around 1560, although Louise and Renée de Bourbon were placed at the foot of Christ's deposition from the cross at the start.

Off the cloisters, you can wander through further empty chambers which sometimes contain exhibitions. The *chauffoir* with fireplace was where nuns executed embroidery rather than manuscript copying. The interminably long dormitories are reached by a coffered Renaissance staircase. The cellar is given over to exhibitions on monastic life. A doorway takes you out into the massive courtyard of the **St-Benoît infirmary**, its architecture dating mainly from the end of the 16th century to the beginning of the 17th. It has a secular, almost château-like look, no symbols of religion clearly visible, except in the little Chapelle St-Benoît to one side, dating back to the abbey's early days. This chapel's architecture was terribly mangled when half of it was annexed off to create apartments for the abbesses, but it retains part of its Angevin Gothic vaulting. You don't visit any of the other buildings around the courtyard, but you can marvel at the sheer size of the place. With over 600 people living at the abbey at one period, St-Benoît didn't just accommodate the sick but also the aged who needed care.

Next comes the massive **refectory**. Strict refectory rules were that the nuns should eat facing away from others. A sister would read in monotone through the meal. Silence was imposed, noise punished. The splendid, bizarrely byzantine octagonal roofed building at the end of refectory remained a mystery for a long time, its original purpose forgotten. Some reckoned it to be a mortuary chapel, others a baptismal parlour; one story even claimed it to be the tower where the legendary bandit Evraud had lived. Those stone fish scales and mushroom chimney pots on the roof might provide you with some clues as to the building's real medieval use, as a **kitchen**. This charcterful and rather comical building was possibly built around the time of the abbey's founding and is now unique in France. The roofing was in fact redone at the start of the 20th century and the disposition of the chimney pots may be somewhat contrived. Inside, Fontevraud's kitchen is quite staggering with its eight hearths. The play of octagons and squares in the architecture makes for a lesson in the joys of geometry. Amusing little sculptural details add to the pleasure of the place. Probably different fireplaces were used according to the direction of the changing wind.

To give you some idea of the cooking that might have gone on here, the lord of Boulogne had apparently in one period to supply the abbey with 100,000 herrings! Beyond the Romanesque kitchen, pleasant gardens have been recreated. The way through them leads to the separate **Prieuré St-Lazare**, once for lepers and those who tended them, now reserved for hotel and conference guests (*see* 'Where to Stay and Eat', pp.361–2). The abbey runs an excellent **musical programme** from September to June, and sells recordings made here.

In the **village of Fontevraud** that spreads star-shaped down the valley roads surrounding the abbey, you might care to take a look inside the **Eglise St-Michel**, founded by Henri Plantagenêt no less, around 1180. He and Eleanor of Aquitaine may even be represented on two of the vaults' bosses. Several later artistic treasures adorn the Angevin Gothic space, including riches from the abbey and a Crucifixion by Etienne Dumontier, painted in the 1560s, and which has been interpreted as an allegory of the Wars of Religion, featuring many royal figures of the day. The abbess in the picture is probably the less than tolerant Louise de Bourbon, who received a visit from King Charles IX in 1565, during which she apparently exhorted him to massacre the Protestant 'heretics'.

From Montsoreau to Saumur

A line of amazing villages built into the limestone cliff runs west from Montsoreau to Saumur. Nowhere will you see finer troglodyte dwellings on the riverbanks of the Loire region. Some of the houses have several levels of rock rooms. In certain parts, the neatly cut stone blocks of the windows and doors look almost as though they've become overgrown with a kind of rock ivy. Look out for the particularly elegant troglodyte houses at La Maumenière, La Vignole, Turquant and Le Val-Hulin.

Champignonnière du Saut aux Loups

Open March–11 Nov daily 10–6.30.

Climb the cliffside of **La Maumenière** to reach the impressive network of quarrying caves of this mushroom farm-cum-restaurant and tourist sight. The quarries around here were principally exploited between the 14th and 17th centuries, but quarrying continued, by hand, right up until the 1950s. Among the places to be built from the local stone was the grand church of Les Ardilliers in Saumur. The troglodyte dwellings at the front of Le Saut aux Loups, now partly converted into a restaurant, were lived in up until just after the war. In the hillside beyond lie kilometres of quarries, many of the corridors and chambers devoted to mushroom growing. On the guided tour, you're shown around 700m.

You're first treated to an explanation of the quarrying work which lasted for so many centuries. Mushroom-growing began at the start of the 20th century, and the

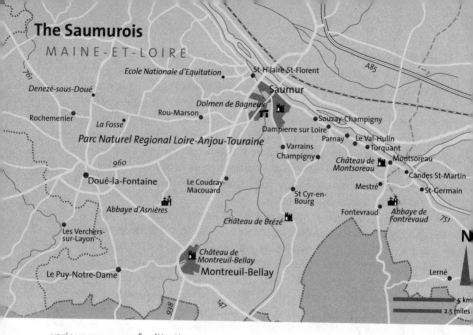

Ecole Nationale d'Equitation

St-Hilaire-St-Florent

A85

Denezé-sous-Doué

Saumur

Dolmen de Bagneux

Rochemenier

Rou-Marson

La Fosse

Souzay-Champigny

Dampierre sur Loire

Parnay

Le Val-Hulin

Parc Naturel Regional Loire-Anjou-Touraine

Turquant

960

Varrains

Montsoreau

Champigny

Château de
Montsoreau

Candes St-Martin

Doué-la-Fontaine

Le Coudray-
Macouard

Mestré

St-Germain

St Cyr-en-
Bourg

Abbaye d'Asnières

Fontevraud

Abbaye de
Fontevraud

Les Verchers-
sur-Layon

Château de Brézé

751

Château de
Montreuil-Bellay

Montreuil-Bellay

Lerné

Le Puy-Notre-Dame

938

147

N

5 km

2.5 miles

various manners of cultivation are presented. The quarries dug into the Loire cliffside and terrain in the Saumurois provide lots of cool, dark, humid spaces, all essential elements in good mushroom growing. With such advantages, the area produces the edible fungi on a fabulous scale. It also has a couple of working museums on the subject, this one and one in St-Hilaire-St-Florent, just west of Saumur. The horse manure produced in vast quantities by that horsey town, mixed with straw and pasteurized before use, makes the compost on which the mushrooms grow, once the mushroom spores have been sewn in sterilized rye and millet grain. The oldest method was to grow the mushrooms on mounds or beds of compost. Then growing in big bags took off in the 1960s, while now the main method is of growing mushrooms in boxes. Old photographs help give an interesting historical view of the changing practices. The mushroom-pickers wear miners'-style helmets with built-in lamps to do their job.

The main production in the Saumurois is of button mushrooms, known in French as *champignons de Paris*. But given that some three-quarters of the national production come from the Saumurois, you'd have thought that the locals might press for a change in name to *champignons de Saumur*. Other mushrooms are also cultivated in the Saumurois caves. *Pleurotes*, oyster mushrooms, grow yellow, blue and pink. *Pieds-bleu*, or bluets, and *shitake* are further exotic-looking, tasty specialities. *Galipettes* are the big open mushrooms which are often served, stuffed with extra ingredients, in Saumurois restaurants. Le Saut aux Loups also displays a selection of very wacky mushrooms from around the world.

At **La Vignole**, you can climb up to an extraordinary manor with a pretty little pepper-pot tower, its openings embellished with classical ornamentation. La Vignole is one of three sites along this stretch of river which lays claim to the distinction of being the place where Marguerite d'Anjou, the ill-fortuned wife of King Henry VI of

England, died. **Turquant**, too, has some very fine houses that emerge from the rock-face, notably La Grande Vignolle (*open Easter–Oct 10–6*).

At **Le Val Hulin** next door, the main attraction is the Troglo des Pommes Tapées (*open July–Aug Tues–Sun 10–12 and 2.30–6; second half of June and Sept Tues–Sun 2.30–6, plus 10–12 weekends; Easter–mid-June and mid-Sept–mid-Nov weekends only 10–12 and 2.30–6*). The First World War tiger of a French prime minister Georges Clemenceau apparently liked to eat these carefully squashed apples with his gloves on during his frequent visits to the area; the British Royal Navy was the locals' best customer. American production put an end to the Saumur trade, but Alain Ludin revived the tradition recently. He shows you how the *pommes tapées* are carefully hammered into shape in a splendid cave with a *pommes tapées* oven which atmospherically fills the place with smoke at times. You're given a tasting at the end of the tour.

At **Parnay**, a little track by the town hall leads down to the river, with views onto a Loire sandbank which attracts an exceptional number of birds in season. Climb to the charming church on the cliff and you get fine wider views. The Château de Parnay

The Wines of Saumur-Champigny

Generally recognized as the best of the reds produced across the Saumurois, and probably Anjou, Saumur-Champigny wines come from nine parishes on the limestone plateau in the triangle of land between the Loire and the Thouet south of Saumur town. The vines extend over roughly 1,000 hectares south from the cliff-face by the Loire.

To go with its cranberry, or even ruby, richness of colour, Saumur-Champigny often smells of cherries. It has the sweet bouquet of Cabernet Franc, by far the most important grape here, although winemakers may use some Cabernet Sauvignon or Pineau d'Aunis. To taste, it's a fruity wine which may sometimes have a slightly dry aftertaste with hints of sloes. It generally has more complexity than the ordinary Saumur red, developing spicy aromas.

The wine cooperative or **Cave des Vignerons de Saumur St-Cyr-en-Bourg** (*t 02 41 53 06 08; open May–Sept 9.30–6.30, rest of year Mon–Sat 9–12 and 2–6*) produces a healthy percentage of the *appellation*'s wine, up to as much as 40 per cent. A good individual property to visit would be the **Château de Villeneuve** at Souzay-Champigny. It's an estate around a 19th-century château that benefits from an attractive setting as well as making good wine. It sells both Saumur-Champigny and some Saumur Blanc.

Some of the best Saumur-Champigny wines come from producers at Varrains, almost due south of Saumur. The **Domaine des Varinelles** again has more than its vinous attractions, with splendid troglodyte cellars resembling a Romanesque chapel. The winery is equipped with modern vats which help produce wines which regularly win medals. This well-known Saumur estate sells both Saumur reds and white, as well as sparkling. The **Domaine des Roches Neuves**, also at Varrains, has the highest of reputations, one of the very finest of producers of Saumur-Champigny.

became the property of Antoine Cristal in the 1880s as phylloxera was killing off France's vines. The Parisian textile merchant, in his 50s, became an important local figure, obsessed with reviving Saumur's viticultural fortunes. Rather than replanting white grape varieties, which had dominated Saumur production until then, he chose red ones and so helped radically change the course of the area's winemaking. So successful was he that he ended up supplying the British court and regaling Clemenceau, whom he had befriended. The name of the next cliffside village, **Champigny**, has been affixed to that of Saumur to particularly distinguish wine production in this area (*see* box on previous page).

Souzay's troglodyte charms are better hidden than those of the more showy cliffside villages to the east, but are worth going to explore. From here on to Saumur, the roadside unfortunately becomes increasingly cluttered with billboards advertizing Saumur's commercial attractions, but beautiful houses hide behind high walls. And up on the hillside, **Gratien et Meyer**'s (*open mid-June–mid-Sept 9–6, rest of year 9–1.30 and 2–5.30; t 02 41 83 13 32*) Art Deco façade stands out before you arrive in Saumur. This is one of the handful of very large Saumur sparkling wine-producing houses, with spectacular cliffside caves for cellars. The others have gathered close together in St-Hilaire-St-Florent, on the western side of Saumur, so you'll find a fuller description of Saumur sparkling wine on p.390. The collection of thousands of miniature model figures once held in the Château de Saumur has recently moved to Gratien et Meyer as a further tourist attraction of the house.

Château de Brézé

Open May–Sept 10–6; t 02 41 51 62 06.

The Château de Brézé is a staggering place, an enormous castle on a wood-topped hillock above the vineyards south of Champigny and some 10km from Saumur along the D93. The place isn't just immense overground, but also underground. In fact the first fortified dwelling, the Roche de Brézé, was totally hidden in the rock. It was developed into quite a sophisticated subterranean maze in the 10th and 11th centuries. Wells were dug to bring light and air into the underground chambers, built in the shape of clover leaves around the wells. Such Roches were common in Anjou, maybe as many as 300 being dug in the region, but this one was clearly a particularly important, lordly one. For example, it was provided with four large silos to receive grain. The corridors into and out of the underground network were generally narrow, built with chicanes and other devices to help in the defence of the place should it be attacked.

A first overground fort went up from 1063. But the one you see now is a major 16th-century Loire Valley Renaissance castle. Exceptionally, Brézé has only known two lordly families in almost 1,000 years. For the first six centuries the proprietors were the Maillé-Brézés. Then the Dreux-Brézés took over. They still own the château, the present proprietors bearing the title of the Comte et Comtesse de Colbert.

Visiting the place, you'll first be overwhelmed by the size of the castle above ground, approached past a dovecote, built to fit the scale of the property, and the

17th-century outbuildings where wine tastings take place. The huge 16th-century pile beyond was much restored in the 19th century by Hodé. The impressive three wings around their courtyard are decorated with classical features. A few of the rooms inside are open to the public, but the main interest of a visit to Brézé is to see the underground chambers.

These are reached via the largest dry moat in Europe, isolating the castle on its square platform. The moat was dug between the 13th and 15th centuries. Actually it looks more like a gorge than a moat, it's so deep. On the guided tour you learn about the uses to which the different subterranean chambers were put. There was basically a whole underground village operating here, with the largest underground bakery in the country. You can also look inside what are thought to have been a forge and a silk-making room. Winemaking has been important here for centuries, so it's no surprise to find winemaking equipment below ground, including massive 15th-century presses said to have been used up to the 1970s. The Château de Brézé still has some 30 hectares under vine.

In the mid-17th century the troglodyte quarters were briefly occupied by 500 soldiers, troops of Louis II de Bourbon, better known as Le Grand Condé, one of the leaders of the Fronde, the French aristocrats' uprising against the young King Louis XIV. The Grand Condé had married into the family which owned Brézé. The tour ends in the so-called Cathédrales d'Images. Three of the largest underground galleries have been transformed into the setting for an outsized slide show of famous and extraordinary subterranean sights from around the world. Striking images are cleverly projected on to the walls, ceilings and even floors of the chambers.

Saumur

Two famous French works of art depict Saumur. The first is a page from one of the most famous illuminated manuscripts in the world, the supremely beautiful medieval Book of Hours, the *Très Riches Heures du Duc de Berry*. Painted by the Flemish Limbourg brothers for Jean Duc de Berry in the early 15th century, it shows a fantastic fairytale fortress with a dreamscape of towers and pinnacles, the archetype of the castle taken up by Walt Disney. The other famous depiction of Saumur in French art appears in Balzac's great novel, *Eugénie Grandet*, set in the heart of old Saumur in the period after the Revolution. The fictional inhabitants don't come out as white and clean in Balzac's description as their château does in the medieval manuscript; provincial avarice and greed characterize the pinnacles of Balzac's caricatural society, although Eugénie's noble sentiments stand apart, along with those of her faithful servant Nanon.

Saumur does look the archetypal squeaky clean, white, bourgeois Loire town. And under its long-serving right-wing mayor, beggars were swept off its streets in the 1990s. The town's conservative image is even reflected in its informal title of 'La Perle d'Anjou'. Pearls are of course associated with a certain social class. So too are horses, and the town's other nickname is the 'Ville du Cheval'. Saumur has long been home to a nationally famous cavalry regiment, along with the associated Cadre Noir riding school, France's answer to Austria's Spanish Riding School. The Ecole Nationale d'Equitation and the Cadre Noir have now been moved a few kilometres outside town, on to the hillside above St-Hilaire-St-Florent, a parish closely attached to Saumur. With advances in military warfare, Saumur military training switched from horses to armoured mounts in the 20th century, and the place has a surprisingly fascinating museum of tanks. Given its military and horsey traditions, it's no surprise to find large numbers of men in stiff military garb wandering round Saumur, and numerous women in Sloane Ranger-type gear. But to national surprise, in the March 2001 elections, the Saumurois voted in a Green candidate to become their new mayor!

For tourists, Saumur is an utterly enchanting town, one of the very finest on the Loire. It presents a cheerful, well-scrubbed face to visitors, and has a magnificent architectural heritage for such a small place. It also has a more signifi- cant history than might be imagined, for a time a Protestant stronghold, with a famous teaching academy that led to yet another title for the town, that of a second Geneva. The château is the obvious sight to make for, but there are several grandiose churches among the rich town houses. A couple of these churches are topped by viciously sharp-pointed steeples that look like great upturned tacks, puncturing the skyline almost as dramatically as the château's towers; another boasts a big breast of a dome, built in the Counter-Reformation to seduce the locals back to Catholicism.

St-Hilaire-St-Florent has a clutch of attractions of its own beyond the Ecole Nationale d'Equitation, including a mushroom museum, a traditional bowling centre, and, above all, a handful of big producers of Saumur sparkling wine, who vie with each other almost as competitively as the horseriders in the local show-jumping contests in their attempts to woo tourists.

History

In the less inspiring southern outskirts of Saumur, the Dolmen de Bagneux provides a fine example of the Neolithic constructions of Anjou, with the largest dolmen chamber in France. You have to wait a long time to find further evidence of Saumur civilization, so let's jump to the 9th century. The monks of St-Florent, west of the present town, were given a villa here after their monastery had been wrecked by the Breton leader Nominoë. Scarcely had they settled than they had to flee from the Vikings coming up the Loire, taking St Florent's bones with them. A castle was built on Saumur's site around this time, known by the charming name of *le vieux tronc* (the old trunk).

By the middle of the 10th century some monks had returned, with a few relics in hand. Thibaud le Tricheur, count of Blois, was the lord of the land; his presence this far west shows how extensive the lands of the counts of Blois and Touraine were at one stage. Thibaud offered the monks protection behind the castle walls. The name of the settlement that grew up here is first recorded around this time as Salmurus, from the Latin for 'safe' rather than 'dirty' wall. It wasn't safe enough to protect the Blois

Getting There and Around

Saumur's **train** station lies on the north side of the Loire, on the line from Angers to Tours. Saumur has direct TGV links with Paris now, the journey taking just 1 hour 50mins. There are **bus** links with the surrounding area going out in all directions, but virtually no services on Sundays.

To tour the town with children or to save on walking Saumur's slopes, you could take the little **tourist train** which runs from the tourist office Easter–Sept. Or in July and Aug you can hire a **horse and carriage** in the afternoon. You can even go out on a **boat** on the Loire mid-June–mid-Sept (except Mon) from Quai Gautier. Make reservations via the tourist office. To go **canoeing** on the Loire, contact Saumur Canoë, Base de Loisires de Millocheau (on the western tip of the Ile Offard), **t** 02 41 50 62 72.

Tourist Information

Tourist office: Office de Tourisme de Saumur, Place de la Bilange, B.P.241, 49418 Saumur Cedex, **t** 02 41 40 20 60, **f** 02 41 40 20 69, *infos@ot-saumur.fr, www.saumur-tourisme. com*.

Market Days
Hauts: Wednesday morning.
Quartiers: Wednesday morning.
Place Pompidou: Wednesday morning.
St-Hilaire-St-Florent: Wednesday morning.
Av du Général de Gaulle: Thursday morning.
Chemin Vert: Friday morning.
Place Angibault: Friday morning.
Place St-Pierre and beyond, plus flower market
  Place de la Bilange: Saturday.

Place de la Déportation, Bagneux: Sunday morning.

Where to Stay and Eat

Saumur ✉ **49400**
★★★**Hôtel Anne d'Anjou**, 32–34 Quai Mayaud, **t** 02 41 67 30 30, **f** 02 41 67 51 00, *anneanjou@ chateauxhotels.com, www.hotel-anneanjou. com* (*expensive*). Absolutely splendid three-star hotel in very elegant 18th-century premises on the Loire's southern bank. The rooms are reached via a staircase so fine that it's been classed a *monument historique*, as has the hotel's façade. Several of the first-floor rooms have amazing features, the most extravagant covered with moulded figures. The second-floor rooms are very comfortable but much more conventional. The rooms at the front look out onto the Loire, but the views from the rooms at the back are almost better, onto the château, which is stunningly illuminated at night. The very elegant restaurant, **Les Ménestrels**, lies at the bottom of the garden. It's reckoned by many to have the best cuisine in town (*menus €25–52*). Restaurant closed Sun Oct–Easter.
★★★**Hôtel Saint Pierre**, Rue Haute-Saint-Pierre, **t** 02 41 50 33 00, **f** 02 41 50 38 68, *www. saintpierresaumur.com* (*moderate*). This is the other stylish hotel in the delightful historic quarter of Saumur, although the 15th–17th-century house itself had to be restored from a ruin at the start of the 1990s. The rooms have been very nicely designed, with excellent facilities, such as air conditioning and well-kitted-out bathrooms, one designed by Paloma Picasso.

counts' stronghold from that Angevin troublemaker Count Foulques Nerra; he destroyed the place in 1026.

Under Geoffroy Martel, next count of Anjou, the settlement grew up again, only to be devastated by Guy Comte de Poitiers in 1067. Geoffroy Plantagenêt then set up a new castle, while the monks opted for a retreat back in what is now St-Hilaire-St-Florent, and the district of Nantilly was blessed with a parish church. The Plantagenet dynasty lost Anjou to the Capetians at the start of the 13th century. Charles d'Anjou, brother of King Louis IX (alias St Louis), had a much larger castle and city wall erected around Saumur in 1230, extending the town's fortifications down to the river. Later,

Some rooms are on the small side, if cute, and one side of the hotel stands opposite a less inspiring tall, modern apartment block. It doesn't have a restaurant, but does have a lovely bar, sitting room and breakfast room.

★★★**Loire Hôtel/Restaurant les Mariniers**, Rue du Vieux Pont, **t** 02 41 67 22 42, **f** 02 41 67 88 80 (*moderate*). Located on the Ile Offard, it benefits from views onto the old town and the château from its excellent riverside position. This modern hotel has bright, well-furnished rooms. You can try tasty experimental cooking in the dining room with a view (*menus €18–32*).

★★**Central Hôtel**, 23 Rue Daillé, **t** 02 41 51 05 78, **f** 02 41 67 82 35 (*inexpensive*). As its name indicates, it's in the middle of the town, only a short distance from the tourist office. The rooms are neat, quiet, well equipped and good value. *No restaurant*.

★★**Le Volney**, 1 Rue Volney, **t** 02 41 51 25 41, **f** 02 41 38 11 04 (*inexpensive*). Also centrally located, a smaller family hotel where you should get a warm welcome. The place has personal touches, including home-sewn embroideries.

Les Délices du Château, Les Feuquières, in the château courtyard, **t** 02 41 67 65 60. Has the privilege of being located in the outhouses of the castle, high on the hill. The furnishings are Louis XVI style in a 14th-century frame. The cook prepares extravagant dishes, such as *sandre* in potato 'scales' with a Champigny wine sauce (*menus €28–45*). *Closed Sun–Tues out of season, and late Dec–early Jan.*

L'Orangeraie, same address as Les Délices, **t** 02 41 67 12 88, **f** 02 41 67 74 60. Attached to Les Délices but less expensive, offering an equally excellent setting with views on to the château, but simpler cuisine (*menus €13.5–19*). *Same closure as Les Délices*.

Le Relais, 31 Quai Mayaud, **t** 02 41 67 75 20. A lovely restaurant down by the Loire, with a pretty dining room with stained-glass windows and a courtyard for summer dining outside. The cuisine is refined and light (*menus €19–27.5*). *Closed weekends and Feb.*

Auberge St-Pierre, 6 Place St-Pierre, **t** 02 41 51 26 25. Best option among many on the wonderful square in front of the church of St-Pierre. This restaurant occupies part of a dramatic house. The place has plenty of atmosphere, waiters rushing round. The food is fairly ordinary, competent Loire Valley cooking (*menus €8.5–12.5*). *Closed Sun and Mon.*

St-Hilaire-St-Florent ✉ 49400

★★**Le Clos des Bénédictins**, 2 Rue des Lilas, **t** 02 41 67 28 48, **f** 02 41 67 13 71, *clos@symphonie-fai.fr* (*moderate*). The name of the hotel is misleading as the house is modern, set in a pleasant housing estate up the hill from St-Hilaire-St-Florent. It has comfortable, well-kept rooms with a modern French homely feel and fine views across to Saumur's major monuments in the distance. The swimming pool in the centre of the buildings also benefits from the fine views. In the restaurant, you may well find yourselves eating next to show-jumpers discussing their latest equine triumphs, and many of the tables are decorated with little sculptures of horse-riders. The cuisine is extremely refined, the chef paying great attention to detail (*menus €20–64*). *Closed mid-Dec–20 Jan.*

when King Jean le Bon famously distributed great appanages to his competitive sons, Louis was given Anjou and developed Saumur's château according to his extravagant tastes (Jean Duc de Berry, who ordered the ravishing illuminated depiction of Saumur castle, was one of Louis' brothers). Louis' interest in the town encouraged traders to settle here.

Louis' successor, Louis II d'Anjou, married Yolande d'Aragon, who proved to be an extremely influential court figure and patron. In art history, she's known for commissioning the magnificent *Rohan Book of Hours*. The guardian of the future French King Charles VII for a time, she became his mother-in-law. Although relatively overlooked because of history's obsession with Joan of Arc, she sustained the work of encouraging Charles VII against the English invaders after Joan had been burnt at the stake; and she had earlier lent her support to Joan, who came to visit her in her early 15th-century Saumur house (one of the few historic houses to survived the Second World War bombings of the town's main island in the Loire) – Yolande even defended Joan's adoption of male dress against the fanatical Bible-bashers of the time. René d'Anjou, the chivalric count who became known as Le Bon Roi René, was a son of Louis II and Yolande. He scarcely visited the castle at Saumur, but did order building work on it between 1454 and 1472. His properties eventually reverted to the French Crown and a royal garrison was posted to Saumur.

The merchants of Saumur continued to trade successfully, even if they seem to have felt some tensions with the mighty and privileged abbeys in the area, St-Florent and Fontevraud lying so close by. This may help explain why Protestantism caught on so readily among the town's merchants in the 16th century. In the Wars of Religion, Saumur's Huguenot contingent was so strong that in 1589 King Henri III granted the town the status of a Protestant safe haven, the theologian Philippe Duplessis-Mornay becoming its leader. A friend of Henri de Navarre, future King Henri IV, Duplessis-Mornay founded the internationally reputed Académie Protestante in the town. Its main task was to train Protestant preachers before they set off around Europe, although it was considered much more moderate than certain other notorious Reformation schools. Among the scholars and teachers who came to Saumur was the admired Scottish doctor and polymath Mark Duncan. He didn't only lecture here; curiously, he also looked after one of the Bourbon abbesses of the abbey of Fontevraud. Such was the academy's international reputation that it was at this time that Saumur became spoken of as a second Geneva, with Protestants making up around a fifth of the population and printing houses flourishing.

The Catholic faction in Anjou was deeply disturbed and fought back strongly through the 17th century, encouraged by the extreme Jansenist bishop of Angers, Henri Arnauld, with the support of the Virgin Mary, whose cult was strongly promoted. Seven different religious institutions were set up around Saumur at the start of the 17th century. In 1615 one Catholic group, the Oratorians, was given the task of promoting the pilgrimage to the Virgin based around the miraculous fountain at Ardilliers, just west of the town. Duplessis-Mornay, nicknamed the 'Huguenot pope', was deposed from his Saumur throne by Louis XIII in 1621. To combat the Protestant learning that was still thriving, a Catholic theology school was established in Saumur in 1649. For a brief period, the heads of the rival factions got on civily, but the Catholic campaign was gaining greater and greater strength and the pilgrimage to the sumptuous Notre-Dame des Ardilliers was acquiring more and more importance across France. In 1685, even before Louis XIV's Revocation of the Edict of Nantes of that year, which would suppress Protestantism in the country, Saumur's Protestant Academy was forced to close and the Protestant church (or *temple* in French) was destroyed. Many Protestants traders were forced to leave.

The château became by turns a barracks, a prison and an arsenal as Saumur became an increasingly important military town. In 1763 a cavalry training school was set up and by 1771 Saumur had become the centre for training cavalry officers from across France. At the start of the Revolution, in 1790, the Saumur authorities pressed unsuccessfully for the town to be made the head of a separate *département*. Anti-Revolutionary, pro-royalist troops from the Vendée uprising briefly occupied Saumur over the month of June 1793, and in 1822, General Berton tried to mount an abortive Bonapartist conspiracy from here. After a rocky period through the Revolution and the First Empire, in 1825 the cavalry training school was properly re-established as the French Ecole de Cavalerie, becoming the national centre for equestrian military training. As to mercantile Saumur in the first half of the 19th century, Balzac cruelly fictionalized and caricatured it in *Eugénie Grandet*.

After the First World War, horses were replaced by tanks in the military training here and the town is still where the French mobile armoured divisions are instructed in the art of war – on maps you can see how a big military camp stretches out below Fontevraud. When the Germans reached Saumur in 1940, the school mounted a defence of the town. Despite the bravery of the act, it proved to no avail and much of Saumur's riverfront was devastated. Further bombing in 1944 caused more destruction; the buildings on the islands in the middle of the Loire, L'Ile Offard and L'Ile Millocheau, and the suburb on the north bank where the railway station is, were worst affected.

After the war Saumur regained its international prestige through tourism. A wealth of architecture had survived the bombings and was gradually restored. The Cadre Noir riding school became a part of the Ecole Nationale d'Equitation established in St-Hilaire-St-Florent in 1972 and numerous prestigious riding events are held in the town. The right-wing mayor Jean-Pierre Hugot held office for several terms, encouraging projects to make Saumur a prestigious, up-market town. Despite a dramatic shock during the rainy spring of 2001, when part of the outer fortifcations of the château collapsed on houses below, the town looks very well maintained indeed now. But perhaps in reaction to having seen so much attention lavished on its image over the last decades, the majority of Saumurois voted for the Green candidate Jean-Michel Marchand in the latest mayoral elections, a real turn-up for the books.

Château de Saumur

Open June–Sept 9.30–6, with night-time visits Wed and Sat in July and Aug; April–May 9.30–12 and 2–5.30; rest of year Wed–Mon 9.30–12 and 2–5.30.

The Château de Saumur still dominates the town's skyline today, but it looks rather simple in comparison with the ornately roofed version in the Duc de Berry's medieval manuscript. From afar, it's still a joy to spot its silhouette on the horizon, its corner towers stretching into the sky like thick upturned pencils. These octagonal towers and many of the walls date in great part as far back as the 1360s, built for Louis Duc d'Anjou on the remnants of Charles d'Anjou's castle. Louis' brothers King Charles V and Jean Duc de Berry both built sumptuous palaces for themselves, Charles V the early Louvre in Paris, Jean his castle at Mehun-sur-Yèvre in the Berry; these two are also illustrated in the *Très Riches Heures du Duc de Berry*. Louis clearly wished for a château to match those of his brothers. A vineyard has recently been planted on the plateau outside it to help copy the image presented in the medieval manuscript.

Up close to the château, you'll see that it's much sterner-looking than it appears from a distance. This impression of sternness comes in part from the fact that an outer range of fortifications with sharp angled protrusions was added for Duplessis-Mornay in the 1590s, at a time when the whole realm was on the defensive due to the upheaval of civil war. These carefully calculated outer defences foreshadow the characteristic work of Vauban and were designed by an Italian, Bartolomeo. After the Protestant governor's enforced departure from Saumur, the castle was neglected. The place was originally enclosed on all four sides, but the western façade crumbled. The château went on to serve first as a barracks, then as a prison from Louis XIV's reign onwards; the Marquis de Sade was even held captive here for a time. During the 19th century the army took over the place, once again turning it into barracks. The town managed to buy it in 1906. Much restoration work has been carried out since then, and Saumur's rather specialized museums installed here.

The inner courtyard still looks quite a mess. From the west side which collapsed, you get excellent views down onto the town. It's inevitably a bit disappointing that the richness of detail and decoration to be seen on the château in the *Très Riches Heures du Duc de Berri* doesn't really exist. You have to take solace in the **Musée des Arts Décoratifs** (guided tour compulsory), on the first floor. This museum includes hundreds of fine ceramic pieces, donated by Charles Lair in 1919. This is one of the most important collections in the country. The first room contains some beautiful Limoges early medieval enamel work. Then the displays trace the development of French ceramics, concentrating on the work of Bernard Palissy in developing glazes, the evolution of regional variations, and the frustratingly long search to reproduce Chinese porcelain. Chests, religious statues and tapestries are among the other works on display, roughly ordered by period.

The **Musée du Cheval**, a fitting museum for this horse-crazy town, occupies the floor above, with its timberframe roof in the shape of an upturned hull. As you follow the history of the horse through different periods, a mass of saddles, stirrups, bits and boots add detail. The elaborate metalwork decoration is staggering at times, especially, for instance, on the knights' chamfers. The collections aren't only French, but range across the continents; one of the main pieces on display is an extravagant sled from Eastern Europe decorated with mermaids and helmeted putti.

A Tour of Central Saumur

Start by Saumur's main bridge over the Loire, the **Pont Cessart**, which connects the main part of Saumur to the Ile d'Offard and gives you a fine view of the château. From the bridge you can also admire the substantial riverside quays which saw so much trade in centuries past. Now in summer you can take a river trip in an old-fashioned Loire boat from in front of the tourist office. This occupies part of the plush 19th-century Italianate **theatre** at the southern end of the Pont Cessart. The lively

Place de la Bilange beyond is full of shops and cafés. This is the busy heart of Saumur. A *bilange*, by the way, was a kind of scales on which taxes in kind were once publicly measured.

Historic Saumur lies both sides of Place de la Bilange and the long line of shopping streets heading due south towards the Thouet river, a tributary which joins the Loire at Saumur. To the west of this axis, the atmosphere is dominated by military and cavalry Saumur. To the east, grand old churches and houses stand out below the castle. We start on the eastern side. Go along the river bank to **Place de la République** just beyond the theatre. The restored **Hôtel de Ville** (town hall) in bright white stone looks over the large car park taking up this square. The remarkable old building itself, with its machicolations and little towers, dates back to 1508. It was once incorporated into the city walls, hence its defensive elements. The façade holds a *pierre de la Bastille*, a stone from the famous Parisian prison whose storming signalled the start of the French Revolution in 1789. This stone was donated by Paris to the Saumurois Aubin Bonnemère, described as one of the four 'heroes of the Bastille'. Within the building, at the back of the courtyard, two sorry arches constitute the sad remnants of the Protestant Academy of Saumur.

Behind the town hall lie some of Saumur's most stylish shopping streets. Take the road on the east side of the town hall or the curving Rue de la Tonnelle off Place de la République to reach **Place St-Pierre**, a delightful sloping square with delicate trees providing some shade. The **church of St-Pierre** at the end has a misleading classical façade, added on to a late 12th- and early 13th-century church after the front was struck by lightning. The belfry is 14th century, but the spire 19th. Within, the church is built on surprisingly wide arches, Gothic to the right, Renaissance to the left. The choir stalls are decorated with splendid late Gothic angels, dragons and fighters, while the 17th-century organ also boasts superb carving. You may be tempted to linger a while on Place St-Pierre, with its half-timbered 15th- and 16th-century houses, its café terraces shaded by tall branches, and a choice of restaurants.

Off the square, the **Montée du Fort** leads up to the château, fine old houses clambering up the hillside. This quarter was the setting for the Grandet house, the building almost a character in itself in Balzac's *Eugénie Grandet* (*see* box). Some modern apartments have been built along the way slightly spoiling the effect.

At the top of the Grandets' road you come out in front of a splendid 15th–16th-century house, beautifully restored by the Compagnons du Devoir du Tour de France, a kind of national crafts guild. Head back down the hillside via the **Chemin de l'Echelle**, past grandiose old town houses to the **Rue Dacier**. Walking along this street and those heading south from it, admire the grand *portes cochères*, the gateways into the Saumur mansions made for carriages to pass through.

Saumur's Two Churches to Our Lady

The churches of Notre-Dame de Nantilly and Notre-Dame des Ardilliers, two splendid religious buildings on the edges of Saumur centre, reflect two different periods of strong campaigning and building by the Catholic Church. It's a fair walk in different directions from the centre to reach them.

Eugénie Grandet, The Saumur Tale the Saumurois May Not Tell You

Which jaundiced writer could attack the greed and pettiness of the French provinces and set his tale in such a pretty blonde bourgeois town as Saumur? Balzac of course. The author was himself obsessed with money throughout his career, or rather the shortage of it to pay for his failed enterprises and profligacy (see Château de Saché, p.329). But in Monsiuer Grandet he created a monster of meanness, tyrannically, obsessively, cruelly avaricious, a man literally in love with gold. A barrel-maker and vineyard owner, jumping at the unexpected opportunities created by the upheaval of the Revolution and the Empire, this miser amasses a huge fortune, until it seems to some in Saumur that he might be able to buy up the whole town.

Eugénie Grandet is a story about inheritance as well as about greed. Not just business rivals suffer at Grandet's hands. His family is shown enduring the most, his lone child, his daughter Eugénie, the principal victim. As her father's millions grow, she's hunted by *la meute*, the pack, seeking the best marriage contract in town. The main battle for her hand and inheritance draws the Cruchotins against the Grassinistes, described pitting their petty wits against each other with some masterly comedy.

The female characters in *Eugénie Grandet* merit separate study. The particular vulnerability of many of their number, especially because of their tendency to kind-heartedness and love, is a recurring theme in Balzac. Men's lives, by contrast, are shown to be dominated by economic obsessions here, with no room for love. The arrival of Eugénie's cousin Charles comes like a thunderbolt to disrupt the order of events in her life. The naive girl falls utterly in love with her foppish cousin, who brings the latest fashions from Paris. He finds what he considers to be a dismal town and a very drab house when he's sent to the Grandets by his bankrupt father. Ambitious young Charles decides his only option is to go and try to make his fortune in the Indies. Eugénie, to start him off, lends him the precious gold coins that her father has given her for each of her birthdays, expecting to marry him once he has proved himself. It's then all sharply downhill, almost 90 degrees, as so often in Balzac, as the battle between avarice and amour plays itself out.

Notre-Dame de Nantilly, south of the château, is a basic Romanesque block with a late Gothic south aisle tacked on. As you arrive, a solid rectangle of defensive wall greets you by way of a façade. Within, the carved Romanesque capitals are hard to discern way up columns supporting the barrel vault. After the size comes the surprise of the church's **tapestry collection** from the 16th and 17th centuries. In fact, the place looks like a tapestry museum. Some came from Flanders, others from Aubusson, while a few are even attributed to the Ateliers des Bords de Loire, regional craftsmen. The trouble with tapesteries is that they can look crudely unrefined, but many of the pieces here, although in various styles, are of superb quality. In the Capture of Jericho the triumphant Israelite army has been transformed into a big Flemish country dance party. The Crowning of the Virgin shows her surrounded by flowers and flames. A huge Tree of Jesse dresses up the only transept, Jesse with his hand on his head in seeming horror at the inheritance he's created. In 1619 the church commissioned a series of eight Aubussons depicting scenes in the Virgin's life; they present the stories in dignified pastoral scenes, the characters ennobled by their rich draperies.

Other notable features to look out for in this highly decorated church interior include the **statue of Notre-Dame-de-Nantilly**, a 12th-century painted Virgin with child. Pilgrims flocked to pay homage to her in medieval times, including King Louis XI, who payed for the addition of the south aisle of the church. The keystones there display the arms of the king, his second wife Charlotte de Savoie, and his son, the dauphin Charles.

To get to **Notre-Dame-des-Ardilliers**, east of the château, you pass through the Quartier de Fenet, wedged in between the Loire cliffside and the river. The pilgrimage to the church was greatly encouraged in the 17th century by the Catholic Church to combat the deep-rooted Protestantism of the town, and the whole quarter became devoted to the manufacture of rosaries and other religious objects to sell to the pilgrims. The 17th-century church itself shows Catholicism stamping its forceful mark by way of outrageously seductive architecture – in the form of a propagandist breast-shaped dome. In fact, Notre-Dame-des-Ardilliers looks like a Venetian temptress imported into the Loire. The building is certainly stunning.

The origins of the church were slightly humbler than this. A small stone Pietà was supposedly unearthed in the clayey (*argilleux* in French, hence *ardilliers* presumably) ground here in the mid-15th century. A century later, a first chapel was built on the spot. The fame of the Virgin spread far and wide and the royal authorities then exploited her popularity in the fight with Saumur's Protestantism. In 1614 the sanctuary was designated a royal chapel and the Oratorians in charge built their church and a convent. The church was subsequently added to under Cardinal Richelieu, who himself believed that the Virgin of Notre-Dame-des-Ardillers helped cure him of an illness once. The dome was planned in the 1650s, but it took until the end of the century to finish it.

You enter an awe-inspiring circular space, a kind of Pantheon to the Counter-Reformation. The cupola is over 20m in diameter. The geometric black-and-white patterning of the floor and the coffered ceiling add to the thrill. Double columns lead up to medallions between the windows depicting the four Evangelists and the four Doctors of the Church. Four corner chapels lie at the square corners added on. The miraculous Pietà stands on the altar in the north aisle, which also contains a notable retable and two sculptures of Christ on the cross. But the most dramatic and anachronistic sculpture decorates the choir, with putti and God popping their heads out of garlands and clouds.

Military and Equestrian Saumur

Saumur is still horse- and military-mad. West of Place de la Bilange stand the town's smart, formal cavalry buildings. On the western side of the square itself, the neoclassical **Hôtel Blancler**, built just before the Revolution, became by turns the brief quarters for the head of the Vendéen army and then the Republican one. A little later, Napoleon stayed here when he came to Saumur in 1808.

Before concentrating on the cavalry, **Rue Beaurepaire** has a couple of alcoholic distractions worth mentioning: the **Maison du Vin de Saumur** (*open June–Sept Mon–Sat 9–12.30 and 2–6.30, rest of year Tues–Sat 9–12.30 and 2–6.30;* **t** *02 41 51 16 40*), a good place to get an introduction to the wines of the area, and the **Distillerie Combier** (*open July–Aug 10–7; June and Sept Wed–Mon 10–12 and 2–6; May and Oct Mon, Fri, Sat and Sun 10–12 and 2–6;* **t** *02 41 40 23 00*), which makes a heady orange liqueur similar to Cointreau (the latter made in Angers, west along the Loire).

The quarter around **Rue St-Nicolas** was once home to Loire fishermen as well as merchants. It leads to a series of squares, including the vast **Place du Chardonnet**. This area is still packed with cavalry buildings, mainly from the 18th century, although several were added later. The Manège des Ecuyers, an 18th-century ring, was where the celebrated Cadre Noir used to perform its equestrian gymnastics; the showmen have now moved to the Ecole Nationale d'Equitation (*see* below). The stables from the early half of the 19th century house the EAABC (the Ecole d'Application de l'Armée Blindée et de la Cavalerie – the long-winded title of the school since cavalry practice was superseded by tank training). Exhibitions are regularly held here on specialist themes.

Stands line the sides of the monumental Place du Chardonnet for much of the summer in readiness for several important equestrian events staged here. The most elegant building giving onto the square, with its noble façade, is the 18th-century neoclassical **Ecole de Cavalerie** itself. This school came into existence in 1763, when Louis XV asked his minister the Duc de Choiseul to reorganize the French cavalry. West from here, busy main roads lead you quickly into St-Hilaire-St-Florent, but as we're on military matters, we focus in first on the tank museum, just southeast of Saumur centre.

With an extensive international collection of over 150 tanks, the **Musée des Blindés** (*open 9–12 and 2–6*) presents something of a history of the major European wars of the 20th century. Tanks came into existence to replace the horse-drawn gun in the First World War and in an attempt to combat the effectiveness of increasingly sophis-ticated artillery against defenceless footsoldiers. In that war of technological advances, with planes taking to the air and submarines to the seas, Churchill described the tank as 'the land battle ship'. One of the few light moments in this pretty horrifying museum comes from seeing the St-Chaumont, basically little more than a gun put on a tractor. Little Willy, the prototype of all modern tanks, came into existence in Lincoln in Britain in 1915, introducing the caterpillar track. As technology developed at lightning speed, tanks became increasingly feared weapons of war. The details on the terse explanatory panels make for grim reading.

A lesser curiosity further south of the centre is the **Dolmen de Bagneux** (*open mid-March–Sept 9–7, 20 Jan–15 March and Oct–20 Dec 9–6*). This impressively sized prehistoric burial chamber, probably erected around 3000 BC, now sits in a café garden way down the long string of boulevards leading towards Cholet. The chamber, made up of 15 monumental pieces of stone, once served as a barn, it's so spacious.

St-Hilaire-St-Florent

St-Hilaire-St-Florent, now effectively a western suburb of Saumur, has a batch of tourist attractions. These include a cluster of sparkling wine houses, the Cadre Noir riding school, a mushroom museum and a newly carved cavern.

Saumur's prestigious National Riding School, the **Ecole Nationale d'Equitation** (*open April–Sept 9.30–11 and 2–4 except Mon am, Sat pm and all day Sunday – note that you can only see the Cadre Noir training in the morning and that they are often away on tour;* **t** *02 41 53 50 60*), was built in the 1970s on the heights above St-Hilaire-St-Florent. It is home to the **Cadre Noir**, France's most glamorous horse-riding circle. This is an extremely exclusive band, with just 24 members drawn from the 50 trainers working at the school. Its origins lie in the development of a team of elite horse-riding officers to instruct the French cavalry.

The Cadre Bleu was formed to instruct how to ride into battle, the Cadre Noir the more peaceable arts of riding. The trademark of the Cadre Noir's displays is three

The Sparkling Wines of Saumur

The parish of St-Hilaire-St-Florent boasts four out of the five big producers of sparkling Saumur. This is the Loire's best-known bubbly, much better recognized than the still relatively obscure Crémant de Loire. Saumur *mousseux* offers a much cheaper celebratory alternative to Champagne, but tastes much simpler too, with a fruity, fresh openness, rather than any biscuity dryness. It has a fair amount of fizz, although the bubbles don't seem to be nearly as well behaved as in Champagne. You could say that it can be petulant as well as *pétillant* (French for bubbly).

Any of the five houses around Saumur makes for an interesting visit, such is the lively competition between them. **Gratien et Meyer**, just west of Saumur, has already been mentioned on p.378. **Bouvet-Ladubay** (**t** *02 41 83 83 83; open June–Sept 9–6.30, rest of year 9–12 and 2–6*) possibly comes out best of all through the number and diversity of its attractions. Not only does it have its fine cellars; in the 1990s it also opened a beautiful Galerie d'Art Contemporain, with four shows a year, some of a high quality. For children there's the distraction of a museum of masks, more interesting than a tour of a wine cellar for most younger ones. There's also the restored late 19th-century theatre built for Etienne Bouvet, where entertainment was put on for him and his employees, crossed wine glasses standing out among the elaborate period decorations. **Ackerman** (**t** *02 41 53 03 21; open April–mid-Nov 9.30–6.30, rest of year Tues–Sun 9.30–6.30*) has the longest history of Saumur's sparkling wine houses, dating back to 1811. It has enormous underground cellars.

The other two major houses are **Veuve-Amiot** (**t** *02 41 83 14 14; open April–mid-Oct 10–6; rest of year Mon–Thurs 10–6, Fri am only*) and **Langlois-Château** (*open April–Oct 10–12 and 2–6.30, otherwise by appointment;* **t** *02 41 40 21 40*), the last associated to Bollinger in Champagne.

Several of these houses produce special *cuvées* which are more selectively made and some aged in oak barrels. The St-Cyr wine cooperative (*see p.377*) and other smaller producers also sell the Saumur *mousseux*.

spectacular jumps of horsey aerobics, the *courbette*, the *croupade* and the *cabriole*, explained on the tour. On a visit on an ordinary morning you may not see the famed jumps being executed, but at least you can watch the trainers executing the perfect *piaffe* in what is described as the largest specialist horse-training ring in Europe. You will also be shown round the stables, which have room for some 400 horses in quite luxurious individual boxes, and can admire some of the other outstanding facilities.

If you prefer more relaxing sports, consider going to watch a game of **boules de fort** on Thursday evenings in the special long, low shed in the centre of St-Hilaire-St-Florent. *Boules de fort*, Anjou's answer to bowls, is played on a curve-edged track with curved wooden balls which wander somewhat drunkenly in search of the jack.

The horses of the riding school provide a lot of manure and the quarries dug into the Loire cliffside lots of dark cool corridors, both essential elements in good mushroom growing, which you can learn about in the **Musée du Champignon** (*open early Feb–15 Nov 10–7*), west out of St-Hilaire-St-Florent along the Loire. At the end of the tour, which is similar to that at Le Saut aux Loups west of Saumur (*see* pp.375–6), separate rooms house a display of hundreds of types of wild mushroom, including the poisonous ones.

A cave or two west from the Musée du Champignon you'll find a new visitor attraction, a specially carved cavern, the **Parc Miniature Pierre et Lumière de Loire** (*open Feb–Dec 10–7*). Using a chainsaw and a dentist's drill among other tools, a contemporary sculptor by the name of Philippe Cormand has transformed the walls of a disused stone quarry into a quite engrossing and amusing new troglodyte sight. He worked inside the place for over two years before it opened in 2000. A Breton used to working with Brittany's tough granite, he says that carving the Loire limestone was like working with butter!

Strolling round the underground galleries, you can go and admire the twenty or so works Cormand has carved out, which recreate beautiful tourist sights along the Loire Valley. All the places featured lie between Amboise and Angers and are clearly labelled. They include many churches, some major, such as those of Fontevraud, Candes-St-Martin, Cunault or the cathedral of Tours, some surprisingly small, such as those of Restigné, Pontigné, Chênehutte-les-Tuffeaux, Le Thoureuil and St-Georges-des-Sept-Voies. Seeing these charming little churches in miniature may perhaps incite you to go exploring the eastern Anjou countryside to see them for real. Clearly Cormand has had to compromise on certain details; for example, the delicate pillar that holds up the beautiful entrance porch of the church of Candes St-Martin has vanished in his sculpture. But in his rendition of Tours cathedral you can make out almost as much detail on this small-scale model as you can in front of the real façade. The most spectacular carved scenes are the townscapes of Amboise, Chinon, Saumur and Angers, remarkably detailed, and reflected in pools of water in which Cormand had to work, adding to the challenge for him, as well as to the beauty of the scenes. If your children are inspired by Cormand's work, the shop in front of the sight sells stone-sculpting kits for children.

The Troglodyte Territory of the Southern Saumurois

To discover a land where chimneys sprout out of the ground, where the houses consist of caves dug around craters sunk into the earth, where people once lived protected and comfortably underground – or hid there – and where a hardy handful still live, head southwest out of Saumur for Le Coudray-Macouard and Montreuil-Bellay, or take the D960 to Doué-la-Fontaine. This is the area where *troglodytisme de plaine* comes into its own. Beyond the caverns, other attractions include the splendid-towered Château de Montreuil-Bellay and the formidable pilgrimage church of Le Puy-Notre-Dame.

Le Coudray-Macouard and La Magnanerie

Set on a rise in the plain south of Saumur, **Le Coudray-Macouard** (off the N147 to Montreuil-Bellay) is a rather frustratingly secretive troglodyte place, as so many of its attractive properties are hidden behind high stone walls. You can get a glimpse of the underground village by visiting **La Magnanerie du Coudray** (*open July–Aug Sun–Fri 10–6, Easter–June and Sept–All Saints' Day Sun–Fri 2–6*), where you can learn about the history of silk and the way it's produced. For centuries, silk-making was a thriving industry in the region. A mulberry tree or two grows on the flowered path down to the pretty cave; the tree's leaves provide the food for the silkworms, caterpillars of the now completely domesticated moth, the *bombyx mori*. The silkworms' cocoons, when unwound, provide the threads of silk.

While the Chinese had discovered the secret of making silk thousands of years before, the French only worked it out in medieval times, first in the south of France. The word *magnanerie* derives from a Provençal word for a worm. King Louis XI made Tours the predominant silk-producing area in France and mulberries were widely planted in the region under Henri IV. The major period for Anjou silk production was from the mid-18th to the mid-19th century. The silk was spun in Saumur or Angers and then taken to the weavers of Tours. An epidemic in 1855 brought a sudden end to the silkworms and the silk trade on the Loire. Since the 1980s a small-scale programme has begun to redevelop silk production, of which La Magnanerie forms a part. While in Le Coudray-Macouard, you might take a look at another curiosity, the **Atelier de la Girouetterie**, devoted to making weather vanes.

Château de Montreuil-Bellay

Open April–Oct Wed–Mon 10–12 and 2–5.30; **t** *02 41 52 33 06.*

Go to Montreuil-Bellay if you're looking for the satisfaction of a dreamy Disney-towered château. But this is the real thing, dominating the fortified medieval town below it. The château boasts 13 towers, making a splendid sight glimpsed from afar. A deep ditch separates the château from the town on one side, adding to the drama of its complicated defences, while on the other side a steep embankment slides down to

Getting Around

There's a regular **bus** service from Angers to Doué and rarer buses as far as Le Puy-Notre-Dame and Montreuil-Bellay. From Saumur, there are occasional buses to Doué and Montreuil-Bellay as well.

Tourist Information

Montreuil-Bellay: Place du Concorde, 49260 Montreuil-Bellay, t 02 41 52 32 39, f 02 41 52 32 35.

Le Puy-Notre-Dame: 16 Rue des Hôtels, 49260 Le Puy-Notre-Dame, t 02 41 38 87 30, f 02 41 38 89 99.

Doué-la-Fontaine: 30 Place du Champ de Foire, 49700 Doué-la-Fontaine, t 02 41 59 20 49, f 02 41 59 93 85.

Market Days

Montreuil-Bellay: Tuesday.
Doué-la-Fontaine: Monday.

Where to Stay and Eat

Montreuil-Bellay ✉ 49260

**Splendid'Hôtel et Relais du Bellay, 2 Rue du Dr Gaudrez, t 02 41 53 10 00, f 02 41 52 45 17 (*inexpensive*). A stone's throw away from the château in elegant Loire buildings, with a variety of styles of rooms and a swimming pool in the large back garden. There's plenty of room for diners in the brashly wall-papered dining rooms serving traditional French cuisine (*menus €13–27*).

Auberge des Isles, 312 Rue du Boëlle, t 02 41 50 37 37. Down by the river, offers a tranquil setting and a delightful terrace where you can sample fish of all sorts (*menus €8–30.5*). *Out of season closed Sun pm and Mon.*

Le Puy-Notre-Dame ✉ 49260

La Tour Grise B&B, t 02 41 38 82 42, f 02 41 52 39 96 (*inexpensive*). Delightful winemakers' property set around a charming courtyard in the village.

Rou-Marson ✉ 49400

Les Caves de Marson, Rue Henri Fricotelle, t 02 41 50 50 05. You couldn't get a much more atmospheroic troglodyte setting than here. A pretty garden leads to the three main candlelit caves where you can taste the old-fashioned Angevin *fouaces*, dough balls which you can see being cooked in the troglodyte oven before being stuffed with various fillings (*menus €18–26*).

Doué-la-Fontaine ✉ 49700

**Hôtel de France, 19 Place du Champ de Foire, t 02 41 59 12 27, f 02 41 59 76 00 (*inexpensive*). A typical unpretentious French provincial hotel in the centre of town (*menus €11.5–35*). *Out of season closed Sun pm and Mon, and late June–early July and 20 Dec–20 Jan.*

Le Dagobert, 14 Place du Champ de Foire, t 02 41 83 25 25, f 02 41 59 76 51 (*inexpensive*). The proprietors have made a big effort to redo their rooms to an excellent standard in this hotel on a slightly dull square. The big dining room is a bit vacuous, but the proprietor-chef is so full of enthusiasm that it can be fun to come here to try his old-fashioned recipes and fine cuisine (*menus €12–38*).

Auberge Bienvenue, 104 Route de Cholet, t 02 41 59 22 44. Stands opposite the zoo, and offers good cuisine and a warm welcome (*menus €13–45.5*).

Rochemenier ✉ 49700

Les Caves de la Genevraie, 13 Rue du Musée, t 02 41 59 34 22. Another good troglodyte address offering *fouaces* (*menu €16*).

the Thouet river. In the magnificent hotchpotch of towers, turrets and fortifications, the vast majority of what you see dates from the 15th century.

The ubiquitous Foulques Nerra had of course already spotted the defensive potential of the hilltop setting in the 11th century, and built a keep here to protect his territories from the county of Poitou to the south. He put his vassal Berlay in charge, whose name was corrupted to Bellay through time. The word 'montreuil' signalled the presence of a little monastery, established in the same century.

The Berlay family are described as a difficult line, rebelling against their overlords on several occasions. The Plantagenets laid siege to the place a few times to bring them into line, and once, so the story goes, to rescue a woman who had been raped by a Berlay. The château was greatly damaged by the consequences of these feudal misdemeanours and was rebuilt. At the end of the 12th century, the lord allied himself to the English. This time troops of the French Capetian King Philippe Auguste came to destroy the château. The Melun-Tancarville family later resurrected the place and ruled it for two centuries, to be replaced by the Harcourts. It's in this family's time that the château took on its present appearance, expanding through the 15th century. The Duchesse de Longueville, sister of the Grand Condé, the prince who organized the mid-17th-century rebellion against royal power (*see* Brézé, pp.378–9), stayed here when she was sent into exile for her part in the uprising. The grandson of Louis-Philippe also stopped here briefly when the Loire army retreated before the Prussian invasion of France in 1870.

The visit starts with the barbican, one of the few remnants from the 13th century, an impressive piece of defensive architecture. Then, passing under the splendid pepper-pot gateway towers, you enter the inner courtyard. Several buildings vie for your attention with their variety of roofscapes. The first part as you enter is the **Château-Vieux**, the first Harcourt edifice, built from 1420 on, with two octagonal towers and big *lucarnes* (dormer windows). The small freestanding building with the curious roof, a throwback to Fontevraud, is the 15th-century kitchen. Behind it lies the **Petit-Château**, which it's believed was built for canons to serve the collegiate church within the château's fortifications. You don't visit this building but you do see inside the kitchen, provided with three impressive fireplaces.

The visit inside the **Château-Neuf** starts underground, as befits the region, with some splendid vaulted cellars. Apparently this was one of the largest arsenals in France before the 16th-century Wars of Religion. In the 20th century it has found more amicable use as the meeting place of Montreuil-Bellay's wine fraternity, with its comically rueful motto which plays on words:

Lorsque le verre est plein je le vide,
Lorsqu'il est vide, je le plains.

(When the glass is full I empty it/When it's empty I feel full of regret.)

The rooms above are fully furnished, in the main with works from the 16th–18th centuries. The most moving part of the visit is to the painted **oratory**. The art dates from the end of the 15th century. On the ceiling, the vault is covered with depictions of delightful angels singing a musical score – should you not recognize it, composed by a Scottish monk, Walter Fry. Below, some of the pictures, though faded, have a moving power, in particular that of Christ's suffering on the cross.

Among an overwhelming catalogue of interesting objects pointed out to you on the rest of the tour, look out for Marie de' Medici's wedding chest; some fine tapestries; a superb Boulle bureau, made of copper encrusted with tinted turtle shell, showing decorative scenes; and a *bourdaloue*, apparently a church chamber pot, passed around the congregation during those unbearably long sermons! After you've visited the inside, you can wander round the lovely *chemin de ronde* and garden and then go and cast an eye into the collegiate church with its extraordinary spiky silhouette.

The **town** around the castle has retained a great part of its medieval fortifying wall, erected between the 13th and the 15th centuries and curiously pimpled with protruding stones. Anjou used to have 32 walled cities in medieval times, but Montreuil-Bellay is the only one to have retained such substantial ramparts. Although Montreuil-Bellay can seem somewhat lifeless nowadays, relegated to a southern outpost of modern Anjou, after medieval times it remained an important town, an administrative centre for a large area, until decline set in from the mid-18th century. With the Revolution, Saumur took over its administrative responsibilities. At **La Soie Vivante** (*open July–Aug daily exc Mon am 10–6, mid-May–June and Sept–mid-Oct Tues–Sun 10–12 and 1.30–6*) you can learn about silk-making (*see* Le Coudray-Macouard, p.392, for more details).

Le Puy-Notre-Dame

The magnificent **collegiate church** of Le Puy-Notre-Dame, a short way west of Montreuil-Bellay, has front towers which could be disconcertingly confused with giant rabbit ears from a hazy distance. As you come up close to the west front it becomes extremely daunting, a sheer wall of a façade above the five arches. This massive church seems way oversized for the quiet village among the vineyards. The reason for its grandeur lies in the Girdle of the Virgin Mary, which it still claims to hold on to. This immeasurably precious object was brought back from the Crusades by Guillaume, Comte de Poitiers, a grandfather of Eleanor of Aquitaine, in the 12th century. The church you see only dates from the first half of the 13th century, and the first recorded mention of the girdle here only from the end of the 14th, but it's assumed that the vast religious edifice was spawned from this miraculous little garment. Pilgrims flocked to the place, ensuring wealth for Le Puy-Notre-Dame, while women were thought to be assured a safe childbirth through visiting it.

The Angevin vaulting inside creates a brilliant effect. At the base of the ribs in the nave stand beautiful little statues, while the keystones of the aisles also attract the attention. The choir, with its ceiling of wonderful fan vaulting, contains some hilarious and finely carved choir stalls of the 16th century, with many depictions of sins, reminding one of the old French saying that monks '*s'assoient sur leurs péchés* (monks sit on their sins)'! Unfortunately the vast majority of the treasure that the church once held, in particular gifts from wealthy pilgrims, was lost through time. The supposed girdle remains, heavily protected in the south transept. Even royals had to write for permission to get hold of the thing, as a letter on display from Queen Anne, wife of Louis XIII, demonstrates.

Taking the step up to the top of the west front, you can get fine views onto the tops of the Angevin vaults and then wander along the parapet connecting the two front towers to appreciate the lovely views over the picturesque vineyards around Le Puy-Notre-Dame. The tourist office has a *dégustation* bar for tasting local wines. While it doesn't sell wine, the guides there can accompany you to visit a proprietor and will act as translator.

Abbaye d'Asnières

The stump of the church of the abbaye d'Asnières (*open July–Aug Wed–Mon 2–6.30*) is a sad and charming ruin off the D761 between Montreuil-Bellay and Doué-la-Fontaine. The establishment was devastated by Huguenots in 1566 and much of its stone sold off for other construction work in the 19th century. The substantial choir and transepts which remain show that the church must have been grand in its time. It was built at the end of the 12th century and beginning of the 13th for the Tironensian order (close to the Benedictines) which settled here in 1114. The choir contains particularly elegant Angevin vaulting with highly ornate keystones and ribs. Take a look at the medieval enamel tiles by the altar. Several tomb stones and effigies add to the atmosphere.

Doué-la-Fontaine

Doué-la-Fontaine may look superficially uninspiring, but dig a little deeper and unusual riches reveal themselves. The town has a couple of spectacular troglodyte sites you can visit, Les Perrières and the zoo, plus a handful of smaller subterranean surprises.

The rock of Doué is not the Loire Valley's best known limestone, tufa, but *faluns*, a different type of limestone filled with organic debris and shells in particular, deposited when a warm shallow sea covered this area back in the mists of time. In Merovingian times sarcophagi made from *faluns* were highly prized. At **La Cave aux Sarcophages** (*open April–Oct 10–12 and 2–7*) you can see an extraordinary archaeological site from which monolithic sarcophagi were extracted from the 6th to the 9th centuries.

Some quite substantial, if not exactly attractive, ruins of a **Carolingian house**, dating from the start of the 10th century, still stand on the outskirts of Doué. By the turn of the next century, the unavoidable Foulques Nerra had built a fortification here. Some *faluns* strong enough to be used in building, as the centre of old Doué shows, the stone known as *grison*, giving an idea of its greyish colour.

Faluns were also quarried for road-building and for extracting lime, and disused quarries were later put to practical housing purposes. Craters form the courtyards for a good number of the underground houses in the town. One very large crater was transformed into a place of amusement, **Les Arènes**. With its roughly elliptical ranks of seats, for a long time the story went that this was a vestige of Gallo-Roman civilization in these parts, hence the name. Now it's known that it was in fact a medieval quarry, converted for entertainment as early as the 15th century. Rabelais set the mock Doué Games in *Pantagruel* here.

The Inverse Architecture of Les Caves Cathédrales

The **Rue d'Anjou** and the **Rue des Perrières** are more curious still than the Arènes. Some of the craters form the core of rather poor-looking households. You may feel a little uncomfortable peering down into these often rather tatty yards, but it's fascinating all the same.

Do go and visit the **Caves Cathédrales of Les Perrières** (*open mid-April–mid-Oct Tues–Sun 10–12.30 and 1.30–7*), a phenomenal series of interconnecting underground quarries. The comparison to underground cathedrals may sound exaggerated, but that doesn't mean it isn't quite accurate in this case, even if the place has no spiritual history, and no windows whatsoever – it's just architecturally very grand and church-like.

The reason for the extraordinary shapes of Les Perrières stems from the way these quarries were excavated. The land had a double use here. The topsoil could be used for agriculture, the stone beneath exploited. So that the agricultural land could be left relatively unspoilt once a quarry had been opened up, the *caviers-cultivateurs*, or quarrying cultivators, here developed an ingenious system of excavation. They dug narrow trenches in the soil. Then they extracted the stone to form an underground arch, but working from the top downwards to create it as they quarried. This inverse architecture resulted in bottle-shaped spaces. Once the *faluns* had been extracted, the underground chambers could be put to practical uses while the thin trench in the roof was simply covered up by blocks of stone, 80cm of earth placed on top and the land was once again ready for cultivation.

Les Perrières dates back to the 18th century, and the site was quarried until 1930. The chambers left were then put to different uses: some for habitation, some for farming needs. For 50 years, from 1930 to 1980, mushroom-growing went on here. Left impressively empty, the place is now open to the public. The interconnecting series of chambers gives the most superb architectural perspective. The shapes of the arches and bays certainly aren't regular as in a cathedral, but they are awe-inspiring. Great rather phallic-shaped openings lead from one bay to the next, the dim lighting casting fantastic shadows. You can imagine that the ingenious Spanish architect Antonio Gaudí might have appreciated the magnificent eccentricity of the forms and structure.

Zoo de Doué

Open Easter–Sept 9–7, Feb–Easter and Oct–mid-Nov 10–6; t 02 41 59 18 58.

Doué's other truly spectacular troglodyte site is its underground zoo, out to the southwest of town in the direction of Cholet. This again will amaze you. If you don't object to visiting zoos, it's probably the most extraordinary and attractive one you'll ever see.

The visitors' path first takes you through a trail of interconnecting craters devoted to different creatures. The first barren crater offers the bizarre sight of giraffes seemingly trying to stretch their necks up far enough to see what might be going on up at ground level. In the next craters you enter a world of lush vegetation, planted with bamboo, acacias and wild flowers. Exotic birds greet you with their songs and squawks. You quite forget you're in the middle of a slightly dull plain by the time you reach the feline enclosures, again densely planted, with crooks and caverns in which the great cats can lounge. Although the craters don't offer enough room for these animals to have a good run, they do make for unusually spacious and cages. You can often get quite a close look at the big cats by using the hides, which mimic the effects of a safari.

The zoo has a programme of breeding endangered species with the aim of reintro-ducing them to the wild, among which snow panthers and Sumatra tigers feature. There's also a hothouse for reptiles in the underground section.

On the zoo's overground trail, once again the place so densely planted that you feel in a different region. Raised observation posts allow you to see rare wolves and, on the well-landscaped islands, several types of lemur, monkeys and a host of other animals. This dreamworld is the realization of the Gay family's imagination. Louis Gay started the zoo in 1961, his son Pierre continuing to add to it.

Back in the centre of Doué, two other troglodyte sites we'd recommend are **La Rose Bleue**, a small-scale craft pottery recently installed in its lovely cave setting, and **La Sablière**, which contains a rose-water distillery – which brings us to Doué's other claim to fame.

The Roses of Doué

The soil in the area has also proved particularly suited to growing roses and Doué is now the capital of rose cultivation in France. Millions of them thrive on the land around the town. Outside Doué you may pass whole fields of roses, cultivated in rows like vegetables. **Les Chemins de la Rose** (*open May–Sept 9.30–7*) is a rose garden planted in the mid-1990s off the road to Cholet, specializing in rare and botanical roses. Some 900 varieties are represented among the 8,000 rose bushes on the site.

The man who really made rose cultivation bloom in Doué was Joseph-François Foulon, in the second half of the 18th century. He also had a grand château built for himself in Doué. Foulon was deadheaded at the Revolution, and most of his château disappeared. But the grounds have been converted into the town's permanent, demo-cratic **Roseraie**, or rose garden.

Next to it, in the former stables of the town's vanished château, there's another rose-water distillery and the substantial **Musée des Commerces Anciens** (*open July–Aug 9–7; May–June and Sept–Oct 9.30–12 and 2–7; rest of year Wed and Fri–Sun 10–12 and 2–6, Thurs 10–2*), another Doué site that attracts large numbers. There's such a wealth of detail displayed in these artificially recreated rows of olde shoppes that it does help to have to follow a guided tour, even if that leaves you at the mercy of the prepackaged bad joke.

A fantastic congregation of roses takes place each year in the Arènes. During the **Journées des Roses**, the town's festival of roses, thousands upon thousands of the plants adorn the town.

Troglodyte Sites North of Doué-la-Fontaine

La Fosse de Forges Maisons Troglodytes (*open June–Sept 9.30–7, March–May and Oct 9.30–12.30 and 2–6.30, Nov weekends only 10–12.30 and 2–6*) is an underground complex which is different from virtually all the other troglodyte sites in the region in that it didn't serve as a quarry first, but was purpose-built in the 17th century. Chimneys and garden walls stick out above the ground, but otherwise the hamlet is totally hidden underground. You can visit the typical, cleverly conceived underground houses run by the extremely enthusiastic curator-cum-troglodyte dweller. He came to live here with his family in 1979, bringing back to life the household dwelling around the sunken 'patio'. You also see the agricultural side, with grain silos, a hemp drying room and a well.

The visit round the **Village Troglodytique de Rochemenier** (*open April–Oct 9.30–7; Nov, Feb and March weekends only 2–6*), west of La Fosse, reveals a good deal about life in such a troglodyte village. You can look into old barns, a wine cellar, bedrooms, a cowshed and stable, all decked out appropriately with old machinery, utensils and decoration, while Gélines de Touraine, the rare black hens of the region, cluck around. The subterranean community hall is one of the most atmospheric rooms, where people would gather for winter *veillées* or evenings spent in each other's company between All Saints's Day and Carnival. Although there was no fireplace, apparently the stable temperature of the cave was warmer than outside and a good number of bodies would help to take the chill off the air as the small community wove baskets, span or prepared their walnut oil together.

There aren't just the living rooms and farm outhouses down here, but also a secretive **underground chapel**. This is actually situated underneath the overground church. It was a quarry originally, but during the 16th-century Wars of Religion became the religious meeting place, the extraction well transformed into the church dome. Niches dug into the rock may have been made to contain statues, while the three Gothic arches and cross carved into the wall make clear its adopted purpose. The whole thing also has the shape of a cross. Above ground, the church of St-Emerance is from the 17th century and has a quaint old atmosphere to it.

The **Caverne Sculptée of Dénezé-sous-Doué** (*open June–Aug 10–7, Sept 10–6, April–May Tues–Sun 2–6*), a mysterious cave containing badly battered sculptures, lies below an uninspiring courtyard. Many of the crude carvings have had to be reconstituted as they've suffered through time and neglect, but the underground scenes still present an intriguing enigma.

The carvings were only discovered by local children in 1950, and no one's quite sure who executed them, when, or why. The preferred theory is that they were the work of a secret society, perhaps a protest group. The most famous scene depicts a Pietà, but the cross has been cleverly turned into an axe, while the woman at the cross, rather than looking the part of the Virgin, bears a noted resemblance to Catherine de' Medici. Such a cutting caricature brings to mind the Wars of Religion, which divided French Catholics and Protestants in the second half of the 16th century. Saumur in that troubled period became the site of a strong Protestant community, while Angers remained staunchly Catholic. The whole area and its leaders were deeply divided.

Although the carving is naive, with a touch of medieval coarseness, the fashions on many of the figures are decidedly 16th century. An American Indian appears among the figures and in fact the first native American settled in Anjou at the start of the 16th century. Certain motifs recur in the sculptures, such as figures astride heads, heads in others' hands, or three people standing intimately in a row. For some, supposedly degenerate or even satanistic scenes are depicted. Was some kind of ritual tied up with these sculptures and this cavern? Until now, it's been hard to assign any certain meaning to these sculptures, so wild speculation can run riot.

The Layon and Aubance Valleys

The landscape changes greatly just west of the flats around Doué-la-Fontaine and two delightful wine-producing valleys make their way north to the Loire. The Layon wines have made the name of this valley, its beautiful slopes worth discovering, although there are only small tourist sites to visit along the route. Windmills mark the way. The Aubance wines remain relatively obscure, the valley best known for the enormous pile of the Château de Brissac.

The Layon

The Layon river rises just south of Anjou in the *département* of Deux-Sèvres. Having provided the waters for the lake of Beaurepaire, which runs along the regional border, it then heads off on an arc of some 75km to the Loire. First the Haut-Layon heads determinedly northeastwards towards Doué-la-Fontaine, but repelled by a geological barrier before reaching that town, it swings round to head off northwest, the so-called Bas-Layon, roughly paralleling the Aubance for its pretty run into the Loire, which it reaches at Chalonnes, southwest of Angers.

The Layon valley has sometimes been seen slightly simplistically as a line dividing different regions, not just geologically, with the change from limestone to schist, nor simply regionally, with the shift from Poitou to Anjou and from southern tiles to slate roofs, but also politically – it was one of the frontiers of the 1793 anti-Republican Guerres de Vendée, the people to the southwest of here, Les Blancs, pro-Catholic and pro-royalist, rising against the Republican army, Les Bleus. Battles were fought here and destruction wrought in 1793 and 1794 (see Les Mauges and Cholet; pp.450–51). The Layon valley was split by that conflict, as was the Aubance, while to the west, in Les Mauges, the populace was unified in its staunch anti-Republicanism. The valley's name is nowadays familiar to French people because of the sweet white wines it produces (*see p.404*). The steep slopes on which the vines grow certainly make for splendid landscapes.

A large number of windmills once turned on the Layon heights, as you'll see, and the odd vestige of a château reminds of a certain importance this little region must have

Angers

Trélazé

Loire

Juigné-sur-Loire

Gohier

St-Saturnin sur-Loire

St Rémy-la-Varenne

Coutures

Loire

Chalonnes-sur-Loire

Brissac-Quincé
Château de Brissac

Aubance

Château de la Haute Guerche

St-Aubin-de-Luigné

Chaume

Beaulieu

MAINE-ET-LOIRE

Grézillé
Château de Pimpéan

St-Lambert-du-Lattay

Rablay

Faye d'Anjou

Louerre

Chanzeaux

Le Champ-sur-Layon

Layon

Bonnezeaux

Thouarcé

Parc Naturel Régional Loire-Anjou-Touraine

160

Chemillé

Faveraye-Mâchelles

Martigné-Briand

Aubigne-sur-Layon

St-Georges-sur-Layon

960

Doué-la-Fontaine

N

Vihiers

960

Les Verchers-sur-Layon

Neuil-sur-Layon

Les Cerqueux-sous-Passavant

Passavant sur Layon

5 km
2.5 miles

had in medieval times. There aren't any major tourist sites to visit, but the villages along the valley's length often have a quiet charm, the roads fine views, and as well as vineyard stops, there's the odd curious attraction.

Les Cerqueux-sous-Passavant, southwest of Doué, pays homage to the Wild West with Bisonland, where you can see bison being reared and then eat some, while the children get a chance to play in tepees. This tourist attraction reveals the methods some French farmers are having to resort to in order to make a living. The village boasts a couple of art galleries, the Galerie Les Z'Arts ('Lizzarts') and the Galerie Les

Getting Around

By **bus**, Brissac-Quincé is on the line between Angers and Doué-la-Fontaine/Montreuil-Bellay. A couple of other services from Angers serve stops along the Layon valley.

Tourist Information

Beaulieu-sur-Layon: 3 Rue St-Vincent, 49750 Beaulieu-sur-Layon, t/f 02 41 78 65 07.
St-Lambert-du-Lattay: Les Etangs de la Coudraye, 49750 St-Lambert-du-Lattay, t 02 41 78 44 26.
St-Aubin-de-Luigné: Place de l'Eglise, 49190 St-Aubin-de-Luigné, t 02 41 78 59 38, f 02 41 78 66 34.
Brissac-Quincé: 8 Place de la République, 49320 Brissac-Quincé, t 02 41 91 21 50, f 02 41 54 25 31.

Market Days

Vihiers: Wednesday.
Martigné-Briand: Saturday.
Thouarcé: Tuesday.
St-Lambert-du-Lattay: Wednesday.
Brissac-Quincé: Thursday.

Where to Stay and Eat

Thouarcé ✉ 49380

★★Le Relais de Bonnezeaux, Route d'Angers, t 02 41 54 08 33, f 02 41 54 00 63, *relais*. bonnezeaux@wanadoo.fr. In the converted railway station, with panoramic views onto vineyards, this has a high reputation for its cuisine and some great vintage wines from the region (*menus €15–40*).

Faye d'Anjou ✉ 49380

Au Logis de la Brunetière B&B, t/f 02 41 54 16 24 (*inexpensive*). These new B&B rooms are set in one wing of a lovely open farm courtyard, the buildings in typical local schist. The rooms are cosy and charming.

Le Champ-sur-Layon ✉ 49380

Auberge de la Contreche, t 02 41 78 48 18 (*inexpensive*) Makes for a charming rustic stop in the Layon for good solid home cooking (*menus €16–33.5*). *Closed Mon and mid-Sept–mid-Oct.*

Grézillé ✉ 49320

Le Clos des Roches, Le Bourgneuf, t 02 41 45 59 36. Eat as many traditional *fouaces* as you can in this troglodyte setting (*menu €18*).

Brissac ✉ 49320

★★Le Castel, 1 Rue Louis Moron, t 02 41 91 24 74, f 02 41 91 71 73 (*inexpensive*). The owner of Le Castel has done wonders transforming a dull modern cement block of a building into a charming hotel with extremely comfortably and stylishly presented rooms.

Maréchaux, both with local and international art on sale, the latter displaying the works of Ted S. Jacobs and his pupils – this American runs an art school eight months of the year.

Passavant-sur-Layon's good position dominating the Layon valley not surprisingly appealed to Foulques Nerra, who ordered that a château be built here. From the heights of the village you can look onto the remains of a 13th-century fortress that succeeded it. The vineyards of the Coteaux du Layon have already begun to embellish the countryside here. The next village, **Nueil**, has the rarity for the area of a monument to Republicans – a dozen villagers took refuge in the church bell tower when the Vendéen troops came to attack them in 1794 and rang and rang for help while the enemy set fire to the church. The bell tower didn't burn, however, and Revolutionary troops arrived to save the Republicans in the belfry the next day.

On the way to Les Verchers you might notice the Château d'Echeuilly, a splendid 18th-century château on the banks of the river, which supplies water for the moat.

Around **Les Verchers-sur-Layon** admire the melting vineyard valley scenery. You could think yourself in southwest France.

From here the Layon switches dramatically in direction, from northeast to northwest. Following the road to St-Georges, the vines grow on slopes that once produced coal. The chimneys and towers of the ruined château of **Martigné-Briand** strangely mark this place. This castle, dating from the end of the 15th century, was terribly scarred by fighting in 1793. Martigné is known for its Cabernet d'Anjou rosé wine. On the opposite bank, the smart, walled properties show what a rich parish **Aubigné** was for many centuries. The 11th-century church of St-Denis has a surprising interior decoration of Italian grotesque paintings, done by Paolo Baronni in the 18th century.

Just above these two villages, around Faveraye, the architecture changes with the geology, schist and slate taking over from limestone and tiles. The land around Thouarcé becomes particularly sharply undulating. Above Thouarcé lies **Bonnezeaux**, one of the Layon's two tiny specialized *appellations* which produce rare sweet white wines (*see* box on next page).

From here north to the Loire you can go through the six wine villages allowed to add their names to distinguish themselves from the run-of-the-mill Coteaux-du-Layon. Faye d'Anjou and Rablay are two of them. **Rablay** has attracted a number of craftspeople (you can visit them any afternoon in July and August, and weekend and holiday afternoons from Easter to June and September to December).

Beaulieu-sur-Layon retains the choir end of a Romanesque church with a 12th-century wall painting of Christ in Majesty against a background of red stars. Around here splendid views towards the Mauges open up to the southwest. In that direction, **St-Lambert-du-Lattay** was devastated by Republican troops in the Vendée war. A chapel, statues and crosses stand in memory of this event, but for foreigners the main point of interest in the village nowadays is the Musée de la Vigne et du Vin d'Anjou (*open July–Aug 10–6.30, April–June and Sept–Oct Tues–Sun 10–12 and 2.30–6.30*). This covers the history of the vine in Anjou from the Middle Ages to the 20th century with a well-set-out series of rooms and displays.

St-Aubin-de-Luigné, a pretty vinegrowers' village set in a vast amphitheatre of and, has a good number of wealthy homes. People go boating on the Layon here in summer. Up above, you can take in the views from the belvedere at the Moulin Guérin. On the other side of the valley the ruined châteaux de Guerche look intriguing. The older **Château de la Haute-Guerche**, from the 13th and 15th centuries, was razed to the ground by Republican troops in 1794. This was the château whose lords claimed the right to a quarter of the production of the local vineyards, Chaume which gave rise to the *appellation* of that scarce sweet wine, Quarts-de-Chaume.

The Layon runs into the Loire at Chalonnes. This town on the Corniche Angevine, as well as Rochefort, another place associated with Layon wines (and Quarts-de-Chaume in particular), is covered in a later chapter (*see* pp.458–9).

The Wines of the Coteaux du Layon and the Coteaux de l'Aubance

In the **Coteaux du Layon**, Bonnezeaux and Quarts-de-Chaume are the crème de la crème, Anjou's answer to the sweet successes of Sauternes in the Bordelais. But these areas are minute. The Bonnezeaux *appellation* only covers 80 hectares, Quarts-de-Chaume still less, only 50 or so. Their wines are doubly rare then, as they're only produced from grapes painstakingly selected if and when so-called noble rot, *botrytis cinerea*, sets in late in the season. The resulting wines can be magnificent, only to be tasted after 10 years of ageing at the very least. The most famous address for Bonnezeaux is the **Château de Fesles** (*t 02 4168 94 00*), dating back to the 11th century, but given the rarity of its sweet whites, you'll taste other Anjou wines if you visit it.

The more run-of-the mill Coteaux du Layon vineyards extend over quite some distance, covering around 1,500 hectares in all. They produce widely varying qualities of wines from the Chenin Blanc grape variety, dependent in good part on the lie of the land. To distinguish further particularly good territories, the Coteaux du Layon Villages denomination has been created to allow growers in six further parishes (Beaulieu, Faye, Rablay, Rochefort, St-Aubin and St-Lambert-du-Lattay) to stand out from the crowd. They have to achieve certain criteria, in particular making wines that attain an alcoholic strength of 12 per cent rather than the normal 11 per cent required. At Beaulieu, the **Château Soucherie** (*t 02 41 78 31 18*) is a good address to find good Layons, including Chaume, to be tasted in splendid cellars. Another property well used to receiving visitors is the **Domaine de Mihoudy** (*t 02 41 59 46 52*) at Aubigné-sur-Layon, the local produce giving good results.

The **Coteaux de l'Aubance** wines aren't widely known in France, unlike the neighbouring Coteaux du Layon. Mind you, production of this medium-sweet wine is miniscule, around 3,500 hectolitres a year. Peachy, with tastes of honey and hints of camomile or lime blossom, you could try it at the **Domaine de Montgilet** (*t 02 41 91 90 48*), Juigné-sur-Loire, with its architecture which couldn't show better the shift in the region from limestone to schist. The Lebreton brothers are dynamic and enthusiastic and can offer a wide range of other Anjou *appellations* to taste.

The Aubance

The Aubance runs north from above the troglodyte lands around Doué-la-Fontaine to the Loire south of Angers, passing from the limestone lands into schist. Caves dug into the limestone rock line the road from Louerre to Grézillé. Up the gorgeous sloping valley here, the **Château de Pimpéan** (*open mid-July–Aug 10–6, June–mid-July and Sept 10–5*) looks like a big fortified farm. The original château was built around 1440 for Bertrand de Beauvau, *sénéchal d'Anjou* and a friend of the Bon Roi René. It was much changed through time and had become terribly run-down in recent times, but a Paris impresario, Mme Tugendhat, has been bringing life back to the place. You get a little tour of some of the parts being renovated. The château's main attraction is the painted ceiling of the little chapel housed in one of the property's four corner towers. A very graceful Nativity scene stands out among the beautiful depictions, including angels and the animals representing the four Evangelists. This delightful room serves as cadre for a series of summer evening concerts (*t 02 41 68 95 90/95*) by young musicians, preceded by a tour and a simple *foué* dinner.

Château de Brissac

Open July–mid-Sept 10–5.45, April–June and mid-Sept–Oct Wed–Mon 10–12 and 2.15–5.15; t 02 41 91 22 21.

...un château neuf à moitié construit dans un château vieux à moitié détruit (a new château, half-built, in an old château, half-destroyed)
> description of Brissac attributed to the present duke

The Château de Brissac looks like a classical body trying to squeeze out of a medieval one. It has very nearly succeeded, but has remained trapped before completing the effort to liberate itself. The clashing styles make Brissac a very peculiar hybrid to look at, but certainly give the architecture a dynamic feel. Built on the sloping hillside down to the Aubance, the château is enormous, an unashamedly swaggering eccentric of a castle. It advertises itself as the tallest along the Loire Valley, reaching seven storeys in one part.

The two medieval towers, what's left of the late Gothic castle, date back to the mid-15th century. In the left-hand tower the Gothic tracery of the chapel window stands out clearly. The schist stone mainly used reminds you that at Brissac the so-called Parisian limestone plateau has given way to the Armorican *massif*. The openings, however, are surrounded by lighter limestone.

The original Gothic château was built for Pierre de Brézé, a courtier who served both King Charles VII and, albeit very briefly, King Louis XI. He died in 1465, fighting to quash the rebellion against Louis, the Ligue du Bien Public. Pierre's nephew, who inherited the Gothic pile, sold it in 1502 to René de Cossé, a powerful minister under King Charles VIII. The same family, with several illustrious members, has kept hold of the castle since then.

Charles II de Cossé (*see* box on next page) wanted to mark his elevated rank on his château, and he and his architect or master mason, Jacques Corbineau, are responsible, to blame or to be congratulated, according to your taste, for the transformation of the family home. The main neoclassical wing and staircase are quite extraordinary in their detail. It seems as though no one was able to tell the architect Jacques Corbineau where to stop. Just look at the windows of the stair tower above the main entrance, built like monumental gateways. The Mannerist slate roof rises triumphantly above the medieval and adds further to the extravagant incompatibility of the effects. The architectural historian Marcus Binney very nicely described Corbineau's work as 'restless masonry'. Charles II's successor Louis then embarked on a new different wing to the right of the main façade, a massive block rising to seven storeys.

Moving inside, in the entrance hall, heavily decorated coats of arms imprint the family honours. You then tour some of the splendid rooms. The Grand Salon sets

A Model of a Courtly Family

The Cossé family is an example of the pure *noblesse d'épée*, military nobility, of France's Ancien Régime, even if several members directed their attention to fighting battles with the fabric of their home. René's son Charles was conferred the title of count. The latter's son, Charles II de Cossé, went one stage better and became a duke, Brissac becoming the centre of his duchy. Charles II de Cossé turned out to be an impressive late 16th-century figure. A formidable fighter in the Wars of Religion, he was also reputed as an orator, and in the national crisis at the end of the 1580s, represented the nobility in the meeting of the Estates General at the Château de Blois in 1588, not mincing his words with King Henri III.

Under King Henri IV, Charles II de Cossé would be rewarded with the highest honours in the land, as governor of Paris having opened the gates to the capital to the reconciling king. Charles became a *maréchal de France* as well as a duke, the two titles indicated by the symbols of the baton and the coronet respectively. Ian Dunlop, an historian of the Loire châteaux, even advances the speculative notion that he might have had higher ambitions still during the turmoil of the Wars of Religion – to become First Consul of a first French Republic. The time wasn't ripe. In all, from his time, the family counts 13 dukes, four of whom became *maréchaux de France*.

the tone with its 17th-century grandeur; it's highly decorated, with an ornate fireplace, coffered ceiling and Venetian glass candelabra. A Gobelin tapestry depicts Don Quixote, but most of the figures around the room are hard-headed family members who knew how to hold on to real power. The bust on the mantlepiece shows Charles II de Cossé. Several of the ceilings in the main rooms are painted, as in the Salle à Manger, the interlacing Cs referring immodestly to Charles de Cossé again. The wealth of decoration is too rich to take in on a guided tour, but you can't fail to miss the vast painting of the now vanished Château de Bercy, or the musicians' gallery.

Up the staircase, you enter the elongated Salle des Gardes, the ceiling beams all the way down painted with miniature pastoral scenes, decorative motifs and gilded putti. You can gaze at bucolic views onto the Aubance from the windows, while noting that even the shutters have been painted with scenes. Splendid tapestries line the walls, some in lovely faded blues and greens.

In the rich atmosphere of a crimson bedroom hung with gold and blue tapestries depicting the heroics of Alexander the Great in battle, the guide tells of King Louis XIII's little war on his mother, Marie de' Medici, and their connection with the locality. Marie de' Medici was the daughter of King François I and became the widow of the assassinated King Henri IV. She had served as regent from 1610–17 while her son was too young to rule and surrounded herself with exploitative favourites, her Italian lover Concini the best known. She also advanced the young Armand du Plessis, alias Cardinal Richelieu. When Louis XIII took power, he had Concini assassinated and banished his mother to the provinces, leaving her to govern Anjou. But her shenanigans led the king to take action and he came to quell her rebelliousness, beating her troops at the Ponts-de-Cé, just south of Angers. Peace was sought, Armand du Plessis, then bishop of Luçon, acting as one of the mediators. The Duc de Brissac found himself someone sandwiched between the two protagonists. He supported the king, but had already entertained the queen mother on several occasions at his château. It now served as the place where she and the king retired to make up properly after the public reconciliation at a village nearby.

The best tapestries of all remain protected from the light in the Chambre de Chasse. These exquisite 16th-century pieces were made in Flanders and show forest hunts after different wild animals, in minute detail. Rarely do you see tapestries of such refinement. Apparently they were once owned by royalty.

You'll be relieved to hear you don't have to visit all 203 rooms the château is said to contain. After the family picture gallery you get a chance for a quick sit-down in the theatre. Yes, without any hint of it showing from the outside, this château conceals a stage with auditorium for an audience of almost 200. This was incorporated into the castle on the whim of an absurdly rich 19th-century woman, Jeanne Say. Great-grand-mother of the present duke, amateur opera singer, spoken of as friend of Gounod, Massenet, St-Saens, Debussy and Wagner, she had a floor removed from part of the château to indulge her passion. Abandoned with the First World War, the theatre was restored in the 1980s and its spacious, rich crimson setting serves once more. At the end of the tour you'll be taken down to the cellars for a semi-enforced wine tasting, hardly much of an imposition.

In the picturesque **village of Brissac-Quincé** up the hill, you can see René de Cossé and his wife at the base of the stained-glass depiction of the Crucifixion in the church. You can then follow the broad meandering, wine-producing river valley via St-Melanie and Mûrs-Erigné to the Loire.

The Loire from Saumur to Angers

Two utterly splendid stretches of Loire-side road compete for your attention between Saumur and Angers. You're strongly recommended not to miss either the south bank or the north bank route.

From Saumur to Angers via the South Bank of the Loire

After a scrappy exit from St-Hilaire-St-Florent, the D751 finds the wonderful, restful company of the Loire at Les Mimeroles. The road on to Gennes is delightfully wooded, offering tempting glimpses of the river through tree trunks and foliage. **Chênehutte-les-Tuffeaux**, the first in a string of utterly charming Loire-side old villages, has a 12th-century church much restored in the 19th. Joined to Chênehutte, **Trèves** is distinguished by the romantic ruin of a tufa tower, left over from a 15th-century fortress. Equally charming is the 12th-century Romanesque church of St-Aubin beside it.

Cunault

Neigbouring Cunault, like Trèves, once had a very active port on the Loire. It also had an important religious community. Christianity stuck here in the 5th century, when a follower of St Martin of Tours, one St Maxenceul, who had been converting the local populace, died here. His memory was later upstaged by the arrival here in the 9th century of St Philibert's relics to escape the grasp of the destructive Vikings. The Vikings continued to advance further inland, however, so the monks ran off east again, carrying the saintly remains with them. By the start of the next century, some of the order were back. They had added to their substantial collection of relics – this time with a real whopper, a ring which had supposedly belonged to the Virgin Mary, plus a phial of her milk! Enough to entice more than your fair share of medieval pilgrims, when a magnificent new church was built.

The belfry of the **priory church of Notre-Dame** dates from the mid-11th century, with some exceptionally imaginative stone carvings at its base, including a mermaid that looks rather like a nun with a fish's tail fighting a man in a Loire boat. A remarkable Annunciation also graces this belfry. But the bulk of the church you now see was built through the 12th century. The fortified elements on the west front were added in the troubled 15th century, although the Virgin and Child of the tympanum probably date from the end of the Romanesque campaign.

Descending the steps into the church, you peer into a vast tomb-like nave. On a sunny day, it's like a brief, dark vision of the underworld, the initial blackness within contrasting with the blinding lightness of the stone outside. You then enter one of the largest Romanesque edifices in western France. Once your eyes have adjusted to the dimness inside, the view towards the apse is elevating. The main church was constructed from the choir to the west end. The increasing richness of the carved capitals going westwards reflects an artistry that was developing in this period. A staggering number of scenes (more than 200, it's claimed) decorate the nave capitals. A bishop caught between two open-mouthed scaly dogs, dragon faces with gaping red mouths, men with legs splayed, vegetation covering their private parts, a choir of monks singing, combat scenes, armoured soldiers in preposterously precarious poses fighting a lance-carrying devil...these and many more show the medieval imagination fighting its monsters.

In the beautiful apse ambulatory, pretty plain leaves adorn the capitals. One of the apse's side-chapels contains St Maxenceul's reliquary chest, a beautiful poly-chrome piece with depictions of the Ascension, Pentecost and the Apostles. To make a visit to Cunault's church even more uplifting, come during the *Heures Musicales* in

Getting Around

The **bus** service between Saumur and Angers offers you the choice between the south bank and the north bank routes, but there are only a few services a day.

Tourist Information

Cunault: Mairie, Place V. Dialland, 49350 Cunault, t 02 41 67 92 55/or 70, f 02 41 67 91 94.

Gennes: Square de l'Europe, 49350 Gennes, t 02 41 51 84 14, f 02 41 51 83 48.

St-Rémy-la-Varenne: Le Prieuré, 49250 St-Rémy-la-Varenne, t 02 41 57 32 32.

Blaison-Gohier: Mairie, 49320 Blaison-Gohier, t 02 41 57 17 57.

St-Martin-de-la-Place: Mairie, 49160 St-Martin-de-la-Place, t 02 41 38 43 06.

Les Rosiers: Place du Mail, 49350 Les Rosiers, t 02 41 51 90 22.

La Ménitré: Place Léon Faye, 49250 La Ménitré, t 02 41 45 67 51.

St-Mathurin-sur-Loire: 20 Rue Roi René, 49250 St-Mathurin-sur-Loire, t 02 41 57 01 82.

Market Days

Gennes: Tuesday.
Les Rosiers: Monday.
La Menitré: Saturday.
St-Mathurin: Tuesday.

Where to Stay and Eat

Chênehutte-les-Tuffeaux ✉ 49350
★★★★**L'Hostellerie du Prieuré**, t 02 41 67 90 14, f 02 41 67 92 24, *prieure@wanadoo.fr* (*expensive*). The rooms in this converted priory hidden in woods just above the Loire are splendid, some with wonderful fire-places, but be warned: there are also some hideous, if comfortable, maisonnettes in the grounds – make sure you're not given one of those. The views onto the Loire Valley are so spectacular from the luxurious terrace and dining room that the place makes a memorable stop for a special meal. Needless to say cuisine and Anjou wine list are top notch (*menus €23–84*). There's a swimming pool, tennis court and mini-golf in the grounds. *Closed early Jan–early Mar.*

Les Bateliers B&B, 28 Rue de Beauregard, t/f 02 41 67 94 49, *marie.voleau@worldonline.fr* (*inexpensive*). Delightful atmospheric troglodyte suite as well as two rooms in the owner's typical limestone home by the Loire (*table d'hôte €13.5*).

Gennes ✉ 49350
★★**Aux Naulets d'Anjou**, 18 Rue Croix de Mission, t 02 41 51 81 88, f 02 41 38 00 78 (*inexpensive*). Peaceful modern hotel set back in grounds away from the road (*menus €15–25*). *Closed Feb–mid-Mar.*

July and August. A concert takes place here every Sunday afternoon at 5pm during those months.

From Gennes Towards Angers

Gennes, too, has its Romanesque legacy, with two early medieval churches, one standing either side of the Avort stream, but it also has a Gallo-Roman past. The amphitheatre (*open July–Aug 10–12.30 and 3–6.30, April–June and Sept Sun only 3–6.30*) lies well hidden in woods south of town. It was only officially rediscovered in 1847, excavated in 1985 and is still quite overgrown and wild. It may date from as early as the 1st century and could probably seat up to 5,000 spectators. The builders made good use of the hillside for the partial circle of seats to oversee the oval arena. Some parts of the chambers below the stage also remain. It may have been used up until a devastating fire in the 3rd century, possibly caused by a revolt of Gaulish slaves.

L'Aubergade, 7 Av des Cadets, **t** 02 41 51 81 07, **f** 02 41 38 07 85. Distinguished Angevin cuisine served in a beamed setting (*menus €21–33.5*).

Le Thoureil ✉ 49350
*Au Cabernet d'Anjou, 2 Place de l'Eglise, **t** 02 41 57 95 02, remy-deretar@wanadoo.fr. A former Loire mariners' bar, with a glorious terrace from which to watch the Loire (*menus €14–15*).

St-Rémy-la-Varenne ✉ 49250
La Riviera, **t** 02 41 57 02 19. A typical Loire-side *guinguette* (or mainly open-air restaurant with evening dances) right by the bridge to St-Mathurin, looking lazily onto the Loire and serving *fritures*, fried fish (*simple menus*). *Closed Nov–March*.

St-Saturnin-sur-Loire ✉ 49320
Auberge La Caillotte, 2 Rue de la Loire, **t/f** 02 41 54 63 74. Adorable inn up on the heights above the Loire. Splendid views over the Loire's valley to accompany good food and a good atmosphere (*menus €17.5–32.5*).
Guinguette à Jojo, Chaloché, **t** 02 41 54 64 04. Go down to the Loire from St-Saturnin via increasingly small lanes and you finally end up on a rough track for this restaurant. The food may not be anything special, but this *guinguette* is all about the location,

with hundreds of plastic seats set out under drooping branches in summer for diners to appreciate the Loire (*menu from around €19*).
Guingette Port la Vallée. Accordion music may be playing when you arrive at this other characterfully scruffy shack with outdoor seating right by the Loire (*menus €13–16*).

Les Rosiers ✉ 49350
***Auberge Jeanne de Laval/Les Ducs d'Anjou, 54 Rue Nationale, **t** 02 41 51 80 17, **f** 02 41 38 04 18 (*moderate*). The cuisine has made the name of this high-quality establishment. The comfortable rooms are in a grand building (*menus €30.5–68.4*).
Au Val de Loire, Place de l'Eglise, **t 02 41 51 80 30, **f** 02 41 51 95 00 (*inexpensive*). Neat, smart little rooms and a dining room which wouldn't look out of place on a 1970s poster, with spacious round tables. The food is carefully prepared, using lots of fresh local produce (*menus €11.5–29.5*).

St-Mathurin-sur-Loire ✉ 49250
Les Mûriers B&B, 4 Grande Rue, **t** 02 41 57 04 15 (*inexpensive*). Typical limestone house close to the Loire, with a delightful garden. The little rooms have a slightly old-fashioned appeal.

From the church of St-Eusèbe you can enjoy a great view of the Loire, but also look out for a plaque recalling the vain but valiant resistance put up here by Saumur's cavalry trainees against the advancing Germans at the start of the Second World War.

Le Thoureil is a lovely village fully exposed to the beauty of the Loire. In summer, when the river dwindles in size, the children's swings planted in the firm sand banks make for a comic sight. There's even a Loire sailing school here. Prehistoric men liked the spot too; it's yielded many finds of tools, while menhirs and dolmens litter the hinterland. Now visitors from abroad seem to have colonized the Loire-side village, to go by the car numberplates. That's nothing new; the 17th-century houses along the river bank were built by Dutch merchants who came to trade along the Loire, exporting the local wines.

You can only appreciate the full extent of the grandeur of the **Abbaye de St-Maur-de-Glanfeuil**'s riverside façade from the Loire's north bank, and it can't be visited, but the late 17th-century building on the riverbank is superb. Continuing to **St-Rémy-la-Varenne**, the Logis du Prieuré may be run down, but it is very charmingly so. You can support the valiant efforts at restoration by having a look round at the carvings, including the monkeys at the entrance gate. Exhibitions are held here in summer.

The countryside around **Gohier**, **Blaison** and **St-Sulpice** is reassuringly peaceful. Various tracks lead down to shaded riverside spots opposite Loire islands on which birds fish. But here, the limestone gives way to schist, as you'll see immediately in the architecture.

Artistic Treasures South of Gennes

Gennes has a hinterland of small delights. Seek out the delightful Romanesque chapels at **St-Pierre-en-Vaux** and **St-Georges-des-Sept-Voies**. Contemporary artists have also created fascinating curiosities in caves in these parts.

L'Hélice Terrestre, L'Orbière (*open May–Sept 11–8, rest of year Wed–Sun 2.30–6.30*), close to St-Georges-des-Sept-Voies, is a wacky troglodyte dwelling transformed into a work of art. Actually, there are several galleries of art here, created by the passionate Jacques Warminski, who died in the mid-1990s. One of his massive works in fact lies out of doors, a concretion of sculptures collected in a small amphitheatre. You can wander up around the science-fiction forms emerging from it. Underground, the sculpture takes on the warm light tones of the limestone. The entrance is like a spiral into the earth, hence the name of *l'hélice terrestre*. The caverns have walls covered with marvellous patterning. Whereas outside the shapes stand out, inside they indent the walls. As well as patternings of bricks, human forms too have been set like shadows in the wall. Nothing is straight or clear down here. The narrow paths wind round in a head-spinning confusion. Shapes are turned upside down. Gymnastics seem a theme. The most fabulous experience awaits you in the Sphere, which emits a musical note when you stamp around in it.

The artist Richard Rak displays his intriguing works in his Etrange Galerie caves at the **Manoir de la Caillère** (*open May–Sept Tues–Sun 10–7, Oct–April weekends only 10–7*) in Coutures, just northwest of St-Georges-des-Sept-Voies. Rather than carving pieces into the rock, Richard Rak uses the maze of corridors at his enchanting property as walls on which to hang his art works. Caves have often been places where remnants of older and different civilizations from our own have been discovered. Richard Rak's art works seem to be built up in good part from remnants and scraps he has culled from here, there and everywhere in modern society, but which he transforms to give a feel of a different culture. For example, he can make a battered old case look like the skin of a strange animal. The paintings, often involving collage, mix the playful elements of surreal and naive art into strangely intelligent concoctions.

From Saumur to Angers Via the North Bank of the Loire

While ancient cultural sites cram the southern, wooded Loire bank from Saumur to Angers, the northern one long lay uninhabited, vulnerable to flooding. It's still harshly exposed to the sun in summer, with few trees to offer any shade. The D952 along the north bank of the Loire is, however, probably the more ravishing of the two competing riverside routes from Saumur to Angers, perhaps even deserving the prize for the prettiest of all roads along the Loire. This is because it runs along the medieval *grande levée*, looking over to the gorgeous southern side of the river with its richer architectural heritage, limestone villages and churches peering out of the woods.

Views onto the romantic sweeps of the river itself are unhindered by foliage from the northern side. So you can appreciate the full the glory of the river. With its islands and sandbanks, the Loire plays tricks on the imagination, making you think you're reaching the coast. In centuries past this was a busy shipping lane, many of the villages along this stretch developing thriving ports. Nowadays, in the middle of the river you may still spot the occasional reed-covered hut on the water, duck hunters' hides. The only marring aspect can be the weight of slow traffic in summer; many cars slow to the pace of carthorses to take in this route.

North of the *levée*, the land looks flat as a crêpe, the richly sandy earth providing excellent fruit, vegetables and flowers. This extensive flat river plain wasn't always so uncomplicatedly fertile and giving. Henri Plantagenêt, in one of the most helpful decisions he took for the Loire, in 1168 ordered the building of a very extensive bank – *grande levée* – from Bourgueil to Angers to hold in the river waters. Henri's plan wasn't totally disinterested of course. Any more cultivable land would also bring in tax revenues for him to spend on further adventures. The alluvial sands were certainly extremely well suited to agricultural exploitation. The Authion river runs along the flats north of the Loire, parallel to it, borrowing a bit of the wide valley. Before the *grande levée*, in flood periods, the Loire could spread out and join the Authion, creating a massive stretch of water referred to as the Vallée d'Anjou.

Stops Along the *Grande Levée*

The villages along the *grande levée* look splendidly sun-bleached in summer. The Loire dwindles in size in this season, exposing large sandbanks. Go down to admire the scene from the cobbled quays in the villages, reminders of how they used to thrive on river trade. They've now turned into popular Loire holiday resorts, with some delightfully situated camp sites. To go on a trip on the river from one of the villages along this route in summer, contact **Loire de Lumière** (*open June–Aug Tues–Sun; t 02 41 45 69 01*).

Pass through **St-Martin-de-la-Place** and **St-Clément-des-Levées**, the latter with substantial quays, although the finest are probably at the next village, **Les Rosiers**, a thoroughly delightful place with a trellised iron bridge over the Loire and a church tower you can climb in summer for fine views. At the next village, **Port-St-Maur** by **La Ménitré**, you can go canoeing on the Loire from the *base nautique*.

At **St-Mathurin-sur-Loire** you might stop at the Observatoire de la Vallée d'Anjou (*open July–Aug Tues–Sun 10–12 and 3–6, April–June and Sept–Oct weekends only 3–6*) to find out more on the ecology and rich bird life of the area. Set in the disused railway station at the back of the village, the place unfortunately doesn't look onto the Loire itself. But it does run organized ornithological trips from here (*contact them well in advance if interested; t 02 41 57 37 55, f 02 41 57 08 02*). The D952 continues to follow the splendid stretch of river for several kilometres until it branches off towards Angers, the area then becoming rapidly more built-up.

Northeastern Anjou

Heading north across the Loire from Saumur, you cross the open, fruit-and-vegetable-growing Authion valley and soon come into woods. These parts are relatively untouristy and very restful. Northeast from Saumur across the Loire, **Brain-sur-Allonnes'** fort was probably destroyed by English soldiers in the Hundred Years' War, around 1360. It was then forgotten for six centuries, until archaeologists uncovered underground caves laid with thousands of 14th-century tiles. These form the main attraction of the little Musée d'Histoire et d'Archéologie (*open Tues–Sun 10–12 and 2–6*). The medieval site of the Maison Forte can also be visited (*open mid-April–mid-Oct Tues–Sun 10–12 and 2–6*).

Continuing north from Brain and you can enjoy religious stops at **Vernoil**, **La Boissière**, **Broc** and **Genneteil**, the last two with Romanesque churches containing religious murals. The major sight in these parts, the **Château du Lude** (*open April–Sept, gardens 10–12 and 2–6, castle 2.30–6*) lies just across the Anjou border, by the Loir (without an 'e') river. This very grand building competes in scale with some of the grandest Loire Valley châteaux. Each corner is marked by a massive round tower covered with Renaissance decoration. The place was substantially modified in the 18th century, and the classical façade and inner courtyard have the air of a great Parisian town house. In the library stands a bust of the Marquis de Talhouët-Roy, finance minister to kings Louis XVIII and Charles X, who initiated many

Getting Around

From Angers, there are occasional **buses** to Beaufort-en-Vallée, Baugé and Noyant. Likewise from Saumur.

Tourist Information

Brain-sur-Allonnes: 12 Place du Commerce, 49650 Brain-sur-Allonnes, **t** 02 41 52 87 40.
Baugé: Place de l'Europe, 49150 Baugé, **t** 02 41 89 18 07.
Beaufort-en-Vallée: Place Joseph Denais, 49250 Beaufort-en-Vallée, **t** 02 41 57 42 30.

Market Days

Baugé: Monday afternoon.
Le Vieil-Baugé: Thursday.
Beaufort-en-Vallée: Wednesday.

Where to Stay and Eat

Bocé ✉ 49150
Le Chant d'Oiseau B&B, Les Rues, **t/f** 02 41 82 73 14 (*inexpensive*). Enchanting little place a short way south of Baugé, run by enchanting hosts. This is a picture-book little farm with lovely blue shutters. The small rooms have been recently done up and are very cheerful, while the main part of the barn has been converted into a dining area. You can also make the most of the hot tub in the garden (*table d'hôte €15*).

Brion ✉ 49250
Le Logis du Pressoir B&B, Villeneuve, **t/f** 02 41 57 27 33 (*inexpensive*). Extremely stylishly modernized farm buildings, with very charming rooms, salons and garden, just east of Beaufort-en-Vallée (*table d'hôte €18*).

of the internal modifications. From the spectacular ballroom, with its floral marquetry floor, you trip through a series of spacious salons. An intimate surprise awaits you in a jewel-box of a room covered with paintings and grotesques in the Italian Mannerist style. The terraced gardens by the Loir are embellished with dramatic statues, while in summer the château serves as the sumptuous backdrop to a grand *son-et-lumière* show.

Baugé

Baugé can feel more than a little subdued outside its market day. It enjoyed its golden days many centuries ago, when Le Bon Roi René (*see* Angers, p.425) adopted the town in the 15th-century. Foulques Nerra had left his mark here before him, of course, having built a fortification here. And earlier in the 15th century, in 1421, a significant battle in the second half of the Hundred Years' War saw the French carry off a much-needed victory after so many early setbacks, this a good few years before Joan of Arc came on the scene. Apart from the little château in the centre of town at which René enjoyed staying with his first wife Isabelle de Lorraine, Baugé's claim to fame is a piece of the cross on which Christ died – if you believe in the absurdity of medieval relics.

The **Château de Baugé** (*open July–Aug 11–1 and 3–7, second half June and first half Sept Tues–Sun 2.30–6, April–mid-June and mid-Sept–Oct weekends only 2.30–6*) stands on the vast, barren market square at the centre of the town. Its rough, almost yellow, plaster façade gives it a very pleasing look. It's essentially a 15th-century construction, built in great part for Yolande d'Aragon, mother of René d'Anjou, from the 1430s and 40s. The château, for a short time under René, held the magnificent Apocalypse tapestry now in Angers castle, René protecting it from Louis XI's grasp. The **Musée d'Art et d'Histoire** within contains a modest collection of earthenware and household objects, regional coiffes and decorative items, 17th- and 18th-century utensils, archaeological finds (including prehistoric items), coins and, the best being reserved for last, a fine selection of armour.

You can view what's said to be a piece of Christ's cross at the **Chapelle de la Girouardière** (*open Wed–Mon exc major Christian festivals 2.30–4.15*). This extraordinary relic, with its two distinctive horizontal bars, is guarded in a room off an unremarkable modern chapel. A medieval crusader from Anjou, one Jean d'Alluye, was apparently given the fragment of the cross by the bishop of Crete by way of thanks for protecting the island. Jean d'Alluye returned home in 1241 with his invaluable relic and a parchment from the bishop of Constantinople vouching for its authenticity. But d'Alluye soon sold the piece to the monks of the Cistercian abbey of nearby La Boissière for 550 livres. Pilgrims flocked to see it and derive strength from it.

Some time later, because of the dangers of the Hundred Years' War, the monks took the relic to Angers for safekeeping under Duke Louis I d'Anjou. From 1359 it graced the castle chapel. Louis decided to embellish the piece. The duke and his royal brothers adored gorgeous objects and King Charles V's Parisian jewellers were asked to beautify the relic. Placing it on a gilded silver base, covering the top and arms with pure gold, they then went overboard, setting 17 rubies and 19 sapphires in it. The most exquisite parts, exquisitely painful, are the two small statues of Christ on either side, his agony caught in solid gold.

Treasuring the cross in his chapel, Louis decided to make it the emblem of a new chivalric order, the Confrérie de la Vraie Croix, in the 1370s. The form of the cross appears on the vast tapestry cycle of the Apocalypse he ordered, which hangs in Angers castle. His grandson René would adopt the cross as his symbol, placing it on his coat of arms and on his money. René not only held the titles of Duc d'Anjou, Comte d'Anjou and Roi de Sicile; having married Isabelle de Lorraine, he became duke of that region too. The cross stayed in Angers castle until the mid-15th century, when it was sent back to La Boissière. At the Battle of Nancy of 1477 in eastern France, the shape of the cross served as the banner under which troops fought, led by René's eponymous grandson – after that, the cross became known as the Croix de Lorraine, the emblem of that eastern region of France. During the Revolution, the cross was taken from La Boissière and auctioned at Baugé. Anne de la Girouardière, founder of the hospice for incurables of Baugé, bought it for 400 livres and it has stayed here ever since, although the community has changed to that of the Community of the Heart of Mary.

Why did a small Christian community spend so much money on what you might consider a vain piece like this, perhaps more appropriate for the posturing vanity and hypocrisy of princes? A document the sisters hand out offers another view of the relic: 'Christians venerate this vestige or tangible sign of the Passion of Christ of their Redemption. To all, this relic proposes reflection on the origins and permanence of our history and our civilization. Hail O Cross, unique hope, glorious cross of Jesus Christ. That in you all men may find grace and life!' In June 1940, at the start of the German occupation of France in the Second World War, the shape of the cross was adopted as the symbol of the French Resistance.

From Baugé to Beaufort-en-Vallée

A series of churches with twisting spires marks the Baugeois countryside. The most obvious one is at **Le Vieil-Baugé**, a sweet old village next to Baugé, where the spire not only spirals, but also goes all crooked! **Pontigné**, a short way east of Baugé, has an equally startling church. Apart from the surprise of its twisted spire, the interior conceals splendid carved capitals and rich wall paintings of New Testament scenes by the wonderfully nicknamed Master of the Big Feet. Other of these delightfully eccentric churches can be seen at **Mouliherne** and **La Fontaine-Guérin**. How or why these spires came about is not known for certain, although it may be that an accidental discovery of the technique led to its adoption.

From the heights of **Beaufort-en-Vallée**, you can look down over the fertile plains back south to the Loire. This pleasing town has a fine church bristling with late Gothic decoration. The Musée Joseph Denais (*open July–Aug 11–1 and 3–7, second half of June and first half of Sept Tues–Sun 2.30–6, April–mid-June and mid-Sept–Oct weekends only 2.30–6*) is crammed with the collections of a local journalist and writer from the end of the 19th century who, as well as compulsively amassing the kinds of treasures people store in their attics, also gathered old weapons and Egyptian artefacts.

Château de Montgeoffroy

Open mid-June–mid-Sept 9–6.30, mid-March–mid-June and mid-Sept–early Nov 9.30–12 and 2.30–6.30.

This is a rarity in the Loire Valley, an 18th-century château left pretty well intact. In fact the place is pretty well pickled in time. It was built on its gentle slope above the Authion west of Beaufort-en-Vallée for a very successful military man, the Maréchal de Contades, at a time when France was endlessly at war with Britain. The marshal's presence is still to be felt in the château, the interiors containing much of the original decoration.

The marshal only decided to rebuild the family property late in life, when he was already 67 and, as Commander-in-Chief of Alsace, not often at home. The architect, Jean Barré, was Parisian, but also worked on the Château du Lude (*see pp.413–4, above*). While incorporating styles of the time, the plan also keeps some older elements to underline the ancestry of the family. The work was executed between 1773 and 75, Louis XVI coming to the throne in 1774. The guide says that some 4,000 workers were employed on the site, which seems almost unbelievable, but the vast numbers may explain how it was completed so fast. Two perpendicular wings run down from the main building. Each ends in a powerful, squat, conical-roofed tower, solid reminders of the 16th-century château.

The chapel, too, dates from this earlier period. The exterior doesn't present a wealth of decoration. It's simply, soberly symmetrical, with just the occasional arched window to break the monotony of the rectangular openings, the only sculpture the frieze of the Contade arms in the pediment. This is subdued neoclassicism. The wealth of detail lies within.

On entering the château you're greeted by the 18th-century marshal himself, beaming down at you, admittedly from a painting. This is still a proudly kept family home, full of refined period pieces and of course family portraits. The household inventory drawn up before the end of the 18th century has survived and, astonishingly for a French château, the rooms today still contain the furniture that was recorded at that time, most of it bought in Paris.

The Salle de Billard was deliberately designed to show the two 17th-century Aubusson tapestries to good advantage. The Petit Salon Bleu served more as the games room. A portrait here shows the marshal's wife, whose father was president of the massively powerful Companie des Indes, France's equivalent to the British East India Company, which explains some of the exotic objects to be found later on the tour. The painting of Pompon, the couple's dog, a poodle of royal pedigree, rather curiously represented Anjou at the Seville Expo 92. The royal connections are emphasized by typical portraits of Louis XIV and chubby-cheeked Louis XVI.

The Grand Salon, set out with period chairs, the *bergères* broad enough to cope with the ballooning fashion of ladies' dresses, would have been the centre of social occasions. Apparently seven different shades of grey were employed to decorate the walls. The quality of the original panelling and marquetry floors stands out. Plaster mouldings decorate this and the other ground floor ceilings. The Grand Salon contains more fine portraits, not only another picture of the marshal, but also one of his father, by Rigaud, in shining armour and fine periwig. The little boy of seven with a Boucher-like sweetness was the ill-fated Marie-Jean Héros de Seychelles, who briefly became a leading figure in the French Revolution and was guillotined along with Danton in 1794, at the age of 35. Photos of contemporary family members and European royalty accompany these grand pictures.

The table remains permanently set in the most elegant oval dining room. The disproportionate size of the chairs was once again designed to accommodate the large dresses of the time. The plates bear the insignia of the Companie des Indes, while an exotic glazed earthenware stove takes the shape of a palm tree. Desportes executed the masterly still life, Van Loo the portrait of Louis XV, which has the place of honour here. It may surprise you to learn that formal dining rooms were most uncommon in the Ancien Régime – rather, *châtelains* would have movable tables set up in a room that pleased them. This dining room, therefore, was relatively innovative, but perhaps not surprising given the marshal's liking for food – he's credited with making foie gras the height of fashion in France. You then enter a series of private chambers with precious household objects displayed behind glass.

You see the very poshest rooms in the château, of course, but the inventory went into more basic detail, revealing even some of the differences in lifestyle between the staff. While a *valet de chambre* could sleep in a room adjoining the master's bedroom provided with, say, a canopied bed upholstered with blue and white fabric, an ordinary manservant, for whom no bed is listed at all, would most likely sleep in the master's *garderobe* among the toiletries, on a straw mattress.

After the grand *salons*, you're taken out to see the stables and saddle room, having first passed through the kitchen, supremely well equipped with copper pans, and through the chapel. The latter, with its light vaulting, two bright rows of painted bosses and Renaissance stained-glass windows, also contains a plaque commemorating the marshal's life. He died at the ripe old age of 91, surviving the Revolutionary Terror, as his château would.

Angers

19

Apocalyptic Angers, black Angers...the titles aren't reassuring to this city which saw the birth of the Plantagenet dynasty of western France and later, most famously, of England. The obvious English mispronunciation of the town's name makes the place sound unsettling too – in French, the 'g' is soft of course, the word sounding closer to angels than angers. The town's nickname of 'black Angers' derives from its reputation for slate mining rather than a filthy character. The Apocalypse here comes in the form of two fabulous tapestry cycles, one from the 14th century, the other from the 20th, the first shown in Angers' heavyweight château, the second in surely the most elegant, as well as the oldest standing, hospital in France.

Angers doesn't quite lie along the Loire, but stretches across both banks of the Maine, a tributary just north of it. Two chains used to be drawn across the river at night to stop boats trying to slip by and avoid paying taxes to the town. The river

Maine isn't always so easily controlled. Even in recent years, huge floods have swamped the lands north of the town where the Loir, Sarthe and Mayenne join to form the short and stocky Maine. Most of Angers' historic sites were sensibly built on the slopes well above the river. The east bank rises particularly sharply, and it's here that you'll find the oldest part of the city, with the majority of the historic buildings, museums and shopping quarters. But even in the early medieval period, the town developed on the other side of the Maine, the mainly religious quarter on that side taking the name of La Doutre (roughly, a contraction of *de l'autre côté*, 'the other side'). The main draw on the outskirts of town is the Cointreau factory, but there's also a slate-mining museum and an early aviation museum, among further attractions.

History

As with Tours and Orléans, so with Angers – the centre of a Celtic tribe, the Andes or Andecaves, provided the site for the subsequent important Gallo-Roman centre. The town of Juliomagus oversaw a territory which became known as the Civitas Andecavorum. A good section of wall remains of the fortifications of Gallo-Roman Juliomagus, built to protect the town from the advancing hordes from the east at the end of the 3rd century. A Christian community emerged maybe as early as the 3rd century too, but despite the known appointment of bishops who also held civic power in the 4th century, it was only in the 5th that a cathedral was built within the town walls. A number of religious institutions were set up in ensuing centuries: St-Aubin in the 6th, St-Serge and St-Martin in the 7th.

On the western border of the Angevin territory the Bretons would constitute a threat for many centuries to come, but it was the Vikings who wrought havoc in the mid-9th century. Pillaged in 853–4, occupied in 872, Angers was only liberated after a long siege by King Charles the Bald. After his death in 877, the Carolingian empire's central authority crumbled, and the regional counts set up under the Carolingian kings became much more independent. The Ingelgérien family took power in Angers and Anjou under Foulques le Roux in 898. He was the first in a string of Angevin counts to go by the name of Foulques, or Falcon. The most famous name in this line is Foulques Nerra, very much blacker than the town from which he ruled. Angers expanded greatly under these galvanizing characters, with the important new quarter of La Doutre growing on the west bank of the Maine. St-Nicolas was begun there around 1010, Notre-Dame de la Charité in 1028. The latter became known as La Ronceray.

The chroniclers of the period, ever so slightly prone to exaggeration, wrote of Foulques Nerra as 'another Caesar'. While his forebears had appropriated southern Maine and brought the counts of Nantes under their control, he took the Mauges, southwest of Angers, and then decided to expand to the east, clashing with the mighty counts of Blois, and taking over the Saumurois and most of Touraine by the time of his death. Towards the close of the 11th century, around 1089, Robert d'Arbrissel (*see* pp.369–71), a charismatic preacher, came to Angers, where he taught theology for a time before founding his Fontevrist order, urged on by Pope Urban II, himself come to the city to rally support for the First Crusade.

Getting There and Around

By Air

The airport (t 02 41 33 50 00) is northeast of the centre, at Marcé. International Air France flights to Angers-Marcé pass via the hub of Clermont-Ferrand.

For taxis to and from the airport, you can contact Taxi Marcé – Aéroport Angers-Marcé, t 06 09 71 71 08 or Accueil Taxi Radio – Aéroport Angers-Marcé, t 02 41 73 98 20.

By Train

The TGV between Angers and Paris takes almost exactly 1½ hours. The train station, the Gare St-Laud, is just south of the centre.

By Bus

The Gare Routière (t 02 41 88 59 25) is set to move to beside the railway station. Bus lines radiate out from Angers, serving Anjou quite well, except on Sundays, when there are very few services.

By Car

Angers lies on the A11 motorway, 'l'Océane', which comes down from Paris via Chartres and Le Mans. This continues on to Nantes. The non-paying alternative from Paris is to branch off at the N10 at Chartres and then take the N23.

A large amount of the A85 motorway between Angers and Tours has now been completed.

By Taxi

Beyond the airport taxi numbers given above, you can try **Allo Anjou Taxi**, t 02 41 87 65 00, *allo-anjou-taxi@wanadoo.fr*.

Tourist Information

Tourist office: Office du Tourisme, Place Kennedy, B.P.5157, 49051 Angers Cedex 02, t 02 41 23 51 11, f 02 41 23 51 10, *angers.tourisme@ville-angers.fr*.

Market Days

Place M Vigne: Tuesday and Friday.
Bd Allonneau: Wednesday and Sunday.
Square Jeanne d'Arc: Thursday.
Bd des Deux Croix: Friday.

Festivals

The year starts with the **Premiers Plans**, the festival for first-time film-makers in January. **Les Estivales du Lac de Maine** are a series of open-air concerts in this modern lake near the centre of town in June. In July Angers hosts one of the best French theatre festivals, the **Festival d'Anjou**. Throughout July and August is the **Festival Angers l'Eté**, a world music, classical music and dance programme, while there is **Les Accroche-Cœurs**, street theatre and entertainment, in mid-September.

Contemporary art can be seen at the **Salon d'Angers, L'Art Vous Interpelle** in October, and there's a much-loved Christmas fair, **Soleils d'Hiver**, in December.

Where to Stay

Expensive

***Hôtel d'Anjou, 1 Bd M. Foch, t 02 41 88 24 82, f 02 41 87 22 21. On a major, busy boulevard, a Best Western hotel with rooms renovated to quite a high standard. The **Salamandre** restaurant (t 02 41 88 99 55) serves accomplished cuisine in a neo-Gothic setting (*menus €22–36.5*).

Foulques V, who became king of Jerusalem, also won the rather closer province of Maine (between the Loire Valley and Normandy) by marriage, and had a son called Geoffroy, nicknamed Plantagenêt because of his predilection for placing a piece of broom (*genêt* in French) in his helmet. Foulques V organized for his boy to be married in 1128 to Mathilda, daughter of King Henry I of England, who also ruled Normandy at that time. Impatient upstart that he was, Geoffroy forced Normandy to accept his rule in 1144.

His son Henri Plantagenêt most famously married Eleanor of Aquitaine in 1152, after her divorce from the French King Louis VII. Eleanor's Aquitaine included not just the

Moderate
★★★**Hôtel Bleu Marine**, 18 Bd M Foch, **t** 02 41 87 37 20, **f** 02 41 87 49 54, *www.Bleu-Marine@ angers.fr*. Slightly more basic than Hôtel d'Anjou, on the same boulevard (*menus €12–23*).
★★★**Quality Hôtel de France**, 8 Place de la Gare, **t** 02 41 88 49 42, **f** 02 41 86 76 70, *hotel.de. france.anjou@wanadoo.fr*. Opposite the train station, which is an easy walk from the centre, a substantial hotel with a grand façade and rooms with decent facilities (*menus €9–38*).
★★★**Hôtel Mercure**, 1 Place Mendès France, **t** 02 41 60 34 81, **f** 02 41 60 57 84, *HO540@ accor-hotels.com*. Reliable chain hotel (*menus €18–20.5*).

Inexpensive
★★**Hôtel du Mail**, 8 Rue des Ursules, **t** 02 41 25 05 25, **f** 02 41 86 91 20. The most characterful hotel in Angers, in a 17th-century town house set around a gravel courtyard. The place has a justifiably good reputation. Not only are the rooms atmospheric and good value, but the place is also well run.
★★**St-Julien**, 9 Place du Ralliement, **t** 02 41 88 41 62, **f** 02 41 20 95 19. Nicely located and central, with simple but pleasant rooms giving onto this lively square.
★★**Continental**, 12 Rue Louis de Romain, **t** 02 41 86 94 94, **f** 02 41 86 96 60, *le.continental@ wanadoo.fr*. Another friendly smallish hotel in the centre of town, this has recently been renovated.
★★**Progrès**, 26 Rue Denis Papin, **t** 02 41 88 10 14, **f** 02 41 87 82 93. Opposite the train station, a rather dull modern building but it's well looked after.

Cheap
Hôtel du Centre, 12 Rue St-Laud, **t** 02 41 87 45 07. An excellent central location for a cheap hotel, even if some of the rooms may be a bit run down. There's a brasserie attached.

Avrillé ✉ 49100
★★**Le Cavier**, Route de Laval, on the road north out of Angers to Laval, **t** 02 41 42 30 45, **f** 02 41 42 40 32, *lecavier@acom.fr* (*inexpensive*). Even if it stands just off a busy roundabout in the commercial belt, this unusual hotel built around a traditional Angevin windmill makes for a memorable stay. You can eat by the pool, but better still have dinner in one of the chambers in the heart of the windmill itself (*menus €14.5–27.5*).

Eating Out

Moderate
La Rose d'Or, 21 Rue Delaâge, **t** 02 41 88 38 38. A diminutive restaurant which doesn't have a *menu*, but does offer a good choice of well-prepared dishes at relatively reasonable prices (*menus €16.5–27.5*).
La Ferme, 2 Place Freppel, **t** 02 41 87 09 90. Plenty of dishes incorporating Anjou wine at this popular restaurant with a terrace in the shadow of the cathedral (*menus €10–27*).
Auberge Belle Rive, 25 bis Rue Haute de Reculée, **t** 02 41 48 18 70. By the Maine on La Doutre's side, chic cuisine and Cointreau-coloured materials at this bright, refined riverside restaurant (*menus c.€15–38*).
Les Trois Rivières, 62 Promenade de Reculée, **t** 02 41 73 31 88. On the Doutre side again, with views of the Maine too and good fish on the menu (*menus €12.5–27.5*).

Périgord and Gascony, but also Toulouse, the Saintonge, the Angoumois, the Limousin and Poitou! Henri suddenly found himself ruling an extensive western European empire. A year later he forced Etienne de Blois, better known as King Stephen of England, to recognize him as the heir to the English throne and Henri Plantagenêt became King Henry II of England in 1154.

This expansion of power rather made Angers lose its position as centre stage for the Angevin counts. Geoffroy had already shown a preference for Le Mans in Maine anyway, while Henri preferred Chinon to Angers. He didn't neglect the family town, however, and had the superbly elegant Hôpital St-Jean built in the Doutre in 1175.

Le Lucullus, 5 Rue Hoche, t 02 41 87 00 44. Fish specialities in vaulted rooms (*menus €15–45.6*).

Le Toussaint, 7 Place Kennedy, t 02 41 87 46 20. With its chic façade by the château, this numbers among the most reputed restaurants in town, with some interesting touches of eccentricity to the cooking (*menus from c.€15*).

Cheap

L'Auberge Angevine, 9 Rue Cordelle, t 02 41 20 10 40. An amusing medieval-style restaurant, in a church with stained-glass windows. You can try traditional Angevin *fouaces*, the local answer to pizza. Angevins come here for a laugh (*menus €9–23*).

Le Petit Mâchon, 43 Rue Bressigny (a popular street for restaurants, east of Boulevard Foch), t 02 41 86 01 13. Simple, family-French restaurant (*menu c.€10.5*).

Le Bouchon Angevin, 44 Rue Beaurepaire, t 02 41 24 77 97. A pleasant option in a wine cellar in La Doutre.

For a range of cheap, ethnic restaurants look along the streets north of the cathedral such as Rue St-Laud, Rue Baudrière, Rue Plantagenêt, Rue Parcheminerie and Rue Boisnet. Terraces spill out from them onto the street in summer.

Entertainment and Nightlife

Cinema

Cinéma Les 400 Coups, 12 Rue Claveau, t 02 41 88 70 95. For those who are passionate about cinema, classic films and foreign films in their original language.

Gaumont Multiplexe, Quai Félix Faure. New 12-screen complex in the central modern quarter of St-Serge, just north of the historic centre.

You'll find a clutch of further cinemas along Boulevard Foch.

Theatre

Grand Théâtre d'Angers, Place du Ralliement, t 02 41 24 16 30, f 02 41 24 16 49. Wonderfully over-the-top Italianate theatre with a diverse programme of cultural events.

Nouveau Théâtre d'Angers Beaurepaire, 12 Bd Dumesnil, t 02 41 88 99 22, f 02 41 24 16 49. In La Doutre, another major theatre and cultural venue.

Théâtre du Champ de Bataille, 10 Rue du Champ de Bataille, t 02 41 72 00 94. Lively new little theatre dating from the mid-1990s. Some jazz events too.

La Comédie, 1 Rue Cordelle, t 02 41 87 24 24. Another successful little theatre set up in the mid-1990s.

Music

Chapelle de l'Ancien Couvent des Ursulines, 175 Bd de Strasbourg, t 02 41 44 33 80. A Baroque music and Renaissance dance programme is performed in this Romanesque chapel.

Auditorium du Centre de Congrès, 1 Place Mendès-France, t 02 41 96 32 32. The main venue for the Orchestre National des Pays de la Loire.

Le Chabada, 56 Bd du Doyenné, t 02 41 96 13 40, f 02 41 96 13 49. For all manner of contemporary music concerts.

La Coursive, 7 bis Bd Foch, t 02 41 25 13 87. A little venue for jazz, blues, rock and Celtic music.

Religious institutions would flourish in Angers under the Plantagenets, monks descending in great number on the town. Henri also ordered the building of a second bridge across the Maine river. Tolls raised on river traffic provided substantial revenues and the bridge was covered with opulent shops.

The massive Angers cathedral you see today was mostly constructed through the 12th century, with its fabulous new-style Angevin vaulting. Four Plantagenets would end up being buried not in Angers, but at the abbey of Fontevraud (*see* pp.368–75). King John of England, Plantagenet heir after Richard the Lionheart, came to besiege Angers when troops of his Breton nephew Arthur laid claim to the town. But disastrously for the family fortunes, John would go on to lose his French territories to the French Capetian King Philippe Auguste at the start of the 13th century. In 1214, John returned to try to grasp back this land, but he failed at the Battle of La Roche-aux-Moines, just west of Angers at Savonnières.

Even after the Plantagenets, Angers remained an important strategic position, its protected promontory close to the Brittany and Poitou borders. Blanche de Castille, widow of King Louis VIII and regent for her son Louis IX, took a great interest in the town. She commissioned the building of a new castle in 1230 and had the city protected by a great wall on both sides of the Maine. Louis IX then made Anjou an appanage for his brother Charles in 1246. But this ambitious prince neglected Angers for his foreign forays. Spurred on by the pope, he concentrated his warring attentions on Naples and Sicily, he and his descendants laying claim to the royal title over these distant parts. (Their effective control of Sicily would be ended by the bloody Sicilian Vespers of 1282.)

In the next century, King Jean le Bon of France offered Anjou as an appanage and dukedom to his son Louis. Louis vied with his brothers King Charles V, Jean Duc de Berry and Philippe le Hardi of Burgundy to see which could lead the life of the most sickening extravagance. Louis is the man who commissioned the over-100m Tapestry of the Apocalypse (now displayed at Angers castle), among other little luxuries. But under him civic schemes were also encouraged in Angers, including the development of the town's government and of a university.

The Hundred Years' War would distract attention eastwards along the Loire from Anjou, but the Battle of Baugé in 1421, not that far away from Angers, constituted an important early victory for the French in the second half of the terrible dispute before Joan of Arc hit the scene. Joan would be supported by Yolande d'Aragon, wife of Louis II d'Anjou, who extended the castle of Angers. Yolande and Louis produced a son called René, famously connected with the Angevin capital.

René has a reputation which has survived rather too well through time, for he is commonly referred to as Le Bon Roi René (Good King René) in France. The royal bit in this title simply harked back to the Angevin claim, which he adopted, to the kingdom of Sicily, not to the the French Crown. However, as well being duke of Anjou, René did also hold the significant positions of count of Provence and of Piedmont. René is often simplistically portrayed as a paragon of 15th-century chivalric culture, encouraging artists, himself composing poetry and music, speaking a handful of languages, and showing enough sensitivity to introduce new flowers to northern France, in particular roses. He organized grand tournaments and created l'Ordre du Croissant (as in a crescent, not a pâtisserie). But in the general medieval lordly way he also bled his subjects dry with his extravagance and his grandiose dreams of kingship in Sicily. After the death of his first wife, Isabelle de Lorraine, he married his popular mistress, Jeanne de Laval. He was often absent from Angers, but his administration saw to it that new plans for the city were executed, and significant changes were made to the château from 1435. He also encouraged the growth of the law faculty of the university. King Louis XI, however, forced René to pass Anjou back into the hands of the French monarchy in 1474 and René left for Provence.

Granted a new royal charter and acquiring the first printing press on the Loire in 1476, Angers continued to grow commercially and academically. Many beautiful and grand late Gothic and early Renaissance town houses were built by the wealthy in the region, such as the acrobatically carved Maison d'Adam, the more sober Logis Barrault and the ornamental Hôtel Pincé. Famous humanists studied here, although the nickname of Angers as 'l'Athènes de l'Ouest' sounds just a tad overblown.

Trade prospered in the 17th century in particular, as Anjou's wines and fruit were very successfully exported to England and Holland. Naval sails and rope were produced in large quantities here from around the mid-century, using the hemp widely grown in the region. Slate, too, was being successfully extracted around the town, both for local use and for export.

The anti-Revolutionary tide which swept up in 1793 from the Vendée, southwest of Anjou, reached Angers, where fierce fighting occurred between the Republican army and the rebellious pro-Catholic, pro-royalist Vendéens (see Les Mauges and Cholet, pp.450–51, for more on this painful episode in Anjou's history). A couple of thousand Vendéens were shot on Angers' Champs des Martyrs. The Revolutionaries wrought changes to the town's fabric. The Place du Ralliement, for example, replaced three churches. But much religious architecture survived in town. On a more edifying note, David d'Angers, the famous 19th-century sculptor born in the city, left a detailed record of the major French figures of the first half of the 19th century to his birthplace.

Following the times of upheaval, the 19th century wasn't particularly successful for Angers. However, the city not only expanded at last beyond its medieval city walls, but these were finally destroyed to make way for the spacious boulevards which now ring the older city on both sides of the Maine. The railway reached Angers in 1849, leading to further urban development but also to the rapid decline of the port. Catholicism reasserted itself in a big way and a specialist Catholic university was set up by Monseigneur Freppel in 1875, its theology faculty becoming renowned in the country. Still today the Catholic university holds its own against the newer lay university. Angers never saw the development of much heavy industry. Instead, flower-growing became a charming 'industry' to flourish around the city, and in 1842 the place held the first national rose exhibition in France. But Angers is also a military centre of some importance.

During the Second World War, Angers was damaged by bombs, but in contrast to the big cities further east along the Loire the historic centre remained relatively unscathed. As you'll see from the outskirts of Angers, the town has spread in all directions since the war. With its two universities, research and culture have bloomed. In theatre, the Angers festival was briefly managed by Albert Camus; in recent times it's been under the guidance of Jean-Claude Brialy. With the installation of Jean Lurçat's tapestry of the Apocalypse, this art has also grown in importance since the late 1960s, while a young film-makers' festival encourages new talent in that field. The town today is a bit of a curious mix between the progressive and the conservative. For visitors, it is above all an underrated town, full of interesting sights, and very attractive in the centre.

Château d'Angers and the Medieval Tapestries of the Apocalypse

*Open June–Sept 9.30–7, mid-March–May and mid-Sept–Oct 10–6,
rest of year 10–5.*

This rough medieval pentagon is the most imposing of all the Loire Valley's military fortifications, better preserved and more intimidating than the enormous Château de Chinon even. The outer castle was built by order of Blanche de Castille between 1228 and 1238. The widow of King Louis VIII, she was serving as regent for the young King Louis IX, the future Saint Louis, at the time. The walls protect a high platform of land above the Maine. This corner lay within the Gallo-Roman ramparts and was the spot where the early Anjou counts had built a castle as early as 851 to defend themselves against Viking raids. This was also the site for Foulques Nerra's great hall, his headquarters of stone built in the early 11th century, but virtually nothing remains of them.

Seventeen massive towers stick out around the 13th-century castle's edges. They're quite aptly compared to elephant's feet by many – only these measure between 40 and 60m in height, and are firmly planted in a wide dry moat. Most of the walls are made of local schist, repellent to invaders and not the most appealing of stone to the eye. To beautify the towers somewhat, however, bands of light limestone were added, imported from further east along the Loire. Originally, the towers would have been crowned with pepper-pot towers. They lost their heads as early as the Wars of Religion, to make way for artillery platforms. Peering down into the deep dry moat you can admire formal French parterres in one part, prancing deer in another.

The outer castle's dark penitentiary looks must have helped it adapt quite easily to playing the part of a prison from Louis XIV's reign on. Apparently, a good number of captured British sailors were banged up here. In 1856 the fortification came into the hands of the military, but by 1875 it had received the classification of *monument historique*, protecting it for the future and handing it over to tourism.

Once across the drawbridge and through the formidably fortified gateway, you enter the extensive bailey, where you'll find a château within a château. Lightness prevails here. With its charming gardens and corners protected by the massive ramparts, you'll definitely feel detached from hoi polloi in this bailey. Unfortunately, signs of the cement age have left their ugly mark all too obviously in parts.

The inner castle goes back to Duc Louis I d'Anjou and the 14th century. Not a vast amount remains of the Logis Royal, which was mainly built by his successor, Louis II, and then extended for Le Bon Roi René with an elegant north gallery. René's gallery was completely devastated by bombing in 1944, so what you see is a postwar recreation. On the guided tour, you only view a few rooms within the Logis Royal, and they contain virtually no furniture – instead the visit concentrates on glorious tapestries.

Before starting on the guided tour of the Logis Royal, though, you can look into the Ste-Geneviève chapel, built for Louis II d'Anjou early in the 15th century. A light, airy room stripped of most of its religious features, it now contains a clear display of models of the château and explanations of how it's changed through time. The chapel served for a period as something of a strongroom too, guarding a supposed piece of Christ's True Cross (*see* Baugé, p.415).

The rooms in the Logis Royal contain some enchanting tapestries, giving a foretaste of the Apocalypse ones to come, although these ones are of later date. The guide describes the scenes being depicted, but also concentrates usefully on explaining the methods of making a tapestry, an art form that apparently made it to western Europe in the 12th century.

A couple of the works here illustrate miracles by St Maurice and St Martin. Texts in medieval script are included both on these and on the tapestries in the next room, the flower-strewn millefiori. These hangings are particularly beautiful and rich, the central theme that of angels holding the instruments of Christ's Passion, but the abundance of flora and fauna all round is a pure delight. These pieces were made in Flanders around 1500, but some claim that the little poems may have been the work of Good King René himself. Other imaginative period pieces depict a lady playing an organ and the Queen of the Amazons.

Yet another tapestry cycle in a further room devotes its attention once again to Christ's Passion. Packed with figures, horses and architecture, the wealth of detail overwhelms.

Tapestries of the Apocalypse

The major tapestry cycle at the Château d'Angers is housed in a separate underground bunker, a postwar monstrosity. But the massive medieval work, the most monumental decorative enterprise of northern European 14th-century art, is spectacular. It was commissioned by Duc Louis I d'Anjou. To remind you a of little what this tapestry cycle is about, here's one telling piece from the *Apocalypse*, one of the nuttiest of the many nutty biblical texts. Its influence over the medieval imagination is reflected in the number of times it's interpreted in medieval art, although lords more traditionally commissioned tapestry cycles depicting courtly scenes or legendary tales and left it to the religious as a favourite topic. In the *Apocalypse*, or *Book of Revelation* (well worth reading before any trip to see French medieval Church art), the evil dragon for a time overcomes the good. John narrates:

Then the dragon was enraged with the woman [delivered of a boy, the son who was to rule all the nations with an iron sceptre] and went away to make war on the rest of her children, who obey God's commandments and have in themselves the witness of Jesus.

And I took my stand on the seashore.

Then I saw a beast emerge from the sea: it had seven heads and ten horns, with a coronet on each of its ten horns, and its heads were marked with blasphemous titles. I saw that the beast was like a leopard, with paws like a bear and a mouth like a lion; the dragon had handed over to it his own power and his throne and his immense authority. I saw that one of its heads seemed to have had a fatal wound but that this deadly injury had healed and the whole world had marvelled and followed the beast. They prostrated themselves in front of the beast, saying, 'Who can compare with the beast? Who can fight against him?' The beast was allowed to mouth its boasts and blasphemies and to be active for forty-two months; and it mouthed its blasphemies against God, against his name, his heavenly Tent and all those who are sheltered there. It was allowed to make war against the saints and conquer them, and given power over every race, people, language and nation; and all the people of the world will worship it, that is, everybody whose name has not been written down since the foundation of the world in the sacrificial Lamb's book of life. Let anyone who can hear, listen; those for captivity to captivity; those for death by the sword to death. This is why the saints must have perseverance and faith.

With such a heady source of inspiration for the tapestries, first prepare yourselves for a couple of banal disappointments. The cruddy underground cement cavern really is unbefitting to the work; and the background reds and blues of the tapestries look jaded because in the 1950s and 60s the tapestries were exposed to the damaging effects of sun- and moonlight.

Mind you, it's a miracle that this tapestry cycle survived at all, as its chequered history reveals. The work was commissioned by Louis I d'Anjou in the mid-1370s. Where it was meant for isn't entirely clear. Louis preferred the Château de Saumur to Angers as a residence, but he had renovated Foulques Nerra's great Angers hall, so the plan may have been to show it off here regularly. However, it should be recalled that tapestries were viewed as movable objects, transported from one place to another to be used for decoration, show and ceremony. This one, for example, is known to have been displayed in Arles, in the south of France, in 1400 for the splendid marriage of Louis' eponymous son to Yolande d'Aragon. When not on display or on tour, it was seemingly kept in a special *salle de la tapisserie*, where it was rolled up. René d'Anjou moved it to the castle of Baugé for a time to keep it out of Louis XI's reach, and left it in his will to the cathedral of Angers. Almost until the Revolution it was looked after by the canons there and brought out for display in the church just four times a year.

However, the cathedral authorities became disenchanted with this difficult work, whose subject matter had become outmoded, not to say frowned upon, and they tried to sell it off in 1767. The trouble was that they couldn't find a buyer and the tapestry cycle was sadly neglected. After a brief period when it was confiscated during the Revolution, it was restored to the bishopric in 1806. But by 1825 the bishop found that it was too cumbersome and the work was cut into its individual panels. Various tales are told about the demeaning uses to which they were then subjected. The stories (some possibly apocryphal?) claim that certain sections served as horse blankets, others to cover melons and pumpkins from frost. The most decadent tale goes that some were used as bedside rugs. At any rate, many of the pieces were dispersed and maltreated, but the quality of the workmanship helped them to survive. The true hero of this tale is a certain Canon Joubert, who rescued them in 1848 and undertook the monumental task of putting the tapestry cycle back together as it should have been and having it restored. Seventy-six out of the original 84 scenes remain today.

The cartoons, or drawings, on which the tapestries were based were the work of King Charles V's court painter, or rather, his manuscript illuminator, Jean Bondol, otherwise known as Hennequin de Bruges, of the Flemish school. He apparently took as his inspiration illustrations of the Apocalypse from a 13th-century manuscript in Charles V's library. The tapestries were executed extremely rapidly, under the direction of Nicolas Bataille of Paris. It's thought that it took only seven years to execute the whole series, which is a little over 100m in length!

The scale of the artistic enterprise may seem overwhelming to you at first. There are sensible ways of considering it in more digestible parts. The pattern of alternating background colouring stands out immediately, and certain recurring characters begin to emerge quite quickly.

The ensemble starts with a large vertical panel depicting Christ, John at his feet. Then the rest of the cycle is displayed in two rows along the wall, in the original sections of seven panels (as far as that's still possible), the number seven associated with divine will in the *Apocalypse*, with its references to the seven spirits of God, the seven seals and the seven angels who stand in the presence of God and trumpet in the punishments on wrongdoers. The biblical text isn't followed entirely accurately, but the scenes were derived from the manuscript, which was slightly inaccurate. The narrator John stands by in all the panels, often under a kind of sentry box, and his reactions reflect the different tones of the scenes. The tale is essentially of the fight between Good and Evil. Originally, a Latin text in tapestry ran along the whole length, explaining the action. This has disappeared, but a little frieze decorated with comically innocent details from nature has survived, while the museum provides explanations on modern panels.

The panels can be divided into six main sections. In the **first section**, Christ comes, sword in mouth, to announce to John that he will receive the revelations of the Apocalypse. The 24 Elders who sit around God appear with the four Evangelists. The sacrificial lamb symbolizes Christ, while the horses and riders of the Apocalypse make their appearance. The monstrous creatures of the Apocalypse take on extreme attributes, such as a horse given a monster's tail and a dog's hanging tongue.

In the **second section**, the seven trumpeting angels come out, calling out the plagues, John at one point hiding in horror in his sentry box. The angel with the book recording the names of those to be saved arrives, while St John literally gobbles up the messages from God to take them in properly.

The **third section** tells the story of the witnesses come to spread the word of Christ. They are taunted and killed, but then resurrected. The angels under St Michael take on the dragon, St Michael depicted with the most beautiful of faces.

The **fourth and fifth** sections concentrate in particular on the fall of Babylon, symbolized by the great vain prostitute – only two women feature in the *Apocalypse*, two extremes of good and evil, the one symbolizing the virtuous Church, the other vile decadence and irreligiousness, or Babylon and Rome. The just sleep, and the chosen are saved. The beast of the earth and the sea, the many-headed hybrid described in the quotation above, makes its extraordinary entrance, the devil's number six appearing on its tail, one of the many symbols with which this overloaded monster is charged.

Finally, in the **sixth section** (although more of the panels are missing in this final section than elsewhere), Christ arrives dynamic and triumphant, long hair swept back, to push the evil into a lake of fire. The judges are put to work, while the devil makes a final terrible assault on the castle of the just. They resist and the New Jerusalem comes down, a magnificent apparition from the sky.

All the details in the Revelation to John had potential for many layers of symbolic interpretation, including the contemporary political reading of the persecution of Christians by the Romans, and the desire for the latters' comeuppance. It isn't known why Louis chose the Apocalypse as the theme for the tapestry. Religious themes weren't generally interpreted for lordly tapestries. Maybe the melodrama of the story appealed to him. Maybe he was swayed by his Christian imagination.

Interestingly, some scholars think that they've detected in the cycle elements of medieval historical symbolism that may have prompted Louis' choice. He lived in deeply troubled times. The terrible Black Plague had hit Europe in 1348 and was recurring periodically. The English had invaded France, a very real beast from across the sea, and started what would become known as the Hundred Years' War. Some recent commentators on the tapestry have detected what they believe to be pointed references in the tapestries to the early part of the Hundred Years' War with England. For example, in one or two spots the guides can point to places where the evil knights appear to bear the helmets of English soldiers (look at panel 69 for instance). In panel 38, the sea monster might even be read as a symbol of the English crossing the Channel. Other enemies of France and Christianity may be evoked elsewhere, for example in panel 23, with its Saracen signs.

The Revelation to John emphasizes rescue or salvation soon to come, and the overthrow of the terrifying evil enemy which appears in so many guises. It is a text which carries a message of hope. Aspects of these tapestries could be interpreted then as both religious and political, emphasizing divine authority and the eventual victory not simply of Christianity, but also of the divinely ordained French royal family, of which Louis was of course a part, against all manner of enemy forces: the infidel, the English, horrific plagues, and evil generally.

The detail should absorb you, fantastical and fascinating as it is, often distinctly weird, sometimes extraordinarily beautiful. You may notice the Cross of Anjou or Lorraine (see p.415) stamped on the series, symbol of the lord who commissioned the work. The tapestries were beautifully executed on both sides, so that both were worthy of display. On an official tour, the guide may lift a section to show you how much better preserved the colours and their gradations are on the concealed side and how the sharpness of the figures comes out all the more for that.

After such stirring and disturbing stuff, the remnants of the 12th-century apse of the **Chapelle St-Laud**, unearthed at one end of the digging to make the ugly bunker, may seem like a very minor distraction. Before heading out of the castle's protective walls, take some time to wander through the bailey gardens or go to mull over what you've seen in the delightful café at the eastern end of the fortifications, tables set out beneath a weeping willow.

Cathédrale St-Maurice

Three towers soar up from the façade of St-Maurice, Angers' fearsome cathedral, a short way from the castle along Rue St-Evroult. It looks especially daunting when viewed from way down below on the the Maine bank. A startlingly long stairway, cut through the old quarters in the 19th century, leads up from the river to the church front. The first cathedral on this spot was dedicated to a local bishop of the 4th century by the name of St Maurille. The change of name to honour the Egyptian Christian fighter Maurice (said to have been killed for rejecting pagan ritual at the start of the 4th century) only occurred at the end of the 12th century.

Most of the cathedral dates from the 12th century, built on top of an 11th century structure. The lower parts of the façade are from the middle of the 12th century. The single west portal is filled with magnificent sculpture reminiscent of some at Chartres cathedral. Royal biblical figures count among the major sculptures, while lines of Elders of the Apocalypse and angels surround Christ and his Apostles. Moving up the façade, you can't fail to be struck by the row of eight mighty statues below the towers. These formidable saints in battle gear are copies of the 1537 works by Jean Giffard and Antoine Desmarais, referred to collectively as the 'Galerie St Maurice'. They represent St Maurice and some of the men who died with him. The Latin inscription below is translated as: 'Grant us peace in our time, Lord, and disperse those nations seeking war'. The three towers were also added in the 1530s, even if they've been somewhat altered since.

Stepping inside, the cavernous church has a great aisle-less nave standing on just three broad bays. The place is admired in architectural circles for its domed ceiling, held up on graceful so-called **Angevin vaults** (sometimes known in French as Plantagenet vaults). Such was the success of their design that the fashion spread far and wide and quite affected the development of Gothic church building in the west of France from the end of the 12th century and through the 13th.

A fine collection of **stained glass** dating from the 12th to the 15th centuries embellishes the bulky and sombre interior. On the north side of the nave look out for the three windows dedicated to St Vincent, St Catherine and the Virgin, with a deep intensity of colours and scenes. The most westerly north bay Virgin and Child from the early 13th century is another particularly imposing piece. The stained glass in the transept goes back to the late medieval period; André Robin is the man credited with the glorious rose windows, made between 1434 and 1465. The south transept rose window shows Christ in Majesty, signs of the Zodiac and music-making angels around him. That in the north transept depicts Christ's Passion, as well as symbols of the months and, it being Angers, the Apocalypse. The east window is also a reputed work of art, the Pietà added in 1499.

Most of the remaining 13th-century stained glass of the cathedral has been gathered in the imposing aisleless choir. The depiction of St Martin originally adorned the west front. As well as a Tree of Jesse and scenes from Christ's and saints' lives, some of the glass tells the story of that great Plantagenet friend then foe, Thomas à Becket.

Several monumental furnishings embellish parts of the vast interior. The altar of the 1570s, with its red marble columns and golden baldaquin, was the work of Denis Gervais, architect to Louis XV. The massive Gothic-revival pulpit, sculpted with symbols of the militant Church triumphant, was made in René Choyer's studios in Angers. The vast 18th-century organ is held up by colossal atlantes, straining so much under the weight that they give the unnerving impression that the whole thing might collapse. The choir hides some more subtle treasures. Behind the altar, a sculpture of St Cecilia is a touching piece by the Angers sculptor David (*see* below). Caught behind the choir stalls are rare wall paintings of St Maurille, which can only be viewed on special tours.

Maison d'Adam

On picturesque Place Ste-Croix, just at the back of the cathedral, stands one of the most extraordinary and outrageous houses in the Loire Valley, the Maison d'Adam. You're unlikely ever to see a more splendidly carved building. It dates from around 1500. Half-men half-beasts, a mermaid and a three-balled man count among the weird wooden cast clambering over the beams of this remarkable half-timbered house. Biblical scenes also feature, Samson (presumably with his hand in a lion's mouth), and the Virgin Mary receiving her message from God. The house was known in the past as the Maison de l'Arbre de la Vie, and on the corner you can easily make out this Tree of Life, a superb work heavy with fruit. The statue in the middle of the square represents the late 19th-century Bishop Freppel, who looks nowhere near as amusing as the exuberant late Gothic characters on the Maison d'Adam. The pedestrianized **Rue St-Aubin** leading southwestwards from the square is one of the busiest shopping streets in Angers.

Galerie David d'Angers

Open mid-June–mid-Sept 9–6.30, rest of year Tues–Sun 10–12 and 2–6.

J'ai du marbre et du bronze pour le génie, la vertu, le courage héroïque. Je n'en ai point pour les tyrans (I have marble and bronze for genius, virtue and heroic courage. I have none for tyrants).
        David d'Angers

Angers' Musée des Beaux-Arts is closed for several years to come for the complete renovation of the enormous Logis Barrault in which it's housed, but the city has a couple of other specialized fine arts museums. From Place Ste-Croix, go back towards the château along **Rue Toussaint**, a pretty street lined on one side by the old city wall dating back in part to Gallo-Roman times. Fine old houses look down from their protected platform above the wall. On the opposite side of the street you come to the **Eglise de Toussaint**, tucked away behind a walled entrance and a large portal.

In part vandalized during the Revolution, this church of All Saints lost its roof early in the 19th century and fell into a terrible state of disrepair. The town authorities finally got round to restoring it in the early 1980s, but rather than reviving it for religious use they turned it into the Galerie David d'Angers, a museum to the glory of one of Anjou's most successful artistic sons, the sculptor after whom it is named.

As so often in Angers, it's the architecture that first makes you gasp. However, no attempt was made to redo the lovely Angevin vaulting that the church was probably given in the 1230s, although the fine Gothic windows and some delightful biblical statues protected by stone canopies remain. The modern architect Pierre Prunet instead decided on a replacement roof of tinted glass and steel girders, allowing a beautiful light to fall onto the display of sculptures within.

You enter the gallery to find yourself in the former church nave, cluttered with casts. They're all the work of David d'Angers. Born in 1788, he was baptized Pierre-Jean David. Grateful to his home town for its early support of his endeavours, he referred to Angers as his mother and took its name in 1828. Going on to work in Paris, he dutifully and happily sent back plaster casts of his output as he progressed. The man who turned down the commission to sculpt Napoleon's tomb for the Invalides in Paris, David d'Angers was a man of strong principle, motivated by politics as well as art. In the mid-1830s he presented himself as a Democratic candidate in the Anjou elections. He played an active role in the 1848 revolution and briefly held posts as the mayor of a Paris *arrondissement* and MP for Anjou, but he was exiled with the imposition of the Second Empire early in the 1850s. Making clear his priorities he stated that: '*Avant d'être artiste, il faut être citoyen, voilà ma devise (Before being an artist you have to be a good citizen – that's my motto).*'

But it's his art that he's remembered for. The original of the most famous of all his works, the funeral statue of Bonchamps, a hero of the anti-Revolutionary Guerres de Vendée, rises full of desperate hope from a tomb in the church of St-Florent-le-Vieil, west along the Loire (see pp.460–61). But here you can view a copy of it along with the extensive collection of plaster casts. David d'Angers won the prestigious French art prize, the Prix de Rome, in 1811, for the rather ungainly *Mort d'Epanminondas*, and went to the Italian capital until 1816, where he fell under the spell of the classical influence and of Canova in particular.

D'Angers executed a great number of public monuments to heroic historical person-alities, and medallions of leading figures of the day. He portrayed many a famous native figure for individual French provincial towns: Johannes Gutenberg, the man regarded as the father of printing, holding a sheet freshly curling from the press, for the town of Strasbourg; Jean Bart, a slightly grotesque-sized corsair, sword raised, hair blowing, for Dunkerque; Fénelon for Cambrai; Racine for La Ferté-Milon; and of course Le Bon Roi René for Angers. You can observe some of the history of Anjou depicted in stone in the statuettes at the base of this monument. He also did many commissions in Paris, including, most famously, the pediment of the Panthéon (in this gallery reduced to one-third the real scale). Some of his relatively early important commis-sions, for monuments to Bourcke and Foy, were made for the Père Lachaise cemetery in Paris, where he himself would be buried in 1856.

David d'Angers' medallions are displayed in the choir. Although generally much less dramatic, these works are finely executed and have the great historical value of illustrating many of the important figures of his times. Among them are the likes of Victor Hugo, Balzac, Lamartine, Chateaubriand, Goethe, Washington and Lafayette. D'Angers also executed, among others, a statue of Jefferson, while his rendering of Jeremy Bentham graces Senate House of the University of London. With or without visiting the museum, you can wander out into the pleasant **cloister gardens** by the church.

Hôpital St-Jean and the *Chant du Monde* Tapestries

Open mid-June–mid-Sept 9–6.30, rest of year Tues–Sun 10–12 and 2–6.

Across the river lies **La Doutre**. One sturdy tower, known as the **Tour des Anglais**, survives from Angers' medieval defences here. A great line of tall plane trees stretches down the Maine's bank, making this side of the river much more picturesque than the other which is marred by a very busy road. Behind the towering curtain of trees you'll find one of the most beautiful of all early French medieval buildings, the **Hôpital St-Jean**.

This hospital is presumed to be the oldest one in France. The main **Salle des Malades** looks much more like a religious building than a secular one. It was built from 1175 for Etienne de Marsay, *seneschal* to King Henry II (Henri Plantagenêt), on the latter's orders, the charter stipulating that it should be governed by laymen. Some say that this was one of the institutions Henry established in penance for Thomas à Becket's murder.

The Salle des Malades is supremely graceful. Two rows of slender sandstone columns hold up the beautiful ceiling of Angevin vaults. The vaults look as though they've been filled with air and have puffed out almost like parachutes. The lightness and grace of the architecture in this splendidly elegant room make it hard to imagine the agony of the sick who were treated here. Copies of old engravings give some notion of this aspect of the building's past. It served as a hospital for seven centuries, from its foundation up until 1865.

Although the hospital started out as a lay foundation, in the 13th century Augustinian monks took over its management and a priory was built around it. The Augustinians may have been welcoming, the late 13th-century statutes promising a place for patients of whatever nation or religion, but they often had to cram in three or four patients to a bed. The chances were that by staying here you would catch more diseases than you came in with. Apparently the medical treatment improved slightly when lay authorities regained control of the institution in the mid-16th century, but medicine in those days was still very much hit and miss.

The town built a large new hospital in the 1850s, and after that the Hôpital St-Jean served briefly as an archaeological museum. Nowadays, bits and pieces of the town's ancient fabric lie scattered outside in the garden at the front of the hospital, while within the walls have been hung with the second stupendous cycle of Apocalypse tapestries in Angers, **Jean Lurçat's *Chant du Monde* cycle**.

Jean Lurçat came to Angers at the end of the 1930s and was profoundly moved by the tapestries of the Apocalypse (see pp.428–31). He decided to embark on another vast tapestry series, this one interpreting man's potential for evil and for good in the 20th century. Having looked closely at the medieval work, he revived some of the techniques used in that period's tapestry-making. But rather than being inspired by a biblical text, the left-wing artist was moved by real things, such as the Hiroshima bomb and Champagne. You may find some of the imagery rather hackneyed and the colours garish, but the 10 panels certainly make a great impact. The violently bright colours almost shine out from their black backgrounds. The images are much more familiar and clear to us than those of the medieval Apocalypse.

These tapestries were woven at Aubusson by the workshops of Tabard, Goubely and Picaud. The work commenced in 1957, but wasn't complete by the time the artist died in 1966. Of the 125m of tapestries planned, some 80m were executed.

The positive gets the upper hand over the negative in what was executed. The first four panels, however, are disturbing; the horrors scream out at you. In *La Grande Menace* (*The Great Threat*) an evil eagle flies overhead, while a bull ejaculates atomic poison over the globe. A man with an arc steers through this messy scene accompanied by his dog. *L'Homme d'Hiroshima* (*Hiroshima Man*) presents a terrible image of a man like a plucked bird, shredded by the atomic bomb. *Le Grand Charnier* (*The Great Charnel House*), a *ronde macabre*, centres round a tank with skeletons. *La Fin de Tout* (*The End of Everything*) shows plant life dying in an ashen snow.

The tone then changes, with some of the images of the negative series recurring in a quite different context. *L'Homme en gloire avec la paix* (*Man in Glory and in Peace*), using the juxtaposed motifs of the globe and man again, also shows an owl of wisdom and feet bathing in the sun. *L'Eau et le feu* (*Water and Fire*) features the image of the salamander, part of the Lurçat bestiary. The fish in pastel colours swimming down the tapestry make for one of the most beautiful images in this cycle. *Champagne*, rather than being of uniform, subdued tastefulness, bursts out in unbridled colours, butterflies bubbling up the work. *La Conquête de l'espace* (*The Conquest of Space*) makes reference to Sputnik I, launched in 1956, the first man-made satellite to orbit the earth; the archer Sagittarius hits the bull's eye. *La Poésie* (*Poetry*) displays all the signs of the Zodiac. As an atheist, Lurçat apparently saw salvation in the poetic. The series ends with *Ornamentos Sagrados* (*Sacred Ornaments*), a hymn to the sun and the planets, as well as to domestic life.

At the end of the Salle des Malades you can go through to see the cloister and chapel. The stern north and east sides of the cloister date from the late 12th century, while the south side is 16th century. The chapel contains two differing types of Angevin vaulting, tomb effigies and stained glass of different periods cobbled together.

Angers was chosen as the place to show Lurçat's cycle after the artist's death, and Lurçat's widow donated further works, to be found in a neighbouring building now housing the **Musée de la Tapisserie Contemporaine** (*same ticket and times as for the Lurçat museum*). This serves mainly as a setting for temporary tapestry exhibitions. In yet another building in the ensemble, you can go to watch weavers at work in the

Centre Régional d'Art Textile (CRAT) (*workshop open Sept–July Mon, Tues, Thurs and Fri 10–12 and 2–4; exhibition open all year Tues–Sat 10–11.30 and 2–6*), where an artist at the loom explains working techniques to visitors, revealing the complexity of the craft. It's worth wandering round to one last section of the foundation, the **Greniers St-Jean** on Place du Tertre, the 13th-century storerooms for the foundation. They have an extraordinary schist façade, while the sides are tufa.

While in La Doutre, go and wander round its squares. **Place de la Paix** has several notable 17th-century houses. A short way south, **Place de la Laiterie** was the religious and commercial centre of the quarter in medieval times. The **abbaye du Ronceray**, or abbey of the Bramble Patch, dates back to Foulques Nerra's time, founded by his wife Hildegard in 1028 as the Benedictine establishment for women in the town. Most of the buildings that have survived to this day are 17th century and house the Ecole des Arts et Métier, a prestigious technical college. During special tapestry exhibitions, you can look inside the somewhat battered abbey church interior. The adjoining **church of La Trinité** has suffered from 19th-century over-restoration, but retains its pure and simple Romanesque form on the outside, except for the addition by Jean de l'Espine of the 16th-century belfry.

The most notable secular building on the square, the **Logis Simon Poisson**, boasts sculpted wooden beams which show off the wealth and generosity of the 17th-century pharmacist who commissioned it. The caryatids represent Science, Magnificence, Friendship and Generosity, the latter striking a surprisingly humble note, the bare-footed woman in rags donating money.

A Walk Around Angers

The obvious point to start on a tour of Angers is in front of the castle and the tourist office on Place Kennedy. The statue clearly visible along the 19th-century Boulevard du Roi René off the square represents Good King René. His chivalric dress may make him seem slightly comical today, but the piece is a 19th-century interpretation by the famed David d'Angers (*see above*). Up on the north side of the castle, the **Maison du Vin de l'Anjou** (*open April–Sept Tues–Sun 9–1 and 3–6.30, rest of year Tues–Sat 9–1 and 3–6.30*) is a showcase shop for the wide selection of Anjou wines. This is probably the best place to go to to find out about the whole province's production, although you'll also find other wine shops in the centre.

From the **Promenade du Bout du Monde** in front of the castle's entrance, head into the quietly atmospheric network of cobbled streets, between castle and cathedral. Walk down **Rue St-Aignan** and **Rue Donadieu de Puycharic** in particular to appreciate a fine array of late medieval and Renaissance houses. This little quarter also contains many buildings which once belonged to religious institutions settled close to the cathedral.

After visiting the cathedral (*see p.432*), pass round the back of it, through the delightful adjoining squares, Place Freppel and Place Ste-Croix, then go a short way along **Rue Toussaint**, which contains the Galerie David d'Angers. Branch off before the gallery on to Rue du Musée, where you can see the immense block of the Logis Barrault, being renovated for the revamped fine arts museum.

Next you pass under the massive **Tour St-Aubin**, an isolated 12th-century tower which was never actually attached to other buildings; it was once part of Angers' most important Benedictine abbey. This institution, which claimed roots going back to the 6th century, was named after a bishop of Angers from that period. During the 12th century, the abbey expanded considerably to become one of the largest in western France. Most of the rest of the medieval abbey buildings haven't survived. They were replaced in the late 17th century and early 18th with sober architecture for the monks of the Congregation of St-Maur, who became very powerful in these parts. The abbey has long been used as the seat of local government – the Préfecture – for Anjou (or the *département* of Maine-et-Loire, as it's been officially known since the Revolution). During working hours, you can have a look inside at the cloister, which contains some wonderful little vestiges of Romanesque art in the form of delicately carved capitals and fragments of faded wall paintings. In the vicinity lie the early medieval chapel and cloisters of St-Martin's (*not open to the public at the time of writing*).

From here, head up to the heart of Angers' central shopping district, **Place du Ralliement**. There's no sign of medieval Angers on this square, which looks sparklingly clean following its mid-1990s renovation. Several large 19th-century buildings surround the square, with their ornate façades and wrought-iron work. The churches that once stood here disappeared with the Revolution, while the guillotine was sinisterly set up in their place; the name of the square derives from the fact that Republican (that is, Revolutionary) conscripts gathered in this place. Now the extravagant late 19th-century **theatre** dominates, with elaborate ceiling paintings by Jules Lenepveu, an Angevin artist responsible for much of the excessive decoration inside the Paris Opéra.

Shopping streets head out in all directions from the square. One of these streets, named after Lenepveu, contains the **Musée Pincé** (*open mid-June–mid-Sept 9–6.30, rest of year Tues–Sun 10–12 and 2–6*). Behind the richly decorated Renaissance façade you can visit a surprising international collection, with classical, Egyptian and Oriental works. Around this quarter, explore the lively network of streets, with their shops and restaurants. Rue Lenepveu leads up to Place du Pilori, where medieval public punishments were meted out. Parallel to Rue Lenepveu, **Rue St-Laud** has been turned into a very appealing pedestrian street packed with shops and restaurants, chairs and tables spilling out onto the pavement in summer. Look up to admire several medieval half-timbered façades along the way, as well as one Art Nouveau block.

East of Place du Ralliement, you hit the **19th-century boulevards**. Boulevard Foch, lined with modern cafés and restaurants, leads up to the town hall, which stands in front of the vast combined open spaces of the **Jardin du Mail** and Place du Général Leclerc, with the neoclassical law court (Palais du Justice) on the far side. If the old medieval quarters were forced to develop rather too tightly within the constraining city walls, then this 19th-century breakout suffers from being rather too spacious and sterile. Boulevard Bessoneau leads on up to Place Mendès-France, with Angers' conference centre straight ahead.

Just off the square, down Rue Guitton, you'll find the **Muséum d'Histoire Naturelle** (*open Tues–Sun 2–5*), with a large ornithological collection.

Behind the conference centre, the **Jardin des Plantes** is the town's lovely botanical garden. The well-ruined church of St-Samson provides walls for plants to climb over. This church was attached to the Benedictine monastery here, of which the **church of St-Serge**, opposite the gardens, has survived. It contains some of the most elegant of Angevin vaulting in the choir. Beyond it, you might explore the modern quarter of St-Serge, with some innovative architecture and impressive fountains. West from here, you can cross the Maine via the Pont de la Haute Chaîne, which you into La Doutre (*see* above).

The Outskirts of Angers

One of the most famous liqueurs in the world, Cointreau, is made in Angers. The **Cointreau factory and museum** (*open Feb–Dec, tours daily at 10.30, 2.30 and 4.30*) was once centrally located in La Doutre, but moved some time ago into the eastern suburb of St-Barthélemy-d'Angers. It's signposted off Angers' ring road, or *périphérique*. You come to a typical modern, uninspiring industrial estate, hardly a place to conjure up exotic Haiti, where the all-important green oranges for making Cointreau come from. Mind you, this former French colony is a difficult place to do business with, and is barely alluded to on the tour of the distillery and its museum, recently colourfully jazzed-up in bright oranges and yellows to make the place still headier. Seville oranges are also used in vast quantities in Cointreau's preparation. Come on one of the 120 days of the year when distilling takes place and the factory is suffused with the most intense smell of the liqueur. It's quite delicious and overpowering. On the tour you'll learn about how the drink is made, about the Angers family which created the drink, and its marketing success.

At the eastern edge of St-Barthélemy-d'Anjou, the elegant 18th-century neoclassical **Château de Pignerolle** contains a specialist Musée de la Communication (*open July–Oct 10–12.30 and 2.30–6.30, April–June Tues–Sun same times*), where old radios, telephones and other means of communication have been collected together. It also looks to the future of communications. There are plans to make more of this place in the future, set as it is in very beautiful grounds.

Just south of St-Barthélemy-d'Anjou, at **Trélazé**, you can visit Angers' **Musée de l'Ardoise** (*open July–mid-Sept Tues–Sun 2–6*), or slate museum. You don't go underground, but you can be shown round by former slate miners (*guided tour at 4pm*) and can often see an old-fashioned slate cutting expert, or *fendeur*, at work, as well as looking round the museum, which covers the history of slate-mining in the region. Sculptural pieces lovingly made out of slate add an artistic touch.

Les Ponts-de-Cé, southwest of Trélazé, has some pretty spots despite having been bombed in the war because of its important bridges across the broad Loire. It has a small museum dedicated to old *coiffes* from the region (*open in July and Aug at regular times, June and Sept 2–6*).

Northeast of Angers centre, at the city's airport at Marcé, the **Musée Régional de l'Air** (*open mid-Feb–mid-Nov daily 2–6, rest of year weekends only 2–6*) contains a substantial collection of early aircraft, including some pioneering pieces, all on display in a light, modern new hall.

The Loire from Angers to Nantes

20

Western Anjou

Pouancé
La Petite Couère
Châteaubriant
La Mine Bleue
Noyant-la-Gravoyère
La Jaille-Yvon
Chenillé-Changé
Segré
Châteauneuf-sur-Sarthe
Le Lion d'Angers
Champigné
Haras National
Cheffes
Écuillé
Tiercé
LOIRE-ATLANTIQUE
Grez-Neuville
Château du Plessis-Bourré
Candé
La Pouèze
Briollay
St Émérance
Le Plessis-Macé
Avrillé
Nort
Brest
Angers
Château de Pignerolle
E60/A11
St-Georges-sur-Loire
Bouchemaine
Ancenis
Ingrandes
Varades
Les Ponts de Cé
Oudon
Montjean
Savennières
Mûrs-Érigné
Champtoceaux
St-Florent-Le-Vieil
Chalonnes-sur-Loire
Denée
St-Saturnin-sur-Loire
Le Cellier
Drain
Liré
La-Chapelle-St-Florent
Rochefort-sur-Loire
La Varenne
Courrossé
La Haie Longue
St-Aubin-de-Luigné
Carquefou
Les Mauves
St-Sauveur-de-Landemont
St-Laurent de la Plaine
Chaume
Beaulieu
La Pierre Percée
Le Fuilet
St-Lambert-du-Lattay
Rablay
Faye d'Anjou
MAINE-ET-LOIRE
Montrevault
Le Pin-en-Mauges
Chânzeaux
Thouarcé
Le Loroux-Bottereau
Nantes
Le Landreau
Beaupréau
Chapelle de la Sorinière
Faveraye-Mâchelles
Vallet
Chemillé
St-Fiacre-sur-Maine
Le Pé de Sèvre
Mouzillon
St-Macaire-en-Mauges
Vihiers
Clisson
Maine
St-André-de-la-Marche
Les Cerqueux-sous-Passavant
Nuaillé
Forêt de Nuaillé-Vezins
Sèvre Nantaise
Cholet
Chapelle des Martyrs
Tiffauges
Maulévrier
Montaigu
Parc Oriental
VENDÉE
St-Laurent
Argenton Château
N
Le Puy du Fou
Les Herbiers
Bressuire
La Flocellière

10 km
5 miles

Highlights

1 The gorgeous blond Château du Plessis-Bourré
2 The dramatic banks of the Loire
3 The rough with the smooth at the Château de Serrant
4 Palais Briau – 19th-century luxuries and follies
5 St-Florent-le-Vieil's cliffside church

The south bank route along the Loire from Angers to Nantes, with its dramatic roads high above the river, is more popular with tourists than the busy main roads of the north bank. But don't ignore the north side – it has its own moments. Before heading west along the Loire from Angers, we propose little detours into north-western and southwestern Anjou.

Northwestern Anjou

Three rivers, the Loir, Sarthe and Mayenne, come together a little north of Angers to form the Maine. Two contrasting medieval châteaux lie in this area, both confusingly carrying the name of Plessis. Le Plessis-Bourré, west of the Sarthe, is a welcoming château built in fine white limestone, while Le Plessis-Macé, west of the Mayenne, is a forbidding schist fortification. You can go boating up the Sarthe and the Mayenne from various villages on their banks.

In the Segréen, the northwest corner of Anjou, you move away from the aristocracy that is such a focus of Loire tourism to some surprisingly working-class sites, in particular the slate mine near Noyant-la-Gravoyère.

Château du Plessis-Bourré

Open July–Aug 10–6; April–June and Sept Fri–Tues 10–12 and 2–6, Thurs 2–6; Feb–March and Oct–Nov Thurs–Tues 2–6.

You'll find the invitingly formal Château du Plessis-Bourré between the Mayenne and the Sarthe rivers, near Ecuillé. Inside, it offers the shock of the weirdest ceiling in the Loire Valley. As you approach this château along an alley of tall, noble trees, imagine King Charles VIII's representatives arriving on horseback at this rather remote but extremely refined country house to greet the king of Hungary's emissaries in 1487; the place would have provided a suitably ambassadorial setting. A cavalcade consisting of some 200 horses came, the Hungarians bringing their own musicians to provide entertainment.

In 1487 Le Plessis-Bourré was the swanky modern home recently built for Jean Bourré, faithful minister to King Louis XI, 'most trusted master of an untrusting king', as the writer Ian Dunlop summarized him neatly. Under Louis XI, not only was Bourré given royal finances to oversee, he was also in charge of the education of the dauphin, the future King Charles VIII. What's more, he was asked by the king to organize the construction of the Château de Langeais by the Loire (*see* pp.315–17). Meanwhile, the minister went ahead with two châteaux for himself, Le Plessis-Bourré and Jarzé, the latter east of Angers, sadly disappeared. Busy man that Bourré was, he appears to have had a great zest for the good things in life.

The nature of Bourré's work meant that he was usually running after the king, and he left it to his wife, Marguerite de Feschal, to manage the building site. Their tender correspondence has survived, providing some idea of the way the building of the château progressed. Begun in 1468, it was completed by 1473, and demonstrates a much more advanced taste in planned architecture than Plessis-Macé close by.

Getting Around

Bus lines from Angers serve the Sarthe valley, with stops at Cheffes and Châteauneuf-sur-Sarthe; the Mayenne, with stops at Grez-Neuville and Le Lion d'Angers; and the Segréen, with stops at Segré, Noyant-la-Gravoyère and Pouancé. The occasional bus stops at Le Plessis-Macé.

Tourist Information

Le Lion-d'Angers: Square des Villes Jumelées, 49220 Le Lion-d'Angers, **t** 02 41 95 83 19, **f** 02 41 95 17 82.
Châteauneuf-sur-Sarthe: Quai de la Sarthe, 49330 Châteauneuf-sur-Sarthe, **t/f** 02 41 69 82 89.
Segré: 5 Rue David d'Angers, 49500 Segré, **t** 02 41 92 86 83.
Pouancé: 2 bis Rue de la Porte Angevine, 49420 Pouancé, **t** 02 41 92 41 08, **f** 02 41 92 45 86.

Market Days

Segré: Wednesday.
Pouancé: Thursday.

Where to Stay and Eat

Briollay ✉ 49125
★★★★**Château de Noirieux**, 26 Route du Moulin, **t** 02 41 42 50 05, **f** 02 41 37 91 00, noirieux@relaischateaux.fr, www.relais-chateaux.fr/noirieux (luxury). The height of luxury in Anjou, in a soberly elegant castle above the Loir. Refined cuisine. Swimming pool, tennis court and helipad in the grounds (menus €29.5–73.5).

Châteauneuf-sur-Sarthe ✉ 49330
Hôtel de la Sarthe, 1 Rue du Port, **t/f** 02 41 69 85 29 (inexpensive). With a terrace looking on to the river. You can try a steak of Maine-Angevin here, a special breed developed across the two regions (menus €10.5–32).

Champigné ✉ 49330
Château des Briottières B&B, **t** 02 41 42 00 02, **f** 02 41 42 01 55, briottieres@wanadoo.fr, www.briottieres.com (luxury). Extremely elegant 18th-century property. Heated swimming pool (table d'hôte €45).

Grez-Neuville ✉ 49220
La Croix d'Etain B&B, 2 Rue de l'Ecluse, **t** 02 41 95 68 49, **f** 02 41 18 02 72 (moderate). Delightful 19th-century property by the banks of the Mayenne (table d'hôte from €23).

Chenillé-Changé ✉ 49220
La Table du Meunier, **t** 02 41 95 10 83/98. A restaurant in an intriguing schist property close to the river, with curious sculptures set around it. Not only do Anjou wines feature in certain sauces, but also cider, reflecting the closeness of cider-producing Maine (menus €15.5–38).

La Jaille-Yvon ✉ 49220
Château du Plessis-Anjou B&B, **t** 02 41 95 12 75, **f** 02 41 95 14 41, www.perso.wanadoo.fr/plessis, (expensive). A really appealing mix of 16th- and 18th-century architecture, just north of Chenillé-Changé on the Mayenne. You can go up in the château's hot air balloon as well as playing tennis in the grounds (table d'hôte €42.5).

Pouancé ✉ 49420
Le Vieux Logis, 53 Rue de la Libération, **t** 02 41 92 40 15. An unpretentious restaurant by the Breton border, with cheap and tasty food (menus €11–23.5).

Although set in flat, slightly uninspiring land, the château makes for the prettiest of moated pictures. The moats were once even more elaborate than they are today, but you still have to cross three bridges to reach the main entrance. These waters provided one form of defence, and the château itself sits on an island, with just enough room for new types of artillery. Each corner is marked by a round tower, one more imposing than the others, referred to as the donjon and providing a viewing post for the countryside around. While defence certainly wasn't ignored, nor were the possibilities for gracious living. The walls were pierced with generous mullion windows, making the rooms light and airy. In the *corps de logis*, the windows were neatly arranged in vertical rows, even if symmetry of the whole façade doesn't appear to have been an objective. All in all, it is an extremely attractive house, especially as particularly light stone from a quarry near Saumur was chosen for its construction. What a difference there is in the brightness of Plessis-Bourré compared with the grim greyness of Langeais, which was built for the king at roughly the same time.

As you enter the large inner courtyard, the lord's wing confronts you. It lacks ornamentation, its three storeys topped by a row of plainish *lucarnes*, three bearing arms: those of France, of the Roi René and of Jean Bourré. Although Jean Bourré seems to have had the interior decorated, he and his family spent little time at Le Plessis-Bourré, making Jarzé their main residence.

To the left, the substantial building is the chapel. A pleasant arcade, a new architectural touch for the times, runs along this side.

Most of the interior has been substantially altered since Bourré's time, but many of the rooms have a lovely feel to them. The wood panelling in the Louis XV and Louis XVI salons was put in by the family that acquired the château at the start of the 20th century and still lives here. The floral carvings in the Louis XVI room were made by David d'Angers, father of the renowned 19th-century sculptor of the same name (*see* Angers, pp.433–5). The high-relief wood carving in the Grand Salon elaborately depicts hunting scenes. By contrast, the Salle des Parlements, vaulted with splendid stone ribs, the floor of tiles made at Les Rairies nearby on the Loir river, takes you back to Bourré's period. The monumental fireplace off centre apparently bears symbols of alchemy.

Upstairs, the stunning painted ceiling of the Salle des Gardes awaits. For those among you with delicate sensibilities, it might be better not to look up too carefully. The hexagonal panels in the coffered wood include pictures of a woman sewing up a magpie's anus and of Venus peeing, standing up, into a bowl a man holds out below her. One prudish owner's wife covered up the offending ceiling before the Revolution, which may have helped it to survive. Her husband was not so lucky; despite local pressure and protests in his defence, he was executed in Angers in 1794. In the middle of the 19th century the château was put up for sale and almost fell into the hands of the destructive *bande noire*, ruthless opportunists wanting to sell off the stone, but an Angers lawyer stepped in to buy it. He ordered much restoration work in the castle, not always in the best taste, but also had this ceiling restored to its former glory.

The meanings of the 24 scenes still remain shrouded in mystery, although they're considered to date back to Bourré's day and to reflect the great period taste for alchemy. The booklet available at the château gives a rather abstruse and inadequately explained reading of the symbols. Eight of the panels contain verses in old French reflecting popular wisdom. They include further absurd scenes, such as a goose which a couple are earnestly trying to put shoes on, and eels which another couple are attempting to break in two.

After such a bizarre experience, the hotchpotch of articles in the last few rooms is a bit of an anticlimax. You're rushed through the corridor of a wing connecting the lord's dwelling to the chapel, converted into a library, but also containing a large collection of fans. The chapel itself holds a memorable naive depiction of the Last Supper.

Up the Sarthe

A short way north of Le Plessis-Bourré, at Cheffes and Châteauneuf-sur-Sarthe, you can take a **river trip** with a running commentary giving you the history of river navigation, trade and the life of mariners in the past across Anjou. The highlights along the Sarthe river lie just across the border, in the *département* of the Sarthe. The pleasant riverside town of Sablé, the renowned abbey of Solesmes, the splendid tiny medieval village of Asnières-sur-Vègre and the pottery town of Malicorne are just a short drive away.

Château du Plessis-Macé

Open July–Aug 10.30–6.30, June and Sept Wed–Mon 10–12 and 2–6.30, March–May and Oct–Nov Wed–Mon 1.30–5.30.

From Angers, head towards Laval on the N162 to reach Le Plessis-Macé. On the edge of a plateau, Le Plessis-Macé stands at a high point in the region and in historical terms; it lies in Anjou's frontier territory with Brittany. The name Macé refers to an 11th-century lord. On arrival outside the castle, you're confronted by the forbidding schist fortifications, the overgrown moat with just a trickle of a stream running through it. The surrounding walls date back as far as the 12th century, making them older than those of Angers castle.

At the end of the Hundred Years' War, the château proper was in good part devastated, but the substantial keep survived, overdone with later decoration. Rebuilding work took place in the 1450s. As at Angers castle, once you're through the imposing outer walls, a much more graceful, light, expansive courtyard opens up before you, although the architecture isn't harmonious or unified; in fact it looks an appealing shambles. The castle follows the traditional plan, with the lord's chambers on one side, his followers' and servants' quarters on the other.

Louis de Beaumont was the most significant of Le Plessis-Macé's 15th-century lords. He served King Louis XI as chamberlain and as *seneschal* of Poitou, and devoted quite some attention to his château in the last quarter of the 15th century. He repaired the walls and added certain elements within, including turrets and staircases. The inner château mixes rugged schist with smooth limestone in almost comical fashion, the latter used to frame the windows and corners, but also for the bits and pieces of decoration. It was Louis de Beaumont who ordered the striking, quirky balconies in their elegant sculpted limestone. A knight of the Order of St-Michael (created by Louis XI at Amboise in 1469; *see* p.241), his chapel is dedicated to the dragon-slaying military saint. The bottom half was built in rough schist, the top half in well-prepared limestone.

During Louis XI's time the independent province of Brittany was still a force to contend with for the French Crown. Louis XI is recorded setting out from here to attack Pouancé to the northwest and to take Ancenis, west along the Loire, then the major town on the Anjou–Brittany line. Brittany would effectively be joined to the French royal possessions by the marriage of Louis XI's successor, Charles VIII, to Anne de Bretagne. The guides claim that in one of Le Plessis-Macé's rooms, in 1532, François I signed the last clause of the Treaty of Vannes, definitively joining Brittany to the royal French realms.

Le Plessis-Macé turned into a country residence for the powerful Du Bellay family, serving the house of Anjou and the Valois, from the mid-16th to the mid-17th centuries. The 1627 inventory gives an idea of the wealth of the interiors, listing Aubusson tapestries, Turkish rugs, fine furniture, bookshelves and a mass of gold brocade and crimson velvet. What you see today is less ostentatious, much altered by the 19th-century owners, with many window openings along the outer château walls and defences, added by them to let in more light. The furniture varies in quality, especially the tapestries.

Among the more interesting pieces on the tour, you'll see a rare tapestry with a red parrot, one of the oldest pianos in France, and a great Charles X bookshelf containing vast tomes on Egypt, reflecting the period fascination with that place. The chapel preserves original late Gothic carved wood panelling, with the lords' box on the first floor an exceptional piece of carpentry work.

In the over-cemented outhouses, space is given over to local exhibitions, while during the Anjou theatre festival (see Angers, p.422), the courtyard serves as a venue for performances. From the outside of the fortifications there are some lovely views onto the château.

A short way west of Le Plessis-Macé, the little **chapel of St-Emérance** is delightfully decorated in Flamboyant Gothic style in royal recognition of the relief the saint apparently brought Louis XI when he was caught short while out hunting.

Up the Mayenne and Oudun

Above Le Plessis-Macé, the Mayenne river has a couple of particularly attractive little riverside villages from which you can take a river cruise. **Grez-Neuville** lies just east of the N162 a few kilometres north of Le Plessis-Macé.

At the confluence of the Mayenne and Oudon, by **Le Lion d'Angers**, lies a national stud farm, the **Haras National** (*open Easter–mid-Sept 10–12 and 2–6, mid-Sept–Dec and Feb–Easter weekends only 2–5*), and a beautiful race course. Even outside the racing season you can go and visit the stud. There's no guide, but details on the wide variety of stallions in their stalls are clearly stated. Continuing up the Mayenne, the village of **Chenillé-Changé** makes a particularly picturesque river stop. The Mayenne is a beautiful river, with wooded banks protected from roads, and towpaths you can walk along. You can hire a cruiser from Chenille-Changé to discover it.

La Mine Bleue

Open April–Sept 10–5, Feb–April and Oct–Dec 2.30–5.

West of the town of Segré, and beyond the mean mine-workers' cottages of Noyant-la-Gravoyère, a former slate mine has been converted into an interesting tourist sight. The conversion has been well done, combining industrial history with mild theme park attractions. Former miners lead the tour. You have to don a mining hat to go down the shaft, where you're herded into a miniature train to go to the mines.

The underground caverns don't feel at all claustrophobic. They're vast atmospheric spaces. The former slate-mining work is explained in a kind of son-et-lumière as you're led from one hall to another. The taped dialogue between workers explains their craft through everyday gossip. Although fairly simple, the French may be hard to follow as the actors speak with heavy accents and their conversation is peppered with specialized phrases and jargon. The tour underlines the difficult working conditions and the all-too-slow social reforms for the miners. The 19th-century writer Zola was most famously among those who campaigned for better working conditions for such miners. One cavern is appropriately enough devoted to literature and mythology inspired by the underworld.

Above ground, you can visit the well-planned museum. Explanatory panels, with texts in English as well as French, trace the development of the slate industry in Anjou. Opencast mining was the way initially. By the 18th century, sizeable opencast mines had developed, dug downwards in a system of layered steps. The advent of the steam engine enabled mining at a much greater depth and in the 19th century production became much more efficient, the mines turning into the great underground chasms you visit. Lively videos take you through the story of slate-mining at the start of the 20th century, mimicking a silent film. Technology and labour costs have caused dramatic changes since the war. After a severe crisis in the French industry, the demand for natural slate for roofing has returned. Traditional methods have been replaced by high-tech ones, but you can watch a traditional slate-splitter at work outside, the craftsman slowly but satisfyingly slicing off neat tiles from the slabs.

Just a little northeast of La Mine Bleue, the **Domaine de la Petite Couère** (*open May–mid-Sept 10–7, March–April and mid-Sept–mid-Nov Sun only 10–6*) is a rural museum on rural ways. It recalls ordinary life in the countryside, as well as displaying some more curious collections. The vast array of objects are well presented and include horse-drawn carriages, tractors, old engines, old cars and model cars, most of them lined up in long purpose-built barns. You can then walk or take a little train to the farm turned fake olde village.

The character of northwestern Anjou turns markedly Breton around **Pouancé**, with its landscape of agricultural ridges broken up by hedgerows and its much darker stone. Fragments of an old, extremely ruined **château** (*open July–Aug Tues–Sat 10–12 and 2–7, Sun 2–7*) are being restored little by little each year by enthusiastic young volunteers. The vestiges date from the 13th to the 15th centuries. The castle was abandoned when Brittany was effectively attached to the French Crown after Anne de Bretagne's marriage to Charles VIII in 1491.

Southwestern Anjou

In southwestern Anjou, an area known as Les Mauges or the Choletais, when locals mention the 'Grande Guerre', the Great War, they may not be referring to the First World War but to the Guerre de Vendée. This bitter regional anti-Revolutionary uprising lasted from 1793 to 1795. Although the Vendée is a separate *département*, the southwest of Anjou was deeply involved in this painful civil war (*see* box overleaf). There certainly weren't celebrations here for the bicentennial of the French Revolution in 1989. Instead, Cholet, for example, organized a commemoration of the Vendéen War.

Getting Around

Buses from Angers to Cholet stop at Chanzeaux and Chemillé. There are also buses to Le Pin-en-Mauges.

Tourist Information

Chemillé: Parc de l'Hôtel de Ville, 49120 Chemillé, t/f 02 41 46 14 64.
Cholet: Place Rougé, B.P.636, 49300 Cholet, t 02 41 49 80 00, f 02 41 49 80 09.
Maulévrier: Rue St-Pierre des Echaubrognes, 49360 Maulévrier, t 02 41 55 09 60.
Beaupréau: Centre Culturel de la Loge, 49600 Beaupréau, t 02 41 71 38 31, f 02 41 75 38 28.

Market Days
Chemillé: Thursday.
Cholet: Tuesday, Wednesday, Thursday and Saturday.
Beaupréau: Monday.

Where to Stay and Eat

Chemillé ✉ 49120
Auberge de l'Arrivée, 15 Place de la Gare, t 02 41 30 60 31, f 02 41 30 78 45 (*inexpensive*). Has cheap rooms and a pleasant restaurant set in a large town house (*menus €10.5–26.5*).

Cholet ✉ 49300
***Château de la Tremblaye, Route des Sables, t 02 41 58 40 17, f 02 41 58 20 67, tremblaye@chateauxhotels.com, www.chateauxhotels.com/tremblaye (*expensive*). Stylish 19th-century pastiche of a Loire Valley château outside Cholet, on the site of the battle of Cholet in the Guerre de Vendée (*menus €18–33*).

**Grand Hôtel de la Poste, 26 Bd Gustave Richard, t 02 41 62 07 20, f 02 41 58 54 10 (*moderate*). Traditional-style, well-run French family hotel with restaurant (*menus €15–48.5*).
Le Stofflet, 8 Bd Gustave Richard, t 02 41 62 26 50 (*menus €8.5–19.5*). A popular place, serving typical Vendée dishes, such as Vendée ham with white beans or *marquins* (little eels) (*menus €15–48.5*).

La Flocellière ✉ 85700
Château de la Flocellière B&B, t 02 51 57 222 03, f 02 51 57 75 21, erika.vignial@wanadoo.fr (*expensive*). Just 7km south of the Le Puy du Fou, a dramatic amalgam of bits of castle from different periods, and surely the best choice near the big tourist sight (*table d'hôte €38*).

Maulévrier ✉ 49360
**Château Colbert, Place du Château, t 02 41 55 51 33, f 02 41 55 09 02, colbert@chateaux-hotels.com, www.chateauxhotels.com/colbert (*moderate*). A big, jolly, slightly tackily decorated but very good-value castle above the wonderful Oriental garden. Boasts a series of splendidly over-the-top *salons* to go with its very loud owner, who sometimes puts on his own shows with *dîners-spectacles*. There's some amazing wood panelling to admire along the main corridor outside the posher bedrooms (*menus €12–38*).

Nuaillé ✉ 49340
**Le Relais des Biches, Place de l'Eglise, t 02 41 62 38 99, f 02 41 62 96 24 (*inexpensive*). Once a hunting lodge, this has been neatly done up, with a swimming pool in the garden (*menus €11.5–23*).

The Guerre de Vendée

What sparked off the so-called Guerre de Vendée? First and foremost, the defence of the Catholic faith and the popular local priests, persecuted by the new Republic. Second, the execution of the king early in 1793 led to more protest. Third, the European powers were menacing the French borders and the Republican authorities enforced conscription by lottery of 300,000 bachelors across France aged between 18 and 40 who hadn't already signed up to become members of the Revolutionary forces. This not only created deep and widespread resentment, but also caused large bands of rebellious young men to be gathered together. Riots broke out in many parts of France. While they were quickly stamped out elsewhere, incompetent French Revolutionary forces in this part of western France failed to suppress the disorder.

Resistance leaders had appeared from among the ordinary people, notably Cathelineau and Stofflet. Independently, certain aristocrats had led actions against the Revolutionary guards. In the course of the uprising, a few army officers would even join the Vendéen side, notably D'Elbée and Bonchamps. Republican troops came to quell the uprisings, but the 'Vendéen' protesters knew early victories, taking control briefly of Cholet, Saumur and Angers. Towards the end of June 1793 they attacked Nantes. But the old Breton capital resisted. With the death of Cathelineau – virtual leader of the chaotically ordered Vendéens by this stage – in Nantes on 29 June, the Vendéens' fortunes were reversed. At the battle of Cholet in October, the Vendéens suffered a bruising defeat. They retreated northwards, well over 50,000 in number many estimate, crossing the Loire at St-Florent-le-Vieil. Their leader by this time, Bonchamps, had been mortally wounded in action, but in a memorable act of mercy asked for the lives of 5,000 captive Republican soldiers to be spared. This act of forgiveness is interpreted in David d'Angers most famous and moving sculpture, at St-Florent-le-Vieil.

Cholet's history and art museum, a martyrs' chapel in the forest of Nuaillé-Vezins and the church of Le Pin-en-Mauges count among the sites to be visited which are most closely linked with this war in Anjou, along with St-Florent-le-Vieil. There are also other, more light-hearted, things to see in the area, such as the surprising Oriental gardens at Maulévrier.

Angers to Cholet

Heading southwest from Angers, the N160 leads to Cholet. It passes close to **Chanzeaux**, which has a church containing stained-glass windows and frescoes recalling the Guerre de Vendée. The sacristan and some friends hid for a time up the tower as their village was being burned in the vile war. **Chemillé** has a medicinal herb garden, while the **Chapelle de la Sorinière**, a few kilometres east, has interesting 16th-century murals.

Some way west of Chemillé, the stained glass in the church of **Le Pin-en-Mauges** tells the story of the Guerre de Vendée, and in particular the part played by Jacques

The action then moved north of the Loire, in a campaign known as the Virée de Galerne. The Vendéens, under a young hotheaded would-be hero Henri de La Rochejaquelin, general at the tender age of 21, swept into the province of Maine. The civil war entered a bloodier phase in the winter of 1793–4. Some 15,000 men were killed in the terrible defeat of the Vendéens at Le Mans in December 1793, and they suffered a further massive loss at Savenay, near Nantes.

Early 1794 saw the most awful devastation of the Vendéens' territories. The Republican leader Turreau was put in command of vicious troops, who tore through the rebellious lands into Vendée. These men were so destructive that they became known as the *colonnes infernales*. They tortured, killed, pillaged and burned as they went along, and many towns and villages across the Mauges were completely destroyed. Among the dispersed and divergent Vendéen leaders, Stofflet was the main figure in Les Mauges. He had established a refugee camp and hospital in the forest of Nuaillé-Vezins at the start of the year. A traitor gave away its whereabouts and the people there were massacred. In Nantes, Carrier organized ritual drownings in the Loire.

The mass anti-Revolutionary fighting would die down, to be replaced by the actions of small bands known as the Chouans. In 1795 peace was negotiated between the Vendéens and the Republic and several treaties were signed, for example by Stofflet in May in St-Florent-le-Vieil, bringing an end to the major part of the war, although the Chouannerie would go on longer, particularly in Brittany. Some of the Vendéen leaders continued guerilla actions, but Stofflet and Charette captured and shot in early 1796. In 1801, the Concordat passed laws guaranteeing Catholic freedoms. The brutal repression of the Vendéen pro-Catholic Blancs (the Whites) by the Revolutionary or Republican *colonnes infernales* of the Bleus (the Blues) has scarred a whole seam of this part of western France.

Cathelineau, a native of the place, described as the *généralissime de la Grande Armée Catholique Royale qui fit trembler la Convention*. The depictions of the stages of his fight against the irreligious evil of the Republic make him into a militant saviour figure. In a curious postscript, other windows tell the story of a couple of Jacques Cathelineau's descendants. His son, Count Jacques-Joseph Cathelineau, was assassinated in his attempt to help the royalist cause in the abortive uprising in support of the Duchess of Berry in the 1830s. Jacques' grandson, General Henri de Cathelineau, is shown being blessed, in military uniform, by a bishop. The themes of royalty and Catholic militancy shine through. Where, you might ask, have God and Jesus disappeared in all this?

Cholet isn't an obvious tourist stop, but it has several interesting features which are unusual and attractively presented. The Musée d'Art et d'Histoire (*open Wed–Mon 10–12 and 2–6*) occupies a purpose-built swanky modern building of some size. A miscellany of items aims to recreate a feeling for Guerre de Vendée times, with weapons, maps, pamphlets and all manner of little period objects and memories on display. The most striking room contains portraits of the main Vendéen leaders. These pieces were commissioned by King Louis XVIII with the restoration of the monarchy.

The fine arts collection of the town is also housed in this building, the modern section concentrating on geometrical abstraction, the older works mainly 18th- and 19th-century French pieces.

At the Musée du Textile Choletais (*open June–Sept Wed–Mon 2–6.30, Oct–May Wed–Mon 2–6*), set in an old factory that has been freshly restored, you can learn something of the importance of textiles in Cholet's history, and a guide will explain the way that mechanization developed the process of working cloth. You're accompanied by the clatter of the old machines on the tour, which is given by enthusiastic young volunteers. Cholet is rather strangely associated across France with its chequered handkerchiefs in particular.

A short way northwest of Cholet at **St-André-de-la-Marche**, the Musée de la Chaussure (*open July and Aug Tues–Fri 10–12 and 2.30–6, rest of week pm only; March–June and Sept–Oct 2.30–6*) celebrates the fact that the Choletais is western France's top footwear region.

Cholet also serves as the dormitory town for the vast son-et-lumière of **Le Puy du Fou**. This place lies just across the regional frontier, in Poitou, a short distance east of Les Herbiers. This is a major tourist attraction, with the popular appeal of ersatz culture on a grand scale. The artificial medieval village and attractions in the Grand Parcours are open during the day (*open June–mid-Sept 10–7*), with craftspeople in period costume called upon to play their part. But the main performance, the Cinéscénie, takes place after dark on summer evenings (*mid-June–1st weekend in Sept Fri and Sat only at around 10.30pm*). The story once again revives the memories of the Guerre de Vendée. It was written by Philippe Devilliers, a highly popular right-wing politician in these parts, who rather disastrously stood for election as president in the 1990s. The show ends with an impressive fireworks show.

Southeast of Cholet, beyond the reservoirs popular for swimming, water sports and ornithology, **Maulévrier** boasts a surprisingly luxuriant Asian **Parc Oriental** (*open July–Aug 10.30–7.30, March–June and Sept–mid-Nov Tues–Sun 2–6*), laid out at the start of the 20th century in the steep Moine valley. The Château Colbert, named after the brother of Louis XIV's famous minister, stands above the gardens. The original edifice was destroyed at the Revolution, but rebuilt according to the original plans. It's now a hotel (*see* 'Where to Stay and Eat', p.449).

Si l'on pressait le sol comme une éponge, il en jaillirait le sang des martyrs (If you squeezed the ground like a sponge, the blood of the martyrs would gush out).
words of Pierre l'Ermite on the massacres in the Forêt de Nuaillé-Vezins

Take the D25 northeast from Maulévrier and then turn left onto the D196 to reach the **Chapelle des Martyrs** in the **Forêt de Nuaillé-Vezins**. This is a moving place for the descendants of the supporters of the Vendée uprising, deathly calm. At the beginning of 1794, Stofflet had set up a well-hidden camp next to his headquarters to take in refugees running from the Republican *colonnes infernales* and to treat the sick. On 25 March the enemy, led by Grignon and Crouzat, two villains in local history, sniffed out the population in hiding, given away by a traitor. The defenceless families, with numerous women, children and the old, were massacred. Behind the chapel (originally made for the Maulévrier Colbert family) you'll find a modest further chapel listing the martyrs' names, a touching reminder of the victims of a war too easily forgotten in France. The collective memory of the people of Les Mauges has certainly not let the atrocities be forgotten. Statues of the Vendéen leaders Stofflet and Cathelineau stand on the façade of the main chapel.

The North Bank of the Loire from Angers to Nantes

Although the high-perched villages of the Corniche Angevine on the south bank of the stretch of the Loire between Angers and Nantes get more tourist attention than the north bank, there are some wonderful things to see along this route, from Bouchemaine to Le Cellier via the splendid Château de Serrant.

From Bouchemaine to Béhuard

Bouchemaine, or 'Mouth Maine', rather basically signals by its name where the short and stocky river Maine meets the long-legged Loire. You can easily reach this marvellous confluence from Angers. Follow the signs to Bouchemaine and then

Getting Around

A **bus** service covers the villages strung along the north bank. Ancenis is on the Angers–Nantes **train** line.

Tourist Information

Bouchemaine: Mairie, 49080 Bouchemaine, t 02 41 22 20 00.
Savennières: 1 Rue de la Mairie, 49170 Savennières, t 02 41 72 84 46 or t 02 41 72 85 00.
Béhuard: Mairie, 49170 Béhuard, t 02 41 72 84 11.
Ingrandes-sur-Loire: Rue Michel, B.P.14, 49123, t 02 41 39 29 06 or t 02 41 39 20 21.
Ancenis: Place du Millénaire, 44150 Ancenis, t/f 02 40 83 07 44.
Oudon: Rue du Pont Levis, t 02 40 83 80 04.

Market Days

St-Georges-sur-Loire: Thursday.
Ingrandes-sur-Loire: Friday.
Varades: Saturday morning.
Ancenis: Thursday morning.

Where to Stay and Eat

Bouchemaine ✉ 49080
La Terrasse, Place Ruzebouc, La Pointe de Bouchemaine, t 02 41 77 11 96. The wide windows of this restaurant's bright dining room have a great view out over the confluence of the Maine and the Loire. It's a very good stop at which to try Loire fish and Angevin wines (*menus c.€15–45.5*).
★**L'Ancre de Marine**, 2 Place Ruzebouc, La Pointe de Bouchemaine, t 02 41 77 14 46, f 02 41 77 25 71 (*inexpensive*). Hotel run by the same proprietor as La Terrasse, quite basic by comparison, with a bar below. But it's still very well located, and serves food produced in the same kitchens as at La Terrasse.

Béhuard ✉ 49170
Les Tonnelles, 12 Rue du Chevalier Béhuard, t 02 41 72 21 50. An enchanting stop on this secretive Loire island, with a deeply shaded terrace for summer dining. Fine fish dishes with wine sauces (*menus €20.5–53*).
Notre-Dame, 12 Place de l'Eglise, t 02 41 72 20 17. May be much simpler, but its terrace also offers a delightful spot at which to sample Loire fish (*menus from c.€15*).

the **Pointe de Bouchemaine**. Here you get expansive views onto the merging river masses and can wander down to the very pleasant old cobbled quayside which recalls busier trading days. In winter and spring the expanse of water can seem almost Amazonian; in summer it dwindles considerably as the riverbank flowers and the *épis*, or dykes, emerge. Fishermen colonize these *épis* or take to the water in little boats in the warm season.

Following the winding narrow rocky road along the Loire, you pass through **Epiré**, a charming village with a couple of churches and very narrow walled streets. You're entering the very prosperous vineyards of **Savennières**, which produce a superlative dry white wine, one of the very greatest from the Loire, extremely exclusive and elusive. It's relatively hard even to see the vines for that matter, as many of the vineyards are enclosed behind high stone walls. The centre of the village has a sweet old Romanesque church off the lovely green. The TGV rushes by like a serpent through the grass down by the river.

Go down to the Loire to cross onto the **Ile Béhuard**, a delightful island named after a companion of Geoffroy Martel. The place is regularly submerged in winter, the houses finding themselves *les pieds dans l'eau*, their feet in the water. You can understand why the adorable little church here was perched on top of a rock. The houses cluster around below it. Pilgrims gathered on the Ile Béhuard in centuries past to pay their respects to the local Virgin, who was supposed to look after the well-being of Loire mariners and travellers in these potentially treacherous waters. The story goes that King Louis XI ordered the church after he escaped drowning around here. One of the two parts to the nave in the 15th-century building was quarried out of the rock. A couple of Virgins star within, while the chains of a galley slave inside are said to be an *ex voto* left by a prisoner of the Moors who escaped from captivity on the seas.

Back on the north bank of the Loire, from Béhuard you can follow a small but pretty route westwards, continuing along right by the river up to the bridge almost as far as Ingrandes. The more obvious but less attractive way from Angers to Ingrandes is the busy N23. This takes you right past the aristocratic gates of the Château de Serrant, just east of St-Georges-sur-Loire.

Château de Serrant

Open July–Aug 9.30–6 and 2–5.20, April–June and Sept–mid-Nov
Wed–Mon 9.30–12 and 2–5.20.

Mixing the rough with the smooth as so often in western Anjou, the outer sides of the Château de Serrant are built principally of irregular pieces of schist, with just the windows solidly surrounded by finely cut limestone. But within the courtyard, the walls are pure tufa, blinding in the summer sunshine. This is a substantial, magnificent château, which really deserves to be better known. Though begun in the middle of the 16th century, building work on it extended over more than 150 years, being completed in the 18th century, but the harmony of the Renaissance design was maintained.

The project goes back to the Brie family. One Pontus de Brie, a chamberlain to Louis XI, had already built a castle on the site of an earlier one here around the 1480s. His grandson Charles decided on a complete rethink of the family home. The name of the great architect Philibert de l'Orme has been linked to the plans, although there's no concrete evidence of his involvement. The detail of the design looks rather sober and serious, Ionic pilasters on the ground floor giving way to Corinthian ones on the first. Further important changes were made to the roof in the 19th century by the architect Lucien Magre. He added the *lucarnes* and the balustrade with decorative stone urns which runs right round to the two massive southern towers. Topped by elegant, round, helmet-like slate roofs, these are crowned with a little domed observation tower.

One of the elements that points most strongly to De l'Orme's involvement is the splendid central staircase by which you enter the château, with its layers of openings, the last divided up caryatids. But first you're taken to see the **chapel** incorporated into the end of one wing. This grandiose room is linked with another of the most famous names in French architecture, Hardoin Mansart, most notably associated with Versailles. Inside, superb black-and-white effects set the clean tone, black pilasters framing the white walls. The chapel serves as a mausoleum for the Marquis de Vaubrun, son-in-law of the second member of the De Bautru family to own the château; Guillaume de Bautru bought the property in 1636. The Marquis de Vaubrun died a supposedly glorious death at the Battle of Altenheim in 1675. He it is depicted in the laudatory sculpture by Antoine Coysevox, winged Victory floating down from on high to crown him. He reclines periwigged, togaed, semi-naked, seemingly unaware of the laurel wreath Victory has destined for his head. This chapel is a place charged with family emotion, heightened by the panels recording the death of five children from tuberculosis.

An exiled Irish family, the Walshes, became the next proprietors of Serrant. They had moved to Nantes, faithful to the fleeing James II. Antoine, an arms dealer, acquired the home for his brother François. The imposing stone arch gateway marking the principal entrance to the château courtyard carries the family coat of arms, with three swans, one pierced by an arrow. These arms recall the romantic story of an ancestor wounded in battle and left in the water to die, who was rescued by two of the birds. François' son, also named Antoine, continued to support the Stuarts, financing two ships for Bonnie Prince Charlie to sail across the Channel in the course of his 1745 rebellion.

As you enter the château by the stairway, the barrenness of the outer courtyard gives way to some extremely sumptuous rooms, full of the extravagance of Ancien Régime noble living. From the start, fine tapestries, paintings and a diversity of *objets d'art* adorn the rooms. The number of *écritoires* (writing cases) and writing tables might make you imagine that these aristocrats had nothing better to do than to pass their days writing letters to each other. In the Prince de Tarente's room you're shown how discreetly modern comforts were later installed. One corridor displays a genealogy of the very ancient noble family of La Trémoille, who married into the Walsh family in 1830.

The finest rooms are on the first floor. The Grand Salon contains a marvellous set of tapestries specially made for this room, rich with forest scenes and fabulous animals. The Emperor Napoleon visited the château in 1808. He only stayed a few hours, but the room specially prepared for him has stayed shrine-like intact to this day. The Countess of Serrant of the time had been a lady-in-waiting to Josephine, but it's a bust by Canova of Napoleon's second wife, Marie-Louise of Austria, which looks over the room. The aristocratic line continues, the person in charge of the château carrying the pretty title of the Princesse de Mérode, recently returned with her husband from life in Kenya. After the guided tour, enjoy a walk around the charmingly landscaped property.

From Ingrandes to Le Cellier

Ingrandes is the pretty, exposed village that marks the end of present-day Anjou on the north bank of the Loire. The *département* to the west is the Loire Atlantique, formerly an important part of Brittany, but since the 1960s changes in regional boundaries, part of the Pays de la Loire region. Ingrandes' extraordinary communal swimming pool lies on the Loire bank, or more accurately, in the Loire bank, as you'll see. Seen from the south side of the river, Ingrandes has a typical Angevin silhouette – portside slate roofs, a mill, a 19th-century limestone church and big bourgeois houses. Only the ugly modern block of the Ingrandes cooperative and the *château d'eau* slightly mar the picture. One of the grand houses in the centre is the Hôtel de la Gabelle, a reminder of the much resented, unequal and compulsory salt tax of the Ancien Régime. In Brittany, a salt-producing region, the *gabelle* wasn't payable; in Anjou it was often extortionate, salt costing up to 10 times more than in Brittany. To stop contraband trade, a separate police force made up of 'gabelous' patrolled the border territories looking to catch the *faux-sauniers*, as the smugglers were known. This is the *frontière du sel*, the old salt frontier.

The pretty village of **Varades** in the Loire Atlantique stands on the slope of the Loire's bank. Below it lies the Loire fishermen's village of **La Meilleraie**. A plaque commemorates the death here from his war wounds of the Marquis de Bonchamps, considered a hero of the anti-Revolutionary Guerres de Vendée (*see p.450*).

Close to Varades, the **Palais Briau** (*open April–Oct, the house at weekends only, the grounds daily 10–12 and 2–6*) is a sumptuous brick and limestone château of the 19th century, commissioned by François Briau, a model of a 19th-century engineer. He had made his fortune planning the regional railway lines from Tours to Nantes and from Nantes to Pornic. He also worked in Italy, overseeing the construction of the Bologna–Ancona track. When he returned to the Loire, he decided to build his own *palazzo* along Italianate lines, but incorporating the latest modern comforts of the day. The architect Edouard Moll planned the stocky building in 1854, following Palladian models. Inside, money was lavished on the stucco decoration, the elaborate wall coverings, the odd fresco and such features as the monumental staircase. But on the tour of the beautifully proportioned interiors, you also get an excellent feel for life at the cutting edge of design and engineering in France's Second Empire. Many pieces of period furniture have been retained inside, but the walls are also hung with paintings by the present owner, who has been restoring the property. Wonderful views open up onto the church of St-Florent-le-Vieil on the other side of the Loire (*see* p.460). Various follies lie scattered in the grounds, for you to discover.

Ancenis is most appealing to visit for its huge traditional market, which brings a good deal of life to its renovated heart. In medieval times this was an important Breton frontier post. The castle grew to substantial proportions through medieval times, although it has long lain in ruins. For centuries, boats passing this way had to pay tolls to cross the frontier between Brittany and Anjou.

Vineyards slope down to the Loire in this area, producing **Coteaux d'Ancenis** (Slopes of Ancenis) wines. The wide local range includes VDQS wines made from Cabernet, Gamay, Pinot or Gros Plant. The Coteaux d'Ancenis Malvoisie VDQS is a rare sweet white made from either Pinot Beurot or Pinot Gris. The one wine given the added distinction of its own *appellation* in this area is the Coteaux de la Loire Muscadet. Ancenis town has a Maison des Vins where you can learn about, taste and buy the local wines. You can also organize vineyard visits from here.

A many-sided keep rises high above the village of **Oudon**, a landmark along this stretch of the Loire. It formed part of a medieval castle built here for the Malestroit family under Duke Jean IV of Brittany. You can climb the tower at certain times of year to appreciate the superb views onto the river. You can also enjoy some dreamy glimpses of the Loire from around **Le Cellier**, near which the Château de Clermont boasts the finest views of all. This mid-17th-century castle was built in brick in archetypal Louis XIII style. In recent times it was owned by one of France's best-loved comedians, Louis de Funès.

The South Bank of the Loire from Angers to Nantes

The most spectacular piece of road south of the Loire between Angers and Nantes is known as the Corniche Angevine – strictly speaking the stretch between Rochefort and Chalonnes – but further west, Montjean, St-Florent-le-Vieil and Champtoceaux all boast very fine views down onto the Loire.

Getting Around

Local buses stop at the villages along the south bank of the Loire.

Tourist Information

Rochefort-sur-Loire: 20 Av d'Angers, 49190 Rochefort-sur-Loire, t 02 41 78 81 70.
Chalonnes-sur-Loire: Place de l'Hôtel de Ville, 49290 Chalonnes-sur-Loire, t 02 41 78 26 21, f 02 41 74 91 54.
Montjean-sur-Loire: Quai des Mariniers, 49570 Montjean-sur-Loire, t 02 41 39 07 10 or t 02 41 39 80 46.
St-Florent-le-Vieil: Rue de Rénéville, 49410 St-Florent-le-Vieil, t 02 41 72 62 32, f 02 41 72 62 95.
Champtoceaux: Le Champalud, 49270 Champtoceaux, t 02 40 83 57 49 or t 02 40 83 52 31.
La Varenne: Mairie, 49270 La Varenne, t 02 40 98 51 04.

Market Days

Chalonnes-sur-Loire: Tuesday and Saturday.
Montjean-sur-Loire: Thursday.
St-Florent-le-Vieil: Friday afternoon.

Where to Stay and Eat

Rochefort-sur-Loire ✉ **49190**
★★**Le Grand Hôtel**, 30 Rue René Gasnier, t 02 41 78 80 46, f 02 41 78 83 25 (*inexpensive*). Signals its discreet presence by palm trees. The rooms may be basic, but the cuisine is delicate, in summer served in the very pretty back garden. The place is being redone by an enthusiastic young couple (*menus €16–31*).

Montjean-sur-Loire ✉ **49570**
Auberge de la Loire, 2 Quai des Mariniers, t/f 02 41 39 80 20 (*inexpensive*). Really likeable unpretentious Loire-side inn, with good-value very tasty cooking and four rooms recently freshened up.
Les Cèdres B&B, 17 Rue du Prieuré, t/f 02 41 39 39 25, les.cedres@wanadoo.fr (*inexpensive*). Up in the town, a walled property with a pretty garden in which one cedar is left standing. The three stylish rooms carry the names of composers, a sign of the owners' passion for music. This is a cultured stop.

St-Florent-le-Vieil ✉ **49140**
★★**Hostellerie de la Gabelle**, 12 Quai de la Loire, t 02 41 72 50 19, f 02 41 72 54 38 (*inexpensive*). In a delightful location by the Loire, a

From Murs-Erigné to Montjean

You'll cross a confusing number of branches of water south of Angers to reach Murs-Erigné, beyond Les Ponts-de-Cé. The cliff of schist at **Mûrs-Erigné** (sandwiched between the Louet, a wayward branch of the Loire, and the end of the Aubance river) was where the anti-Revolutionary Vendéen troops pushed 600 Republican fighters to their deaths on 26 July 1793. Surprisingly for this anti-Revolutionary region, a monument to the Republicans, in the form of Marianne, symbol of the French Republic, was put up here in 1889.

Before **Denée**, you might like to cross briefly onto the long island formed between the Louet and the Loire to appreciate the pretty and little known sites of **Les Jubeaux** and **St-Jean-de-la-Croix**.

Rochefort-sur-Loire could just as well be called Rochefort-sur-Louet, while its vines produce Layon wines. From the Louet's island here, three brothers called St-Offrange caused chaos in the late stages of the Wars of Religion. The royal troops failed to dislodge them, so in 1598 King Henri IV bought peace with them, giving them court positions. Their fort, whose remnants you can see, was destroyed, as Rochefort had been.

traditional French provincial hotel in bright stone. The interiors are a bit old fashioned. There are some delicious sauces on the menu (*menus €13–38*).

La Chapelle-St-Florent ✉ 49410
Le Moulin d'Epinay, Rue de l'Evre, t/f 02 41 72 70 70. You can try the flour produced by this windmill in crêpes and *galettes* at the modern restaurant in front of it which enjoys spectacular views.

Drain ✉ 49530
Le Mésangeau B&B, t 02 40 98 21 57, f 02 40 98 28 62, *le.mesangeau@wanadoo.fr*, *www.anjou-et-loire.com/mesangeau* (*moderate*). An enormous, long, 19th-century farm building on the scale of a castle, with big, square, beamed rooms and very well-kitted-out bathrooms, run by an energetic couple who will look after you over dinner, too, if you reserve in advance (*table d'hôte €18*).

Champtoceaux ✉ 49270
★★★Les Jardins de la Forge, 1 Place des Piliers, t 02 40 83 56 23, f 02 40 83 59 80 (*expensive–moderate*). The most highly reputed restaurant in the area. People come from far and wide to sample Paul Pauvert's cuisine, some

particularly delicate fish sauces among the specialities (*menus €23.5–58.5*). All is beautifully prepared in the stylish contemporary dining rooms. In addition, a few superbly designed and air-conditioned rooms are now available in the misleadingly dull-looking house opposite the restaurant. There's a swimming pool too, by the cemetery!

★★Chez Claudie, Le Cul du Moulin, t 02 40 83 50 43, f 02 40 83 59 72 (*inexpensive*). Some rooms with views of the Loire in this quite characterful, traditional French hotel down the slope below the town (*menus €10–33.5*).

★★Le Champalud, Promenade du Champalud, t 02 40 83 50 09, f 02 40 83 53 81 (*inexpensive*). Good restaurant with French country cooking in a rustic setting. The basic rooms are being redone (*menus €10–38*).

St-Sauveur-de-Landemont ✉ 49270
★★★★Château de la Colaissière, t 02 40 98 75 04, f 02 40 98 74 15, *colaissiere@chateauxhotels.com*, *www.chateauxhotels.com/colaissiere* (*expensive*). Splendid medieval castle behind fortified farm walls. Very smart rooms and sumptuous cuisine. Heated pool and tennis court in the grounds (*menus €27.5–48.5*).

The beautiful road west through the countryside leads you up to **La Haie Longue**, with its spectacular views all around – a picturesque place for the aviation pioneer René Gasnier to have set off on his first flights in September 1908. To the south of La Haie Longue, the Layon river draws slowly and reluctantly closer to the Loire, which it reaches at **Chalonnes**, where the Louet is also reunited with its parent. Down at Chalonnes' atmospheric old quays, lined by trees, Loire *barques* rest in the shade. Wine and coal from the Layon once used to depart from here. The church has its feet in the water. This was where the new bishops of Angers came after their ceremony of consecration – the episcopal palace long stood in Chalonnes. Gilles de Rais, companion to King Charles VII and Joan of Arc, and notoriously executed for hundreds of child murders, was married here in 1422. From the quayside near the church you can look up to see a typical Angevin view, a windmill on the vine-covered hill above a curve in the river.

To the south, **St-Laurent de la Plaine** has a substantial, well-presented museum devoted to old crafts, the Cité des Métiers de Tradition (*open April–Sept daily exc all Tues–Sat 10–12.30 and 2.30–7, Sun 2.30–7; rest of year Tues–Fri 10–12 and 2–5*). In the Guerre de Vendée, half the inhabitants of this village died at the hands of the Republicans.

Montjean

From the top of Montjean, with its landmark neo-Gothic church on a height, you can walk over to a typical panoramic view from the Angevin Corniche, with a tufty Loire island far below. The village descends prettily to the very extensive Loire **quays** below, which stretch over some 600m and from which a traditional **Loire** *gabare* sets sail regularly for tourists in the summer season.

Loire navigation and trade of the past is the main theme of the scruffy **Ecomusée de la Loire Angevine** (*open Easter–All Saints' Tues–Sun 2.30–6.30*), in a former ironworks. Actually, it looks rather like a school crammed with inexpertly presented sixth-formers' projects – and it has a certain confused adolescent charm. Limestone, salt, coal, hemp, sails, wine, flour and sugar...all manner of important materials were shipped up and down the Loire around here. Montjean had an important boat-building community. When the time came for the boats to be split up after service, their timber was sometimes used in the local houses.

St-Florent-le-Vieil

St-Florent-le-Vieil is another cliff-top village with particularly spectacular views next to its church. As the old bit added on to the town's name implies, little St-Florent has a long and noble history. It was a Celtic site and an early Christian one. The evangelical story has it that the hermit Florent settled here in the 4th century and travelled around to spread the Christian message to the people of the Mauges, successfully converting them. An abbey venerating his relics was founded on the site by the 7th century, but Breton and then Norman attacks in the mid-9th century caused the monks to flee a long way east, taking the saint's bones with them. They would only return some one hundred years later. The new abbey in honour of the saint was established just outside Saumur and this site of St-Florent relegated to a priory, albeit a powerfully independent one.

The grandiose neoclassical **church** you now see dates in the main from the early 18th century and should definitely draw you inside. It was a fortunate survivor of the Republican wrath. The architecture within is a model of Loire brightness. Religious memories are once more eclipsed in Les Mauges by memories of the Guerre de Vendée, and the church contains a moving, even heroic, statue of a local hero. With windblown, flowing hair, veins standing out on the veined marble, the beautiful young Marquis de Bonchamps props himself up, semi-recumbent, on his tomb. The lower part of his perfect body, paler than a sheet, is draped with a toga. Bonchamps looks like a combination of classical virtue and a Christ of the Resurrection. His head is raised, his right hand stretching up to the sky in a powerful peace-making gesture. Below him, on the slab on which his body lies, are his words of restraint: '*Grâce aux prisonniers*'.

This statue, with its mixture of political and religious tones, recalls just about the only noble moment in the Guerre de Vendée (*see pp.450–51*). Its nobility probably sums up the general feelings of many in the region towards the pro-Catholic cause in the anti-Revolutionary uprising. The sculptor of this work, one of the most famous French sculptures of the 19th century, was David d'Angers (*see pp.433–5*). His father is said to have been among the Republican prisoners saved by Bonchamps's clemency. The piece was executed only some 30 years after the act of mercy.

Go down via a monumental internal staircase into the blinding neo-Gothic **crypt**, which has been turned into something of a museum, attractively exhibiting old stones from St-Florent, religious finery and some recuperated relics of the saint himself. The church and its gardens serve as the setting for a highly regarded programme of music concerts in July.

The local museum, the **Musée d'Histoire Locale et des Guerres de Vendée** (*open July–mid-Sept 2.30–6.30, rest of period between Easter and Nov weekends only 2.30–6.30*), set in a former 17th-century chapel, relentlessly pursues the theme of the war of Vendée, as well as devoting little sections to Loire boats and Loire birds.

Beyond St-Florent-le-Vieil towards Nantes

At **La Chapelle-St-Florent**, on the heights to the south of St-Florent-le-Vieil, the **Moulin de l'Epinay** (*open July–Aug Tues–Fri 10–12.30 and 2.30–7, Sat and Sun 2.30–7; May–June and Sept Tues–Sun 2.30–6.30; March–April and Oct–Nov Sun only 3–6.30*) stands in a spot with fantastic views, 18 church towers visible on clear days. Built in the mid-19th century, this towering windmill was restored by enthusiasts in the parish and started producing flour again in 1989. A small museum recalls the windmills of Anjou of the past. Nearby, at the **Cirque de Courrossé**, the Evre river has formed a dramatic amphitheatre of slopes which you can walk down; the Catholic Church turned the path into something of a religious route. Just a short way further southwest, the village of **Le Fuilet** is devoted to pottery. Go and visit the Maison du Potier (*open July–Aug Tues–Fri 10.30–12.30 and 2.30–7, Sat–Mon 2.30–7; April–June and Sept–Oct Sun only 2.30–7*) to appreciate the local tradition.

Back close to the Loire, the sleepy village of **Liré** is proud of its connections with the great 16th-century Pléiade poet, a native of the area, and has seen its Musée Joachim du Bellay (*open late Feb–Christmas Tues–Sun 10–12 and 2–6*) recently brought into the modern age. The poet was actually born at the Château de la Turmelière, now a picturesque ruin just west of the village. But the substantial 16th-century village mansion holding his museum is a fitting place to remember him. From an illustrious Angevin family with many members who became important military and religious figures in France, he was able to travel widely, notably to Italy, which features prominently in his poems. He was disillusioned by what he discovered in the capital of the Catholic Church, finding Rome the capital of ambition and prostitution; in contrast, he found his native Anjou a joy. He enchantingly said that he considered poetry as a sumptuous banquet. His works are beautifully crafted classical pieces, following Petrach's sonnets, but importantly written in French. The displays incite you to read some of Du Bellay's pieces, as well as to learn something of the importance of his times.

Continuing west along the Loire, **Champtoceaux** looks dramatically down on the river and across to Oudon on the north bank, the latter standing out with its lone tall castle tower. The whole medieval town of Châteauceaux was laid to waste by Jean V Duc de Bretagne in warring over the Breton succession. Some ruins of the fortifications remain. Still further back in time, in the Dark Ages, Pépin le Bref received the ambassadors of the caliph of Baghdad here! There's a delightful walk, the Coulée de la Luce, you can take down to the Loire via an amphitheatre of a public garden.

La Varenne makes the last, most westerly stop in Anjou. You can climb the freckled square church tower for splendid views of the surrounding area. Vines slope gracefully down into the Loire Atlantique and the Muscadet wine-making area of the Pays Nantais. Curiously, the valley of the Loire reaches its narrowest point here since its long descent into the plains around Roanne, near Lyon. At Varenne, it's reduced to only 1km in breadth. It broadens out again as it heads for Nantes and the sea.

Seamlessly entering the Loire Atlantique following the Loire's southern bank, look out for the tiny Romanesque chapel at **St-Simon**, just past a striking metal-lattice bridge over the Loire. Opposite it lies **Les Mauves**, depicted in a couple of Turner's most magical watercolours of the Loire. **La Pierre Percée**, beyond St-Simon, presents a particularly beautiful Loire-side picture, a big cobbled slope running down to the old port. A miniature modern port has been constructed on the island in the Loire opposite. You pass through extremely fine sandy fields ideal for market gardening and through patches of vineyards before reaching the Nantes suburbs.

The Loire from Nantes to the Atlantic

21

10 km
5 miles
N

LOIRE-ATLANTIQUE

Ile-de-Fédrun

St-Nazaire **4**
Mindin **5**
Paimbœuf
St-Brévin

St-Michel-Chef-Chef

Pornic

Nantes **3**

Trentemoult
Rezé
Haute-Maison
St-Fiacre-sur-Maine
Château-Thébaud

La Haye-Fouassière

Oudon
Carquefou Le Cellier
La Varenne
Les Mauves
La Pierre
Percée

Ancenis
Champtoceaux
St-Sauveur-de-Landemont

Le Loroux-Bottereau
Château de Goulaine
Haute-Goulaine Le Landreau
1 *Château de la Noé de Bel-Air*
Le Pé de Sèvre Vallet
Monnières Le Pallet Mouzillon
Clisson **2** Maine

Highlights

1 The Muscadet vineyards
2 Clisson, where the Loire meets Italy
3 Nantes' glamorous quarters and museums
4 St-Nazaire's startling maritime musuems
5 The high drama of the Loire's estuary at St-Nazaire

Nantes

We would go to the Pommeraye Arcade to buy Chinese shades, Turkish sandals or Nile baskets, to be able to take our time examining all the knick-knacks brought back here from overseas, to touch them with our own hands: the gods, the shoes, the parasols, the lanterns, the splendid, futile, colourful objects that make us dream of other worlds, useless frivolities which we take so seriously.

Gustave Flaubert

The cosmopolitan city that Flaubert conjured up still exists within the modern urban sprawl of Nantes. Nantes has an ocean feel to it – even if the Atlantic lies some 50km away, and even if most of the shipping trade that brought the place such riches in the Ancien Régime moved out towards the sea a long time ago. Despite the destruction of Second World War bombs, large portions of historic Nantes have survived, including the massive castle of the late medieval dukes of Brittany, the medieval cathedral where the last Breton duke was buried, and the grand streets and squares which the young Jules Verne would have known in his childhood.

The centre of Nantes shines brightly now. It's a delightful, vibrant, inspiring place, teeming with students in term time. However, a huge historical shadow casts its darkness over the place. The vast 18th-century wealth of the merchants of Nantes was built on the triangular slave trade. Clusters of ornate 18th-century town houses are the most obvious legacy. The finest are typically decorated with *mascarons*, appropriately grotesque stylized masks. To date, the slave-trading part of Nantes' past appears to have been almost totally ignored in the town museums, of which there are many. The best ones include the fine arts museum and the Musée Dobrée. It's somewhat ironic, given the city's forgetfulness about those slaving expeditions, that Nantes is best known in French history for a famous edict of tolerance, signed here by King Henri IV of France in 1598 at the end of the terrible French Wars of Religion.

History

The Gaulish tribe of the Namnetes had a port at the spot where the Erdre river joins the Loire. The Gaulish Pictones seem to have favoured the south bank. Few signs remain of Gallo-Roman Nantes, however. Christianity came early to the place, with its usual tale of cruel martyrdom. Donatien and Rogatien were the children of Aurlien, a Gallo-Roman governor of the town in the late Roman Empire, who converted to the new faith. Donatien had already been baptized, Rogatien had not, by the time the persecutors hounded them down at the very start of the 4th century. The imprisoned Rogatien is said to have uttered the tender words: 'If my brother, who is baptized, will deign to kiss me, his kiss will serve as a baptism for me.' The two were viciously tortured before having their heads cut off in 304. Christianity soon got the upper hand, however, the bishops of Nantes becoming powerful figures.

During much of the Dark Ages, the county of Nantes was fought over by Franks and Bretons. In Merovingian times, this county formed a part of the Frankish Marches. Nomenoë, appointed leader of Brittany by one Frankish king, made his successful bid for Breton independence under another. He conquered Nantes and its territories. But soon the Vikings sailed up the Loire to wreak havoc. Gohard, the bishop of Nantes of the time, had his throat cut at the cathedral altar.

In the Breton War of Succession in the mid-14th century, the city switched hands several times between the Penthièvres and the De Montforts. Nantes competed with Rennes as ducal capital through the later Middle Ages; under the De Montfort dukes, it got the upper hand. In the chaotic, war-torn, superstition-riddled first half of the 15th century, Gilles de Rais, or de Retz, became one of the most powerful and noto-rious Frenchmen of his age. He owned substantial estates south of Nantes and along the Loire, and he became a major figure at the French court under King Charles VII, where he is supposed to have sported a blue beard. Having fought alongside Joan of Arc, he was later accused of raping and murdering scores of young boys in his castles, using them in satanic rituals, including writing prayers to the devil in their blood. He may have been framed, but was certainly hanged and then burnt in Nantes, in 1440.

Under Duke François II, who was to be the last duke of Brittany, Nantes thrived as capital of that province. A prestigious university was inaugurated here in 1460, with the papacy's blessing. Duke François II's famed daughter, Duchess Anne de Bretagne,

L'Erdre

QUAI CEINERAY

PLACE
SALENGRO

RUE DU ROI ALBERT

RUE SULLY

RUE ST-ANDRÉ

COURS ST-ANDRÉ

PLACE M.
FOCH

RUE MARÉCHAL JOFFRE

St-Clément

RUE GAMBETTA

Chapelle de
l'Oratoire

Musée des
Beaux-Arts

RUE GEORGES CLEMENCEAU

RUE GAMBETTA

RUE S. BALDY

Jardin
des
Plantes

ÎLE DE STRASBOURG

RUE ST-DENIS

RUE DE VERDUN

PLACE
ST-PIERRE

COURS ST-PIERRE

RUE HENRI IV

Cathédrale
St-Pierre

RUE RODIER

Chapelle de
l'Immaculée
Conception

RUE DE RICHEBOURG

BOULEVARD DE STALINGRAD

To Angers,
Le Mans
& Paris

PLACE
PILORI

RUE DE LA JUIVERIE

RUE P. ÉCURIES

PLACE DE LA
DUCHESSE
ANNE

Château de
Nantes

COURS JOHN KENNEDY

Gare
SNCF

FFAY

RUEL

TRÉ

SQUARE ELISA
MERCŒUR

ALLÉE BACO

RUE CRUCY

Canal St-Félix

QUAI MALAKOFF

AVENUE CARNOT

RUE EMILE PÉHANT

RUE DE VALMY

Palais des
Congrès

PONT DE TBILISSI

Stade
Marcel Saupin

CHAUSS. DE LA MADELEINE

BD JEAN MONNET

RUE FOURÉ

RUE DES OLIVETTES

La Loire

PONT A. BRIAND

BD L. BARTHOU

QUAI MONCOUSU

QUAI MAGELLAN

PONT GAL. AUDIBERT

BD GASTON DOUMERGUE

ÎLE DE NANTES

To Jardin
des Cinq Sens

QUAI HOCHE

To Bordeaux

Getting There and Around

Nantes-Atlantique (t 02 40 84 80 00) is an international airport receiving flights from London-Gatwick. You can also fly to Nantes from Paris, but the super-fast TGV **train** is really more convenient as it amazingly takes you from one centre of town to the other in a mere 2hrs.

Tramway lines crisscross the centre of town, complementing the **bus** service (call **t** 02 40 29 39 39 for information on both).

Tourist Information

Tourist office: Office de Tourisme de Nantes Atlantique, 7 Rue de Valmy, 44041 Nantes Cedex, **t** 02 40 20 60 00, **f** 02 40 89 11 99, *office@nantes-tourisme.com*. The main tourist office is on Place du Commerce.

Market Days
Talensac: Tuesday to Sunday mornings.
Place Bouffay: Food market; Tuesday to Sunday mornings.
Place du Commerce: Flower market; daily.
Place de la Petite Hollande: Saturday morning.
Place Viarme: Flea market; Saturday morning.

Festivals
Many of Nantes' festivals have a distinctly cosmopolitan flavour. **La Folle Journée**, first weekend in February, concentrates on honouring the works of one or a school of composers. There is a big **carnival** every March. **Le Printemps des Arts** celebrates Baroque music and dance in venues across the area in April, May and June. The **Festival International d'Eté** features traditional folk music, dance and theatre from across the globe. It takes place the first week in July. **Nantes l'Eté** involves a whole programme of free cultural events, concerts and street entertainment throughout July and August.

All manner of boats and jazz musicians gather in Nantes for the **Rendez-Vous de l'Erdre**, the last weekend in August or first weekend in September.

The **Festival des Trois Continents** focuses on films from Africa, Asia and South America every November.

Where to Stay

Nantes ✉ 44000

Moderate
***La Pérouse, 3 Allée Duquesne, **t** 02 40 89 75 00, **f** 02 40 35 74 50. This is the most exciting hotel in Nantes, built in ultramodern style by architects Barto & Barto, with walls at gravity-defying angles – the best of modern design. The hotel is well located, close to the main shopping and restaurant quarters.
***Hôtel de France, 24 Rue Crébillon, **t** 02 40 73 57 91, **f** 02 40 69 75 75. The smartest of the old-style hotels in town, the rooms quite cosy (*menus €12–23*).
***Le Jules Verne, 3 Rue de Couëdic, **t** 02 40 35 74 50, **f** 02 40 20 09 35. A member of the reliable Best Western chain of hotels, in the heart of Nantes.

Inexpensive
***L'Astoria, 11 Rue de Richebourg, **t** 02 40 74 39 90, **f** 02 40 14 05 49. Large rooms reached by the fanciest of staircases behind its prewar façade.
***L'Hôtel, 6 Rue Henri IV, **t** 02 40 29 30 31, **f** 02 40 29 00 95. In a modern block right opposite the château, this has neat, good-value, comfortable if slightly characterless rooms.
Cholet, 10 Rue Gresset, **t 02 40 73 31 04, **f** 02 40 73 78 82. Close to the theatre, with pleasant recently renovated rooms which seem good value.

was born at the Château de Nantes in 1477. Nantes would remain a city close to her heart for all her life – and after it was over. She would marry two French kings in a row; the first, Charles VIII, she was wedded to at the Château de Langeais (*see* pp.315–17); the second, Louis XII, she married in the chapel of the Château de Nantes in 1499. Anne died at another château on the Loire, Blois, in 1514. While most of her

★★Les Colonies, 5 Rue du Chapeau Rouge, t 02 40 48 79 76, f 02 40 12 49 25. Quiet rooms close to the central pedestrian area of Nantes.

Cheap

★St-Daniel, 4 Rue du Bouffay, off Place du Bouffay, t 02 40 47 41 25, f 02 51 72 03 99. Extremely well located and good value for central Nantes.

★Fourcroy, 11 Rue Fourcroy, t 02 40 44 68 00. Basic, but in a posh part of town.

Auberge de Jeunesse, Cité Universitaire Internationale, 2 Place Manu, t 02 40 20 57 25 (you must present your youth hostelling card; beds €8–10). North out of the centre.

Eating Out

Central Nantes has a much wider choice of restaurants than of hotels. In summer, specially constructed restaurant terraces are built out into the streets, many of them covered with green baize like fake lawn.

Moderate

La Cigale, 4 Place Graslin, t 02 51 84 94 94. Not just a classic French brasserie, but a tourist site in itself for its outstanding and extravagant hundred-year-old Art Nouveau decor. It is set in one of Nantes' most elegant squares (menus c.€11.5–23).

Auberge du Château, 5 Place de la Duchesse Anne, t 02 40 74 31 85. An intimate little restaurant opposite the massive castle. It has a warm atmosphere in which to try classic Nantes food (menus €20–35).

Le Chiwawa, 17 Rue Voltaire, t 02 40 69 01 65. On a typically elegant Nantes square, this has a typical summer terrace and cosy dining rooms inside where Claude Vallée cooks up inventive dishes (menus c.€13–36.5).

L'Esquinade, 7 Rue Saint Denis, t 02 40 48 17 22. Traditional Loire gastro cuisine with

menus du marché and a speciality of sea bass cooked in potato skins (menus €15–33.5).

Le Galion – Les Boucaniers, 28 Rue Kervégan, t 02 40 47 68 83. Good French food in an atmospheric 18th century building. The set up here is a restaurant in one half and a more informal buffet in the other, serving rapide versions of the same food for a fraction of the price (menus €9–36.5).

Lou Pescadou, 8 Allée Baco, t 02 40 35 29 50. Serves tasty fish dishes (menus €13.5–45.5).

Le Carnivore, 7 Allée des Tanneurs, t 02 40 47 87 00. Traditional meat lovers might prefer this place, but might be surprised to see bison and ostrich meat on the menu (menus c.€9–39.5).

Cheap

La Poissonnerie, 4 Rue Léon Maître, t 02 49 47 79 50. A good fish restaurant which has a light, nautical look and aquarium inside (midday menu at c.€12).

L'Atlantide, 16 Quai Ernest-Renaud, t 02 40 73 23 23. Michelin-star Nantes cuisine from a chef who has returned to his roots with the benefiting influence of his travels. Roof-top view over Nantes and the Erdre (menus €22–53).

Chez l'Huître, 5 Rue des Petites Ecuries, t 02 51 82 02 02. A tiny green-check brasserie with fresh and fast seafood specialities served by an eccentric host. There's a little terrace and humorous blackboard drawings!

Ile Verte, 3 Rue Siméon Foucault, t 02 40 48 01 26. A rarity – French vegetarian food (menus €7.5–12).

Pommier Laprugne, 3 Allée de l'Ile Gloriette, t 02 40 47 78 08. A crêperie that serves up some interesting fillings.

La Baguett', 19 Rue Paul Bellamy, t 02 40 48 15 20. Almost a pastiche of the traditional Breton crêperie.

mortal remains were taken to the French royal resting place of the abbey of St-Denis, outside Paris, she had specifically asked for her heart to be returned to Nantes to be buried in the most gorgeous of inscribed gold reliquaries. Anne's daughter Claude de France was married to King François I, who organised Brittany's official union with France in 1532.

During the French Wars of Religion in the second half of the 16th century, Nantes fell under the control of the ultra-Catholic governor of Brittany, Philippe-Emmanuel de Lorraine, Duc de Mercœur, but at the end of the torments, the 1598 Edict of Nantes worked out by King Henri IV famously granted some freedom of worship for Protestants in France. At the close of the 17th century, King Louis XIV revoked the edict, rekindling the persecution of the Huguenots. In between times, Nantes was rapidly growing into one of the major French colonial ports.

Nantes and the Triangular Slave Trade

The most prosperous times for Nantes came with the acquisition of France's Caribbean colonies. By 1633, Guadeloupe and Martinique were in French hands. With the 1697 Treaty of Ryswick, France gained the western half of Santo Domingo (present-day Haiti), which became the most lucrative of all of France's colonies. Before long, Nantes was possibly the largest centre in Europe for the triangular slave trade, outstripping all others in the 18th century. The first leg of the journey took the ships from Nantes to the east African coast. Goods such as guns, powder, alcohol, jewellery, trinkets and cloth were exchanged with the local slave traders for the human cargo that filled the vessels on the second leg of the journey. The slaves had to undergo the crossing of the Atlantic in the most appalling and degrading conditions. The horror of their treatment is painful to conceive. Many slaves died on these journeys; those who survived were sold to the colonial plantation owners of the Caribbean in exchange for the precious goods other slaves were already busily helping to produce, notably sugar, coffee, cotton and indigo. On the third and final leg of the triangular journey, these luxuries were brought back to Europe.

Between 1715 and 1775, the return to port of 787 slave ships was registered in Nantes, half the number recorded for the whole of France. However, the sailing ships grew too large to travel right up to the city's quays. Much of the merchandise imported and exported was loaded and unloaded at Paimbœuf, west along the Loire. New industries developed in and around Nantes on the back of the Caribbean imports. Sugar was refined here to be sold across Europe. Cotton was turned into printed calico, known in French as *indiennes*, much of which went back to Africa to be bartered for more slaves.

Hugh Thomas, in his fascinating recent book *The Slave Trade*, gives many telling insights into the activities of the Nantes shipping merchants. Apparently, the Montaudoins held the ignoble record in Nantes slave-trading. Between 1694 and 1791, they equipped 357 ships for the triangular journeys. Far behind in second place, the De Luynes prepared some 182, and in third place came the Boutelhiers with 171. One of the most significant players was Antoine Walsh, an Irish Catholic immigrant, who organized some 57 slaving trips to Africa in the mid-18th century. With the backing of Parisian bankers, he set up the Société d'Angola, specializing in buying men from traders on the Loango coast. The company exported some 10,000 slaves in a mere seven years, but proved a financial failure as the Angolan slaves were considered inferior, less valuable workers to those bought from the Gold Coast.

Black African slaves became a common sight in wealthy Nantes households. Hugh Thomas describes the casual attitude some of the rich merchants had towards their human chattels: 'Slave merchants, living in their fine town houses...would give such "négrillons" or "négrittes" to members of their household as tips. In 1754, an ordonnance provided that colonials could bring into France only one black apiece. But that rule was often forgotten.'

From the end of the 17th century to the end of the 18th, Nantes' population doubled, from 40,000 to 80,000. The successful merchants, putting their sickening wealth to aesthetic use, built their grand town houses (known as *hôtels* in French) in the Louis XV and Louis XVI styles. A concentration of particularly fine mansions went up on the Ile Feydeau, then still an island. Hugh Thomas notes how 'the one-time slave-trading residents of the mansions on the Ile Feydeau, in the 1780s, sent their dirty linen to be laundered in Saint-Domingue [Santo Domingo] where the mountain streams were said to wash whiter than any in Brittany.' Many of the period houses there still survive, even if the Loire river has disappeared underground. Before the Revolution, in the second half of the 18th century, new town planning on a large scale was carried out across the centre of Nantes by the architect Ceineray. Grand streets, squares and perspectives were added to the city. The architect Mathurin Crucy was also influential around the time of the Revolution.

The Revolution banned the slave trade for a time. This was a catastrophe for many Nantes merchants, poor things. When the slaves of St Domingo rose up in revolt in 1791, the Nantes shipowners wrote in protest to the king. The terrifying Carrier was sent to Nantes by the Committee of Public Safety; his mission, to make some of the pig-headed royalists of Nantes wed the cause of the Revolution. The so-called 'republican marriages' were cruel mock ceremonies: the un-Revolutionary offenders were tied in pairs and bundled onto a boat with a hole in the bottom. The boat sank and the 'couples' drowned in the Loire. Charette, a nobleman from the Loire-Atlantique and one of the main leaders of the anti-Revolutionary, pro-Catholic and royalist Vendée uprising (*see* pp.450–51), led a desperate attack on Nantes in 1793. But it failed. Cathelineau, another of the heroes of the anti-Revolutionary cause, was mortally wounded in the battle. Charette was eventually executed in Nantes in 1796.

The arrest a few decades later of the pro-royalist Duchesse de Berry at the foot of the château after she had tried unsuccessfully to spark off another Vendée uprising was much more farcical. But a sign of renewed royalism in Nantes stands atop a column close to the château. It's a figure of King Louis XVI in Roman dress, the original statue inaugurated in 1823, 30 years after the royal had been executed.

Nantes Post-Slavery

Turner came to paint here and along the Loire in 1828, the year that Jules Verne was born. Rather less glamorously, the modern techniques of tinning fish were developed in Nantes at this time. Canning became a big industry in Brittany as a consequence, and played an important part in employment as well as culinary culture. The slave trade, reinstated after the Revolution, petered out in the middle of the 19th century.

Nantes' prosperity didn't entirely drain away after the Revolution, as you can see for example in the glamorous mid-19th century shopping arcade of the Passage Pommeraye. Although the main Loire estuary shipping activity had moved still further west from Paimbœuf to St-Nazaire, the import and export of goods along the train line to and from Nantes provided plenty of work. Trams started operating in town as early as 1874 and have recently been revived.

Aristide Briand, one of the major French political figures of the early 20th century, came from Nantes. He became general secretary of the French Socialist Party in 1901 and framed the extremely important bill separating the Church from the French State in 1905. In the turbulent times at the start of the last century he would serve as prime minister no fewer than 11 times. After the First World War, as part of the German war reparations, most of the seven channels of the Loire that had flowed through the city centre for so long were filled in by German workers. Aristide Briand continued to be a major political figure in France after the war, when with Jean Jaurès he founded the left-wing newspaper L'Humanité. From 1925 to 1932, he served as French foreign minister and worked hard for reconciliation and disarmament, proposing a form of United States of Europe. In 1926 he and the German foreign minister Gustav Stresemann were awarded the Nobel Peace Prize. Unfortunately their efforts would prove fruitless, although Aristide Briand can be considered one of the forefathers of the European Union. The Allied bombing raids on Nazi-occupied Nantes during the Second World War have left their scars, and the wide modern road artery through the centre, known as the Cour des 50 Otages, commemorates the execution of 50 hostages in 1942.

Postwar, several figures from the French art world have paid homage to Nantes, including the much-respected film-maker Jacques Demy, whose movie Lola was shot here, and the writer Julien Gracq, whose work La Forme d'une ville is devoted to the city. The university, closed at the Revolution, was reinstated in 1962, giving youth to the streets. High-tech industries have settled here. Nantes is close to the heart and stomach of many a French child, being a major centre of the French biscuit industry; this industry grew up to cater for the shipping expeditions. Many of France's best-known biscuit brands are still made here, while sugar from the Caribbean still arrives in Nantes in large quantities.

A Tour of Nantes

Nantes does not have an obvious heart, but several quarters that are worth exploring. The most obvious place to start is with the massive Château de Nantes.

Château de Nantes (Château des Ducs de Bretagne)

Open July–Aug daily 10–12 and 2–6, rest of year Wed–Mon 10–12 and 2–6.

This château is massive, forbidding and an architectural mess, to put it mildly. The thick dark outer walls enclose some slightly more graceful, whiter wings. A deep broad dry **moat**, where many Nantais now take their dogs for a walk, separates the

ramparts and their seven artillery towers from the surrounding boulevards, but origi-
nally the Loire lapped at the château's walls. The castle you see today, known as the
Château des Ducs de Bretagne, was in fact built in the main for the last duke of
Brittany and his daughter, although their forbears did have a castle on the spot.

This castle might be regarded as the most westerly of the châteaux of the Loire.
It might also be described as the least harmonious of them all. On entering the
enormous **inner courtyard** it's hard to know where to focus your attention, what with
the irregular shape of the site, the diversity of buildings from down the centuries, and
the miserable misleading alley of trees which goes nowhere in particular. The two
main wings of the castle show reasonably well the change from French late Gothic
architecture to French Renaissance forms so characteristic of the Loire châteaux of
the late 15th and early 16th centuries. The soaring vertical lines, the slight lack of
symmetry in the windows, and the ornate *lucarnes*, or dormer windows, fit the bill. In
the corner between the two main wings rises the **Tower of the Golden Crown**, light-
ened by Renaissance loggias high up. The name of the tower refers to the elaborate
covering on top of the well in front of it. This crown in wrought iron was once gilded
and was meant to represent the crown of the kings of Brittany of the Dark Ages.

The **Petit Gouvernement** is the small 16th-century building added for King François I
and covered with restored French Renaissance detail, such as the shells in the
dormers and the slate inlaid in the chimneys. The large rectangular building stranded
in the inner courtyard is the 18th-century **Bâtiment du Harnachement**. This is the
architectural equivalent of a sore thumb, but it reminds you of the fact that the
château served as an army camp from the beginning of the 18th century to the
start of the 20th. In between times, in 1800 to be precise, the military managed to
blow up a whole section of the castle by accident, including the chapel. You can
climb some of the castle ramparts, but the views of the roads and modern town
are disappointing.

The château used to house several museums. Now major work is under way to
create one single much grander museum, but this will not be ready until 2008. In the
meantime, temporary **exhibitions** will be held each year in the swishly restored
Harnachement building.

To the Cathedral of St-Pierre

From the château you might take the Rue Rodier (named after the man who
planned the castle for Duke François II) straight up to the front of the cathedral on
Place St-Pierre. Or if you prefer something a little grander, opt for the wide, mid-18th-
century boulevard of the Cours St-Pierre, running up from the Place de la Duchesse
Anne to the choir end of the cathedral. This Cours is of Parisian proportions and
elegance. It takes you to the imposing **Place Maréchal Foch**, where the column
commemorating King Louis XVI stands in the centre, traffic circling balletically round
it. The big building on the north side was where Napoleon stayed on a visit to Nantes
in 1808. The Hôtel Montaudoin, built for that infamously wealthy Nantes shipping
family, stands out, the family arms proudly showing. The grand Cours St-André, the
extension northwards of the Cours St-Pierre, leads to the Erdre boat station. Clashing

with the careful classical planning of the rest of the square, the massive Porte St-Pierre is a remnant of Nantes' 15th-century town walls, built on much earlier Gallo-Roman vestiges.

While the exterior of the bulky, squat **Cathédrale St-Pierre** looks rather grey, the inside is superbly white. This is the cleanest cathedral you're ever likely to see, and one of the emptiest. The interior had in fact to be restored and cleaned after a terrible fire in 1972. Only a few patches of humidity marks remain on certain pillars holding up the white Gothic arches. Some of the uncluttered monuments appear even whiter than the Loire limestone used in the building of this cathedral. Work began in 1434, financed by Jean V Duc de Bretagne and the bishop Jean de Malestroit. It was constructed on the site of the previous Romanesque cathedral, and possibly of Bishop Félix's 6th-century church. Only the Romanesque crypt under the present choir was kept from the previous structures. The 15th-century architects were Guillaume de Dommartin-sur-Yèvre and Mathelin Rodier. The building work would prove laborious and lengthy, but the façade was completed before the end of the 15th century and the towers were added by 1508. The nave and the aisles slowly went up in the 16th century, worship in the building only starting in 1577.

The major artistic interest within lies in the **tomb of François II** Duc de Bretagne and his two wives. This moving work is generally said to have been executed in the Tours workshops of the sculptor Michel Colombe between 1502 and 1507, although an Italian artist of great ability may have carried out some of the work. The two main effigies represent the duke and his second wife, Marguerite de Foix, mother of Anne de Bretagne. The large corner statues show personifications of Justice (thought to be a portrait of Anne de Bretagne), Fortitude, Temperance and Prudence, the last with its double-faced head, the one of a young woman, the other of an old man. This grand and beautiful tomb was commissioned by Anne de Bretagne. She asked for her heart to be placed in it after her death and her wish was granted. Another remarkably fine tomb in the cathedral dates from the 19th century. It was made by Paul Dubois in 1879, in honour of the formidably moustached military commander General Lamoricière. A Nantais by birth, he was celebrated for his role in the French taking of Algeria, and in particular for his capturing of the Algerian leader Abd-el-Kader. Almost all of the cathedral's original stained-glass windows have been destroyed by explosions and fire. Some striking modern ones have replaced them, for instance that above Duc François II's tomb, the figures representing Nantes and Breton saints.

The Rue du Roi Albert leads north from the cathedral square up to the **Préfecture**. This is Ceineray's classical masterpiece in the town, built from 1763. On the cathedral side, the arms of France have been sculpted in the pediment. On the side of the Erdre river, the arms of Brittany feature.

The best way to appreciate the beautiful Erdre river is on a **cruise**. The Gare Fluviale de l'Erdre from which the boats depart lies on the west bank of the river, near the Ile de Versailles. Contact Bateaux Nantais, **t** 02 40 14 51 14, *www.bateaux-nantais.fr*, for cruises on slick modern boats. They now operate a variety of different tours, including meals and cabaret performances, child-orientated cruises and floodlit tours of the Erdre's chateaux.

Musée des Beaux-Arts
Open Mon, Wed, Thurs, Sat 10–6; Fri 10–9; Sun 11–6.

The splendid Nantes fine arts museum lies on the other side of Cours St-Pierre from the cathedral. Allegorical statues on the façade represent the arts; architecture, with temple and measuring rod in hands is represented over the main entrance. The museum building is a beautiful, cleanly planned work by the architect Josso, built in 1900 for the elevating educational purposes of the French Third Republic. The founding collection was actually donated to the town a century earlier, in 1801, or the Year IX as it was known under the Consulate; this was one of 15 major provincial museums set up around France after the Revolution. Some of the works came from war booty. Another large number arrived in 1810 from the collections of the Cacault brothers and their lovely Italianate villa in Clisson, southeast of Nantes. They had been on a wild art shopping spree in Italy in the late 18th century. Further generous 19th-century donations and the 20th-century legacy of Gildas Fardel added to the riches on display. If you want a crash course in the history of Western art from 13th-century religious works to present-day conceptual projects, this would be as fine a place as any to come. The 19th- and 20th-century collections are exceptionally good.

The galleries are very neatly set out on two levels, around an arcaded courtyard. This courtyard is even whiter and brighter than the interior of the cathedral. Twentieth-century work is given pride of place on the ground floor. The patio at the centre of the museum is often put to good use for contemporary exhibitions. The upper storey takes you round from the Italian Early Masters to the end of the 19th century in France. The chronological sequence is easy to follow.

There are so many masterpieces in the museum that it isn't possible to single them all out here. Among the highlights, of the three famous De la Tours held by the museum, two show his archetypal candlelit effects cast on waxen faces and figures. The best pieces from the 18th century include a typical Watteau inspired by commedia dell'arte – *Arlequin, Empereur de la Lune* – several Greuzes, and a whole series of portraits of rich families by Tournières. Gros's work *Le Combat de Nazareth* was an early 19th-century piece which had a profound effect on Delacroix and has been viewed as a precursor of the Romantic movement. The same room contains two exceptional sculptures, one by Canova of Pope Clement XIII; the other, by Ceracchi, of Washington. Ingres' *Madame de Senonnes* of 1814 is another of the major pieces.

Courbet's *Les Cribleuses de Blé* counts as one of the most famous works of the second half of the 19th century in the museum. There is a fair representation of wildly over-the-top, sickly French Romanticism for you to be revolted by too. You might view with some irony, given Nantes' history, *L'Esclave blanche* (The White Slave) by Lecomte du Nouy. *Le Sorcier Noir* by Herbert Ward shows a typical European vision of the black man as witch. On the ground floor, while Monet takes you off to Venice and the otherwordly visions of his *Nymphéas*, Emile Bernard's *Le Gaulage des pommes* depicts a typically Breton landscape in the style of the Pont-Aven school. Local artist

Metzinger gives a Pointilliste interpretation of the Château de Clisson. A whole room is devoted to Kandinsky's abstract work, while Chagall's *Le Cheval Rouge* is a typical piece by that great artist. You can interpret some of the thought-provoking conceptual art on display as seriously or comically as the mood takes you. Raymond Hains, a well-known conceptual artist, pays homage to the Nantes biscuit industry via a barcode.

The pretty **Jardin des Plantes** lies at the eastern end of the Rue Clemenceau, beyond the fine arts museum.

The Bouffay Quarter

Make your way back to the very centre of historic Nantes; west of the castle lies the Bouffay quarter. The tightly packed network of old streets makes this the liveliest and most charming part of old Nantes. The area is mainly pedestrian, taking you away from the terrible city traffic. Several street names recall the medieval activities along them, but only a few timberframe houses remain from the 15th and 16th centuries. In the Ancien Régime, grander town houses were built here in what became the lawyers' quarter in particular. Nowadays, this is a neighbourhood of chic boutiques, restaurants and apartments.

Wandering around you will come across several little squares. The **Place du Pilori** served for executions and other public punishments until the Place Bouffay took over that role. **Place Bouffay** now plays host to a lively and smelly daily fish market. The former town belfry has been affixed to the **church of Ste-Croix** in Place Ste-Croix nearby. The church is a quirky mix of architectural styles. Angels trumpet out the Christian message from the top of the belfry.

North of Rue de la Marne and Rue de la Barillerie (the two forming one of the main shopping arteries in Nantes), several further elegant-looking streets lead to the town hall, for instance those leading north from the **Place du Change**, once the hub of historic Nantes. The **Hôtel de Ville** (town hall) is a mix of 17th-century mansions and modernity.

Ile Feydeau

On the opposite side of the Allées from Place Bouffay, the Ile Feydeau was once an exclusive residential island on the Loire. It's now sadly isolated by wide roads. This is where some of the very grandest Nantes shipowners had their town houses and offices from the mid-18th century. You can only really get a good impression of their wealth by wandering along the **Rue Kervégan**. The finest features on the façades are the grotesque Baroque masks, or *mascarons*, carved above the windows, each one showing a different grimacing face. Look out, too, for the wrought-iron balconies and the interior staircases.

Squares and Museums West of the Cours des 50 Otages

To the west of the broad curving Cours des 50 Otages lie many elegant squares and streets from the late 18th and early 19th centuries. More chic shops line many of the streets. The Rue d'Orléans leads to **Place Royale**. This sober-sided square was planned by the architect Crucy. Personifications of certain of the Loire's tributary rivers adorn the granite fountain in this square.

Just to the northeast of Place Royale lie the **Place Fournier** and the **Basilique St-Nicolas**. The latter is a neo-Gothic church from the mid-19th century, its soaring spire reaching 85m in height. A fair way further north rises the much taller **Tour de Bretagne**, Nantes' isolated central skyscraper, visible from afar as you approach the city. A modern shopping and business precinct surrounds it.

South of the Place Royale, a wonderful array of cafés lines up opposite the **Bourse** on Place du Commerce. The Bourse, or exchange building, with its impressive row of monumental Ionic columns, was again planned by Crucy and completed in 1812 . A few of the original statues of famous Breton sailors (some notorious corsairs in fact) remain in place. The Loire used to flow by here and the quay was reserved for the Nantais wine trade. Now it's the domain of the beautiful, trendy student set who come here to forget about their studies.

The **Passage Pommeraye**, Nantes' most elegant shopping arcade, heads up to Rue Crébillon from Rue de la Fosse. You won't find Passage Pommeraye as exotic as Flaubert did in his day, but the mid-19th-century sweeps of stairs have a kitsch romance to them. Rue Crébillon links Place Royale with the more serious **Place Graslin** to the west. This square was again planned by Crucy. It's dominated by the theatre, which saw its first performance in 1788. Statues of muses stand on top of the Corinthian columns. The **Cours Cambronne**, off the southwest corner of Place Graslin, could hardly be more refined.

Musée Thomas Dobrée and Manoir de la Touche

Open Tues–Sun exc public hols 10–12 and 1.30–5.30.

The golden reliquary for the heart of Anne de Bretagne stands on public display in this museum. Little can the last duchess of Brittany have imagined that it would one day be on view for all to see. It's the most striking piece of fine craftsmanship in a museum crammed with the finest stonework, woodwork and enamel work. Thomas Dobrée was a dedicated collector through the 19th century, the son of an extremely wealthy industrialist and shipowner. Among other objects, he amassed sculptures, paintings, furniture, art objects, manuscripts, and correspondence from royals, nobles and literary figures in an obsessive manner. He decided to build a grand house in which to install these collections, next to the Manoir de la Touche. Dobrée even oversaw much of the construction work on this building, with its neo-Romanesque look. It was built in brown-bear coloured stone, with figures of carved bears added onto the corners. Dobrée also had the Manoir de la Touche restored. This manor had been constructed for Bishop Jean de Malestroit as his country retreat outside the city walls at the start of the 15th century. It later served as a Huguenot hospital in the Wars of Religion and from 1695 until the Revolution as a religious refuge for Irish priests who had been driven out of their country.

The museum contains religious sculptures of great beauty. You can observe close up several huge statues originally made for Nantes' cathedral front, carved in Loire tufa, and a collection of Romanesque capitals with some weird grotesque faces. A magnificent length of wooden stringbeam shows a bizarre mix of particularly graceful faces and crudely gesturing figures. Among the exquisite medieval church ceremonial objects on display, the collection of enamel-decorated *pyxides* from the Limousin stand out, as do various encrusted altar crosses, the reliquary of St-Calminius and a staurothique, a reliquary for a fragment of the True Cross. As well as admiring some beautiful and significant old manuscripts, you can also see an extensive collection of ornate weapons.

The Manoir de la Touche contains a mixed bag of collections. The ground floor is devoted to Nantes at the time of the Revolution. Upstairs are archaeological finds from around the Loire-Atlantique, including some interesting Bronze Age, Celtic, Gallo-Roman and Merovingian pieces.

Jules Verne's Museum and Other Specialist Museums in Nantes

Nantes has at least another half-dozen smaller museums. The **Muséum** (*open Tues–Sat 10–12 and 2–5, Sun 10–12, closed public hols*), east of the Musée Dobrée on Rue Voltaire, is Nantes' respected natural history museum. Nearby, down on the quays with the modern Médiathèque, the **Musée de l'Imprimerie** (*open Wed and Sat 10–12 and 2–6; Tues, Thurs and Fri 2–6; closed Aug; 24 Quai de la Fosse*) covers the development of printing in the region, with an impressive collection of old printing presses. Looking further west along the Quai de la Fosse, it's hard to miss the **Maillé Brézé** (*open June–Sept daily 2–6; rest of year Wed, weekends and school hols 2–5*), a decommissioned naval squadron escort vessel which has been turned into a museum. Enthusiastic guides race up and down the decks showing you the nooks and crannies of the ship.

Head west for the Ste-Anne quarter, on a hill, and there you'll find a further cluster of sights. The little **Musée Jules Verne** (*open Mon and Wed–Sat 10–12 and 2–5, Sun 2–5, closed public hols; 3 Rue de l'Hermitage, t 02 40 69 72 52*) pays its respects to the great French visionary 19th-century science fiction writer from Nantes with old editions, posters and topical displays, and has recently been redecorated to modern effect. Jules Verne was the author of such worldwide classics as *Le Tour du monde en quatre-vingt jours* (*Around the World in Eighty Days*), *Voyage au centre de la terre* (*Journey to the Centre of the Earth*) and *Vingt Mille Lieues sous les mers* (*Twenty Thousand Leagues Under the Sea*). You can easily imagine what an inspiration cosmopolitan Nantes must have been to him, even if it hardly features in his writing. Americans might also particularly enjoy his *De la Terre à la lune* (*From the Earth to the Moon Direct in 97 Hours 20 Minutes*), an hilarious story about Americans competing to becoming the first men on the moon – but in the 19th century! It seems appropriate enough that the **Planétarium** (*showings Mon–Fri at 10.30, 2.15 and 3.45, Sun at 3 and 4.30, closed Sat and public hols; 8 Rue des Acadiens, t 02 40 73 99 23*) should stand close by, presenting the skies and constellations.

The **Musée des Compagnons du Devoir**, in the Manoir de la Hautière in the same area (*open Sat 2–6; 14 Rue Guillon Verne, t 02 40 69 30 55*), presents masterpieces by

French master craftsmen. Some distance north, the **Musée de la Poste** (*open Mon–Fri 9–12 and 2–4; 10 Bd Auguste Pageot, by the Parc de Procé*) is dedicated to the French postal services down the centuries.

The **Parc de Procé** is another of what the French call an 'English garden', that is, not as formal as a French garden. This one has collections of rhododendrons, fuchsias, dahlias and magnolias.

South Across the Loire

On the **Ile de Nantes**, a hard-working island just south of the historic city, you might sniff out the **Jardin des Cinq Sens**, a garden which plays on the five senses with its different-textured paths and its musical fountain. Head right around the western tip of the island and you come to an astonishing industrial landscape of hills of scrap metal.

Cross south from the Ile de Beaulieu for **Rezé**, which had a Gallo-Roman settlement like Nantes, but which is known nowadays for its modern architecture. The most famous piece in town is **Le Corbusier**'s crumbling cement experiment in new urban living, the *unité d'habitation de grandeur conforme*, or **Cité Radieuse**, now looking shaky on its stilts. It was built in the mid-1950s to provide a new concept in council housing. The striking curve of Rezé's modern town hall was conceived by the Romanian architect Anselmi.

Following the Loire bank west from the centre of Rezé, you hit upon the roughly charming old fishermen's village of **Trentemoult**, to which many Nantes captains used to retire, often planting exotic trees and shrubs in their little gardens.

Muscadet Vineyards Southeast of Nantes

The Loire-Atlantique makes one very well-known wine, Muscadet, confusingly produced from a grape variety called Melon de Bourgogne. Although much good Muscadet is produced, the region has received a bit of a bashing in the press over recent years for failing to maintain quality across the board.

A good place to start touring the Muscadet vineyards is the Maison des Vins de Nantes at **La Haye-Fouassière** (*open weekdays 8.30–12.30 and 2–5.45, July and Aug daily 10.30–12.30 and 2.30–6*), overlooking hectare upon hectare of vines. You can taste a wide selection of Muscadets here and get general information on the wines of the Loire-Atlantique. If you wish to visit a winery, it's always wise to telephone in advance to see if you can fix a time.

Also near La Haye-Fouassière, the **Domaine Bonneteau-Guesselin** (*t 02 40 54 80 38*) has a welcoming ivy-covered courtyard. Here Olivier Bonneteau, young, eloquent and very pleasant, will give you a good introduction to Muscadet and his characterful wines, which he makes to have a strong impact and good aromas.

Getting Around

Trains go down through the Muscadet area to Clisson, and there are bus services around this area from Nantes.

Tourist Information

Le Pallet: 26 Rue St-Vincent, Le Pallet, t 02 40 80 40 24, f 02 40 80 42 48.
Clisson: 6 Place de la Trinité, Clisson 44190, t 02 40 54 02 95, f 02 40 54 07 77.

Where to Stay and Eat

St-Fiacre-sur-Maine ✉ 44690
Le Fiacre, 1 Rue des Echicheurs, t 02 40 54 83 92. You'll eat with loads of locals at this lively, simple village bistrot-cum-bar. The *patron* is passionate about Muscadet and has a list of over 100 different producers' wines.

Château-Thébaud ✉ 44690
Domaine de la Pénissière, t 02 40 06 51 22 (*inexpensive*). Offering smart B&B rooms in

an atmospheric old house set on a wine estate on the opposite bank of the Maine, with good views of the vineyards (*table d'hôte €12*).
Le Petit Douet, t 02 40 06 53 59 (*inexpensive*). Run by Thérèse Méchineau, a vine-grower's wife who provides wine books and wine conversation in her modern B&B (*table d'hôte c.€13.5*).

Monnières ✉ 44690
Château de Plessis-Blézot , t 02 40 54 63 24, f 02 40 54 66 07, a.calonne@online.fr (*moderate*). Little 17th-century property set above the Sèvre Nantaise at Monnières. A reputed wine domain and a luxury B&B.

Clisson ✉ 44190
La Bonne Auberge, 1 Rue Olivier de Clisson, t 02 40 54 01 90. Stylish gastronomic restaurant (*menus c.€18–47*).
Restaurant de la Vallée, 1 Rue de la Vallée, t 02 40 54 36 23 (*menus c.€13–20*). Delightfully located over the river with a summer dining terrace. Recently come under new ownership, the *salle* has been completely redone, and the cooking is fresh – good local fish.

Among some recommendations of other good Muscadet vineyards to see, if you're looking for a spectacular property, try the **Château de Goulaine** (*t 02 40 54 91 42; open 15 June–15 Sept, daily Wed–Mon 2–6; otherwise Easter–Oct weekends and public hols 2–6*), both a reputed Muscadet-producing estate and an historic castle you can visit just east of Haute-Goulaine, relatively close to the southeastern suburbs of Nantes. The history of the family of Goulaine goes back almost one thousand years. A beautiful new château arose in the last two decades of the 15th century. The present marquis, Robert de Goulaine, a crime and wine writer as well as a promoter of his beloved Muscadet, is described as the eleventh one in a row. Inside the château you only see a small number of rooms, but they are sumptuously decorated.

Or try the **Château du Coing** (*t 02 40 54 81 15 for an appointment*), by St-Fiacre-sur-Maine. The vineyards lie on some of the prettiest slopes in the Muscadet region. The place, a true château, has impressive cellars where you can sample the wines. The winemaker is Véronique Günther Chéreau, a member of a well-known Muscadet-making family. She is willing to experiment with her wines, ageing some in barrel since 1986. Among other major producers, the **Château de la Galissonnière** (*t 02 40 80 42 03*), by Le Pallet, is well known and well used to receiving foreign visitors. With attractive cellars around a courtyard, this place has links with a French admiral and botanist who served as governor of Quebec in the 18th century. De la Galissonnière supposedly planted the first magnolia in Europe here. The **Château du Cléray** (*t 02 40 36 22 55*), by Vallet, is less attractive to look at, but it is run by one of the families with the best reputations in Muscadet country, the Sauvions. (Just north of Vallet, you might like to visit the grounds of the 19th-century **Château de la Noé de Bel Air**, with its follies and English-style gardens as well as its vineyard. The place is still owned by the Malestroit family, descendants of the bishop of Nantes who started the cathedral and presided over the court which condemned Bluebeard to death.)

Among lesser-known addresses, you might try the **Domaine des Perrières** (*t 02 40 03 92 14*), at Mouzillon, south of Vallet or due east of Le Pallet. This is a clean, relatively small-scale winery set by a modern house. The grapes are still harvested by hand and brought to the wine vats set in the ground. Many of the wines have a good length to them, as well as being fruity. Mouzillon also has a charming Gallo-Roman bridge.

Christophe Maillard (*t 02 40 80 44 92*) is a charming Vigneron-Récoltant with some very good Muscadet Sèvre and Maine Sur Lie, and Gros-Plant. He is based near Le Pallet at Le Pé-de-Sèvre. Sale and tasting is on site, sitting on top of the underground vats of wine. Between Le Loroux-Bottereau and Vallet, at Le Landreau, the Couillauds at the **Domaine du Haut Planty** (*t 02 40 06 42 76*) produce good wine and one of the Madame Couillauds can greet you in English, being American.

There's an excellent book, *Découvertes en terroir du Muscadet*, published by Ouest-France for the wine and tourist authorities of the Loire-Atlantique, which introduces some 200 Muscadet vineyards you can visit, as well as providing much more historical and practical information on the region's wines.

Clisson

Clisson is the town where Brittany and Italy meet, although the feudal **Château de Clisson** (*open Wed–Mon 9.30–12 and 2–6*) looks French enough. Its ruins dominate the slopes of the valley where the Maine joins the Sèvre Nantaise. The church and town, however, look as though they've been shipped straight from Italy. Clisson was devastated by the Vendée uprising (*see pp.450–51*), and what arose afterwards was the work of Pierre and François Cacault of Nantes and their friend, the sculptor Frédéric Lemot. All had travelled in Italy and they decided to build Roman-style homes. The church of **Notre-Dame** is typical of Clisson's Italianate style, with a *campanile*. From the Pont de la Vallée bridge you get beautiful views.

The wonderful Italianate villa of **La Garenne-Lemot** and its park (*park open April–Sept daily 9–8, Oct–Mar daily 9.30–6.30; Maison du Jardinier open Tues–Sun 10–1 and 2–6; villa open during exhibitions*) lie on the other bank of the Sèvre Nantaise. Frédéric Lemot, best known for his statue of Henri IV on the Pont-Neuf in Paris, bought La Garenne in 1805. The Maison du Jardinier is built in rustic Italian style and houses an exhibition that ranges widely over the Italian influence on French artistic circles in the 18th century. The villa is reached by a garden lined with statues, its front courtyard formed by a semicircle of granite columns. The house contains Lemot's prize-winning sculpture, the *Judgement of Solomon*, while the grounds offer a treasure hunt of follies.

The Loire from Nantes to St-Nazaire

The north bank of the Loire from Nantes to St-Nazaire is heavily industrial, and unless you're on a specialist industrial tour of the Loire, you're unlikely to find it appealing. The **south bank** offers a more appealing route to St-Nazaire, passing via the once-bustling port of **Paimbœuf**. The scene here is very, very flat indeed. Small boats congregate in what was once a substantial French port. Paimbœuf knew much more lively days in slave-trading times. As ships grew in size through the 18th century, this became the important stop where much merchandise was transferred onto smaller vessels to be taken upstream to Nantes. Apparently, Jules Verne came to Paimbœuf to dream of sailing to the Indies. Now the unpretentious, unhurried harbour streets can induce the most soporific daydreaming.

St-Nazaire

Hard hit by war bombs, hard hit by the recent decline of shipbuilding in western Europe, traditionally hard hit by guidebooks, St-Nazaire does in fact have plenty of character. And it has cleverly turned its attentions to tourism in recent years. The famed St-Nazaire shipbuilding yards were developed from the 1860s on, at first in association with the Scottish company of John Scott. Penhoët, in the east of town, was chosen as the site for the shipyards. The ship *L'Impératrice Eugénie* was the first to be built there, during the French Second Empire. St-Nazaire became one of the major European ports to operate transatlantic services. Many sailed off from here to seek a new life in the Americas. During the First World War, thousands of North American soldiers arrived here before being sent out to the front.

The supposedly glorious ship-building period came between the two world wars. The most famous of France's massive ocean liners were built here, the *Paris*, the *Ile-de-France*, the *Champlain* and, most impressive of the lot, the misleadingly named *Normandie*, launched in 1932. But this was also a time of major world economic recession. The shipyard workers suffered terribly from the cyclical nature of their work, and in 1933 went on an important hunger march to Nantes. Between the wars, the port stretched ever further east.

Most notoriously, when the Nazis occupied France, they turned St-Nazaire into one of their most important submarine bases. St-Nazaire was also the only French Atlantic port large enough to take German battleships. The town became a crucial target for the British air force to wipe out; operation Chariot in 1942 wrought much damage. Several of the major St-Nazaire ocean liners were destroyed in the war. As for the *Normandie*, requisitioned by the US government during the conflict, it caught fire and sank in New York harbour in 1942. Intensive bombing of St-Nazaire continued into 1943, but the Nazis hung on doggedly to this vital harbour. While most of France was liberated in the summer of 1944, St-Nazaire was one of the pockets of territory which the Nazis defended right through to May 1945 and the end of the Second World War in Europe. By then, St-Nazaire lay in ruins, 80 per cent destroyed.

Getting There

St-Nazaire has a **train** station. For information about **buses** around the area, call **t** 02 40 11 53 00.

Tourist Information

Tourist office: Office de Tourisme, Place François Blancho, B.P.178, 44613 St-Nazaire Cedex, **t** 02 40 22 40 65, **f** 02 40 22 19 80.

Market Days

Daily except Monday.

Eating Out

St-Nazaire ✉ **44613**
L'An Deux, 2 Rue Villebois Mareuil, **t** 02 40 00 95 33. Serves good food in an Art Deco dining room with spectacular views onto the mouth of the Loire (*menus €15–44*).

The town was rapidly rebuilt along a grid plan in the 1950s, and naval and aeronautical construction took off again. The ocean liner the *France* is the most glamorous vessel to have been built here since the war, although cruise ships are still made in the yards east of town. The stunning bridge across the mouth of the Loire from St-Nazaire to Mindin was inaugurated in 1975 and was at the time the longest bridge in France.

Escal' Atlantic

Open July–Aug 9.30–12.30 and 1–7, nocturnal visits on Tues and Sat; April–June and Sept–Oct 9.30–12.30 and 2–6; Feb–Mar and Nov–Dec Wed–Sun 10–12.30 and 2–6.

The glamour of the *paquebot*, or ocean liner, inspired the gargantuan new enterprise of Escal' Atlantic. Inside a massive hangar at the former German submarine base, this 'floating city' is quite unlike most sea museums. Dispensing with the tradition of inhabiting a crabby old authentic vessel, here you enter an entirely recreated world of the ocean liner – all 3,500 sq m of it – made with the aid of top architects and theatre set designers. The project was 17 years in the planning, so the appearance of the film *Titanic* a few years ago must have been the happiest of coincidences.

Every conceivable part of a liner is supposedly represented, including the hair salon, the emigrants' quarters and the engine room, and everywhere are bits of complementary movie footage (excerpts from the era's biggies that have only the vaguest connection to the ocean liner) on porthole screens. You get a fascinating idea of the cabins of each era, including the 1860s Jules Verne model, complete with *vomitoire*. The set design is at its most impressive inside the bar and dining room. Your tour should end inside the movie theatre, where more multimedia japes will have you swaying (forcibly) in your seats to archive film footage. If you're not feeling involved enough, the journey back to the real world requires the donning of a life jacket and a slightly hair-raising proximity to water, so you've been warned.

On coming out and regaining your senses, it's worth taking a moment to nip up to the roof of the submarine base. Apart from affording a great viewing point of the area, it's grimly fascinating to see how this last Nazi stronghold was designed to be bomb-proof, with its ugly great skin of concrete pimples.

The Ecomusée and the Espadon Submarine

Open July–Aug 9.30–12.30 and 1–7, nocturnal visits on Tues and Sat;
April–June and Sept–Oct 9.30–12.30 and 2–6; Feb–Mar and Nov–Dec
Wed–Sun 10–12.30 and 2–6.

The town museum and submarine make for quite an engrossing visit, too. Outside, a moving sculptural group, *A l'Abolition de l'Esclavage*, put up in 1991 by the sculptor J-C. Mayo, recalls the slave trade that brought such wealth to the Loire estuary in the 18th century (*see* pp.470–71) and remembers the importance of the abolition of slavery.

The Ecomusée retells the prehistory and history of St-Nazaire, while the guided tour around the *Espadon* is a unique experience in France. The submarine lies in the water in a heavily fortified concrete lock built by the Nazis in 1943. It was donated to the town in 1986, having served the French navy for 25 years. Built in Le Havre in 1957, the *Espadon* became the first French submarine to cross the North Pole under the ice fields, in 1964. Some 60 sailors lived down here for up to 45 days at a time. Just a half-hour visit can make you feel claustrophobic. If you're lucky the guided tour will be given by a man who did his military service on board a submarine.

You might consider proceeding to one of the port's 'working' museums. The **Chantiers de l'Atlantique** offers you the chance to explore the actual construction of the ocean liners by stepping on board the *Alstom*. More industrial terrain is explored at **Aerospatiale**, essentially a massive aircraft factory where you can see St-Nazaire's technological industry in action. (*Both open summer season and school hols daily, four to six visits a day, and low season by reservation; t 0810 888 444 for reservations and information on all the port's sites.*)

From the Centre to the Sea

In the **centre of town**, a slick shopping centre has been built to mimic some of the forms of an ocean liner. You could go in search of the Place du Dolmen, too, actually boasting a neolithic menhir and lech as well as the table of stone.

To the west of the centre, St-Nazaire has a long **sea front** which turns its back on the docks and looks out to the ocean. It is an interesting stretch of coast. Along Bd Président Wilson, some 19th-century villas survived the bombs. Further west you come to a string of beaches which are comfortably wide at low tide. Curious *carrelets*, square fishing nets left suspended in the air while not in action, add a picturesque note, as do the lighthouses. Some of the best beaches in Brittany lie just to the west, but they're covered in the Cadogan guide to Brittany.

To the south of the Loire estuary, the flat beaches are more typical of the Vendéen coast. To reach them you have to cross St-Nazaire's splendid serpent of a bridge, which provides a spectacular ending to the Loire.

Language

Everywhere in France the same level of politeness is expected: use *monsieur, madame* or *mademoiselle* when speaking to everyone (and never *garçon* in restaurants!), from your first *bonjour* to your last *au revoir*.
See pp.75–9 for menu vocabulary.

Pronunciation

Vowels

a, à, â between *a* in 'bat' and 'part'
é, er, ez at end of word as *a* in 'plate' but a bit shorter
e, è, ê as *e* in 'bet'
e at end of word not pronounced
e at end of syllable or in one-syllable word pronounced weakly, like *er* in 'mother'
i as *ee* in 'bee'
o as *o* in 'pot'
ô as *o* in 'go'
u, û between *oo* in 'boot' and *ee* in 'bee'

Vowel Combinations

ai as *a* in 'plate'
aî as *e* in 'bet'
ail as *i* in 'kite'
au, eau as *o* in 'go'
ei as *e* in 'bet'
eu, œu as *er* in 'mother'
oi between *wa* in 'swam' and *wu* in 'swum'
oy as 'why'
ui as *wee* in 'twee'

Nasal Vowels

Vowels followed by an **n** or **m** have a nasal sound.
an, en as *o* in 'pot' + nasal sound
ain, ein, in as *a* in 'bat' + nasal sound
on as *aw* in 'paw' + nasal sound
un as *u* in 'nut' + nasal sound

Consonants

Many French consonants are pronounced as in English, but there are some exceptions:

c followed by *e, i* or *y*, and *ç* as *s* in 'sit'
c followed by *a, o, u* as *c* in 'cat'
g followed by *e, i* or *y* as *s* in 'pleasure'
g followed by *a, o, u* as *g* in 'good'
gn as *ni* in 'opinion'
j as *s* in 'pleasure'
ll as *y* in 'yes'
qu as *k* in 'kite'
s between vowels as *z* in 'zebra'
s otherwise as *s* in 'sit'
w except in English words as *v* in 'vest'
x at end of word as *s* in 'sit'
x otherwise as *x* in 'six'

Stress

The stress usually falls on the last syllable except when the word ends with an unaccented *e*.

Vocabulary

General

hello *bonjour*
good evening *bonsoir*
good night *bonne nuit*
goodbye *au revoir*
please *s'il vous plaît*
thank you (very much) *merci (beaucoup)*
yes *oui*
no *non*
good *bon (bonne)*
bad *mauvais*
excuse me *pardon, excusez-moi*
My name is... *Je m'appelle...*
What is your name? *Comment t'appelles-tu?* (informal), *Comment vous appelez-vous?* (formal)
How are you? *Comment allez-vous?*
Fine *Ça va bien*

I don't understand *Je ne comprend pas*
I don't know *Je ne sais pas*

Could you speak more slowly? *Pourriez-vous parler plus lentement?*
Can you help me? *Pourriez-vous m'aider?*
How do you say ... in French? *Comment dit-on ... en français?*
Help! *Au secours!*

WC *les toilettes*
men *hommes*
ladies *dames* or *femmes*
drinking water *eau potable*
non-drinking water *eau non potable*

doctor *le médecin*
hospital *un hôpital*
emergency room *la salle des urgences*
police station *le commissariat de police*
tourist information office *l'office de tourisme*

No Smoking *Défense de fumer*

Shopping and Sightseeing

Do you have...? *Est-ce que vous avez...?*
I would like... *J'aimerais...*
Where is/are...? *Où est/sont...*
How much is it? *C'est combien?*
It's too expensive *C'est trop cher*

entrance *l'entrée*
exit *la sortie*
open *ouvert*
closed *fermé*
push *poussez*
pull *tirez*

bank *une banque*
money *l'argent*
traveller's cheque *un chèque de voyage*
post office *la poste*
stamp *un timbre*
phone card *la télécarte*
postcard *une carte postale*
public phone *une cabine téléphonique*
Do you have any change? *Avez-vous de la monnaie?*

shop *un magasin*
covered food market *les halles*
tobacconist *un tabac*
pharmacy *la pharmacie*
aspirin *l'aspirine*
condoms *les préservatifs*

insect repellent *crème anti-insecte*
sun cream *la crème solaire*
tampons *les tampons hygiéniques*

beach *la plage*
booking/box office *le bureau de location*
church *l'église*
museum *le musée*
sea *la mer*
theatre *le théâtre*

Accommodation

Do you have a room? *Avez-vous une chambre?*
Can I look at the room? *Puis-je voir la chambre?*
How much is the room per day/week? *La chambre coûte combien par jour/semaine?*
single room *une chambre pour une personne*
twin room *une chambre à deux lits*
double room *une chambre pour deux personnes*
... with a shower/bath *... avec douche/salle de bains*
... for one night/one week *... pour une nuit/une semaine*

bed *un lit*
blanket *une couverture*
cot (child's bed) *un lit d'enfant*
pillow *un oreiller*
soap *du savon*
towel *une serviette*

Directions

Where is...? *Où se trouve...?*
left *à gauche*
right *à droite*
straight on *tout droit*

here *ici*
there *là*
close *proche* or *près*
far *loin*
forwards *en avant*
backwards *en arrière*
up *en haut*
down *en bas*
corner *le coin*
square *la place*
street *la rue*

Transport

I want to go to... *Je voudrais aller à...*
How can I get to...? *Comment puis-je aller à...?*
When is the next...? *Quel est le prochain...?*
What time does it leave (arrive)? *A quelle heure part-il (arrive-t-il)?*
From where does it leave? *D'où part-il?*
Do you stop at...? *Passez-vous par...?*
How long does the trip take? *Combien de temps dure le voyage?*

A (single/return) ticket to... *un aller* or *aller simple/aller et retour) pour...*
How much is the fare? *Combien coûte le billet?*
Have a good trip! *Bon voyage!*

airport *l'aéroport*
aeroplane *l'avion*
berth *la couchette*
bicycle *la bicyclette/le vélo*
mountain bike *le vélo tout terrain, VTT*
bus *l'autobus*
bus stop *l'arrêt d'autobus*
car *la voiture*
coach *l'autocar*
coach station *la gare routière*
flight *le vol*
on foot *à pied*
port *le port*
railway station *la gare*
ship *le bateau*
subway *le métro*
taxi *le taxi*
train *le train*

delayed *en retard*
on time *à l'heure*
platform *le quai*
date-stamp machine *le composteur*
timetable *l'horaire*
left-luggage locker *la consigne automatique*
ticket office *le guichet*
ticket *le billet*
customs *la douane*
seat *la place*

Driving

breakdown *la panne*
car *la voiture*
danger *le danger*
diesel *gazole/gasoil*

driver *le chauffeur*
entrance *l'entrée*
exit *la sortie*
give way/yield *céder le passage*
hire *louer*
(international) driving licence *un permis de conduire (international)*
motorbike/moped *la moto/le vélomoteur*
no parking *stationnement interdit*
petrol (unleaded) *l'essence (sans plomb)*
road *la route*
road works *les travaux*

This doesn't work *Ça ne marche pas*
Is the road good? *Est-ce que la route est bonne?*

Months

January *janvier*
February *février*
March *mars*
April *avril*
May *mai*
June *juin*
July *juillet*
August *août*
September *septembre*
October *octobre*
November *novembre*
December *décembre*

Days

Monday *lundi*
Tuesday *mardi*
Wednesday *mercredi*
Thursday *jeudi*
Friday *vendredi*
Saturday *samedi*
Sunday *dimanche*

Numbers

quarter *un quart*
half *une moitié* or *un demi*
one *un*
two *deux*
three *trois*
four *quatre*
five *cinq*
six *six*

seven *sept*
eight *huit*
nine *neuf*
ten *dix*
eleven *onze*
twelve *douze*
thirteen *treize*
fourteen *quatorze*
fifteen *quinze*
sixteen *seize*
seventeen *dix-sept*
eighteen *dix-huit*
nineteen *dix-neuf*
twenty *vingt*
twenty-one *vingt et un*
twenty-two *vingt-deux*
thirty *trente*
forty *quarante*
fifty *cinquante*
sixty *soixante*
seventy *soixante-dix*
seventy-one *soixante et onze*
eighty *quatre-vingts*
eighty-one *quatre-vingt-un*
ninety *quatre-vingt-dix*
one hundred *cent*
two hundred *deux cents*
one thousand *mille*

Time

What time is it? *Quelle heure est-il?*
It's 2 o'clock (am/pm) *Il est deux heures*
  (du matin/de l'après-midi)
... half past 2 *...deux heures et demie*
... a quarter past 2 *...deux heures et quart*
... a quarter to 3 *...trois heures moins le*
  quart
it is early *il est tôt*
it is late *il est tard*

month *un mois*
fortnight *une quinzaine*
week *une semaine*
day *un jour/une journée*
morning *le matin*
afternoon *l'après-midi*
evening *le soir*
night *la nuit*
today *aujourd'hui*
yesterday *hier*
tomorrow *demain*
day before yesterday *avant-hier*
day after tomorrow *après-demain*
soon *bientôt*

Glossary

Abside: apse

Absidiole: apsidal chapel

Achever, achèvement: to complete, completion

Arc-boutant: flying-buttress

Arc en plein cintre: semicircular arch

Archère: arrow-slit; loophole

Ardoise: slate

Auberge: inn

Autel: altar

Bas-côté: aisle (which can also be a *collatéral*)

Basse-cour: (for château) outer courtyard; (for farm) farmyard

Berceau: barrel vault (more frequently means either cradle or birthplace)

Bergère: wing chair (more frequently means shepherdess)

Bien national: property of the state

Boiserie(s) (en plis de serviette): (linenfold) wood panelling

Bretèche: gatehouse, bartizan

Cachot: prison cell, dungeon

Canonnière: loophole for gun

Caponnière: (*see* entry for Château de Bridoré, pp.303–4)

Cartonnier: artist who paints cartoons for tapestries or carpets (also a cardboard-maker or seller)

Cave: cellar

Chaire: pulpit

Châtelain(e): lord (lady) of a château

Chemin de ronde: parapet walk, wall walk, rampart walk

Chevet: apse

Choeur: choir (architecturally speaking)

Cintre: arch (also coat-hanger)

Clef (or clé) de voûte: keystone or boss (architecturally speaking)

Cloître: cloister

Colimaçon (escalier en): spiral (staircase)

Collégiale: collegiate church

Colombage: half-timbering (not to be confused with *colombier*)

Colombier: dovecote (*see pigeonnier*; not to be confused with *colombage*)

(les) Combles: attic, loft, garret; roof timbers

(les) Communs: outbuildings

Corps de garde: guard, guardhouse, guardroom

Corps de logis: main building

Cour: court, courtyard (a *cour d'honneur* is the principal courtyard of a château; *see* also *basse-cour*)

Courtine: façade between two pavilions

Croisée: crossing (in church architecture, where nave and transepts intersect)

Croisée d'ogives: intersection of the ribs (of a vault)

Cul-de-four: half dome (of apse)

Cul-de-lampe: sculpted pendant at the bottom of a rib or vault (*cul* in French is a coarse word for backside or bottom)

Dessin: drawing (to be distinguished from *dessein*, meaning intention, design or plan)

Domestique: as an adjective, domestic, but just as commonly used as a noun meaning servant

Donjon: keep (not a dungeon)

Douves (sèches): (dry) moat

Droit de gîte: right to lodgings (a right held by French kings to lodge at their nobles' houses when travelling around the country. The château owners kept a room in constant readiness for that unexpected royal arrival, which virtually never came.)

Echauguette: bartizan or small watchtower projecting from a wall

Eglise: church

Enceinte: defensive enclosure (also means pregnant)

Enfilade: series of linked rooms

Estampe: engraving (**sur bois** = woodcut)

Estampillé: stamped

Etage: storey or floor of a building

Fabrique: folly (more commonly manufacture or factory)

Fenêtre à meneaux: mullioned window

'Fillette': prison cell in the form of an iron and wooden cage, associated with Louis XI (*see* Loches, p.294; normally means a little girl)

Fossé: ditch

Fraise: strawberry, but also ruff

Fusain: charcoal

Gare: station

Géminé: twin

Gisant: recumbent statue on tomb

Grange: barn

Halles: covered market

Herse: portcullis, (in agriculture) harrow

Historié: historiated (decorated with flowers or figures or animals, often telling a story in pictures)

Hôtel: hotel where a tourist sleeps, but also the word for a grand town house

Investir: to invest, but also to besiege

Jubé: roodscreen (screen separating the choir from the nave in a church)

Lavoir: communal fountain, usually covered, used in times past for washing clothes

Logis: dwelling, abode, house

Lucarne: dormer, attic or gable window

Mail: mall (as in avenue)

Mairie: town hall

(la) Maison: ordinary word for the house, but also a euphemism for the château, which it would be too vulgar to refer to directly

Mandorle: mandorla (almond-shaped form)

Mécène: patron

Meurtrière: loophole

Modillon: a stone projecting from the cornice of a church, sometimes carved with a face or animal

Moellon: rubble stone

Moellon d'appareil: ashlar

Motte: earth and wood fort

Nef: nave

Ogive: diagonal rib (in architectural vaulting) (An *arc en ogive* is a lancet arch. An *ogive nucléaire* is a modern instrument of the Apocalypse, a nuclear warhead.)

Pavillon: wing of a building, pavilion, lodge

Pierre de taille: ashlar (i.e. a piece of stone cut with straight edges. Compare with *petit appareil* and *moellon*.)

Particule (nom à): name with a handle (i.e. nobleman's name indicated by a 'de' or 'du' in front of the surname)

Petit appareil: uncut small pieces of stone in building

Pigeonnier: pigeon-house (see also *colombier*)

Pignon: gable (*avoir pignon sur rue* = to be prosperous, or to have a shop in a prime position)

Pleurant: weeper, mourner

Pont-levis: drawbridge

Porche: porch

Porte cochère: carriage entrance

Poudre de succession: 'powder of inheritance' (euphemism for poison)

Poutre: beam

Primitif: early master (in painting)

Retable: retable (a carved or painted altarpiece)

Rez-de-chaussée: (UK) ground floor, (US) first floor

Rinceau(x): ornamental foliage, foliated scroll

Romain: Roman (note difference from *roman* in French)

Roman: Romanesque (note difference from *romain* in French. A *roman*, as a noun, is a novel.)

Sablière: beam, stringer

Sens de la visite: generally not sense of the visit, but direction to follow on the visit

Sens interdit: no entry

Sens unique: one way

Temple: both temple and Protestant church

Toit: roof (*toiture:* roofing)

Tomber en quenouille: to pass into the female line or fall to the distaff

Tour: tower (*tour de guet:* watch tower)

Tour d'escalier: stair tower

Tourelle: turret

Travée: bay (in church architecture), span (of bridge)

Tuffeau: tufa limestone

Vantail: leaf (of a door), folding panel (of a triptych)

Verdure: tapestry representing trees or foliage as the main motif (more commonly means greenery or salad vegetables)

Visite libre: unaccompanied visit, not free visit (which would be *visite gratuite*)

Vitrail (vitraux): stained-glass window(s)

Volée (d'escalier): flight of stairs

Voussure: arch moulding

Voûte: vault or arch (*en anse de panier:* basket-handle arch; *d'arête:* groined vault; *en berceau:* barrel vault; *en éventail:* fan vault; *d'ogives:* ribbed vault; *en plein cintre:* semi-circular arch)

Further Reading

Balzac, Honoré de. The author, born in Tours, set many of his stories in the Loire Valley, most famously *Le Lys dans la vallée*, *Eugénie Grandet*, the *Contes drolatiques*, *Le Curé de Tours*, *L'Illustre Gaudissart*, *La Grenadière* and *La Femme de trente ans*.

Caesar, Julius, *The Conquest of Gaul* (Penguin Classics). Including the Loire Valley.

Cloulas, Ivan, *La Vie quotidienne dans les châteaux de la Loire au temps de la Renaissance*. Offers an excellent evocation of royal life and excesses in the Loire from the time the Valois ran off there to the assassination of Henri duc de Guise at the Château de Blois.

Desbordes, Michelle, *La Demande*. The Clos Lucé in Amboise serves as the main setting for this well-received recent work of French fiction. An atmospheric short story, suffused with the white light of the Loire, it cleverly tells the tale as much of Leonardo da Vinci's serving woman as of the great Italian. Although his work is evoked, Desbordes refrains from referring to Leonardo as a genius for the most of the story, and pays as much attention to the way the old woman devotes herself so wholeheartedly to her chores as to Leonardo.

Dunlop, Ian, *Châteaux of the Loire*. Treating the developments in Loire châteaux chronologically, and full of details on life in many of the major châteaux.

Genevoix, Maurice, *Trente mille jours*. Autobiography of a writer from the Orléanais, who recalls his childhood by the Loire river in the early part of the book.

Gracq, Julien, *La Forme d'une ville*. Homage to Nantes by Gracq, who still lives along the Loire and is regarded as one of the most respected French literary figures of the 20th century, even if he's not well known abroad.

Gregory of Tours, *The History of the Franks* (Penguin Classics). Rip-roaring 'history' from the 6th-century bishop of Tours.

Harris, Joanne, *Five Quarters of the Orange*. A Loire fishing tale, but a horrifying one, looking back at collaboration with the occupying Germans. More sharply written than the bestseller *Chocolat*.

James, Henry, *A Little Tour in France* (first published 1884; published by Penguin, 1985). Perceptive and entertaining tour of the Loire Valley towards the close of the 19th century.

Knecht, R.J., *Renaissance Warrior and Patron: The Reign of Francis I*. If you're looking for a serious historical study of one of the great French kings associated with the greatest period in Loire Valley history, try this excellent book. There is some technical detail, but it's also a good read.

La Loire vue du ciel. A coffee-table book with superb aerial photos taken along the whole length of the Loire.

Lorris, Guillaume de, and Jean de Meun, *Le Roman de la rose*. Written in the 13th century and then a bestseller for several centuries, this is an allegorical poem that every self-respecting medieval lord just had to have a manuscript copy of in his château.

Maxwell, William, *The Château*. A naive young American couple, Harold and Barbara Rhodes, go on holiday to France and the Loire in 1948, to find a country only slowly recovering from the German occupation. The couple spend most of their time as paying guests in a château by the Loire between Blois and Amboise, where they gradually get to know their host Madame Viénot, her family, her guests and their stories.

Rabelais, François. Of the series of comic giant adventures Rabelais wrote, with their intellectual icebergs lurking beneath, *Gargantua* in particular contains numerous references to the Chinon area and to the terrible Picrocholine war.

Ronsard, Pierre de. Supreme French lyrical poet of the 16th century, but also an interesting political poet.

Shaw, George Bernard, *Saint Joan* (first published 1924; Penguin, 1946). Highly spirited interpretation of Joan of Arc's rise and fall, with an interesting preface which surveys other literature on Joan. For more details on Joan in literature, *see* **Warner**, below, and the **Topics** chapter at the start of this guide.

Warner, Marina, *Joan of Arc: The Image of Female Heroism* (Weidenfeld & Nicolson, 1981/Vintage 1991). A fascinating study of the true story of Joan of Arc's life – as far as it's possible to piece it together – and of the multitude of myths she gave rise to and why.

Weir, Alison, *Eleanor of Aquitaine: By the Wrath of God, Queen of England*. Despite the title, much of this history concentrates on Eleanor in France. After her marriage to King Louis VII of France had been annulled, she then married Henri Plantagenêt of Anjou (who of course went on to become the first Plantagenet king of England), which therefore features a bit in the book.

Index

Main page references are in **bold**. Page references to maps are in *italics*.

Acknowledgements

Philippe Barbour

Very many thanks to the tourism professionals in the various *départements* along my route who helped me so greatly in preparing this Cadogan Guide to the Loire. Enormous thanks to Jean-Louis Sureau, Pierre Sabouraud and Hélène Ramsamy for going well beyond the bounds of duty and offering their friendship as well as their assistance and advice, and to Lygie Rothon and Anne Gaborit for their enthusiasm for Cadogan guides. In Anjou, Chantal Bessière, Dominique Dubois and Céline Grasset went out of their way to help with this edition of the guide. A special thank you also to Scott Corregan, *guide-interprète*, for accompanying me round Blois again and for reading through that city's chapter, and to the team at the Orléans tourist office for doing likewise. The support of the Maison de la France in London has been important to me down the years, so thank you once more to the staff there, especially Marie-Thérèse Smith. Lastly, a big thank you to Christine Stroyan at Cadogan for showing so much interest in editing this second edition.

Cadogan Guides

We are grateful to FIVAL (Fédération Interprofessionelle des Vins d'Appellation d'Origine Contrôlée du Val de Loire) for allowing us to use their wine map.

One call...

Car Rental Services
- Over 4,000 locations worldwide
- Travel into Eastern Europe
- Long-term leasing

Prestige and Sports Cars
- Large selection of vehicles
- Available throughout Europe

Chauffeur Services
- Hourly, half day and full day services
- Airport transfers

European Air & Hotel Packages
- Over two thousand 2, 3, and 4-star hotels
- Airfares from major US cities available

Online Reservations
- Browse and request all of our services from our website
- Affiliate program with commissions

Loire touring atlas

PARIS

Nevers

Bourges

Chartres

Montargis

Lorris

Gien

Briare

Sancerre

Pithiviers

Châteauneuf

Sully

Châteaudun

Orléans

Beaugency

Vendôme

Blois

Romorantin-Lanthenay

Vierzon

Selles

Montrichard

St-Aignan

Châtillon-sur-Indre

Châteauroux

Le Mans

Alençon

Tours

Amboise

Bléré

Loches

Ste-Maure

Richelieu

Châtellerault

Poitiers

Saumur

Loudun

Parthenay

Doué-la-Fontaine

Montreuil-Bellay

Bressuire

Angers

Sablé

Laval

Cholet

Rennes

Ancenis

Châteaubriant

Nantes

La Roche-sur-Yon

St-Nazaire

Noirmoutier

Challans

St-Gilles-Croix-de-Vie

Les Sables-d'Olonne

20 km

10 miles

N

1

2

3

4

5

6

Pithiviers

Vrigny

Chilleurs-aux-Bois

Beaune-la-Rolande

Chamerolles

Château de Chamerolles

Artenay

Patay

F o r e t

LOIRET

Ingrannes

Combreux

Vitry-aux-Loges

Canal d'Orléans

d

Fay-aux-Loges

Orléans

St Jean-de-Braye

Combleux

Chécy

E60

O r l é a n s

St Jean le Blanc

Mardié

St-Denis-de-l'Hôtel

Jargeau

Châteauneuf-sur-Loire

Parc Floral

Olivet

Germigny-des-Prés

St Ay

Les Muids

Source du Loiret

Loire

Meung-sur-Loire

St-Benoît

Cléry-St André

La Source

Loiret

Neuvy-en-Sullais

Guilly

Tigy

Bouteilles

Sully-sur-Loire

La Ferté-St-Aubin

Ménestreau-en-Villette

Lamotte-Beuvron

Neung

St-Viâtre

Aubigny

Marcilly-en-Gault

Millançay

Salbris

CHER

Veilleins

Villeherviers

La Ferté-Imbault

Le Vieux-Nançay

Aliotis Aquarium

Romorantin-Lanthenay

Nançay

2

SARTHE

Asnières-sur-Vègre

Solesmes

Sablé

306

Malicorne

La Flèche

23

306

Le Lude

Marcé

Genneteil

Broc

La Boissière

Baugé

Pontigné

Château-la-Vallière

Le Vieil-Baugé

766

Noyant

766

Courcelles-de-Touraine

La Fontaine-Guérin

Bocé

Château de Montgeoffroy

Moulliherne

Savigné-sur-Lathon

Beaufort-en-Vallée

Brion

Parçay les Pins

Rillé

Hommes

St-Mathurin-sur-Loire

La Ménitré

Port-St-Maur

Abbaye de St-Maur-de-Glanfeuil

Longué

Vernoil

Gizeux

INDRE-ET-LOIRE

Le Thoureil

Les Rosiers

St-Pierre-en-Vaux

St-Clément-des-Levées

Planchoury

Gennes

Cunault

St-Martin-de-la-Place

Brain-sur-Allonnes

Chevrette

St Michel-sur-Loire

Château de Pimpéan

Trèves

Chênehutte-les-Tuffeaux

St Nicolas-de-Bourgueil

Restigné

St Patrice

Bréhémont

Louerre

Bourgueil

Ingrandes-de-Touraine

Rivarennes

Ecole Nationale d'Equitation

St Hilaire-St Florent

Saumur

Château des Réaux

Rigny-Ussé

Rou-Marson

Souzay-Champigny

Parnay

Chouzé-sur-Loire

Château d'Ussé

La Fosse

Dampierre sur Loire

Varrains

Le Val-Hulin

Turquant

Champigny

Montsoreau

Candes St-Martin

Avoine

Doué-la-Fontaine

Mestré

St-Germain

Beaumont-en-Véron

Le Coudray-Macouard

St Cyr-en-Bourg

Abbaye de Fontevraud

Fontevraud

Abbaye d'Asnières

Chinon

Cravant-les-Côteaux

Les Verchers-sur-Layon

Château de Brézé

La Devinière

Cinais

Rivière

Montreuil-Bellay

Lerné

Seuilly

La Roche Clermault

Tavant

Le Puy-Notre-Dame

Marcay

Château du Rivau

Champigny-sur-Veude

Candé

La Pouëze
St Emérance

770

878

0

E60/A11

23

St-Georges-
sur Loire

Château de
Serrant

Ingrandes

Ancenis

Varades

Montjean

E60/A11

Oudon

Liré

St-Florent-Le-Vieil

Chalonnes-sur-Loire

Champtoceaux

Drain

La-Chapelle-St-Florent

Loire

Le Cellier

La Varenne

Courrossé

St-Laurent
de la Plaine

Les Mauves

St-Sauveur-de-
Landemont

Le Fuilet

MAINE-ET-LOIRE

A11

La Pierre
Percée

763

Montrevault

752

Le Pin-en-
Mauges

Le Loroux-Bottereau

Château de Goulaine

Le Landreau

Beaupréau

Chapelle de la Sorinière

760

Chemillé

Haute-Goulaine

Château de la Noé de Bel-Air

La Haye-Fouassière

Vallet

aine

Le Pé de Sèvre

Le Pallet

Mouzillon

249

St-Macaire-
en-Mauges

Château-
Thébaud

Monnières

Maine

St-André-de-
la-Marche

Clisson

7

Cholet

Nuaillé

Forêt de
Nuaillé-Vezins

149

Sèvre Nantaise

753

Chapelle des Martyrs

93

Maulévrier

Tiffauges

Parc
Oriental

Montaigu

137

St-Laurent

759

Le Chabotterie

160

VENDEE

Le Puy du Fou

149

E03/A83

6

Les Herbiers

St-Michel-
Mont-Mercure

La Flocellière

137

Loire Wines

N

50 kms
30 miles

Châteaubriant

Le Mans

La Flèche

Orléans

VINS DE
L'ORLÉANAIS

Blois

CHEVERNY
COUR-CHEVERNY

TOURAINE
MESLAND
AMBOISE

VOUVRAY
MONTLOUIS
COTEAUX DE
VILLAGES

TOURAINE

Loches

COTEAUX DU
GÂTINOIS

Sancerre

POUILLY-
FUMÉ

SANCERRE

POUILLY-
SUR-LOIRE

MENETOU-
SALON

Bourges

Vierzon

QUINCY

REUILLY

Cher

Indre

COTEAUX DU
VENDÔMOIS

JASNIÈRES

COTEAUX
DU LOIR

Loir

Tours

TOURAINE
NOBLE-JOUÉ

BOURGUEIL
ST-NICOLAS
DE BOURGUEIL

TOURAINE
AZAY-LE-RIDEAU

CHINON

Poitiers

HAUT-POITOU

Saumur

SAUMUR
CHAMPIGNY

SAUMUR

ANJOU

COTEAUX DE THOUET
ET DE L'ARGENTON

Angers

SAVENNIÈRES

QUARTS DE
CHAUME

COTEAUX DE
L'AUBANCE

ANJOU COTEAUX
DE LA LOIRE

BONNEZEAUX

COTEAUX
DU LAYON

ANJOU

Cholet

Ancenis

COTEAUX
D'ANCENIS

MUSCADET DE
SÈVRE & MAINE

MUSCADET DES
COTEAUX DE LA LOIRE

Nantes

Gros Plant du
Pays Nantais

Muscadet
Côtes de Grandlieu

Muscadet

La Roche-
sur-Yon

FIEFS VENDÉENS

Les Sables-
d'Olonne